9/28/77

EXPERIENCE AND ENVIRONMENT

Major Influences on the Development of the Young Child

VOLUME II

EXPERIENCE
Major Influences on the

VOLUME II

AND ENVIRONMENT,
Development of the Young Child

BURTON L. WHITE
with
BARBARA TAYLOR KABAN
JANE ATTANUCCI
BERNICE BROYDE SHAPIRO

Preschool Project
Laboratory of Human Development
Harvard Graduate School of Education

PRENTICE-HALL, INC., Englewood Cliffs, New Jersey 07632

Library of Congress Cataloging in Publication Data (Revised)

White, Burton L. (date)
    Experience and environment.

    Vol. 2 by B. L. White with B. T. Kaban and others.
    Bibliography: v. 1, p. 249-250.; v. 2, p.
    1.   Child psychology.   I.   Watts, Jean Carew, 1936-
joint author.   II.   Title.
BF721.W43   155.4'13   72-10354
ISBN 0-13-294843-5 (v. 1)
ISBN 0-13-294819-2 (v. 2)

155.413
W582
Vol.2

Prentice-Hall Series in Early Childhood
Bernard Spodek, *editor*

EXPERIENCE AND ENVIRONMENT
Major Influences on the Development of the Young Child Vol. II
Burton L. White with Barbara Taylor Kaban, Jane Attanucci
and Bernice Broyde Shapiro

© *1978 by* PRENTICE-HALL, INC., *Englewood Cliffs, N.J. 07632*

All rights reserved. No part of this book
may be reproduced in any form or
by any means without permission in writing
from the publisher.

PRINTED IN THE UNITED STATES OF AMERICA

10   9   8   7   6   5   4   3   2   1

PRENTICE-HALL INTERNATIONAL, INC., *London*
PRENTICE-HALL OF AUSTRALIA PTY. LIMITED, *Sydney*
PRENTICE-HALL OF CANADA, LTD., *Toronto*
PRENTICE-HALL OF INDIA PRIVATE LIMITED, *New Delhi*
PRENTICE-HALL OF JAPAN, INC., *Tokyo*
PRENTICE-HALL OF SOUTHEAST ASIA PTE. LTD., *Singapore*
WHITEHALL BOOKS LIMITED, *Wellington, New Zealand*

Contents

Preface *ix*

part I
INTRODUCTION AND BACKGROUND

1 Introduction *3*

    Let the Rest of the World Go By? *3*
    The Research Strategy *4*
    Progress to Date *5*
    The Plan of the Book *5*

2 A Revisit to the Source of the Definition of Competence in Three to Six Year Old Children *8*

v

part II
THE LONGITUDINAL EXPERIMENT   13

3   The Study   *15*

The Design   *15*
Data Collection Schedule   *16*
Subjects   *17*

4   The Development of Competence   *25*

Introduction   *25*
Interim Achievement Data (Unmatched Groups)   *27*
   social competence: results and discussion   33
   receptive-language development: results and discussion   33
   sensing dissonance: results and discussion   34
   abstract thought: results and discussion   35
   general development: results and discussion   37
   general discussion   38
Primary Outcome Data (Unmatched Groups)   *39*
   predicted vs. achieved competence levels at three years of age   39
   social competence: results and discussion   42
   receptive-language development: results and discussion   44
   sensing dissonance: results and discussion   45
   intellectual development: results and discussion   47
   general discussion   48
Interim Achievement Data (Partially Matched Groups)   *48*
   social competence: results and discussion   50
   receptive-language development: results and discussion   52
   sensing dissonance: results and discussion   53
   abstract thought: results and discussion   55
   general development: results and discussion   55
   general discussion   56
Primary Outcome Data (Partially Matched Groups at 36 Months)   *57*
   social competence: results and discussion   57
   nonsocial abilities   58
Primary Outcome Data   *62*
   social vs. nonsocial vs. overall competence   62

5   Patterns of Experience During the Second and Third Years of Life: Results and Discussion   *65*

The Complicated Question of the Validity of Data on the Experiences of Young Children   *65*
Experiences of the Second and Third Years of Life   *70*
Other General Points to Ponder   *73*
   social experiences   73
   nonsocial experiences   73

Contents

**6 The Relation of Environmental Factors
to Experiences Associated with the Development of Competence:
Generating Hypotheses About Effective Child-rearing Practices** *75*

Experience During the Second Year of Life
 and Achievements at Three Years *75*
Generating Hypothesis About Child-rearing Practices *77*
Experiences at 12-15 Months and Competence at Three Years of Age *78*
  extreme group analyses 78
  task initiation information 81
  *correlational analyses of the effects of experience at 12-15 months on
  the development of competence at three years of age 81*
  *pattern analyses: experiences at 12-15 months and competence
  at three years of age 88*
Experiences at 18-21 Months of Age and Competence
 at Three Years of Age *94*
  extreme group analysis 95
  task initiation information 96
  *correlational analyses of the effects of experience at 18-21 months
  on the development of competence at three years of age 96*
  *pattern analyses: experiences at 18-21 months of age and competence
  at three years of age 103*
  pattern analyses: concluding remarks 110
The Importance of Process Monitoring *114*
Comparison of Findings *124*
Subsidiary Analyses *127*
  *the effects of socioeconomic status
  on the development of competence 127*
  the effects of sex on the patterns of experience of young children 133
  *the effects of experience on the achievement of competence
  at five years of age 140*
  *intercorrelations among general developmental
  and intelligence test scores 148*

7 Hypotheses About Effective Child-rearing Practices *150*

What Goes into Effective Child-rearing *150*
Discussion and Conclusions *154*
General Guidelines for Effective Child-Rearing Practices *157*

part III
NEXT STEPS 161

8 A Comparative Experiment *163*

9 Creating an Instrument to Assess Child-rearing Effectiveness *170*

Background *170*
The Adult Assessment Scales *173*

10   Creating a Training Program   *176*

   The Experimental Treatment (The Training Program)   *177*

part IV
CONCLUSIONS   183

11   Ramifications for Science of Human Development   *185*

12   Ramifications for Society   *192*

   References   *201*

appendix A
INDIVIDUAL SUBJECT DATA   206

appendix B
SUBSIDIARY ANALYSES   383

appendix C
MEASUREMENT TECHNIQUES: MANUAL AND RELIABILITY STUDIES   401

   Manual for Adult Assessment Scales   *403*

   Manual for Assessing Social Abilities of One to Six Year Old Children   *431*

   Manual for Testing the Language Ability of One to Three Year Old Children   *462*

   Manual for Abstract Ability Test   *488*

   Manual for Assessing the Discriminative Ability of One to Three Year Old Children   *512*

appendix D
A TRAINING PROGRAM TO ASSIST PEOPLE IN EDUCATING INFANTS   523

   Index   *561*

Preface

AUTHORSHIP

Volume I of this series was written by two research groups who had been studying the same subjects. One group was directed by Burton L. White, the other by Jean Carew Watts. Each group reported its work in separate chapters of that volume. Shortly after the publication of Volume I, the two groups discontinued coordinated research. This second report is solely the responsibility of the group directed by White.

ACKNOWLEDGMENTS

We wish to extend our gratitude to the present research staff of the Preschool Project: Mrs. Kitty Riley Clark, Mrs. Mary Comita, and Ms. Eugenia Ware. In addition, we wish to thank all of those who have helped us in the past: Mrs. Jacqueline Allaman, Mrs. Nancy Apfel, Miss Frances Aversa, Mrs. Ellen Cardone Banks, Mrs. Martha Bronson, Mrs. Barbara Rich Bushell, Miss Martha Carroll, Mr. Andrew Cohn, Mrs. Cherry Collins, Mrs. Elizabeth Constable, Mrs. Virginia

Demos, Miss Anna DiPietrantonio, Mrs. Marjorie Elias, Dr. John Guidubaldi, Miss Christine Halfar, Miss Geraldine Kearse, Dr. E.R. LaCrosse, Jr., Dr. Patrick C. Lee, Mrs. Sandra Lin, Mrs. Frances Litman, Miss Maxine Manjos, Mrs. Mary Meader Mokler, Dr. Daniel M. Ogilvie, Mrs. Meredith S. Pandolfi, Mrs. Sylvia Skolnick Staub, Mrs. Ingrid Stocking, Dr. Susan S. Stodolsky, Mrs. Jolinda Taylor, Mrs. Eleanor Wasserman, Mr. Paul Weene, Miss A. Elise Weinrich, Mrs. Louise Woodhead, and Dr. Melvin Zolot.

Particular gratitude is owed to Drs. Theodore Sizer, Gerald Lesser, and Paul Ylvisaker of the Harvard Graduate School of Education and to Dr. Edith Grotberg of the Office of Economic Opportunity and to Mrs. Barbara Finberg of the Carnegie Corporation of New York, who were willing to take risks for this project. Special thanks must go to Dr. Miriam Fiedler of the Maternal Infant Health Project.

In addition, this study has been made possible by the cooperation of several hundred families and many school personnel from nearby public and private institutions.

The research and development reported herein was performed in part pursuant to a contract (OE 5-10-39) with the United States Office of Education, under the provisions of the Cooperative Research Program as a project of the Harvard University Center for Research and Development on Educational Differences, the Carnegie Corporation of New York, and the Office of Economic Opportunity, Head Start Division, and the U.S. Office of Child Development Grant No. OCD-CB-193, 1972-1974. The statements made and views expressed are solely the responsibility of the authors.

part **1**

INTRODUCTION AND BACKGROUND

1
Introduction

This book is the second report on the research of the Harvard Preschool Project. *Experience and Environment*, Volume I, published in 1973, described the origins, methods, and preliminary results of the study. This volume will contain considerably more data on the development of the 39 children of our first longitudinal study, the natural experiment. It will also report on the conversion of hypotheses about effective child-rearing practices generated by the longitudinal study into a training program for those who would educate a baby. Finally, we shall present a new assessment device which may be used to monitor the quality of child-rearing practices in the first years of life. We are currently beginning a test of our hypotheses about effective child-rearing practices. The findings of our new longitudinal experimental study will be reported in a later volume.

LET THE REST OF THE WORLD GO BY?

When we started in 1965, interest in preschool education was booming. Head Start was new, exciting (to some), and generously funded. Most of the new sizable preschool research was directed toward the rapid creation of "compensatory" programs for three- and four-year-old children from low-income families. We chose to initiate a project that might ultimately provide guidance in the education of *all* children from birth to six years of age. It has been with a measure of satisfaction that we have watched early education research evolve into a more comprehensive, family-based study of the sort on which we have been concentrating. Today it has become quite fashionable to talk about education during infancy. Fifteen years ago few professionals gave such a radical idea a thought. Similarly, the conviction that the family is the first and most fundamental educational delivery system has also become commonplace. Correspondingly, professional educators (especially of children older than six years) are now much more willing to admit to a more limited conception of their influence on a child's educational achievement.

We do not mean to say there is now a general belief that going to school is of no use, but rather that if a family does not do a minimally adequate job of rearing and educating a child in the first years of life, professional educators, given our current capabilities, are not often able to overcome the resultant educational weaknesses. To put the issue more directly, the results of Projects Head Start and Follow-Through seem to indicate that if a child of three years is six months behind his peers in the development of language and problem-solving ability, the chance that he will ever become an average or superior student is rather small. The widespread ineffectiveness of all but a handful of remedial programs focuses attention on the prevention of the buildup of educational deficits. Some researchers believe that such deficits are genetically predetermined for the most part (Jensen, 1969). Few people of that persuasion have worked extensively with children and families. Other people believe that the experiences children undergo in the first three years of life determine whether or not a child develops an educational deficit. We don't know of a single thoughtful person who believes in either extreme position—i.e., that inheritance is of no concern or that experiences make no difference. Certainly, educators cannot afford to prejudge the issue, and the available evidence is too sketchy to do more. It is the belief that early experiences may be of central importance to a child's later educational achievement that has motivated and sustained our research.

THE RESEARCH STRATEGY

The Preschool Project has been in existence for ten and a half years as of this writing. During that time we have followed what seemed to us to be a rather straightforward plan. Our purpose has been to determine how to structure experiences during the first six years of life so as to assist each child to maximize the potential he is born with. We talked initially about maximizing the educability of children. More recently we have dropped the term *educability* in favor of the term *competence*. The steps in our long-range plan are:

1. Determine what is meant by a well-developed or educable or competent six-year-old.
2. Plot the course of development of competence during the first six years of life.
3. Identify any time period during those first six years that appears to be particularly important for the development of competence.
4. Create measurement techniques to enable us to monitor the development of competence during such periods.
5. Perform a natural experiment with families who are likely to do an outstandingly good job rearing their children and with families likely to do less well than average. Monitor, in detail, the child-rearing practices of each of the families.
6. Using data on the actual competence levels achieved by the children, generate hypotheses about effective child-rearing practices.
7. Convert those hypotheses into a feasible training program suitable for families.
8. Test the validity of the hypotheses experimentally by having families with apparently average child-rearing capacities put those ideas into practice with their children.
9. Use the results of the experiment to refine the hypotheses about effective child-rearing practices.
10. Retest the modified hypotheses, etc.

PROGRESS TO DATE

We are currently testing our hypotheses about effective child-rearing practices, having spent the last two and a half years developing and field-testing a training program for parents. Also, during this last year the oldest subjects of our natural longitudinal experiment began to turn five years of age. Around their fifth birthday we have revisited them and gathered information about their social and intellectual development. Some of these follow-up data will be reported in this volume.

THE PLAN OF THE BOOK

We do not plan to repeat, extensively, material available in Volume I, which introduced the reader to the project. In particular, we tried to show the evolution of our research strategy as we sought to apply scientific methods to the question of how to structure experiences during the first six years of life so as to help each child make the most of his potential. Because our children had not all reached three years of age, we could only present a part of the data describing their development. Those data are now complete and are presented in this volume for all 39 subjects in the study. We are now, therefore, in a position to examine the data on child-rearing practices and experiences in the light of the actual achievement levels of our subjects at three years of age. Furthermore, we now have information on intellectual competence at five years of age. That too will be presented in this report.

Volume I contained extensive descriptions of the new data-gathering techniques we created for this project. Here we shall report minor revisions in some of those instruments along with a new, potentially very important, instrument to assess quantitatively those aspects of an adult's behavior that we believe are central to the development of competence in young children.

In Volume I, we provided minimal information about the original sample from whose behavior we generated our working definition of the well-developed child. Because of the central importance of our conception of competence, we provide more detail here and show that our definition of competence was not derived from a stereotypical middle-class population and has applicability across many kinds of families.

The purpose of our natural experiment was to generate hypotheses about effective child-rearing practices. It was not *to prove* that child-rearing practices caused a particular effect. The natural experiment produced an array of child-rearing practices and related experiences that accompanied an array of achievement levels in 39 children, thus permitting correlations. Researchers vary in the degree to which they give credence to correlational data. We are inclined to be conservative on the issue. We are treating our correlational results as a source of hypotheses which will then be tested *experimentally* in our next study.

In Volume I, we presented our first generation of hypotheses about effective child-rearing practices. In this book, some five years later, we feel more confident about the refined and extended version of the hypotheses that we will present. Nevertheless, they are still hypotheses, yet to be tested experimentally.

Aside from the problem of the relationship of child-rearing practices to the development of competencies, there are other data that emerge from our study which do not require experimental testing. Our task data describing what children are *actually doing* as they go about the daily business of living during the second and third years of life are the first of their kind (see also Clarke-Stewart and Caldwell) and seem both interesting and useful. Our results on interrelations among test performances may also have utility aside from the major focus of our research. For example, our receptive-language test (given during the second year of life) is a rather impressive predictor of performance on the Stanford-Binet Intelligence Scale at three years and on the Weschler Preschool and Primary Scale of Intelligence (WPPSI) at five years. Indeed, within our data there are quite a number of interesting areas to explore, many of which we will probably pass by.

Toward the end of this book we will deal with converting hypotheses generated in the natural experiment into a feasible training program for average families. We will also present our Adult Assessment Scales. In Volume I the quantitative assessment of environmental factors was dealt with by Dr. Jean

Carew Watts and her staff.* Since then our projects have gone separate ways. We have now inductively devised our own instrument for assessing salient human environmental factors. The design of this instrument was an exercise in induction as was the design of our instruments for assessing experiences (the task instrument) and social competence. *After* observing 39 mothers rear their children for one or two years, and *after* we identified how well each child had developed at three years of age, we then described the behavior patterns common to the mothers of the children who developed the highest and the lowest levels of overall competence. The patterns we agreed upon became the source of the items we selected to include in our Adult Assessment Scales. We hope those scales will help us focus effectively on the behaviors that discriminate a highly competent caretaker from a less competent caretaker.

The book will close with a brief description of the comparative experiment we are now engaged in to test our ideas about effective child-rearing practices and some remarks about possible ramifications of our work.

---

*Dr. Carew Watts has completed her data collection on the 39 subjects of this study. She plans a separate volume on her research in the near future. The interpretations and opinions expressed in this book are not intended to represent Dr. Watts's views, although in many instances she might share our positions.

2

A Revisit to the Source of the Definition of Competence in Three-Six-Year-old Children

In Volume I, we remarked that the psychological literature did not contain extensive research findings on the topic of the competent six-year-old. Aside from Lois Murphy's Sarah Lawrance study (Murphy, 1956) we could find no reports of extensive studies of unusually good development in the first six years of life.[*] We then described briefly how we observed children going about their ordinary activities in nursery schools, in kindergartens or playgrounds, and in their own homes. Although in Volume I we generally characterized the population on whom we gathered such data over an eight-month period, we provided limited detail. Consequently, a few observers of our work have concluded that our definition of competence seems to be a "middle-class" definition. Such is not the case. We have tried to focus on those distinguishing dimensions of competence held *in common* by children across socioeconomic status (SES) and ethnicity within our sample.

Table 1 presents more detailed data on the characteristics of the original sample from which we generated our definition of the competent three to six year old child. We obtained observational access to 21 preschools in and around

---

[*]Terman's studies of gifted children (1925 and 1947), while of great value, contain too little detail about behavior during the first six years of life to be of significance for our research.

TABLE 1. Age, Social Class, Ethnicity, and Sex of Subjects in 1966-67 Sample

	Age				Social Class**			Ethnicity		Sex	
	2	3	4	5	L	M	U	Black	Caucasian	Male	Female
Type A* N = 13	1	4	3	5	4	8	1	4	9	7	6
Type B N = 15	1	5	5	4	6	7	2	4	11	9	6
Type C N = 13	1	5	2	5	5	5	3	4	9	5	8
TOTAL = 41	3	14	10	14	15	20	6	12	29	21	20

*Type A = Highly competent
Type B = Average
Type C = Less competent

**At this early stage of the research, we were using a very simple social-class designation:
L = Lower, M = Middle, U = Upper.

the Boston area and chose 57 children to observe. In our ultimate discussions dealing with the definition of competence, we studied a more select group of 15 preschools and 41 subjects, chosen to maximize the distribution of race, socioeconomic level, community location, and school program. Our sample included 15 lower-class, 20 middle-class, and 6 upper-class children;* 21 were male, and 20 were female.

Although our sample was quite broad in those terms, the primary organizing factor for the sample was the variable we then called *educability*. The teachers were asked to rate the educability of their pupils on a three-point scale. A child was to be rated A if the teacher was quite confident he or she would do very well in elementary school. A child was to be rated C if a teacher was quite confident he would do significantly less well than average in elementary school. All others were to be rated B. We obtained preliminary ratings from teachers early in the school year. At the end of the school year, teachers rerated their classes, and research assistants who had observed each subject for the same period independently rated each child. In addition, we administered to each child the information subtest from the WPPSI, the Peabody Picture Vocabulary Test, and tests of fine and gross motor skills. Finally those subjects on whom *all ratings and test scores agreed* were rerated as either A or C. All others were rated B. The final sample contained 13 A, 15 B, and 13 C subjects. This group of 41 subjects that had been observed for nine months was the source of our description of the competent six-year-old child.

One ten-minute protocol was taken on each subject each week. The day

---

*This simple three-level treatment of socioeconomic class was discontinued in favor of the more refined Hollingshead and Redlich five-level system (1958).

of the week, the time of day, and the research assistant who observed and took the record were rotated in a random fashion from October through February. In March, April, May, and June some records were taken by this standard method. However, research assistants were also assigned to the same few subjects every second week. Every subject had two repeated observers. Observations were made in pairs, both observers taking protocols. One of each pair was a repeated observer making his biweekly observation of this particular subject, and one was observing as a random assignment. The paired protocols gave us a check on reliability. The regular assignment system ensured that at least two members of staff were familiar with each subject, and the continued random assignment kept continuity with the observational method used earlier in the year.

Because of absentee problems we failed to get complete records on all children. Most, however, were fairly complete. In all, at the end of the school year we had over one thousand ten-minute running behavior records.

Data analysis concentrated on the protocols on our A and C subjects. Two subject files (each consisting of about twenty records) were examined and discussed per day, one of an A and one of a C subject of similar age. In the morning each research subgroup read the files and discussed the subjects, comparing their behaviors, temperaments, traits, and abilities. The notes from each subgroup meeting were read at a meeting of the whole project each afternoon, and discussion continued. Lists of differences between A and C subjects were drawn up. As the three weeks of this intensive analysis proceeded, comparisons between C subjects and between A subjects were made and the list refined. In sum, the distinguishing characteristics were identified through an inductive process.

This initial description of the competent three to six year old was subjected to extensive review by our staff during the following year. We again worked in preschools and homes that contained children from the full spectrum of socioeconomic levels and many ethnic backgrounds. The seven observational settings (in addition to private homes) in the second observational series were:

1. and 2. Two Head Start schools, one serving a black low-income population, the other serving an integrated low-income population
3. One Montessori school serving children of academic and professional parents
4. One experimental community school serving ghetto and middle-class* white and black children
5. One traditional public school kindergarten serving lower- and middle-class children
6. One parochial nursery school serving lower-class white children
7. One traditional private nursery school serving middle-class children.

*Class designations here are cruder than in later sections in this report where we used the Hollingshead and Redlich five-point SES scale.

The social ability specialists on the project* confirmed and refined the original definition of social competence on the basis of 120 half-hour protocols on 40 new three to six year old children in these facilities. These observations required six weeks.

The nonsocial ability specialists† confirmed and refined the definition of nonsocial competence on the basis of systematic observations from fall 1967 to July 1968 of 24 other three to six year old children in four other facilities with comparable variability of populations. Their manner of data collection was less formal and more variable than that of the social group.

As a result of the second round of observations, one of the original social competencies—the capability to empathize—was deleted because of its infrequent occurrence in children of this age range. The original descriptions of the nonsocial competencies were made more concise and behaviorally specific.

We did no further work on the definition of competence in the three to six year old child at that time. The degree to which our definition is a middle-class definition is therefore not really known. We could have pursued that topic further in 1968, but we chose not to do so. We were very much aware of the value of a definition that embraced *only* those abilities held in common by very able children across socioeconomic levels. We took pains (as described) to gather data in such a manner as to produce such a definition. Such a goal is, however, far from an easy one, and we realize others may do better than we have in subsequent research.

---

*Led by Dr. Daniel Ogilvie and Mrs. Bernice Broyde Shapiro.
† Led by Dr. Patrick Lee.

part **II**

THE LONGITUDINAL EXPERIMENT

3

The Study

THE DESIGN

Our first longitudinal study is a natural experiment. We wanted to learn the details of excellent child-rearing practices for the second and third years of life. Therefore, we observed two sets of families as they reared their children during those years. One set of families was selected because we had reason to believe that their children would attain high levels of competence as defined by our project. The other set was selected because we believed their children would achieve a less-than-average level of general competence. Of course, our predictions may for any number of reasons turn out to be wrong at times (as indeed some have), and we have acknowledged this likelihood in our plans.

The primary purpose of our planned longitudinal natural experiment was to search for environmental factors that play important causal roles in the early development of human competence. It should be noted that the major contributions to the development of competence need not involve the environment in any significant way. Indeed, some students of the problem (including Jensen, 1969) seem to hold the view that our search would be fruitless. Our view was, and is, that there is good reason to believe that environmental factors do play an important role in early human development, and, further, that the possibility is far too vital an issue to leave untouched by direct inquiry.

After screening each subject for assurance of physical normality,* we conducted an interview with the child's mother to gain a general understanding of household routines, schedules, and other information relevant to the child's everyday experience. Within a few days of his birthday—usually about a week after the interview—we began formal data collection.

We needed to monitor the development of competence to validate the usefulness of both data on the experiences of the child and data on environmental influences on those experiences. Further, if we had guessed wrong about an infant's likelihood for outstanding growth (either positively or negatively), we needed to know as soon as possible, so as to avoid a continuing investment in a family that would be less useful to us than another. Fourteen tests for the development of various aspects of competence were administered during the second year of life. Fifteen or eighteen such tests were administered during the third year of life, depending on whether a child started in the project at one or two years of age.

DATA COLLECTION SCHEDULE

The first assessment measure given to the subjects was the Bayley Tests of Infant Development, administered once to each age group, the younger children at 12 months, and the older at 24 months.

Three other tests, assessing receptive-language ability, the capacity for abstract thinking, and the ability to sense discrepancies, are always administered within the same one- or two-week period. The sequence was begun at 12½ or 24½ months, and the three tests were repeated approximately two and a half months later, at 15 and 27 months, respectively.

Beginning at about 15 months of age and extending into the 20th or 21st month, there arises a period during which testing becomes even more difficult than usual with young children. The child is apt to be unusually shy or stubborn and fussy. This type of behavior is often attributed to the newly developing "age of autonomy," when the child has discovered the word *no* and has little hesitation in using it. He is no longer the generally friendly, cooperative child of 12 to 14 months and has not yet reentered the stage where sociability and curiosity make him eager to try the games the experimenter introduces. Naturally, there are many exceptions of all ages, but we have found it best to postpone testing during these months and to resume at about 21 months of age. The need for postponement occurs far less often for the two-year-olds, and their testing schedule continues at regular intervals, the 22-to-27-month testing being followed by another sequence at 30 months (see Figure 2).

*See Volume I for procedures to screen out handicapped children.

Another problem that arises as the one-year-olds approach 24 months is that they begin to outgrow the 12-24-month version of the tests and are often ready for the 24-36-month adaptation. The experimenter must use his discretion as to the appropriate time to introduce the more difficult material. Many of the subjects can master the more advanced tests to some degree by the 21-month age level. This pertains to the language and abstract abilities tests, which differ for younger and older subjects, but not to the discrepancies test, which has increasingly difficult steps ranging from the 12- to the 36-month-old level of development.

We gather data on the typical experiences of our subjects once every three weeks, six months out of each year. Since we collect three ten-minute continuous records on each visit, we accumulate approximately twenty-seven such protocols each year for one child. Correspondingly, we gather data on the child's social experience, his mother's interactions with him, and his utilization of the physical environment (toys, furniture, areas of rooms, etc.) once every three weeks for six months of the year. The result is a very substantial amount of systematically interrelated data on each child. The schedule of observation and test sessions is illustrated in Figures 1 and 2.

Special note should be taken at this point of the danger of drowning in information. Each ten-minute task record may involve as many as forty or more separately coded and analyzed events. We collect thirty a year for each child. The numbers involved are very large. On the one hand, such an amount of data helps to insure the validity of our findings. On the other hand, many a longitudinal study has collected (at great expense) masses of data, much of which was subsequently not used.

SUBJECTS

Originally we planned to study 48 children as they developed during the second and third years of life. Twenty-four children would have been one year old when

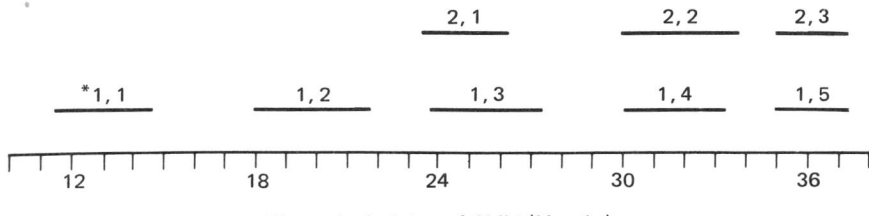

* First number is the starting age of child; second number is the run number.

Figure 1. Schedule of runs

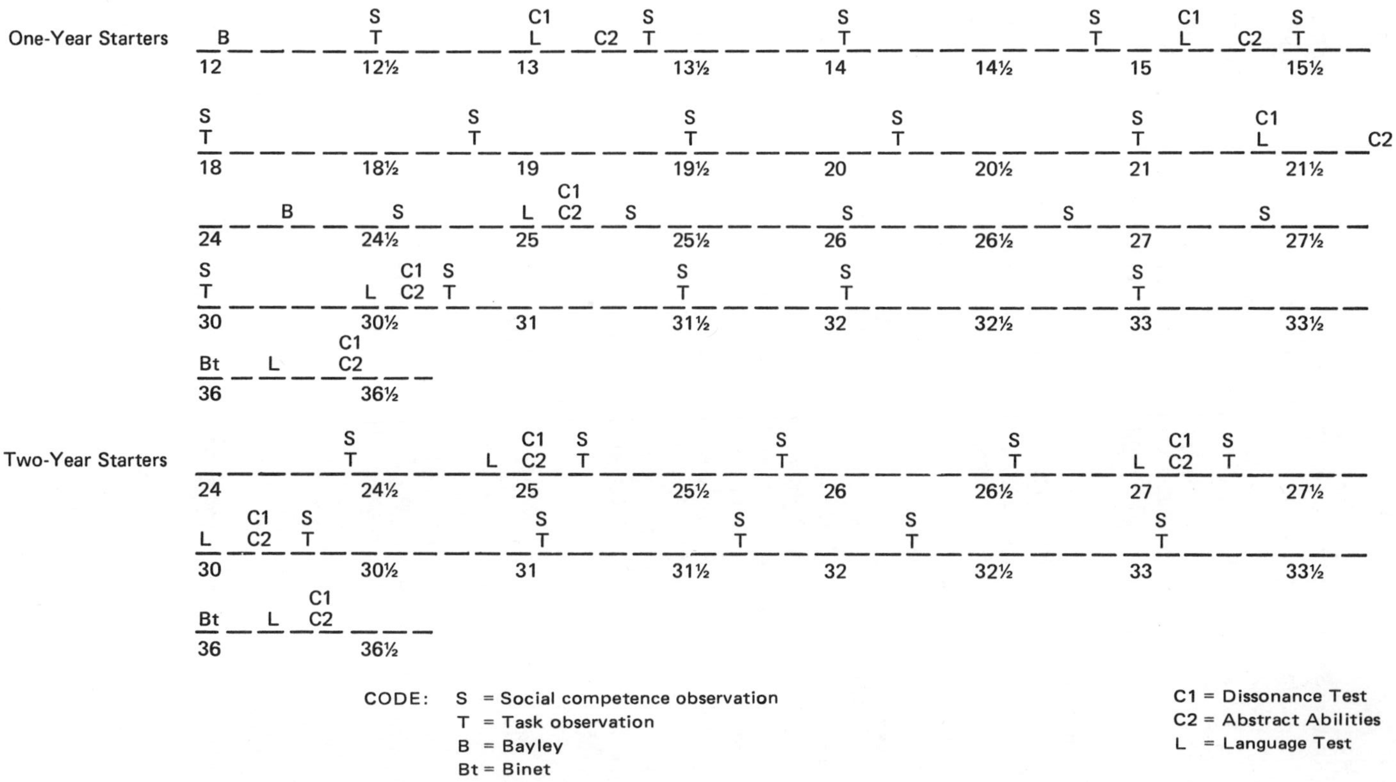

Figure 2. Details of social and task observations and tests within runs

CODE: S = Social competence observation
T = Task observation
B = Bayley
Bt = Binet

C1 = Dissonance Test
C2 = Abstract Abilities
L = Language Test

we began. Half would have come from families that had previously reared children who had attained very high levels of competence; the other half, from families whose older children had developed lower-than-average levels of competence. We planned to follow that group of 24 for two years. The remaining 24 children would similarly have been divided among A and C families but would have been started at two years of age and followed for one year, in order that we might learn something about third-year phenomena sooner than if we had to wait for our one-year-olds to turn two.

We knew, of course, that we would probably lose some of our subjects due to illness, family disruptions, relocations, and the like. We also expected that some of our predictions about how well children would develop would turn out to be false. And, of course, unless a child did develop as either an A or a C, data on his history of experiences would weaken the usefulness of our pool of information on excellent and poor child-rearing practices. We therefore planned to start with 60 families. That plan turned out to be totally unrealistic.

First of all, since we wanted to start all the children in the study within the space of a few months' time and at about their first or second birthday, we could not use children whose birthdays fell at other times of the year. Second, we were planning to deal with special kinds of children, who constituted a small minority of all children. Third, we were fairly sure we would have trouble working with families who were doing a poor job of rearing their children. And finally, since we fully intended to gather extensive data on the average of once a week for at least 26 weeks of each year, we would simply have drowned in the sheer volume of work and information. We therefore resigned ourselves to an upper limit with more A's than C's.

The subject sample to be reported on consists of 39 children (see Tables 2A and 2B). They come from a variety of backgrounds, including Anglo-Saxon, Irish, Italian, and Jewish ancestry. Our subject families can be grouped according to the widely used Index of Social Position developed by Hollingshead and Redlich (1958), which employs occupation, education, and residence as class criteria.

For each child, we predicted an outstanding level of competence at three years of age based upon the levels achieved by their older siblings.* Table 3 portrays the SES and predicted competence of our sample arranged by sex of the child.

---

*There was one only child in the study. It was predicted that he would develop very well, on the basis of the apparently high quality of his mother's child-rearing practices.

TABLE 2A. Demographic Information, One-Year-Old Starters (n = 19)

Sub. ID	Sex	Hollings-head Redlich Code	Family Income	Mother Education	Father Education	Mother[a] Occupation	Father[b] Occupation	Mother[c] Ethnic	Father[c] Ethnic	Mother[d] Religion	Father[d] Religion	No. Children in Household
03	F	I	$20,000 or over	College graduate	Post-col. graduate	Secretary	Chemist	Anglo.	Jewish	None (Prot.)	None	2
17	F	I	$20,000 or over	College graduate	Post-col. graduate	Homemaker	Physicist	Anglo.	Anglo.	None	None	2
24	M	I	$20,000 or over	Post-col. graduate	Post-col. graduate	(Doctor)	Univ. professor	Ital.	Jewish	Prot.	Jewish	4
19	F	I	$12,000-$20,000	Partial/jr. coll.	Post-col. graduate	(Nurse)	Univ. professor	Anglo.	Anglo.	Prot.	Prot.	3
31	M	II	$12,000-$20,000	Post-col. graduate	Post-col. graduate	Restaurant manager	Restaurant owner	Ital.	Ital.	Catholic	Catholic	3
08	M	II	less than $3,000	Post-col. graduate	Post-col. graduate	Teacher	Ph.D. student	Anglo.	Anglo.	Prot.	Prot.	1
20	F	II	$12,000-$20,000	Post-col. graduate	Post-col. graduate	(Teacher)	Architect	Jewish	Jewish	Jewish	Jewish	4
11	F	II	$12,000-$20,000	College graduate	Post-col. graduate	Homemaker	Univ. professor	Ital.	Anglo.	None	None	2
16	M	III	$7,000-$12,000	Partial/jr. coll.	Partial/jr. col.	Homemaker	Physical ed. Teacher	Anglo.	Anglo.	Catholic	Catholic	3
32	M	III	$3,000-$7,000	High sch. graduate	Partial/high sch.	Homemaker	Small repair shop	Irish	Ital.	Catholic	Catholic	8
45	F	III	$7,000-$12,000	Partial/high sch.	High sch. graduate	Homemaker	Owner of small catering service	Anglo.	Anglo.	Catholic	Catholic	2

TABLE 2A. (continued)

44	F	III	$7,000-$12,000	Partial/ jr. col.	College graduate	Homemaker	Bank treasurer	Anglo.	Irish	Catholic	Catholic	3
42	M	III	$7,000-$12,000	High sch. graduate	High sch. graduate	(Bookkeeper)	Route service canteen filler	Irish	Italian	Catholic	Catholic	3
43	M	III	$7,000-$12,000	High sch. graduate	Partial/ voc. col.	Homemaker	Hairdresser	Jewish	Jewish	Jewish	Jewish	3
34	M	IV	$7,000-$12,000	Partial/ high sch.	High sch. graduate	Homemaker	Truckdriver	Anglo.	Anglo.	Catholic	Catholic	3
01	F	IV	$7,000-$12,000	High sch. graduate	High sch. graduate	Homemaker	Maintenance man	Italian	Italian	Catholic	Catholic	13
40	F	IV	$7,000-$12,000	Partial/ high sch.	Jr. high graduate	Homemaker	Crane operator	Anglo.	Anglo.	Catholic	Prot.	3
37	M	V	Under $3,000	Partial/ jr. col.	?	Homemaker	(Prof. soldier)	Anglo.	Anglo.	Catholic	?	3
41	F	V	Under $3,000	Partial/ high sch.	Elementary school	Homemaker	House painter	?	?	None (Catholic)	None	4

[a] Parentheses denote Mother's occupation prior to our study.
[b] Parentheses used when parents are divorced and mother is head of household.
[c] Anglo. used to mean of European background other than Irish, Italian, Jewish, or Spanish.
[d] Parentheses denote the religious background where parents no longer profess a religious faith.

TABLE 2B. Demographic Information, Two-Year-Old Starters (n = 20)

Sub. ID	Sex	Hollings- head Redlich Code	Family Income	Mother Education	Father Education	Mother[a] Occupation	Father[b] Occupation	Mother[c] Ethnic	Father[c] Ethnic	Mother[d] Religion	Father[d] Religion	No. Children in Household
12	M	I	$12,000–$20,000	Post-col. graduate	Post-col. graduate	Prenatal teacher	Physician	Jewish	Jewish	Jewish	Jewish	4
10	F	I	$20,000 or over	Post-col. graduate	Post-col. graduate	Teacher	Lawyer	Jewish	Jewish	Jewish	Jewish	3
21	M	I	$12,000–$20,000	College graduate	Post-col. graduate	Homemaker	Lawyer	Anglo.	Anglo.	Prot.	Prot.	2
05	M	I	$20,000 or over	Partial/ jr. col.	Post-col. graduate	Nurse	Psycho- analyst	Anglo.	Anglo.	Catholic	Episcopal	3
09	F	I	$7,000–$12,000	Post-col. graduate	Post-col. graduate	Social worker	Univ. professor	Anglo.	Spanish	None (Unit.)	None (Catholic)	1
13	M	I	$20,000 or over	Post-col. graduate	Post-col. graduate	(Teacher, college)	Physician	Jewish	Jewish	Prot.	Jewish	3
33	M	I	$20,000 or over	Partial/ jr. col.	Post-col. graduate	Homemaker	Exec., shoe mfg.	Jewish	Jewish	Jewish	Jewish	3
02	M	II	$3,000–$7,000	College graduate	Post-col. graduate	Homemaker	Medical student	Anglo.	Anglo.	Prot.	Prot.	2
38	M	III	$3,000–$7,000	Partial/ jr. col.	High sch. graduate	Homemaker	Travel agent	Latin America	Latin America	Catholic	Catholic	6
35	F	III	$7,000–$12,000	Partial/ voc. col.	Partial/ voc. col.	(Lab. technician)	Sr. lab. technician	Anglo.	Anglo.	Catholic	Catholic	6
18	F	III	$7,000–$12,000	Partial/ jr. col.	Partial/ jr. col.	Homemaker	TV repair shop owner	Italian	Italian	Catholic	Catholic	7

TABLE 2B. (continued)

22	F	III	$3,000–$7,000	Partial/jr. col.	College graduate	Cocktail waitress	(City reg. planner)	Anglo.	Anglo.	None (Catholic)	None (Catholic)	3
36	M	III	—	High sch. graduate	Partial/voc. col.	Homemaker	Industrial tool salesman	Italian	Italian	Catholic	Catholic	2
39	M	III	$7,000–$12,000	Partial jr. col.	High sch. graduate	Homemaker	Machinist	Irish	Irish	Catholic	Catholic	2
28	F	III	$3,000–$7,000	Jr. high graduate	Partial/voc. col.	Homemaker	Accountant	Italian	Italian	Catholic	Catholic	2
27	M	III	$7,000–$12,000	Partial/jr. col.	College	Homemaker	(Antique dealer)	Greek	Irish	Greek Orthodox	None (Catholic)	3
30	F	III	$12,000–$20,000	Jr. high graduate	Partial/high sch.	Maintenance, Ct. house	Court officer	Irish	Irish	Catholic	Catholic	7
14	M	IV	$3,000–$7,000	Partial/high sch.	Partial/high sch.	(Hairdresser)	MBTA bus driver	Irish	Irish	Catholic	Catholic	2
25	M	IV	$3,000–$7,000	High sch. graduate	Partial/high sch.	Homemaker	Painter	Anglo.	Anglo.	None	None	2
07	M	IV	$3,000–$7,000	Partial/high sch.	Jr. high graduate	Waitress	Steel worker	Anglo.	Anglo.	Prot.	Prot.	6

[a] Parentheses denote Mother's occupation prior to our study.
[b] Parentheses used when parents are divorced and mother is head of household.
[c] Anglo. used to mean of European background other than Irish, Italian, Jewish, or Spanish.
[d] Parentheses denote the religious background where parents no longer profess a religious faith.

TABLE 3. Subject Characteristics, Total Population of the Study

		1-Year-Olds					2-Year-Olds				
SES Score		I	II	III	IV	V	I	II	III	IV	V
A's	Boys	1	2	2	0	0	4	1	3	0	0
	Girls	3	2	2	0	0	2	0	3	0	0
C's	Boys	0	0	2	1	1	1	0	1	3	0
	Girls	0	0	0	2	1	0	0	2	0	0
Total		4	4	6	3	2	7	1	9	3	0

All subjects = 39
One-year-olds = 19
Boys = 22
A's = 25

Two-year-olds = 20
Girls = 17
C's = 14

4

The Development of Competence

INTRODUCTION

Our original intention was to learn how some fortunate children develop especially well during their first three years of life. Our recruitment efforts focused on identifying such children from diverse family backgrounds. We were especially interested in such children from lower-income families. Clearly, if a family had to be from the middle or upper socioeconomic classes in order to produce a very competent three-year-old, the practical ramifications would be very great.

Studying only examples of excellent development would have left us with no way of distinguishing between child-rearing practices especially associated with such development and others that might be associated regularly with average or even poor development; nor would we learn about child-rearing practices to be avoided. Because our resources were not unlimited and because we believed the multitudinous forms of average child-rearing practices would be too confusing for us to deal with, we sought families whose child-rearing practices might contrast sharply with our primary group. We especially sought out advantaged families with children developing poorly.*

We labeled the families that we expected would rear their children unusually well A, and those we expected would do less well than average families, C. In Volume I of this series, we presented our preliminary results so as to allow comparisons across the two groups.

In spite of the fact that each of our subjects had an older sibling† who was either of very high or of less-than-average general competence, we could not be certain that he or she would develop the same way. Indeed, though our predictions turned out to be generally accurate, there were several children who either did significantly better or worse than predicted. In addition, as the children reached their third birthdays, it became obvious that though the range of achieved competence was great across the 39 children, we no longer had two distinct groups of children (A's and C's). Our population had achieved a more or less continuous distribution of levels of ability.

What to do? The A-C method of data presentation was no longer as feasible as it seemed at the outset. There were too many apparently average three-year-olds. We tried defining A, B, and C zones. This task was complicated by the fact that we had come to the firm conclusion that our 39 subjects were not all of equal heuristic importance. Put simply, children who started with us at one year of age had become of primary interest because our data, like that of many other recent studies (for a notable example, see Earl Schaefer), indicated that stable precocity or delay was usually well established by the second birthday. To examine the experiential processes that *preceded* the emergence of consistent developmental divergence, we had to look at our data on the second year of life. In effect, we were left with 19 subjects for that purpose.

The result is that we shall continue to use the method of extreme group comparisons but reduce our groups to the best- and the poorest-developed three-year-olds (of our one-year-old starters). Secondary analyses will utilize all of our subjects but with methods of analysis appropriate for continuous rather than for dichotomous distributions. One result of this decision is that statistical analyses on differences between our key groups of one-year-olds are reduced to illustrative functions. For analyses involving larger numbers of our subjects, statistical significance data will be presented. The reader is reminded that the major purpose of this natural experiment was to generate *hypotheses* about the effectiveness of child-rearing practices. Such hypotheses would then be subjected to experimental test. Our current study, to be reported in Volume III, is designed for that purpose.

---

*We had considerably more success finding and working with lower SES level families with well-developing children than we did with advantaged families with poorly developing children. Indeed, in most of the cases where children developed better than we predicted, the families involved were upper-level families.

†Except in one case.

INTERIM ACHIEVEMENT DATA
(UNMATCHED GROUPS)*

We monitored the growth of competence in our subjects according to the schedule as outlined in Figure 2, page 18.

Achievement data gathered during the children's second and third years of life enabled us to plot growth trends and to note the emergence of precocity or delay.

Social Competence: Results and Discussion

In Volume I and in other writings we have described observable behaviors that well-developed three to six year old children engage in when interacting with others. We were most impressed at the skillfulness and maturity shown by advanced children in social encounters. In the intervening years there has been a substantial increase in interest in such phenomena by students of child development research and early education. Impelled partly by urgings from the Federal Office of Child Development, several programs for developing assessment techniques for interpersonal skills are now underway. The most recent survey of instruments available for such purposes (Walker, 1973) indicates that the field is still woefully deficient in such instruments.

Our view of our own procedures for assessing social competence is as follows: The first requirement of any such instrument is conceptual suitability. It is not all that difficult to think of behaviors that can be crudely labeled as social, to assemble a number of them for an observation or rating sheet, and to call it a scale to assess social competence. Indeed, we have had social or personal-social subscales for years as elements of general tests of early development. Our conception of social competence was developed from many hundreds of written protocols describing social behaviors of one to six year old children in a wide variety of natural circumstances. We† analyzed those behaviors with an eye to consistent differences between those exhibited by children rated remarkably adept (in overall competence) and those characteristic of children rated less well developed than most. We are very confident of the general validity of our identification of specific dimensions of social competence. This ethologically based conceptual scheme is the strongest feature of our social competence assessment techniques.

A conceptual scheme is, however, only part of what is needed for first-rate assessment. One needs, in addition, an appropriate procedure for gathering data

---

*Data will be presented first on all children and then on those who achieved the highest and lowest levels of overall competence at three and five years of age regardless of socioeconomic background. A second analysis will deal with differences seen when subjects are partially matched for SES yet still achieve at markedly different levels.

†The development of this assessment technique was the work of Daniel Ogilvie and Bernice B. Shapiro.

on subjects, a method for scoring the raw data, high interobserver and scorer reliabilities, normative data on diverse and sizable populations, and useful predictive validity, for starters.

The Preschool Project, unfortunately, does not have all of the necessary ingredients for the assessment techniques it has devised. For assessing social competence, we do have what looks to be a solid conceptual base, without which all the other requirements are of little use. We also have both a behavior checklist and a rating scale. For the behavior checklist, we had to create items for scoring observed behaviors of relevance. We feel we are on solid ground, here, having invested several years on the topic. We also have a semi-arbitrary scoring procedure (see Appendix C, pages 455-456) designed for computer transformation of raw data into indices of social competence with peers, with adults, and with both (overall). We have minimally adequate intertester and interobserver reliability and modest indications of predictive validity (Guidubaldi, 1969), but no normative data on representative populations.

Our rating scale is a typical "seat of the pants" affair. We ask qualified people to rate a child (in reference to other children his own age) on a scale of one to five on each dimension of social competence, on competence with peers and with adults, and on overall competence.* We also ask them to rate the reference group used (e.g., a kindergarten class, a day-care group) against the levels of such skills they have observed in similar children in the past. Experienced teachers seem to have little difficulty with this procedure, but we suspect a strong halo effect, with bright children sometimes ranked higher by their teachers than by one of our staff specialists.

The data we present must therefore be evaluated in the light of these weaknesses. Social competence was assessed according to the degree to which each child exhibited the particular social skills listed in our definition of the competent three to six year old child. There were five such skills usually exhibited in interactions with adults and three with age-mates:

	1. gaining adult attention
	2. using adult as resource
Adult	3. expressing affection and hostility to adult
	4. engaging in role play
	5. expressing pride in achievement†
	6. showing competition with peers
Peer	7. expressing affection and hostility to peers
	8. leading and following peers

*This rating scale was used only when the children turned five years of age.
†The earliest expressions of pride relate to motor achievements rather than to the creation of products such as drawings or other constructions.

The data were collected with our Checklist for Scoring Social Behavior (see Appendix C, pages 450-452). Since the instrument is used as the child goes about his ordinary in-the-home activities, and since three-year-olds have much more contact with their mothers than with peers, we accumulated much more data on social competence with adults than with peers. We decided to use only the former in assigning social competence scores to our subjects. (Generally, but not always, the level of skills shown with adults paralleled the level shown with peers.) Credit was given for degree of competence in each of the five dimensions and also for the number of such competencies that were well developed.* This factor of breadth of competencies reflected our original finding that very competent children showed *all* of the listed competencies rather than a few well-developed ones.

Tables 4 and 5 present the social competence achievement data gathered from our first contact with the children up to the primary outcome assessment period at three years of age.

Table 4 indicates the level of social competence (with adults) revealed by our subjects between 12 and 27 months of age. Two major groups of children are involved, those we studied from their first birthdays and those we began observing near their second birthdays. The data are organized to show development for those entering the study at one year of age or at two years and for the strongest and weakest of our children (at three years of age). In a second treatment of our results we shall present data on top- and bottom-ranked children matched (to the degree possible) for SES.

For one-year-old starters, a rather remarkable finding surfaces. Children who turn out well at three years of age clearly begin to reveal their future success before they turn 15 months old. Conversely, the one-year-old starters weakest at three have apparently already fallen behind by 15 months. Considering the repeated finding that early testing begins to identify lasting educational deficits no sooner than at 15 to 18 months (see Schaefer and his references) this finding is both surprising and potentially quite useful. At 18-21 months the differences remain, though they appear to be somewhat smaller, not quite achieving statistical significance.

Data on our two-year-old starters at 24-27 months again show a difference favoring the children who are developing well, but again that difference is not as large as the difference at 18-21 months.

We do not have data for 24-27 months on the social competence of our one-year-old starters.

A reminder: Because of our scoring technique, these social competence scores can be compared only within a single age range. The fact that the scores for the entire group of one-year-olds are 13.8 and 22.2 does not imply that

---

*The credit for breadth of skills was not a part of our scoring procedure at the time of the writing of Volume I. We overlooked the necessity for this step until fairly recently. Appendix C contains the amended scoring instructions.

TABLE 4. Extreme Group Comparisons of Social Competence Scores (with Adults,[1] Unmatched SES

	Age (months)			
	12-15[2]		18-21	
Groups	Median	Range	Median	Range
1-Year-Old Starters (n = 19)	13.8	0.7-47.9	22.2	5.5-47.9
Most Competent (n = 8)	25.7**	12.6-47.9	24.0	9.3-33.7
Least Competent (n = 5)	8.5	6.4-17.5	15.4	5.5-47.9

	24-27	
Groups	Median	Range
2-Year-Old Starters (n = 20)	23.2	7.1-44.4
Most Competent (n = 7)	23.7	7.1-44.4
Least Competent (n = 5)	19.1	7.2-28.3

[1] These are weighted scores. See the Appendix C for details.
[2] A two-tailed test of significance was used since we had no reason to expect divergent scores at 12-15 months. All others are one-tailed tests.
**Mann-Whitney U $p \leq .01$

social competence has increased by 8.4 "units." Nor does the score of 22.2 for the 18-to-21 month group mean they are 1.0 "units" less able than the two-year-olds represented in the table.

Table 5 contains data* on the development of the individual social competencies we monitored as the children interacted with adults (usually their own mothers).

Those dimensions were:

AA—gaining attention in socially acceptable ways
R —using an adult as a resource after first determining the task was too difficult to do on his own
HA—expressing affection or mild annoyance when appropriate
RP —engaging in role play fantasy or make believe
PA —expressing pride in achievement

*These data have not been converted to weighted scores. Weighted scores allow comparisons of children with those in the same age group *only*. Unweighted scores allow comparisons (to a limited extent) across the four age periods sampled.

TABLE 5. Extreme Group Comparisons of Individual Social Competence Scores,[1] Unmatched SES

Age (months)	Groups	Dimensions of Social Competence									
		Gaining Attention		Using Adult as Resource		Expressing Hostility/Affection		Engaging in Role Play		Expressing Pride in Achievement	
		Median	Range	Median	Range	Median	Range	Median	Range	Median	Range
12-15[2]	1-Year-Old Starters (n = 19)	27.4*	11.0-49.8	16.8	4.0-36.8	19.7	3.0-77.0	1.0	1.0-2.0	2.0	2.0-10.0
	Most Competent (n = 8)	38.1**	24.1-49.8	25.1**	14.5-34.3	20.9	8.3-33.7	1.0	1.0-2.0	3.5	2.0-10.0
	Least Competent (n = 5)	19.8	11.0-27.8	12.8	8.0-20.3	23.5	9.8-77.0	1.0	0.0	2.0	0.0
18-21	1-Year-Old Starters (n = 19)	33.0	17.7-80.0	28.1	5.2-46.9	24.3	8.7-74.3	2.0	1.0-9.0	2.0	2.0-13.0
	Most Competent (n = 8)	38.1	28.1-53.4	34.2*	20.8-46.9	24.5	8.7-38.0	2.5	1.0-5.0	2.5	2.0-13.0
	Least Competent (n = 5)	23.8	17.7-80.0	23.6	5.2-38.4	33.2	17.3-74.3	1.0	1.0-9.0	2.0	2.0-8.0
24-27	2-Year-Old Starters (n = 20)	28.6	9.3-53.7	26.6	7.3-45.1	16.9	1.2-51.0	1.0	1.0-5.0	2.0	2.0-15.0
	Most Competent (n = 7)	26.5	9.3-53.7	25.0	18.0-31.7	11.0	1.2-22.0	1.0	1.0-5.0	3.0	2.0-15.0
	Least Competent (n = 5)	24.3	15.8-42.3	16.8	7.3-33.4	14.8	7.8-51.0	1.0	1.0-3.0	2.0	0.0

[1] These scores are unweighted. See the Appendix C for details.
[2] A two-tailed test of significance was used since we had no reason to expect divergent scores at 12-15 months. All others are one-tailed tests.
*Mann-Whitney U $p \leq .05$
**Mann-Whitney U $p \leq .01$

At 12-15 months children developing well are already ahead on *gaining attention, using an adult as a resource,* and *expressing pride in achievement.* They are no different from the other children in *expressing their emotions,* nor do they or any of the children *role play* much.

By 18-21 months, the picture has shifted. While still superior in *gaining attention* and *using an adult as a resource,* and still not different on *expressing emotions,* they seem to be beginning to show an edge in *role play behavior.*

With two-year-old starters at 24-27 months, differences that look meaningful are the greater tendency by the well-developing child *to use an adult as a resource* and *to express pride in achievement.*

Data on the tendency of our subjects to comply with requests are presented in Table 6. Well-developing children appear slightly more compliant than poorly developing children during the second year of life. At 18-21 months the difference is substantial ($p = .04$), reflecting (we believe) the easier transition through negativism of children developing well as compared with others.

A point worth remembering is that parents vary in the numbers of requests they make of their children even during infancy and toddlerhood. A good index of this adult tendency is contained in our task data under the heading of "to cooperate" experiences. At 18-21 months, for example, the parents of our

TABLE 6. **Extreme Group Comparisons on Compliance Tendencies (% Compliance), Unmatched SES**

	Age (months)			
	12-15[1]		18-21	
Groups	Median	Range	Median	Range
1-Year-Old Starters (n = 19)	63.0	37.5-88.9	69.7	41.0-94.7
Most Competent (n = 8)	72.0	44.4-88.0	72.0*	54.5-94.7
Least Competent (n = 5)	66.7	41.0-88.9	68.8	41.0-71.4
	24-27			
Groups	Median	Range		
2-Year-Old Starters (n = 20)	65.5	28.6-86.1		
Most Competent (n = 7)	75.0	28.6-86.0		
Least Competent (n = 5)	58.3	37.5-73.0		

[1] A two-tailed test of significance was used since we had no reason to expect divergent scores at 12-15 months. All others are one-tailed tests.
*Mann-Whitney U $p \leq .05$

well-developing children made considerably more requests of their children than did the parents of our poorly developing children. For more details, see later sections on patterns of experience.

The picture we see is of a remarkably early divergence in the development of social competence. A closer look points to two types of behavior as the clearest indicators of what is to come: *gaining attention in socially acceptable ways,* and *using an adult as a resource* (after first determining a task is too difficult to handle alone). The evidence shows that *role playing* and *expressing pride in achievement* surface somewhat later (after the first birthday) and that ease of emotional expression (*expressing affection or hostility*) is not a good early indicator of precocity or delay in social development. We believe the emergence and crystallization of social behaviors is both exciting to study and of fundamental significance in the forming of the personality of the child.

Receptive-Language Development:
Results and Discussion

Receptive-language development appears to be an extremely important process in regard to educational development. It goes without saying that the acquisition of language is fundamental to human competence. Less obvious but only slightly so is the central role of language in cognitive and social development. The former has been thoroughly documented by psychometricians over the years. Language ability correlates very highly with intellectual ability. As for social development, it seems clear to us that the shaping of a child's social attitudes and behaviors is largely accomplished through verbal stimulation, commentary, and control provided by significant adults during late infancy and toddlerhood.

It is now a routine finding that most children who do poorly at school first reveal developmental deficits toward the end of the second year of life (Schaefer, 1969; Halpern, 1969). The widely accepted interpretation is that language deficits are being revealed during that period for the first time. This judgment makes sense in the light of the timing of first language learning. The meaning of words is first understood some time around 7 or 8 months of age. By the age of one and a half years (after 10 or 11 months of potential learning), some children have acquired a substantial language capacity. Some 18-month-old children understand several dozen words, others even more than one hundred words. They also can cope with the many grammatical structures involved in simple linguistic messages. It is not at all unusual for such children, however, to speak very little. While some are quite verbal, many, if not most 18-month-old children, say only a few words and do not speak in long sentences.

Our procedures for assessing language development therefore focus on the growth of the *understanding* of language rather than on its production.

TABLE 7. **Extreme Group Comparisons on Receptive-Language Test Scores,[1] Unmatched SES**

		Age at Testing (in months)			
		13[2]	15	21½	25
1-Year-Old Starters (n = 19)	Median	14	16	21	36
	Range	10-21	10-24	10-42	10-51
Most Competent (n = 8)	Median	16	18	31.5**	37.5*
	Range	10-21	14-24	18-42	24-51
Least Competent (n = 5)	Median	12	16	18	18
	Range	10-16	10-21	10-27	10-40
		Age at Testing (in months)			
		25	27½	30½	
2-Year-Old Starters (n = 20)	Median	30	36	40.5	
	Range	18-42	18-54	18-51	
Most Competent (n = 7)	Median	36**	42**	51***	
	Range	24-42	36-54	42-51	
Least Competent (n = 5)	Median	18	27	27	
	Range	18-30	18-36	21-36	

[1] Scores are expressed in months.
[2] A two-tailed test was used here since we had no reason to expect divergent test scores at 13 months. All others are one-tailed tests.
*Mann-Whitney U p ≤ .05
**Mann-Whitney U p ≤ .01
***Mann-Whitney U p ≤ .001

In Volume I we described our assessment procedures in detail. Because of the importance of the topic and the general efficacy of our procedures we recommend their use. A warning, however: As usual, we have no suitable normative data. Our designations of developmental levels scored by subjects, though expressed as age levels, are only approximations. We believe they are not far from what would be found with a proper representative sample, but as yet no standardization has taken place.

Table 7 presents interim achievement data on our subjects. In general there are no surprises in these results. Our children who come to look remarkably different at three years of age look rather similar until sometime between 15 and 21½ months of age. From then on, the gap in achievement of language skills broadens steadily.

Sensing Dissonance: Results and Discussion

Highly competent three to six year old children are extraordinary observers. They note small discrepancies better than most children their age. These discrepancies can be in an immediately present scene such as an anomaly in a picture or a new piece of clothing worn by another child. They can exist in

TABLE 8. Extreme Group Comparisons on Dissonance Test Scores,[1] Unmatched SES

		Age at Testing (in months)				
		13[2]	15	21½	25	30½
1-Year-Old Starters	Median	1.0	2.0	3.0	3.5	5.0
(n = 19)	Range	0.0-3.0	0.0-4.0	0.0-8.0	2.0-8.0	2.0-8.0
Most Competent	Median	2.0	2.0	3.25	6.5**	7.5**
(n = 8)	Range	0.0-3.0	0.0-3.0	2.0-8.0	3.5-8.0	3.0-8.0
Least Competent	Median	0.0	1.0	2.0	3.5	3.5
(n = 5)	Range	0.0-2.0	0.0-3.5	0.0-5.0	2.0-3.5	2.0-5.0

		Age at Testing (in months)		
		25	27½	30½
2-Year-Old Starters	Median	3.0	3.0	6.0
(n = 7)	Range	0.0-7.0	2.0-8.0	0.0-8.0
Most Competent	Median	3.0	5.0**	7.0*
(n = 5)	Range	2.0-7.0	3.0-7.0	3.5-8.0
Least Competent	Median	3.0	2.0	3.5
(n = 5)	Range	2.0-4.0	2.0-4.0	2.0-7.0

[1] Scores are expressed in levels.

[2] A two-tailed test was used here since we had no reason to expect divergent test scores at 13 months. All others are one-tailed tests.

*Mann-Whitney U $p \leq .05$

**Mann-Whitney U $p \leq .01$

a temporal sequence as when a child goes out of turn in a game. Most subtly they may involve a logical inconsistency in a story told by another person. Our procedure for gauging a child's development in this area is somewhat weaker than we would like. It consists of two choice visual discrimination tasks with a wide range of difficulty (for details see Volume I). We were unable to devote the additional resources necessary to construct a more sophisticated instrument. Empirically, we found our brighter children getting bored with the test just before their second birthdays. (This was the only assessment procedure that was not interesting to most of our subjects throughout the study.)

Table 8 presents data on the development of our subjects' capacity to assess dissonance and on the statistical significance of group differences. The data are expressed in levels of achievement rather than by developmental ages. On this test we find the emergence of stable differences coming between 21½ and 25 months of age. Thereafter, well-developing children maintain a superiority, but the differences are nowhere near as striking as in the case of language development.

Abstract Thought: Results and Discussion

Our techniques for assessing the acquisition of abstract thinking had to focus on prerequisite abilities during the child's second year of life. The reason is simply that infants are not capable of significant higher mental activities. This is why Gesell labeled his infant test score the DQ rather than the IQ. It is why Piaget labeled infancy the period of sensorimotor intelligence. We, therefore, have used Uzgiris and Hunt's scale (1964) for the development of object permanence in testing infants. We used Meyers's cognitive items to test children during the third year of life (see White et al., 1973 for details). Recent findings (Wachs et al., 1967; Golden et al., 1971) suggest that sensorimotor intelligence including object permanence develops adequately across wide variations in early experience. It would appear that tasks of sensorimotor intelligence are not particularly sensitive indicators of good or poor early educational development. Whether we would have acted differently had we known these facts is unclear. At any rate our data on these abilities are presented in Table 9.

Again, developmental divergence becomes stable between 15 and 21½ months. The superiority of well-developing children is maintained; however, it is not as striking as in the case of language development.

TABLE 9. Extreme Group Comparisons on Abstract Abilities Test Scores,[1] Unmatched SES

		Age at Testing (in months)			
		13[2]	15	21½	25
1-Year-Old Starters (n = 19)	Median	2	2	5	6
	Range	<1-3	1-4	<5-7	<5-7
Most Competent (n = 8)	Median	2	2.5	6*	6.5
	Range	1-3	1-4	5-7	5-7
Least Competent (n = 5)	Median	1	1	5	<5
	Range	<1-2	1-3	<5-6	<5-7
		Age at Testing (in months)			
		25	27½	30½	
2-Year-Old Starters (n = 20)	Median	5.5	6	6.5	
	Range	<5-7	<5-7	<5-7	
Most Competent (n = 7)	Median	6*	7**	7**	
	Range	<5-7	6-7	7	
Least Competent (n = 5)	Median	<5	5	6	
	Range	<5-6	<5-6	<5-7	

[1] Scores are expressed in levels.
[2] A two-tailed test was used here since we had no reason to expect divergent test scores at 13 months. All others are one-tailed tests.
*Mann-Whitney U $p \leq .05$
**Mann-Whitney U $p \leq .01$

General Development: Results and Discussion*

We used the Bayley scales of development when our subjects were one and two years of age. Such a yardstick is useful for partial characterization of our sample. It allows other researchers and readers to place our population in relation to others. It also serves as a crude screening device. Children consistently scoring very low on such tests (less than 85), for example, should be considered delayed in light of recent research (Pasamanick et al., 1956). Furthermore, the Bayley Mental Index seems to be a respectable partial indicator of precocity in educational areas by the time children reach two years of age.

Table 10 presents the Bayley Mental Index scores for our children and the statistical data on group comparisons. At one year of age the score for the total group (median value, 103) is unremarkable.†

The group score for children who at three had developed well was slightly lower (106) than the score for children who looked weak at three years of age. This finding is consistent with the long-standing inability to predict IQ scores from DQ scores at one year of age (except in cases of DQ's lower than 85) (Hunt, 1961).

By two years of age, developmental divergence is very clear (125 vs. 94, $p = .002$). The group as a whole scored 112, reflecting the bias in our sample toward better-than-average developmental situations. It is of course also possible that two other factors—test sophistication and sensitization of our subjects' parents—contributed to the high scores. The likelihood of the mentioned inflation factors is further evidenced by the performance of our subjects who entered the study when they were two years old. In every instance, for the groups as a whole, for the top and bottom groups, the scores of our children who entered the study at age one exceed the scores of those who entered at age two (e.g., one-year-old starters at 24 months had a median score of 112; two-year-old starters at 24 months had a median score of 101; difference significant at .05 level). It is possible that the two groups are not from the same population—i.e., that our one-year-old starters are generally more able at two years than our two-year-old starters. In a study such as this, we cannot know for sure.

---

*In Volume I we combined tests of general and intellectual development. In this volume the format change requires separate treatment since our tests of intellectual development were not appropriate for the interim developmental period (12-33 months). Our first tests of intellectual functions (aside from tests of abstract thinking ability) are administered when the children turn three years of age (the Stanford-Binet) and will be reported in outcome data sections.

†One child scores well below our cutoff level (90) but we judged the score invalid; the child looked grossly normal, and we kept him in the study. Subsequently, he has turned out well. Indeed, although below average at age three, by five years of age he seems slightly above average (WPPSI score; 109).

TABLE 10. **Extreme Group Comparisons on the Bayley Scales of Infant Development,[1] Unmatched SES**

		Age at Testing (in months)	
		12[2]	24
1-Year-Old Starters (n = 19)	Median	103	112
	Range	<94-134	66-143
Most Competent (n = 8)	Median	106.5	125*
	Range	100-134	106-143
Least Competent (n = 5)	Median	109	94
	Range	<94-134	66-112
		Age at Testing (in months)	
		24	
2-Year-Old Starters (n = 20)	Median	101	
	Range	69-140	
Most Competent (n = 7)	Median	109**	
	Range	102-140	
Least Competent (n = 5)	Median	84	
	Range	69-94	

[1] Scores are based on performance on the Mental Scale.

[2] A two-tailed test was used here since we had no reason to expect divergent test scores at 13 months. All others are one-tailed tests.

*Mann-Whitney U $p \leq .01$

**Mann-Whitney U $p \leq .001$

General Discussion

Consistently our findings reinforce older research in regard to the emergence of lasting developmental divergence. Scores at about one year of age on several aspects of competence including the Bayley Mental Index do not predict performance at three years of age. The one exception is in the area of social competence. Data gathered during the 12-15-month observation period seem to show that social skills are the earliest useful area in the identification of lasting precocity or delay in our children. Overall social competence with adults, and, in particular, getting and holding their attention in socially acceptable ways, using them as resources (after first determining that a task is too difficult), and expressing pride in achievement (usually a motor achievement at this age) are all better developed before 15 months of age in our subjects who gain the highest levels of competence by three years of age.

Between 14½ and 25 months of age, significant differences emerge in all the other measured areas: language, abstract-thinking ability, sensing dissonance, and the broad range of processes the Bayley Mental Index samples.

PRIMARY OUTCOME DATA (UNMATCHED GROUPS)

Our early work convinced us that three years of age was a very special point in development. We concluded that three-year-olds developing very well had acquired the general pattern of competencies of high-achieving six-year-olds. Development between three and six years of age for such children seemed to consist of refinement of an effective style rather than the emergence of new and different skills. Conversely, the three-year-olds doing poorly seemed to resemble the four-, five-, and six-year-olds who were doing poorly in their general coping styles.

The educational experiments of the last decade—Head Start, Parent-Child Centers, infant tutorial programs, etc.—reinforce the view that by three years of age lasting precocity or delay is usually established if it is going to exist. Older research (Hunt, 1961), especially the large longitudinal studies, reported the first reliable predictive validity of general and intellectual scores at about three years also.

Our design, therefore, featured monitoring of child-rearing practices, children's experiences, and their development between the first and third birthdays.

We considered achievement levels at three years of age to be reasonably stable indicators of where a child was headed (even though the Berkeley Growth Study and the Guidance Study found predictive correlations of only +.5 to +.6 for IQ scores at three years to similar scores at sixteen years).

We knew we could not perfectly predict what a one- or two-year-old would achieve by his third birthday. We selected families whose older children had done either very well or very poorly to heighten the likelihood that our subjects would do similarly. We needed prospective data on the processes of very good or poor development. We had to wait until each child reached three years of age and was tested before we could judge the usefulness of data gathered on the child as he grew.

Predicted vs. Achieved Competence Levels at Three Years of Age

Table 11 shows the relationship of predicted to actual development at three years of age. Later we will present some data on the subjects' development at five years of age.

The procedure for determining the rankings is described below:

Social Competence Rankings. The social competence (with adults) scores were calculated and ranked. Each subject's score represented his facility in each of the five social competencies and an added value was given if a

TABLE 11. Predicted vs. Achieved Competence Levels at Three Years of Age

Sub. ID	Age at Entry to Study	SES	Predicted Development: A (good), C (poor)	Bayley Mental Index Score* 12 Months	Bayley Mental Index Score* 24 Months	Overall Rank at Three Years**	Stanford-Binet Score at Three Years
20	1	II	A	134	132	1	142
8	1	II	A	106	123	2	139
17	1	I	A	100	137	3	139
24	1	I	A	107	116	4	118
3	1	I	A	102	143	5	139
9	2	I	A		109	7	139
16	1	III	A	102	127	7	127
40	1	IV	C	122	106	7	110
22	2	III	A		140	9	134
11	1	II	A	119	119	10.5	144
2	2	II	A		137	10.5	132
39	2	III	A		104	12	108
35	2	III	A		104	13	132
21	2	I	A		111	14	131
12	2	I	A		102	15	122
41	1	V	C	98	91	16	76
43	1	III	C	97	109	17	93
18	2	III	A		100	18	105
19	1	I	A	102	127	19	120
32	1	III	A	94	108	20.5	93
38	2	III	A		94	20.5	95
5	2	I	A		97	22	127
31	1	II	A	112	108	23	118
44	1	III	A	103	132	24	113
36	2	III	A		119	25	90
37	1	V	C	50	84	26.5	64
13	2	I	A		102	26.5	118
10	2	I	A		106	28	127
33	2	I	C		89	29	120
14	2	IV	C		86	30	81
42	1	III	C	103	94	31	98
25	2	IV	C		84	32	117
1	1	IV	C	134	112	33	108
28	2	III	C		94	34.5	88
30	2	III	C		77	34.5	81
34	1	IV	C	109	66	36	<57
45	1	III	A	125	96	37	76
27	2	III	C		88	38	88
7	2	IV	C		69	39	74

*The Bayley was administered to each child at the age of entry to the study. It was repeated at 24 months to those children who entered the study at 12 months.

**
1 = Highest achievement
39 = Lowest achievement

subject showed several or all of the competencies. The resultant indices were then ranked.

Nonsocial Competence Rankings. For each child, his scores for language, abstract thinking, and sensing dissonance were individually ranked. The average of those three ranks was calculated. Each child's Stanford-Binet score was ranked with the others. The nonsocial competence rank was the average of the Binet score rank and the average rank of the three other tests. The Binet score was therefore given three times the weight of each of the shorter tests of language, abstract thinking, and sensing of dissonance.

Overall Competence Rankings. The overall competence rank was produced by taking the average of the social and nonsocial competence ranking for each subject and ranking it with those of all the other children.

Subjects #40, 41, and 43 achieved considerably higher levels of general competence than we predicted. It should be noted that subjects #41 and 43 were much more competent socially than nonsocially (Binet scores were 76 and 93, respectively).

Subjects #36, 13, 10, and 45 looked less well developed at three years than we had predicted. Again, it should be noted that subjects #13 and 10 did well enough on the Binet (118 and 127, respectively).

Subject #44 seems to be marginal as far as our predictions were concerned. The Binet score was 113, and the overall rank was 24 of 39.

In summary, we were reasonably accurate in 31 of 39 cases, wrong in 7, and borderline in 1. Contrast this performance with expectations from Bayley Mental Index scores on these children at one and two years of age (see Table 11). For children entering the project at one year of age, Bayley Mental Index scores predicted their standings on overall competence reasonably well in 7 of 19 instances, incorrectly 11 times, and partially in 1 case. This finding supports the long-held notion that tests of general development at one year of age tell little about how a child will test at three years of age. The Bayley, therefore, was considerably poorer in predicting overall competence than the Preschool Project's reliance, primarily, on the older sibling's achievements (31 accurate, 7 incorrect, and 1 borderline case).

Bayley Mental Index scores at two years of age predicted overall competence at three years correctly 22 times, incorrectly 13 times, and partially 4 times. This greater predictive power is again to be expected in the light of previous research.

Can Binet scores at three years of age be predicted from the general achievement levels of older siblings? We were accurate in 28 cases, inaccurate in 10, and partly accurate in 1 case.

From Bayley Mental Index scores at one year of age there was no ability to predict Binet scores at three years of age (8 accurate, 8 inaccurate, and 3 borderline).

From Bayley Mental Index scores at two years of age, prediction was better: 25 accurate, 11 inaccurate, and 3 borderline cases.

In general our predictions from the first or second birthday to competence levels at the third birthday were fairly good.

Perhaps our most understandable error was in predicting poor development in children from upper SES families. Two such children did very well on the Stanford-Binet at three years of age. Both did poorly on tests of social competence, but such children cannot be classified as uniformly poorly developed. In retrospect we may have engaged in wishful thinking in such cases. We tried to select subjects so as to include families with very modest resources raising very competent children and others with many resources raising less-competent children. We succeeded rather well in the former case, not so well in the latter.

Social Competence: Results and Discussion

Table 12 presents social competence (with adults) data on the various groups of children in the study gathered when they were 30-33 months of age in five, thirty-minute observation sessions. It is quite clear that the gap in achievement level between our most and least competent children is very wide. A reminder is in order, however: We are limited in our ability to interpret this difference because of our primitive knowledge of how to measure social competence. We do not know where our least competent 30-33-month-olds are in respect to the entire population of children that age. Our Bayley and Binet scores on our subjects suggest something about their ability levels, but since the correlation between social competence and such scores is not known, we must remain, for the time being, cautious about interpreting the numerical

TABLE 12. Extreme Group Comparisons on Social Competence (with Adults),[1] Unmatched SES

Age (months)	30-33	
Groups	Median	Range
1-Year-Old Starters (n = 19)	26.0	3.0-45.7
Most Competent (n = 8)	33.1*	14.2-45.7
Least Competent (n = 5)	8.3	3.0-32.0
2-Year-Old Starters (n = 20)	24.0	2.3-45.7
Most Competent (n = 7)	25.0**	21.5-45.7
Least Competent (n = 5)	13.9	2.3-17.4

[1] Weighted scores.

*Mann-Whitney U p ≤ .01

**Mann-Whitney U p ≤ .001

TABLE 13. Extreme Group Comparison on Individual Social Competence Scores,[1] Unmatched SES

	30-33 Months									
	Dimensions of Social Competence									
	Gaining Attention		Using Adult as Resource		Expressing Hostility/Affection		Engaging in Role Play		Expressing Pride in Achievement	
Groups	Median	Range	Median	Range	Median	Range	Median	Range	Median	Range
1-Year-Old Starters (n = 19)	42.1	12.0-75.0	32.0	13.0-72.3	19.7	4.3-77.2	3.0	1.0-13.0	4.0	2.0-18.7
Most Competent (n = 8)	53.0	37.6-68.6	57.0***	30.9-72.3	22.3	17.0-47.1	5.0*	2.0-13.0	5.0	5.0-18.7
Least Competent (n = 5)	42.4	12.0-55.3	14.0	13.0-23.2	16.0	11.0-58.0	2.0	1.0-3.0	2.0	2.0-7.0
2-Year-Old Starters (n = 20)	29.2	8.3-59.0	29.9	6.9-79.0	15.2	3.0-42.0	1.0	1.0-13.0	4.0	2.0-7.0
Most Competent (n = 7)	37.1**	26.8-55.6	30.8	8.0-46.5	20.0	10.3-33.8	2.0	1.0-13.0	5.0	2.0-7.0
Least Competent (n = 5)	18.1	8.3-27.8	17.5	6.9-35.1	11.6	3.0-42.0	1.0	0.0	2.0	2.0-6.0

[1] Unweighted scores.
*Mann-Whitney U p ≤ .05
**Mann-Whitney U p ≤ .01
***Mann-Whitney U p ≤ .001

aspects in social competence data. On a subjective basis it is abundantly clear that all groups of our highly competent children are far more skillful in social encounters than our least able children.

Table 13 presents data on the five individual social competencies (with adults) for the same subjects at 30-33 months of age. For our strongest and weakest one-year-old starters two of the five differences reach significance and one approaches significance: using an adult as a resource ($p = .001$), role playing ($p = .02$), and expressing pride in achievement ($p = .08$). For our strongest and weakest two-year-old starters only one social competency—gaining and holding attention ($p = .005$)—reaches significance. Three others approach significance: using an adult as a resource ($p = .09$), role playing ($p = .06$), and expressing pride in achievement ($p = .06$). In none of the comparisons does expressing affection and hostility discriminate between groups.

Table 14 presents data on the tendency of our subjects to comply with simple requests (almost invariably from their mothers). In each case the more competent children were more compliant, but the group differences were not large enough to reach statistical significance. Recall that our two-year-old starters who developed very well were significantly more compliant during the 24-27-month age span than our less well-developed two-year-old starters.

Receptive Language Development: Results and Discussion

Table 15 presents data on language achievement. Scores are expressed in months, but again the reader is reminded that we have no normative data

TABLE 14. Extreme Group Comparisons of Compliance Tendencies (% compliance) Unmatched SES

Groups	30-33 Months	
	Median	Range
1-Year-Old Starters (n = 19)	67.7	41.0-93.0
Most Competent (n = 8)	77.3*	54.5-93.0
Least Competent (n = 5)	67.7	54.5-81.0
2-Year Old Starters (n = 20)	65.5	28.6-93.0
Most Competent (n = 7)	70.6	52.4-93.0
Least Competent (n = 5)	67.7	52.4-93.0

*Mann-Whitney U $p \leq .05$

TABLE 15. Primary Outcome Data (36 Months):
Extreme Group Comparisons of Receptive-
Language Test Scores,[1] Unmatched SES

Group	Group Median	Range
1-Year-Old Starters (n = 19)	45	16-60
Most Competent (n = 8)	55.5***	45-60
Least Competent (n = 5)	36	16-42
2-Year-Old Starters (n = 20)	48	33-60
Most Competent (n = 7)	54**	48-60
Least Competent (n = 5)	39	33-51

[1] Scores on Preschool Project Receptive-Language Test are expressed in months.

*Mann-Whitney U p ≤ .05
**Mann-Whitney U p ≤ .01
***Mann-Whitney U p ≤ .001

for this test. Our guess is that our working norms probably err on the high side to some extent. Our three weakest subjects, who scored well below 90 on the Binet at three years, were slightly above three years on the Preschool Project language tests. Our more competent children had more consistent Binet and language test scores (see Table 18, page 47).

The difference in language achievement of our most and least competent children at three years was predictably marked. This is, after all, what would be expected from groups of children three to four standard deviations apart on Binet scores. Yet these same children looked (as groups) pretty much alike developmentally at one year of age (Bayley Mental Index median scores were 109 for the bottom five vs. 106.5 for the top eight).

Sensing Dissonance: Results and Discussion

Table 16 presents data on the development of the capacity to sense dissonance. Again, we find significant differences, although not as large as in the area of language. The reader is reminded that our testing staff believes this test is less suitable for able children over two years of age than for those between one and two years. Able children seem to find the procedures somewhat boring once they reach two years of age.

Table 17 presents data on the development of abstract thinking ability. These data are not entirely independent of our Binet data because for our

TABLE 16. Primary Outcome Data (36 Months):
Extreme Group Comparisons of
Dissonance Test Scores,[1] Unmatched SES

Group	Group Median	Range
1-Year-Old Starters (n = 19)	8.0	4.0-8.0
Most Competent (n = 8)	8.0**	8.0
Least Competent (n = 5)	7.0	4.0-8.0
2-Year-Old Starters (n = 20)	7.5	2.0-8.0
Most Competent (n = 7)	8.0*	7.2-8.0
Least Competent (n = 5)	4.0	3.5-8.0

[1] Scores on Preschool Project Dissonance Test are expressed in levels.

*Mann-Whitney U $p \leq .05$
**Mann-Whitney U $p \leq .01$

TABLE 17. Primary Outcome Data (36 Months): Extreme
Group Comparisons and Statistical Analyses
of Abstract Ability Test Scores[1],
Unmatched SES

Group	Group Median	Range
1-Year-Old Starters (n = 19)	9.0	5.0-12.0
Most Competent (n = 8)	11.0*	9.0-12.0
Least Competent (n = 5)	8.0	5.0-9.0
2-Year-Old Starters (n = 20)	9.5	6.0-11.0
Most Competent (n = 7)	11.0**	9.0-11.0
Least Competent (n = 5)	7.0	6.0-8.0

[1] Scores on Preschool Project Abstract Abilities Test are expressed in levels.

*Mann-Whitney U $p \leq .01$
**Mann-Whitney U $p \leq .001$

TABLE 18. Primary Outcome Data (36 Months): Extreme Group Comparisons and Statistical Analyses of Stanford-Binet Intelligence Scales Scores Unmatched SES

Group	Group Median	Range
1-Year-Old Starters (n = 19)	113	57-144
Most Competent (n = 8)	139**	110-144
Least Competent (n = 5)	76	57-108
2-Year-Old Starters (n = 20)	117.5	74-139
Most Competent (n = 7)	132*	108-139
Least Competent (n = 5)	88	74-117

*Mann-Whitney U $p \leq .01$

**Mann-Whitney U $p \leq .001$

strongest three-year-olds we provided selected Binet items to assure an adequate ceiling. Recall that the ability to think abstractly emerges during the first years of life. We therefore tested for probable precursor abilities (object permanence items) in early developmental stages, shifted to pattern completion (C. E. Meyers) items later, and then to Binet items for those who passed all the Meyers items.

As expected, group differences here are quite large.

Intellectual Development: Results and Discussion

The most conservative choice for a test of intellectual ability for three-year-old children seemed to be the recently revised Stanford-Binet. Table 18 presents data on Binet performance by our subjects at three years of age. The bias in our sample toward higher competence levels is apparent in the total group scores: range, 57-144; median, 117. Again, note that the scores for one-year-old starters ranged from < 94[*] to 144 within a median value of 113. Our most competent three-year-olds scored well above the ninety-fifth percentile, while our weakest scored below the twenty-fifth percentile. Such differences are, of course, highly significant statistically. Bear in mind, we did nothing to *cause* such differences, but rather our task was to select families to study where such

[*] One child had an obviously low score, but the test results were considered only partly valid.

differences would *emerge* in the natural course of events. In this important sense we were quite successful.

General Discussion

It seems clear that our most competent children at three years of age were markedly more able than our least competent three-year-olds in just about every dimension of ability we measured. Such was not the case when our children were one year old. Although there were individual differences in abilities among our children, as indeed there are at *all* ages in *all* children, one could not predict the huge differences that emerged by three years of age from their behaviors at age one. The only possible execption to that statement is in our social competence data. *Gaining attention in socially acceptable ways, using an adult as a resource* after first determining the task is too difficult, and *expressing pride in achievement* were already more developed as social skills in our subjects who later would do very well as contrasted with those who would fall behind. If such early signs of developmental divergence are reliable, the finding would have both heuristic and practical value. From what we know about the process of development of infants, the finding makes good sense, but the reader is reminded that many replications are needed in order for it to be considered firm.

INTERIM ACHIEVEMENT DATA (PARTIALLY MATCHED GROUPS)

The subjects of this study came from the full range of socioeconomic backgrounds found in eastern Massachusetts. On the Hollingshead and Redlich scale these families were classed from Class I to V, with Class I the most advantaged in terms of income, educational level, type of work, and type of housing. We sought to balance the expected bias toward better development from higher SES families by studying some lower SES families whose children do very well and some higher SES families whose children do rather poorly. We were fairly successful in regard to the former goal and not very successful in regard to the latter. We were able to find upper SES families whose older children were judged to be generally less competent than their peers, but unlike lower SES families with poorly developing children, higher SES families with such children tended to avoid participation in our study. We told none of the families that we wanted to study their children because of the families' child-rearing successes or failures. We merely expressed an interest in the age range (one to three years) and in natural conditions. This interest has been sufficient as a justification for our overtures with nearly every family we have ever approached.

The best matching of children we could accomplish, given our population, is shown in Tables 19 and 20.

TABLE 19. Subject Characteristics of Extreme Groups of One-Year-Old Starters, Unmatched and Partially Matched for SES

	Unmatched			Partially Matched			
	Sub. Number	SES* Ranking	Sex	Sub. Number	Rank Among All Subjects for Group	SES* Ranking	Sex
Most Competent	20	II	F	20	1	II	F
	08	II	M	08	2	II	M
	17	I	F	16	6	III	M
	24	I	M	40	7	IV	F
	03	I	F	11	8	II	F
	16	III	M				
	40	IV	F				
	11	II	F				
Least Competent	37	V	M	31	13	II	M
	42	III	M	44	14	III	F
	01	IV	F	42	16	III	M
	34	IV	M	01	17	IV	F
	45	III	F	45	19	III	F

*Hollingshead-Redlich Scale.

TABLE 20. Subject Characteristics of Extreme Groups of Two-Year-Old Starters, Unmatched and Partially Matched for SES

	Unmatched			Partially Matched			
	Sub. Number	SES* Ranking	Sex	Sub. Number	Rank Among All Subjects for Group	SES* Ranking	Sex
Most Competent	09	I	F	22	2	III	F
	22	III	F	02	3	II	M
	02	II	M	39	4	III	M
	39	III	M	35	5	III	F
	35	III	F	18	8	III	F
	21	I	M				
	12	I	M				
Least Competent	25	IV	M	25	16	IV	M
	28	III	F	28	17.5	III	F
	30	III	F	30	17.5	III	F
	27	III	M	27	19	III	M
	07	IV	M	07	20	IV	M

*Hollingshead-Redlich Scale.

Social Competence: Results and Discussion

Table 21 presents data on the social competence of our subjects at 12-15, 18-21, and 24-27 months of age. Strongest and weakest three-year-olds, partially matched for SES, are compared. The general pattern of findings is very much like those when unmatched contrasting groups were compared. Differences are present at all times; they always favor the children who turn out best at three years; the difference is significant at 12-15 months and not significant at the later ages. Since our strongest children in these comparisons of partially matched subjects are slightly less competent at three years of age than our strongest children in the total sample, such findings seem reasonable.

Table 22 presents interim data on the development of individual social competencies with adults. Again we find *getting and holding attention* and *use of an adult as a resource* distinguishing the comparison groups at 12-15 months of age. No other differences reach significance in these data, although the trends always favor our stronger children. In general the pattern parallels that seen with unmatched comparison groups; however, the differences are slightly smaller.

TABLE 21. Extreme Group Comparisons of Social Competence Scores (with Adults),[1] Partially Matched for SES

	Age (months)			
	12-15		18-21	
Groups	Median	Range	Median	Range
1-Year-Old Starters (n = 19)	13.8	0.7-47.9	22.2	5.5-47.9
Most Competent (n = 5)	22.1[2]	12.6-45.9	24.4	9.3-32.4
Least Competent (n = 5)	6.6	4.5-13.8	20.1	5.5-47.9
	24-27			
Groups	Median	Range		
2-Year-Old Starters (n = 20)	23.2	7.1-44.4		
Most Competent (n = 5)	27.7	8.7-44.4		
Least Competent (n = 5)	19.1	7.2-28.3		

[1] These are weighted scores. See Appendix B for details.
[2] A two-tailed test of significance was used since we had no reason to expect divergent scores at 12-15 months. All others are one-tailed tests.

TABLE 22. Extreme Group Comparisons of Individual Social Competence Scores,[1] Partially Matched for SES

Age (months)	Groups	Dimensions of Social Competence									
		Gaining Attention		Using Adult as Resource		Expressing Hostility/Affection		Engaging in Role Play		Expressing Pride in Achievement	
		Median	Range	Median	Range	Median	Range	Median	Range	Median	Range
12-15	1-Year-Old Starters (n = 19)	27.4	11.0-49.8	16.8	4.0-36.8	19.7	3.0-77.0	1.0	1.0-2.0	2.0	2.0-10.0
	Most Competent (n = 5)	34.6*	24.1-43.9	31.8*	16.8-34.3	14.8	8.3-29.8	1.0	1.0-2.0	3.0	2.0-6.0
	Least Competent (n = 5)	20.0	11.0-27.8	12.8	11.9-20.3	14.0	9.8-23.5	1.0	0.0	2.0	0.0
18-21	1-Year-Old Starters (n = 19)	33.0	17.7-80.0	28.1	5.2-46.9	24.3	8.7-74.3	2.0	1.0-9.0	2.0	2.0-13.0
	Most Competent (n = 5)	43.3	30.4-55.5	31.7	20.8-46.9	22.4	8.7-38.0	1.0	1.0-4.3	2.0	2.0-13.0
	Least Competent (n = 5)	52.4	20.7-80.0	23.9	5.2-38.4	19.9	17.0-38.0	4.0	1.0-9.0	2.0	2.0-8.0
24-27	2-Year-Old Starters (n = 20)	28.6	9.3-53.7	26.6	7.3-45.1	16.9	1.2-51.0	1.0	1.0-5.0	2.0	2.0-15.0
	Most Competent (n = 5)	28.8	23.9-53.7	29.8	23.9-30.9	19.0	1.2-28.0	1.0	1.0-5.0	3.0	2.0-15.0
	Least Competent (n = 5)	24.3	15.8-42.3	16.8	7.3-33.4	14.8	7.8-51.0	1.0	1.0-3.0	2.0	0.0

[1] These scores are unweighted. See Appendix B for details.
*Mann-Whitney U $p \leq .05$

TABLE 23. Extreme Group Comparisons on Compliance Tendencies (% Compliance), Partially Matched for SES

Groups	Age (months)			
	12-15[1]		18-21	
	Median	Range	Median	Range
1-Year-Old Starters (n = 19)	63.0	37.5-88.9	69.7	41.2-94.7
Most Competent (n = 5)	56.5	44.4-88.0	72.2	63.0-94.7
Least Competent (n = 5)	54.5	41.2-76.7	68.8	58.3-73.0

Groups	24-27	
	Median	Range
2-Year-Old Starters (n = 20)	65.5	28.6-86.1
Most Competent (n = 5)	75.0*	50.0-86.1
Least Competent (n = 5)	58.3	37.5-73.0

[1] A two-tailed test of significance was used since we had no reason to expect divergent scores at 12-15 months. All others are one-tailed tests.
*Mann-Whitney U $p \leq .05$

Table 23 presents data on the tendency of these children to comply with simple requests. The pattern is very much as seen in earlier comparisons between nonmatched groups. Children more competent at three years of age are more compliant between 12 and 27 months of age. The difference is statistically significant only at 24-27 months, reinforcing the finding that more competent children are easier to live with near their second birthdays.

The general picture of the growth of social competence when our comparison groups are matched (partially) for SES is very much like what was seen with our unmatched groups. *Gaining attention in socially acceptable ways* and *using an adult as a resource* once again are apparently the earliest and clearest indicators of later achievement levels. Other differences, especially after the 12-15-month period are smaller, except for the greater compliance tendencies seen at 24-27 months.

Receptive-Language Development: Results and Discussion

Table 24 presents group performance and statistical significance data on interim receptive-language development for partially matched groups. The overall pattern consistently favors the groups who become highly competent

TABLE 24. Interim Data: Extreme Group Comparisons on Receptive-Language Test Scores,[1] Partially Matched SES

		Age at Testing (in months)			
		13[2]	15	21½	25
1-Year-Old Starters	Median	14	16	21	36
(n = 19)	Range	10-21	10-24	10-42	10-51
Most Competent	Median	18*	21	36*	39
(n = 5)	Range	16-21	16-24	18-42	24-42
Least Competent	Median	14	16	18	24
(n = 5)	Range	12-16	16-21	18-27	18-40

		Age at Testing (in months)		
		25	27½	30½
2-Year-Old Starters	Median	30	36	40.5
(n = 20)	Range	18-42	18-54	18-51
Most Competent	Median	36	42*	45
(n = 5)	Range	18-42	27-54	18-51
Least Competent	Median	30	36	40.5
(n = 5)	Range	18-42	18-54	18-51

[1] Scores on Preschool Project Receptive-Language Test are expressed in months.

[2] A two-tailed test was used here since we had no reason to expect divergent test scores at 13 months. All others are one-tailed tests.

*Mann-Whitney U $p \leq .05$

at three years of age. However, there are some differences from the comparison data on unmatched children. Our unmatched groups showed a very simple, standard pattern: no differences at the outset (12-15 months), gradual divergence which became significant at 21½ months, then steady increases in divergence over the following year. With partially matched groups, however, we found divergence present at the outset, less striking at 25 months, and even less so at 27½ and 30½ months. None of these differences is contrary to general expectations, but they do diverge from the classical pattern to an extent worth noting. We have no idea why this pattern occurred.

Sensing Dissonance: Results and Discussion

Table 25 presents interim data on sensing dissonance for partially matched groups. As was the case with unmatched groups, differences between groups were less striking for this ability than for social competencies and language. Indeed, although competent children consistently did better than those developing less well, the differences often failed to reach statistical significance. Once again such results were not unexpected in view of the differences in the groups being compared and the previous comparisons.

TABLE 25. Interim Data: Extreme Group Comparisons on Dissonance Test Scores,[1] Partially Matched for SES

		Age at Testing (in months)				
		13[2]	15	21½	25	30½
1-Year-Old Starters (n = 19)	Median	1.0	2.0	3.0	3.5	5.0
	Range	0.0-3.0	0.0-4.0	0.0-8.0	2.0-8.0	2.0-8.0
Most Competent (n = 5)	Median	2.0	2.0	3.0	7.0*	7.0
	Range	2.0-3.0	0.0-3.0	3.0-4.0	4.0-8.0	3.0-8.0
Least Competent (n = 5)	Median	1.0	3.0	3.5	3.5	3.5
	Range	0.0-2.0	1.0-3.0	2.0-5.0	2.0-7.0	3.5-5.0

		Age at Testing (in months)		
		25	27½	30½
2-Year-Old Starters (n = 20)	Median	3.0	3.0	6.0
	Range	0.0-7.0	2.0-8.0	0.0-8.0
Most Competent (n = 5)	Median	3.5	5.0*	7.0
	Range	2.0-4.0	3.0-7.0	0.0-8.0
Least Competent (n = 5)	Median	3.0	2.0	3.0
	Range	2.0-4.0	2.0-4.0	2.0-7.0

[1] Scores on Preschool Project Dissonance Test are expressed in levels.
[2] A two-tailed test was used here since we had no reason to expect divergent test scores at 13 months. All others are one-tailed tests.
*Mann-Whitney U $p \leq .05$

TABLE 26. Interim Data: Extreme Group Comparisons on Abstract Ability Test Scores[1] Partially Matched for SES

		Age at Testing (in months)			
		13[2]	15	21½	25
1-Year-Old Starters (n = 19)	Median	2	2	5	5
	Range	<1-3	1-4	<5-7	<5-7
Most Competent (n = 5)	Median	2	2	6*	7
	Range	1-3	1-4	5-7	5-7
Least Competent (n = 5)	Median	2	3	<5	<5
	Range	1-3	1-3	<5-6	<5-7

		Age at Testing (in months)		
		25	27½	30½
2-Year-Old Starters (n = 20)	Median	5.5	6	6.5
	Range	<5-7	<5-7	<5-7
Most Competent (n = 5)	Median	6	7*	7
	Range	<5-7	6-7	5-7
Least Competent (n = 5)	Median	<5	5	6
	Range	<5-6	<5-6	<5-7

[1] Scores on Preschool Project Abstract Abilities Test are expressed in levels.
[2] A two-tailed test was used here since we had no reason to expect divergent test scores at 13 months. All others are one-tailed tests.
*Mann-Whitney U $p \leq .05$

Abstract Thought: Results and Discussion

Table 26 presents our findings for interim achievement in abstract ability for partially matched groups. Here the pattern is similar to that found with unmatched groups, although once again the differences are not as great. Divergence appears between 15 and 21½ months, but its degree subsequently is somewhat smaller than was the case with unmatched groups.

General Development: Results and Discussion

Table 27 presents Bayley Mental Index data for our partially matched groups. These data once more crudely conform to those for unmatched groups, but there are notable differences. At one year of age, these groups scored somewhat better than our previously compared groups (median scores, 119 and 112 vs. 106.5 and 109). At two years of age, our one-year-old starters had moved in expected directions (top five from 119 to 123, bottom five from 112 to 108), but the difference was not statistically significant. On the other hand, the differences between groups of two-year-old partially matched starters looked like those found between two-year-old unmatched starters (median scores, 104 and 84 vs. 107 and 84). Again this difference was highly significant.

TABLE 27. Interim Data: Extreme Group Comparisons on the Bayley Scales of Infant Development,[1] Partially Matched for SES

		Age at Testing (in months)	
		12[2]	24
1-Year-Old Starters (n = 19)	Median	103	112
	Range	<94-134	66-143
Most Competent (n = 5)	Median	119	123
	Range	102-134	106-132
Least Competent (n = 5)	Median	112	108
	Range	103-132	94-132
		Age at Testing (in months) 24	
2-Year-Old Starters (n = 20)	Median	101	
	Range	69-140	
Most Competent (n = 5)	Median	104**	
	Range	100-140	
Least Competent (n = 5)	Median	84	
	Range	69-94	

[1] Scores are based on performance on the mental scale.

[2] A two-tailed test was used here since we had no reason to expect divergent test scores at 12 months. All others are one-tailed tests.

**Mann-Whitney U p ≤ .01

General Discussion

Our most competent three-year-old children were from higher SES levels than our very weakest three-year-olds. Tables 19 and 20 show relationships between unmatched and partially matched comparison groups with respect to SES and sex for each starting age.

It is quite clear that our very strongest three-year-olds were from the highest SES levels and our very weakest three-year-olds were from lower SES levels. In attempting to match groups of high and low achievers, we found we could maintain wide differences between groups in achieved competence at three years provided those children were mostly from SES Class III. We repeatedly noted, however, smaller differences between comparison groups when SES differences were minimized. In our population, as in most studied, SES apparently made a difference. Indeed, we and others probably would not believe data that indicated otherwise.

Another way of estimating the relative effect of SES on achieved competence of our subjects is indicated in the correlation data of Table 28.

Although competence is clearly linked to SES, it is just as clear that SES accounts for only a modest proportion of the variance. In other words, highly competent children can come from lower SES levels (at least from Classes III and IV), and children with low competence can come from the higher SES levels. It is also clear that SES relates more to nonsocial (language, intelligence, etc.) than to social competence. Comparisons of extreme groups partially matched for SES, as comparisons with unmatched, revealed developmental divergence during the second year of life, although the findings were less regular and the differences between groups generally smaller. Two exceptions are worth noting: First, the partially matched SES group comparisons confirmed the repeated finding that social competence differences were already present

TABLE 28. Relationships Among Major Demographic Variables and Achieved Levels of Competence by Spearman Rank Correlation (n = 39)

	Overall Rank	Social Rank[1]	Nonsocial Rank[2]
Hollingshead-Redlich SES	.43*	.00	.55**
Income	.16	−.15	.28
Mother's Education	.59**	.27	.77**
Father's Education	.46*	.08	.75**
Mother's Occupation[3]	.11	−.10	.20
Father's Occupation	.44*	.05	.71**

[1] Rank with respect to social skills.
[2] Rank with respect to nonsocial skills—i.e., linguistic and intellectual skills
[3] Only ten of the thirty-nine mothers of the study were employed.
*$p \leq .01$
**$p \leq .001$

at 12-15 months and that language ability differences were also present at 13 months. At 12-15 months the specific social skills that discriminate best are *getting and holding attention in socially acceptable ways* and *using an adult as a resource* after determining the task is too difficult. Unlike the unmatched groups, *expressing pride in achievement* did not discriminate between partially matched groups. Second, differences in language ability were evident at 13 months in the partially matched SES comparison.

PRIMARY OUTCOME DATA (PARTIALLY MATCHED GROUPS AT 36 MONTHS OF AGE)

Our strongest three-year-olds were all one-year-old starters from SES Classes I and II. Our weakest were two one-year-old starters and three two-year-old starters, three from Class III and two from Class IV. The matching process worked out rather well (see Tables 11, 19, and 20) in that for the three sets of groups we had two single level mismatches with one-year-old starters, two single level mismatches with our two-year-old starters, and none with our total population comparisons. These mismatches should not be ignored, nor should they be exaggerated. For most of these groups the modal SES level was III, the middle level of the population.

Our most interesting analyses (in our opinion) will center on our one-year-old starters, for our research has convinced us that by two years of age much has crystallized in the development of early competencies. It is, therefore, unfortunate that even better matching was not obtained with those children. Although we achieved perfect SES matching for children with wide divergence in achievement at three years when all 39 subjects were used, several of those selected for comparison were two-year-old starters for whom we have no data on the processes of development before their second birthdays.

Social Competence: Results and Discussion

Table 29 presents information on the levels of social competence achieved by our partially matched groups at 30-33 months of age. As was the case with nonmatched comparison groups, the gaps in achievement of social skills are quite wide. It is clear that though the most competent children from the highest SES levels in our sample are somewhat more able than our most competent children from lower levels that gap is quite small compared to the achievement level differences between our strongest and weakest children when they are from similar backgrounds, at least in regard to social competence.

Table 30 presents data on the individual social competencies (with adults) for these subjects at 30-33 months of age. For one-year-old starters, significant

TABLE 29. **Extreme Group Comparisons on Social Competence Scores,[1] Partially Matched for SES**

	30-33 Months	
Groups	Median	Range
1-Year-Old Starters (n = 19)	26.0	3.0-45.7
Most Competent (n = 5)	35.5**	14.2-37.0
Least Competent (n = 5)	8.3	3.0-16.0
2-Year-Old Starters (n = 20)	24.0	2.3-45.7
Most Competent (n = 5)	28.4**	23.9-45.7
Least Competent (n = 5)	13.9	2.3-17.4

[1] These scores are weighted. See Appendix B for details.
**Mann-Whitney U $p \leq .01$

differences occurred for *getting and holding attention* (p = .028), *using an adult as a resource* (p = .004), and *engaging in role play* (p = .048). For two-year-old starters, significant differences occurred in *getting and holding attention* (p = .008), *using an adult as a resource* (p = .048), and *expressing pride in achievement* (p = .022). For none of the comparisons was *expressing hostility or affection* a significant discriminator, although the direction of the results all favor our more competent children. These results generally parallel those found with our unmatched groups, again suggesting that the influence of socioeconomic status is not by any means overpowering.

Table 31 presents data on the tendency of our subjects to comply with simple requests (almost invariably from their mothers). Again the findings are very similar to those of the unmatched group. More competent children are consistently more agreeable children though not dramatically so.

Nonsocial Abilities

Tables 32, 33, 34, and 35 present primary outcome data for partially matched groups on nonsocial abilities. In every comparison but one (one-year-old starters, sensing dissonance) the group performances were significantly different and favored the more competent children. Furthermore, in every case but one (bottom five, one-year-old starters) the group scores were close to identical to those of the comparison groups unmatched for SES. In the one case the Binet score differences were substantial (108 vs. 76) and seem directly

TABLE 30. Extreme Group Comparisons of Individual Social Competence Scores,[1] Partially Matched for SES

	30-33 Months									
	Dimensions of Social Competence									
	Gaining Attention		Using Adult as Resource		Expressing Hostility/Affection		Engaging in Role Play		Expressing Pride in Achievement	
Groups	Median	Range	Median	Range	Median	Range	Median	Range	Median	Range
1-Year-Old Starters (n = 19)	42.1	12.0-75.0	32.0	13.0-72.3	19.7	4.3-77.2	3.0	1.0-13.0	4.0	2.0-18.7
Most Competent (n = 5)	41.3*	37.6-61.5	52.5**	37.2-64.8	22.3	7.3-43.0	6.0*	2.3-13.0	4.5	2.0-8.0
Least Competent (n = 5)	33.4	12.0-42.4	23.0	13.0-32.0	11.0	4.3-16.0	3.0	2.0-5.0	2.0	2.0-5.0
2-Year-Old Starters (n = 20)	29.2	8.3-59.0	29.9	6.9-79.0	15.2	3.0-42.0	1.0	1.0-13.0	4.0	2.0-7.0
Most Competent (n = 5)	43.0**	26.8-55.9	31.2*	23.6-46.5	17.0	10.3-33.8	1.0	1.0-2.3	6.0*	4.0-7.0
Least Competent (n = 5)	18.1	8.3-27.8	17.5	6.9-35.1	11.6	3.0-42.0	1.0	0.0	2.0	2.0-6.0

[1] These scores are unweighted. See Appendix C for details.
*Mann-Whitney U p ≤ .05
**Mann-Whitney U p ≤ .01

TABLE 31. **Extreme Group Comparison of Compliance Tendencies (% Compliance), Partially Matched for SES**

	30-33 Months	
Groups	Median	Range
1-Year-Old Starters (n = 19)	67.7	41.2-93.1
Most Competent (n = 5)	77.2*	54.5-93.1
Least Competent (n = 5)	72.2	54.5-81.1
2-Year-Old Starters (n = 20)	65.5	28.6-93.1
Most Competent (n = 5)	74.4	52.4-93.1
Least Competent (n = 5)	67.7	28.6-81.5

*Mann-Whitney U p ≤ .05

TABLE 32. **Primary Outcome Data (36 Months): Extreme Group Comparisons and Statistical Analyses of Receptive-Language Test Scores,[1] Partially Matched for SES**

Group	Group Median	Range
1-Year-Old Starters (n = 19)	45	16-60
Most Competent (n = 5)	60**	45-60
Least Competent (n = 5)	42	30-54
2-Year-Old Starters (n = 20)	48	33-60
Most Competent (n = 5)	54*	39-60
Least Competent (n = 5)	39	33-51

[1] Scores on Preschool Project. Receptive-Lanuage Test are expressed in months.

*Mann-Whitney U p ≤ .05
**Mann-Whitney U p ≤ .01

TABLE 33. **Primary Outcome Data (36 Months); Extreme Group Comparisons and Statistical Analyses of Dissonance Test Scores,[1] Partially Matched for SES**

Group	Group Median	Range
1-Year-Old Starters (n = 19)	8.0	4.0-8.0
Most Competent (n = 5)	8.0	8.0-8.0
Least Competent (n = 5)	8.0	7.0-8.0
2-Year-Old Starters (n = 20)	7.5	2.0-8.0
Most Competent (n = 5)	8.0*	6.0-8.0
Least Competent (n = 5)	4.0	3.5-8.0

[1] Scores on Preschool Project Dissonance Test are expressed in levels.

*Mann-Whitney U $p \leq .05$

TABLE 34. **Primary Outcome Data (36 Months): Extreme Group Comparisons and Statistical Analyses of Abstract Ability Test Scores,[1] Partially Matched for SES**

Group	Group Median	Range
1-Year-Old Starters (n = 19)	9.0	5.0-12.0
Most Competent (n = 5)	11.0*	9.0-12.0
Least Competent (n = 5)	9.0	8.0-11.0
2-Year-Old Starters (n = 20)	9.5	6.0-11.0
Most Competent (n = 5)	11.0**	9.0-11.0
Least Competent (n = 5)	7.0	6.0-8.0

[1] Scores on Preschool Project Abstract Abilities Test are expressed in levels.

*Mann Whitney U $p \leq .05$

**Mann Whitney U $p \leq .01$

TABLE 35. **Primary Outcome Data (36 Months): Extreme Group Comparisons and Statistical Analyses of Stanford-Binet Intelligence Scale Scores, Partially Matched for SES**

Group	Group Median	Range
1-Year-Old Starters (n = 19)	113	57
Most Competent (n = 5)	139*	110-144
Least Competent (n = 5)	108	76-118
2-Year-Old Starters (n = 20)	117.5	74-139
Most Competent (n = 5)	132*	105-134
Least Competent (n = 5)	84	74-117

*Mann-Whitney U $p \leq .05$

ascribable to the SES differences. In the matching process the least competent one-year-old starting comparison group became a predominantly Class III group; whereas, in the unmatched groupings they were between Classes III and IV.

Probably the most interesting and important finding in the achievement data at 36 months is that our strongest three-year-olds from SES Class III (partially matched SES groups) performed just as well as our strongest three-year-olds from Classes I and II and that our one-year-old starters had a small but consistent superiority at three years of age over our two-year-old starters. Such a finding suggests that blue-collar families (at least) may be capable of doing as fine a job of educating their children in the first three years of life as families from the highest SES levels in our society. It also suggests, as does the recent work of many others, that participation in a long-term research study that results in test experience for a child and sensitization to early behavior by parents may produce higher test results than would ordinarily occur.

PRIMARY OUTCOME DATA

Social vs. Nonsocial vs. Overall Competence

The focus of the Preschool Project research is on the fully competent child. "Fully competent" was defined for us through observations of three to six year old children as they coped with the entire range of tasks confronted in daily life. Many of these tasks required the use of intellectual and linguistic abilities. Others involved motor or perceptual skills. Children varied widely in their effectiveness in the social realm. Our behaviorally based description of a competent child therefore featured social skills (or competencies) as well as intellectual, linguistic, and perceptual ones.

Our achievement data were such as to allow us to rank our 39 subjects for social and nonsocial competence separately as well as for overall competence. Our primary focus on overall competence is reflected in the types of analyses in this book. Unfortunately for both the reader and the authors, we have a complicated story to tell. We have huge amounts of detailed data on 39 subjects, which have to be presented in several basic packages as an absolute minimum task. Beyond the achievements and experiences of the 39 children across the age ranges studied, we have to present, separately, data grouped according to age upon entry into the study, standing on overall competence at three and five years of age, and standing on overall competence at three and five years of age with SES level matched to the degree possible. The result is a rather high potential for confusion.

In addition we could present and analyze data on the relationship of experiences to social competence. We could do the same in the case of nonsocial competence. We shall not do so, however, for two reasons. First, we believe this book is going to be complicated enough as it is. Second, the study was designed primarily to generate hypotheses about effective child-rearing practices. We prefer not to push our data too far. Our hypotheses will require experimental testing and in any case are only crude first approximations in a scientific inquiry. The possibilities for correlational analyses and speculations about our data are multitudinous. We prefer to draw the line conservatively. We shall therefore present our social and nonsocial competence rankings at this point and provide data on the experiences of each child in Appendix A. Those wishing to speculate on relationships across the two may do so.

Table 36 presents the achievement levels of all our subjects arranged according to entry into the study and overall, social, and nonsocial competence.

Earlier findings of importance are underlined by this table. For example, some children are ranked consistently at the top (subjects #20 and 8), at the bottom (#7, 27, and 28), or at the middle (#31 and 44) of the groups. A few others (#37 and 41) are quite strong socially but rather weak nonsocially or vice versa (#10 and 11). It is also clear that more lower SES children are in the upper social ranks than in the upper nonsocial ranks.

For data on the experiences each of the children underwent that led to the various levels of achievement, please refer to the Appendix A.

TABLE 36. **Competence Ranks at 36 Months**

	Overall				Social				Nonsocial			
Rank	Sub. #	Age at Entry	SES	Sex	Sub. #	Age at Entry	SES	Sex	Sub. #	Age at Entry	SES	Sex
1	20	1	II	F	24	1	I	M	11	1	II	F
2	8	1	II	M	20	1	II	F	20	1	II	F
3	17	1	I	F	40	1	IV	F	8	1	II	M
4	24	1	I	M	8	1	II	M	17*	1	I	F
5	3	1	I	F	41	1	V	F	22*	2	III	F
6	9**	2	I	F	43	1	III	M	3**	1	I	F
7	16**	1	III	M	39	2	III	M	9**	2	I	F
8	40**	1	IV	F	37	1	V	M	2**	2	II	M
9	22	2	III	F	3	1	I	F	35	2	III	F
10	11*	1	II	F	17	1	I	F	21	2	I	M
11	2*	2	II	M	16	1	III	M	10	2	I	F
12	39	2	III	M	18	2	III	F	19	1	I	F
13	35	2	III	F	38	2	III	M	16	1	III	M
14	21	2	I	M	32	1	III	M	24	1	I	M
15	12	2	I	M	36	2	III	M	5*	2	I	M
16	41	1	V	F	12	2	I	M	13*	2	I	M
17	43	1	III	M	9	2	I	F	33	2	I	M
18	18	2	III	F	2*	2	II	M	12	2	I	M
19	19	1	I	F	14*	2	IV	M	44	1	III	F
20	32*	1	III	M	22	2	III	F	31	1	II	M
21	38*	2	III	M	35*	2	III	F	40	1	IV	F
22	5	2	I	M	21*	2	I	M	25	2	IV	M
23	31	1	II	M	31	1	II	M	39	2	III	M
24	44	1	III	F	11*	1	II	F	1	1	IV	F
25	36	2	III	M	44*	1	III	F	42	1	III	M
26	37*	1	V	M	5	2	I	M	18	2	III	F
27	13*	2	I	M	42	1	III	M	32	1	III	M
28	10	2	I	F	19	1	I	F	38	2	III	M
29	33	2	I	M	13*	2	I	M	36	2	III	M
30	14	2	IV	M	34*	1	IV	M	41*	1	V	F
31	42	1	III	M	25	2	IV	M	43*	1	III	M
32	25	2	IV	M	28*	2	III	F	27	2	III	M
33	1	1	IV	F	30*	2	III	F	14	2	IV	M
34	28*	2	III	F	33	2	I	M	45	1	III	F
35	30*	2	III	F	1	1	IV	F	28*	2	III	F
36	34	1	IV	M	45	1	III	F	30*	2	III	F
37	45	1	III	F	10	2	I	F	37	1	V	M
38	27	2	III	M	7	2	IV	M	7	2	IV	M
39	7	2	IV	M	27	2	III	M	34	1	IV	M

*Two subjects tied and were assigned their average rank value.
**Three subjects tied and were assigned their average rank value.

5

Patterns of Experience During the Second and Third Years of Life: Results and Discussion

THE COMPLICATED QUESTION OF THE VALIDITY OF DATA ON THE EXPERIENCES OF YOUNG CHILDREN

Our procedures for learning about the experiences of children are new and imperfect. Our intention has been to go considerably beyond the method of single-observer observations without systematic procedures. Ideally, we want to gather an absolutely reliable quantitative picture of the experiences of children. Unfortunately, neither we nor anyone else has figured out how to do that yet. Given the current state of the maturity of child development research, the relationship between methods of data collection and quality or usefulness of data is by no means clear. Piaget's entire work on the origins of intelligence was performed by *one* highly involved observer, with no trace of objective recording of data, with no instruments written or otherwise, and on only three subjects (his own children).

Early in our research, one member of a site-visiting team with thirty years of research experience (none of which involved observations under natural conditions) urged us to stay very close to behavior. She seriously insisted that reliable data could be gathered *only* if each identifiable motor pattern was identified, classified, and used to form a complete inventory of actions. That inventory should become our observation instrument, and we should use it to organize *all* behaviors of our subjects as they went about their ordinary business. We estimate that we could create at least a thousand categories in such a system. We find suggestions of that sort *never* come from people who have tried observational research themselves.

Kurt Lewin and his colleagues Roger Barker and Herbert Wright have for decades tried to alert child development researchers to the need for research on the environment and on the intersection of the environment with development: the stream of experience. They used the terms *ecological psychology* and *the stream of behavior* (Barker, 1963, 1968). Mostly their pleas have fallen on deaf ears.

Ethologists have for some time now attempted to gather data on naturally occurring events. Hinde's textbook (1966) contains examples of schemes for quantifying such behavior. Such observational schemes, however, do not attempt to quantify the stream of experience, but rather focus on a small number of specific behavior classes, such as fixed action patterns, instances of physical contact, grooming behavior, etc. We had expected that anthropologists would have developed powerful observational methods but soon learned (Whiting and Whiting, 1960) that they preferred the method of interviewing informants or, at the most, simple forms of participant (informal) observer activity. Recently, there seems to be some interest in quantitative, firsthand observation.

Turning to another area of child development research—evaluation of early educational programs—we find a parallel state of affairs. Early "evaluations" of Head Start programs sometimes consisted of the evaluator's spending a few hours walking through a center. To be sure, one can get an idea of the quality of the physical plant, the types of materials used, and an idea of whether children are under control or not, etc. What could be told about each child's actual experiences? Virtually nothing.

Another common practice was to ask to see the written "curriculum." Presumably, if the center had, for example, a "Montessori" curriculum, an evaluator might learn more of what happened to each child. But what was written and what actually happened were not likely to be the same. Even if they were, would each child's experience be similar if not the same? Obviously not.

There is only one way to know what a child is experiencing in a center, in a home, or anywhere. One has to sample, fairly, his actual experiences. One cannot reliably tell how much television a child watches by calling his mother on the phone and asking her. Even if the TV set is on, he may be attending to something else. Sampling the stream of experience is now called *process monitoring*. It is very difficult work. There is no inexpensive way to do it. It is usually incompatible with a career as a university professor. In a laboratory it cannot be done for any but short-lived atypical processes. Even if an observer goes to the home of a young child to do it properly, his problems are far from extensive data on individual children for readers who care to explore small group topics.

One might think that with this long list of problems, we would not or should not present any data at all on the child's stream of experience. Nevertheless, we will. There is, at this time, no way of knowing how far from the ideal our data have veered. Most of the major categories of experience seem to us *relatively* invulnerable to observer effect. Children, between their first and third birthdays, seem to adapt to the presence of a nonparticipant observer rather quickly in almost all cases. And it must be remembered that we have found that such children spend most of their waking hours in solitary activities. The child, except for glances at the observer, generally acts as if he were alone in most cases. Many of the major categories of tasks are quite rigidly defined in behavioral terms so that the general validity of the patterns we have seen seems to us high enough to be valuable. It should also be kept in mind that this study was designed *to generate hypotheses* about effective child-rearing practices that would then be tested experimentally. Finally, though we believe that quantitative data are the most reliable material on which to build a science in this and most other subject areas, we are not abandoning as useless the remainder of the judgments and observations we have made *without* benefit of formal quantitative techniques. Bearing in mind how easy it is to fool oneself in such areas, we still feel that informally gathered knowledge has at least two important values. First, especially with computer-assisted data processing, it helps one to retain a capability to detect human and mechanical errors in data handling. This is what is often meant by an "intuitive feel for data." Second, the range of general knowledge acquired about any topic studied at length is always far more extensive than the few phenomena and processes on which quantitative data are gathered.

For example, although we never measured the angle to which a young infant could rear his head when placed in the prone position, we still knew from hundreds of casual observations that the newborn could barely clear the surface of the mattress and that over the next four months all healthy children acquire the ability to hold their heads fully erect for several minutes at a time. Likewise, though in our early studies of one- and two-year-olds we did not count the number of minutes mothers spent with their children, we knew that the total time for nearly all families observed was very low, far less than 25 percent of the time. Such general knowledge, while not as precise as quantitatively gathered data, is nonetheless real and indispensable. The problem for the scientifically oriented researcher is to avoid misusing his general informal knowledge, on the one hand, and to avoid the equally common mistake of believing that if he has not measured something he cannot possibly know anything about it.

We shall use both kinds of information in this book. We shall tell you when and the degree to which our analyses are based on quantitative data and when they are based instead on a consensus of our core staff. Bear in mind that three of our core staff members (B. White, B. Kaban, and B. Shapiro) visited the homes of our 39 subjects in more than one half of the over 1,500 observation and test sessions of the study.

EXPERIENCES OF THE SECOND AND THIRD YEARS OF LIFE

Table 37 presents data on the typical experiences of all 39 of our subjects during the 12-33-month period and on the balance of social to nonsocial experiences during that time. Each subject was observed every three weeks (five times). At each observation, three ten-minute continuous observations were performed. After deleting the data gathered by the observer whose protocols differed strikingly from the other three, the resultant data base was reduced to an average of four observations per child. We gathered no data during the second year of life for our two-year-old starters, and although we did gather some during the third year of life for one-year-old starters, none is presented here.

Of particular satisfaction to us in light of all the difficulties of collecting such data is the consistency of our findings. While internal consistency is by no means a total guarantee of the legitimacy of data, it is at least to be expected when orderly developmental processes are monitored with quantitative assessment techniques. The complete data on the 12-15-month period for 19 subjects very closely resembles those reported in Volume I. The same is true for the 24-27-month period except that the complete data indicate slightly more *cooperating* tasks and slightly fewer *gaining information (visually)* tasks. One other small difference is that the complete data indicate a bit more social tasks at 24-27 months than the data in Volume I. Otherwise, the numbers are strikingly similar. Likewise, the new data on the 18-21- and 30-33-month period seem quite consistent with the balance of the data. In addition, the data "feel" right. They line up with our subjective judgments about what actually happened in the lives of these children.

What, then, is the picture we see as we repeatedly sample the experiences of these children as they go about their day-to-day lives? Note the predominance of nonsocial tasks. Regardless of whether a child is developing very well or very poorly, he spends far more time interacting with physical reality than he does trying to affect people during these age ranges (see Table 38).* For 12-15-month-old children the figures are 89.7 percent for nonsocial tasks vs. 10.3 percent for social tasks. By 18-21 months the figures are 83.8 percent nonsocial and 16.2 percent social; at 24-27 months, 80.0 percent nonsocial and 20.0 percent social; and at 30-33 months, 79.1 percent nonsocial and

---

*Some corroboration of our findings has recently appeared in the work of Wenar (1972) and Clarke-Stewart (1973). They, too, find infants at home spending much more time at nonsocial activities than interacting with other people.

TABLE 37. Typical Experiences of One- and Two-Year-Old Children, Median Group Values, Percent of Time Awake

Social Tasks	12-15 Months (n = 19)	18-21 Months (n = 19)	24-27 Months (n = 20)	30-33 Months (n = 20)
To please	0.1	0.0	0.2	0.1
To cooperate	2.8	4.6	3.9	3.5
To gain approval	0.0	0.0	0.0	0.0
To procure a service	1.0	1.0	2.3	1.8
To gain attention	2.2	2.0	2.6	2.8
To maintain social contact	2.2	2.8	5.0	2.7
To avoid unpleasant circumstances	0.0	0.0	0.1	0.0
To annoy	0.0	0.0	0.0	0.0
To direct	0.0	0.1	0.2	0.5
To assert self	0.5	1.5	1.3	1.4
To provide information	0.0	0.0	0.2	0.7
To compete	0.0	0.0	0.0	0.0
To reject overtures	0.0	0.0	0.0	0.0
To enjoy pets	0.0	0.0	0.0	0.0
To converse	0.0	0.0	0.1	0.7
To produce verbalization	0.0	0.0	0.0	0.0
Nonsocial Tasks				
To eat	4.4	10.3	5.5	2.9
To gain information (v)	16.0	10.6	13.7	7.7
To gain information (v & a)	6.0	6.0	9.8	10.6
live language directed to child	*1.7*	*1.4*	*2.8*	*2.8*
overheard language	*0.8*	*1.3*	*2.6*	*2.0*
mechanical language	*0.2*	*0.0*	*0.0*	*1.7*
Sesame Street	*0.0*	*0.0*	*0.0*	*1.2*
Nontask	12.2	11.8	9.5	6.8
To pass time	3.4	3.2	2.3	1.7
To find something to do	0.0	0.0	0.0	0.0
To prepare for activity	1.4	2.0	1.7	2.2
To construct a product	0.0	0.0	0.0	0.1
To choose	0.0	0.0	0.0	0.0
To procure an object	3.3	3.1	1.8	2.0
To engage in large muscle activity	0.0	0.0	0.4	0.0
To gain pleasure	0.0	0.0	0.7	0.1
To imitate	0.0	0.0	0.3	0.1
To pretend	0.0	1.5	0.5	1.8
To ease discomfort	0.6	0.4	0.5	0.2
To restore order	0.7	0.6	0.6	0.9
To relieve oneself	0.0	0.0	0.0	0.0
To dress	0.0	0.0	0.0	0.0
To operate a mechanism	0.0	0.2	0.2	0.2
To explore	12.8	6.6	4.6	2.3
Mastery	8.7	11.4	8.9	12.7
gross	*6.7*	*2.4*	*3.9*	*2.3*
fine	*2.4*	*3.9*	*2.0*	*6.5*
verbal	*0.0*	*0.1*	*0.0*	*0.1*
To eat and gain information (v)	4.2	1.9	1.4	0.7
To eat and gain information (v & a)	0.3	0.4	0.5	0.5
live direct	*0.1*	*0.0*	*0.3*	*0.0*

TABLE 38. Percent of Time Spent in Social vs. Nonsocial Tasks

	Social Tasks	Nonsocial Tasks
12-15 Months (n = 19)	10.3*	89.7
18-21 Months (n = 19)	16.2	83.8
24-27 Months (n = 20)	20.0	80.0
30-33 Months (n = 20)	20.9	79.1

*All values are group median % durations.

20.9 percent social. There is a doubling of social tasks between the first and second birthdays. (Later we will dwell on the rather striking fact that mothers apparently spend rather modest amounts of time in direct interactions with their children during this period.)

A second rather striking feature of these data is that for the most part our subjects initiated their own experiences. There is a remarkable consistency in the task-initiation data throughout the 12-33-month period with scores for self-initiation ranging from 86.5 to 90.9 percent (see Table 39). The only other person to initiate any substantial fraction of a child's experiences during this age range is the mother.* Furthermore, where tasks are initiated by the child's mother, they are likely to be social tasks and, in particular, *to cooperate* experiences consisting of simple requests.

Another rather unexpected finding is that the most frequent experience of most children in this age range is what we call *to gain information (visual)*, which means staring steadily at one object or scene for at least three seconds (see Table 37). (For 12-15-month-olds, 16.0 percent; for 18-21-month-olds, 10.6 percent; for 24-27-month-olds, 13.7 percent; and for 30-33-month-olds, 7.7 percent.)† Of the many child psychologists I have asked, only one guessed correctly that visual inquiry was the most frequent activity of this age range. Little wonder, however, when we realize how few professionals have studied on- to three year old children under natual circumstances.

Nontask behavior (desultory scanning or wandering about) is the second most common activity seen among our one- and two-year-old children (12.2 percent at 12-15 months; 11.8 percent at 18-21 months; 9.5 percent at 24-27 months; and 6.8 percent at 30-33 months). During the period studied this experience seems to be declining gradually.

---

*A reminder is in order: Our data cover only the hours between 9:00 and 6:00 on weekdays. Unquestionably, fathers and others initiate some activities for such children on weekends at least.
†All figures are medians of percent of total duration.

TABLE 39. **All Tasks: % Self- vs. Other-Initiated**

Group	Self-initiated	Mother-initiated	Other Adult-Initiated
12-15 Months (n = 19)	86.5*	13.0	0.0
18-21 Months (n = 19)	87.7	9.9	0.0
24-27 Months (n = 20)	89.7	8.4	0.3
30-33 Months (n = 20)	90.9	7.0	0.2

*All values are group median % durations.

OTHER GENERAL POINTS TO PONDER

Social Experiences

There are only four social tasks that occur rather frequently with our youngest children: cooperating with simple requests, seeking help, seeking attention, and trying to maintain attention or social contact.

With age the picture becomes more complex so that by two and a half years of age, nine social tasks occur with some regularity in contrast to only six at one year of age.

Social developmental themes seem to be reflected in the data. At 18-21 months, children are asked to respond to simple requests (to cooperate) more than at one year or at the later ages. This is the age when we find negativism at its peak. Children are usually harder to live with and higher cooperate scores seem to us to indicate more frequent necessity to control the child of this age.

Similarly, peaks for seeking assistance (procuring a service) and trying to maintain social contact are seen at 24-27 months of age, a time when "clinginess" seems to reach its peak.

Social encounters that feature the child's use of oral language (*providing information and conversing*) emerge at 24-27 months and increase at a rate consistent with our general knowledge of the growth of speech in young children.

Nonsocial Experiences

Nonsocial experiences (in these data) follow the same pattern of increases in types and consistent relations to developing attributes as do social experiences.

The numbers of nonsocial experiences increase from 13 near the first birthday to 18 with our oldest children. (The total number of all experiences grows from 19 to 28 during the period.)

Eating shows an interestingly steep peak at 18-21 months of age. We believe this is again due to the difficulty of coping with *most* children of this age. Offering food is one of the most common methods used by parents when children manifest one or another form of negativism.

Steady staring at scenes (gaining information—visual) seems to be on the decline in these data, although our earlier work suggested that it picks up and remains a very frequent experience throughout the preschool years.

Staring and listening to relevant language (gaining information—auditory and visual) increases at a rate parallel to the normal growth of facility with language.

Idling (nontask behavior) is a rather persistent feature of infancy and toddlerhood, although it seems on the decline as the third birthday approaches. Our earlier work suggests that this type of experience does not usually increase in amount in later years. Rather we find it supplanted by "passing time."

Passing time seems for all our children gradually to decrease over the age range sampled. Our earlier works showed a marked increase in this experience when children entered nursery schools (regardless of type of child or school).

Pretend behavior (making believe, role playing, etc.) is never very common (in the age range we have studied) but does emerge for most children by one and a half years of age. Subsequently it is a fixture (as far as groups of children are concerned).

Constructing products such as primitive drawings or buildings is one of the latest emergents in these data. Some children show none at all until they turn three years of age. It is a rather common experience in the preschool years.

Exploring the properties of objects and practicing simple skills on them (mastery behavior) are two universally common experiences that are best discussed together. They constitute a large percentage of the waking activities of *every* infant we have ever studied. One-year-olds in this study, for example, typically spent from 18 to 21.5 percent of their time engaged in such activities with small portable objects of many kinds. At first (12-15 months) exploration outweighs mastery behavior. By the middle of the second year, the situation is reversed, and this trend continues at least until the third birthday.

Experiences which feature a concentration by the child on language are universal during the second and third years. In our system they take four major forms: (1) live language directed to the child, (2) live language overheard by the child, (3) language from "Sesame Street" television programs, and (4) language from other TV as well as radio and records (mechanical language). The total amount of such experience grows steadily during the period studied.

6

The Relation of Environmental Factors to Experiences Associated with the Development of Competence: Generating Hypotheses About Effective Child-rearing Practices

EXPERIENCE DURING THE SECOND YEAR OF LIFE AND ACHIEVEMENTS AT THREE YEARS

The central purpose of our natural longitudinal experiment was to identify experiences that contribute maximally to the development of competence in children. We selected our sample of children in order to heighten the probability that we would be studying some children who would develop very well and others who would develop at much lower levels of competence. Since groups of such children usually look similar in achievement at about 12 months of age and gradually diverge in achievement sometime late in the second year of life, data on their experiences before they turn two years of age interest us the most.

Table 40 provides socioeconomic status information on the children we observed from their first birthdays and who were most widely separated on measures of competence at three years of age. Our most competent three-year-olds were generally from higher SES levels than our least competent three-year-olds. We shall concentrate our discussion on experiential differences associated with the largest differences in achieved competence. In later sections and in Appendix B we will present parallel information on the influence of SES on the development of competence. The picture changes but not dramatically.

TABLE 40. SES Characteristics of Children with Highest and Lowest Levels of Competence at Three Years of Age

Achieved Competence Level	Hollingshead-Redlich SES Ratings* (# of Ss in Each Category)					
	I	II	III	IV	V	
Highest (n = 8)						Group Median
Female	2	2	0	1	0	II
Male	1	1	1	0	0	
Lowest (n = 5)						
Female	0	0	1	1	0	IV
Male	0	0	1	1	1	

*Classes I and II are upper to middle classes; Classes III, IV, and V are middle to lower classes. A. B. Hollingshead and F. C. Redlich, *Social Class and Mental Illness* (New York: John Wiley and Sons, Inc., 1958).

Although SES clearly influenced the development of competence in our study, the influence was not sufficient to overpower other factors as seen in the following correlation Table 41.

As might be expected, the influence of SES on the level of competence achieved at three years of age is greatest for intellectual and related skills. SES *for these 39 subjects*, however, only accounted for about 30 percent of the variance in such achievements. It is to be remembered that we are not talking about a representative sample of children. For one thing, we sought out children likely to develop either very well or poorer than average. For

TABLE 41. Relationships Among Major Demographic Variables and Achieved Levels of Competence (n = 39)

	Overall Rank	Social Rank[1]	Nonsocial Rank[2]
Hollingshead-Redlich SES	.43*	.00	.55**
Income	.16	−.15	.28
Mother's Education	.59**	.27	.77**
Father's Education	.46*	.08	.75**
Mother's Occupation[3]	.11	−.10	.20
Father's Occupation	.44*	.05	.71**

[1] Rank with respect to social skills.
[2] Rank with respect to nonsocial skills—i.e., linguistic and intellectual skills.
[3] Only ten of the thirty-nine mothers of the study were employed.

*p ≤ .01
**p ≤ .001
Spearman Rank Correlation

another, our selection process produced some lower SES children likely to develop either very well or poorly and higher SES children most of whom were likely to develop well. One cannot claim that results from studies of such children can be generalized to national populations. Nevertheless, in our sample some children from SES Classes III and IV held their own with subjects from SES Classes I and II who at age three were functioning beyond the ninety-fifth percentile in basic academically relevant areas.

Interestingly, SES had no apparent influence whatsoever on the development of social competence in our subjects.

GENERATING HYPOTHESES ABOUT CHILD-REARING PRACTICES

We had considerable difficulty analyzing the effects of experiences on developing competencies. Relating twenty-five to thirty types of experiences sampled at four stages of life to seven types of competence at a later stage is no mean statistical chore. We were assisted in such work by three colleagues—John Frederickson, Richard Light, and Marcus Lieberman—each a specialist in statistics and design. All were consistently modest about the power of current knowledge in the relevant fields of statistical analysis to help us maximize the heuristic yield of our data. It might be asked why we did not design and execute our study so that all such matters might be settled in advance of data gathering. After all that is what is taught in statistic and experimental design courses. The answer is that there did not appear to be any genuinely suitable designs in existence to match our topic.

Our advisors urged us to keep our analyses as simple as possible. Such has always been our preference anyway. We shall perform and present very few analyses in comparison to the number that could be done. Any who would care to go further with these data are welcome to them. Since we are seeking *testable hypotheses* not *proof of causal connections*, we shall try to deal with our data conservatively as a matter of policy.

We shall present our inquiry into effective child-rearing practices in several ways. We shall concentrate on our task (experience) data gathered during the second year of life, especially in the 12-15-months age range because of the repeated finding that lasting developmental divergence seems to first manifest itself for most children late in the second year of life. We shall deal with the most obvious differences in potentially formative experiences between groups of children who looked similar in abilities at one year of age but who diverged most dramatically by three years of age. We shall then provide a correlational analysis using data on all 19 subjects studied from their first birthdays. Finally, we shall present the results of a multiple regression analysis design to identify *patterns* of experience that seem to lead to high levels of competence in young children. These primary analyses will be followed by several others. We will present data that speak to SES and sex effects and achievement at five years of age as measured by the Wechsler Preschool and Primary Scale of Intelligence (WPPSI) as well as the interrelations among achievements at various ages between the first and fifth birthdays.

EXPERIENCES AT 12-15 MONTHS AND COMPETENCE AT THREE YEARS OF AGE

Extreme Group Analyses

Experiential patterns during the second year of life for our children who diverged most in achieved competence at three years of age are shown in Table 42. At 12-15 months of age, the most interesting differences* across the groups are as follows:

	Time Spent (%)		
	Children		Statistical Significance
Experiences	Developing well (n = 8)	Developing less well (n = 5)	Probability Value (Mann-Whitney U two-tailed)
All social tasks	11.2	6.6	.008
To please	0.1	0.0	.030
Procure a service	1.2	0.2	.128
Gain attention	3.0	0.8	.018
Gain information (v)	20.0	10.9	.030
Live language directed to S	4.2	1.0	.004
Live language overheard by S	1.8	0.4	.046
Procure an object	2.0	3.9	.094
Mastery (all)	8.2	15.2	.128

We are particularly interested in the data on experiential differences in the 12-15-month age range because these data are the ones most likely to reveal something of the early processes wherein children begin to move ahead rather well or, on the contrary, to fall behind developmentally. The first experiential difference to note is that children who were most competent at three years of

---

*Task differences may be statistically significant, but the difference is not likely to be important because the particular experience occurs so rarely in the lives of normal children. Conversely, if a group difference does not quite reach statistical significance but involves a very common type of experience, we believe it merits special attention.

age had almost twice as much social experience (11.2 percent) as those who did not do so well (6.6 percent).

Looking at specific social tasks we find that two tasks in particular are substantially related to the development of competence, and there is a trend with respect to a third. The strongest relationships are found across attempts at seeking the attention of someone else (usually the mother) and attempts to please someone else (usually the mother). *Seeking attention* is far more common than attempting to please, but both are strongly associated in this analysis with the development of competence. In addition, there is a trend in respect to the seeking of simple assistance from the primary caretaker; in our system that task is called *procuring a service*.

Though these differences are not very large when expressed as percentages of total waking time, when multiplied out over the twelve or so waking hours each day and the many weeks involved in the 12-15-month period, they mount up to substantial differences in absolute amounts of experience.

Turning to the nonsocial tasks at this age range, we find, interestingly, that the children developing well spent a huge amount of time in steady staring—at objects, people, scenes, at various and sundry items in their worlds. The total amount of time is almost double that of children developing poorly and constitutes a large portion of each day. Twenty percent of all waking time was spent in this manner by our highly competent children.

The next item to note is the amount of live language directed to the children. Children developing well had considerably more of this experience. Here, we believe, we have one of the key clues as to how to rear children well. The differences, in an absolute sense, are modest, but the statistical significance is quite impressive, and we believe the psychological significance to be so as well. In addition to *live language directed to the child*, we found a statistically significant relationship between competence and *live language overhead by the child*.

Procuring objects seems to take more time in the lives of children not developing well than in the others. Gross *mastery* experiences, especially those involving the large muscles, are engaged in somewhat more regularly at this age by children developing not so well. These eight types of experience seem to contain the most striking differences in the total pattern of experience during the 12-15-month age range in this extreme group analysis.

Two general points about these data deserve attention at this time. First of all, the comparisons under discussion have been extracted from a larger group of comparisons, and, therefore, to some extent, their statistical significance has been inflated due to chance factors (see Table 42). The second point is that it would be unrealistic to expect any individual task out of the total matrix of all experiences to be overpowering with respect to the later development of competence. It is more likely that a pattern of tasks distinguishes a healthy course of development from one not so efficacious. Nevertheless, since we are novices at analysis of data such as these, we believe that an examination of

TABLE 42. Typical Experiences of Most and Least Competent One-Year-Old Children, Median Group Values, Percent of Time Awake

	12-15 Months		18-21 Months	
Social Tasks	Most Competent (n = 8)	Least Competent (n = 5)	Most Competent (n = 8)	Least Competent (n = 5)
To please	0.1	0.0	3.4	0.0
To cooperate	2.9	2.5	5.1	3.3
To gain approval	0.0	0.0	0.2	0.0
To procure a service	1.2	0.2	1.9	1.0
To gain attention	3.0	0.8	2.1	2.0
To maintain social contact	2.1	1.5	2.0	1.6
To avoid unpleasant circumstances	0.0	0.0	0.0	0.0
To annoy	0.0	0.0	0.0	0.0
To direct	0.0	0.0	0.1	0.0
To assert self	0.5	0.8	1.8	1.5
To provide information	0.0	0.0	0.0	0.0
To compete	0.0	0.0	0.0	0.0
To reject overtures	0.0	0.0	0.0	0.0
To enjoy pets	0.0	0.0	0.0	0.4
To converse	0.0	0.0	0.0	0.0
To produce verbalization	0.0	0.0	0.0	0.0
Nonsocial Tasks				
To eat	4.2	1.4	9.3	11.9
To gain information (v)	20.0	10.9	10.1	5.8
To gain information (v & a)	6.0	3.3	8.1	4.2
live language directed to child	4.2	1.0	3.1	0.8
overheard language	1.8	0.4	1.3	0.4
mechanical language	0.2	0.4	0.5	0.0
Sesame Street	0.0	0.0	0.2	0.0
Nontask	9.5	13.3	10.8	25.9
To pass time	1.6	3.4	3.6	0.8
To find something to do	0.0	0.0	0.0	0.0
To prepare for activity	1.7	1.3	3.2	1.3
To construct a product	0.0	0.0	0.0	0.0
To choose	0.0	0.0	0.0	0.0
To procure an object	2.0	3.9	4.1	2.7
To engage in large muscle activity	0.0	0.0	0.1	0.0
To gain pleasure	0.0	0.3	0.0	0.0
To imitate	0.0	0.0	0.1	0.2
To pretend	0.0	0.0	1.3	0.0
To ease discomfort	0.6	0.6	0.3	0.4
To restore order	0.7	0.2	1.5	0.1
To relieve oneself	0.0	0.0	0.0	0.0
To dress	0.0	0.0	0.0	0.0
To operate a mechanism	0.2	0.6	0.4	0.2
To explore	12.2	12.5	7.5	7.5
Mastery	8.2	15.2	4.3	7.9
gross	5.5	9.4	2.5	0.9
fine	2.8	2.6	6.8	0.6
verbal	0.0	0.0	0.2	0.0
To eat and gain information (v)	5.7	0.8	1.7	2.9
To eat and gain information (v & a)				
live direct	0.6	0.1	0.2	0.0

individual tasks may complement the analysis of task patterns. Furthermore, we will add to the statistical treatments of our data a less formal discussion of the general shape of the experiences of these children for heuristic purposes. We recognize that less formally based judgments carry different kinds of risks.

Task Initiation Information

Overall, between 85 percent and 92 percent of all tasks are initiated by the children themselves throughout the second year of life regardless of whether the children are developing well or poorly. (Statistical analyses comparing extreme groups revealed no significant differences.) This finding is consistent with our other indications that mothers do not spend the bulk of their day focusing exclusively on their children at this age range.

Turning to the distinction between social tasks and nonsocial tasks, we find that the mother's influence is apparent in the area of social tasks rather than nonsocial tasks. With the most competent children, mothers initiate 33.9 percent of social tasks and 11.4 percent of nonsocial tasks. With the least competent children, mothers initiate 54.3 percent of the social tasks and 6.1 percent of the nonsocial tasks. Though the differences appear substantial, statistical significance is not reached in any case. We do find statistical significance reached in regard to other-initiated tasks in respect to all tasks at 12-15 months of age and also in the case of social tasks. For the most competent children, others initiate 0.2 percent of all tasks and 1.9 percent of social tasks, while for the least competent children, others initiate no tasks. However, the amount of other-initiated experience is so small as to not have much heuristic meaning. There are very few instances where other adults come into the lives of these children.

Correlational Analyses of the Effects of Experience at 12-15 Months on the Development of Competence at Three Years of Age

Overall Competence. Table 43 presents correlation data across experiences during the second year of life* and levels of overall competence achieved by our subjects at three years of age. To gauge the psychological significance of these data, one must consider the level of statistical significance of the correlation figure, the possible psychological significance of the experience, and the amount of time spent in the particular experience. In some instances common tasks seem to bear a strong relationship to later competence, as in the case of gaining information through steady staring (*to gain information—visual*). In other cases, a correlation is statistically substantial, but the experience

---

*Tasks that occurred less than 0.1 percent of the time in any of our group analyses are deleted from these tables.

TABLE 43. Correlation Among Tasks (12-15 Months) and Achievement Variables at Three Years of Age (n = 19)

Social Tasks	Percent Time Spent in Activity (Group Median)	Correlation with Overall Competence[1]	Correlation with Social Competence
All social tasks	10.3	−.49*	−.33
To please	0.1	−.40	−.01
To cooperate	2.8	−.01	−.25
To procure a service	1.0	−.46*	−.31
To gain attention	2.2	−.46*	−.06
To maintain social contact	2.2	−.19	−.17
To assert self	0.5	.05	−.05
Nonsocial Tasks			
To eat	4.4	−.04	−.02
To gain information (v)	16.0	−.49*	−.01
To gain information (v & a)	6.0	−.27	−.14
live language directed to the child	1.7	−.78***	−.39
overheard language	0.8	−.33	.01
mechanical language	0.2	.20	−.17
Nontask	12.2	.42	.13
To pass time	3.4	.33	.24
To prepare for activity	1.4	−.25	.09
To procure an object	3.3	.48*	.24
To gain pleasure	0.0	.11	.24
To ease discomfort	0.6	.21	.35
To restore order	0.7	−.11	.17
To operate a mechanism	0.0	.12	.05
To explore	12.8	−.06	−.39
Mastery	8.7	.40	.08
gross	6.7	.40	.09
fine	2.4	.01	−.26
To eat and gain information (v)	4.2	−.62**	−.42
To eat and gain information (v & a)	0.3	−.30	−.63**
live language directed to the child	0.1	−.36	−.45*

[1] The most competent child is ranked 1, and the least competent child is ranked 19. Therefore, the relationship of high competence and greater task duration is negative.

[2] The relationship between high test scores and greater task duration is positive.

*p ≤ .05
**p ≤ .01
***p ≤ .001
Spearman Rank Correlation

involved rarely occurs at that time in a child's life. Take, for example, *to please* where only 0.1 percent of all time is the typical amount of such experience across all 19 children. With that caveat in mind, let us look more closely at the particular tasks that seem to have promise in respect to the identification of effective child-rearing practices.

Note that the total of all social tasks (at 12-15 months) correlates rather

TABLE 43. (continued)

Correlation with Nonsocial Competence	Correlation with Stanford-Binet Score[2]	Correlation with Receptive-Language Test Scores	Correlation with Abstract Abilities Test Scores	Correlation with Dissonance Test Scores
−.34	.33	.55**	.20	.30
−.41	.55**	.54*	.49*	.59**
−.19	−.12	.22	−.18	−.06
−.26	.39	.37	.30	.55*
−.38	.61**	.53*	.53*	.54*
.10	−.05	.16	−.14	.06
−.14	.04	−.04	.15	.16
.40	−.11	−.23	−.09	−.09
−.81***	.85***	.76***	.82***	.65**
−.29	.21	.26	.11	.04
−.73***	.79***	.88***	.72***	.53*
−.38	.52*	.45*	.43	−.65**
.28	−.50*	−.28	−.53*	−.55**
.38	−.37	−.45*	−.24	−.13
.24	−.25	−.21	−.28	−.30
−.26	.45	.40	.42	.43
.41	−.43	−.71***	−.35	−.24
−.35	.25	.14	.32	−.05
.27	.04	−.26	.09	.07
−.07	.25	.30	.23	.62**
−.06	−.03	−.25	.14	.00
.02	−.21	−.14	−.12	−.18
.27	−.40	−.46*	−.37	−.20
.24	−.36	−.38	−.34	−.16
−.08	−.11	−.20	−.05	−.05
−.28	.45*	.28	.44	.30
−.25	.01	.04	−.08	−.15
−.19	.15	.04	.06	−.09

strongly with competence at three years of age, with well-developing children having a considerably greater amount of social experience than those not developing well (Table 43).

Turning to individual social experiences we find two of the six common tasks achieving statistical significance in this analysis—*procuring a service* and *gaining attention*. *Procuring a service* is of particular interest in that it ties in with one of the major dimensions of competence we have focused on, *using an adult as a resource*. There is one other social experience category which deserves a passing comment and that is the category called *to please*. Experiences under this heading consist of overtures of a friendly nature initiated by the child toward another person. Although such overtures did not happen very often, the correlation figure of $-.40$ is high enough to merit attention.

Turning to nonsocial tasks, we find the following experiences highly correlated with achieved competence levels: *gaining information through steady staring, gaining information through looking and listening (live language directed to the child), eating and steady staring* and, in the opposite direction, *procuring objects*. (Children who spent more time, when they were 12-15 months old, procuring objects developed less well than those who spent small amounts of time in such an activity.) We can think of no obvious reason why *steady staring* should be especially beneficial. *Live language directed to the child* seems to be an obviously important experience since it feeds directly into intellectual and social development. *Eating and steady staring* again seems hard to interpret as efficacious experience. Why children not developing well spend more time *procuring objects* than children who develop well is also something we are not able to interpret with confidence at this time.

Three other experiences seem worthy of special mention, although the correlation figures do not reach statistical significance. *Nontask* experiences which consist of desultory scanning and aimless wandering correlate negatively with high levels of achieved competence. The suggestion that the more *pass time* experience a child has the poorer he develops fits in with other informal observations we have made about restricting the locomobility of the child in this particular age range. By and large it is our judgment that many caretakers routinely restrict the first locomotor activities of their children between 8 and 15 months of age and, in doing so, inadvertently interfere with the development of a child's curiosity and other important related capabilities.

These data also seem to suggest that the child who spends a great deal of time in gross motor activities such as climbing up stairs and onto furniture is less likely to be developing very well than one who engages in such activities less frequently.

Social Competence. Table 43 also presents correlations between all tasks that occurred at least 0.1 percent of the time in the 12-15 month age range and our subjects' social competence rank at three years of age. Again, note the absence of statistically significant correlations. There are only two that reach significance. However, the percentage of time that children engage in such experiences can be seen to be quite low. Among the more prominent central experiences that children have, all we can see are trends which go in the expected direction in just about every instance. For example, we find a small positive correlation between the sheer amount of social behavior and the achievement of social competence. Once again, we find a correlation between *procuring a service* and social competence. Turning to the nonsocial experiences, again we find *live language directed to the child* positively associated with the achievement of social competence. We find *easing discomfort*, an indication of unhappy experiences, negatively associated with the development of social competence. We find *exploratory behavior* positively associated. This is something new in these analyses. We have not seen this kind of relationship before. Among the multiple tasks involving *eating and looking* or *looking and listening*, we find relationships in the predicted direction.

Nonsocial Competence. Table 43 also presents correlational data on this topic. Here we expect stronger relationships between certain experiences and development, and, to some extent, this is so, although not dramatically. We find a trend in the expected direction with respect to the total amount of social tasks and a trend again with respect to *to please* and *seeking attention*, but the trends do not reach statistical significance. In the nonsocial experiences we find two dramatically high relationships. *Steady staring* and *live language directed to the child* are both positively correlated with the development of nonsocial competence. These findings were not unexpected but the size of the relationships are very impressive. As expected from earlier analyses a lot of *eating* in the life of the 12-15-month-old child is not apparently a very good sign; nor is a lot of empty time represented by the score in *nontask* experience. A lot of time spent *procuring objects* is negatively related to the achievement of nonsocial competence at three years of age; all in all, this is a reasonably interesting set of data.

Performance on the Stanford-Binet Test. Table 43 also presents data on these relationships.* We would expect that since nonsocial competence (at three years of age) and Binet scores (at three years of age) are highly correlated, these results would look like the preceding ones. However, we find the relationships generally stronger between experiences and Binet performance. When it is remembered that we are discussing the experiences of the 12-15-month period in life, these data begin to have more interest value than some of the others. In our research we use a number of assessment procedures that are neither standardized nor generally in use in child development research. But the Binet is another story indeed. It is quite commonly used, although we do not believe it is as powerful when used with three-year-olds as it is with older children. Nevertheless, the fact that we can predict Binet scores with the power that we can from sampling the tasks of these children holds great promise.

---

*The reader should be sensitive to the fact that the correlation signs with respect to this column of Table 43 are reversed in their significance as compared to those of the first three columns, as a consequence of the mechanical reversal of scores in our analysis. A negative correlation in the preceding discussions that dealt with overall social and nonsocial competence meant a positive relationship between those competencies and the particular experience. This analysis along with others relating test scores to experiences is constructed so that a positive correlation figure means the more the experience the higher the test score.

There are no fewer than seven statistically significant relationships between individual experiences at 12-15 months of age and performance on the Binet at three years. In addition, there are another seven or eight relationships that do not quite reach statistical significance but are well worth noting.

In regard to social tasks, note the highly significant positive relationships between the experience *to please* and high scores on the Binet at three years and between attempts at *gaining attention* and high Binet scores. In addition there is a positive trend with respect to total amount of social experience and attempts to *procure services*. Moving to the nonsocial experiences, we find a whole host of strong relationships. Those between *steady staring* and Binet performance and between *live language directed to the child* and Binet performance are quite remarkable: +.85, +.79. We also note the statistically significant relationships with respect to *live language overheard by the child* (the more the better), whereas television viewing, other than "Sesame Street," and other related *mechanical language* are negatively associated with Binet performance. Wandering or desultory scanning labeled by us *nontask* is also negatively related with Binet scores. *Preparing for an activity* is positively related and almost reaches statistical significance. *Procuring an object*, as in preceding analyses, is negatively related, fairly strongly, as is *motor mastery*, especially *gross motor mastery. Eating and steady staring* is significantly and positively related to Binet scores. All in all this is a rather impressive collection of striking relationships between the everyday experiences that occur shortly after one year of age in a child's life and his performance on the Binet at age three. The reader should note that in many preceding studies correlations between general development test scores at one year of age and Binet scores at three generally clustered around zero (Hunt, 1961).

Language Capacity. Table 43 also presents data on experiences and language development. As might be expected from the preceding analyses of the relationships across experiences and Binet scores and across experiences and nonsocial competence scores, we find fairly strong relationships in these data. Indeed, these relationships closely parallel those in respect to the Stanford-Binet score at three years of age. This, to some extent, solidifies our confidence in the data. We would be quite perplexed, to say the least, if we did not find this kind of result. At any rate, looking at social tasks we find, if anything, a stronger relationship between certain social tasks and the total amount of social experience and language ability at three years of age. A rich social life at a year or so of age seems conducive to good language learning. That should come as no surprise, but it should at least be comforting to finally have some numbers on the topic. Attempts at *pleasing others* and *seeking attention* again are statistically significant in their relationship to later language learning. *Procuring a service* also seems to be trending in that direction.

Moving to the nonsocial tasks, we find six significantly related to the achievement of language; however, of those six, one represents experience that happens rarely—that is, *live language overheard. Steady staring, live language directed to the child, nontask behavior, procuring an object,* and *exploratory behavior* are all strikingly related to later language achievement. Two additional tasks, *procuring an object* and *mastery experiences*, are negatively related to language scores at three years of age. In addition to the statistically significant relationships, there are strong trends that are worth noting: *preparing for activity* is positively related to language development as is *attempts at restoring order. Gross motor mastery*—that is, large muscle practice in climbing and related activities—is negatively related to language development. All in all, no surprises are present.

The Capacity for Abstract Thinking. With regard to this topic, we expected to see indications similar to those seen in regard to language acquisition, performance on the Binet, and nonsocial rank. Indeed, such is the case, although not with exactness. The relationship between the overall amount of social tasks and the achievement of abstract thinking abilities is smaller than with the preceding analyses and hardly warrants labeling even as a trend. *To please,* however, and *seeking attention* are both positively and significantly related to achievement; and, again, we see a trend, though slightly weaker, in regard to experiences in *procuring a service.*

Turning to nonsocial tasks, once again the ubiquitous *gaining information through steady staring* is very strongly related to this later achievement as is *live language directed to the child.* There are no other frequent experiences that relate significantly to abstract ability at three years. However, there are trends in the expected direction with regard to *preparing for activities, procuring objects, motor mastery tasks,* and *gross motor mastery.* There are also consistent trends in *eating and gaining information,* a multiple task with apparently similar psychological meaning to *simple steady staring.*

The Capacity to Sense Dissonance. We expected to find weaker relationships between tasks and outcomes because of our lower level of confidence in the suitability of this test for the age in question. Yet we do have fairly strong relationships. There is a trend with respect to all social tasks. They are the same findings with respect to the three repeatedly identified tasks: *to please, to procure a service,* and *to gain attention.* Indeed, *procuring a service* relates significantly during this period, whereas in the immediately preceding analyses (except with overall competence) it was only a trend. Turning to nonsocial tasks, we have significant but somewhat lower relationships across *gaining information through steady staring* and *live language directed to the child* in this outcome measure. Interestingly, we find *restoring order* more highly correlated with this particular outcome; perhaps this is because in order to try to set something right one has to first notice that it is awry. The capacity to notice when something is a little off is essentially what this test is tapping. There are trends (in the expected direction) with respect to *passing time, preparing for an activity,* and *eating and steady staring.*

Discussion. All in all it would appear that these correlational data are internally consistent and contain no surprises. The weakest of the analyses has to do with experiences shortly after one year of age and the achievement of social competence at three years of age. We simply cannot tell much from the table in question. However, all the other analyses having to do with the nonsocial skills, either singly or in combination, and with performance on the Stanford-Binet, mutually support each other and strongly suggest that a half dozen or so tasks or experiences at or around the child's first birthday are implicated with respect to the involved developmental processes.

A reminder to the reader is in order: As one can see, quite a number of experiences go into the makeup of a child's waking day. We did not really expect to find that many of these individual experiences would, in isolation, relate very strongly to achievement at three years of age. Nevertheless, several of them have related strongly—for example, live language directed to the child and attempts to procure a service. However, it is more likely that differences in patterns of experiences rather than in one or two types of experiences underlie differential development. Our next manner of data presentation is a rather simple attempt at pattern analysis.

Pattern Analyses: Experience at 12-15 Months and Competence at Three Years of Age

Table 44 presents correlations among all common experiences of our children at 12-15 months of age and the seven major achievement indices we tested for at or near three years of age. There is much overlap across our seven developmental indices. Overall competence is (by our definition) composed of social and nonsocial competence. Social and nonsocial competence are no doubt interrelated, but how much and in which ways we do not know. They only correlate at the +.30 level (in our study), but we are sure that there is some general ("g") factor involved.

We derived nonsocial competence scores by combining scores on the Stanford-Binet test with scores on the language, abstract abilities, and dissonance tests. Clearly each of the separate subtests is positively correlated with nonsocial competence and in turn with overall competence. The correlations range from +.40 to +.79 (see Table 44).

The information in Table 44 could be discussed extensively, but we do not intend to deal with it at any length at this point in the report. It is provided at this time to indicate the basis of our multiple regression analyses. They are shown in Table 45. We selected those experiences that individually correlated most strongly with competence at three years and that also occurred regularly in the lives of our children. We used sufficient numbers of experiences

REGRESSION ANALYSIS OF WPPSI 60 MOS AND 12-15 MOS TASKS
CORRELATIONS OF DATA

POSITION	LABEL	19 EAT.VE.D IRCT	20 EAT	21 GAI.N.IN FO.V	22 G AIN. INFO .V.A	23 LIV E.DI RECT	24 O VERH EARD	25 ME CHAN ICAL	26 NON TASK	27 P ASS. TIME	28 PRE PARE .ACT	29 PR OCUR E.OB JECT	30 G AIN. PLEA SURE	31 EAS E.DI SCOM FORT	32 R ESTO RE.O RDER	33 OPER ATE. MECH	34 EXP LORE	35 MAS TERY
1	LANGUAGE.36.MO	21	-12	70		69	31	-67		-51	40	-55	32	-22	11	-37	-10	-35
2	ABSTRCT.A.36.MO	19	-11	72		63	25	-67		-51	41	-23	39	12			-19	-36
3	DISSONANCE.36.MO		-23	52	-12	38	45	-85	14	-46	49	-14	17		50		-31	
4	BINET.36.MO	26	-12	75		66	36	-65	-14	-44	43	-34	39	20		-18	-30	-35
5	WPPSI.60.MO		-33	70	37	38	33	-23	-52			-18	51	-30			-46	-16
6	ADULT.SOCIAL	35	12		16	37			-18	-26		-24			-19		34	-17
7	OVERALL.RANK	-33		-47	-17	-64	-27	34	26	36	-24	39	-19	21		19	-29	42
8	SOCIAL.RANK	-36	-16		-16	-38	-11		21	29		29		31	21	16	30	24
9	NONSOCIAL.RANK	-27	21	-79	-14	-74	-33	61	26	36	-41	42	-44	-30	14	15		34
10	PLEASE	16	-29	22		20	40	-31	-15	-11		-14	-15	-24	29	-16	23	
11	COOPERATE	26	-20		16	27	25	-17	18	-41	29		20	-14	31	-32	-23	-15
12	PROCURE.SERVICE	20		18		31	69	-49	-12	-45	15	-14		10		-45	-35	-33
13	GAIN.ATTENTION		55	63	-13	15	48	-42		-35	-22	-23		-31		-37		-36
14	MNTN.SCL.CONTACT	-22		-22		-14	16	-13	-18		33	-29	22			11	-26	
15	ASSERT.SELF		-13	13	-19	21		-18				28	-27	48			-20	95
16	MASTERY.GROSS	22	-19	-35	24	-26						14	-17	31	12	59	35	30
17	MASTERY.FINE	19	-27	-23	-13		-12	21			21	-17	-14	-44				-11
18	EAT.AND.G.INFO.V	38	27	22		26		-29	-19	-47				-21	-20		-21	24
19	EAT.A.LIVE.DIRCT	100	-12	-40	43	61	15		-25	-21		-45	-18	-13	-38	-31	-21	-29
20	EAT	-12	100	100	-48	-34	-24	-40	15	-24	17	-15	53	-20		-23	-21	-43
21	GAIN.INFO.V	43	-40		14	54	24	39	-28	48		-37	39		14		-34	
22	GAIN.INFO.V.A		-48	14	100	53	27	-33	-59	-25	46		58	-14	45	-32	-25	-25
23	LIVE.DIRECT	61	-34	54	53	100	18	-37	-29	-18	15						-42	-12
24	OVERHEARD	15	-24	24	27	18	100		-19									18
25	MECHANICAL			-40	39	-33	-37	100	-27	64	-42	13	-13		-52	16	25	
26	NONTASK	-25	15	-28	-59	-29	-19	-27	100	-50	25	42	-24	35	42		34	18
27	PASS.TIME	-21		-24	48	-25	-18	64	-50	100	-39	-14	25	21	-42	19	-23	14
28	PREPARE.ACT	21		17		46	15	-42	25	-39	100	14	-38	52	39	-11	-23	-11
29	PROCURE.OBJECT			-45	-15	-37		13	42	-14	14	100	-38	24	45	34		30
30	GAIN.PLEASURE		-18	53	39	58		-13	-24		25	-38	100	100	-13		-38	-31
31	EASE.DISCOMFORT			-13	-20	-14	45	-52	35	-42	21	52	24	100	20	12	-48	17
32	RESTORE.ORDER		-38			14	-32	16	42	19	39	45	-13	20	100	100	-18	28
33	OPERATE.MECH		-31	-23			-42	25		-23	-11		-38	12		21	100	-12
34	EXPLORE	-21		-21	-34	-25	-12	18	34	14	-23	34	-31	-48	-18	28		100
35	MASTERY	24	-29	-43		-25					-11	30		17			-12	100

REGRESSION ANALYSIS OF WPPSI 60 MOS AND 12-15 MOS TASKS
CORRELATIONS OF DATA

POSITION	LABEL	1 LANGUA GE.3 6.MO	2 ABS TRCT .A.3 6.MO	3 DISS ONAN CE.3 6.MO	4 BIN ET.3 6.MO	5 WPP SI.6 0.MU	6 ADUL T.SO CIAL	7 OVER ALL. RANK	8 SOC IAL. RANK	9 NO NSOC IAL. RANK	10 PL EASE	11 C OOPE RATE	12 PRO CURE .SER VICE	13 GA IN.A TTEN TION	14 .SCL MNTN .CON TACT	15 ASS ERT. SELF	16 M ASTE RY.G ROSS	17 MAST FINE	18 EAT AND. G.IN FO.V
1	LANGUAGE.36.MO	100	80	66	85	52	35	-77	-41	-88	33	26	39	56		24	-24	-19	35
2	ABSTRCT.A.36.MO	80	100	72	96	61	16	-69	-21	-93	35		30	57	-29	35	-27	-13	46
3	DISSONANCE.36.MO	66	72	100	75	41	-10	-40		-72	35	-10	51	50	-18	18			27
4	BINET.36.MO	85	96	75	100	64	20	-76	-26	-98	41		42	66	-23	23	-27	-16	53
5	WPPSI.60.MO	52	61	41	64	100	19	-57	-23	-69		-31	33	60	-10	16		-17	24
6	ADULT.SOCIAL	35	16	-10	20	19	100	-75	-98	-24		22	31		24	-12	-21	31	48
7	OVERALL.RANK	-77	-69	-40	-76	-57	-75	100	80	79	-30		-43	-48	-30	10	39		-58
8	SOCIAL.RANK	-41	-21		-26	-23	-98	80	100	30			-38	-16	18	-24	26	-22	-50
9	NONSOCIAL.RANK	-88	-93	-72	-98	-69	-24	79	30	100	-40	-24	-39	-60	-13	-24	27	12	-47
10	PLEASE	33	35	35	41			-30		-40	100		29	20		21		11	-29
11	COOPERATE	26	30	-10	42	-31	22	-43	-24	-39	29	100	14	-14	18	-19	-14	16	-25
12	PROCURE.SERVICE	39	57	51	66	33	31		-38	-60	20	14	38	38	30	-22	-19	-39	42
13	GAIN.ATTENTION	56	50	18	75	60		-48	-16	-18	-13	-18	30	100		-19	-30	-22	42
14	MNTN.SCL.CONTACT		-29	-18	-23	-10	24		-30		-24	21			100	-22	17	-37	-27
15	ASSERT.SELF	24	35	18	-23	16	-12		10	-24			-19	19	-22	100	17		-12
16	MASTERY.GROSS	-24	-27		-27		-21	39	26	27	11	16	-14	-19	-30	-37	100	100	22
17	MASTERY.FINE	-19	-13		-16	-17	31		-22	12	29	-25		-39	-22	-27	-12	22	100
18	EAT.AND.G.INFO.V	35	46	27	53	24	48	-58	-50	-47	16	26	42	42	-22	-13	22	19	38
19	EAT.A.LIVE.DIRCT	21	19		-12		35	-33	-36	-27	-29	-20	20		55	13	-19	-27	27
20	EAT	-12	-11	-23	-26	-33	12		-16	21	22			-60	-22		-35	-23	22
21	GAIN.INFO.V	70	72	52	75	70		-47		-79			18	63		13	-19	24	-13
22	GAIN.INFO.V.A			-12		37	16	-17	-16	-14			16	-13	-14	21	-26		26
23	LIVE.DIRECT	69	63	38	66	38	37	-64	-38	-74	20	27	31	15	-14			-12	
24	OVERHEARD	31	25	45	36	33		-27	-11	-33	40	25	69	48	-16	-18		21	-29
25	MECHANICAL	-67	-67	-85	-65	-23	-18	34	21	61	-31	-17	-49	-42	-13				-19
26	NONTASK			14	-14	-52	-26	26	26	36	-15	18	-12		-18	33			-47
27	PASS.TIME	-51	-51	-46	-44			36	29	41	-11	-41	-45	-35	-22				
28	PREPARE.ACT	40	41	49	43			-24					29	15	-29		28	14	-17
29	PROCURE.OBJECT	-55	-23	-14	-34	-18	-24	39	29	42	-14		-14	-23		22	-27	-17	-14
30	GAIN.PLEASURE	32	39	17	39	51	-19	21	31	-44	-15		-20	48		48	31	-44	-21
31	EASE.DISCOMFORT	-22	12		20	20	-30		21		-30	-24	-14	10	-31		12		-20
32	RESTORE.ORDER	11		50			-19			15	14	29	-32					59	
33	OPERATE.MECH	-37	-19	-31	-18		34	19	16	30		-16	-23	-45	-37	11	-20	59	
34	EXPLORE	-10			-30	-46			-29			23		-35		-26		35	
35	MASTERY	-35	-36		-35	-16	-17	42	24	34	14		-15	-33	-36		95	30	-11

TABLE 45. Task Experiences (12-15 Months) Predicting Outcome Variables (36 Months), Regression Analysis

Dependent Variables	Multiple r	p*	Regression Equation
Overall Competence Rank (1 = high, 39 = low)	0.8438	.049	Predicted Overall = 23.0248 + % duration (0.1882) + % duration (−2.9090) + Procure a Service Gain Attention Rank % duration (0.3765) + % duration (−1.2073) + % duration (0.3407) + Gross Motor Eat and Gain Info (v) Gain Info (v) Mastery % duration (−1.9713) + % duration (0.0414) + % duration (0.6750) Live Language Pass Time Procure an Object Directed to S
Social Competence Rank (1 = high, 39 = low)	0.7691	.107	Predicted Social = 54.0601 + % duration (−2.8875) + % duration (−1.1046) + Procure a Service Maintain Social Rank Contact % duration (−1.6720) + % duration (−1.7093) + % duration (−0.3008) + Eat and Gain Info (v) Live Language Pass Time Directed to S % duration (−0.7232) + % duration (−1.1852) Procure an Object Explore
Nonsocial Competence Rank (1 = high, 39 = low)	0.9176	.001	Predicted Nonsocial = 37.7065 + % duration (−0.6243) + Procure a Service Rank % duration (−2.2283) + % duration (−0.3873) + % duration (−1.6141) + Gain Attention Gain Info (v) Live Language Directed to S % duration (0.0358) + % duration (−1.1897) + % duration (0.2713) Pass Time Prepare for Procure an Object Activity

*Statistical probability.

TABLE 45 (continued)

Dependent Variables	Multiple r	p*	Regression Equation
Stanford-Binet Intelligence Test	0.8920	.001	Predicted Binet = 67.0602 + % duration (1.5902) + % duration (6.5512) + Score Procure a Service Gain Attention % duration (0.6994) + % duration (2.9799) + % duration (−0.2671) + Gain Info (v) Live Language Pass Time Directed to S % duration (3.1625) Prepare for Activity
PSP Language Test	0.9274	.001	Predicted Language = 46.3204 + % duration (−1.4235) + Score Procure a Service % duration (1.9750) + % duration (0.0715) + % duration (1.1439) + Gain Attention Gain Info (v) Live Language Directed to S % duration (−0.4920) + % duration (1.7519) + % duration (−2.1737) Pass Time Prepare for Procure an Object Activity
PSP Abstract Abilities Test	0.8568	.006	Predicted A.A. = 6.5754 + % duration (0.1240) + % duration (0.1149) + Score Gain Attention Eat and Gain Info (v) % duration (0.0782) + % duration (0.1199) + % duration (−0.0367) + Gain Info (v) Live Language Pass Time Directed to S % duration (0.2776) Prepare for Activity
PSP Dissonance Test	0.7578	.068	Predicted Dissonance = 4.8930 + % duration (0.6075) + Score Procure a Service % duration (0.0382) + % duration (0.0654) + % duration (−0.0644) + Gain Attention Gain Info (v) Live Language Directed to S % duration (−0.0173) + % duration (0.5624) Pass Time Prepare for Activity

*Statistical probability.

to make the analysis heuristically meaningful. Fewer experiences might have predicted just as well but would have left us with too sparse a picture. On the other hand, we kept the numbers of experiences small enough to capture impressive predictive power (at least for our sample).

Overall Competence. Time spent in eight experiences at 12-15 months of age predicts how each of our 19 one-year-old starters ranks in overall competence at three years of age (multiple $r = +.84$, $p = .049$). *Procuring a service* and *gaining attention* among the six common social experiences are apparently key indicators. High scores in such experience are associated with good overall development. Likewise, high scores in steady staring (*gaining information, visual*) while *eating* and *eating and listening to live language* addressed directly to the child are also associated with good development over the second and third years of life. Low scores in *gross motor activity, passing time,* and *procuring objects* round out the pattern of tasks experienced at 12-15 months of age and linked to competence at three years.

Social Competence. Our capacity to predict social competence at three years of age is not as impressive as is the case with overall competence (multiple $r = +.77$, $p = .107$). There is substantial overlap in the predictive tasks (five of eight predictors of overall competence predict social competence). *Maintaining social contact* replaces *seeking attention*; *gross motor activity* drops out; and *exploring* enters the picture. The meanings of the changes are not immediately apparent to us. The major finding is that most of the experiences that lead to general competence apparently also lead to social competence.

Nonsocial Competence. The regression analysis is very strong in respect to the association between early tasks and later nonsocial competence (multiple $r = +.92$, $p = .001$). Seven of the eight tasks are the same as in the case of overall competence. *Gross motor activity* drops out, while *preparing for activities* enters. High scores in the latter experience are associated with high nonsocial competence.

Stanford-Binet Performance. As might be expected, our data are also strong in regard to the prediction of performance on the Stanford-Binet test at three years of age (multiple $r = +.89$, $p = .001$). Again the pattern overlaps with those for the previous analyses, especially for nonsocial and overall competence.

Language Capacity. Once again we find our data predicting with impressive power (multiple $r = +.93$, $p = .001$). And again, we find almost the same pattern of tasks involved.

Abstract Thinking Ability. As before, the predictive power is high (multiple $r = +.86$, $p = .006$), and there is much overlap in the tasks involved.

The Ability to Sense Dissonance. Here we find somewhat lower predictive power (multiple $r = +.76$, $p = .068$). Again, the same core tasks are involved.

Discussion. What we seem to find surfacing repeatedly in our data is a strong relationship between six to ten of the typical experiences of our children when they are 12-15 months old and their achievement of competence at three years of age. According to these analyses, for good general educational development, children at 12-15 months of life should have a good deal of social experience (as we define it), although it need not occupy more than 10-12 percent of their time. In particular, they should be encouraged in their attempts at seeking attention and assistance (after first determining they cannot handle a task themselves). A note of caution should be added in respect to the task of procuring a service: There is an important distinction to be made between procuring a service in order to maintain social contact, on the one hand, and procuring a service in order to cope with a task, having tried it first and failed or having thought about it and concluded it could not be handled alone. It is the latter condition we are talking about rather than the former. By 13 months of age children can use such overtures in a skillful manipulative manner. Between 7 or 8 and 13 months of age such behavioral trends surface in many infants.

A child's listening to language directed at him by another person is clearly centrally involved in all of our analyses. Restrictive practices such as lengthy playpen confinement (which lead to high *pass time* scores) is negatively associated with good development. Less easily understood are the negative correlations of *gross motor activity* and *procuring objects*.

EXPERIENCES AT 18-21 MONTHS OF AGE AND COMPETENCE AT THREE YEARS OF AGE

The reader should be reminded yet another time that we are inclined to think of analyses such as the following, which concentrate on the implications of experiences at 18-21 months of age for later development, as of less value for the heuristic purposes of this study than those having to do with earlier experiences. Although we feel that they continue to provide major causal input, we are also convinced that these experiences reflect the developments that preceded them. It is our judgment (as we have said before) that the child of 12 months of age, within the range of development we are dealing with, has not had the opportunity to acquire marked educational advantage or disadvantage. For example, we feel that the amount of language learning possible between the onset of the process at 6-8 months of life and the test age of 12 months is likely to be, in most cases, comparatively modest. In contrast, after another six months of age, children who have learned a great deal of language are probably markedly ahead of those who have learned less than an average amount. In that sense the data on the experiences of 18-21-month-old children would reflect, in part, the fact that some of the children we are dealing with are already significantly behind or ahead in language; whereas, this would not be the case to any important degree at 12 months of age. With that caveat in mind let us proceed to look at our data on these topics.

Extreme Group Analysis

At 18-21 months of age the most interesting differences across the extreme groups are as follows:

	Time Spent (%)		
	Children		Statistical Significance
Experiences	Developing well (n = 8)	Developing less well (n = 5)	(Mann-Whitney U two-tailed)
All social tasks	17.1	10.2	.222
To please	3.4	0.0	.046
Procure a service	4.1	2.7	.080
To direct	0.1	0.0	.066
To eat	9.3	11.9	.094
Live language directed to S	3.1	0.8	.170
Nontask	10.8	25.9	.024
Prepare for activity	3.2	1.3	.046
Gross motor activity	0.1	0.0	.170
Mastery (fine motor)	6.8	0.6	.094

We found that well-developing children still had greater amounts of social experience, but the gap had narrowed to the point where there was only a fairly strong trend rather than a statistically significant difference. We found three social tasks that seemed to relate positively to the development of competence. The strongest relationship was found in the area of attempts at *pleasing the other person*. That relationship was statistically significant, as it was six months earlier. There was a continued trend in the area of attempts at *procuring services* with the relationship being slightly stronger than six months earlier. And we found surfacing (in modest amounts) attempts on the part of well-developing children at *directing the behavior of others*, the others usually being the primary caretakers, most commonly the mothers.

As for nonsocial tasks, we found the poorly developing children spending more time *eating*. Remember, 18-21 months is a period when children usually engage in a good deal of negativistic behavior and are generally more difficult to live with. Routinely we saw parents of children not developing well resort to food as a near final tactic when they simply could not handle misbehavior on the part of their 18-21-month-old children in any other way. The difference in *live language directed* to the child, so strikingly apparent six months earlier, was still present but was considerably smaller. The previously found difference with respect to *live language overheard* disappeared. One of the most striking characteristics of these data, and a terribly unhappy thing for an observer to witness and for children to undergo, is the huge increase in empty time or *nontask* behavior of children developing poorly at the age of 18-21 months. To think that this group averaged 26 percent of their time in desultory scanning or aimless wandering is remarkable, to say the least. Children developing well spent more time *preparing for activities*, suggesting that they were considerably more focused on tasks than children developing poorly. Children developing well seemed to engage in more *large muscle activity* for the sheer joy of it, although it was only a trend. Finally, there were signs that children developing very well spent more time at this stage in *fine motor mastery* tasks, practicing simple digital skills under the guidance of vision.

Task Initiation Information

Regardless of their level of competence, the children at 18-21 months initiate between 85 and 88 percent of all tasks for themselves. The most competent children initiate slightly more of their tasks than they did at 12-15 months (88.1 vs. 85.3 percent), and the least competent children initiate slightly fewer tasks for themselves (85 vs. 91.5 percent).

The mothers' influence is still apparent in the area of social tasks rather than in the area of nonsocial tasks. Mothers of the more competent children initiate fewer social but more nonsocial tasks for their children than they did at 12-15 months (40.4 and 7.6 percent at 18-21 months vs. 33.9 and 11.4 percent at 12-15 months), while mothers of the least competent group are initiating more social but fewer nonsocial experiences (28.3 and 9.2 percent at 18-21 months vs. 54.3 and 6.1 percent at 12-15 months). No initiation of tasks by others is apparent in the data on this age range.

Correlational Analyses of the Effects of Experience at 18-21 Months on the Development of Competence at Three Years of Age

Overall Competence. Turning to the 18-21-month age range, we find that well-developing children still spend more time in social tasks, although the figure now does not reach statistical significance (see Table 46). Statistical significance is reached once again in the experience of *procuring a service*, usually from the mother. It is also reached in the attempts by children developing well to *direct* the behaviors of other people. Likewise, children developing well continue to exhibit more attempts at *pleasing* others (although, overall, such behavior is rare). Strong trends are present in respect to *seeking approval* and *cooperating* with simple requests. All of these figures strongly suggest the centrality of social experiences in the second year of life for the development of competence in young children. This is a point that seems particularly important for this research.

In the nonsocial area, children in our study who ate a lot, particularly between meals, developed less well. Also at this age the children who developed rather poorly spent a huge amount of time in nontask experiences. This particular piece of information serves as a reminder that we are dealing not only with experiences which have likely consequences for later development but which, in part, reflect the consequences of earlier experiences.

Preparing for activities was more common with well-developing children as was a rare but interesting experience labeled *restoring order*. Typical examples of restoring order include picking up a piece of paper and putting it in a basket or otherwise fixing something that is not quite right, such as a misplaced book or a piece on a table surface.

Moving to the nonsignificant but still strong relationships among other tasks and achieved competence levels, we find that *live language directed to the child* continues to be relatively strongly associated with good development as does *procuring objects, practicing fine motor skills* (on small objects), and *engaging in large muscle activity* for the sheer pleasure of it.

Social Competence. We believe Table 46 is rather remarkable. There is not a single task which correlates significantly with social competence at three years of age. Using the threshold value as plus or minus .30 as an indication of a trend, there are only four of all tasks on this rather long list which represent more than one percent of the children's time and show any trend in this respect. The first is a social task called *asserting oneself* or *resisting domination*. The child of high social competence at three has lower scores in asserting himself at 18-21 months of age. In other words, the more ornery the 18-month-old is on balance the less likely he is to be socially competent at three years. We find a lot of between-meal *eating* and *nontask* experiences are not particularly good omens for the development of social competence. The same is true for low scores in *live language directed to the child*. Finally scores in *exploratory behavior* correlate negatively with scores in social competence at three.

Perhaps the fact that we find children mixed in negativism at 18-21 months has something to do with the lack of relationships among tasks and later social competence. We have found that whether a child is developing very well, very poorly, or somewhere in between, he still, by and large, goes through a period of orneriness between the 15th and 21st months of his life. We also find, generally, that children developing well are a bit easier to live with during this period. Nevertheless, they are always more difficult to live with than at an earlier or a later age. Exactly how that judgment relates to these numbers we do not really know.

Nonsocial Competence. Surely the contrast between what we saw in the previous column of Table 46 and the nonsocial column is dramatic indeed. Quite a number of experiences at 18-21 months of age relate significantly to nonsocial competence at three years of age. The sheer amount of social tasks

TABLE 46. Correlation Among Tasks (18-21 Months) and Achievement Variables at Three Years of Age (n = 19)

Social Tasks	Percent Time Spent in Activity (Group Median)	Correlation with Overall Competence[1]	Correlation with Social Competence
All social tasks	16.2	−.37	.15
To please	0.0	−.50*	.07
To cooperate	4.6	−.34	−.27
To gain approval	0.0	−.41	−.13
To procure a service	1.0	−.45*	−.28
To gain attention	2.0	−.11	.28
To maintain social contact	2.8	.22	.26
To direct	0.1	−.53*	−.15
To assert self	1.5	.00	.32
To enjoy pets	0.0	.22	.29
Nonsocial Tasks			
To eat	10.3	.51*	.32
To gain information (v)	10.6	−.25	.00
To gain information (v & a)	6.0	−.17	−.15
live language directed to the child	1.4	−.36	−.30
overheard language	1.3	−.13	.08
mechanical language	0.0	.15	.21
Sesame Street	0.0	−.34	−.40
Nontask	11.8	.61	.38
To pass time	3.2	−.16	−.20
To prepare for activity	2.0	−.51*	−.11
To procure an object	3.1	−.40	−.12
To engage in large muscle activity	0.0	−.36	.00
To imitate	0.0	.09	.07
To pretend	1.5	−.06	.16
To ease discomfort	0.4	−.02	−.10
To restore order	0.6	−.80***	−.43
To operate a mechanism	0.2	−.24	−.23
To explore	6.6	−.16	−.38
Mastery	11.4	−.29	.01
gross	2.4	−.05	.17
fine	3.9	−.42	−.12
verbal	0.1	−.34	.02
To eat and gain information (v)	1.9	.04	.00
To eat and gain information (v & a)	0.4	.18	−.11
live language directed to the child	0.0	.20	.01

[1] The most competent child is ranked 1, and the least competent child is ranked 19. Therefore, the relationship of high competence and greater task duration is negative.

[2] The relationship between high test scores and greater task duration is positive.

  *p ≤ .05
  **p ≤ .01
  ***p ≤ .001

Spearman Rank Correlation

TABLE 46. (continued)

Correlation with Nonsocial Competence	Correlation with Stanford-Binet Test Scores[2]	Correlation with Language Test Scores	Correlation with Abstract Abilities Test Scores	Correlation with Dissonance Test Scores
−.53*	.60**	.60**	.52*	.27[2]
−.62**	.76***	.55*	.72***	.56**
−.53*	.33	.46*	.26	.09
−.54*	.58**	.51*	.58**	.23
−.47*	.39	.45*	.29	.37
−.20	.35	.24	.24	.15
.34	−.24	−.11	−.22	−.24
−.38	.46*	.50*	.37	−.31
.12	.10	.15	.08	.06
.25	−.15	−.16	−.12	−.22
.47*	−.45*	−.35	−.40	−.11
−.33	.41	.32	.41	.17
−.01	.08	.17	.06	−.07
−.53*	.44	.44	.46*	.33
−.20	.34	.22	.38	.16
.24	−.10	−.08	−.16	.03
.15	−.06	.07	−.11	−.18
.29	−.43	−.46*	−.34	−.32
−.64**	.35	.38	.37	.36
−.49*	.64**	.64**	.56**	.60**
−.47*	.49*	.36	.37	.51*
−.45*	.49*	.44	.40	.44
−.29	.07	.16	.08	.05
.02	.14	.33	.16	.22
−.09	.02	−.13	.01	−.16
−.65**	.72***	.76***	.65**	.53*
−.10	.08	.34	.08	.00
.06	−.19	−.24	−.13	−.23
−.16	.34	.21	.27	.47*
−.21	.27	.12	.24	.41
−.12	.31	.26	.31	.27
−.48*	.60**	.45*	.63**	.21
.13	−.02	−.15	.04	.00
.29	−.04	−.08	−.04	.02
−.37	.45*	.40	.40	.32

is strongly related to this outcome variable. Attempts *to please an adult, to cooperate* with requests, and *to procure a service* are all positively correlated with good development. The child who is too clingy, and who therefore has high scores in *seeking to maintain social contact*, is, on balance, not doing so well. A child who attempts *to direct* another preson, usually the parent, is, on balance, likely to be developing well. This pattern is consistent with our staff's impressions.

Turning to nonsocial tasks, we find the following items significantly related to nonsocial competence in a positive fashion: *live language directed to the child, passing time, preparing for an activity, procuring an object, engaging in large muscle activity, restoring order,* and *verbal mastery.* Negatively, we find *eating* the only category with a statistically significant relationship. In other words, a child of 18-21 months of age who eats a lot is, on balance, less likely to be nonsocially competent at three years of age. In addition to the several statistically significant relationships, we have one trend worth noting in that the more *steady staring* we found, apparently the better the development in relation to nonsocial competence.

A couple of relationships of special interest should be mentioned. We note that unlike the case at 12-15 months of age, here at 18-21 months of age, a child developing well is likely to spend more time as a psychological captive— that is, *passing time*—than the child developing poorly. What seemed to happen was that many of our subjects who were developing not so well found themselves spending a lot of their time at 18-21 months of age by themselves. That is, their parents adopted a laissez-faire orientation toward them. They were no longer using restrictive devices as much. The children were, after all, able to walk about and were not as likely to have accidents because of clumsiness. They could also understand simple prohibitions more readily. They were, however, not encouraged to remain near their parents anywhere near as often as children whose development was proceeding well. Close proximity to an adult for an 18-month-old child inevitably leads to a certain amount of *passing time*. One common type of such experience involved the parents telling the child to wait for them while they went off to check briefly on some food that was cooking or to get a diaper. Under such circumstances the child often entered into a *pass time* episode until the mother returned.

Another very common experience is the ride to the market where, at this age, the child is inevitably put into a car seat. We find that children find it hard to engage in any sustained activity for as much as fifteen seconds at a time. It might be assumed that they would find things to look at outside of the car or that they might engage in sustained conversation or, at least, listen to patter from the parent. In fact, none of these happens. The child generally runs out of things to do very quickly in a car seat, and since he cannot leave the scene he soon lapses into boredom.

At 12-15 months of age *procuring an object* was, on balance, a negative sign. High scores in that category were associated with relatively poor development. Now we find just the opposite. The activities of the 18-21-month-old child are generally much more organized and sophisticated than those of the 12-15-month-old child. Now *procuring an object* is usually instrumental to a relatively well-organized activity, whereas at 12 months of age such was not the case.

We have no comment with respect to the *large muscle activity*. We do not understand what its psychological meaning is.

We made an exception to our habit of working only with high duration experiences by listing *verbal mastery* because it is so germane to nonsocial competence. A child is engaged in *verbal mastery* when he is practicing words, for example, in a labeling experience where a mother points out and names items in a child's book or a magazine; the child may attempt to speak the words. Such an episode is what we mean by a *verbal mastery* experience.

We believe that this collection of data is once more rather remarkable in respect to the relationship of early experiences to the achievement of competence.

Performance on the Stanford-Binet Test. As we might expect from both the comparable data dealing with tasks at 12-15 months and the discussions of social and nonsocial competence at 18-21 months, we see a rather remarkable collection of relationships across experiences at 18-21 months and Binet performance at three years. There is again a very strong positive relationship across the total amount of social experience and performance, indicating that, all things being equal, social experience counts in intellectual growth. We believe that statement needs reiteration. We find *to please, to seek approval,* and *to direct adults* or others are tasks which, in general, are highly related to later performance on the Binet. There are trends with respect *to cooperate, to procure a service,* and *to gain attention.* In each case, the more of such activities at 18-21 months, the better the prospects for the child.

A whole host of nonsocial experiences at this time in life seem to relate to later Binet scores. Among the statistically significant tasks that correlate highly with the Binet are the following: *preparing for activities, procuring objects, engaging in large muscle activity, restoring order, engaging in verbal mastery tasks,* and *eating while listening to live language* directed to the child. There is a significant negative relationship between amount of time spent *eating* and performance on the Binet.

Turning to the trends, we find strong positive relationships across Binet scores at three and the following tasks: *steady visual staring, listening to live language directed to the child* and *overheard by the child, passing time* (which, as we have previously remarked, is a sign of regular proximity to an adult at this age), *general mastery* tasks, and *fine motor mastery* tasks, in particular. In addition we find that there is one strong negative trend: high scores in *nontask* or *empty behavior* are negatively related to Binet scores later on. In passing I would suggest that a multiple regression analysis that utilized the strongest of these relationships would very probably produce most impressive results. Again, because an 18-21-month-old child is not only developing with respect to his 36-month ability levels but is also a child who has undergone rather substantial development already, the interpretation of these data is difficult. For example, the category *to eat*: As far as I can tell, an 18-21-month-old child who is being brought up in a home where the parents love him but are not particularly adept at providing a variety of interesting and age-appropriate experiences will end up, often, being given a rather large number of between-meal snacks. Feeding a child in such circumstances is usually a sign that the parents care about his happiness and contentment. It also is effective in the sense that it keeps the child occupied and tends to reduce the demands he makes on the parents, at least while he is eating. From what we can see in this particular study, while a high amount of such experience is related to low levels of achievement, it is also likely to be a consequence of the relatively ineffective collection of child-rearing practices in the preceding year or ten months.

Experiences at 18 to 21 months and language achievement at three years of age. Table 46 also presents the data on this particular issue. Perhaps the most striking aspect of this column is the almost overwhelming strength of relationship across various social tasks and later language development. Such relationships will not come as a big surprise to anybody interested in early development, but we do believe that the power of the numerical data and the specificity of the types of social experience may very well prove to be quite useful. The sum total of social tasks is strongly associated with later language achievement. Episodes of *trying to please another, cooperating with requests, seeking approval, seeking services,* and *trying to direct the other* are all significantly related to later language achievement. All in all, a rather impressive array.

In nonsocial areas we find that statistical significance is achieved in several places and there are some interesting trends. We find a positive relationship between *preparing for activities, restoring order,* and *verbal mastery* experiences and later language success. We find a negative relationship between *empty time* or *nontask* behavior and later language achievement. We find positive trends between *steady staring, live language directed to the child, passing time, procuring an object, engaging in large muscle activity, make-believe or pretend activity, operating a mechanism,* and *eating and listening to live language directed to the child.* The results once more fall into a reasonable pattern. Finally, there is a negative relationship between *eating* and language achievement.

Experiences at 18 to 21 months and abstract ability test scores at three years of age. Table 46 also presents data on the development of this form of higher mental abilities in our subjects. Once again we find strong relationships across social activities and nonsocial skill, and once again we suggest to the reader that this is a rather important finding. The sum total of social tasks positively correlates with later abstract ability. Attempts at *pleasing others* seems very strongly associated as do attempts at *gaining approval* for one or another achievement. There is also a trend with respect to attempts at *directing another* in activities.

Nonsocially we find positive relationships of statistical significance across abstract ability test scores at three and *live language directed to the child, preparing for activities, restoring order,* and *verbal mastery experiences.* We find no negative correlation figures that reach significance. There are trends with respect to positive relationships in regard to *steady staring, live language overheard, passing time, procuring objects, engaging in large muscle activity, fine motor mastery experiences,* and *eating and listening to live language directed to the child.* In the other direction we find a trend that *nontask* experience is an apparently poor sign with respect to future achievements in the area of abstract ability.

Experience at 18 to 21 months of age and the ability to sense dissonance at three years of age. In the last column of Table 46, we find a pattern that deviates fairly substantially from the preceding analyses. The relationship across social tasks and later achievement in this area is considerably smaller; if we had more confidence in the validity of this test at three years of age, we would be inclined to say that social experiences apparently make less difference in this regard. However, we do not have full confidence in the test at three years of age, so we will be more bearish in our interpretations. At any rate, we do see a statistically significant relationship between this ability and experiences designed to *please* another person, a positive trend in respect to *procuring a service,* and a negative trend with respect to *directing* activities; all in all, considerably less of a relationship than in preceding analyses.

In the nonsocial task area, statistically significant positive relationships occur between the ability to sense dissonance at three years of age and *preparing for activities, procuring objects, restoring order,* and *gross mastery experiences.* There are no relationships of a negative variety that reach significance. Positive trends are in *live language directed to the child, passing time, engaging in large muscle activity, gross motor mastery,* and experiences in *eating and listening to live language directed to the child.* There is one negative relationship that is worthy of mention and that is between *nontask* experience and sensing dissonance.

Pattern Analyses: Experiences at 18-21 Months of Age and Competence at Three Years of Age

Table 47 presents correlations among all common experiences of our children at 18-21 months of age and the seven major achievement indices we tested for at or near three years of age. Table 48 presents our multiple regression analyses on patterns of experience at this age as they relate to outcomes at three years of age. Because of our main focus on experiences at 12-15 months of age, the discussion of the data will be brief.

THE LONGITUDINAL EXPERIMENT

ONE YR OLDS 18-21 MOS TASK CORRELATIONS WITH OUTCOME VARS AND INTERCORS
SYMMETRIC MERGE OF QQQQ.1 , QQQQ.3 , AND QQQQ.2

POSITION	LABEL	1 LA NGUA GE.3 6.MO	2 ABS TRCT .A.3 6.MO	3 DISS ONAN CE.3 6.MO	4 RTN ET.3 6.MO	5 WPP SI.6 0.MO	6 ADUL T.SO CIAL	7 OVER ALL. RANK	8 SOC IAL. RANK	9 NSOC IAL. RANK	10 PL EASE	11 C OOPE RATE	12 G AIN. APPR OVAL	13 PRO .SER VICE	14 GA IN.A TTEN TION	15 MNTN .SCL .CON TACT	16 DI RECT	17 ASS ERT. SELF	18 EN JOY. PETS
1	LANGUAGE.36.MO	100	80	66	85	52	35	-77	-41	-88	40	47	44	21	18	-13	42		-30
2	ABSTRCT.A.36.MO	80	100	72	96	61	16	-69	-21	-93	44	27	49	16	22	-18	31		-15
3	DISSONANCE.36.MO	66	72	100	75	41	-10	-40		-72	32		23	30	14	-11	24		-27
4	RINET.36.MC	85	96	75	100	64	20	-76	-26	-98	46	26	49	22	34		36		-32
5	WPPSI.60.MO	52	61	41	64	100	19	-57	-23	-69	55	20	26	36	74	-40	22		-32
6	ADULT.SOCIAL	35	16	-10	20	19	100	-75	-98	-24			-10	27	-18	-31	32	-25	-37
7	OVERALL.RANK	-77	-69	-40	-76	-57	-75	100	80	79	-37	-31	-23	-35	-15	25	-47		41
8	SOCIAL.RANK	-41	-21		-26	-23	-98	80	100	30		-20		-30	13	32	-38	21	43
9	NONSOCIAL.RANK	-88	-93	-72	-98	-69	-24	79	30	100	-51	-36	-52	-24	-39	12	-44		28
10	PLEASE	40	44	32	46	55		-37		-51	100		29	13	58			32	-18
11	COOPERATE	47	27		26	26	20	-31	-20	-36		100	29		-19	16	44	-11	-29
12	GAIN.APPROVAL	44	49	23	49	36	-10	-23		-52		29	100		29	-26	36	27	-36
13	PROCURE.SERVICE	21	16	30	22	36	27	-35	-30	-24	13	-19		100			39	25	
14	GAIN.ATTENTION	18	22	14	34	74	-18	-15	13	-39	58	16	29		100				
15	MNTN.SCL.CONTACT	-13	-18	-11		-40	-31	25	32	12		44		-26	27	100	-23	25	
16	DIRECT	42	31	24	36	22	32	-47	-38	-44	32	-18	36	39	-36	-23	100	-32	
17	ASSERT.SELF						-25		21			-31		-11		25		100	
18	ENJOY.PETS	-30	-15		-27	-32	-37	41	43	28	32			-29			19	-45	100
19	MASTERY.GROSS						-20	13	18	-19	-18			19	-16	-29			40
20	MASTERY.FINE	14	23	32	17	11	29	-31	-21		11	28	-13	37	22	-11	43	-38	
21	MASTERY.VERBAL	35	35	26	40	47	20	-33	-22	-43		33	49		-10	-51		-29	23
22	EAT.AND.G.INFO.V	-11		17		-10		13			-11			10	44	-20	38	20	-15
23	EAT.AND.A.LIVEDIRCT	33	34		40	43		-34	-12	-41	-67	-23	21	52	-23	-48		-12	42
24	EAT	-19	-27		-34	-36	-30	44	31	38	-27	42	-17		36	36			
25	GAIN.INFO.V	34	38	32	38	30		-19	-28	-37	50	-44	14					-17	-35
26	GAIN.INFO.V.A			-28			27	-17	-23	-46	-24	12	54	-26	27	-18	53	26	-27
27	LIVE.DIRECT	49	47	28	43	17	19	-40		-32		21	40		-16	-21	17		-31
28	OVERHEARD	31	39	18	31	39		-19						-15	18				
29	MECHANICAL	-40	-49	-16	-35	-16	-18	26	19	33	-22	-43	-19	-24	22	40	-22	49	-19
30	SESAME.ST	-11	-14	-37	-10	-21	34	-14	-34	19	-19	-42	-16	-44	-19		-14	12	-13
31	NONTASK	-67	-57	-35	-62	-38	-47	67	51	60	-21	-22	-26		-13	24	-44	22	32
32	PASS.TIME	15	-14	-14		14	14		-14			33			36	-11		-36	-34
33	PREPARE.ACT	62	57	52	65	44		-47	-13	-69	16	11	47	29	47	-18	32		-29
34	PROCURE.OBJECT	28	31	35	45	54		-40	-28	-48	31			47	47	-21	35		-35
35	LARGE.MUSCLE	25	32	33	37	48	14	-34	-10	-39	16	20	22	71		-27	48		-20
36	IMITATE	17					-26	20	29		14	37	-20		-12	42	-19		
37	ROLE.PLAY	26		28		-30				-36		-11	-12	-30	-29	25	-15	53	28
38	EASE.DISCOMFORT	-12	-15		-14		-12	24	12	16		-14	-20	-18	19	-35	-19	-43	
39	RESTORE.ORDER	58	60	37	64	25	32	-68	-38	-70	14	45	39	26			59	14	-12
40	OPERATE.MECH	24				-19	38	-29	-37		18	20	-17	-15	-12		-12	39	11
41	EXPLORE	-42	-31	-36	-28	-19	27		-23	26		-26				30	-14	12	-21
42	MASTERY	26	29	51	30	23		-21		-33		30		43		-33	27	-40	21

The Relation of Environmental Factors 105

ONE YR OLDS 18-21 MOS TASK CORRELATIONS WITH OUTCOME VARS AND INTERCORS
SYMMETRIC MERGE OF QQQQ.1, QQQQ.3, QQQQ.2, AND QQQQ.2

POSITION	LABEL	19 ASTEPY.G ROSS M	20 MAST ERY. FINE	21 MA STER Y.VF RBAL	22 EAT. AND. FQ.V	23 .A.L IVED IRCT	24 EAT	25 GAT N.IN FO.V	26 G ATN. INFO .V.A	27 LIV E.DI RECT	28 O VERH EARD	29 ME CHAN ICAL	30 S ESAM E.ST	31 NON TASK	32 P ASS. TIME	33 PRE PARE .ACT	34 OCCU E.OR JECT	35 LARG E.MU SCLE	36 IMI TATE
1	LANGUAGE.36.MO	14	35	-11	33	-19	34		49	31	-40	-11	-67	15	62	28	25	17
2	ABSTRCT.A.36.MO	23	35		34	-27	38		47	39	-49	-14	-57		57	31	32	
3	DISSONANC.36.MO	32	26	17	32		12	-28	28	18	-16	-37	-35	-14	52	35	33	-26
4	BINET.36.MO		17	40	40	-34	38		43	31	-35	-10	-62		65	45	37	-20
5	WPPSI.60.MO	11	47	-10	43	-36	30		17	39	-16	-21	-38	14	44	54	48	29
6	ADULT.SOCIAL	-20	29	20		-30		27	19		-18	34	-47	14		14		
7	OVERALL.RANK	13	-31	-33	-34	44	-19	-17	-40	-19	26	-14	67		-47	-40	-34	-20
8	SOCIAL.RANK	18	-21	-22	-12	31		-28	-23		19	-34	51	-14	-13	-22	-10	20
9	NONSOCIAL.RANK		-19	-43	-41	38	-37		-46	-32	33	19	60		-69	-48	-39	29
10	PLEASE		11		67	-27	50	-24			-22	-42	-21	33	16	31	16	14
11	COOPERATE		28	33	21	-23	42	-44	12	21	-43	-42	-22		11		20	37
12	GAIN.APPROVAL		-13	49		-17	14		54	40	-19	-16	-26		47		22	-20
13	PROCURE.SERVICE	19	37	22	52	-23	36	-26		18	-15	-24	-44		29	47	71	-12
14	GAIN.ATTENTION		-16	-10	44	-48	36			-21		-19	-13	-11	47	47		42
15	MNTN.SCL.CONTACT	-29		-11	-20	-12	-17	26	-18	17	40	12	24	-36		-24	-27	-19
16	DIRECT	19		43	38	42	-35	-27	53		-22	-14	22	-34	32	35	48	
17	ASSERT.SELF	-45	40	-38	20	47	-15	-33			49	-13	-44	-14	-29	-35	-20	-12
18	ENJOY.PETS				-15			-45	-31		-19	-21	32	-28	25	52	21	
19	MASTERY.GROSS	100	-18	40	14	-36	37	-36		-27	-23	-21	-29	-14	25		12	-11
20	MASTERY.FINE	-18	100	31		69			33	52	-34	-27	-22	-28	15			-25
21	MASTERY.VERBAL		-16	100					-36	18	-22	-16	-19	18	-14	33	-23	-23
22	EAT.AND.G.INFO.V	40	31	-17	100	-36	69	20	10		-47	-20	-20	-34	24	14	36	14
23	EAT.A.LIVEDIRCT			14	100		-43	-21	-27		-19	100	-32		-15		-12	46
24	EAT	47		-36		100	-30	100	-30	41	-24	-15	-30	-28	14	-24		38
25	GAIN.INFO.V	-15	-22	-19	20	-43	100	-23	43	22	-40	-22	-14	-12	33		19	-24
26	GAIN.INFO.V.A	-33	-18		-21	-30	100	43	100	100	37	89	-34	36	14	-23	32	-11
27	LIVE.DIRECT	-27	-45	33	10	-27	-23		43	22	-24	18		13	14	-13	13	
28	OVERHEARD	-23	-36	52			41		100	22	100	-29	59	-10	-22	-21	-17	-23
29	MECHANICAL	-21	-34	18	-19	-24	-40	37	18	-24	100	12	-27	-24	-54	-32	-30	14
30	SESAME.ST	-29	-27	-22	-20	-15	-22	89	-34	-29	12	100	100	19	100	43		46
31	NONTASK	-14	-22		-32	-28	-30	-14	36		59	-27	100	19				-17
32	PASS.TIME	25	-28	-19	24		25	-12	33	13	-10	-24	-54	100	100	56	19	
33	PREPARE.ACT	52	15	18	43	-15	14			14	-13	-22	-32		56	100	46	
34	PROCURE.OBJECT	21		-14	36	-12	38	-24	-24	-23		-21	-30	46	19	100	100	
35	LARGE.MUSCLE	-12		-11	-23	-11	-20	-14	-11	13		-17	14	-23		46	100	
36	IMITATE		12	-25					32	-15	24	-23	-30	-13		-17		100
37	ROLE.PLAY	-34	-11	-31	-24	49	-20	24	-20		-34	20	13	-23		-35		-16
38	EASE.DISCOMFORT	78	-24	48	-24	-29		-14		-15			-22	-13	63	25	-27	-14
39	RESTORE.ORDER		26	-14	20	17			38		-17	-17	-43			49	-17	-19
40	OPERATE.MECH	-34	38	16	-33	-44	-17	14	-22	10			31	-26	-12	-35	44	
41	EXPLORE	-32	-19	-21	-33	-44			-11	-41	43	12	-46	-28		-35	-27	-42
42	MASTERY	66	59		53	33	-17		-60	-18		-51	-40		-28	36	42	24	

ONE YR OLDS 18-21 MOS TASK CORRELATIONS WITH OUTCOME VARS AND INTERCORS
SYMMETRIC MERGE OF QQQQ.1 , QQQQ.3 , AND QQQQ.2

POSITION	LABEL	37 ROLE.PLAY	38 EAS E.DISCOMFORT	39 R ESTORE.ORDER	40 OPERATE.MECH	41 EXPLORE	42 MASTERY
1	LANGUAGE.36.MO	26	-12	58	24	-42	26
2	ABSTRCT.A.36.MO		-15	60		-31	29
3	DISSONANCE.36.MO	28		37		-36	51
4	BINET.36.MO		-14	64		-28	30
5	WPPSI.60.MO	-30		25	-19	-19	23
6	ADULT.SOCIAL		-12	32	38	27	
7	OVERALL.RANK		24	-68	-29		-21
8	SOCIAL.RANK		12	-38	-37	-23	
9	NONSOCIAL.RANK		16	-70		26	-33
10	PLEASE			14	18		
11	COOPERATE	-11	-14	45	20	-26	30
12	GAIN.APPROVAL	-12	-20	39	-17	-17	
13	PROCURE.SERVICE	-30	-18	26	-15		43
14	GAIN.ATTENTION	-29	19		-12		
15	MNTN.SCL.CONTACT	25	-35			30	-33
16	DIRECT	-15	-19	59	-12	-14	27
17	ASSERT.SELF	53	-43	14	39	12	-40
18	ENJOY.PETS	28		-12	11	-21	21
19	MASTERY.GROSS	-34	78		-34	-32	66
20	MASTERY.FINE		-24	26	38		59
21	MASTERY.VERBAL					-19	-21
22	EAT.AND.G.INFO.V	-31	48	-14	16	-33	53
23	EAT.A.LIVEDIRCT		-24	20			
24	EAT		49	-29	17	-44	33
25	GAIN.INFO.V	-20				-17	
26	GAIN.INFO.V.A	24	-14			14	-60
27	LIVE.DIRECT		-20	38	-22	-11	-18
28	OVERHEARD		-15	10	-41		
29	MECHANICAL	24	-34	-17		43	-51
30	SESAME.ST	20		-17		12	-40
31	NONTASK	13	-22	-43		31	-46
32	PASS.TIME	-23	-13		-26		-28
33	PREPARE.ACT			63	-12		36
34	PROCURE.OBJECT	-35	25	49	-35		42
35	LARGE.MUSCLE	-27	-17	44	-35	-27	24
36	IMITATE	16	-14	-19		-42	
37	ROLE.PLAY	100	-36		50	-11	-29
38	EASE.DISCOMFORT	-36	100	-23	-15	-32	43
39	RESTORE.ORDER		-23	100			28
40	OPERATE.MECH	50	-15		100		
41	EXPLORE	-11	-32			100	-28
42	MASTERY	-29	43	28		-28	100

TABLE 48. Task Experiences (18-21 Months) Predicting Outcome Variables (36 months), Regression Analysis

Dependent Variables	Multiple r	p*	Regression Equation
Overall Competence Rank (1 = high, 39 = low)	.8706	.010	Predicted Overall = 1.9361 + % duration(−0.2743) Procure a Service + % duration(0.7023) Eat + % duration(−0.2081) Live Language Directed to S + % duration(0.8023) Nontask + % duration(1.8026) Prepare for Activity + % duration(−0.7822) Procure an Object + % duration(−4.7436) Restore Order
Social Competence Rank (1 = high, 39 = low)	.8429	.023	Predicted Social = −5.6683 + % duration(−0.9452) Procure a Service + % duration(2.5151) Maintain Social Control + % duration(−6.1659) Direct + % duration(1.3517) Eat + % duration(0.3726) Nontask + % duration(1.3073) Restore Order + % duration(−7.4465) Operate a Mechanism
Nonsocial Competence Rank (1 = high, 39 = low)	.8302	.032	Predicted Nonsocial = 25.3951 + % duration(−1.2897) Cooperate + % duration(−1.1832) Gain Attention + % duration(0.5013) Eat + % duration(0.0446) Gain Info (v) + % duration(0.4686) Nontask + % duration(−2.8643) Prepare for Activity + % duration(−1.0310) Procure an Object
Stanford-Binet Intelligence Test	.8412	.052	Predicted Binet = 69.8329 + % duration(2.2485) Gain Attention + % duration(0.0084) Eat + % duration(1.6575) Live Language Directed to S + % duration(2.5818) Gain Info (v) + % duration(−0.7456) Nontask + % duration(0.9828) Prepare for Activity + % duration(2.7133) Procure an Object + % duration(9.0339) Restore Order

*Statistical probability

TABLE 48. (continued)

Dependent Variables	Multiple r	p*	Regression Equation
PSP Language Test	.8540	.007	Predicted Language = 40.2673 + % duration(1.2658) + % duration(1.0794) + Score Cooperate Live Language Directed to S % duration(−0.4007) = % duration(2.4005) + % duration(1.0485) + Nontask Prepare for Activity Restore Order % duration(−0.5808) Explore
PSP Abstract Abilities Test	.8068	.025	Predicted A.A. = 7.1344 + % duration(0.0976) + % duration(0.1540) + Score Gain Info (v) Live Language Directed to S % duration(0.1511) + % duration(−0.0447) + % duration(0.1469) + Overheard Language Nontask Prepare for Activity % duration(0.5951) Restore Order
PSP Dissonance Test	.6191	.224	Predicted Dissonance = 6.3143 + % duration(0.0068) + % duration(0.4137) + Score Nontask Prepare for Activity % duration(0.1084) + % duration(0.1254) + % duration(−0.1128) Procure an Object Restore Order Explore

*Statistical probability

As with the earlier analysis, a small number (seven) of common experiences predicts well the rank in overall competence at three years of age for our sample (multiple r = +0.87, p = .010). Predictive power is even greater in the area of social development (multiple r = +0.84, p = .023). It remains high in regard to nonsocial competence (multiple r = +0.83, p = .032); drops slightly in regard to performance on the Stanford-Binet test (multiple r = +0.84, p = .052), the language capacity test (multiple r = +0.85, p = .007), and the abstract-thinking ability test (multiple r = +0.81, p = .0025); and drops considerably in the area of the ability to sense dissonance (multiple r = +0.62, p = .224).

It seems to us that the most powerful result of these multiple regression pattern analyses is simply the magnitude of the relationship between small groups of tasks during the second year of life and achievement at 36 months of life. Multiple regressions that range from the 70's to the mid-90's have to be considered impressive. Statistical probabilities of the sort that we have associated with those regression figures are also imposing. What this seems to mean is that we have captured some important relationships in this particular study. We, of course, never knew with any confidence that we would. To some extent, the creation of our task instrument involved arbitrary decisions. In particular it covers only one level of the process of development. One could certainly find far more complicated schemes for analysis. After all *seeking attention*, for example, could be subdivided into at least a half dozen specific ways of seeking attention. To name a few, a child may use sound or understandable language, or may tug on another person's clothing or body, or may strike another person. The number of mechanisms that could and are used as a child changes over time and as situations vary is great. We felt that an approach that was strictly linked to behavior would have been hopeless from a practical data-gathering standpoint. As it is, we barely had respectable success in gathering reliable data with approximately 36 primary categories of the instrument we use. On the other hand, one could envision a coding system that would have far fewer categories, with the categories we talk about subsumed under more molar purposes. For example, from time to time a child will be seeking attention in order to procure a service, in order to get something to eat or drink, in order to eat or drink. We could subsume each of the instrumental tasks within the more molar purpose and ultimately end up with a system that had no more than seven or eight categories. That is, one major molar category might be to play, another might be to interact socially, and another might be to be essentially passive, etc. It, therefore, was with the awareness of some risk that we invested in the particular level of analysis that we use in our task instrument.

To say that our study found very strong relationships across early task patterns and later achievement is, of course, not to say that such relationships will hold for the population at large. The size of any correlation depends not only on the strength of the actual developmental relationships within the data but also upon the nature of the population worked with, among other things.

We deliberately sought out children who were likely to develop in rather divergent directions. We clearly did not succeed completely. Our well-developing children did quite well, as expected. But our poorly developing children were nowhere near as weak as we assumed they would be at the outset of the study. In general they achieved better than we had predicted.* The population of 19 one-year-olds on whom we have concentrated our analyses nevertheless could not be construed as anything like a representative sample of children in eastern Massachusetts, let alone in the United States. Our sample contains one group of children who achieved the very highest levels of achievement short of genius and others somewhere around the middle or slightly above the middle of the population. We have therefore the kind of population from which one would expect fairly strong correlational results.

We have, on several occasions, remarked that we believe that most children in the first 7 months of life live in adequate environments with respect to the modest kinds of educational achievements attained during this period. We have repeatedly noted in the literature that children who end up doing rather poorly at school (when they are six or seven years and older) do not look weak by any general developmental standards during the first year of life but begin to lag behind (in academically relevant areas, at least) sometime during the second year of life. Given that general picture of development along with what we have known and newly learned about the growth of central educational processes (such as language), the data on the process of learning that come earliest among those that we collected (namely, the data on the 12-15-month period of life) would appear to be the most purely causative with respect to divergent development of competence. This is a cumbersome way of saying that because we are looking for differences in experience that are consequential for educational development, we are more interested in our 12-15-month data than we are in experiential data on our children when they were older.

Pattern Analyses: Concluding Remarks

In all of our analyses—whether they are of the experiences of our children in the groups most extremely separated at three years of age in competence levels, the correlational analyses that we dealt with in our second type of analysis in this chapter, or the pattern analyses based upon multiple regression procedures—we find consistencies that seem to have substantial heuristic value. First of all, we find that even though over 36 primary types of experiences are engaged in by children when they are three years of age, it is a considerably smaller number of experiences than children engage in during their 12-15-month age period. Of this smaller number (which may range from 15 to 20), a par-

---

*For example, see our follow-up Wechsler Test Performance data for the subjects when they were five years of age, page 149.

ticular, even smaller group seems to be repeatedly implicated with respect to the development of competence.

The best single way of focusing in on those potentially critical experiences is to look at the pattern analysis of the 12-15-month task data as it relates to general competence at three years of age. There are eight tasks that are implicated. In most instances the same tasks crop up in each of the analyses of child-rearing practices, resultant experiences, and later achievement. Two of the eight tasks are social experiences: the first is *procuring services,* and the second is *seeking attention. Procuring services* ties in conceptually with the social ability of *using an adult as a resource* and as such is particularly likely to be of heuristic value. Both experiences cannot happen in great quantities unless there is another human being around who is susceptible to, and indeed encourages, such overtures by the child. Bear in mind that throughout these various analyses on relationships of experiences to development, we find that children developing well are children who have a richer and larger amount of social interaction in this period shortly after the first birthday. We believe that as trite as that finding might appear to some, to have quantified it is very important, and its message should not be lost, either scientifically or for humane purposes. A one-year-old child who is kept away from close proximity with his mother (or other primary caretaker) because that person has too many other things to do or because the cultural life style is incompatible with close interchanges or because the mother is working and the primary caretaker is not there to interact with the child is, on balance, in a situation that is not likely to be good for development to the extent that these data turn out to be valid.

Turning from the social experiences, we find six nonsocial experiences are implicated. *Gross motor mastery* tasks—for example, practice in throwing and retrieving a ball or difficult climbing—represent one category. We distinguish such large muscle practice from *fine motor mastery* in which the child is usually concentrating on some form of hand-eye activity. In addition to *gross motor mastery,* the other nonsocial experiences of special interest are *eating and steady staring, steady staring, listening to live language directed at the child, passing time,* and *procuring objects.* These nonsocial tasks fall into two groups, those that are positively associated with good development and those that are negatively associated with good development. *Steady staring* and *listening to language* are positively associated with good development. The difference between *eating and staring steadily* at something vs. merely *staring steadily* at something is probably not psychologically meaningful. The significance of *listening to live language directed specifically to the child* seems obvious. On the other hand, practice in *gross motor skills,* time spent *trying to procure objects* of one sort or another, and time spent as a psychological captive *with little to do,* as is often the case when a child is confined to a playpen, are all negatively associated with the development of competence and are apparently to be avoided.

None of these ideas violates common sense. Time spent procuring objects would, on balance, seem to be good for the development of a child in comparison to time spent doing nothing at all. However, in the overall economy of experiences of children we have studied, a child who spends more time procuring objects is a child who is not having as rich a social life as some of the other children nor developing as well as they are. The correlational matrix (see page 147) indicates that the common social tasks and the task of *procuring an object* are indeed negatively related. With *to please*, the correlation is −.14, with *procure a service* it is −.14, with *gain attention* it is −.23, and with *maintain social contact* it is −.29. In our sample, if a 12-15-month-old child spent more time than the average for the group trying to get objects, that child was less likely to engage in social experience.

Looking at *gross motor mastery*, we find a similar pattern: negative correlations with the major social tasks of *procuring a service*, −.14; *gaining attention*, −.19; and *maintaining social contact*, −.30. There is a positive correlation with only one social task: *asserting self*, +.17. Asserting oneself is likely to involve a child resisting a suggestion by an adult or some other person.

Looking at the secondary multiple regression analyses, we find that whether we are talking about later social or nonsocial competencies, we find a strong relationship between at least one, sometimes two or three, social experiences in the 12-15-month age range and later achievements. We believe this repeated finding warrants special emphasis. People in child development research, by and large, have not studied the relationships among the social experiences of infants and toddlers and their intellectual and linguistic achievements. Beyond simple generalizations to the effect that adults have to provide love for children, detail, information, and supporting data have been lacking, in our opinion. That is not to say that no one has ever found such a relationship. However, the emphasis of past work seems to have been on the links between nonsocial experiences and nonsocial achievements. For example, people have often talked about the amount of language heard and the later level of language skill. The fact that language learning takes place in an atmosphere that involves a great deal of affect and human interaction has generally been less featured in analyses and reports than we believe is appropriate.

When we looked for patterns of tasks for 12-15-month-old children that best predicted nonsocial achievement at three years of age, we found two social tasks plus five nonsocial tasks. Those two social tasks were the same found in the analysis having to do with overall achievement. When we looked at the pattern of tasks that would best predict social competencies at age three, we again found two social tasks out of the seven experiences that were implicated. *Procuring a service* appears repeatedly in these analyses whether we are focusing on overall, nonsocial, or social achievement. Now, instead of *seeking attention*, we find *maintaining social contact* in that analysis. We do not intend to probe into the various possible meanings of the varieties of the tasks involved. We do not believe we are in a position to do a great deal of reliable speculating about these patterns, but a few things seem quite obvious. For a child to score well on a Binet at three years of age (and few parents would prefer to have their children not do well on a Binet at three years of age, although we do not mean to imply that it is more than it is), six tasks, according to our data, seem to be of special relevance. Once again, two of them are the key social tasks of *procuring a service* and *gaining attention*; and, once again, *steady staring* shows up prominently. *Live language directed to the child, preparing for activities,* and *pass time* experience were substantially related to the achievement of high scores on a Binet at three years for our subjects. To the extent that these relationships persist across the different analyses, it would seem to us that one should feel even greater confidence in their likely salience.

All in all, these analyses suggest that for a child to develop well, he should have extensive human contact during the 12-15-month age range. He should be encouraged to use another person to help him succeed in tasks when the requirements are beyond his abilities. He should also be encouraged in his natural tendencies to gain attention. It appears that there are two major ways in which children can be discouraged from seeking attention. One is the obvious way: when there is nobody nearby, there is less inducement for the activity and no chance of success. On the other hand, a second way to slow the growth of effective attention-seeking skills is to spend so much time with the child, anticipating his every need that he never *needs* to seek anybody's attention because he has *always had some*. The fact that our successful children did have high scores in seeking attention means that someone was not always hovering over them. We believe this point is very important.

In all of our analyses, *live language directed to the child* appears very likely to be beneficial for the development of competence. Later we will describe, at greater length, the particular style in which such language was delivered to the children who were developing well. We found repeatedly that the child whose movement about the home was regularly limited by confinement in playpens, cribs, or jump seats, had high *pass time* scores at 12-15 months of age. It would seem that a child should not be chronically restricted in his opportunities to explore the environment and to engage in the normal interchanges with people and objects which inevitably result.

How to facilitate the *steady staring* behavior of children which we routinely find associated with good development is not clear to us. We do know that the apparently effective adults in our sample habitually point out and comment on interesting events to their children. *Gaining information through steady staring* is focused visual attention.

The other tasks that crop up in the analyses seem to be either signs that things are not going well, in the case of negative correlations, or tasks that particularly relate to the specific outcome measure involved. Examples of tasks that do not appear to be good signs for later development are the already discussed *pass time* task, *gross mastery* experience (if unusually frequent), and seeking to *procure objects* (if unusually frequent). Tasks that seem particularly associated with certain of the measured competencies are, for example, *preparing for activities*, which is strongly related to Binet scores, and *maintaining social contact*, which is strongly related to social development.

THE IMPORTANCE OF PROCESS MONITORING

How to help children develop well has been a longstanding interest in the field of child development research. Over the last decade or so that interest has increased substantially. Investigators who have studied the general topic of learning have been active for quite a long time. Indeed, the work of pioneers such as Pavlov and Thorndike and Skinner all relate, in a very fundamental way, to the current, very strong interest in helping the young child to develop well. In spite of the fact that many efforts of diverse kinds have been pursued over several decades, a solid science of early human development does not yet exist. There are very special problems associated with the study of human learning, and a brief discussion of those problems seems in order at this point as a basis from which to discuss our results in the light of other relevant work.

One can study the "learning process" from learning experiences that cover a few minutes in the life of a subject or, in contrast, that go on for several weeks or for even longer periods of time. Some learnings take place rather quickly, and other learnings take place over very long periods of time. For example, the learning of a foreign language will take months, perhaps even years, of part-time study, whereas learning to operate one's new tape recorder is likely to take something less than an hour; there are even simpler learning tasks that take only a minute or two. While learning a foreign language would seem to be considerably more complicated than the very brief and simple kinds of learning, the sizable problem facing anybody who would study human development is that human beings seem to be learning from the time they are born on through as many as eighty *years* or so. This mind-boggling range of durations of time for various learnings to take place does not seem often to be reflected in the work of investigators on the topic of learning. By far, the most substantial efforts of a serious, scientific kind of study of human learning have been focused on processes that transpire over rather small durations of time. The impressive array of findings in the area of conditioning studies, typified by the work of Pavlov and Thorndike, Skinner and thousands of others, by and large focuses on learning events that cover very brief periods of time in the lives of the subjects involved. Occasionally long-term effects of circumscribed experiences are examined (e.g., the work of J. McVicker Hunt on the hoarding behavior of adult rats as related to their early experiences). In a sense, such studies do span a substantial portion of a life of the animal. But no attempt is made in such studies to monitor learning experiences *throughout* the lifetime. Indeed, except for species with relatively short life spans, this kind of task would seem to be beyond doing by any individual investigator for many obvious reasons. Yet, if an observer studies closely the development of young children as they go about their everyday activities, he cannot fail to be impressed by the astronomical number of learning events in any child's life.

We have found that the typical infant usually focuses on a task for considerably less than one minute of time. Now, what do we mean by focusing on a task? A one-year-old child may enter a room, walk to a window, and look out. The child may stare steadily at an object off in the distance, or he may turn around and move to an object on the floor. He may sit down with the object, gum it, finger it, handle it, then move off and start to climb the sofa, change his mind, turn around, seek out his mother, and so forth and so on. We believe there is a certain reasonableness in talking about each of these activities as having its own distinctness and therefore qualifying as a separate event. Exactly how much learning a child does in each of those events is anyone's guess, but we know too little as yet to conclude that such common experiences have no educational significance. A more conservative judgment is that each experience constitutes some kind of learning event. If one grants that kind of notion (and, admittedly, some will not), then in the space of an hour such a child is likely to average about 120 such events. Since the typical one-year-old is likely to be awake about twelve hours a day, he experiences about 1,400 such learning events each day. Multiply that number by 365 days in a year, and multiply that total by the number of years in a lifetime, or even in a preschool lifetime, or for that matter in infancy and toddlerhood, and it is clear that we are dealing with astronomical sums.

To watch the movements from one target of attention to the next in a young child is to watch the process of development. To the best of our knowledge, formal research of this kind has rarely been done. To trace the history of efforts at the study of the process of learning is beyond our competence, to say nothing of the limitations of a book such as this. Certainly, in the recent past, one historical strand of great importance can be traced. It began with the work of Kurt Lewin (1935, 1951), who, several decades ago, introduced the topic of topological psychology and the concept of the psychological life-space. Lewin's work stimulated that of Roger Barker and Herbert Wright and their students, most especially Philip and Maxine Schoggen.

Observational work in the Lewinian tradition seemed to have two particularly important distinguishing features. On the one hand, there was the interest in the scientific analysis of the continuous flow of behavior. On the other, there was an interest in what was called *ecological* or *environmental* psychology. The latter interest was an equally formidable challenge in that these investigators took seriously the undeniable reality that in addition to a continuous stream of behavior and learning there was a continuous stream of environmental input to each living creature. These notions are quite compatible with ideas about interactionalism, strongly implied in the work of Piaget (1952), spelled out in the work of J. McVicker Hunt (1961), and argued forcibly in the work of Thomas et al. (1964) and Escalona (1968), among others. It is one thing to point to the obvious reality of the continuity of behavior and its infinite number of elements. It is another thing to point to the parallel flow of environmental factors. It is yet another to point to their interaction. But identifying these several realities is some distance away from dealing with them in scientific terms. Valiant and substantial attempts have been made, but so far this particular topic seems to be beyond the grasp of our comparatively primitive scientific methods. Birch, for example, working with Thomas, Chess, and others lamented the lack of interactionism in early longitudinal studies of personality development but then made relatively little headway in his own longitudinal study in spite of his commitment to the approach. Escalona's recent report, too, effectively emphasizes the necessity of an interactionist understanding, but we find that her progress in coping with issues like the complementary qualities of a baby and his mother, combined with the difficulty of sequential analyses, has been very modest. We, for that matter, do not pretend to have made any greater progress. Indeed, we have not even seriously attempted a true interactionalistic approach to early human development.

The early massive longitudinal studies, initiated in the 1920s and 1930s in the United States, have been summarized in a most useful article by Kagan (1964). He describes the kinds of data collection and analysis they performed. In the Berkeley Growth Study, for example, 61 young children were recruited during their first months of life and then some 50, on the average, were studied for the next 26 years. The prime focus was on the growth of intelligence. The children were seen monthly during their first fifteen months of life, and then less frequently thereafter. Attempts have been made, over the last two decades, to determine what was learned about the influence of maternal behaviors on the growth of intelligence of the children in the studies. The method consisted mainly of correlational analyses of maternal characteristics and the intellectual achievement of the children. The bulk of the time the observers spent in the presence of each infant was time when the infant was being tested on a standard test of general achievement, in this case the California First Year Mental Scale. Subsequently, ratings of the mother's behavior toward the subject were made. In addition, the observational notes that were made during the testing sessions were converted to numerical scores having to do with the mothers' behavior, and presumably having to do with the consequential experiences that the children underwent every day. This kind of approach to the question of how early experiences influence development has been used by a number of investigators. It is, in many basic ways, the same approach that Marjorie Honzik and others used in the Guidance Study, another of the major longitudinal studies. Again, ratings of parental characteristics were made from the behavior of parents during interviews and test sessions. Maternal concern, worrisomeness, and achievement orientation were some of the major dimensions studied. Such information about parents was presumed to be germane to the experiences the children were undergoing and was therefore examined through correlational procedures for its significance for later scores on standard IQ tests. In such studies the child's stream of experience is not dealt with directly. The examination of what the child is learning is indirect in that it is approached through observations of parental behavior; it is a remarkably limited examination in the sense that the contact with the child is very brief, usually amounting to no more than an hour or an hour and a half per year.

This kind of approach to the study of the effects of experience on human development has worried a number of students of the subject, and recently quite a few thoughtful analyses on this issue have appeared. In particular, Wenar (1972), Caldwell (1968), Escalona (1968), Sander (1974), Bronson (1974), Yarrow et al. (1975), Schoggen and Schoggen (1968), and Clarke-Stewart (1973) have all written about the necessity for close monitoring of the stream of experience. Each of these authors went on to do substantial work of this type. Interestingly, three of them (Escalona, Sander, and Wenar) came to the study of the stream of behavior from an interest in personality development and related topics. The Schoggens come out of the tradition of Lewin, Barker, and Wright, which was more methodological than substance oriented. Caldwell, Clark-Stewart, and Yarrow et al. seem especially concerned with the avoidance of educational underachievement. We are interested both in the avoidance of developmental underachievement and also in the maximizing of achievement.

Even though these and other talented people have begun to invest in the methodological problems involved in process analysis, we still face a situation where the comparison of findings in the subject area is very difficult. Not only do the various investigators have diverse foci, but the methods they chose to build are also diverse. Since each of these investigators is committed to the use of quantitative procedures in dealing with the problem of understanding ongoing development, one inevitably has to start to convert a continuous flow of behavior into a form that is amenable to statistical analysis. This question leads us to several kinds of problems.

In our research, we start with the ultimate goal of understanding how early experiences can influence the development of overall competence during the first three years of life. The definition of overall competence that we use came from extensive field observations by a staff of well over a dozen people. These observations led us to a definition of a well-developed three-year-old which included conventional abilities in the area of intellectual and linguistic skills, as well as a number of social competencies and certain aspects of nonsocial functioning that are not conventionally tested in three-year-olds. As an example of the latter, I refer to the capacity to take the perspective of another person and the capacity to organize activities and perform as an effective executive, among several others. In our selection of outcome variables we were guided by this home-grown definition of outstanding development in three-year-old children; and, although we did not manage to develop assessment techniques for all seventeen dimensions of overall competence, we did cover social competence and several of the nonsocial abilities. In contrast, in the work of Clark-Stewart there is a relatively conventional approach to outcome measures with language assessment and general mental status assessed with conventional instruments at 17 and 17½ months. As is the case with other studies, Clark-Stewart created new measures of other outcomes by forming subscales from conventional scales. The Cattell was used to generate a subscale to measure ego strength, imaginativeness, and other characteristics much as Yarrow et al. have used the Bayley Scales of Infant Development to produce eight clusters of items to evaluate aspects of child achievement such as social responsiveness, goal directedness, secondary circular actions, etc.

Escalona assessed developmental outcome using ratings which she and her colleagues created on five "adaptation indices": developmental status, irritability, pleasure in functioning, adequacy of vegetative functioning, and excitability. Sander, also coming from a background of interest in personality development, was particularly interested in "characterological" outcomes in children at six years of age. There are no standardized ways of assessing characterological outcomes, and Sander's project lost its financial support midway through its design, so they never did come to a determination of how they would measure such an outcome. The first point to be made, therefore, is that it is rare to find two research studies interested in the influence of early experience and development that use the same outcome measures at the same ages of children.

The next consideration is the question of what kinds of children were studied in each of the various programs. In our program we seriously attempted to find subjects from the entire socioeconomic spectrum, given the fact that we were limited to eastern Massachusetts. In particular we aimed for two kinds of situations: one in which the child was very likely to develop much better than most children and one in which the child was likely to develop considerably less well—indeed, perhaps even less well than the average child. We sought out especially those cases that went against the ordinary findings in respect to the influence of socioeconomic status—that is, well-endowed families with poorly developing children and poorly endowed families with well-developing children. In that pursuit we were only marginally successful. Nevertheless, we do have children who come from modest backgrounds doing as well as those that come from the most richly endowed. All in all, 19 of our subjects were seen from their first birthday through their third, and 20 more were seen from their second birthday on to their third.

In the case of the Yarrow study, there were 41 subjects seen between 5 and 6 months of age. They were recruited from well-baby clinics in Washington, D.C., and they were all black and physically normal. In the case of the Clarke-Stewart study there were 36 lower-class children, all first-born, 18 white, 18 black; 22 of the parents were married, 14 were not. The children were seen between the ages of 9 and 18 months. In the case of the Caldwell study, data are reported on only 5 children, 9 to 48 months of age, because the report (1968) focused on the potential value of a new observation instrument. These were children attending a day-care center at Syracuse University directed by

Caldwell. We believe they were all black and low income, but we are not certain of that. Carew et al. report on the same subject sample that we report on with the addition of seven children that our group did not study (1976). All in all, what one learns from this kind of information is that these studies vary quite substantially with respect to the number of subjects reported on and also with respect to their home backgrounds. Ever since 1965, the year that saw the initiation of Project Head Start, a host of studies of preschool development have been done, including most of those mentioned here. In the majority of cases the children studied were from low-income families. Of those, a disproportionate number were black families. This nonrepresentative quality of populations studied is important and should not be overlooked.

The next order of business has to do with how much data people reported on in the small number of pioneering studies on process analysis. Starting with the Schoggens' work, the only written report we have been able to find provides examples of the use of the procedure with 3 children. For each of the 3 subjects about twenty minutes of behavior is reported, and since the recording style was continuous the amount of data offered totals about one hour. In the Caldwell study data are reported for 5 subjects. The samples range from twenty to thirty minutes in length. The recording was continuous, so the total amount of data was about a hundred minutes. In the Wenar study there were two home visits that covered four or five hours each, of which forty-five minutes were selected for analysis. There were 26 one-year-old subjects; therefore, there were 19½ hours of data reported on. In the Yarrow study there were two home visits, a week apart, when the children were 5½ months of age. The method of data collection was time sampling. For every minute and a half there were thirty seconds of observation and sixty seconds of writing. Forty-one children were observed during a total of eighty-two hours. In the Clark-Stewart study 36 children were observed on seven different occasions for an hour and a half each time, which led to ten and a half hours of data on each of the children. The technique was time sampling. All told, that meant a possible maximum of 378 hours of observational data. It is to be expected in the case of repeated observations that not all the data would be collectable. Children get sick and so do researchers and so forth and so on. We can assume, however, that the amount of data collected by Clark-Stewart et al. represents one of the largest amounts of process analysis to date. Data collection by the Preschool Project consisted of three ten-minute sessions, five times for each three-month observational period, twice a year for all subjects. Data were collected for more than one year with 19 subjects who started when they were one year of age, and for one year with the remaining subjects who started when they were two years of age. All told, there were about two hundred hours of data; in this report only about 20 percent of the data is used in the primary analyses since they concern the period of life that we judge to be salient for the developments we have been studying.

In contrast, in the older longitudinal studies cited earlier (the Guidance

Study and the Berkeley Growth Study), no data were gathered on the stream of experience, even though numerical data that presumed to deal with the child's early experience were utilized in analyses of the effects of early experience on development. In the Escalona study each infant was studied only once for a period of about a week; within that week a variety of material was collected on each infant. There was a running record kept during the four- or five-hour session at research headquarters that included, along with "all significant events" occurring during the entire session, some detailed information on the behavior of the infant. There were detailed observational records kept on the baby's behavior while the mother was being interviewed, during a home visit, and during tests of general developmental status, of physical health, and so on. However, when Escalona talks about the influences of experiences on the child's development, she is not referring to data of the sort just listed but rather to eight "stable patterns of experience" that were chosen by her staff because they were considered important for infants in the age range and because they lent themselves to derivation from the various assessments that they had done. Those "patterns of experience" were rated for each child in terms of their intensity of frequency in each child's daily life based in turn on that one week of study of the child. Some of those patterns were the frequency of strong bodily arousal, the prominence of internal somatic sensations, the balance between behavior activations responsive to internal somatic causes and those responsive to external stimulation, and so forth and so on. Obviously this is a different way of conceptualizing patterns of experience than used in any of the other studies.

We find then, when looking at the amount of data that is being reported upon in these various studies, that the range is very wide, going as it does from a total of about one hour up to a maximum of almost four hundred hours of data.

We have found repeatedly that the effect of a professional observer in the home influences the behavior of those being observed, most especially the mother. The problem of observer effect is an old one. No one has yet figured out an effective way to eliminate it. Earlier, we indicated how we attempt to reduce it. One of the major ways we believe one can reduce observer effect is to go to a home many times. If investigators gather data in a home only once or twice, or even only three times, it is our judgment that the resultant view of the home will be substantially distorted. Many adult subjects seem either self-conscious or anxious to either please or impress the observer. Of all the process analysis studies that we have listed, the only groups that gather data in homes more than one or two times are those of Clarke-Stewart, Carew, and the Preschool Project. In the case of Clarke-Stewart there were twelve visits over a nine-month period. In the case of our program there were twenty-six visits over a one-year period and an average of forty in the case of children who were studied for two full years. Carew's project was construed by most of the families involved as part of the Preschool Project.

The next item to consider is the scheduling of home visits. In our study an attempt was made to get a somewhat *representative* sample of the child's experiences. We therefore attempted, within the limits set by the hours our staff worked, to sample fairly the bulk of a child's experience. We scheduled visits at several time periods between nine and five during weekdays. We cannot claim to have succeeded fully. In the Clarke-Stewart study an effort was also made to sample the full day; whereas, in contrast, Carew made a special effort to be in the home when mother and child would be interacting. For a study focusing on mother-child interactions, this kind of scheduling makes sense. On the other hand, if one is interested in getting data representative of a child's total experience, the procedure is not as appropriate. Caldwell also reports scheduling at what she calls "useful" times of the day, suggesting that representative sampling was not her goal. In the Bronson study (1974), subjects (the children and their mothers) were always seen in a play group situation and the focus was primarily on mother-child interactions. Some of the other studies do not indicate when they scheduled their observations.

The central purpose of our natural experiment was to generate quantitative and nonquantitative observational data on environmental influences on experiences in order to generate hypotheses about effective child-rearing practices. We were, therefore, interested in histories of experiences associated with excellent or comparatively poor development. We tried to obtain quantitative data on the stream of experience. We could find no tried and true instruments to sample the stream of experience. One common approach to the problem is to use one's own intuitions about the impact of various experiences on development to form a classification system. This is best exemplified in the work of Carew, who created an observation scale on the basis of her personal evaluation of the degree of intellectual value in one or another type of experience.

Yarrow et al. created an observational procedure with only three major categories of infant behavior with nine subcategories (in contrast to 36 in the Preschool Project Task Instrument). The three major headings are *vocalizations, visual attention,* and *focused exploration.* The subheadings are *positive vocalizations or indications of distress, visual attention to a primary giver or to someone else,* and *focused exploration on toys, household furnishings, caretaking materials, another person, or on the self.* Why these particular behavioral categories were selected is unclear; the fact that the Yarrow population was between 5 and 6 months of age probably had something to do with the design of the observational categories. Children at that age are much simpler creatures than they will become a few months later. They are not yet usually capable of locomotion. They have very limited language ability, if any at all, and comparably limited intellectual power. Indeed, we consider this to be one of the quieter times during infancy and toddlerhood.

The Caldwell Approach scale represents a heroic attempt in the area of process monitoring. It is quite unique in that the unit of observation is determined not by time, nor by the type of event, nor by the direction of interest of the child, but rather by grammar. The behavior that is being observed is described in a sentence and the verb that is used in the sentence is the heart of the unit. If Johnny picks up an object and then gums it, there are two units involved because two verbs have been used. In this interesting grammatical approach Caldwell's group found 65 activities to include. These activities represent behaviors by the child that range from *information processing* through *bodily activities* and on to *control techniques* with another person. The system has room for at least 34 more kinds of activities of children; and if anyone thinks of others that would be useful, he is advised to put them into the system. From that description we get the impression that the system is not meant to be inclusive of all experiences that children engage in at this point, but we cannot be sure. The individual categories are carefully defined, such that the behavior of the child is meant to determine the particular label that is used. In contrast, in the work of the Schoggens, which came much earlier, there is no standard category system to guide the observer. One records, using simple language, the continuous events the child engages in, and later analyzes the protocol in terms of *behavior episode units* and *environmental force units*. The behavior episode units refer to what the child is actually doing from moment to moment. They are the natural units of molar behavior. The child's goals, aims, or molar purposes determine the size of the unit; these, of course, have to be inferred from the observed behavior and context.

The Preschool Project instrument to sample behavior is similarly based upon inferences about the child's molar purposes. However, in the Preschool Project system the categories are meant to include all things the children do in the age ranges studied. The first form of the instrument was generated from about 1,000 written thirty-minute protocols that we believe encompassed any and all behavior children six months to six years engage in. It also follows that other people creating instruments that aspire to be inclusive might improve on what we have done.

In the Clarke-Stewart study there are 23 infant behaviors listed. They seem to be the most elementary and short-lived of those observed in the various studies. For example, they are named *holds, affectionate tactual contact, expressive physical, hurts, appropriate response, goes, looks, looks at mother, smiles, drops, gives, shows, eats, takes,* etc. The categories for the Clarke-Stewart observational technique were selected for their apparent suitability from published observation schedules of other mother-infant studies. It was then noted that there was not sufficient detail in the observation schedule, and a developmental checklist was devised to complement it. All in all, there are some 32 infant variables in the study, 23 of them being infant behaviors with others having to do with test scores, ratings, behaviors during a special test of attachment and so forth. Clark-Stewart reported that she had a hundred different measures at one stage of her study. Since the resultant data were unmanageable from an analytical perspective, she consolidated them into 76 measures, and followed that consolidation with a factor analysis that led to five infant and six maternal factors. From our perspective, this route to the understanding of what infants are actually doing leaves us somewhat concerned about the relationships of the condensed indices to the actual observable behaviors of children. Nevertheless, clearly the most sophisticated and lengthy statistical treatment of data in this kind of work is in the report by Clarke-Stewart.

In summary, the kinds of quantitative techniques that people use to gather data on the process of learning are highly variable. They range from observational procedures with a handful of categories to those with as many as 65; some are designed for narrow purposes, and others for broad purposes but in a semi-arbitrary manner. Our task instrument is the only procedure for which nonarbitrary comprehensiveness is claimed. These distinctions among data-gathering procedures are absolutely fundamental in the evaluation of work of this kind.

Another consideration of importance has to do with the gauging of reliability of the instruments. There do not appear to be more than two reports among those cited wherein the reporting of methods for gauging reliability are the same. Each investigator uses his own approach, thereby making comparisons more difficult. In our project, reliability is calculated using the most primitive kind of procedure, the simple percentage of agreement. The best agreement we have managed to achieve is slightly less than 70 percent. Traditionally, behavioral research with instruments whose reliability fall much below r's of .85-.90 are considered too weak to be used. Yet here we are, reporting at great length with a considerably weaker reliability index, albeit not a correlation figure. In our reliability study we compare two ten-minute running records, each of which is likely to contain 30-40 units of behavior. For 100 percent reliability there has to be perfect correspondence between the label for each unit of experience and the time spent in that experience, moment by moment, to within five seconds of accuracy. Considering that the individual unit of experience has to be selected from over 36 possibilities, and considering that the recording is continuous and meant to be inclusive of all experience, we believe that this is a rather stringent requirement. We felt, however, that a straightforward presentation of the sort that we have made would be the most informative and indicate the substantial difficulty of doing continuous recording of the sort we are talking about. That same difficulty is clearly indicated in the Caldwell report where the agreement on infant behaviors, before coding, is reported as 55 percent, and the intercoder agreement, from a single protocol, is 76 percent. Bear in mind that our procedure covers both steps at once. Clarke-Stewart reports a mean agreement between different pairs of observers of 75 percent. This we consider a substantial achievement considering the complexity of her observational procedures.

A final consideration, before we go on to a comparison of reported results, has to do with whether the observer uses a tape recorder or a writing instrument to record data. We have found that trying to produce a written record of continuous behavior means that the observer must spend approximately one third of the time looking at the record sheet rather than at the child. This we consider to be too risky a procedure. We, therefore, dictate our observations into a small tape recorder and then convert them to written form later. Yarrow et al. dealt with the problem by time sampling and by spending thirty seconds observing and sixty seconds recording. The Clarke-Stewart observational data were both time sampled and written. No indication is given as to what fraction of each ten seconds was spent writing and what fraction was spent looking at the child. The Caldwell procedure is like that of the Preschool Project, and also that of the Carew study, in that the observer tape-records the observation for later transfer to a written form. Like us, Caldwell has found that very young children adapt very quickly to such observational circumstances, treating the observer as a piece of movable equipment, provided that the observer has convinced the child promptly that he is not there to play with the child. The Schoggens' observations were written as they were collected. In the Yarrow study a special recording sheet was created which enabled the observer to enter raw data into a computer directly from the observation sheet. The entries, therefore, did not employ ordinary language but rather that kind of notation required by computer processes. In both the Wenar study and the Bronson study written records were taken. The Bronson study recorded simple frequency data of the various preselected types of behavior of the child germane to interaction with the mother.

COMPARISON OF FINDINGS

We have dealt extensively with background information about data collection on the process of development because we do not think it is possible to do a meaningful job of comparison of findings without an awareness of these facts. The Preschool Project analyses and interpretations suffer from some obvious liabilities. First of all, we have a social class bias of some degree in our population. We did not find children from the poorest and least well-educated families developing as well as some of those from well-endowed families. We did not find children from our strongest families at the very bottom levels of achievement in our population. Furthermore, the reliability of our observational procedure is admittedly less than we would like it to be. That, along with the traditional problems of observer bias, must be considered in interpreting any of the judgments we put forth. The same sort of caution is necessary, however, in dealing with the reported findings of every one of the studies we have cited. Each as its own strengths and weaknesses, and the reader is advised to examine carefully the background aspects of each of these studies before deciding how much faith to put into their conclusions. However, the reader should also remember two other things: First, in the case of Piaget (who was admittedly a genius) observational work led to a general description of the behavioral events of the first two years of life which has proven to be generally accurate in spite of the fact that the investigator used no other observers at all and was working with just three subjects, each of whom was his own child. True, there was only one Piaget. On the other hand, in our opinion, you do not have to be brilliant to gather useful information through observational methods, provided that you have a good deal of patience and a reasonable amount of accuracy in your reporting. Second, we believe that information on the actual moment-to-moment process of development is simply indispensable in the building of the science of human development. What we have described represents much of the best that is available. It is obviously relatively easy to locate weaknesses in each of these approaches. What would be far more useful would be for people to apply themselves seriously to the creation of improved techniques. We are convinced that the material that we have reported is neither perfectly accurate and true nor terribly far from wrong in some very important ways. History will tell how accurate that appraisal is.

In the meantime, our findings that infants between one and three years old spend far more time exploring the nonsocial world than they do in direct interaction with their primary caretakers are confirmed in the studies of Wenar, who reports a surprising and impressive predominance of nonsocial pursuits as compared to approaches to the mother by one-year-old children. It is also confirmed by Clarke-Stewart, who points out that considering the high proportion of time mother and child spend together, it was interesting that only about 36 percent of the time the infant was awake were he and his mother interacting *in any way*, and that included simply looking in the direction of the other. In our approach to these data, if a child were merely looking at his mother, we did not consider that he was engaged in any social task because we defined a social task as one where the child was actually attempting to create an affect on another person. Even in a play group situation, Bronson found a surprisingly small amount of orientation from infant to mother. In general, all the data included among these studies is consistent with the notion that previously held views that infants and toddlers spent large amounts of time in active interaction with their mothers is simply not borne out by reality. The only study that tends to go in a somewhat slightly different direction is that of Carew, who reports somewhat higher amounts of time spent in active interaction than the rest of the studies do. Here, it seems to us that her particular interest in interactions between mother and child seems to have affected the scheduling of observational times in a manner that would predispose the observer to be in the home precisely at those times when the child and the mother were most likely to be interacting—for example, around the time of feeding or bathing.

We have reported, in several places, that the single most common activity of groups of children between their first and third birthday is steady staring at (looking or visual regard) one or another scene. In the reports of Caldwell and Clarke-Stewart, the same finding is reported. We have reported that hand-eye activities in the form of exploring small objects or practicing simple skills on them is a prominent, everyday activity in the lives of very young children. Caldwell's and Clarke-Stewart's work again confirm that notion. We have reported that television viewing does not occupy much of the day before a child's second birthday, with scores averaging considerably less than 3 and 4 percent of all waking time. Clarke-Stewart reports a figure of 2 percent for an eight-hour day with a maximum (in rare cases) of about one hour.

We have reported that the period between 15 and 21 months of age is a particularly stressful one for parents since children seem to be in a period of negativism at this point; Sander, coming from an altogether different orientation to these issues, reports that the period from 14 to 20 months of age is "one that requires an adjustment between infant and caretaker in terms of those new, self-assertive behaviors the infant deliberately initiated against the wishes and limitations of the caretaker." Sanders also reports that this development was suggested earlier by Spitz (1957), when he claimed that the emergence of the self occurs somewhere around 15 months of age.

In our analyses of the relationship of experience to development, we repeatedly found that the social experiences between 12 and 15 months of life were linked to later development. Briefly, we found the more the better. A rich social life at that time seems to be consistent with a good course of development. The same sort of finding is reported by Clarke-Stewart along with an emphasis on verbal input by the mother to child. The concept she uses to describe the factor involved in the social realm is "social attention."

Clarke-Stewart's attempts to explore the issue of causality with data from a purely correlational study are not convincing to us. The notion that "cross-lagged panel correlational techniques" will help determine the plausibility of causal hypotheses seems to us a bit farfetched, yet others who are more familiar with such statistical procedures may disagree. It is worthwhile to note that Clarke-Stewart of course recognizes the limitations of any such statistical technique. In one of her final comments, she states, "a sound approach, integrating basic and applied research, would be the application of conclusions based on observational studies to programs of experimental intervention." This is precisely what we have been doing for the last few years, and the next report on our long-term research will include the results of just such a study.

Certainly the field of child development research owes a substantial debt to the work of people like Lewin, Barker, Wright, and the Schoggens for urging that we move in the direction of process analysis as a fundamental necessity in trying to understand the long-term learning course of a young child. The work of the last few years seems to have made some inroads into the complex methodological problems involved. Furthermore, we believe we know considerably more today about the fabric of ordinary day-to-day experiences in the first years of life than we have ever known before. We also have some fairly decent hypotheses about the causal relations among child-rearing techniques, child experiences, and the development of various processes in children. Our current study, generated from this natural experiment, may take us an additional small step farther, but the amount that needs doing with respect to methodology and data collection and data analysis is monumental compared to the numbers of people seriously applying themselves to this kind of research. If we do not proceed at a more rapid pace and with greater success, it will take another fifty years before we have the kind of knowledge about the process of development that we need to have in order to have a mature science and in order to do the kind of educational job that each child deserves.

In the next section of this chapter, we move on to a variety of subsidiary analyses that we believe are worthy of note. However, we will not treat them anywhere near as extensively as we have treated the preceding primary analyses. First of all, we believe that we are presenting so much data that the reader could easily get lost; second, we would prefer to maintain a proper perspective about the differential importance of these many analyses by allocating discussion and space on the basis of our judgments about the dependability of the analyses and the importance of each of them. What follows then will be a discussion of subsidiary issues such as the influence of socioeconomic status (SES) and sex on our findings. We shall also present data on the performances of our subjects at five years of age on the Wechsler test of intelligence. Finally, we shall describe the intercorrelations among our major test results. In Appendix B several further analyses of our data will be presented.

SUBSIDIARY ANALYSES

The Effects of Socioeconomic Status on the Development of Competence

It has long been understood, on the basis of extensive study, that academic achievement at least, in this country, is clearly linked to a person's socioeconomic status. Put simply, that means the stronger the family that the young child comes from in terms of the amount of education, type of occupation of the parents, and the amount of wealth, the higher his achievement level is likely to be. In the design of the research we are reporting on, we made a special effort to study families from lower SES levels who somehow manage to produce children who excel both in school and in general competence. We also sought to study families from upper SES levels whose children do not do so well. As noted earlier, we were more successful in respect to the former type of family than in regard to the latter. We found an understandable sensitivity to the presence of observers on the part of middle- and upper-income families whose children were not developing well. It should be remembered that these two groups were not the only groups we studied. The major part of our sample consisted of families from the upper SES levels whose children developed rather well and others from the lower SES levels whose children developed rather poorly.

TABLE 49. Relationships Among Major Demographic Variables and Achieved Levels of Competence (n = 39)

	Overall Rank	Social Rank[1]	Nonsocial Rank[2]
Hollingshead-Redlich SES	.43**	.00	.55***
Income	.16	−.15	.28
Mother's Education	.59***	.27	.77***
Father's Education	.46**	.08	.75***
Mother's Occupation[3]	.11	−.10	.20
Father's Occupation	.44**	.05	.71***

[1] Rank with respect to social skills.
[2] Rank with respect to nonsocial skills—i.e., linguistic and intellectual skills.
[3] Only ten of the thirty-nine mothers of the study were employed.

*p ≤ .05
**p ≤ .01
***p ≤ .001
Spearman Rank Correlation

In Table 49, we present information on the general relationships among demographic variables and various types of competence achieved at three years of age. We see several noteworthy points in this table. First of all, there is a strong relationship in our subject group (small though it may be) between SES and overall competence achieved at three years of age: +.43 (significant at the .01 level). On the other hand, it is obvious that we appear to have been, to some extent, successful in studying families where factors other than those linked to socioeconomic status play a significant role in the development of achievement. In retrospect, common sense would indicate that this was likely to be the case anyway. Still, it is comforting to know that in our sample something less than 20 percent of the variance involved in respect to overall competence is attributable to SES factors. We find that linguistic and intellectual skills are more strongly associated with socioeconomic status that social skills. Indeed we see no relationship whatsoever between SES and social competence.

At 12-15 Months. Table 50 presents data on the correlations found between tasks of that particular age among all 19 of our one-year-old starting subjects and their socioeconomic status level. We find that several common experiences are linked with socioeconomic status. In general, the total amount of social experience seems independent of socioeconomic level; the tendency of the young child to make overtures to an adult of a kind that we label *to please*—that is, friendly overtures with no immediately obvious ulterior motive in mind—seems to be considerably greater the higher one goes up the SES scale. Bear in mind two things: This particular task is not among the more common ones, but it is implicated in preceding analyses in the development of

TABLE 50. Correlation Among Tasks at 12-15 Months and Hollingshead-Redlich SES Levels (n = 19)

Social Tasks	Percent Time Spent in Activity (Group Median)	Correlation with SES[1]
All social tasks	10.3	.01**
To please	0.1	−.56**
To cooperate	2.8	.39
To procure a service	1.0	−.20
To gain attention	2.2	−.38
To maintain social contact	2.2	.24
To assert self	0.5	−.03
Nonsocial Tasks		
To eat	4.4	.17
To gain information (v)	16.0	−.70**
To gain information (v & a)	6.0	−.14
live language directed to child	*1.7*	*−.60***
overheard language	*0.8*	*−.32*
mechanical language	*0.2*	*.35*
Nontask	12.2	.22
To pass time	3.4	.26
To prepare for activity	1.4	−.35
To procure an object	3.3	.11
To ease discomfort	0.6	−.03
To restore order	0.7	−.34
To operate a mechanism	0.0	−.35
To explore	12.8	−.03
Mastery	8.7	.11
gross	*6.7*	*.04*
fine	*2.4*	*.05*
To eat and gain information (v)	4.2	−.44
To eat and gain information (v & a)	0.3	.15
live language directed to child	*0.1*	*−.06*

[1] The Hollingshead-Redlich Scale designates upper class as I and lower class as V. Therefore, a positive correlation indicates that lower-class children show greater task duration.
**$p \leq .01$

competence. *Cooperate* tasks—that is, those that reflect simple requests by an adult (usually the mother)—seem to be linked in the other direction; more demands are made of children of this age by lower SES mothers than by higher SES mothers. *Seeking attention* seems to be somewhat linked with SES; children from the higher SES levels engage in more of such activity.

In the area of nonsocial tasks, we have a rather striking finding in regard to *steady staring*. Again, this particular experience at 12-15 months of age, which has cropped up repeatedly in our analyses, is very strongly associated positively with SES. The fact that *live language directed to the child* is strongly associated with SES does not surprise us; nor are we surprised that *overheard live language* is positively associated as well. We do have a trend with respect to *listening to language* off a television set that is inversely related to SES. *Preparation for activity* seems to be positively associated with SES, as are *restoring order, operating a mechanism,* and *eating and steady staring.*

It would appear that there are substantial numbers of experiences that at 12-15 months of age were dependent, in part, upon the SES level of the family involved. The most conspicuous were the occasional social task of making pleasant overtures (*to please*), *steady staring,* and *listening to live language directed to the child*; all three of these achieved fairly substantial statistical significance.

At 18-21 Months. Table 51 shows that the influence of SES on experience is similar at 18-21 months of age to what it was at 12-15 months; if anything, the influence seems a bit stronger. Once again we find the social experience of *to please* significantly related to SES in a positive manner along with several others. However, the others, in this instance, were not those that were significantly related at 12-15 months of age. During this age we find no fewer than five nonsocial tasks significantly related, only one of which (*eating*) is negatively related to SES. The lower SES children do considerably more eating than the upper SES children. The remaining tasks are positively associated with SES; that is, the higher the SES level, the more *preparation for activity*, the more *motor mastery* in general, the more *fine motor mastery* in particular, and the more *verbal mastery*. The categories of *steady staring* and *live language directed to the child* have shifted with respect to SES by this time. We still have the same generally positive trend with respect to *steady staring*. Very interestingly, the amount of *live language directed to the child* is no longer strongly associated with SES.

We see that whereas there was nothing in the way of substantial difference in the total amount of social tasks linked with SES at 12-15 months of age, there is considerably more social experience if the child is from a higher SES level by the time he is a year and a half of age. However, not many of the individual social experiences are very strongly related to SES. We do find more *seeking of approval* and more *seeking of attention*, but neither reaches statistical significance.

Turning to the nonsocial tasks, we find positive trends with respect to *procuring of objects* and *restoring order*, and negative trends with respect to watching "Sesame Street" and empty time, *nontask* behavior. In other words, children from the higher SES levels watched *less* "Sesame Street," and children from the higher SES levels had less empty time (nontask). The former is a surprise; the latter is not.

At 24-27 Months. Table 52 presents data on the association of SES with experience when the children have reached their second birthdays. By now we would expect a considerably more striking association, but we find just the opposite is true. With the exception of one nonsocial experience, *to explore*, we find no statistically significant relationship across any task and SES.

TABLE 51. Correlation Among Tasks at 18-21 Months and Hollingshead-Redlich SES Levels (n = 19)

Social Tasks	Percent Time Spent in Activity (Group Median)	Correlation with SES[1]
All social tasks	16.2	−.43
To please	0.0	−.63**
To cooperate	4.6	−.20
To gain approval	0.0	−.34
To procure a service	1.0	−.25
To gain attention	2.0	−.36
To maintain social contact	2.8	.09
To direct	0.1	−.27
To assert self	1.5	.06
To enjoy pets	0.0	.15
Nonsocial Tasks		
To eat	10.3	.52*
To gain information (v)	10.6	−.44
To gain information (v & a)	6.0	.21
live language directed to child	*1.4*	*−.16*
overheard language	*1.3*	*−.16*
mechanical language	*0.0*	*.31*
Sesame Street	*0.0*	*.30*
Nontask	11.8	.44
To pass time	3.2	−.29
To prepare for activity	2.0	−.62**
To procure an object	3.1	−.38
To engage in large muscle activity	0.0	−.26
To imitate	0.0	−.14
To pretend	1.5	−.02
To ease discomfort	0.4	−.17
To restore order	0.6	−.44
To operate a mechanism	0.2	−.03
To explore	6.6	.03
Mastery	11.4	−.48*
gross	*2.4*	*−.25*
fine	*3.9*	*−.48**
verbal	*0.1*	*−.47**
To eat and gain information (v)	1.9	−.01
To eat and gain information (v & a)	0.4	.22
live language directed to child	*0.0*	*−.18*

[1] The Hollingshead-Redlich Scale designates upper class as I and lower class as V. Therefore, a positive correlation indicates that lower-class children show greater task duration.

*p ≤ .05
**p ≤ .01

Considering the number of correlations being calculated that one statistically significant number is not likely to mean much. In other words, the best judgment one could make of these data is that SES hardly influences the pattern of experience at two years of age, although it does at earlier ages. What that means we really have no idea.

TABLE 52. Correlation Among Tasks at 24-27 Months and Hollingshead-Redlich SES Levels (n = 20)

Social Tasks	Percent Time Spent in Activity (Group Median)	Correlation with SES[1]
All social tasks	20.0	.18
To please	0.2	.21
To cooperate	3.9	−.22
To procure a service	2.3	.18
To gain attention	2.6	.24
To maintain social contact	5.0	.30
To avoid unpleasant circumstances	0.1	.39
To annoy	0.0	.39
To direct	0.2	−.15
To assert self	1.3	.09
To converse	0.2	−.20
To provide information	0.1	−.19
Nonsocial Tasks		
To eat	5.5	.21
To gain information (v)	13.7	.07
To gain information (v & a)	9.8	−.17
live language directed to child	*2.8*	*−.10*
overheard language	*2.6*	*.01*
Nontask	9.5	.23
To pass time	2.3	−.03
To prepare for activity	1.7	−.14
To construct a product	0.0	−.36
To procure an object	1.8	.20
To engage in large muscle activity	0.4	.10
To gain pleasure	0.7	.07
To imitate	0.3	.04
To pretend	0.5	−.25
To ease discomfort	0.5	.22
To restore order	0.6	.09
To dress	0.0	.04
To operate a mechanism	0.2	−.30
To explore	4.6	.54*
Mastery	8.9	−.17
gross	*3.9*	*−.37*
fine	*2.0*	*.23*
To eat and gain information (v)	1.4	.24
To eat and gain information (v & a)	0.5	.09
live language directed to child	*0.3*	*.01*

[1] The Hollingshead-Redlich Scale designates upper class as I and lower class as V. Therefore, a positive correlation indicates that lower-class children show greater task duration.
*$p \leq .01$

Looking at the trends, we find that lower SES children seek *to maintain more social contact*, to some extent. They are obliged *to avoid unpleasant circumstances* more, and they engage in more *annoying* behavior. Those are the major differences among social tasks. We would suggest that since there were more likely to be more siblings around in the case of our lower SES children, those experiential differences are linked to family size as much as to SES.

Turning to the nonsocial tasks, we find that upper SES children engage in more *construction of products,* although there really is very little activity by any child at this age. They engage in somewhat more attempts at *operating a mechanism* and a bit more *gross motor mastery.* We have a rather consistent pattern in this table, and we believe that the most dramatic meaning of it is that the differences, as a function of SES, are quite modest indeed.

At 30-33 months. In Table 53 we find something of a reversal in that we do have a considerably greater number of relationships across experiences and SES at 30-33 months of age. Statistically significant differences were found with respect to the social category *to converse* and with respect to the nonsocial categories *to pretend, verbal mastery,* and *to eat and live language overheard.* We find in every instance that the relationship is positive. That is, the higher the child's socioeconomic level, the more likely he was to engage in conversation and each of the other listed tasks. It should be noted from the column on the table indicating the amount of time spent in the activity that many of these activities were quite rare.

Turning now to trends, we find that low SES children engaged in more attempts at *seeking services* at this age. On the other hand, there were many more attempts at *directing* other people and *providing information* by higher SES children.

Turning to nonsocial activities, there is a continued trend for a positive relationship across SES in *preparation for activities* along with *eating* and *steady staring* and *operating of mechanisms.* Also the same trend is present with respect to *eating and looking* and *listening to language* from all sources. In sum, this is a relatively substantial collection of relationships.

The Effects of Sex on the Patterns of Experience of Young Children

Just about every study of the development of young children that has been done in the last thirty years will report on differences found between boys and girls with respect to the topic at hand. The reader should note that we have not made a major issue of sex differences in any of our preceding writings nor in this one. This avoidance is partly due to our belief that the tendency to spend so much time on sex differences, particularly in studies concerning infants and toddlers, has often substituted for more imaginative approaches to the data. It is also partly explained by our failure, over a long period of research on young children, to find dramatic sex-linked differences in behavior. Nevertheless, we feel that the presentation of data on this topic is a responsibility that must be met in any study of this sort. Therefore, Tables 54, 55, 56, and 57 present data on correlations among tasks and sex for our 39 subjects between one and three years of age.

TABLE 53. Correlation Among Tasks at 30-33 Months and Hollingshead-Redlich SES Levels (n = 20)

Social Tasks	Percent Time Spent in Activity (Group Median)	Correlation with SES[1]
All social tasks	20.9	−.15
To please	0.1	−.28
To cooperate	3.5	.02
To gain approval	0.0	−.17
To procure a service	1.8	.42
To gain attention	2.8	.02
To maintain social contact	2.7	.11
To direct	0.5	−.39
To assert self	1.4	−.09
To converse	0.7	−.48*
To provide information	0.7	−.41
Nonsocial Tasks		
To eat	2.9	−.04
To gain information (v)	7.7	.25
To gain information (v & a)	10.6	.00
live language directed to child	2.8	−.21
overheard language	2.0	−.21
mechanical language	1.7	.28
Sesame Street	1.2	.05
Nontask	6.8	.20
To pass time	1.7	−.11
To find something to do	0.0	.13
To prepare for an activity	2.2	−.43
To construct a product	0.1	.05
To procure an object	2.0	.20
To gain pleasure	0.1	−.11
To imitate	0.1	−.20
To pretend	1.8	−.53*
To ease discomfort	0.2	−.02
To restore order	0.9	.04
To relieve oneself	0.0	.21
To operate a mechanism	0.2	−.34
To explore	2.3	.17
Mastery	12.7	−.15
gross	2.3	−.21
fine	6.5	.15
verbal	0.1	−.48*
To eat and gain information (v)	0.7	−.43
To eat and gain information (v & a)	0.5	−.37
overheard language	0.1	−.55**

[1] The Hollingshead-Redlich Scale designates upper class as I and lower class as V. Therefore, a positive correlation indicates that lower-class children show greater task duration.

*p ≤ .05
**p ≤ .01

Table 54 presents the data on children 12-15 months of age. There are six individual social tasks plus one category for all combined; sixteen individual

TABLE 54. Correlation Between Tasks at 12-15 Months and Sex (n = 19)

Social Tasks	Percent Time Spent in Activity (Group Median)	Correlation with Sex[1]
All social tasks	10.3	.22
To please	0.1	.30
To cooperate	2.8	.03
To procure a service	1.0	−.08
To gain attention	2.2	.28
To maintain social contact	2.2	.15
To assert self	0.5	−.09
Nonsocial Tasks		
To eat	4.4	.01
To gain information (v)	16.0	.45*
To gain information (v & a)	6.0	−.27
live language directed to child	*1.7*	*.13*
overheard language	*0.8*	*−.09*
mechanical language	*0.2*	*−.42*
Nontask	12.2	.23
To pass time	3.4	−.09
To prepare for activity	1.4	.05
To procure an object	3.3	−.46*
To ease discomfort	0.6	−.05
To restore order	0.7	.05
To explore	12.8	.02
Mastery	8.7	−.45
gross	*0.7*	*−.36*
fine	*2.4*	*−.42*
To eat and gain information (v)	4.2	−.12
To eat and gain information (v & a)	0.3	−.49*
live language directed to the child	*0.1*	*−.41*

[1] Point biserial correlation coefficients were computed. Males were assigned a value of 1, females 2. Therefore, a positive correlation indicates females show greater task duration.
*p ≤ .05

nonsocial tasks and three overriding categories. By that we mean, for example, that we have lumped all *gaining information, visual and auditory* categories into one total score as well as presenting subscores. The same is true for *mastery* experience and *eating and gaining information, visual and auditory*. Of the grand total of twenty-six categories, we find that three correlations reach the .05 level of statistical significance. One could reach that level of statistical significance on the basis of chance alone. Therefore, the general conclusion one has to come to is that sex per se does not seem to have an overpowering effect on the pattern of experiences of children 12-15 months of age, at least among our 19 subjects. Looking more closely, we find that the only category that even represents a trend of any sort among the social experiences of our children is the category *to please*, or to make friendly overtures. We see a trend indicating that girls made more such overtures than boys in our population. We have been using .30

as a threshold with respect to trends; anything less than plus or minus .30 we have not considered worth discussing. This is of course a somewhat arbitrary cutoff point, and the reader may decide that other cutoff points would be more appropriate.

Among nonsocial experiences we find that three were significantly correlated with sex: *gaining information through steady staring, procuring an object,* and *eating and gaining information by looking and listening.* The first was positively correlated. Girls apparently did more *steady staring. Procuring an object* is negatively correlated, meaning that boys spent more time *procuring objects* than girls. Boys also spent more time *eating* and simultaneously *listening to language.*

There are a number of fairly strong trends in the data, and they are worth looking at. *Listening to language* from a television set and from other mechanical sources were experiences engaged in more often by boys than by girls. *Mastery* activities of all kinds were engaged in more by boys than by girls. These *mastery* experiences were predominantly *motor mastery* experiences: climbing and hand-eye skills for the most part. *Gross motor mastery* experiences were more often engaged in by boys than girls as were the fine motor skills. Finally, *eating and listening to live language directed to the child*, while it was a scarce experience, was more common among males than among females. All in all, we see a small collection of trends in these data.

The picture at 18-21 months of age is seen in Table 55. It was our expectation, of course, that as children got older the influence of sex on experiences would be greater. Everyone assumes that the culturally influenced behaviors of parents with their children inevitably influence the types of experiences children have at some point in their early development. Looking at Table 55, however, we find that there are still only four statistically significant relationships to be found. First of all, we find that young girls have significantly more social experience than young boys. Second, we find that young girls are apparently a bit testier in this negativistic period; the *assert self* score is significantly higher for them.

Turning to trends within the social data, we find several. Girls continue to engage in more *to please* behavior. They are asked to perform more simple tasks as reflected in the *to cooperate* scores. They ask for help (*procure a service*) less than boys. They cling more. The *maintain social contact* category scores are higher for girls. In our sample, girls *enjoyed their pets* a bit more.

Turning to the nonsocial tasks, we find that *make-believe behavior* (*to pretend*) was considerably higher in girls than in boys as was the relatively rare task of *operating a mechanism*, an example of which might have been an attempt to open a drawer or cabinet door.

The trends in the nonsocial data are considerably more scarce than in the social data. We find girls *overhearing more live language* than boys. We find boys continuing to *procure objects* more often than girls and also to *explore* such objects more often. Furthermore we find boys, as in the earlier data, engaging in more *gross motor mastery*, but now the tendencies with respect to *fine motor*

TABLE 55. Correlation Between Tasks at 18-21 Months and Sex (n = 19)

Social Tasks	Percent Time Spent in Activity (Group Median)	Correlation with Sex[1]
All social tasks	16.2	.51*
To please	0.0	.32
To cooperate	4.6	.30
To gain approval	0.0	.29
To procure a service	1.0	−.40
To gain attention	2.0	.17
To maintain social contact	2.8	.30
To direct	0.1	−.12
To assert self	1.5	.53*
Nonsocial Tasks		
To eat	10.3	−.11
To gain information (v)	10.6	.28
To gain information (v & a)	6.0	−.03
live language directed to child	*1.4*	*.01*
overheard language	*1.3*	*.33*
Nontask	11.8	.03
To pass time	3.2	−.16
To prepare for activity	2.0	.12
To procure an object	3.1	−.32
To engage in large muscle activity	0.0	−.18
To imitate	0.0	.26
To pretend	1.5	.68**
To ease discomfort	0.4	−.27
To restore order	0.6	.13
To operate a mechanism	0.2	.50*
To explore	6.6	−.32
Mastery	11.4	−.17
gross	*2.4*	*−.37*
fine	*3.9*	*.11*
verbal	*0.1*	*.22*
To eat and gain information (v)	1.9	−.27
To eat and gain information (v & a)	0.4	−.31

[1] Point biserial correlation coefficients were computed. Males were assigned a value of 1, females 2. Therefore, a positive correlation indicates females show greater task duration.

*p ≤ .05
**p ≤ .01

mastery no longer favor the boys. Finally, we find in *eating and listening to language* a tendency for boys to continue to engage in more of such activity.

Comparing the patterns at 18-21 months to those seen earlier at 12-15 months, we find about the same overall influence of sex on behavior, on experience. However, it would appear that the influence has increased by 18-21 months of age with respect to social experience and decreased somewhat with respect to nonsocial experience.

Table 56 presents data on the influence of sex on experience at 24-27

TABLE 56. Correlation Between Tasks at 24-27 Months and Sex (n = 20)

Social Tasks	Percent Time Spent in Activity (Group Median)	Correlation with Sex[1]
All social tasks	20.0	−.01
To please	0.2	.06
To cooperate	3.9	.15
To procure a service	2.3	.06
To gain attention	2.6	.06
To maintain social contact	5.0	−.21
To avoid unpleasant circumstances	0.1	−.29
To annoy	0.0	−.34
To direct	0.2	.07
To assert self	1.3	.17
To provide information	0.2	.49*
To converse	0.1	.14
Nonsocial Tasks		
To eat	5.5	.66**
To gain information (v)	13.7	−.01
To gain information (v & a)	9.8	−.11
live language directed to child	2.8	.13
overheard	2.6	.04
Nontask	9.5	−.06
To pass time	2.3	.31
To prepare for activity	1.7	.13
To construct a product	0.0	−.24
To procure an object	1.8	.03
To engage in large muscle activity	0.4	−.33
To gain pleasure	0.7	−.16
To imitate	0.3	.06
To pretend	0.5	.11
To ease discomfort	0.5	−.03
To restore order	0.6	.06
To dress	0.0	−.18
To operate a mechanism	0.2	−.39
To explore	4.6	−.06
Mastery	8.9	−.28
gross	3.9	−.24
fine	2.0	−.21
To eat and gain information (v)	1.4	.17
To eat and gain information (v & a)	0.5	.50*
live language directed to child	0.3	.54**

[1] Point biserial correlation coefficients were computed. Males were assigned a value of 1, females 2. Therefore, a positive correlation indicates females show greater task duration.

*p ⩽ .05

**p ⩽ .01

months of age. The reader should be reminded that these 20 subjects are not the same subjects that we talked about in the preceding tables. Here we find, once again, that the number of statistically significant relationships is rather small, showing that in general sex is not a major determinant of types of experiences, even as late as 24-27 months of age. Among the social experiences only one reaches statistical significance and it is a rare category, the category of *providing information*, which refers to a child's trying to explain something to another person at great length. In our sample girls engaged in considerably more of this activity than did boys. Looking at the other social categories, we find that boys tended to engage in somewhat more *annoying* behavior than girls, although there is only a trend.

Turning to nonsocial tasks, we find three categories that reach statistical significance. Girls apparently do considerably more *eating* than boys at this point in life. Two considerably less common experiences also reach statistical significance, with girls also doing more *eating and looking and listening* and more *eating and looking and listening to live language directed to them.*

Looking at the trends in the data we find that girls have a bit more *pass time* experience. Boys engage in somewhat more *large muscle activity* at this age. They also spend more time *operating mechanisms*, although again, it is an infrequent experience. None of the other relationships seems to be strong enough to be worthy of mention. All in all, a rather unimpressive testimony to the influence of sex on experience.

The data on the influence of sex on experience in the 30-33-month period is presented in Table 57. Looking at social experiences, we find that none of the relationships reaches statistical significance. There are, however, two or three trends worthy of notice. Boys attempt *to procure services* a bit more than girls at this age. Girls *attempt to direct others* a bit more than boys and also *to provide more information.* In general, there is nowhere near the influence of sex on social experience that was seen at 18-21 months of age.

Turning to nonsocial experiences, three of this long list reached statistical significance. We find boys watching a bit more television and apparently listening to television and records. We find girls engaging in significantly more *motor mastery* than boys. On closer examination, it is *fine motor mastery* that is involved rather than *gross motor mastery* such as climbing, running, and riding tricycles, etc.

Looking at the trends, we find little. There is a slight trend for girls to engage in more make-believe activities (*to pretend*).

We don't know what other researchers will make of these data, but as far as we are concerned the influence of sex on patterns of activities in the one- to three year age range, on the basis of what we have seen in our population, seems rather modest. We would not go so far as to say that sex had no influence at all; but, on the other hand, it is our judgment that those who would claim that cultural attitudes toward sex play a dominant role in the types of experiences children undergo in the first three years of life would not be supported in their views by these data.

TABLE 57. Correlation Between Tasks at 30-33 Months and Sex (n = 20)

Social Tasks	Percent Time Spent in Activity (Group Median)	Correlation with Sex[1]
All social tasks	20.9	−.15
To please	0.1	.20
To cooperate	3.5	−.21
To gain approval	0.0	−.20
To procure a service	1.8	−.31
To gain attention	2.8	−.16
To maintain social contact	2.7	−.16
To direct	0.5	.42
To assert self	1.4	.13
To provide information	0.7	.32
To converse	0.7	−.09
Nonsocial Tasks		
To eat	2.9	.08
To gain information (v)	7.7	.00
To gain information (v & a)	10.6	−.18
live language directed to child	2.8	−.10
overheard	2.0	−.05
mechanical	1.7	−.45*
Sesame Street	1.2	−.01
Nontask	6.8	−.23
To pass time	1.7	−.24
To find something to do	0.0	−.14
To prepare for activity	2.2	.15
To construct a product	0.1	−.15
To procure an object	2.0	−.06
To gain pleasure	0.1	−.10
To imitate	0.1	−.03
To pretend	1.8	.30
To ease discomfort	0.2	−.27
To restore order	0.9	.02
To relieve oneself	0.9	.22
To operate a mechanism	0.2	−.11
To explore	2.3	.05
Mastery	12.7	.53**
gross	2.3	.08
fine	6.5	.54**
verbal	0.1	.27
To eat and gain information (v)	0.7	−.02
To eat and gain information (v & a)	0.5	.22
overheard	0.1	.15

[1] Point biserial correlation coefficients were computed. Males were assigned a value of 1, females 2. Therefore, a positive correlation indicates females show greater task duration.

*p ⩽ .05
**p ⩽ .01

The Effects of Experience on the Achievement of Competence at Five Years of Age

We, of course, were interested in how well our children did later in life than their third birthdays. Therefore, we made arrangements as the children approached their fifth birthdays to recontact the families and engage in assessments parallel to those we had done earlier. We then faced the problems of assessment techniques. There were several. Bear in mind that the prime focus of this research is on the concept of overall competence, and we have defined overall competence on the basis of distinguishing abilities of very talented three to six year old children. Unfortunately, however, there are no established procedures, that we know of, for assessing such abilities in five-year-old children; as usual, we have had to make do.

In the area of nonsocial abilities we felt that the Wechsler Preschool and Primary Scales of Intelligence Test, which had been recently modernized, was, as far as we could tell, one of the most powerful instruments available. We decided that even though it would not conceptually cover all the areas of development we are interested in, it did seem to relate to each of them, at least to some degree, and in any case the test was about all we could afford, given our resources and our focus.

In the area of social competence, we were in considerably more difficulty. We had and continue to have a good deal of confidence in the legitimacy of the concepts that we have created and used in the area of social competence; but we have not, to date, found a reliable method of assessing the social competence of a child in one sitting. In the research that we have done we have generally collected a minimum of two and a half hours of frequency data on a child's social interchanges; then, in a rather cumbersome manner, we have calculated indices of social competence with peers, with adults, and with both. We were not about to invest in a parallel amount of effort with the subjects when they turned five years of age. We did gather data from their teachers if the children had gone to a school regularly, using a simple rating scale we contrived for the occasion.

We knew, however, that the use of the rating scale was a relatively poor manner in which to proceed. First of all, teachers, as talented as they are in many areas, are not necessarily reliable data gatherers or reporters, especially when it comes to the children they work with on a day-to-day basis. Second, there was the question of variability across groups of children with respect to social competence. A teacher who rated child A in context B might be inclined to rate child A quite differently in context C or D. Our rating system was simply too crude to allow us any power in respect to control for such variability. Nevertheless, we gathered the data on the individual child with respect to his classmates, and we also asked the teachers to rate their groups in comparison to all other children of that age that they had known. The resulting information seemed to us to be too fraught with weaknesses to be worthy of inclusion in this report. We mention it only to explain that we tried but failed with respect to the assessment of both social and overall competence at five. We only feel justified, therefore, in presenting information about the WPPSI scores of our subjects, even though we would much prefer to be able to present more.

SOCIAL COMPETENCE RATING SCALE

Name _____ Age _____

Date _____ Rater _____

Place of Observation: _____

School _____ Day care _____ Home _____ Other _____

Number of students in comparison group _____

Compared to others in the same age group, how often does subject behave in the following ways:

Interaction with Adults

1. Getting an adult's attention through socially acceptable means.

5	4	3	2	1	0
top 10% of the group	somewhat above average	average	somewhat below average	bottom 10% of the group	unable to decide

Comments: _____

_____

2. Using an adult as a resource, emotional or instrumental.

5	4	3	2	1	0
top 10% of the group	somewhat above average	average	somewhat below average	bottom 10% of the group	unable to decide

Comments: _____

_____

3. Expressing *both* affection and hostility to adults.

5	4	3	2	1	0
top 10% of the group	somewhat above average	average	somewhat below average	bottom 10% of the group	unable to decide

Comments: _____

_____

4. Expressing pride in creations, possessions, or actions.

5	4	3	2	1	0
top 10% of the group	somewhat above average	average	somewhat below average	bottom 10% of the group	unable to decide

5. Engaging in adult role play, or otherwise expressing the desire to grow up.

5	4	3	2	1	0
top 10% of the group	somewhat above average	average	somewhat below average	bottom 10% of the group	unable to decide

Comments: _____

Interaction with Peers

1. Leading *and* following peers and children.

5	4	3	2	1	0
top 10% of the group	somewhat above average	average	somewhat below average	bottom 10% of the group	unable to decide

Comments: _____

2. Expressing *both* affection and hostility to peers and children.

5	4	3	2	1	0
top 10% of the group	somewhat above average	average	somewhat below average	bottom 10% of the group	unable to decide

Comments: _____

3. Competing with peers and children for equipment or adult attention.

5	4	3	2	1	0
top 10% of the group	somewhat above average	average	somewhat below average	bottom 10% of the group	unable to decide

Comments: _____

Ranking of General Social Competence

Compared to others in the same age group, how would you rank this student's general level of social competence?

5	4	3	2	1
top 10% of the group	somewhat above average	average	somewhat below average	bottom 10% of the group

Comments: _____

_____

Ranking of Present Class as a Group

Compared to other classes in this age group you have taught, how would you say the present class compares as a whole with them on the dimensions of social competence?

5	4	3	2	1
very much above the competence level of other classes taught	somewhat above the competence level of other classes taught	about the same as other classes	somewhat below the competence level of other classes taught	very much below the competence level of other classes taught

Comments: _____

_____

TABLE 58. Secondary Outcome Data: Weschler Preschool Primary Scale of Intelligence,* Unmatched SES Groups

Group	Median	Range
1-Year-Old Starters (n = 18)	117.5	98-149
Most Competent (n = 8)	128	106-149
Least Competent (n = 4)	109.5	98-120
2-Year-Old Starters (n = 19)	112	74-134
Most Competent (n = 6)	120	106-127
Least Competent (n = 5)	99	74-116

*Full score

Table 58 describes the test scores of 37 of our 39 subjects on the Wechsler intelligence test when the subjects were approximately five years of age. Two of the subjects were untestable—one because we had lost contact with the family, the other because the child is apparently burdened with a fairly significant emotional handicap that precludes standardized testing.

We thought it might be interesting to list with the WPPSI scores the scores that the children achieved on the Bayley instrument of general development when they were one and two years of age and the scores the same children attained on the Stanford-Binet Intelligence Scale at 36 months. The scores are arranged according to the standing of the children on overall competence at three years of age, the one-year-old starters ranked on Table 59, the two-year-old starters on Table 60.

Perhaps the most interesting analysis with respect to these results at five years of age would concern the relationship of patterns of experience at 12-15 months of age and achievement as indicated by WPPSI scores at five years of age. We did such an analysis, starting first with correlations across individual types of experience and WPPSI scores at five years of age (Table 61) and proceeding to a multiple regression analysis (Table 62). We found five types of experience that individually were highly correlated with the five-year WPPSI scores. Not surprisingly they were categories that had been implicated in preceding analyses. The five are *gaining attention* (the only social experience); *gaining information through steady staring*; *gaining information by listening*

TABLE 59. Individual Scores on Measures of General Development and Intelligence, One-Year-Old Starters, (n = 19)

Sub. #	Bayley* 12 Months	Bayley* 24 Months	Stanford-Binet 36 Months	WPPSI Full Score 60 Months
20	134	134	142	149
8	106	123	139	113
17	100	137	139	140
24	107	116	118	123
3	102	143	139	119
16	102	127	127	133
40	122	106	110	106
11	119	119	144	136
41	98	91	76	106
43	97	109	93	116
19	102	127	120	122
32	94	108	93	120
31	112	108	118	116
44	103	132	113	116
37	50	84	64	109
42	103	94	98	120
1	134	112	108	98
34	109	66	<57	Unavailable
45	125	96	76	110

*Bayley Scales of Infant Development Mental Scale Score

TABLE 60. Individual Scores on Measures of General Development and Intelligence, Two-Year-Old Starters, (n = 20)

Sub. #	Bayley* 24 Months	Stanford-Binet 36 Months	WPPSI Full Score 60 Months
9	109	139	116
22	140	134	Unavailable
2	137	132	127
39	104	108	106
35	104	132	124
21	111	131	134
12	102	122	111
18	100	105	109
38	94	95	102
5	97	127	112
36	119	90	110
13	102	118	123
10	106	127	123
33	89	120	118
14	86	81	90
25	84	117	116
28	94	88	95
30	77	81	99
27	88	88	99
7	69	74	74

*Bayley Scales of Infant Development Mental Scale Score

to live language directed to the child; *nontask experience* (that is, empty time); and *exploratory experience*.

As can be seen from Table 61, the correlations were all rather substantial, ranging from .38 up to .70. Three of the tasks were positively correlated with later WPPSI scores, and two were negatively correlated. Once again we find no surprises. *Seeking the attention* of another person is positively correlated as is *steady staring* and *listening to live language directed to the child*. Nontask experiences and *exploratory* experiences, mostly with small objects, were negatively correlated as they have been in all the preceding analyses.

TABLE 61. Correlations of Most-Predictive Task Experiences (12-15 Months) and Weschler Preschool and Primary Scale of Intelligence (60 Months)

Tasks	Percent Time Spent in Activity (Group Median)	Correlation with WPPSI
To gain attention	2.2	.60
To gain information (visual)	16.0	.70
live language directed to child	1.7	.38
Nontask	12.2	−.52
To explore	12.8	−.46

TABLE 62. **Task Experiences (12-15 Months) Predicting Weschler Preschool and Primary Scale of Intelligence (60 Months), Regression Analysis**

Dependent Variable	Multiple r	p*	Regression Equation
WPPSI	.8331	.008	Predicted WPPSI = 118.7795 + % duration (1.8797) + Gain Attention
			% duration (0.5974) + % duration (−0.1365) + % duration (−0.5769) + Gain Info (v) Live Language Directed to S Nontask
			% duration (−0.4996) Explore

*Statistical probability

For a variety of reasons we do not intend to belabor this analysis. We do feel, however, that in spite of the limitations of the sample size and characteristics, there is potentially a good deal of heuristic value in this last analysis. Especially because the many preceding analyses tend to reinforce this one, we think that we are on to something of special significance with respect to the core problem of the process of the development of competence. The simple social experience of *seeking attention* is, in the light of the preceding analyses in this report, symptomatic again of the importance of a rich social life for the achievement of later competence. Here we find a direct line between a very early experience and performance on a reliable standardized instrument to assess intellectual ability at age five years. Furthermore, we know that there is predictive power with respect to future academic achievement from the WPPSI scores at age five. The suggestion here is that a rich social life at 12-15 months of age very possibly is causative with respect to academic achievement, at least as far forward as the elementary grades.

Turning to the nonsocial tasks, once again we find that *steady staring* at all the various and sundry things that infants look at is very strongly correlated with later intellectual success. Again, this poses, for us, the question of the meaning of this particular experience and its relationship to mechanisms of development. It would appear that we are referring here to a capacity for focused attention, and we have to look once again at what it is that families do that might enhance such a capacity in the one-year-old child. Once again, *live language directed to the child* is positively related to later intellectual achievement. This comes as no surprise. *Empty time* and *exploratory* behavior are both negatively related, and the interpretation in each case is, as usual, obviously speculative. Empty time for a 12-15-month-old child is, as far as we can see, associated with the freedom to roam but with the lack of interesting things to interact with and perhaps also with a lack of guidance and encouragement by another person. *Exploratory* behavior is an experience that can be done alone. While it is quite consistent with a child's natural tendencies to explore his world, when this task is expanded to occupy a larger percentage of the child's activities than usual, the pattern apparently reflects the absence of other experiences that would be more efficacious. We would doubt, for example, that the total absence of exploratory behavior would be a good sign with respect to the future development of competence.

Intercorrelations Among General Developmental and Intelligence Test Scores

The preceding discussion indicated a rather dramatic capacity of the data on the typical daily experiences of our subjects at 12-15 months to predict their performances on the Wechsler tests of intelligence when they were five years of age. We know of no precedent for figures of this sort. Yet, there have been a great number of other studies that have attempted to relate scores on general developmental tests, such as the Gesell, to scores on the Binet, on the Wechsler, and on many other tests. For the reader's information, Tables 63 and 64 show the state of affairs with respect to those topics among all our subjects. Note that with respect to the children who started with us when they were one year of age, the Bayley mental index scores at one year of age do not correlate at all with WPPSI scores at five years of age nor, for that matter, with the Bayley index scores at two years of age. There seems to be a slight, insignificant trend with respect to the Binet score at three years. Bayley scores at two years of age correlate very highly with Binet scores at three and with WPPSI scores at five. This finding is consistent with previous work. The Binet scores at three years correlate strongly with the WPPSI scores at five. In general there are no surprises in the matrix. We remind the reader, however, that the experiential data on these same 19 children gathered at 12-15 months of age correlate extremely highly with WPPSI scores at five years of age as well as with Binet scores at three years of age. Turning to the second half of the table, we find a corroboration of what we had in the first half of the table—similar scores. If anything, there is an even stronger predictive capacity of the Binet at three toward WPPSI scores at five. Another reminder is in order here: Our subjects were selected to form a dichotomous distribution. While the outcomes at three years of age clearly indicated more continuity in the distribution than we had originally predicted, we are still talking about the kind of population that is much more likely to yield high correlation values than a representative population. Given such a caveat, it is noteworthy that we find the Bayley scores at 12 months to behave with our population exactly as they behave with representative populations; the remainder of the relationships seen in this particular table also are consistent with previous findings on representative populations. For us, this is clear support of a very impressive kind for the heuristic power of information on the experiences of young children for predictive purposes and for helping us to understand causality with respect to the development of competence.

TABLE 63. Intercorrelation of Intelligence Tests, One-Year-Old Starters

	Bayley 12 Months	Bayley 24 Months	Binet 36 Months	WPPSI 60 Months
Bayley 12 Months (n = 19)	1.00	.04	.25	−.03
Bayley 24 Months (n = 19)		1.00	.85***	.60**
Binet 36 Months (n = 19)			1.00	.68**
WPPSI 60 Months (n = 18)				1.00

**$p \leq .01$
***$p \leq .001$

TABLE 64. Intercorrelation of Intelligence Tests, Two-Year-Old Starters

	Bayley 24 Months	Binet 36 Months	WPPSI 60 Months
Bayley 24 Months (n = 20)	1.00	.75***	.68***
Binet 36 Months (n = 20)		1.00	.89***
WPPSI 60 Months (n = 19)			1.00

***$p \leq .001$

7

Hypotheses About Effective Child-Rearing Practices

WHAT GOES INTO EFFECTIVE CHILD-REARING?

A brief review of one or two major points is necessary in order to set the stage for a discussion of child-rearing practices. We have pointed out on more than one occasion, in this volume, that we believe that the data we gathered on the process of development between 12 and 15 months of age are the best data for us to look at in our attempt at identifying those learning experiences that contributed maximally to the achievement of high levels of competence in our subjects. In retrospect, we invested too heavily in gathering of comparable data on children beyond that age. In particular, we have made considerably less use of the task data for children who started in our study when they were two years of age. Also, in retrospect, we believe we might have been wiser in executing this study had we arranged to gather task data on children from the time they were 7 or 8 months of age rather than from the time they were 12 months of age. We hope the following discussion will make the reasons for that statement clear.

The second major point worth reiteration at this time is that our quantitative procedures to sample the experiences of children must be regarded as considerably less than perfect. We have described the instrument we have used.

Although it was constructed from extensive data on the types of experiences children in this age range undergo, our findings are still subject to several kinds of errors: (1) The reliability of the instrument is far from perfect; (2) the accuracy of our analyses is no doubt less than perfect; and (3) we operate at only one level of a child's experiences. There are a number of other levels that should be looked at and might have been more useful than the one we chose. We are however, on balance, comfortable with what we have done and feel it has provided us with the kind of wedge into the problem of early development that we had aspired to.

A third major point to be reiterated at this time is that in addition to the quantitative data we have gathered on children's experiences, we utilize in our analyses and discussions the nonquantitative, or subjective, data that we collected as an inevitable accompaniment to our quantitative procedures.

With those caveats in mind, let us now proceed to our interpretation of what these data and our general experience has taught us about effective child-rearing practices. From our task data, regardless of how we analyze it, we come away with the conclusion that a close social relationship, particularly during the first few months that followed their first birthday, was a conspicuous feature in the lives of our children who developed best. The suggestion is that the parent who for any reason spends a minimum amount of time in free and easy social interchange with the one-year-old child is not likely to be providing as rich an educational experience as the one who makes himself or herself regularly accessible to the baby. To expand on that point, we have to state that in this study several of the mothers of babies developing very well had part-time jobs or for other reasons spent a good deal of time out of the home. There are two notions suggested by such a statement. One is that a rich social experience can be provided by someone other than the child's parents. In a few instances there were very skillful substitute parents available. Second, it would appear that a parent or parents do not have to spend the entire day providing a rich social life for the young child in order to provide enough of such experience.*

Looking at individual social experiences, we repeatedly find that a task called *procuring the service of another* seems to be involved with good development. Here we are referring to situations in which a child wants something done that he cannot do for himself. He asks someone else to do it for him in order to achieve a desired goal. Now what does this mean? First of all, it means that the child has access to other human beings for a fair period each day. Second, it means that another human being facilitates what the child wants to do. In other words, the adult is acting as a resource or a tool for the child. Later we will talk about how this sort of tendency on the part of the young child

---

*In more recent studies, we have found that total time spent in direct contact with one-year-olds is rarely more than 10 percent of the child's waking hours, or about 70 minutes per day.

can get out of hand. We have come to believe that there can be too much of this type of experience in a child's life. For the time being, suffice it to say that the child who is not attended to regularly by an older person, or who may be seen as a burden to be dealt with as quickly and as little as possible, would appear to be less well off from a basic educational standpoint than the child who is freely offered assistance by sympathetic older persons. More subtly, but probably just as important, is the notion that an adult who is giving such assistance to the young child is an adult who is interested in what the young child is interested in. This may seem terribly obvious, but we have found in subsequent programs that some adults, for one reason or another, are not inclined to be genuinely interested in an infant's focus of the moment. This lack of interest often precludes their acting as an effective resource for the child.

The second major social task that recurs in our analyses and warrants discussion at this point is *attempting to gain attention*. This category reflects the natural gregariousness of the 12-month-old child. Once again, a child cannot have large amounts of such experience if, by and large, he is not near an adult fairly often during the day. Nor would he have a fair amount of such experience if he were repeatedly rebuffed in his attempts at achieving social contacts. Furthermore, a child who is hovered over by an adult has less of a need to develop attention-seeking skills. Both of these social experiences suggest a style of living that we believe has substantial importance with respect to effective early education.

In nonsocial experiences (those where the child is not trying to create an affect on another person), we find the interesting and somewhat perplexing category of *gaining information through vision* or of *steady staring* highly significant from a statistical point of view. We have learned, from the work of Phyllis Dollinow, that young infrahuman primates also engage in a great deal of staring behavior. *Steady staring*, as we define it, is focused attention in contrast to desultory scanning. This simple behavior apparently has an important role to play in the process of development. Obviously, if a person never dwells for long on any scene, he is going to get less out of it than if he examines it carefully. Beyond that simple statement, we do not feel that we can safely speculate about the special significance of the behavior. It is conceivable that the behavior of the parent has something to do with the frequency of the activity. It is possible that the tendency of the parent to instruct the child, to talk about things seen, to draw the child's attention to one or another interesting aspect of the environment affects the probability of the behavior.

The next most interesting and powerful nonsocial experience is listening to *live language directed to the child*. As explained, we make distinctions among the different kinds of listening-to-language experiences that children have. A child can be concentrating on the language that two nearby people are addressing to each other. Such a task would be coded as *live language overheard*. He may be listening to a record machine or a radio in which case we would code the activity as *mechanical language*. In the case of a child looking at and listening to a "Sesame Street" program on television, we code the experience as *language from Sesame Street*. The category *live language directed to the child* is the one most strongly associated with good development.

What does that mean? First of all no television program, no matter how excellent it is, can custombuild its language to the child's interest of the moment. In contrast, any adult responding to a child's overtures can, in a perfectly natural way, usually identify the child's interest of the moment (during this period of life) and talk about it to the child. This kind of event was repeated many times every day in the lives of our well-developing subjects. We believe live language on the topic the child is actually thinking about at that moment probably plays a key role in the achievement of language facility, social skills, and higher mental abilities. In other words, we believe that this particular experience is especially germane to good development. It may be asked, Where is the surprise in that? After all, we have always known that adults should talk to children; indeed, there is no basic surprise. We hope that by describing, with some precision, how and when this language experience is delivered, we can add to the general appreciation of the importance of talking to children. Not all speech to children appears equally effective. For example, speaking to children while trying to redirect their attention turns out to be much more difficult than identifying a child's interest of the moment and interesting him in talk about *that* interest. That distinction may seem like a modest one, but it has several practical consequences.

We found that in some homes, especially those of the children doing least well, restriction of their locomotor efforts was a routine practice; that is, playpens were used for the bulk of the day. If it was not a playpen that was being used, then it was long "naps," morning and afternoon. A child would be put into his crib for a nap shortly after breakfast and kept there whether he was awake or asleep for two or three hours. The same thing would be repeated after lunch. Repeatedly we found that children rather quickly became bored under such circumstances. They also became habituated to them in a matter of a few weeks. Ordinarily there would be toys available in the playpen or crib, sometimes quite a few; but it was a very rare child who managed to find enough to keep himself interested. Such children spent as much as three or more hours a day *passing time*, in a state of boredom and unable to alter their circumstances. Regular confinement to either a small room, a crib, a jumpseat, or a playpen, was consistently associated with comparatively poor development. On the other hand, relative freedom from these restrictive experiences was a routine feature in the lives of one-year-old children developing very well. This, in retrospect, should not come as much of a surprise. The child who is restricted in such a manner simply cannot satisfy his curiosity in any persistent way, nor can he readily practice newly emerging motor skills. The child who is not restricted, in our experience, finds it relatively easy to become involved in many kinds of sustained activities, both social and nonsocial. Furthermore, it is the child who has high *pass time* experience at 12-15 months of age who has enormous nontask experiences at 18-21 months of age. What seems to happen is that restriction is used at 12-15 months of age to avoid the work, the physical danger, the breakage, and the other unpleasant consequences of free locomobility of the 12-month-old. The resultant inability to satisfy and build upon one's curiosity seems to lead to a generally less interested child some 6 months later. That less interested 18-month-old then understands enough language and is steady enough on his feet so that he need not be restricted to the playpen as often. However, he no longer has quite the same zest for exploration that other children have when that zest has been nourished by the opportunity to explore during the earlier age range.

We found that children, who at 12-15 months of age spent an above average amount of time *practicing large muscle skills*—especially those having to do with pulling to stand, cruising and climbing onto and off objects—were not, on balance, developing as well as others. It is open to speculation whether this reflects simple maturational lag or genetically determined individual differences or the consequences of having been kept in a playpen to the point where the normal achievement of gross motor skills has been delayed, or whether the lack of regular human interaction has somehow resulted in more emphasis being placed upon motor development.

The other task that tends to be negatively correlated with good development is *procuring objects*. Again, we are left in a situation where we really have no lines of analysis and interpretation that we are happy with. All 12-15 month old children have more difficulty getting to things that they want and actually grasping them than do adults or older children. Yet, in the case of children not developing very well, we find that the sheer amount of time spent trying to procure objects is greater than with children developing well.

What does that mean? Perhaps the opportunity to procure the assistance of a human is less available, and therefore their task becomes one in which they have to depend on their own resources more exclusively or perhaps, again, the relatively low level of social interaction predisposes them more toward a greater investment in physical reality.

DISCUSSION AND CONCLUSIONS

What follows next is an attempt not only to stay fairly close to the quantitative results on the relationship of experiences to the development of competence, but also to add our subjective agreed-upon judgments about styles of child-rearing as they related to the numerical data. We repeatedly find in longitudinal work that we learn considerably more than what is contained in our quantitative data. It was certainly not possible to anticipate all the things that could be profitably measured in advance of executing this study. It seems to us, from these years of natural longitudinal experimentation, that effective child-rearers essentially perform three major functions in a manner that distinguishes them from other child-rearers. These three functions are:

1. Designing the child's world
2. Consulting for the child
3. Disciplining or controlling the child

In a design function, the effective child-rearer makes the living area as safe as possible for the naive newly crawling or walking child and then provides maximum access to that living area. This immediately allows a process of development that will lead naturally to the satisfaction of and further development of the child's curiosity and the opportunity to learn much more about the world at large. It also provides the child with the opportunity to enter into natural, useful relationships with people. The child-rearer not only provides maximum access to the living area but, in addition, makes kitchen cabinets attractive and available, and in general pays attention to the safety and interest qualities of the kitchen area since the child will spend more time in that room than in any other for the next year or so. The child-rearer also keeps a few materials in reserve for those times when the child becomes a bit bored. These materials do not have to be special toys. They can be half-gallon ice cream containers filled with a variety of 2-3-inch objects of one shape or another. They can be empty plastic measuring devices or empty thread spools. Children at this age are particularly interested in collections of small objects, so anything that is small and has a diverse form or interesting pictures becomes a suitable object for exploration. Other good items to keep in reserve are collections of plastic jars with covers and containers that can be used by the child to pour water back and forth.

An effective child-rearer functions as the child's consultant when he needs comforting or assistance, or when the child would simply like to share an exciting discovery. For example, one common consequence of an infant's explorations is a degree of minor frustration. A door may be stuck shut or two items that the child has been putting together and taking apart may refuse to come apart on the fortieth attempt. In instances such as these, the child may move toward the primary caretaker to get help with whatever it is that is frustrating him. Given such a situation, if there is someone around, there seems to be a rather special opportunity for teaching. In our sample, when a child was developing well there was someone close by rather commonly, and that person was someone who was particularly interested in that child. On other occasions we saw instances where someone was around but not readily available nor terribly interested. In some instances we saw that while the mother was unavailable the person left in the house was assigned the task of keeping the house clean as well as making sure that the baby was safe, fed, and not in any trouble. Under such circumstances the common tendency of the child to share enthusiasm or get assistance was often not met appropriately. In the case of the more fortunate child, someone was there, someone was interested, and that someone usually responded very quickly to the overture. The quick response usually was followed by whatever it was that the child was interested in getting. At times, adding a touch of realism to the life of this very young child, the adult would say, "I'm busy now. You are going to have to wait a moment." This seemed, to us, to be a symptom of the kind of fair-minded and even-handed treatment that young children got in homes where they were developing well. In contrast, in some homes, adults dropped everything the moment that the child wanted any kind of attention, almost regardless of what they were doing.

The next step in the apparently effective child-rearing pattern involved the attempt by the adult to identify what it was the child was interested in at the moment. The attempt was almost invariably successful since children between one and two years of age do not seem to be terribly devious and their intentions seem very easy to read. One cannot be certain that the identification was always accurate, but usually the succeeding behaviors tended to confirm that it was so. Once the interest of the child was accurately identified, the adult had what would seem to be the ideal teaching situation—a motivated student and knowledge of exactly what it was the student was focusing on. The adult then responded with what was needed and generally used some words at or above the child's apparent level of understanding, incorporated a related idea such as "Oh yes, you squeezed your little finger," "You remember Daddy banged his elbow this morning," or "Look at my finger, see the boo-boo I have." At times a certain kind of realistic teaching was possible. If, for example, the child wanted the stuffed rabbit to eat some food, the mother would have the chance to explain that while they could make believe that the rabbit would eat food, the rabbit simply would not swallow, etc. Once the child showed a lessened interest in the interchange, he was released, allowed to then return to whatever it was he was doing or wanted to do. The entire episode rarely took more than twenty or thirty seconds, although at times there were much longer interchanges. Our impression was that no more than 10 percent of a child's waking time was spent in direct interactions of all kinds with the parent. But quite a number of twenty-second interchanges can be included in the hour or so that represents 10 percent of a one-year-old child's waking time.

These brief episodes precipitated by the child rather than by the adult seem to us to be the core teaching situations involved in good development. None of the children in our studies underwent any other kind of regular didactic sessions beyond an occasional brief adult-initiated teaching session focusing on a magazine or a small book. There were no protracted didactic experiences of adults insisting on teaching reading readiness skills or anything of that sort.

The third core function we saw with apparently effective child-rearers consists of setting limits or disciplining the child. We found that apparently effective child-rearers were extraordinarily firm and consistent with their children, while simultaneously showing deep love and respect for the child's interests. Different types of discipline seemed necessary at different stages within infancy and toddlerhood, and a minority of child-rearers in some fortunate way have stumbled across procedures that work. Children less than 13 months of age can usually be controlled by distraction. Out of sight is often out of mind. Apparently, children 13-18 months of age require distraction and physical removal from circumstances at times, or, on the other hand, removal of the object from the child's vicinity. Children from 18 months on require distraction, physical distance, and firm verbal restrictions.

In sum, then, these three functions seem to be at the heart of effective child-rearing and, for us, form the nucleus to which we can add other ideas generated from our quantitative data to create a training program.

GENERAL GUIDELINES FOR EFFECTIVE CHILD-REARING PRACTICES

These guidelines represent the conversion of hypotheses to recommendations for child-rearers.

1. *Provide access to as much of the house as possible so that the child has the maximum opportunity to exercise his curiosity and explore his world.* The hypothesis involved is that the opportunity to explore the world around the child is basic to the nourishment of his curiosity and instrumental to the development of social relationships as a natural outcome.

2. *Provide a wide range of materials for the child to explore.* Common household objects such as plastic jars with covers, large containers filled with smaller interesting objects, a baby-proofed kitchen cabinet with pots, pans, and canned goods, are all perfectly suitable for a child between 7 and 18 months of age. The hypothesis involved is that the newly crawling child will, for several months, have a very special interest in the physical properties of small objects and the characteristics of motion they display when pushed, dropped, rolled, etc.

3. *Be available to your child for at least half of his waking hours.* Do not hover over him constantly but be available to provide attention, support, or assistance as it is needed. The hypothesis involved is that a child needs the direction provided by a more experienced person to support his curiosity, to instruct in the area of language, and to encourage the development of using and interacting with other people.

4. *Utilize the following pattern of response to the degree it is possible when your child begins to make overtures to you from age 9 or 10 months on:*
   a. Respond promptly as often as possible.
   b. Respond favorably as often as possible.
   c. Make some effort to understand what the child is trying to do.
   d. Set limits; do not give in to unreasonable requests.
   e. Provide encouragement as often as possible.
   f. Provide enthusiasm as often as possible.
   g. Provide assistance as often as possible.

h. Use words as often as possible.
   i. Use words the child understands or words that are a little too hard for him.
   j. Provide a related idea or two.
   k. Do not prolong the episodes if a child wants to leave; the interchange will usually last less than one minute.
   l. Encourage make-believe or pretend activities.

The hypothesis involved is that this particular pattern of response is especially suited to the developmental needs of the very young child.

   5. *If the child seems bored, and if it is convenient, provide things for him to do.* The hypothesis involved is that substantial periods of time spent doing little of anything in the way of organized activities is, on balance, a poor sign with respect to the development of the young child.
   6. *If a child is misbehaving, discipline him firmly and consistently.* The hypothesis involved is that children require that limits be set to their behavior in order to develop into socially acceptable individuals who feel comfortable with other people.
   7. *Allow a child to try to do something that seems somewhat unsafe but would not be unsafe if he were closely supervised.* Give the child the chance to try the activity, under supervision, rather than stop him completely. The hypothesis involved is that if the child wants to try a new activity, it probably is a naturally interesting and a potentially beneficial one. Such activities, when encouraged, lead to better development.

In addition to these positive guidelines and related hypotheses, the following list of practices to be discouraged tends to round out our picture of an effective set of child-rearing circumstances.

   1. Do not cage the child or confine him regularly for long periods during the day.
   2. Do not allow him to concentrate his energies on the primary caretaker to the point where he spends most of his time following that person around or standing nearby, especially during the second year of life.
   3. Do not allow tantrums.
   4. Do not worry that he will not love the primary caretaker if the primary caretaker says *no* from time to time.
   5. Do not try to win all the fights with him, especially from the middle of the second year on, when the baby may start becoming negative.
   6. Do not try to prevent the baby from cluttering the house. It is an inevitable sign of a healthy, curious creature.
   7. Do not be overprotective. Babies are more careful than people think.
   8. Do not overpower the child. Let him do what he wants to do as often as possible.
   9. Do not take a full-time job or otherwise make yourself unavailable. A caretaker should not take a full-time job or otherwise be largely unavailable to the baby during this period of life.
   10. Do not bore the baby if it can be avoided.

Hypotheses About Effective Child-Rearing Practices 159

11. Do not worry about when the baby learns to read, count numbers, or say the alphabet, or even if he is slow to talk as long as he seems to understand more and more language as he grows.
12. Do not try to force toilet training. By the time he is two or two and a half, it will happen rather easily.
13. Do not let the baby think the whole world was made just for him.

The preceding collection of guidelines, hypotheses, and cautions seems to us to spring directly from the quantitative data we gathered and the subjective judgments that we as a staff agreed upon. Of course, they are not likely to be perfectly accurate, but they seemed to relate to each other in a consistent manner. In the time since those determinations were made, we created a training program and went on to perform a comparative experiment utilizing these hypotheses. Much more has been added in the course of piloting the training program. Details on those additional features of our experimental treatment will be presented in Volume III of this series.

part **III**

NEXT STEPS

8

A Comparative Experiment

We have been gaining confidence in dealing with the puzzle of the relationship of early experiences to developing competence. We feel that the various parts of the picture we have identified relate to each other in a coherent way; therefore, we think we know something about the likely causes of development, good and poor. Nevertheless, we are fully aware that the kind of research that we have performed in our natural longitudinal experiment only produces correlational data with respect to the relationships across experiences and development. We made a commitment, when we first started this line of research in 1965, to the maximum feasible utilization of the scientific method in our research; as a result, we have moved from the stage of natural experimentation to the stage of true experimentation. In a sense there is a humanistic incompatibility between the topics of true experimentation and the development of the young child. Indeed, many people flinch when they hear anything at all about plans for experiments with young children. While mindful of the controversy involved, we feel that experimentation in the lives of young children can be done in an ethical way. Furthermore, we know of no other way in which to advance the state of reliable knowledge about how to raise a child. We, therefore, remain committed to the method.

How, then, does one go about putting to experimental test the hypotheses generated by our natural experiment? Our plan involved one preliminary step and then the design of an experiment. The preliminary step took us two years. It consisted of the creation of a training program that in scientific terms is equivalent to the experimental treatment. A major factor we had to be aware of in designing an experiment is the potential array of important influences in the development of competence of the children we would work with. We knew, for example, that the educational background of families had been repeatedly found to be associated with the level of development of competence. We also were concerned with ancillary or secondary factors that could contribute significantly to developing competence in children. For example, from previous experience and from the experience of others, we knew that the kind of attention that we, as a professional group from a high prestige university, would lavish on a family would heighten the family's self-consciousness and interest in the rearing of their young children. J. McVicker Hunt reports that in Earladeen Badger's recent parent-training program just this factor of increased attention to the family without any accompanying detailed information about how to raise a child seemed to result in improved test performance for very young children. We, therefore, had to do something in our design to allow us to cope with such sensitization and prestige-type effects, which could be confounded with true experimental effects. Our answer was to provide in the design, in addition to the core experimental group who would receive assistance and guidance from us, a second group, known as the pediatric control group, and two additional control groups.

The pediatric control group would receive guidance in comparable quantities to that provided by our staff. In addition the group would receive, it was hoped, a collection of ideas about child-rearing that were substantially different from ours. This group would also receive a degree of attention somewhat parallel in its power to that received by the experimental families. We were fortunate enough to enlist the assistance of a pediatrician with over twenty years of experience. This gentleman holds an appointment at the Harvard Medical School and is held in very high regard by both his academic colleagues and the parents in his practice, many of whom are professionally trained. He has over the years built up a huge amount of experience and a rather high degree of frustration in respect to guiding young families in rearing their children. His feeling was that he never had quite enough time to do the job as well as he would like because of the size of his practice and other extraneous factors. We asked him if he would be willing to enter into this experimental design with us. We provided him with the same amount of money we were using in our program and, in essence, tried to equate his support for the families he tutored with ours in every respect aside from the specificity of the child-rearing ideas transmitted in the two training programs.

In the next report of this research, the details of his curriculum will be presented. Suffice it to say they are much more oriented toward the centrality of the mother-child relationship than our program is, although we certainly paid a good deal of attention to that topic.

In the flurry of activity in the area of research on infant development over the last decade, it has been found by several researchers (although not published frequently) that repeated testing of children during infancy leads to higher test scores than one would expect. Infants and toddlers, in other words, seem to become test savvy. In particular, this topic has been explored by Mark Golden of the State University of New York at Stony Brook, who has found that a thorough acclimatization period prior to testing a naive infant makes for a very substantial difference in test scores (personal communication). Others have remarked about this phenomenon to us, and indeed we seem to see evidence of it in our own data. This factor of beneficial effects of repeated testing along with the extra sensitization of parents to child-rearing caused by participation in the research project even if only as a control had to be coped with. Therefore, we have in our design a second control group of families who receive no outside support from either our training group or the pediatric counselors. However, the children in those families are tested on the same schedule as the other two groups, and data are gathered on their experiences and on the parent's child-rearing styles, etc., on precisely the same schedule. A fourth group of children is seen only before the study and when the study is over, for final evaluation. This last group as compared to the third group should give us some sense of contribution of repeated testing and the presence of an observer in the home to the achievement scores of the child. The second group should give us information about the addition of the prestige factor and increased sensitization perhaps to the preceding factors and also some unknown degree of impact that might follow from the particular ideas espoused by that team. The experimental group, presumably, will have an effect that is made up of all those factors combined, along with the particular ideas that we hope to put to test. The reader should be aware that certain risks are involved here. We and/or the pediatric group could very well end up with children who developed less well than those in the other groups. Nevertheless, we know of no other way of putting these ideas to a reasonably fair test in the real world.

We do not pretend that what we have just described represents an airtight experimental design. Many flaws are likely to develop. We have very limited control over the degree to which experimental families we work with actually execute what we want them to do with their children. We have no sure way of knowing precisely how well the families would have done without our help. We are not ideally positioned to select the families so that they really meet the criteria that we created for eligibility. There is no way of seeing to it that the ideas for the experimental group are kept fully from the pediatric group or from the other control groups. But, as in all our previous work, our feeling is that if we were to wait for the perfect research opportunity, we would wait a very long time.

Because we had planned to work closely with families for a fair period of time, we knew there was a rather modest limit to the numbers of families we could work with. Since there were four groups, the likelihood of substantial numbers in the experimental group was significantly lowered. We began with 18 families in each group and narrowed that number down to 15 for the ultimate sample. Therefore, the study includes 60 families.

The question of when we would work with the children was a rather difficult one. We noted earlier that the first consistent deviations in the development of competence seemed to be occurring routinely for many children sometime during the second year of life. Since our hope was to prevent the underachievement in children, we wanted to start early enough for such purposes. On the other hand, we were not anxious to invest heavily in the process well before it made much sense. We were quite convinced that the first 6 or 7 months of life were months when most families managed to get through the task of educating their young children rather well. From our previous work on the development of abilities in the first 6 months of life (White, 1971), we were reasonably well acquainted with what went on during that time. In addition, from the results of a whole host of studies on the effects of maternal deprivation in the first few years of life (UNESCO publication, the World Health Organization publication, Bowlby, ed.), we knew that if a child spent his first 6 months in an institution, away from his mother and in generally inferior substitute circumstances, he did not usually sustain lasting harmful effects. We knew from the studies of Nancy Bayley and MacFarlane on the longitudinal development of children (see Hunt, 1961) that scores on infant tests for general development in the first year of life did not seem to predict later achievement terribly well. We knew that children from all parts of the world who did poorly on tests when they were six, seven, eight years of age, on the whole, tended to look perfectly normal well into the second year of life (Brown and Halpern, 1971; Schaefer, 1968 and 1969).

Therefore, we knew from the data from the cited sources and from our own experience that there were no obvious signs of persistent deficiencies showing up before the middle of the second year of life. Yet, others claimed and continue to claim that educational development from birth is very often at risk and that people routinely get their children off to a very poor start from the child's first days. Some have claimed that eye contact patterns in the first weeks of life are very important and do not work out too well unless the parent is either lucky or receives some sort of special guidance. Others have claimed that certain kinds of stimulation are necessary and not at all assured in the first months of life, etc. When confronted with the fact that these children who supposedly have not had just the right kind of early mother-child interactional pattern test perfectly well in the first year of life, such advocates remarked, "Ah, but our tests are very weak and indeed the children really are in trouble, but we just have no way of measuring the trouble. We dare not assume that there are no difficulties just because we can't measure them." Such a disagreement will only be resolved as more and more specific evidence on the topic becomes available. We simply are much less impressed by the evidence to support this position than some other people are.

Added to this kind of thinking are the following kinds of notions about what happens at 7 months or so in the lives of children which would lead families to do a considerably less effective job of rearing their children. As we have pointed out earlier, true language learning begins in earnest at 6-8 months of age and then moves ahead very rapidly through the next few years. Unlike the process of the acquisition of visually directed reaching skill (which is one of the major achievements of the first 6 months of life), language development is directly dependent on a good deal of input from other human beings. Learning to reach can be done without help from anyone else. In fact, institutionally reared children tend to learn reaching just as well and just as rapidly as those who are reared in the most advantaged of homes.

In addition to the development of language (which is fundamental to educability and socialization) there is the development of curiosity, which seems to us to be present in great quantities in all but a very few 7-8 month old children but which, in the course of the next couple of years, seems to, in many cases, become either less intense or less catholic. By that we mean that while many children retain a fresh and broad interest in learning right through their second and third years of life, others end up at those ages with considerably less interest or with interests that have been misshapen. The most frequent form of misshaping that we have seen among our children is a concentration of curiosity and interest and exploration on the behavior of the primary caretaker, such that by two years of age some children no longer "play alone well" but insist on close proximity with the primary caretaker for as many hours of the day as possible.

In addition to curiosity and language there is the process of social differentiation and development in the period between 7 and 24 months of age. We have been repeatedly amazed and delighted as we have watched the relatively undifferentiated 7-month-old become a complicated social creature by his second birthday. We find more and more of the skills that we have identified in very talented three- to six year old surfacing in that period, starting with varied attempts at *getting and holding attention,* moving on through *use of an adult as a resource, expression of pride in achievement, engagement in make-believe or fantasy activities, expression of affection and mild annoyance,* and on to incipient attempts at *directing other people* and the surfacing of *leadership and fellowship roles.* All these skills surface fairly rapidly under the best of circumstances between 7 and 36 months of age and can lead to a complicated, delightful three-year-old. On the other hand, the process can easily go sour and produce a three-year-old who is relatively low on social competencies and not terribly pleasant to live with.

Finally, starting at 7 months or so the infant routinely moves from the first exploration of his own simple hand-eye and body skills on to the beginning of interest in the object world around him. The growth of interest in objects, their motions, their characteristics, their other physical characteristics and in simple cause-and-effect phenomena has been beautifully detailed by Piaget. This growth seems, from our research, to be intimately involved in the foundations of intelligence and highly susceptible to environmental effects that result from various child-rearing practices during the 7-36-month period.

This view of four fundamental educational processes that seem to be undergoing very rapid development between 7 and 36 months of age and that, at the same time, seem to be at risk, underlies our conviction that the time to begin to structure experiences that might help a child develop well should be no later than 7 months.

There are other less theoretical reasons for starting at that point. The difficulties involved in rearing children begin to escalate from 6 or 7 months on as that child begins to be able to crawl about the home. Locomobility markedly increases the likelihood that the child will get hurt or into mischief or damage things in the home or annoy an older sibling, etc. Children who are just beginning to crawl are quite naive about danger. They are incredibly curious. They use their mouths to explore many things. They are impulsive, they are clumsy, they are forgetful. All these characteristics lead to danger and extra work. A parent who is trying to cope with such stresses is less able to be concerned with the child's educational development. Indeed, one of the most common ways of coping with the onset of locomobility is to confine the child for the better part of the day, to prevent the extra work and the danger, etc. Prolonged restriction to playpens and jumpseat or long "naps in the crib" morning and afternoon, etc., are often used for these purposes. Simultaneously, from the research we have just reported, such practices seem to get in the way of the development of abilities in children.

For all these reasons we started our program of intervention with the experimental group when the children were 5 months of age. By the time the children turned 8 months, we entered into more intensive support for the family that lasted until the children were 17 months of age. By that time the children would have been well into negativism and the parents would have adopted whatever styles of adjustment they deemed suitable.

We could not tell the pediatric control group when they should make their inputs into the families they were guiding. All we asked was that they make their inputs before the child was two years of age because by two we assumed that we could get reasonably stable indications of how well the children had done in the study. The design for data collection is presented in Figure 11.

This experiment is now nearing completion, and further details and results will be presented in Volume III in this series.

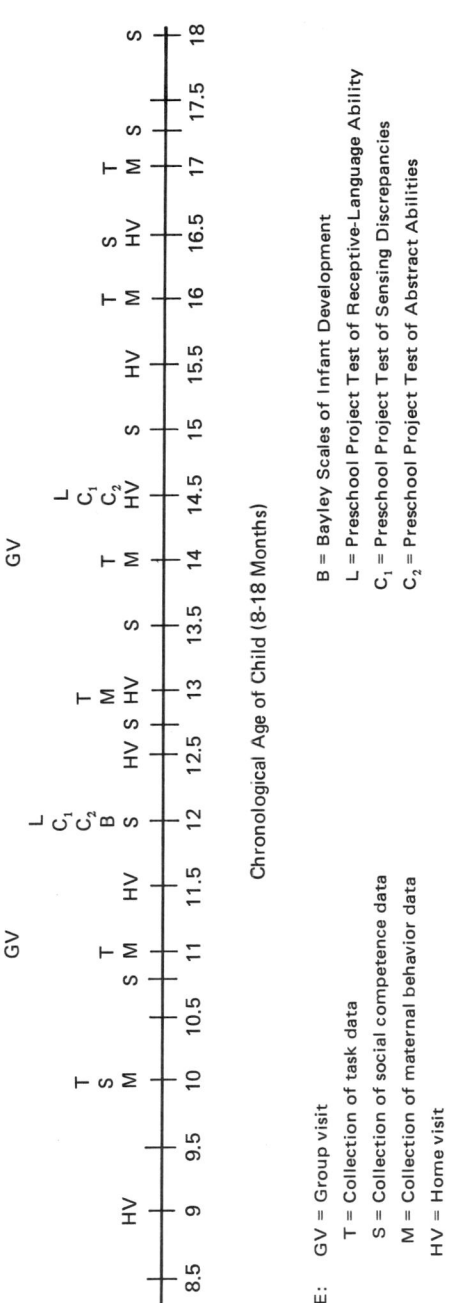

Figure 11. Schedule for intervention program and process monitoring

9
Creating an Instrument to Assess Child-Rearing Effectiveness

BACKGROUND

To the extent that a child's development is significantly influenced by his environment, it is necessary to be able to gauge the educational quality of that environment in reliable ways. Ultimately, if we are to have first-rate early education, we must have accurate and reliable ways to measure the salient factors that affect development. In experimental terms, if competence is the desired outcome or dependent variable, then the relevant environmental influences on the child are the independent variables. A child's experiences (or tasks) are partially shaped by environmental factors such as available physical materials and the child-rearing practices of his parents. Those experiences constitute the *process* of learning or educational development and lead in turn to changes in abilities of the child. A child's competencies at any age are, in part, determined by his history of experiences and by the environmental factors that shaped those experiences as well as his genetic endowment, etc.

Several years ago, when we began our longitudinal natural experiment, we divided our staff into subgroups. Some people were assigned to monitor the growing achievements of the children. Others were to sample the experiences of the children. One group was assigned the task of gathering data on the environments of the children. This latter group had to cope with an enigma of special importance. The central assumption of our work is that the environment plays a major role in determining the level of competence a child will achieve in the first years of life. Furthermore, our ultimate goal is an understanding of how the environment actually affects the child so that we may design methods of child-rearing that will help each child make the most of the potential he is born with.

The problem we faced at the outset was that neither we nor anyone else (as far as we could tell) knew *which* of the infinite aspects of a child's environment were important to his educational development. True, many people, professionals and others, had opinions on the subject. Few topics have had more written about them than how to raise a child. Opinions, however, are not necessarily truths or even high probabilities. For example, in *our* opinion, Piaget's explanation of the ontogenesis of mental abilities is the most accurate view that exists to date. If one would like to understand how the mind of an infant works, one must read about Piaget's views. Yet, nowhere in Piaget's writing does one find more than a brief treatment of the environmental factors that are most salient to the development of intelligence. True, the interactionistic nature of the theory implicates the environment. Also, Piaget's examples of behavior (*The Origins of Intelligence in Children*) identify whatever immediate environmental factors are involved in the episode. However, the central issue for educational practice and for progress toward the completion of the scientific picture of the early development of intelligence is a coherent analysis of the causal connections between the organism (the child) and *all* the influential elements of his surround (environment). Progress to date on this issue seems to us still modest. In other words, thanks to Piaget, we have a fairly good general understanding of how the mind of the young child works. Neither he nor anyone else, however, has yet discovered how to help it develop to its fullest. Furthermore, there are other important developmental processes—i.e., curiosity, language, social skills, etc.—about which we know even less than we know about the development of intelligence.

Under the circumstances, we found ourselves in a dilemma. We were about to begin a long-term study of both excellent and comparatively poor development in a search for hypotheses about the most important environmental influences on the development of the young child. Yet not knowing (in advance) their identity, we were unable to design a focused assessment technique to use to monitor those forces quantitatively. We were confident, of course, that the effects of the primary caretaker were somehow going to be significant. We were also sure it was necessary to sample the influences of other people who contacted the child. Also, characteristics of the physical surround such as toys, television, and, in fact, any element of the life span that was involved in the child's stream of experience had to be considered. Yet, if we knew in any detailed sense which environmental aspects made significant impacts, we probably would not have had to do the research. Ours was intended to be an *inductive* study. We hoped to identify the most salient environmental factors *from the data of the study*. That identification would, of course, not be definitive, but would rather serve as the basis for subsequent experimental tests.

We decided to cast a broad, loose net over the "environment" hoping that some of the resulting quantitative data would be germane and assuming that when our subjective judgments were added we would then be prepared for the inductive process.

The least fortunate subgroup on our project therefore was the *Environment* group. Their first task was to create an instrument to assess the impact on the child's development of the primary caretaker's behavior. They labored mightily for many months. Their first product was a 99-item observational scale. They had no great confidence in its design and they were doubtful that it was usable. Try as they might, they never managed to reduce its size to anything manageable, and ultimately it was discarded. Shortly thereafter, the subgroup head left for other work,* and his position was taken by Dr. Jean C. Watts. Dr. Watts began her work with new financing and soon began to proceed vigorously with the task of dealing with environmental factors. She and her staff created new instruments to gather quantitative data on the subjects of our longitudinal study (see Volume I).

It rather soon became clear that Dr. Watts' approach to the research was, in many ways, quite different from that of Dr. White. Over a period of months it became clear that the unified nature of the Preschool Project could not be maintained. One result was that Volume I of this series was authored by two quite separate teams, one directed by Dr. Watts, the other by Dr. White. A second result was that each group was thrown more upon its own resources. This volume, for example, makes no use of Dr. Watts' data. Our staff did not, however, feel bereft of information on the environments of our subjects for two reasons. First, it is impossible for a large research staff to observe and discuss the development of 39 children intensively for up to five years without learning quite a bit about what the children interact with in the physical surround and about the major differences among the various child-rearing styles of families, etc. Second, in the process of sampling the stream of experience, we gathered a good deal of data on moment-to-moment environmental inputs. If a child was exploring an object, we recorded what it was as well as how long and in what ways it was played with. If the child's task was imposed by another human, we noted who the person was, etc. If he sought attention or assistance, we recorded the person involved and the type of response, etc.

It was from these sources that we ultimately were able to design an instrument to assess the effectiveness of child-rearing patterns.

*Dr. Robert LaCrosse left to become president of Pacific Oaks College in California.

THE ADULT ASSESSMENT SCALES

Our scales focus primarily on the behavior of the child's caretaker. There are four scales in all. The first and most important concerns the *responses* of the caretaker to *overtures by the child*. The second concerns behaviors directed toward the child but *initiated by the caretaker*. The third and fourth will be described, but we have not found them to be very useful. They are both rating scales, one dealing with the behavior of the caretaker in regard to each of the social and nonsocial competencies we study; the second dealing with seemingly important child-rearing practices such as child-proofing of the home, provision of access of the living area, etc. (see Adult Assessment Scales pages 424-430).

Checklist I is the heart of this instrument, and it is used in a manner parallel to our social behavior checklist in the sense that we spend one-half hour watching a child and we only record data when events of relevance occur. For example, if the child was left totally alone for any thirty-minute span, there would be almost no recording. The only data we would record would occur if a child, while alone, makes a clear overture to another person. Such an overture would not be responded to, but we would record its occurrence provided that we were confident that it was indeed directed toward another person. Of course, if another person is around and the child makes an overture that is not responded to, we would record it as well. Overtures are recorded in both cases to get an indication of the frequency of overtures and the degree of responsiveness to such behaviors by children.

At the top of the data sheet are categories designed to give us fairly specific information on a child's overtures. The balance of the eight categories have to do with the quality of the adult's response.

Item 1 tells us whether or not there was a response and, if so, how quickly it was delivered.

Item 2 indicates how well the responder has perceived the particular purpose of the subject.

Items 3 and 5 have to do with the language involved in the response, if any.

Item 4 has to do with whether or not ideas related to the primary topic were provided in the response.

Item 6 deals with the factor of motivational support for the activity at hand.

Item 7 has to do with whether the child was given any instruction about reality as a result of the overture.

Item 8 has to do with whether or not the subject's needs seem to have been satisfied.

These items are neither very elaborate nor complex nor in retrospect do they violate common sense. They were selected on the basis of our staff's conception of the type of responding that especially seemed to characterize the most effective mothers we have ever observed (regardless of SES, etc.). The instrument was refined somewhat as all instruments are as we moved into the trial stages with it. Its reliability is high (see Appendix C, pages 419-422).

From our earlier writing on this topic it might be assumed that only a modest fraction of any thirty-minute observation time is likely to be occupied by events that would merit scoring on Checklist I. Such does turn out to be the case. We find that the numbers of overtures that children under two years of age make to their parents are relatively modest. In a pilot study that we have since performed, we used this instrument with children between 8 and 17 months of age from 11 families.

Table 65 presents information to give the reader some sense of the kind of data one generates with the instrument. As can be seen, children ranging from 8 to 17 months of age were likely to make something in the order of five overtures to an adult during a thirty-minute span of time. Most of the overtures were responded to. An average of less than two minutes of the thirty were spent by the mothers responding to the children. This amounts to significantly less than 10 percent of the time and is consistent with our earlier observations as to the amount of time spent by a mother in direct interactions with her child. In order to get the total amount of such time, one has to include

TABLE 65. Adult Behavior in Response to a Child-Initiated Interaction[1]

Category	Range	Median
Frequency of S's overtures to A[2]	1-13%	5.0%
Frequency of overtures responded to by A[2]	1-13	4.5
Total duration of responses[2]	40-463 sec.	105.0 sec.
Mean duration of response time[2]	13-40 sec.	26.0 sec.
Timing and direction of A's response:[2]		
a. immediate	67-100%	82.0%
b. delayed	0-20	0.0
c. no response	0-33	0.0
d. rejected	0	0.0
A's perception of S's needs:[2]		
a. accurate	81-100%	100.0%
b. partial	0-50	0.0
c. none	0	0.0
Level of difficulty of A's words:[2]		
a. appropriate	0-100%	67.0%
b. too complex	0	0.0
c. too simple	0-50	10.0
d. baby talk	0	0.0
e. none	0-25	0.0
A's satisfaction of S's needs:[2]		
a. yes	20-100%	82.0%
b. no	0-20	0.0
c. partial	0-60	7.0

[1] This data summarizes observations on 11 Ss from the age of 8 to 17 months. The number of 30-minute observations on each S range from 5 to 10 with a median of 8-9 observations.
[2] Mean per 30-minute observation.

time involved in adult-initiated interactions. Checklist II deals with that issue. Checklist II is considerably simpler than Checklist I and reflects our lower interest in the events precipitated by the adult rather than by the child. Of course, it is only our judgment that leads us to the conclusion about the relative importance of the two types of interaction. Others might choose to construct an instrument differently. At any rate, on Checklist II all we record is the type of interaction, its emotional tone, and the miscellaneous aspects of the interaction.

Table 66 describes the kind of data we collected with the same sample reported on in Table 65. Table 66 shows that the typical number of adult-initiated interactions is slightly less than the number of child-initiated interactions. Also, total interaction time is shorter. All in all, when one adds the 65 seconds found for adult-initiated interactions to the 105 seconds adults spent responding to overtures from children, the total comes to just under three minutes, or approximately 10 percent of the observation time.

These sample data are presented simply to provide the reader with a better understanding of what kind of data one collects using such an instrument. We have gone on to use this instrument not only in the preparation of a training program for parents but also in the longitudinal experiment that will be described in the sections to follow.

TABLE 66. Adult Behavior When Initiating Interaction with a Child[1] ($n_{Families} = 11$)

Category	Range (of Mean Scores)	Median (of Mean Scores)
Frequency of A-initiated interactions[2]	3-9	4.0
Total duration of interactions[2]	55-215 sec.	65 sec.
$\overline{X}$ duration per interaction	13-30 sec.	16 sec.
A's purpose[2]		
a. to stimulate	40-86%	60%
b. to control	14-60	40

[1] This data summarizes observations on 11 Ss from the ages of 8 to 17 months. The number of 30-minute observations on each S range from 5 to 10 with a median of 8 observations.

[2] Scores represent mean values across all observations.

10

Creating a Training Program

After the several years of research of our natural longitudinal experiment, we had come to believe we had some promising ideas on how to raise a child well. Our staff was quite anxious to enter into an experimental test of the hypotheses. Indeed, we went ahead and asked a federal agency for support for such research. The agency was the Office of Child Development, and a senior staff officer did us a rather substantial service at the time. We discussed the proposed research with Mrs. Esther Kresch. She pointed out to us that though we had had many years of experience in research in child development, we had no prior experience actually training nonprofessional people. It was her recommendation that instead of attempting a comparative experiment immediately that we accept the likelihood of significant difficulties in creating a feasible training program and in working with the lay public. Therefore, Mrs. Kresch recommended support from her agency for a two-year period during which time we could work out a pilot training program and get our feet wet in working with parents.* The training program research lasted some two years; and, when it was over, our staff unanimously concluded that Mrs. Kresch

*Harvard Preschool Project, Child-rearing Practices and the Development of Competence, Final Report Grant No. OCD-CB-193 (9/1/72-8/31/74).

had been quite accurate in judging the kinds of difficulties we would run into. We have therefore been quite grateful to her for her counsel and support.

THE EXPERIMENTAL TREATMENT (THE TRAINING PROGRAM)

The experience of the longitudinal study along with previously established information on early growth and development led our staff to focus on that period in life between the onset of crawling and language learning ability (6-8 months of age) and the second birthday. We became convinced, from all that we had learned, that children generally manage to get to the crawling stage reasonably intact (from an educational point of view) but that few managed to get the most, educationally, out of the balance of infancy and toddlerhood. We, therefore, felt that the first priority of any course of research oriented toward the maintenance of optimal development in the early years was to prevent the falling off of development in the 8-36-month period.

We had come to believe that there were four educational foundations that were at risk between 8 and 24 months of age:

1. Language development
2. Curiosity development
3. Social skills and attachment development
4. Development of the roots of intelligence

Our experimental treatment-training program was therefore designed to: (a) make parents more aware of the course of development of these four educational foundation processes, (b) help parents emulate the child-rearing practices of apparently successful parents, (c) help parents avoid child-rearing practices of apparently unsuccessful parents.

Further shaping of the experimental treatment came from the actual experiences we had in attempting to work with a small group of families as their children grew from 5 to 17 months of age.

Through the mechanism of regular staff discussions of the experiences of working with parents on their child-rearing practices, we believe we strengthened our experimental treatment. For example, we knew that there would be a good deal of verbal interchange between staff and families throughout the pilot period and the training program in general. Therefore, we decided we would relieve the stress that might be caused by long-term verbal interchange by using a few well-chosen movies. We screened quite a number before we selected some for trial, but we could not know in advance how effective the various movies would be. Final judgment on films was the kind of practical problem that could only be resolved by trial and error.

Similarly, the optimal frequency of visits to homes was something that we found difficult to anticipate in advance; we learned how to space the visits through experience. Numerous other related kinds of learnings were met and coped with through the actual piloting of the project. Some of the more interesting aspects will be discussed further on.

We wanted to work with about a dozen families in this pilot phase. We were confident that not every family we began to work with would turn out satisfactorily for the purposes of the research. We were concerned, for example, that if a young couple was not getting along well the family discord might interfere with the utilization of ideas about child-rearing that we sought to test. We also were concerned with the possibility of families being unreliable. From our previous work with families we knew that there were some who failed to keep appointments. For these reasons we started with a few extra families (n = 16) and reduced the number to 12 between the fifth and eighth months of their children's lives. Subsequently, one additional family dropped out because of health reasons. We will report on our experiences with the remaining 11 families from the time their children were 8 months old.

We chose families in a rather special way. We did not want families who were likely to do such a good job with their children that there was not much room for improvement, nor did we want families where conditions were such that the ideas would not be given a fair chance. So, we aimed for families with average child-rearing abilities. We tried to determine the child-rearing capacity of each family as carefully as we could, although it is clear that we had no very reliable yardstick to measure that capacity in each family.

The goal of this pilot study was the creation of an effective training program to assist people in educating infants, one which would help us to put the hypotheses generated from the natural experiment to a proper experimental test. We have produced such a training program (see Appendix D). We have also piloted it and, in the process, refined it. We feel confident that this is a feasible, though imperfect, training program. It concentrates on the age range of 5-17 months because we feel that a powerful input into the development of the young child can be made at that time to preclude the loss of potential we claim is generally happening. We believe that most families do a perfectly adequate job with their children until the children get to be of crawling age, but very few families do an exceptionally good job from the onset of crawling through the second birthday. We were particularly concerned with certain natural developments of the second year of life. We knew that sometime between 14 and 16 months of age most children enter into negativistic behavior, and that families find this difficult to deal with. We therefore continued our input to these families until the seventeenth month in order to provide assistance during those months when the family is learning to cope with the problems generated by negativism.

From Schedules I and II outlined in Figures 12 and 13 it can be seen that we have treated the 5-8 month period separately from the 8-17 month period. We reasoned that the 5-8 month period is a relatively easy one for most families and could be used as a time to prepare them, at a relatively leisurely pace, for what was going to happen when the child began to crawl about the home. We used two kinds of activities to introduce the training program to families during this time period. We had group visits at the university featuring discussions and films, and we had follow-up visits to discuss the films and to get to know the individual circumstances in the home. Descriptions of what went on in each of the group and home visits are presented in Appendix D, as part of the description of the training program.

Once the baby turned 8 months of age, we shifted into high gear in our training program. The frequency of home visits was raised such that we were contacting families in their own homes approximately every other week. Simultaneously, the frequency of group get-togethers at the university was reduced. In addition, we began to monitor closely the processes of development.

We were particularly interested in the stream of experiences of these children and such data collection is represented in Schedule II by the symbol T. We were also interested in the behavior of the mothers and especially the degree to which it corresponded to the behaviors we were advocating. The frequency with which we sampled those behaviors is represented by the placement of the letter M. We collected data on the details of the child's social life (S), and we were assessing the growth of competence periodically throughout the time period (B, L, C_1, and C_2). As the child approached two years of age, we initiated our final assessment measures, which can be seen in Schedule III, Figure 14.

After each of the home visits, a relatively brief report of what transpired was produced by the particular home visitor. We routinely held meetings to discuss our views of how things were going in each of the family situations. The home visit reports were very important elements in those discussions. Samples of those home visit reports are presented with the training program material in Appendix D.

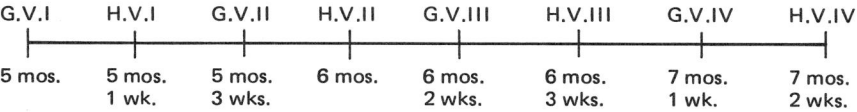

Chronological Age of Child (5-8 Months)

CODE: G.V. = Group Visit
H.V. = Home Visit

Figure 12. Schedule I

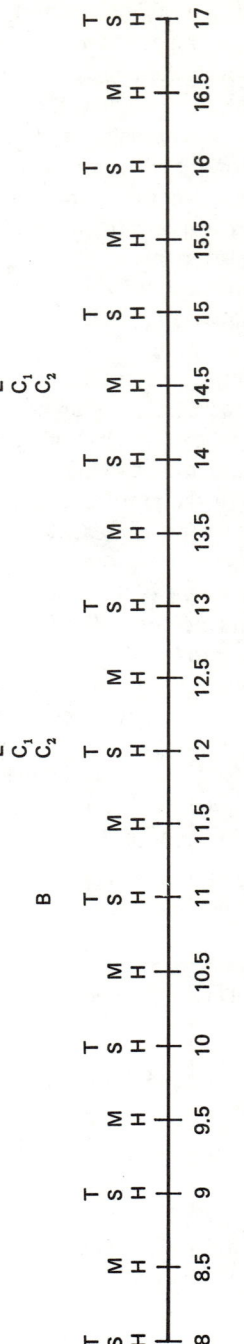

Figure 13. Schedule II

CODE: S = Collection of social competence data
        B = Bayley Scales of Infant Development
        L = Preschool Project Test of Receptive-Language Ability
        C_1 = Preschool Project Test of Sensing Dissonance
        C_2 = Preschool Project Test of Abstract Abilities

Figure 14.   Schedule III

part IV
CONCLUSIONS

11

Ramifications for Science of Human Development

In many places both written and spoken we have gone on record as being skeptics with respect to the track record of the science of child development research. We have repeatedly claimed that surprisingly little has been established through child development research that would help us fully understand the psychological growth of the very young child. We have been chided for these statements by our colleagues on numerous occasions. Regardless of that criticism, our position still stands: especially for the child five days to three years of age, the amount of relevant fundamental and applied research that has actually been done in proportion to the amount of esoteric and relatively impractical work that has been done is distressingly small. When the Congress of this country votes funds to research-oriented agencies such as the National Institutes of Child Health and Human Development, the National Institutes of Mental Health, and the Office of Child Development, it does not vote them primarily because it wants faculty members in developmental psychology to advance the science of psychology. While some legislators unquestionably value science for science sake, the vast majority of them seem to be more interested in research that has either immediate or near-term applicability to the problems of society. We do not believe that those purposes have been well served by the field over the last thirty years or so.

186   CONCLUSIONS

Our work is an attempt at bridging basic research and applied research on current social problems. We have tried to combine what seems most powerful about the research of Piaget and Lorenz and others in ethology with some form of experimental method as best developed in recent years within psychology and statistics. We believe we have made real, though modest, progress. Piaget in his pioneering studies of the development of intelligence in the first few years of life studied only three subjects, his own children, but he studied them in an incredibly powerful manner. First of all, he did not oversimplify the processes he was studying. His conceptualizations about the evolution of complicated forms of mental life are in comparison to the theoretical models involved in many other systems—especially those of association theory—far more sophisticated and (in our opinion) far more appropriate. His stage theory of development (which postulates several qualitatively different kinds of functioning in the first 18-24 months of life) is tied closely to actual behavior. That intensity of examination of the process of development is something we have attempted to use as one guideline. In the work of Lorenz and Tinbergen and others in ethology, one sees another source of guidance for our research: the attempt to understand how the subject under study copes with life on a day-to-day basis in respect to all kinds of waking experiences. Whereas Piaget focused on the adaptational processes facilitated by preintellectual mechanisms, the ethologists look at adaptation to the environment in a total fashion, and this comprehensive look is a feature we have attempted in our work. Finally, neither Piaget nor the ethologists are particularly well known for their use of quantitative procedures in the study of development of young animals, including man; yet, it has been our judgment from the outset that the use of quantitative procedures, both to assess abilities and to monitor the process of development and to design and analyze research studies is necessary.

Our work is clearly only a very small beginning. Although we have spent more than eighteen years at it to date, it still represents an extremely small investment compared to what is needed. After all, in the study reported in this volume we have examined the lives of only 39 children, of whom only 19 started in our project when they were one year of age. This is an extremely small group for consideration of an issue as important as the development of human competence. We know that the procedures we have used have in every instance been flawed. In some instances—in particular, in the case of the instrument for monitoring the process of development (the task instrument)—the flaws are almost great enough to destroy the usefulness of the procedures. The instrument is too complicated in a sense, and the result has been too low an interobserver reliability correlation. We are aware of that, but we simply could not do any better given the limits of our talent and time. A tremendous amount needs to be done to follow up on a study such as ours. We are of the opinion that the role of the environment in human development is far more complicated than the topics covered by most child development research. The same can be said of the study of the process of development, the stream of experience, or whatever one chooses to call it. In comparison, for example, the work involved in plotting the growth of abilities strikes us as being a scientific problem of considerably less complexity. Yet, comparatively few of our research people have either prepared themselves for such work or actually executed it. Conspicuous exceptions came from the tradition of Kurt Lewin with Roger Barker, Herbert Wright, Maxine and Philip Schoggen and their students examples of pioneers in the field of environmental psychology. They were pioneers who received relatively little support from the vast majority of people in child development research. They continue to this day to receive relatively little support. It is hard to see how a science of human development can ever become mature with such an emphasis on the scientific study of the plotting of the growth of human characteristics and a dearth of studies on the independent variable side of the ledger.

Not only are studies of the environment and the process of development comparatively rare and very much needed, but so are studies of normal or superior development in comparison to studies of the pathological. We believe it fair to say that over the last three decades studies of personality growth, for example, have much more emphasized the study of children in severe difficulty than those who developed well. Support for this point of view can be mustered very easily. All one has to do is to try to think of research associated with the study of the gifted child and then compare that modest number of studies with the amount of research associated with children or adults in difficulty. Think of the Freuds, Sullivans, Eriksons, and Rogerses of the world as compared to the Termans and the Maslows. Actually this imbalance is a bit more understandable than the preceding one in that the emergency situation should get attention before the long-term concern. Nevertheless, there is no justification for either putting off the study of good development indefinitely or for believing that by studying pathological processes we somehow have come to the position where we understand good development. An example of the latter is the case of the hospital department that specializes in evaluation. Such departments generally deal predominantly with referred patients. Those referrals are in response to situations in which someone thinks a child is in trouble. The evaluations done by such personnel will therefore, in most instances, involve children in trouble. Children living and functioning well or unusually well are not very likely to ever be referred for evaluation. Where, then, would people in such a center get their experience with good development with which to round out their professional perspective? The answer is nowhere.

When one specializes for many years in the analysis of the differences in experiences that young children undergo and the relationships among those differences and the development of abilities, it is extremely hard to take seriously current public arguments about the nature-nurture controversy. For anyone to report that x percent of achievement is due to genes or to any other innate factors on the basis of research that has so far been done is to us patently silly. For example, examine the studies of identical twins reared apart. To say that because one of them goes to one middle-class family and the other goes to another middle-class family you have somehow or other equated the environment they will be reared in is simply nonsense. The variations in moment-to-moment learning experiences across middle-class families is huge. No amount of studies of a correlational nature and focused on the degree of genetic similarity of individuals can lead to an adequate scientific explanation of the differential effects of nature and nurture on the development of abilities. What has to be done to supplement the work that involves genetic differences is a tremendous amount of difficult work on the environmental factors that affect the development of abilities. Until the time arrives when we can arrange experiments where environmental factors can be manipulated along with genetic input, we will never have anything like the substantial evidence required for responsible policy judgments on the issue.

In all the years that we have been involved in this study, certain things have become very clear to us on the nature-nurture issue:

1. What a child is born with physically sets upper limits to his ultimate achievement. A child with a congenital anomaly of major consequences given the finest conceivable early education cannot possibly reach levels of human competence reached by a physically normal or gifted individual.
2. The child with a fine physical constitution at birth has no guarantee whatsoever that regardless of the experiences he moves through during the first years of life that he will, at three years of age, have fully realized the potential he started with.

The lack of studies of the influences of the environment on the process of development and the lack of studies of normal and the better-than-normal-developing children prohibit the full development of a mature science of human growth. We believe that this notion will not remain unheeded indefinitely. It is just a shame that it is taking us so long to deal with it.

Our experience in the field has led us to the identification of several fundamental needs. First of all, we need much better tools to monitor the process of development. Our task instrument is only one tool. It is not a bad beginning, but it is far from perfect. The recent procedures generated by Clarke-Stewart also look promising for this fundamental purpose. Aside from those, plus whatever heuristic value the work of Lewin, Barker, and Wright, and the Schoggens have, we know of relatively little that is available in this area. There have been, of course, numerous other studies of which we are not aware. Among others, we believe comparative psychologists, such as Robert Hinde of Cambridge, have done valuable work with other animal species. William Mason, Phyllis Dollinow, and other American comparative researchers have made impressive beginnings in these areas. However, by and large, our capacity to sample the stream of experience in a scientifically respectable way seems to be at a very primitive stage of development. Second, we need many more techniques to assess human abilities in the first years of life. Just about everything we decided we needed to measure in our natural longitudinal study needed or required assessment techniques that did not exist or, if they did, were not particularly good. We are reasonably well off with respect to the assessment of general development in the first three years of life. The pioneering work of Gesell has led to many descendant forms of his instrument, which we believe do a perfectly adequate general screening job for us. In addition to Gesell, of course, Charlotte Bühler performed pioneering work in this field. Nowadays we have several useful instruments in the Bayley, Griffiths, and Denver scales.

We are in considerably worse shape when it comes to assessing language development. In spite of brilliant work by the psycholinguists, we are not well positioned in this area. We believe that our receptive-language scale constitutes a good beginning. Yet, much remains to be done with respect to test construction and the establishment of norms on large representative samples before that instrument will be as useful as it might be. We feel we have made a decent beginning with our Adult Assessment Scale in the area of the assessment of the effectiveness of an adult in child-rearing. Nevertheless, it too is an amateur performance with respect to test construction, and we have no norms for general usage. The Adult Assessment Scale is an example of a procedure focused on a major environmental complex and, as such, is relatively rare. The Lewinian movement created approaches to this topic. The Environmental Force Unit was a concept that came out of such work. However, Lewin and his students have never gone much further in attempting to dissect elements in the environment that have psychological salience for developmental processes. Much more work of this sort is required. An instrument that will allow one to assess the utilization of the physical surround is sorely needed. With respect to social abilities, we believe that our scales represent a reasonably good beginning as far as conceptualizing early social abilities. But our conceptions are only one of a number of conceptual schemes. Our instruments for assessing a child's competence in social areas are even less impressive to us than some of our other instruments, and, of course, we have no normative data, etc. As weak as our instrument seems to be, we do not know of any other that can compare favorably with it. The one most in use in the recent past in this country is the Vineland Social Maturity Scale. It was not designed to assess social competence. It was an attempt to help understand how well a retarded child has progressed toward independence. That problem is an important one in its own right, but it is very different from the identification of social skills in nonretarded young children.

Many another topic of obvious importance has had no substantial quantitative assessment work done with it. For example, the development of curiosity or the intrinsic interest in learning is acknowledged by all who study development to be at the heart of the achievement of competence. Yet, we have neither a serious plotting of the different manifestations of curiosity during the first three years of life nor a proper conceptualization of it nor, therefore, any way at all of assessing it quantitatively. This, to us, is clear evidence of the immaturity of the field, the lack of fundamental information that has to be acquired before we are truly knowledgeable.

In addition to basic knowledge of the course of development and reliable assessment techniques to monitor process and to evaluate the environment, etc., this field seems to lack basic strength in research design and statistical analysis. We are surrounded by exceptionally talented people in those areas in the several schools nearby. Almost invariably their training has been exclusively in the area of parametric statistics. Parametric statistics is fine when dealing with conventional child development research done in the laboratory or at least done where control over nearly all but a small number of the experimental variables is possible. Such is not the case when it comes to studies of development in the natural worlds of children or studies of the environment that go beyond one or two variables. As a result, our consultants in design and statistical analysis have to give us advice that they find in the footnotes to their classical designs and procedures for parametric statistics. This lefthanded treatment of the statistical needs of environmental research is unfortunate. We believe that the situation will inevitably change and more attention will be devoted to the problems of this more complicated work. For the time being, however, we operate under a rather serious handicap.

A more ultimate source of difficulty for the science is the lack of personnel who are oriented toward this kind of research in child development. It is a relatively rare graduate training program in this country that turns out people who are familiar with the work of Lewin, Barker, Wright, or any other people who choose to take seriously the scientific study of the environment. The much more conventional approach to the topic of child development research is represented in the thousands of reports of research of a highly focused nature dealing with small pieces of functions. That particular kind of training is obviously not the most suitable for someone who would choose to approach these relatively neglected spheres of the problem.

In comprehensive treatments of child development research, it soon becomes clear that among quite a number of different professions involved in the creation of the science of human development we have conventional child development research people with a background in psychology. We have people in educational research. But, in addition to those who are to some extent closely related, there are people in the field of ethology (most of those in Europe), people in child psychiatry, and people as far removed from laboratory psychologists as Erik Erikson, the famed personality theorist. Trying to relate the orientations and findings of people from seven or more different disciplines is no mean epistemological task. It is our judgment that what is centrally lacking is some sort of guidance from people skilled in philosophy of science with respect to this heterogeneous collection of ideas and work. After all, these are the people who should be positioned some distance from all the skirmishes and emotionalism and stresses of child development research. Not only do we need guidance from philosophers of science in methods and in weighing the relative values of different types of evidence, but we also need to have our new research personnel undergo some sort of exposure to principles of epistemology and to different aspects of the scientific method. It seems to us quite unfortunate that the typical doctoral student in child development research rarely is exposed to studies in philosophy or, for that matter, in comparative or physiological psychology. We recognize that it is no small task for all of these requirements to be met, but there seems to be no avoiding the need. The problem of building a science of human development seems to us far more complicated than the building of the older sciences such as physics or chemistry. It is this difficulty that seems somehow or other not to be appreciated by so many people in child development research. The result is a turning away from the realities of the situation, an oversimplification of issues down to what is "manageable," or an abandoning of the desire of the principles of scientific study altogether. In neither case do we profit; nevertheless, we remain somewhat optimistic. The importance of the problem is so great and the centrality of it so obvious that we believe that gradually progress will be made.

12

Ramifications for Society

It seems to us that the area of the education of the very young child is not only one of great importance to society as a whole and especially to parents, but also one where there is a special state of confusion. We are of the opinion that parents find it very difficult to procure reliable advice as to how to educate their young children. The difficulty that professionals have in trying to find solid information about the educational development of young children may be even more profoundly important. It is our impression that people directing parent education programs and education center-based programs have enormous difficulty sorting out all the ideas purported to be useful in this area. We have talked with numerous people in such positions. We have examined curricula in use. By and large, we have been repeatedly surprised at both the degree of confusion and the tendency of people to take as fact recommendations that do not seem to us to be rooted in substantial evidence. A major case in point is the previously discussed nature-nurture controversy. Many professionals are simply confused on the topic, but another large number are not so much confused and are more inclined to think that one or another answer has been thoroughly, or impressively, supported by substantial evidence. What seems to be happening is that a need to have an answer is overpowering the good sense of people in areas having to do with early education.

In the mid-1940s when René Spitz published his first work on the apparently devastating consequences of extensive separation of an infant from his mother during the first years of life (hospitalism), a great deal of research activity followed. Several years later the World Health Organization commissioned a summary volume to collect, in one place, the results of all research on that most fundamental topic (Bowlby monograph). Hundreds of studies had been done in the intervening years. When put together the results tended generally to go in the same direction. Although many of the individual studies were subjected to serious criticism because of one or another scientific inadequacy, the consistency of the findings across the hundreds of studies convinced people that policy in respect to institutional rearing of young children should be influenced by the studies. What happened was that the weight of evidence was sufficient so that that one topic, the necessity for a continuous emotional bond between mother and child, was *to some degree* clarified by research. The research on maternal deprivation, as it had come to be called, was circumscribed. It dealt primarily with the caretaker-infant emotional bond and did not pretend to cover much more. It has since been extended, but originally it was rather narrowly defined. Turning to topics like the nature-nurture controversy, or how to rear a young child, one finds that from a scientific point of view the scope of the topic is substantially greater and that the evidence necessary to constitute a significant quantity is therefore correspondingly greater. Unfortunately, the evidence, as far as we can tell, does not exist in anything like the amount necessary to deal with either issue with confidence. The question of what constitutes sufficient weight of evidence seems to us to be basically a question that requires clarification from people who specialize in the philosophy of science and in particular in the topic of epistemology. While these may be highly technical pursuits, it is our judgment that when it comes to the well-being of future generations of children, the idea that sophisticated thinking will be required should not be a deterrent to its utilization.

We believe that the research we have engaged in over the last eleven years has several important ramifications for society. First of all, we are totally convinced that it is a relatively rare child who gets off to the kind of beginning, educationally, that is maximally likely to help him make the most of his innate potential. We have had the opportunity to make extensive observations of several hundred children in their ordinary daily learning experiences. We are convinced that only a small fraction of those children receive the kind of day-to-day experiences that mesh well with their developing interests and needs. A conservative estimate would be that something in the vicinity of 9 children out of 10 are undergoing early experiences that are considerably less suited to their needs than they should and could be. Even when a child has developed into a person of rather high levels of competence by three years of age, it is not necessarily the case that his preceding learning experiences were especially well designed for him. We have examples of children who were 14 and 15 months of age before the adults in their environment did any extensive talking to them. Yet, at age three, these children turned out to be quite skillful with respect to language. It might be concluded that it was not necessary for such children to have extensive language experiences before 14 months of age. We, on the other hand, are more inclined to think that if those particular children had been given significantly more language, suitably delivered, from the time they were 7 months of age, they would have achieved even more than they had in the untutored course of events. Their mothers were very talented individuals who, by and large, were not given to chatter. Until the children began to say a few words, the mothers said next to nothing to them. Once the children started to say two or three words at age 14 or 15 months, the mothers began to use language increasingly with them.

By far, the more common kind of child-rearing practice that seems to us significantly inconsistent with the educational needs of an infant is the restricting of the child's locomobility from the time he is 7 months of age to at least through the middle of the second year. Families usually use playpens for this purpose but may also use other restricting items such as high chairs, jump seats, cribs, gates, etc. Restricting an infant's locomobility makes very good sense as a procedure to reduce the likelihood of accidents and breakage of fragile family items, etc. It seems, from what we have observed however, to result in patterns of experience that are much less likely to lead to high levels of achievement than are other patterns of experiences. Results of this kind are numerous within our data. Even though we have dealt with a very small population, the relationships are so striking that we cannot help but feel there is substance to the position.

If experiential patterns of the sort we find strongly associated with excellent development by three years of age were made available on a widespread basis to new children as they came along, the standards of achievement of three-year-olds that we have become accustomed to would ultimately be considered subnormal. It seems to us that the chances for considerably greater yield in terms of the development of human resources are very substantial. Surely anyone who seeks to understand the influence on achievement of experiences compared to influences of other factors (such as genes, diet, etc.) has to consider the rather broad experiential differences that we seem to be finding. Until studies are done where desirable experiential patterns are made available to groups of children with different constitutional characteristics, one cannot really make much scientific headway on the nature-nurture issue.

For several decades, we have known that the higher achievement levels on tests of intelligence, such as the Weschler or the Binet, are associated with better performance in school and that school performance, in turn, bears some positive relationship to other achievements of human beings. Our research has dealt with more abilities than those measured by intelligence tests. We place a great deal of emphasis upon the social skills of a child. Nevertheless, we are not among those who would discard standardized intelligence tests; in fact, we would like to dwell at this point on our results in the area of such tests. Of the 39 children we have studied in this project, 21 ended up with Weschler scores over 116 when they were five years of age. Five of them scored over 130. From what we know about the predictive power of such scores on the WPPSI at age five, the children who scored over 115 are very likely to continue to do outstandingly well in intellectual pursuits. Intelligence test scores at age five tend to correlate somewhere around +.70 with intelligence test scores given at age eighteen to the same children (Hunt, 1961; Jones, 1954). We know from the research we have done that certain kinds of experience are related to certain kinds of child-rearing practices and *also* to these very substantial performances on the Weschler intelligence test at age five. The conclusion seems to be that there is at least a good chance that if family practices were modified in the directions that would lead to the kinds of childhood, infancy, and toddlerhood experiences we have isolated, more intellectually talented adults would develop. This, to us, is a very heady proposition, but it does not seem unreasonable.

With respect to the broader concept of competence, we are in somewhat murkier waters. For all that one would say against the psychometricians and the whole field of intelligence testing, that field has an impressive track record. In the seventy years of its existence, the field has done some very useful things, especially when dealing with large groups of people rather than with individuals. Without it the United States Army during World Wars I and II would have had substantial difficulty in identifying personnel who were unable to absorb training. Without intelligence tests, we would have been less able to begin programs of remedial and compensatory education. With respect to non-intellectual or extraintellectual abilities of children, we simply are in a very weak state as far as assessment goes. Anastasia (1976) has pointed out how poorly we do when we try to assess the mental health status of adults or children using instruments such as the Rorschach or the TAT. She has indicated that our studies of musical talent and other less easily defined psychological characteristics are also very weak. People in psychological research have attempted to create assessment techniques with respect to sex role identity (Brown, 1956), the self concept (Henderson, 1967), creativity (Baron, 1958). What most seem to have discovered is that the ease with which one can create powerful assessment techniques seems to be inversely related to the attractiveness of the topic. For example, while many people value the human attribute of creativity, our capacity to measure or even define the quality turns out to be quite meager, certainly in comparison to our results in the area of intellectual testing. In the area of social abilities we believe we have made a modest dent in the problem; yet we are well aware that it is only a small beginning. We believe that our conceptualization of important social skills is basically sound. We are not at all comfortable, however, with our translations of our behavioral data into an assessment scale. We think a great deal of solid test construction remains to be done to modify our crude instrument. Furthermore, it will then be necessary to gather normative data and perform other standard psychometric work. All those qualifications considered, however, we feel that in our studies we have developed some reliable ways for making distinctions with respect to social competence among children less than six years of age. To the extent that we are capable of making such distinctions, we have information parallel to that previously discussed on intellectual achievement. We have studied a modest number of children who became quite talented in social situations by three years of age. We have information on their experiences between their first and third birthdays. Furthermore we have a general picture of the child-rearing practices that seem, in part, to lead to those experiences. Putting all those together, it seems that the results of this research tend to indicate something about how to raise a socially competent young human. Unfortunately, we had no way of gathering powerful information about social competence with our sample when they reached five years of age. Nor, do we have, as in the case of intellectual testing, any data from other studies suggesting that the socially outstanding five-year-old will be an outstanding adult in social skills.

We have attempted analyses that combine our fairly standard assessments in the area of intellectual function with our relatively primitive instruments in the area of social functioning, and perhaps, to some extent, the combination has unique value. Children identified at age three as being especially talented in both areas would seem to us to be a particularly important group. We should point out that it is not the case that all children who do beautifully on intelligence tests at three (even in our sample) are at the top of our ranks with respect to social competence. Nor is the converse true; that is, not all our children who did beautifully in social competence tested very highly in intellectual tests at three. We have several cases of cross instances. Nevertheless, there were some who were strong in both areas. The kinds of experiences they had around their first birthdays seem to us to form the most conservative picture, given what we know today, of how experiences should be structured in order to lead to a fully developed three-year-old.

We believe these data are precious in some ways. After all, it is a rare family that does not want to raise its children to get the most out of their early years. As far as we can tell, the majority of families do the best they can. Because our educational system has defaulted with respect to the training of families for this function, there has surfaced, here and elsewhere in the world, an infinite supply of recommendations about how one should raise a child. It is our judgment that people who provide recommendations on this topic are rarely in a position to do so on the basis of directly relevant scientific evidence. We do not claim that our results are overwhelming in the light of standard scientific criteria nor that scientific evidence is the only basis for good practice. However, we do want to point out that we know of no other research that could have produced quite the same kinds of results that we have on the topic of the early education of a child. For example, we know of no way in which one or two laboratory sessions with a young child, of any age, could lead to much useful data on the topic of how to educate an infant or a toddler.

Without a substantial body of scientifically respectable information on the process of educational development in the first two years of life, what can be used for societal policy? It is our judgment that information from extensive, acceptable experience on the topic is a second-best choice. As a case in point, one should consider the long-term experience of kibbutz life in Israel. Joseph Stone of Vassar recently produced three superb documentary films on the functioning of several kibbutzim for infants and toddlers. In these handsome films, one sees warm, skillful treatment of young children by the staff. One cannot help but be impressed by the professionalism that is manifested. Since kibbutzim have existed for very young children for quite a number of years, and since there have been no reports of major harmful consequences for the children involved, it follows that someone wishing to learn something about how to deal with a very young child, in an all-day center, could do worse than emulate the most impressive of the kibbutz operations. These films and the kibbutz movement are mentioned here because they seem to represent one of the few conservative alternatives that are available to people who are interested in educational policy for children under three years of age.

Our research has attempted to use scientific methods to generate reliable information on good education for infants and toddlers by observing families who seem to be unusually successful with their children. This approach has sought to analyze some of the results of nature's experiments. It owes very little to theory, although there are always some crude theoretical assumptions embedded in any research. It does not, for example, owe much to the work of previous students of child development such as Freud (1957) or Erikson (1950) but, rather, seeks to be as atheoretical as possible given the conviction that theories are limited in their likely utility by the amount of existing relevant empirical data. Therefore, on the one hand, we have information on the process of early education generated by an examination of what is actually happening when the process goes well (using the best of the sparse collection of appropriate scientific methods) and, on the other hand, the wisdom that comes from experience found in long-established operations such as those of the kibbutzim.

What more is available? We believe that anyone who is interested in the educational process in the first three years of life must ask that question of any new recommendations that are presented by anyone on the topic. Currently, in the United States and, indeed, in other parts of the world, there is rapidly growing enthusiasm for the importance of education in the first three years of life. Concurrently, new programs to educate parents are springing up in great numbers. It is a rare program that uses the kibbutz experience as a basis for its curriculum. A few programs use our research. The question in our minds is, What bases are other programs using and how legitimate are those bases?

For those who would conjure up the research of Piaget as the core of any curriculum for infancy, we would point out a number of things. First of all,

Piaget was only interested in the development of intelligence to the explicit exclusion of all other facets of human development. Second, Piaget was not interested in the study of the education of a child. He was strictly interested in the study of the emergence of mental power; the two topics are not identical. In other words, Piaget was not very much interested in *how you helped the growth of mental power*, and one cannot find explicit guidelines within his system on that topic. Furthermore, the few studies that had tested for the development of sensorimotor intelligence à la Piaget seem to have found that children who would be expected to do rather poorly in their early education looked surprisingly strong with respect to the development of sensorimotor intelligence (Golden et al., 1971; Hunt, 1961). It is our judgment that the sensorimotor stages of Piaget represent deep structures of the sort that develop with a relatively small assist from the environment. In other words, as with the emergence of locomobility, reaching skills, walking and climbing, almost any kind of environment is sufficient to support the normal development of sensorimotor intelligence. In marked contrast, language skills seem to be particularly sensitive to environmental variation; although some language skills will surface in almost any kind of environment, the range of skill is very great and apparently quite sensitive to environmental variation.

For those who would suggest that the work of Erikson forms the basis for curriculum-building in early education, we point out that Erikson dealt with a relatively small population of children growing up with emotional distress. He spent no time with children developing well. Although his thinking and his writing is clearly of very high quality, it does not deal extensively with good development in childhood and it certainly does not lean on any evidence of any consequence with respect to that topic. Finally, in the description of the psychosocial development of children, Erikson presents no specific guidelines of any consequence that would help anyone to design the day-to-day educational input for a young child.

Both Erikson and Piaget offer useful background material for the design of the curriculum. Piaget's material is far more useful in our opinion than Erikson's because there is no way of designing any educational curriculum with infants and toddlers without proper consideration of the intellectual level of the child. That level changes dramatically throughout the first years of life; the only way to understand those changes is to understand the work of Piaget. Therefore, as a tool with which to understand the student (in this case, the infant and toddler), Piaget's work is an absolute essential. As a director of educational practice in the first years of life, Piaget is not running for office, nor should he be elected.

We have concluded from our research and that of others that the experiences of the first three years of life seem especially important to the development of human competence. For most young children in Western society, and certainly in the United States, the nuclear family provides those experiences. It follows logically that families need to know what to provide and need to be able to provide what is needed. The first order of business is to ask, Do they generally know? The second question is, Are they generally able? The answer to the first question as far as we can tell is, No, they do not know what to provide their children. That answer is germane to their ability to provide beneficial experiences. Our data show that people from socioeconomic levels that are as low as Level IV in the Hollingshead and Redlich system are perfectly capable of producing well-developed three-year-olds (even at times without elaborate preparation or assistance). True, such good circumstances prevail all too rarely, but it is important to find they do exist because this suggests that whatever is necessary in the way of intellectual and fiscal resources to do a solid job of educating a young child is available to the vast majority of families in this society. Unfortunately, however, the current educational system neglects the task of preparing and assisting families to do this task. There are discernible historical reasons for this state of affairs. The first six years of life have always been considered to be a time for childhood, a time for play, a time when one cannot teach children much of anything having to do with school, etc. The first six years have also been considered a time when the child's place is in the home, and the home has always, in the United States at least, been considered a sanctuary—one that should not be intruded on, except in rare instances, by the society at large. It is only recently that historical events and social evolution have led us to the point where we have come to see how important the events that transpire within the home are for a growing young child. Currently, there is very clearly a strong case for the treatment of education in the first three years of life as *the very first priority for any national educational system.* As support for that statement we cite the recent survey of the effects of intervention programs done by Bronfenbrenner (1974) and recent declarations by the former Commissioner of Education T. H. Bell (1974). Further support for this notion comes from the recent meetings in Paris of UNESCO member nations on the topic of education in the first six years of life as it relates to lifelong education. The following is an excerpt from the draft of the final report (sections of pages 1-5 on recommendations of the UNESCO talks):

> It is felt that preschool education, as is now increasingly recognized in most countries, should be an integral part of complete educational structures and should therefore in no way be viewed as a luxury. It takes on a new significance in the perspective of life-long education and has a special contribution to make towards the democratization of education.
>
> All countries saw the need to help parents to become educators of their own children, also the need to employ well-qualified personnel to work with children and parents.
>
> 1. The first three years of life are of critical importance in the development of language, approaches to problem-solving and social behavior and emotional growth.
> 2. Basic motivation to learn is inherent in children but it is nourished as a result of the influence of adults within the environment. Thus children learn to learn or learn not to learn as a result of how adults handle their development during the first three years of life.

3. The period after 7 months appears to be of critical importance for the development of language, curiosity, social behavior, and the beginnings of intelligence and emotional growth.
4. Language plays an important role in concept development and social behavior. It begins to develop rapidly about the age of 7 or 8 months and especially during the two years or so that follow. Most of the basic language acquisitions—grammar, syntax, basic vocabulary, etc.—are already present by the end of the third year.
5. The parents, particularly the mother or the person most in contact with the child, influence the acquisition of language by the way in which explanations are made to the child and the way in which verbal behavior is reinforced, rewarded, punished, or ignored.
6. Deep curiosity is invariably present in all but seriously damaged children at the age of 8 months, but unless this curiosity is encouraged and rewarded, it can easily be somewhat retarded by the age of two years, or even sharply reduced.
7. Social development is particularly noticeable at the age of 8 months, and by the age of two years it is being used to acquire attention, utilize adults as a resource, and seek the support of others.
8. The roots of intelligence as described by Piaget are nourished by the environment and in favorable environments intelligence is well developed by the age of four years (cf. Benjamin Bloom).

This draft was signed unanimously by the representatives of twenty nations from all parts of the world and reflected the unified attitudes toward the importance of preparing and assisting families to educate their children in the first three years of life.

References

Anastasi, A. *Psychological Testing*, 4th edition: New York. Macmillan Co., 1976.

Barker, R. C. *The Stream of Behavior*. New York: Appleton-Century-Crofts, Division of Meredith Publishing Company, 1963.

———. *Ecological Psychology: Concepts and Methods for Studying the Environment of Human Behavior*. Stanford, Calif.: Stanford University Press, 1968.

Barron, F. "The Psychology of Imagination." *Scientific American*. 199; 50, September 1958, pp. 150-156.

Bayley, N. "Comparisons of Mental and Motor Test Scores for Ages 1-15 Months by Sex, Birth Order, Race, Geographical Location, and Education of Parents." *Child Development* 36 (1965): 379-411.

Bayley, N., and Schaefer, E. S. "Correlations of Maternal and Child Behaviors with the Development of Mental Abilities: Data from the Berkeley Growth study." Monographs of the Society for Research in Child Development, serial no. 97, vol. 29, no. 6 (1964). University of Chicago Press, Chicago, Illinois.

Bell, T. H. "The Family, the Young Child, and the Schools." Paper presented at the 10th Annual Conference of South Carolina School Officials, Myrtle Beach, July 12, 1974.

Bowlby, J. "The Nature of the Child's Tie to his Mother," *International Journal of Psycho-Analysis*, 1958, part V, vol. XXXIX, pp. 1-23.

REFERENCES

Bronfenbrenner, U. "Is Early Intervention Effective?" A Report on Longitudinal Evaluation of Preschool Programs, vol. 2, DHEW Publication No. (OED) 74-25, 1974.

Bronson, W. C. "Mother-Toddler Interaction: A Perspective on Studying the Development of Competence." *Merrill-Palmer Quarterly* 20 No. 4 (1974): 275-302.

Brown, D. G. "Sex Role Preference in Young Children". *Psychological Monographs General and Applied*, Vol. 70, No. 14, 1956. pp. 1-19.

Brown, R. E. and Halpern, F. "The Variable Pattern of Rural Black Children." *Clinical Pediatrics* 10 (1971): pp. 404-409.

Bühler, C., and Hetzer, H. *Testing Children's Development from Birth to School Age*. New York: Farrar and Rinehart, 1935.

Caldwell, B. "A New 'Approach' to Behavioral Ecology." In *Minnesota Symposia on Child Psychology*, edited by J. P. Hill, vol. 2. Minneapolis: University of Minnesota Press, 1968. pp. 74-109.

Carew, J. V.; Chan, I.; Halfar, C. *Observing Intelligence in Young Children*. Englewood Cliffs, N. J.: Prentice-Hall, Inc., 1976.

Clarke-Stewart, A. K. "Interaction Between Mothers and Their Young Children: Characteristics and Consequences." Monographs of the Society for Research in Child Development, serial no. 153, vol. 38, nos. 6-7 (1973). University of Chicago Press: Chicago, Illinois.

Erikson, E. H. *Childhood and Society*. New York: W. W. Norton & Co., Inc., 1950.

Escalona, S. *The Roots of Individuality*. Chicago: Aldine Publishing Co., 1968.

Freud, S. "Three Essays on the Theory of Sexuality (1905)." New York: Basic Books, Inc. 1962.

Gesell, A. et al. *The First Five Years of Life. A Guide to the Study of the Preschool Child*. New York: Harper, 1940, xiii & 393.

Gesell, A. and Amatruda, C. S. *Developmental Diagnosis: Normal and Abnormal Child Development*. New York: Paul B. Hoeber, Inc., 1960.

Gesell, A.; Ilg, F. L.; Bullis, G. E. *Vision: Its Development in Infant and Child*. New York: Paul B. Hoeber, Inc., 1949.

Golden, M; Birns, B.; Bridger, W.; and Moss, A. "Social Class Differentiation in Cognitive Development Among Black Preschool Children." *Child Development* 42 (1971): 37-45.

Guidubaldi, J. "Social competence of preschool children as a predictor of social and academic competence two years later." A thesis presented to the Faculty of the Graduate School of Education at Harvard University, in partial fulfillment of the requirements for the degree of Doctor of Education, 1969.

Halpern, Florence. "The Mental Development of Black Rural Southern Children Aged One Week to Thirty-Six Months." Paper presented at the Society for Research in Child Development at Santa Monica, Calif., March, 1969.

Henderson, R. W. "Influences on Cognitive and Motivational Conditions for Acculturation." Paper presented at the Annual Meeting of American Education Research Association, New York City, February 16-18, 1967.

Hinde, Robert A. *Animal Behavior: A Synthesis of Etiology and Comparative Psychology*. New York: McGraw-Hill Book Co., 1966.

Hollingshead, A. B., and Redlich, F. C. *Social Class and Mental Illness*. New York: John Wiley & Sons, Inc., 1958.

Honzig, M. P. "Environmental Correlates of Mental Growth: Prediction from the Family Setting at 21 Months." *Children Development* 38 No. 2 (1967): 337-64.

Hunt, J. McV. *Intelligence and Experience.* New York: Ronald Press Co., 1961.

Jensen, A. R. "How Much Can We Boost IQ and Scholastic Achievement?" *Harvard Educational Review* 39, no. 1 (1969).

Jones, H. E. "The Environment and Mental Development." In *Manual of Child Psychology* edited by L. Carmichael. New York: John Wiley and Sons, Inc., 1954.

Kagan, J. "American Longitudinal Research on Psychological Development." *Child Development* 35 (1964): 1-32.

Lewin, K. *Dynamic Theory of Personality.* New York: McGraw-Hill Book Co., 1935.

———. *Field Theory in Social Science.* New York: Harper & Row, Inc., 1951.

Murphy, L. B. *Personality in Young Children.* Vols. 1 and 2. New York: Basic Books, 1956.

Pasamanick, B.; Knobloch, H.; Lilienfeld, A. M. "Socio-Economic Status and Some Precursors of Neuropsychiatric Disorder." *American Journal of Orthopsychiatry* 26 (1956): 594-601.

Piaget, J. *The Origins of Intelligence in Children.* New York: W. W. Norton, & Co., Inc., 1952.

Sander, L. W. "Infant and Caretaking Environment: Investigation and Conceptualization of Adaptive Behavior in a System of Increasing Complexity." In *The Child Psychiatrists as Investigators*, edited by E. J. Anthony. New York: Plenum Press, 1974.

Schaefer, E. "Intellectual Stimulation of Culturally Deprived Infants." Excerpted from Mental Health Grant Proposal No. MH-09224-01, Laboratory of Psychology, National Institute of Mental Health, July 1968.

———. "Need for Early and Continuing Education." Paper presented at the War Memorial Auditorium, Boston, Mass., December 28, 1969.

Schoggen, P., and Schoggen, M. "Behavior Units in Observational Research." Paper presented as part of the symposium *Methodological Issues in Observational Research*, American Psychological Association, San Francisco, Calif., 1968.

———. "Environmental Forces in the Home Lives of Three-Year-Old Children in Three Population Subgroups." *DARCEE Papers and Reports*, vol. 5, no. 2 (1971).

Spitz, R. A. *No and Yes: On the Genesis of Human Communication.* New York: International Universities Press, 1957.

Terman, L. M., et al. *Genetic Studies of Genius.* The Mental and Physical Traits of a Thousand Gifted Children, vol. 1. Stanford, Calif.: Stanford University Press, 1925.

Terman, L. M., and Merrill, M. A. *Stanford Binet Intelligence Scale.* Boston: Houghton Mifflin Co., 1960.

Terman, L. M., and Oden, M. H. *Genetic Studies of Genius.* The Gifted Child Grown Up, vol. IV. Stanford, Calif.: Stanford University Press, 1947.

Thomas, A.; Chess, S.; Birch, H. F.; Hertzig, M. E.; Korn, S. *Behavioral Individuality in Early Childhood*, New York: New York University Press, 1964.

REFERENCES

United Nations Eductional, Scientific and Cultural Organization, Meeting on PreSchool Education as the First Phase of Life Long Education, Final Report, Paris, March 15, 1976.

Uzigiris, I. C., and Hunt, J. McV. "A Scale of Infant Psychological Development." 1964 mimeographed.

──────. *Assessment in Infancy, Ordinal Scales of Psychological Development.* Urbana, Ill.: University of Illinois Press, 1975.

Wachs, T. D.; Uzigiris, I. C.; Hunt, J. McV. "Cognitive Development in Infants of Different Age Levels and from Different Environmental Backgrounds." Paper presented to biennial meeting of the Society for Research in Child Development, New York, March 29-April 1, 1967.

Walker, D. *Socioemotional Measures for Preschool and Kindergarten Children.* San Francisco, California: Jossey-Boss, 1973.

Watts, J. C.; Barnett, I. C.; Halfar, C. "Environment, Experience, and Development in Early Childhood." The Harvard Preschool Project Final Report, Grant No. CG-9916, Office of Economic Opportunity, Head Start Division, January 1973.

Wenar, C. "Competence at One." *Merrill-Palmer Quarterly* 10, no. 4 (1964).

──────. *Personality Development from Infancy to Adulthood.* Boston: Houghton Mifflin Co., 1971.

──────. "Executive Competence and Spontaneous Social Behavior in One-Year-Olds." *Child Development* 43 (1972): 256-60.

White B. L. *Human Infants: Experience and Psychological Development.* Englewood Cliffs, N.J.: Prentice-Hall, Inc., 1971.

White, B. L., et al. "Child-rearing Practices and the Development of Competence," The Harvard Preschool Project Final Report, Grant No. OCO-CB-193, U.S. Office of Child Development, December 1974.

White, B. L.; Watts, J. C.; et al. *Experience and Environment: Major Influences on the Development of the Young Child.* Vol. 1. Englewood Cliffs, N.J.: Prentice-Hall, Inc., 1973.

Whiting, J. and Whiting, B. "Contributions of Anthropology to the Methods of Studying Child Rearing." In *Handbook of Research Methods in Child Development* edited by P. Mussen. New York: John Wiley & Sons, Inc., 1960.

Winer, B. J. *Statistical Principles in Experimental Design.* New York: McGraw Hill, 1962.

Yarrow, L. J.; Rubenstein, J. L.; Pederson, F. H. *Infant and Environment.* New York: John Wiley & Sons, Inc., 1975.

Appendix **A**

INDIVIDUAL SUBJECT DATA

SUBJECT #1

Subject #1 is a one-year-old SES Level IV[1] predicted C girl. She is the youngest of thirteen children who range in age from one to nineteen years. Both parents are high school graduates, and the oldest child is at present attending a state university.

The family lives in a small, well-worn seven-room house that is sparsely furnished. The major source of entertainment for the family seems to be the large color television, which is often on most of the day.

This subject is a sturdy little girl who is physically and socially mature for her age. In the mornings she is at home with her mother and two-and-a-half-year-old sister. The mother is a warm, loving woman who is usually busy with household chores. Most of her interaction with the subject is centered around food.

By noontime, different siblings and the father start arriving home. The subject is the recipient of a lot of affectionate hugging and kissing, but very little interaction of any other type occurs. She is usually left to roam freely around the house, and since there are very few toys available to her—and even fewer that are appropriate for a one-year-old—she spends most of her time watching television or wandering from room to room.

[1] The socio-economic status (SES) levels are derived from the Index of Social Position developed by Hollingshead and Redlich (1968), which implies occupation, education, and residence as class criteria. There are five Hollingshead and Redlich levels with I as highest class position and V as the lowest.

Summary of Test Scores

Subject #1   Group: One-Year-Old Starters (n = 19)

Tests	Age at Testing (Months)	Score	Group Median
Bayley Mental Developmental Index	12	134	103
	24	112	112
Stanford-Binet IQ	36	108	113
WPPSI IQ	60	98	117.5
Lanugage Test[1]	12	16	14
	15	21	16
	21	27	21
	24	40	36
	27	not tested	—
	30	42	43.5
	36	42	45
Abstract Abilities[2]	12	1	2
	15	3	2
	21	6	5
	24	7	6
	27	not tested	—
	30	7	7
	36	9	9
Discrimination Test[2]	12	0	1
	15	3	2
	21	5	3
	24	3.5	3.5
	27	not tested	—
	30	3.5	5
	36	7	8

[1] Scores in Months
[2] Scores in Level Achieved

Individual Subject Data 209

SOCIAL COMPETENCE FOR SUBJECT 1

```
                              T
GAIN            O
ADULT           O
ATTENTION       O
                      T
                        T
USE             O
ADULT           OXXXXXXXXXXXXXXXXXXXX
RESOURCE        OXXXXXXXXXXXXXXXXXXXXX
                O       T
                    T
HOSTILITY,      O
AFFECTION       OXXXXXXXX
TO ADULT        OXXXXXXX
                        T
                T
ROLE PLAY       O
                O
                    T
                T
PRIDE IN        O
PRODUCT         O
                    T
                            T
COMPETES        O
WITH            OXXXXXXXXXXXXXXXXXXXXXXXXXXXXXXXXXXX
PEER            OXXXXXXXXXXXXXXXXXXXXXXXXXXXXXXXXXX
                        T
                O       T
HOSTILITY,      O
AFFECTION       OXXXXXXXXXXXXXX
TO PEER         OXXXXXXXXXXXX
                O   T
                O       T
LEADS AND       OXXXXXXXXXXXXXXXXXXXXXXXXXX
FOLLOWS         OXXXXXXXXXXXXXXXXXXXXX
PEER            O
                    T

                0   1   2   3   4   5   6   7   8   9   10

                    TOTAL SCORES    MEDIANS AT 12/15 MONTHS
                        FOR S 1         FOR ALL SUBJECTS

ADULT COMPETENCE        6.6                 13.8
PEER COMPETENCE        17.9                  9.0
OVERALL COMPETENCE     24.5                 20.5
```

T INDICATES THE MEDIAN FOR ALL SUBJECTS FOR EACH COMPETENCE FACTOR.

SOCIAL COMPETENCE FOR SUBJECT 1

```
                            T
GAIN            O
ADULT           OXXXXXXXXXXXXXXXXXXXXXXXXXXXXXXXXXXXXXXXXXXXXXXXXX
ATTENTION       OXXXXXXXXXXXXXXXXXXXXXXXXXXXXXXXXXXXXXXXXXXXXXXX
                O
                                T
USE             O
ADULT           OXXXXXXXXXXXXXXXXXXXXXXXXXXXXXXXXXXXXXXXXXXXXXX
RESOURCE        OXXXXXXXXXXXXXXXXXXXXXXXXXXXXXXXXXXXXXXXXXXXXXX
                O           T
                    T
HOSTILITY,      O
AFFECTION       OXXXXXXXXXXX
TO ADULT        OXXXXXXXXX
                    T
                    T
ROLE PLAY       O
                OXXXXXXXXXXXXXXXXXXXXXXXXXXXXXXXXXXXXXXXXXXXXXXXXX
                OXXXXXXXXXXXXXXXXXXXXXXXXXXXXXXXXXXXXXXXXXXXXXXX
                O   T
                T
PRIDE IN        OXXXXXXXXXXXXXXXXXXXXXXXXXX
PRODUCT         OXXXXXXXXXXXXXXXXXXXXXXXXX
                T
                                T
COMPETES        O
WITH            O
PEER            O
                                T
HOSTILITY,      O
AFFECTION       O
TO PEER         O
                                    T
LEADS AND       O
FOLLOWS         O
PEER            O

                0   1   2   3   4   5   6   7   8   9   10

                    TOTAL SCORES    MEDIANS AT 18/21 MONTHS
                        FOR S 1         FOR ALL SUBJECTS

ADULT COMPETENCE       47.9                 22.2
PEER COMPETENCE         0.0                 13.5
OVERALL COMPETENCE     47.9                 23.5
```

T INDICATES THE MEDIAN FOR ALL SUBJECTS FOR EACH COMPETENCE FACTOR.

APPENDIX A

```
              SOCIAL COMPETENCE FOR SUBJECT  1

GAIN          0                         T
ADULT         0
ATTENTION     0
              0                     T
---------------------------------------------------------------
USE           0             T
ADULT         OX
RESOURCE      OX
              0                 T
---------------------------------------------------------------
HOSTILITY,    0         T
AFFECTION     OXXXXXX
TO ADULT      OXAXXXX
              0             T
---------------------------------------------------------------
              0     T
ROLE PLAY     OXXXXXXXX
              OXXXXXXXX
              0         T
---------------------------------------------------------------
              0     T
PRIDE IN      0
PRODUCT       0
              0     T
---------------------------------------------------------------
COMPETES      0                                 T
WITH          0
PEER          0
              0                             T
---------------------------------------------------------------
HOSTILITY,    0             T
AFFECTION     0
TO PEER       0
              0             T
---------------------------------------------------------------
LEADS AND     0         T
FOLLOWS       0
PEER          0
              0     T
---------------------------------------------------------------
              0   1   2   3   4   5   6   7   8   9   10

                     TOTAL SCORES      MEDIANS FOR 30/33 ONE YEAR STARTER CHILD.
                        FOR S  1         FOR ALL SUBJECTS

ADULT COMPETENCE          3.0                26.0

PEER COMPETENCE           0.0                12.2

OVERALL COMPETENCE        3.0                33.6

T INDICATES THE MEDIAN FOR ALL SUBJECTS FOR EACH COMPETENCE FACTOR.
```

Subject #1

	% Duration	
Social Tasks	12-15 Months	18-21 Months
To please	0.1	0.1
To cooperate	2.6	5.2
To gain approval	0.0	1.7
To procure a service	1.2	1.1
To gain attention	2.7	2.1
To maintain social contact	3.0	6.8
To avoid unpleasant circumstances	0.0	0.0
To annoy	0.0	0.1
To direct	0.1	0.0
To assert self (protect domain)	0.5	1.5
To provide information	0.0	1.1
To compete	0.0	0.0
To reject overtures	0.0	0.0
To enjoy pets	0.0	1.3
To converse	0.0	0.2
To produce verbalizations	0.1	0.8
Nonsocial Tasks		
To eat	12.9	12.0
To gain information (v)	18.5	14.8
To gain information (v & a)	3.3	4.5
live language directed to child	2.3	1.4
live language overheard by child	0.1	1.4
mechanical language	0.2	0.4
Sesame Street	0.0	0.0
Nontask	20.6	16.7
To pass time	0.9	0.9
To find something to do	0.0	0.0
To prepare for an activity	2.5	1.5
To construct a product	1.1	0.0
To choose	0.0	0.0
To procure an object	2.5	1.7
To engage in large muscle activity	0.0	0.0
To gain pleasure	1.0	0.0
To imitate	0.3	0.2
To pretend (role play)	0.3	3.2
To ease discomfort	0.7	0.2
To relieve oneself	0.2	0.2
To dress/undress	0.0	0.0
To operate a mechanism	0.0	0.0
To explore	13.8	7.6
To improve a developing skill (mastery)	3.5	8.0
gross	0.8	3.4
fine	2.2	3.0
verbal	0.0	1.6
To eat and gain information (v)	5.3	2.9
To eat and gain information (v & a)	0.1	0.3
live language directed to child	0.2	0.4
overheard	0.0	0.0

SUBJECT #2

Subject #2 is a two-year-old SES Level II predicted A boy. He is the younger of two children (sister, aged four) of well-educated parents. The family lives in a large, comfortable apartment in an urban area.

S's mother is an affectionate, gentle woman who is very aware of her child's interests and abilities. Often, she will offer suggestions and help him set up a particular activity (e.g., doing puzzles). Although she is usually busy with household chores, she is always available to S and ready to answer his questions or help him.

There are many interesting and appropriate toys available for S. He makes extensive use of the materials, often engaging in very sophisticated activities. However, at other times he will be observed wandering around the house holding his favorite blanket.

Summary of Test Scores

Subject #2   **Group: Two-Year-Old Starters (n = 20)**

Tests	Age of Testing (Months)	Score	Group Median
Bayley Mental Developmental Index	12	—	—
	24	137	101
Stanford-Binet IQ	36	132	117.5
WPPSI IQ	60	127	111
Language Test[1]	12	—	—
	15	—	—
	21	—	—
	24	42	30
	27	54	36
	30	51	40.5
	36	57	—
Abstract Abilities[2]	12	—	—
	15	—	—
	21	—	—
	24	7	5.5
	27	7	6
	30	7	6.5
	36	11	—
Discrimination Test[2]	12	—	—
	15	—	—
	21	—	—
	24	7.0	3.0
	27	7.0	3.0
	30	7.0	6.0
	36	8.0	—

[1] Scores in Months
[2] Scores in Level Achieved

APPENDIX A

SOCIAL COMPETENCE FOR SUBJECT 2

```
                              T
GAIN            OXXXXXXXXXXXXXXXXXXXXXXXXXXXXX
ADULT           OXXXXXXXXXXXXXXXXXXXXXXXXXXXXXXXXX
ATTENTION                T
                O
USE             OXXXXXXXXXXXXXXXXXXXXXX
ADULT                              T
RESOURCE        OXXXXXXXXXXXXXXXXXXXX
                               T
                O
HOSTILITY,                  T
AFFECTION       OXXXXXXXXXXXXXXXX
TO ADULT        OXXXXXXXXXXXXXXXX
                          T
                O
                T
ROLE PLAY       O
                O
                T
                T
PRIDE IN        OXXXXXXXX
PRODUCT         OXXXXXXXXX
                T
COMPETES        O      T
WITH            O
PEER            O
                T
                O       T
HOSTILITY,      OXXXXXXXXXXXXXXXXXXX
AFFECTION       OXXXXXXXXXXXXXXXXXXXX
TO PEER              T
                O
                O   T
LEADS AND       OXXXXXXXXX
FOLLOWS         OXXXXXXXXX
PEER            T
                O
                |---|---|---|---|---|---|---|---|---|---|
                0   1   2   3   4   5   6   7   8   9   10
```

	TOTAL SCORES FOR S 2	MEDIANS FOR 24/27 TWO YEAR STARTER CHILD. FOR ALL SUBJECTS
ADULT COMPETENCE	27.7	23.2
PEER COMPETENCE	7.4	5.1
OVERALL COMPETENCE	35.2	28.6

T INDICATES THE MEDIAN FOR ALL SUBJECTS FOR EACH COMPETENCE FACTOR.

SOCIAL COMPETENCE FOR SUBJECT 2

```
                              T
GAIN            OXXXXXXXXXXXXXXXXXX
ADULT           OXXXXXXXXXXXXXXXXXX
ATTENTION                T
                O
                         T
USE             OXXXXXXXXXXXXXX
ADULT           OXXXXXXXXXXXXXX
RESOURCE                    T
                O
HOSTILITY,              T
AFFECTION       OXXXXXXXXXXXXXXXXXX
TO ADULT        OXXXXXXXXXXXXXXXXXX
                              T
                T
                OXXXX
ROLE PLAY       OXXXX
                T
                                           T
                OXXXXXXXXXXXXXXXXXXXXXXXXXXXXXXXXXXXXXXXXXX
PRIDE IN        OXXXXXXXXXXXXXXXXXXXXXXXXXXXXXXXXXXXXXXXXX
PRODUCT                        T
                O
COMPETES        O    T
WITH            OXXX
PEER            OXXX
                O    T
                O                  T
HOSTILITY,      OXXXXXXXXXXXXXXXXXXXXXXXXXXXXXXXXXXXXXXXXXXXXXXXXXXXX
AFFECTION       OXXXXXXXXXXXXXXXXXXXXXXXXXXXXXXXXXXXXXXXXXXXXXXXXXXXX
TO PEER                       T
                O            T
LEADS AND       OXXXXXXXXX
FOLLOWS         OXXXXXXXXX
PEER
                O
                |---|---|---|---|---|---|---|---|---|---|
                0   1   2   3   4   5   6   7   8   9   10
```

	TOTAL SCORES FOR S 2	MEDIANS FOR 30/33 TWO YEAR STARTER CHILD. FOR ALL SUBJECTS
ADULT COMPETENCE	28.4	24.0
PEER COMPETENCE	12.6	11.9
OVERALL COMPETENCE	41.0	28.9

T INDICATES THE MEDIAN FOR ALL SUBJECTS FOR EACH COMPETENCE FACTOR.

Subject #2

Social Tasks	% Duration	
	24-27 Months	30-33 Months
To please	0.0	0.9
To cooperate	1.9	1.8
To gain approval	0.4	3.3
To procure a service	3.2	1.6
To gain attention	1.6	2.1
To maintain social contact	7.4	6.6
To avoid unpleasant circumstances	0.0	0.0
To annoy	0.0	0.6
To direct	0.4	3.2
To assert self (protect domain)	0.6	1.1
To provide information	0.3	0.8
To compete	0.0	0.0
To reject overtures	0.0	0.0
To enjoy pets	0.0	0.0
To converse	2.1	1.8
To produce verbalizations	0.0	0.0
Nonsocial Tasks		
To eat	2.8	3.6
To gain information (v)	11.6	9.2
To gain information (v & a)	6.6	8.1
live language directed to child	2.8	6.2
live language overheard by child	3.2	1.9
mechanical language	0.0	0.0
Sesame Street	0.0	0.0
Nontask	10.7	10.4
To pass time	2.4	1.8
To find something to do	0.2	0.0
To prepare for activity	4.7	4.4
To construct a product	5.1	4.1
To choose	0.0	0.0
To procure an object	1.1	3.1
To engage in large muscle activity	2.5	0.0
To gain pleasure	4.9	1.7
To imitate	1.2	0.0
To pretend (role play)	0.0	4.0
To ease discomfort	0.6	1.2
To restore order	1.0	0.3
To relieve oneself	0.0	0.0
To dress/undress	0.1	0.0
To operate a mechanism	0.2	0.4
To explore	6.3	1.9
To improve a developing skill (mastery)	7.9	20.3
gross	7.7	1.1
fine	0.0	17.3
verbal	0.0	1.9
To eat and gain information (v)	3.6	1.5
To eat and gain information (v & a)	0.4	0.0
live language directed to child	0.4	0.0
overheard	0.0	0.0

SUBJECT #3

Subject #3 is a one-year-old SES Level III predicted A girl. She is an active, alert little girl. Both parents are college graduates, and the father has advanced degrees.

At the outset of the study, the family lived in a six-room apartment in a residential area. The apartment was functionally furnished but not elaborate. She shared a bedroom with her sister, and this room seemed to overflow with their toys. She was not restricted within the apartment, and her toys were usually scattered throughout. During the study, the family moved to a large private home with spacious grounds. In addition to their bedroom, the children now have a very large playroom, which seems to contain every toy imaginable. Again this child has access to the whole house but spends most of her time in the playroom. Her mother is easily available and will often spend time reading or playing with her.

Summary of Test Scores

Subject #3 Group: One-Year-Old Starters (n = 19)

Tests	Age at Testing (Months)	Score	Group Median
Bayley Mental Developmental Index	12	102	103
	24	143	112
Stanford-Binet IQ	36	139	113
WPPSI IQ	60	119	117.5
Language Test[1]	12	14	14
	15	16	16
	21	36	21
	24	51	36
	27	not tested	—
	30	54	43.5
	36	51	45
Abstract Abilities[2]	12	2	2
	15	3	2
	21	6	5
	24	7	6
	27	not tested	—
	30	7	7
	36	11	9
Discrimination Test[2]	12	2	1
	15	2	2
	21	8	3
	24	7	3.5
	27	not tested	—
	30	8	5
	36	8	8

[1] Scores in Months
[2] Scores in Level Achieved

APPENDIX A

SOCIAL COMPETENCE FOR SUBJECT 3

```
                         T
GAIN              OXXXXXXXXXXXXXXXXXXXXXXXXXXXXXXXXX
ADULT             OXXXXXXXXXXXXXXXXXXXXXXXXXXXXXXXXX
ATTENTION         O              T

                         T
USE               OXXXXXXXXXXXXXXXXXXXXXXXXX
ADULT             OXXXXXXXXXXXXXXXXXXXXXXXXX
RESOURCE                       T

                         T
HOSTILITY,        OXXXXXXXXXXXXXXXXXXXX
AFFECTION         OXXXXXXXXXXXXXXXXXXXX
TO ADULT          O       T

                  T
ROLE PLAY         O
                  O
                  T

                  T
PRIDE IN          OXXXXXXXXXXXXXXXXXXXXXXXXXXXXX
PRODUCT           OXXXXXXXXXXXXXXXXXXXXXXXXXXXXX
                  T

                         T
COMPETES          OXXXXXXXXXXXXXXXXXXXXXXXXXXXXXXXXX
WITH              OXXXXXXXXXXXXXXXXXXXXXXXXXXXXXXXXX
PEER              O       T

                  O       T
HOSTILITY,        OXXXXXXX
AFFECTION         OXXXXXXX
TO PEER           O       T

LEADS AND         O   T
FOLLOWS           OX
PEER              OX
                  O   T

                  0  1  2  3  4  5  6  7  8  9  10

                TOTAL SCORES       MEDIANS AT 12/15 MONTHS
                 FOR S  3             FOR ALL SUBJECTS

ADULT COMPETENCE     34.0               13.8
PEER COMPETENCE      11.7                9.0
OVERALL COMPETENCE   45.7               20.5
```

T INDICATES THE MEDIAN FOR ALL SUBJECTS FOR EACH COMPETENCE FACTOR.

SOCIAL COMPETENCE FOR SUBJECT 3

```
                         T
GAIN              OXXXXXXXXXXXXXXXXXXXXXXXX
ADULT             OXXXXXXXXXXXXXXXXXXXXXXXX
ATTENTION         O

                                    T
USE               OXXXXXXXXXXXXXXXXXXXXXXXXXXXXXXXX
ADULT             OXXXXXXXXXXXXXXXXXXXXXXXXXXXXXXXX
RESOURCE                                      T

                         T
HOSTILITY,        OXXXXXXXXX
AFFECTION         OXXXXXXXXXX
TO ADULT          O

                         T
ROLE PLAY         OXXXXXXXXXXXXXXXXXXXXXXX
                  OXXXXXXXXXXXXXXXXXXXXXXX
                          T

                  T
PRIDE IN          OXXXXXXXX
PRODUCT           OXXXXXXXXX
                  T

COMPETES          O              T
WITH              O
PEER              O

                                    T
HOSTILITY,        O
AFFECTION         O              T
TO PEER           O

LEADS AND         O           T
FOLLOWS           O
PEER              O       T

                  0  1  2  3  4  5  6  7  8  9  10

                TOTAL SCORES       MEDIANS AT 18/21 MONTHS
                 FOR S  3              FOR ALL SUBJECTS

ADULT COMPETENCE     33.7               22.2
PEER COMPETENCE       0.0               13.5
OVERALL COMPETENCE   33.7               23.5
```

T INDICATES THE MEDIAN FOR ALL SUBJECTS FOR EACH COMPETENCE FACTOR.

Appendix A - Individual Subject Data

SOCIAL COMPETENCE FOR SUBJECT 3

```
GAIN           O                   T
ADULT          OXXXXXXXXXXXXXXXXXXXXXXXXXXXXXXXXXXXXXXXX
ATTENTION      OXXXXXXXXXXXXXXXXXXXXXXXXXXXXXXXXXXXXXXX
               O                   T
---------------------------------------------------------
USE            O            T
ADULT          OXXXXXXXXXXXXXXXXXXXXXXXXXXXXXXXXXXXXXXXXXXXXX
RESOURCE       OXXXXXXXXXXXXXXXXXXXXXXXXXXXXXXXXXXXXXXXXXXXXX
               O            T
---------------------------------------------------------
HOSTILITY,     O          T
AFFECTION      OXXXXXXXXXXX
TO ADULT       OXXXXXXXXXXX
               O          T
---------------------------------------------------------
               O      T
ROLE PLAY      OXXXX
               OXXXX
               O      T
---------------------------------------------------------
               O   T
PRIDE IN       OXXXXXXXXX
PRODUCT        OXXXXXXXXX
               O   T
---------------------------------------------------------
COMPETES       O                            T
WITH           O
PEER           O
               O                            T
---------------------------------------------------------
HOSTILITY,     O                T
AFFECTION      O
TO PEER        O
               O           T
---------------------------------------------------------
LEADS AND      O      T
FOLLOWS        O
PEER           O
               O      T
---------------------------------------------------------
               0   1   2   3   4   5   6   7   8   9   10
```

	TOTAL SCORES FOR S 3	MEDIANS FOR 30/33 ONE YEAR STARTER CHILD. FOR ALL SUBJECTS
ADULT COMPETENCE	30.7	26.0
PEER COMPETENCE	0.0	12.2
OVERALL COMPETENCE	30.7	33.6

T INDICATES THE MEDIAN FOR ALL SUBJECTS FOR EACH COMPETENCE FACTOR.

Subject #3

Social Tasks	% Duration	
	12-15 Months	18-21 Months
To please	2.1	0.4
To cooperate	1.9	5.3
To gain approval	0.7	0.2
To procure a service	1.6	0.5
To gain attention	2.9	2.5
To maintain social contact	1.6	6.2
To avoid unpleasant circumstances	0.0	0.0
To annoy	0.0	0.0
To direct	0.0	0.1
To assert self (protect domain)	0.3	1.8
To provide information	0.1	0.1
To compete	0.0	0.0
To reject overtures	0.0	0.0
To enjoy pets	0.0	1.1
To converse	0.2	0.0
To produce verbalizations	0.0	0.1
Nonsocial Tasks		
To eat	4.5	2.4
To gain information (v)	18.9	12.1
To gain information (v & a)	5.6	4.0
live language directed to child	3.4	1.3
live language overheard by child	2.2	1.0
mechanical language	0.0	1.0
Sesame Street	0.0	0.0
Nontask	9.3	13.8
To pass time	5.9	0.6
To find something to do	0.2	0.6
To prepare for an activity	0.6	4.6
To construct a product	0.8	0.0
To choose	0.0	0.0
To procure an object	2.3	4.7
To engage in large muscle activity	0.0	0.0
To gain pleasure	0.0	0.1
To imitate	0.1	0.0
To pretend (role play)	0.0	3.6
To ease discomfort	0.5	0.8
To restore order	0.4	3.2
To relieve oneself	0.2	0.0
To dress/undress	0.0	0.0
To operate a mechanism	0.7	0.7
To explore	17.5	13.1
To improve a developing skill (mastery)	12.3	16.9
gross	8.6	3.6
fine	3.1	13.1
verbal	0.0	0.2
To eat and gain information (v)	7.9	0.3
To eat and gain information (v & a)	0.8	0.0
live language directed to child	0.9	0.0
overheard	0.0	0.0

SUBJECT #5

Subject #5 is a two-year-old SES Level I predicted A boy. He is the youngest of three children (a brother is five; a sister is three and a half). Both parents are professional people; the mother works part-time.

S lives in a large, lovely home (at least fifteen rooms) close to the city. Although the home is furnished with valuable antiques, the children have access to all areas of the house. They are frequently observed in the living room using the furniture for climbing and imaginative play.

Next to S's bedroom there is a large playroom in which he spends a great deal of time watching television. When his mother is at home, S will often be observed playing word games with her or including her in his activities. She takes part in these activities willingly and will often expand and encourage the games.

Summary of Test Scores

Subject #5   Group: Two-Year-Old Starters (n = 20)

Tests	Age at Testing (Months)	Score	Group Median
Bayley Mental Development Index	12	—	—
	24	97	101
Stanford-Binet IQ	36	127	117.5
WPPSI IQ	60	112	111
Language Test[1]	12	—	—
	15	—	—
	21	—	—
	24	36	30
	27	51	36
	30	51	40.5
	36	57	—
Abstract Abilities[2]	12	—	—
	15	—	—
	21	—	—
	24	<5	5.5
	27	5	6
	30	7	6.5
	36	10	—
Discrimination Test[2]	12	—	—
	15	—	—
	21	—	—
	24	3.0	3.0
	27	5.0	3.0
	30	3.0	6.0
	36	2.0	—

[1] Scores in Months
[2] Scores in Level Achieved

Individual Subject Data

SOCIAL COMPETENCE FOR SUBJECT 5

```
                      0
GAIN                  OXXXXXXXXXXXXXXX       T
ADULT                 OXXXXXXXXXXXXXXX    T
ATTENTION             0
                  ----+----+----+----+----+----+----+----+----+----+
                      0                                  T
USE                   OXXXXXXXXXXXXXXXXXXXXXXXXXXXXXXXXXXXXXXXXXXXX
ADULT                 OXXXXXXXXXXXXXXXXXXXXXXXXXXXXXXXXXXXXXXX
RESOURCE              0                              T
                  ----+----+----+----+----+----+----+----+----+----+
                      0                 T
HOSTILITY,            OXXXXXXXXXXXXXXXXXXX
AFFECTION             OXXXXXXXXXXXXXXXXX
TO ADULT              0               T
                  ----+----+----+----+----+----+----+----+----+----+
                      T
ROLE PLAY             OXXXXXXXXXXX
                      OXXXXXXXXXX
                      T
                  ----+----+----+----+----+----+----+----+----+----+
                      T
PRIDE IN              0
PRODUCT               0
                      T
                  ----+----+----+----+----+----+----+----+----+----+
                      0    T
COMPETES              OXXXXXX
WITH                  OXXXXXX
PEER                  0    T
                  ----+----+----+----+----+----+----+----+----+----+
                      0        T
HOSTILITY,            OXXXXXXXXXXXXXXXXXXXXXXXXXXXXXXXXXXXXXXXXXXXX
AFFECTION             OXXXXXXXXXXXXXXXXXXXXXXXXXXXXXXXXXXXXXXXXXXXX
TO PEER               0        T
                  ----+----+----+----+----+----+----+----+----+----+
                      0  T
LEADS AND             OXXXXXXXXX
FOLLOWS               OXXXXXXXXX
PEER                  0      T
                  ----+----+----+----+----+----+----+----+----+----+
                      0    1    2    3    4    5    6    7    8    9    10

                              TOTAL SCORES    MEDIANS FOR 24/22 TWO YEAR STARTER CHILD.
                                 FOR S 5               FOR ALL SUBJECTS
ADULT COMPETENCE                  27.5                      23.2
PEER COMPETENCE                   13.0                       5.1
OVERALL COMPETENCE                40.5                      28.6
```

T INDICATES THE MEDIAN FOR ALL SUBJECTS FOR EACH COMPETENCE FACTOR.

SOCIAL COMPETENCE FOR SUBJECT 5

```
                      0
GAIN                  OXXXXXXXXXXXXXXX          T
ADULT                 OXXXXXXXXXXXXXXX       T
ATTENTION             0
                  ----+----+----+----+----+----+----+----+----+----+
                      0                   T
USE                   OXXXXXXXXXXXXXXXXXXXX
ADULT                 OXXXXXXXXXXXXXXXXXXXX
RESOURCE              0                 T
                  ----+----+----+----+----+----+----+----+----+----+
                      0        T
HOSTILITY,            OXXXXXXXX
AFFECTION             OXXXXXXXX
TO ADULT              0
                  ----+----+----+----+----+----+----+----+----+----+
                      T
ROLE PLAY             OXXXXXXXXX
                      OXXXXXXXXX
                      T
                  ----+----+----+----+----+----+----+----+----+----+
                      0                     T
PRIDE IN              OXXXXXXXXXX
PRODUCT               OXXXXXXXXXX
                      0
                  ----+----+----+----+----+----+----+----+----+----+
                      0    T
COMPETES              OXXX
WITH                  OXXX
PEER                  0    T
                  ----+----+----+----+----+----+----+----+----+----+
                      0                       T
HOSTILITY,            OXXXXXXXXXXXXXXX
AFFECTION             OXXXXXXXXXXXXXXX
TO PEER               0                       T
                  ----+----+----+----+----+----+----+----+----+----+
                      0                       T
LEADS AND             OXXXXXXXXXXXXXXXXX
FOLLOWS               OXXXXXXXXXXXXXXXXX
PEER                  0                 T
                  ----+----+----+----+----+----+----+----+----+----+
                      0    1    2    3    4    5    6    7    8    9    10

                              TOTAL SCORES    MEDIANS FOR 30/33 TWO YEAR STARTER CHILD.
                                 FOR S 5               FOR ALL SUBJECTS
ADULT COMPETENCE                  24.4                      24.0
PEER COMPETENCE                    4.6                      11.9
OVERALL COMPETENCE                29.0                      28.9
```

T INDICATES THE MEDIAN FOR ALL SUBJECTS FOR EACH COMPETENCE FACTOR.

Subject #5

Social Tasks	% Duration	
	24-27 Months	30-33 Months
To please	0.6	0.0
To cooperate	0.8	1.5
To gain approval	0.4	0.1
To procure a service	0.4	1.8
To gain attention	1.9	2.9
To maintain social contact	6.3	1.2
To avoid unpleasant circumstances	0.0	0.0
To annoy	0.1	0.0
To direct	0.3	0.1
To assert self (protect domain)	1.1	1.4
To provide information	1.1	0.9
To compete	0.0	0.0
To reject overtures	0.0	0.0
To enjoy pets	0.0	0.0
To converse	0.0	2.6
To produce verbalizations	0.1	0.0
Nonsocial Tasks		
To eat	5.7	3.9
To gain information (v)	10.9	5.1
To gain information (v & a)	40.2	52.9
live language directed to child	1.8	4.6
live language overheard by child	1.8	3.6
mechanical language	4.7	15.8
Sesame Street	29.7	27.2
Nontask	7.8	1.3
To pass time	2.1	3.3
To find something to do	0.6	0.0
To prepare for an activity	1.3	1.1
To construct a product	0.5	0.0
To choose	0.0	0.0
To procure an object	0.1	0.6
To engage in large muscle activity	0.1	0.0
To gain pleasure	0.8	0.2
To imitate	0.1	0.3
To pretend (role play)	0.9	2.6
To ease discomfort	0.1	0.1
To restore order	1.1	0.0
To relieve oneself	0.0	0.0
To dress/undress	0.2	0.0
To operate a mechanism	1.6	0.0
To explore	2.5	3.5
To improve a developing skill (mastery)	4.2	2.9
gross	4.2	0.9
fine	0.0	2.1
verbal	0.0	0.0
To eat and gain information (v)	1.3	3.1
To eat and gain information (v & a)	4.4	5.5
live language directed to child	4.4	1.1
overheard	0.0	3.1

SUBJECT #7

Subject #7 is a two-year-old SES Level IV predicted C boy. This child is an average-looking boy whose most outstanding feature is his blank expression. He is the youngest of six children in a family that seems generally overwhelmed by the daily problems of living. The father, a semiskilled laborer, was unemployed during the period under discussion. The mother worked several evenings a week as a waitress.

The family lives in a six-room duplex that is part of a public housing project. The living room is usually cluttered with large piles of laundry. The television is on most of the day, and the child spends a good deal of his day watching it.

He is rarely encouraged to do anything and is often severely threatened for something he has done. Most of his mother's interactions with him are disciplinary in nature, although there is little consistency or follow-through in her approach. Even friendly exchanges are worded aggressively (for example, "Hey, bad boy, get over here," said with a smile).

Summary of Test Scores

Subject #7   Group: Two-Year-Old Starters (n = 20)

Tests	Age at Testing (Months)	Score	Group Median
Bayley Mental Development Index	12	—	—
	24	69	101
Stanford-Binet IQ	36	74	117.5
WPPSI IQ	60	74	111
Language Test[1]	12	—	—
	15	—	—
	21	—	—
	24	21	30
	27	18	36
	30	21	40.5
	36	33	—
Abstract Abilities[2]	12	—	—
	15	—	—
	21	—	—
	24	<5	5.5
	27	6	6
	30	<5	6.5
	36	6	—
Discrimination Test[2]	12	—	—
	15	—	—
	21	—	—
	24	4.0	3.0
	27	2.0	3.0
	30	2.0	6.0
	36	3.5	—

[1] Scores in Months
[2] Scores in Level Achieved

Individual Subject Data

SOCIAL COMPETENCE FOR SUBJECT 7

```
GAIN                    O                    T
ADULT                   O
ATTENTION               O              T
-------------------------------------------------
USE                     O              T
ADULT                   O
RESOURCE                O        T
-------------------------------------------------
HOSTILITY,              O              T
AFFECTION               OXXXXXXXXXXXXXXXXXXXXXXXXXXXXXX
TO ADULT                OXXXXXXXXXXXXXXXXXXXXXXXXXXXX
                        O           T
-------------------------------------------------
ROLE PLAY               T
                        O
                        O
                        T
-------------------------------------------------
PRIDE IN                O                    T
PRODUCT                 O
                        O        T
-------------------------------------------------
COMPETES                O  T
WITH                    OXXXXXXXXXXXXXXXXXXXXXXXX
PEER                    OXXXXXXXXXXXXXXXXXXXXX
                        O T
-------------------------------------------------
HOSTILITY,              O        T
AFFECTION               OXXXXXXXXXXXXXXXXXXXXXX
TO PEER                 OXXXXXXXXXXXXXXXXXX
                        O  T
-------------------------------------------------
LEADS AND               O  T
FOLLOWS                 OXXXXX
PEER                    OXXXXX
                        O  T
-------------------------------------------------
                        0  1  2  3  4  5  6  7  8  9  10

                        TOTAL SCORES       MEDIANS FOR 30/33 TWO YEAR STARTER CHILD.
                        FOR S 7            FOR ALL SUBJECTS
ADULT COMPETENCE        10.0               24.0
PEER COMPETENCE         11.9               11.9
OVERALL COMPETENCE      21.9               28.9
```

T INDICATES THE MEDIAN FOR ALL SUBJECTS FOR EACH COMPETENCE FACTOR.

SOCIAL COMPETENCE FOR SUBJECT 7

```
GAIN                    O
ADULT                   OXXXXXXXX
ATTENTION               OXXXXXXXX
                        O
-------------------------------------------------
USE                     O                    T
ADULT                   O              T
RESOURCE                O
                        O
-------------------------------------------------
HOSTILITY,              O              T
AFFECTION               OXXXXXXXXXXXXXXXXXXXXXXXXXXXXX
TO ADULT                OXXXXXXXXXXXXXXXXXXXXXXXXXX
                        O           T
-------------------------------------------------
ROLE PLAY               T
                        O
                        O
                        T
-------------------------------------------------
PRIDE IN                T
PRODUCT                 O
                        O
                        T
-------------------------------------------------
COMPETES                O  T
WITH                    OXX
PEER                    OXX
                        O  T
-------------------------------------------------
HOSTILITY,              O        T
AFFECTION               O
TO PEER                 O              T
                        O
-------------------------------------------------
LEADS AND               O
FOLLOWS                 OXX          T
PEER                    OXX
                        O
-------------------------------------------------
                        0  1  2  3  4  5  6  7  8  9  10

                        TOTAL SCORES       MEDIANS FOR 24/27 TWO YEAR STARTER CHILD.
                        FOR S 7            FOR ALL SUBJECTS
ADULT COMPETENCE        7.2                23.2
PEER COMPETENCE         0.7                5.1
OVERALL COMPETENCE      7.9                28.6
```

T INDICATES THE MEDIAN FOR ALL SUBJECTS FOR EACH COMPETENCE FACTOR.

Subject #7

	% Duration	
Social Tasks	24-27 Months	30-33 Months
To please	0.6	0.2
To cooperate	2.3	5.4
To gain approval	0.0	0.0
To procure a service	0.9	2.1
To gain attention	2.6	0.9
To maintain social contact	4.2	4.2
To avoid unpleasant circumstances	0.3	0.3
To annoy	0.4	0.3
To direct	0.0	0.1
To assert self (protect domain)	0.7	0.8
To provide information	0.0	0.1
To compete	0.0	0.0
To reject overtures	0.0	0.1
To enjoy pets	0.6	0.4
To converse	0.0	0.0
To produce verbalizations	0.1	0.0
Nonsocial Tasks		
To eat	7.6	9.5
To gain information (v)	23.4	8.0
To gain information (v & a)	12.1	38.2
live language directed to child	1.3	0.3
live language overheard by child	4.4	1.7
mechanical language	1.7	12.4
Sesame Street	4.4	23.7
Nontask	14.3	10.8
To pass time	0.8	2.9
To find something to do	0.0	0.0
To prepare for an activity	1.0	1.2
To construct a product	0.0	0.0
To choose	0.0	0.0
To procure an object	1.4	0.7
To engage in large muscle activity	3.9	0.0
To gain pleasure	4.5	0.3
To imitate	1.6	0.0
To pretend (role play)	0.0	1.4
To ease discomfort	0.2	0.2
To restore order	0.9	0.2
To relieve oneself	0.0	0.0
To dress/undress	0.0	0.0
To operate a mechanism	0.3	0.0
To explore	7.9	1.5
To improve a developing skill (mastery)	1.5	8.3
gross	1.4	1.2
fine	0.1	7.1
verbal	0.0	0.0
To eat and gain information (v)	4.3	0.5
To eat and gain information (v & a)	0.7	0.0
live language directed to child	0.8	0.0
overheard	0.0	0.0

SUBJECT #8

Subject #8 is a one-year-old SES Level II predicted A boy who is the only child of a graduate-student couple. He is a bright, assertive, active child, exposed to unusually frequent interaction with his mother, who engages his attention with a variety of interesting learning experiences ranging from books to live animals. She is a mother who manages to extract a learning experience from the most mundane task and make it come to life. Subject #8 has access to all parts of the home, which, although small, has been arranged to provide the maximum in enjoyment for the child. The mother is totally child-centered in philosophy and very devoted to shaping the child's interests and awareness of the world around him. The home is fairly well equipped with toys suitable to S's age and interest level.

Summary of Test Scores

Subject #8   Group: One-Year-Old Starters (n = 19)

Tests	Age at Testing (Months)	Score	Group Median
Bayley Mental Developmental Index	12	106	103
	24	123	112
Stanford-Binet IQ	36	139	113
WPPSI IQ	60	113	117.5
Language Test[1]	12	18	14
	15	24	16
	21	36	21
	24	36	36
	27	not tested	—
	30	51	43.5
	36	60	45
Abstract Abilities[2]	12	2	2
	15	2	2
	21	6	5
	24	6	6
	27	not tested	—
	30	6	7
	36	11	9
Discrimination Test[2]	12	3	1
	15	3	2
	21	3.5	3
	24	6	3.5
	27	not tested	—
	30	3	5
	36	8	8

[1] Scores in Months
[2] Scores in Level Achieved

Individual Subject Data

SOCIAL COMPETENCE FOR SUBJECT 8 (12/15 MONTHS)

Category	Score (0-10)
GAIN ADULT ATTENTION	xxxxxxxxxxxxxxxxxxTxxxxxxxxxxxxxxx (T at ~3.5)
USE ADULT RESOURCE	xxxxxxxxxxxxxxxxxTxxxxxxxxxxxxxxxxxxx (T at ~3)
HOSTILITY, AFFECTION TO ADULT	xxxxxxx T (T at ~1)
ROLE PLAY	xxxxxxxxxxxxxxxxxxxxxxxxxxxxxxxxxxxxxxxxxxx T (T at ~0.5)
PRIDE IN PRODUCT	xxxxxxxxxxxxxxxxxxxxxxxxxxxxx T (T at ~0.5)
COMPETES WITH PEER	T (T at ~2.5); other T at ~1
HOSTILITY, AFFECTION TO PEER	T ~2; T ~1
LEADS AND FOLLOWS PEER	T ~1.5; T ~1

TOTAL SCORES FOR S 8 / MEDIANS AT 12/15 MONTHS FOR ALL SUBJECTS

	Total Scores for S 8	Medians at 12/15 Months for All Subjects
ADULT COMPETENCE	45.9	13.8
PEER COMPETENCE	0.0	9.0
OVERALL COMPETENCE	45.9	20.5

T INDICATES THE MEDIAN FOR ALL SUBJECTS FOR EACH COMPETENCE FACTOR.

SOCIAL COMPETENCE FOR SUBJECT 8 (18/21 MONTHS)

Category	Score (0-10)
GAIN ADULT ATTENTION	xxxxxxxxxx T (T at ~2)
USE ADULT RESOURCE	xxxxxxxxxxxxxxxxxxxxxxxxxxxxxxxxxxxxxxTxxxxxx (T at ~7); T at ~3
HOSTILITY, AFFECTION TO ADULT	xxxxxxx T; xxxxxxx (T at ~2)
ROLE PLAY	T (T at ~2); T at ~1
PRIDE IN PRODUCT	xxxxxxxxxxxxxxxxxxxxxxxxxxxxxxxxxxxxxxxxxx; T at ~0
COMPETES WITH PEER	T (T at ~4); T at ~4
HOSTILITY, AFFECTION TO PEER	T ~4; T ~3
LEADS AND FOLLOWS PEER	T ~3.5; T ~3

TOTAL SCORES FOR S 8 / MEDIANS AT 18/21 MONTHS FOR ALL SUBJECTS

	Total Scores for S 8	Medians at 18/21 Months for All Subjects
ADULT COMPETENCE	32.4	22.2
PEER COMPETENCE	0.0	13.5
OVERALL COMPETENCE	32.4	23.5

T INDICATES THE MEDIAN FOR ALL SUBJECTS FOR EACH COMPETENCE FACTOR.

APPENDIX A

```
                    SOCIAL COMPETENCE FOR SUBJECT  8

GAIN              O                         T
ADULT             OXXXXXXXXXXXXXXXXXXXXXXXXXXXXXXXX
ATTENTION         OXXXXXXXXXXXXXXXXXXXXXXXXXXXXXXXX
                  O                         T
------------------------------------------------------------
USE               O            T
ADULT             OXXXXXXXXXXXXXXXXXXXXXXXXXXXXXXXXXXXXXXXXXX
RESOURCE          OXXXXXXXXXXXXXXXXXXXXXXXXXXXXXXXXXXXXXXXXXX
                  O            T
------------------------------------------------------------
HOSTILITY,        O         T
AFFECTION         OXXXXXXXXXXXX
TO ADULT          OXXXXXXXXXXXX
                  O         T
------------------------------------------------------------
                  O    T
ROLE PLAY         OXXXXXXXXXXXXXXXXXXXXXX
                  OXXXXXXXXXXXXXXXXXXXXXX
                  O    T
------------------------------------------------------------
                  O  T
PRIDE IN          OXXXXXXXXX
PRODUCT           OXXXXXXXXX
                  O  T
------------------------------------------------------------
COMPETES          O                              T
WITH              O
PEER              O
                  O                              T
------------------------------------------------------------
HOSTILITY,        O             T
AFFECTION         O
TO PEER           O
                  O             T
------------------------------------------------------------
LEADS AND         O      T
FOLLOWS           O
PEER              O
                  O   T
------------------------------------------------------------
                  0  1  2  3  4  5  6  7  8  9  10


                  TOTAL SCORES      MEDIANS FOR 30/33 ONE YEAR STARTER CHILD.
                  FOR S  8          FOR ALL SUBJECTS

ADULT COMPETENCE      35.5              26.0

PEER COMPETENCE        0.0              12.2

OVERALL COMPETENCE    35.5              33.6

T INDICATES THE MEDIAN FOR ALL SUBJECTS FOR EACH COMPETENCE FACTOR.
```

Subject #8

	% Duration	
Social Tasks	12-15 Months	18-21 Months
To please	0.6	0.2
To cooperate	5.2	7.4
To gain approval	0.2	1.1
To procure a service	1.4	2.1
To gain attention	1.6	0.9
To maintain social contact	1.4	2.8
To avoid unpleasant circumstances	0.0	0.0
To annoy	0.0	0.0
To direct	0.2	1.4
To assert self (protect domain)	1.1	0.0
To provide information	0.2	0.2
To compete	0.0	0.0
To reject overtures	0.0	0.0
To enjoy pets	0.0	0.6
To converse	0.0	0.8
To produce verbalizations	0.0	0.2
Nonsocial Tasks		
To eat	1.0	9.1
To gain information (v)	21.4	6.7
To gain information (v & a)	15.9	10.6
live language directed to child	13.3	6.9
live language overheard by child	2.7	0.3
mechanical language	0.0	0.0
Sesame Street	0.0	3.3
Nontask	7.5	4.3
To pass time	0.8	5.2
To find something to do	0.0	0.0
To prepare for an activity	2.1	4.0
To construct a product	0.0	0.4
To choose	0.0	0.0
To procure an object	3.2	4.8
To engage in large muscle activity	0.0	0.2
To gain pleasure	0.6	0.0
To imitate	0.1	0.2
To pretend (role play)	0.0	0.8
To ease discomfort	0.1	0.3
To restore order	1.4	3.4
To relieve oneself	0.0	0.0
To dress/undress	0.0	0.1
To operate a mechanism	0.4	0.1
To explore	9.7	6.7
To improve a developing skill (mastery)	11.4	17.1
gross	6.4	10.8
fine	4.4	4.6
verbal	0.6	1.7
To eat and gain information (v)	6.1	2.1
To eat and gain information (v & a)	4.1	0.3
live language directed to child	4.2	0.3
overheard	0.0	0.0

SUBJECT #9

Subject #9 is a two-year-old SES Level I predicted A girl who lives in a comfortable, modern home in a woodsy, suburban setting. She is an only child, but spends a great deal of time in the company of a two-year-old playmate.

Her parents are college educated and are often away from the home. S's mother has an active career and works several days a week. During her absence, S is cared for by several regular babysitters, usually along with her two-year-old girlfriend (Subject #10). This setup (with the girlfriend) was carefully arranged by S's mother, who feels that it is in the best interest of her child's development. S's father also takes part in his daughter's care when he is at home. He has a warm and affectionate relationship with her that contrasts somewhat with his wife's cooler but active approach. The mother often both directs and takes part in S's play, setting up games and puzzles or reading to S. She also treats her daughter in an adult manner.

S herself is a mature child who gets along well with adults. She tends to dominate her playmates and is pushy and stubborn, insisting on getting her own way. She spends a great deal of time playing outdoors, riding a bicycle and playing on her backyard jungle gym.

Summary of Test Scores

Subject #9   Group: Two-Year-Old Starters (n = 20)

Tests	Age at Testing (Months)	Score	Group Median
Bayley Mental Development Index	12	—	—
	24	109	101
Stanford-Binet IQ	36	139	117.5
WPPSI IQ	60	116	111
Language Test[1]	12	—	—
	15	—	—
	21	—	—
	24	30	30
	27	36	36
	30	51	40.5
	36	51	—
Abstract Abilities[2]	12	—	—
	15	—	—
	21	—	—
	24	5	5.5
	27	6	6
	30	7	6.5
	36	11	—
Discrimination Test[2]	12	—	—
	15	—	—
	21	—	—
	24	3.0	3.0
	27	3.0	3.0
	30	3.5	6.0
	36	8.0	—

[1] Scores in Months
[2] Scores in Level Achieved

APPENDIX A

SOCIAL COMPETENCE FOR SUBJECT 9

```
                         T
GAIN          0XXXXXXXXXXXXXXXXXXX
ADULT         0XXXXXXXXXXXXXXXXX
ATTENTION     0
                              T
USE &         0
ADULT         0XXXXXXXXXXXXXXX
RESOURCE      0XXXXXXXXXXXXX
              0          T
HOSTILITY,    0
AFFECTION     0XXXXXXXXX
TO ADULT      0XXXXXXXX
              0              T
              T
ROLE PLAY     0
              0
              T
PRIDE IN      0
PRODUCT       0
              T
                 T
COMPETES      0XXXXXXXXXXXXXXXXXXXXXXXXXXXXXXXX
WITH          0XXXXXXXXXXXXXXXXXXXXXXXXXXXXXXXXXX
PEER          0     T
              0  T
HOSTILITY,    0XXXXXX
AFFECTION     0XXXXXXX
TO PEER       0    T
              0    T
LEADS AND     0XXXXX
FOLLOWS       0XXXXX
PEER          0      T

              0   1   2   3   4   5   6   7   8   9   10
```

	TOTAL SCORES FOR S 9	MEDIANS FOR 24/27 TWO YEAR STARTER CHILD. FOR ALL SUBJECTS
ADULT COMPETENCE	13.8	23.2
PEER COMPETENCE	12.5	5.1
OVERALL COMPETENCE	26.4	28.6

T INDICATES THE MEDIAN FOR ALL SUBJECTS FOR EACH COMPETENCE FACTOR.

SOCIAL COMPETENCE FOR SUBJECT 9

```
                         T
GAIN          0XXXXXXXXXXXXXXXXXXXXX
ADULT         0XXXXXXXXXXXXXXXXXXX
ATTENTION     0          T
              0                 T
USE &         0X
ADULT         0X
RESOURCE      0
              0               T
HOSTILITY,    0XXXXXXXXXXXXXXXX
AFFECTION     0XXXXXXXXXXXXXX
TO ADULT      0       T
              T
ROLE PLAY     0XXXXXXXXXXXXXXXXXXXXXXXXXXXXXXXXXXXXXXXXXXX
              0XXXXXXXXXXXXXXXXXXXXXXXXXXXXXXXXXXXXXXXXX
              T
PRIDE IN      0
PRODUCT       0
              0
              0  T
COMPETES      0XXXXXXXXXXXXXXXXXXXXXXXXXXXXXXXXXXX
WITH          0XXXXXXXXXXXXXXXXXXXXXXXXXXXXXXXXXX
PEER          0 T
                 T
HOSTILITY,    0XXXXXXXXXXXXXXXXXXX
AFFECTION     0XXXXXXXXXXXXXXXXXXX
TO PEER       0
              0
LEADS AND     0XXXXXXXXXXXXXXXXXXXXXXXXXXXXXXXXXXXXXX
FOLLOWS       0XXXXXXXXXXXXXXXXXXXXXXXXXXXXXXXXXXX
PEER          0

              0   1   2   3   4   5   6   7   8   9   10
```

	TOTAL SCORES FOR S 9	MEDIANS FOR 30/33 TWO YEAR STARTER CHILD. FOR ALL SUBJECTS
ADULT COMPETENCE	24.2	24.0
PEER COMPETENCE	21.6	11.9
OVERALL COMPETENCE	45.8	28.9

T INDICATES THE MEDIAN FOR ALL SUBJECTS FOR EACH COMPETENCE FACTOR.

Subject #9

	% Duration	
Social Tasks	24-27 Months	30-33 Months
To please	0.4	1.2
To cooperate	5.6	2.6
To gain approval	0.5	0.3
To procure a service	2.1	0.6
To gain attention	2.7	3.8
To maintain social contact	2.8	5.1
To avoid unpleasant circumstances	0.3	0.1
To annoy	0.7	0.4
To direct	1.9	5.7
To assert self (protect domain)	2.2	4.8
To provide information	0.9	1.3
To compete	0.0	0.3
To reject overtures	0.0	0.0
To enjoy pets	0.6	0.3
To converse	3.3	3.2
To produce verbalizations	0.0	0.0
Nonsocial Tasks		
To eat	8.0	1.7
To gain information (v)	11.2	7.7
To gain information (v & a)	18.4	2.8
live language directed to child	13.4	2.7
live language overheard by child	1.9	0.1
mechanical language	0.2	0.0
Sesame Street	1.6	0.0
Nontask	5.6	5.9
To pass time	2.3	1.5
To find something to do	0.0	0.0
To prepare for an activity	3.9	5.6
To construct a product	0.2	0.2
To choose	0.0	0.4
To procure an object	4.9	2.2
To engage in large muscle activity	0.6	1.1
To gain pleasure	0.0	0.1
To imitate	0.7	0.4
To pretend (role play)	3.9	15.0
To ease discomfort	0.1	0.7
To restore order	0.0	1.0
To relieve oneself	0.0	0.0
To dress/undress	0.0	0.0
To operate a mechanism	0.3	0.9
To explore	3.5	1.5
To improve a developing skill (mastery)	3.8	14.7
gross	3.2	3.4
fine	0.6	11.2
verbal	0.0	0.1
To eat and gain information (v)	1.1	0.8
To eat and gain information (v & a)	3.8	0.3
live language directed to child	3.8	0.0
overheard	0.0	0.3

SUBJECT #10

Subject #10 is a two-year-old SES Level I predicted A girl, the youngest of three children; she has an eight-year-old sister and a six-year-old brother. Her family lives in a comfortable, warmly furnished home in an attractive suburban neighborhood. The home has a well-equipped playroom. There is a piano that S often uses and an enclosed backyard complete with swing set and bicycles.

Subject #10 is an outgoing and friendly child with a generally sunny disposition. She gets along well with peers and has grown up in frequent contact with a girlfriend of the same age. Her older siblings are very affectionate toward S and often include her in their play. When they are at school, S plays well by herself.

Subject #10's parents are well educated and show concern for their children's development. This is particularly true of S's mother. She is a busy, efficient woman dedicated to interests outside the home as well as to the upbringing of her children. She frequently takes S along on errands but spends much time away from the home, with S being cared for by several regular babysitters, usually together with her two-year-old playmate. S's mother has gone to some trouble to set up an arrangement so that her child can be cared for in the company of her little friend.

When at home, S's mother does not set up or participate in S's play, as a rule, but encourages her independence, frequently checking on her and praising her activities. The mother provides comfort and affection when S shows a need for this.

Summary of Test Scores

Subject #10 Group: Two-Year-Old Starters (n = 20)

Tests	Age at Testing (Months)	Score	Group Median
Bayley Mental Development Index	12	—	—
	24	106	101
Stanford-Binet IQ	36	127	117.5
WPPSI IQ	60	123	111
Language Test[1]	12	—	—
	15	—	—
	21	—	—
	24	33	30
	27	45	36
	30	51	40.5
	36	51	—
Abstract Abilities[2]	12	—	—
	15	—	—
	21	—	—
	24	6	5.5
	27	6	6
	30	6	6.5
	36	10	—
Discrimination Test[2]	12	—	—
	15	—	—
	21	—	—
	24	3.0	3.0
	27	2.0	3.0
	30	7.0	6.0
	36	8.0	—

[1] Scores in Months
[2] Scores in Level Achieved

APPENDIX A

SOCIAL COMPETENCE FOR SUBJECT 10

```
                                    T
GAIN            OXXXXXXXXXXXX
ADULT           OXXXXXXXXXXXX          T
ATTENTION       O

                                            T
USE             OXXXXXXXXXXXXXXXXXX
ADULT           OXXXXXXXXXXXXXXXX
RESOURCE                    T
                O

                                T
HOSTILITY,      OXXXXX
AFFECTION       OXXXXX
TO ADULT                T
                O

                T
ROLE PLAY       O
                O
                            T

                            T
PRIDE IN        OXXXXXXXXXX
PRODUCT         OXXXXXXXXXX    T
                O

COMPETES        O    T
WITH            OXXX
PEER            OXX
                O    T

                              T
HOSTILITY,      OXXXXXXXXXXXXXXXXXXX
AFFECTION       OXXXXXXXXXXXXXXXXXXX
TO PEER                    T
                O

                      T
LEADS AND       OXXXXXXXXXXXXXXXXXXXXXXXXXXXXXXXX
FOLLOWS         OXXXXXXXXXXXXXXXXXXXXXXXXXXXXXXXX
PEER                T
                O

                O   1   2   3   4   5   6   7   8   9   10

                    TOTAL SCORES        MEDIANS FOR 30/33 TWO YEAR STARTER CHILD.
                      FOR S 10                   FOR ALL SUBJECTS

ADULT COMPETENCE          13.4                        24.0
PEER COMPETENCE           15.4                        11.9
OVERALL COMPETENCE        28.8                        28.9
```

T INDICATES THE MEDIAN FOR ALL SUBJECTS FOR EACH COMPETENCE FACTOR.

SOCIAL COMPETENCE FOR SUBJECT 10

```
                O
GAIN            OXXXXXXXXXXXXXXXXXXX         T
ADULT           OXXXXXXXXXXXXXXXXXX
ATTENTION       O                T

                O                                T
USE             OXXXXXXXXXXXXXXXXXXXXXXXXXXXXX
ADULT           OXXXXXXXXXXXXXXXXXXXXXXXXXXX
RESOURCE                          T
                O

                O
HOSTILITY,      OXXXXXXXXX              T
AFFECTION       OXXXXXXXXX
TO ADULT        O                T

                T
ROLE PLAY       O
                O
                    T

                T
PRIDE IN        OXXXXXXXXXXX
PRODUCT         OXXXXXXXXXXX
                        T

COMPETES        O   T
WITH            OXXXXX
PEER            OXXXX
                O   T

                O         T
HOSTILITY,      OXXXXXXXXXX
AFFECTION       OXXXXXXXXXX
TO PEER                 T

                O    T
LEADS AND       OXXXXXXXXXXX
FOLLOWS         OXXXXXXXXXXX
PEER            O
                    T

                O   1   2   3   4   5   6   7   8   9   10

                    TOTAL SCORES        MEDIANS FOR 24/27 TWO YEAR STARTER CHILD.
                      FOR S 10                   FOR ALL SUBJECTS

ADULT COMPETENCE          22.6                        23.2
PEER COMPETENCE            6.2                         5.1
OVERALL COMPETENCE        28.0                        28.6
```

T INDICATES THE MEDIAN FOR ALL SUBJECTS FOR EACH COMPETENCE FACTOR.

Subject #10

	% Duration	
Social Tasks	24-27 Months	30-33 Months
To please	1.0	0.7
To cooperate	4.4	6.5
To gain approval	0.9	0.7
To procure a service	3.6	2.7
To gain attention	2.3	4.3
To maintain social contact	1.5	1.5
To avoid unpleasant circumstances	0.0	0.0
To annoy	0.0	0.1
To direct	0.8	0.5
To assert self (protect domain)	1.1	1.7
To provide information	0.7	4.6
To compete	0.0	0.0
To reject overtures	0.0	0.0
To enjoy pets	0.0	0.1
To converse	0.4	0.8
To produce verbalizations	0.4	0.0
Nonsocial Tasks		
To eat	8.6	2.9
To gain information (v)	13.3	5.4
To gain information (v & a)	10.8	10.5
live language directed to child	3.4	4.4
live language overheard by child	3.9	2.3
mechanical language	0.0	0.0
Sesame Street	2.8	2.3
Nontask	12.8	4.3
To pass time	4.2	1.7
To find something to do	0.6	0.0
To prepare for an activity	5.2	2.8
To construct a product	0.0	2.0
To choose	0.0	0.0
To procure an object	0.5	1.4
To engage in large muscle activity	0.5	4.8
To gain pleasure	0.9	2.9
To imitate	0.2	0.5
To pretend (role play)	1.2	7.2
To ease discomfort	0.6	0.5
To restore order	0.7	0.1
To relieve oneself	0.5	0.3
To dress/undress	0.2	0.5
To operate a mechanism	0.5	0.5
To explore	4.1	0.5
To improve a developing skill (mastery)	10.8	17.7
gross	8.7	8.6
fine	2.0	7.1
verbal	0.1	2.0
To eat and gain information (v)	2.1	0.9
To eat and gain information (v & a)	3.7	2.9
live language directed to child	3.7	1.7
overheard	0.0	1.3

SUBJECT #11

Subject #11 is a one-year-old SES Level II predicted A girl. She has one older sister, aged five. The family lives in an airy, pleasant, five-room apartment in an academic area. The father does research and teaches at the college level, and the mother, although active in volunteer activities, spends much of her time at home with the children.

S spends each morning at home alone with her mother while her sister attends school. She is a physically mature child and enjoys climbing on furniture and exploring household objects. Her mother does not restrict her in these pursuits but does keep a watchful eye on S to make sure she does not get into trouble. S's mother is easily accessible to her and will often make suggestions to her. In addition to household objects, there are many toys, books, and dolls that S is encouraged to play with.

Summary of Test Scores

Subject #11 Group: One-Year-Old Starters (n = 19)

Tests	Age of Testing (Months)	Score	Group Median
Bayley Mental Developmental Index	12	119	103
	24	119	112
Stanford-Binet IQ	36	144	113
WPPSI IQ	60	136	117.5
Language Test[1]	12	18	14
	15	21	16
	21	39	21
	24	42	36
	27	not tested	—
	30	54	43.5
	36	60	45
Abstract Abilities[2]	12	2	2
	15	4	2
	21	7	5
	24	7	6
	27	not tested	—
	30	7	7
	36	12	9
Discrimination Test[2]	12	2	1
	15	2	2
	21	4	3
	24	7	3.5
	27	not tested	—
	30	8	5
	36	8	8

[1] Scores in Months
[2] Scores in Level Achieved

APPENDIX A

SOCIAL COMPETENCE FOR SUBJECT 11

```
                              T
GAIN           0XXXXXXXXXXXXXXXXXXXXXXXX
ADULT          0XXXXXXXXXXXXXXXXXXXXXXXXX
ATTENTION      0          T

                              T
USE            0XXXXXXXXXXXXXXXXXXXX
ADULT          0XXXXXXXXXXXXXXXXX
RESOURCE       0          T

                   T
HOSTILITY,     0XXXXXXX
AFFECTION      0XXXXXXXX
TO ADULT       0       T

               T
ROLE PLAY      0
               0
               T

               T
PRIDE IN       0XXXXXXXXXXXX
PRODUCT        0XXXXXXXXXXXX
               T

                   T
COMPETES       0XXXXX
WITH           0XXXXX
PEER           0    T

                   T
HOSTILITY,     0XXXXXXXXXXXXXXXXXXXXXXXX
AFFECTION      0XXXXXXXXXXXXXXXXXXXXXXXXX
TO PEER        0            T

               0   T
LEADS AND      0X
FOLLOWS        0X
PEER           0  T

               0  1  2  3  4  5  6  7  8  9  10
```

	TOTAL SCORES FOR S 11	MEDIANS AT 12/15 MONTHS FOR ALL SUBJECTS
ADULT COMPETENCE	22.1	13.8
PEER COMPETENCE	7.0	9.0
OVERALL COMPETENCE	29.1	20.5

T INDICATES THE MEDIAN FOR ALL SUBJECTS FOR EACH COMPETENCE FACTOR.

SOCIAL COMPETENCE FOR SUBJECT 11

```
               0         T
GAIN           0XXXXXXXXXXXXXXXXXXXXX
ADULT          0XXXXXXXXXXXXXXXXXXXX
ATTENTION      0       T

               0                             T
USE            0XXXXXXXXXXXXXXXXXXXXXXXXXXXXXXX
ADULT          0XXXXXXXXXXXXXXXXXXXXXXXXXXXXXXXX
RESOURCE       0                         T

               0               T
HOSTILITY,     0
AFFECTION      0
TO ADULT       0        T

               0      T
ROLE PLAY      0
               0
               0    T

               T
PRIDE IN       0XXXXX
PRODUCT        0XXXXX
               T

               0                T
COMPETES       0
WITH           0
PEER           0          T

               0                  T
HOSTILITY,     0
AFFECTION      0
TO PEER        0              T

               0          T
LEADS AND      0
FOLLOWS        0
PEER               T

               0  1  2  3  4  5  6  7  8  9  10
```

	TOTAL SCORES FOR S 11	MEDIANS AT 18/21 MONTHS FOR ALL SUBJECTS
ADULT COMPETENCE	11.7	22.2
PEER COMPETENCE	0.0	13.5
OVERALL COMPETENCE	11.7	23.5

T INDICATES THE MEDIAN FOR ALL SUBJECTS FOR EACH COMPETENCE FACTOR.

SOCIAL COMPETENCE FOR SUBJECT 11

```
GAIN            O                         T
ADULT           OXXXXXXXXXXXXXXXXXXXXXXX
ATTENTION       OXXXXXXXXXXXXXXXXXXXXXXX
                O                         T
-------------------------------------------------------------------
USE             O                     T
ADULT           OXXXXXXXXXXXXXXXXXXXXX
RESOURCE        OXXXXXXXXXXXXXXXXXXXXX
                O                     T
-------------------------------------------------------------------
HOSTILITY,      O           T
AFFECTION       OXX
TO ADULT        OXX
                O           T
-------------------------------------------------------------------
                O       T
ROLE PLAY       OXXXXX
                OXXXXX
                O       T
-------------------------------------------------------------------
                O   T
PRIDE IN        O
PRODUCT         O
                O   T
-------------------------------------------------------------------
COMPETES        O                             T
WITH            O
PEER            O
                O                             T
-------------------------------------------------------------------
HOSTILITY,      O                     T
AFFECTION       O
TO PEER         O
                O                     T
-------------------------------------------------------------------
LEADS AND       O       T
FOLLOWS         O
PEER            O
                O           T
-------------------------------------------------------------------
                0   1   2   3   4   5   6   7   8   9   10
```

	TOTAL SCORES FOR S 11	MEDIANS FOR 30/33 ONE YEAR STARTER CHILD. FOR ALL SUBJECTS
ADULT COMPETENCE	14.2	26.0
PEER COMPETENCE	0.0	12.2
OVERALL COMPETENCE	14.2	33.6

T INDICATES THE MEDIAN FOR ALL SUBJECTS FOR EACH COMPETENCE FACTOR.

Subject #11

Social Tasks	% Duration	
	12-15 Months	18-21 Months
To please	0.1	0.5
To cooperate	3.0	3.8
To gain approval	0.0	2.5
To procure a service	0.1	1.7
To gain attention	4.0	4.7
To maintain social contact	0.3	1.4
To avoid unpleasant circumstances	0.0	0.1
To annoy	0.0	0.1
To direct	0.0	0.3
To assert self (protect domain)	3.2	3.0
To provide information	0.3	1.4
To compete	0.0	0.0
To reject overtures	0.0	0.1
To enjoy pets	0.0	0.0
To converse	0.0	0.0
To produce verbalizations	0.0	0.0
Nonsocial Tasks		
To eat	2.7	9.5
To gain information (v)	30.0	9.5
To gain information (v & a)	8.1	17.3
live language directed to child	6.9	7.6
live language directed to child	1.4	5.0
mechanical language	0.2	1.4
Sesame Street	0.0	0.0
Nontask	7.9	9.3
To pass time	15.0	6.0
To find something to do	0.0	0.3
To prepare for an activity	2.3	5.7
To construct a product	0.0	0.0
To choose	0.0	0.0
To procure an object	1.9	3.4
To engage in large muscle activity	1.2	0.3
To gain pleasure	2.0	0.6
To imitate	0.1	0.1
To pretend (role play)	0.0	0.9
To ease discomfort	2.3	0.5
To restore order	0.3	2.7
To relieve oneself	0.4	0.0
To dress/undress	0.0	0.0
To operate a mechanism	0.5	0.3
To explore	5.0	3.4
To improve a developing skill (mastery)	8.5	8.0
gross	8.5	3.5
fine	0.0	4.0
verbal	0.0	0.5
To eat and gain information (v)	0.0	1.0
To eat and gain information (v & a)	0.0	0.2
live language directed to child	0.0	0.3
overheard	0.0	0.0

SUBJECT #12

Subject #12 is a two-year-old SES Level I predicted A boy. The family lives in a spacious home in a suburban area close to the city. S has three siblings—a sister (five years old) and two brothers (one four years old, and an infant three months old). Both parents are well educated. Although the mother does not work, she is out daily, and the children are left in the care of the live-in maid.

S is a lively child who enjoys playing with vehicles: trikes, wagons, cars, trucks. He has free access to most areas of the house and is encouraged to play outside as well.

Although S's home is well equipped with toys, the atmosphere is not particularly child-centered. S's mother is usually busy with her own activities and restricts her interactions with S to checking up on what he is doing.

Summary of Test Scores

Subject #12   Group: Two-Year-Old Starters (n = 20)

Tests	Age at Testing (Months)	Score	Group Median
Bayley Mental Developmental Index	12	—	—
	24	102	101
Stanford-Binet IQ	36	122	117.5
WPPSI IQ	60	111	111
Language Test[1]	12	—	—
	15	—	—
	21	—	—
	24	36	30
	27	36	36
	30	42	40.5
	36	51	—
Abstract Abilities[2]	12	—	—
	15	—	—
	21	—	—
	24	5	5.5
	27	6	6
	30	7	6.5
	36	10	—
Discrimination Test[2]	12	—	—
	15	—	—
	21	—	—
	24	2.0	3.0
	27	3.0	3.0
	30	7.0	6.0
	36	7.0	—

[1] Scores in Months
[2] Scores in Level Achieved

Individual Subject Data

SOCIAL COMPETENCE FOR SUBJECT 12

```
                                                   T
GAIN             O
ADULT            OXXXXXXXXXXXXXXXXXXXXXXXXXXX
ATTENTION        O                           T
                 O
-------------------------------------------------
                 O                T
USE              OXXXXXXXXXXXXXXX
ADULT            OXXXXXXXXXXXXXXX
RESOURCE         O              T
-------------------------------------------------
                 O                                    T
HOSTILITY,       OXX
AFFECTION        OXX
TO ADULT         O         T
-------------------------------------------------
                 T
                 O
ROLE PLAY        O
                 O
                 T
-------------------------------------------------
                 T
PRIDE IN         OXXXXXXXXXXXXXXXXXXXXXXX
PRODUCT          OXXXXXXXXXXXXXXXXXXXXXXX
                 T
-------------------------------------------------
                 O     T
COMPETES         O
WITH             OX
PEER             O    T
-------------------------------------------------
                 O          T
HOSTILITY,       OXXX
AFFECTION        OXXX
TO PEER          O       T
-------------------------------------------------
LEADS AND        O      T
FOLLOWS          OX
PEER             OX
                 O    T
-------------------------------------------------
                 0    1    2    3    4    5    6    7    8    9    10

                TOTAL SCORES        MEDIANS FOR 24/27 TWO YEAR STARTER CHILD.
                  FOR S 12            FOR ALL SUBJECTS

ADULT COMPETENCE    7.1                    23.2
PEER COMPETENCE     0.8                     5.1
OVERALL COMPETENCE  7.9                    28.6
```

T INDICATES THE MEDIAN FOR ALL SUBJECTS FOR EACH COMPETENCE FACTOR.

SOCIAL COMPETENCE FOR SUBJECT 12

```
                                     T
GAIN             O
ADULT            OXXXXXXXXXXXXXXXXXXXXXXXXXXXXX
ATTENTION        OXXXXXXXXXXXXXXXXXXXXXXXXXXX
                                          T
                 O
-------------------------------------------------
                 O
USE              OXXXXXXXXXXXXXXXXXXX
ADULT            OXXXXXXXXXXXXXXXXXXX      T
RESOURCE         O                T
-------------------------------------------------
                 O                                               T
HOSTILITY,       OXXXXXXXXXXXXXXXXXXXXXXXXXXXXXXXXXXXXXXXXXXXX
AFFECTION        OXXXXXXXXXXXXXXXXXXXXXXXXXXXXXXXXXXXXXXXXXXXX
TO ADULT         O        T
-------------------------------------------------
                 T
ROLE PLAY        OXXXX
                 OXXXX
                 T
-------------------------------------------------
                 O                             T
PRIDE IN         OXXXXXXXXXXXXXXXXXXXXXXXXX
PRODUCT          OXXXXXXXXXXXXXXXXXXXXXXXX
                 O                        T
-------------------------------------------------
                 O   T
COMPETES         OXXX
WITH             OXX
PEER             O T
-------------------------------------------------
                 O                   T
HOSTILITY,       OXXXXXXXXXXX
AFFECTION        OXXXXXXXXXXX
TO PEER          O                T
-------------------------------------------------
LEADS AND        O       T
FOLLOWS          O
PEER             O
                 O        T
-------------------------------------------------
                 0    1    2    3    4    5    6    7    8    9    10

                TOTAL SCORES        MEDIANS FOR 30/33 TWO YEAR STARTER CHILD.
                  FOR S 12            FOR ALL SUBJECTS

ADULT COMPETENCE   30.5                    24.0
PEER COMPETENCE     2.8                    11.9
OVERALL COMPETENCE 33.3                    28.9
```

T INDICATES THE MEDIAN FOR ALL SUBJECTS FOR EACH COMPETENCE FACTOR.

Subject #12

Social Tasks	% Duration	
	24-27 Months	30-33 Months
To please	0.0	0.3
To cooperate	2.7	7.3
To gain approval	0.0	0.7
To procure a service	2.1	1.2
To gain attention	1.5	1.6
To maintain social contact	3.8	2.6
To avoid unpleasant circumstances	0.4	0.9
To annoy	1.7	0.4
To direct	0.0	0.3
To assert self (protect domain)	2.9	3.7
To provide information	0.1	0.8
To compete	0.0	0.0
To reject overtures	0.0	0.0
To enjoy pets	0.0	0.0
To converse	0.0	0.8
To produce verbalizations	0.1	0.3
Nonsocial Tasks		
To eat	3.3	1.6
To gain information (v)	19.9	5.1
To gain information (v & a)	8.5	23.4
live language directed to child	4.2	1.2
live language overheard by child	3.1	3.0
mechanical language	0.0	7.5
Sesame Street	0.0	10.8
Nontask	18.0	13.4
To pass time	1.4	0.0
To find something to do	0.0	0.0
To prepare for an activity	2.2	2.4
To construct a product	0.0	2.6
To choose	0.8	0.0
To procure an object	2.4	2.3
To engage in large muscle activity	3.6	0.0
To gain pleasure	0.8	0.7
To imitate	0.3	0.0
To pretend (role play)	0.2	2.3
To ease discomfort	0.6	0.5
To restore order	0.8	2.6
To relieve oneself	0.0	0.0
To dress/undress	0.2	0.0
To operate a mechanism	0.1	2.3
To explore	4.1	2.3
To improve a developing skill (mastery)	11.7	12.1
gross	4.8	6.3
fine	6.9	5.2
verbal	0.0	0.6
To eat and gain information (v)	4.4	0.8
To eat and gain information (v & a)	0.0	1.2
live language directed to child	0.0	0.3
overheard	0.0	0.1

SUBJECT #13

Subject #13 is a two-year-old SES Level I predicted A boy. His family lives in a lovely, spacious home in an affluent suburban area close to the city. S is a middle child, the only boy; his sisters are six years old and one year old. Both parents are well educated. Although S's mother does not work, she is very busy at home and goes out on frequent errands, usually bringing S along.

When at home, she usually lets S occupy himself with his many toys and books rather than participate in or direct his play. S's mother particularly encourages gross motor activities and shows concern for the healthy physical development of her children. An indoor exercise bar for the children's use and a jungle gym set outdoors reflect this interest.

Subject #13 tends to seek out his mother for emotional support; perhaps his position as a middle child, with a new baby in the home and an older sister who often excludes him from her play, encourages this "babyish" behavior. At such times, S's mother is quite willing to cuddle him and allow him to tag along after her with his blanket in hand.

Summary of Test Scores

Subject #13   Group: Two-Year-Old Starters (n = 20)

Tests	Age at Testing (Months)	Score	Group Median
Bayley Mental Developmental Index	12	—	—
	24	102	101
Stanford-Binet IQ	36	118	117.5
WPPSI IQ	60	123	111
Language Test[1]	12	—	—
	15	—	—
	21	—	—
	24	36	30
	27	39	36
	30	39	40.5
	36	48	—
Abstract Abilities[2]	12	—	—
	15	—	—
	21	—	—
	24	6	5.5
	27	6	6
	30	6	6.5
	36	10	—
Discrimination Test[2]	12	—	—
	15	—	—
	21	—	—
	24	3.0	3.0
	27	8.0	3.0
	30	8.0	6.0
	36	8.0	—

[1] Score in Months
[2] Score in Level Achieved

Individual Subject Data 253

SOCIAL COMPETENCE FOR SUBJECT 13

Category	Score (0–10)
GAIN ADULT ATTENTION	~9 (T at ~4)
USE ADULT RESOURCE	2 (T)
HOSTILITY, AFFECTION TO ADULT	3 (T)
ROLE PLAY	7 (T at 0)
PRIDE IN PRODUCT	6 (T at 0)
COMPETES WITH PEER	0 (T at 1)
HOSTILITY, AFFECTION TO PEER	0 (T at 2)
LEADS AND FOLLOWS PEER	0 (T at 3)

	TOTAL SCORES FOR S 13	MEDIANS FOR 24/27 TWO YEAR STARTER CHILD. FOR ALL SUBJECTS
ADULT COMPETENCE	33.6	23.2
PEER COMPETENCE	0.0	5.1
OVERALL COMPETENCE	33.6	28.6

T INDICATES THE MEDIAN FOR ALL SUBJECTS FOR EACH COMPETENCE FACTOR.

SOCIAL COMPETENCE FOR SUBJECT 13

Category	Score (0–10)
GAIN ADULT ATTENTION	~9 (T at ~4)
USE ADULT RESOURCE	2 (T)
HOSTILITY, AFFECTION TO ADULT	3 (T)
ROLE PLAY	1 (T at 0)
PRIDE IN PRODUCT	0 (T at 4)
COMPETES WITH PEER	0 (T at 1)
HOSTILITY, AFFECTION TO PEER	0 (T at 3)
LEADS AND FOLLOWS PEER	0 (T at 3)

	TOTAL SCORES FOR S 13	MEDIANS FOR 30/33 TWO YEAR STARTER CHILD. FOR ALL SUBJECTS
ADULT COMPETENCE	15.1	24.0
PEER COMPETENCE	0.0	11.9
OVERALL COMPETENCE	15.1	28.9

T INDICATES THE MEDIAN FOR ALL SUBJECTS FOR EACH COMPETENCE FACTOR.

Subject #13

Social Tasks	% Duration	
	24-27 Months	30-33 Months
To please	0.1	0.9
To cooperate	6.9	5.3
To gain approval	0.2	1.1
To procure a service	1.8	3.7
To gain attention	5.4	2.2
To maintain social contact	6.2	7.6
To avoid unpleasant circumstances	0.0	0.0
To annoy	0.0	0.2
To direct	0.0	2.3
To assert self (protect domain)	1.3	0.9
To provide information	0.2	0.9
To compete	0.0	0.0
To reject overtures	0.0	0.4
To enjoy pets	0.0	0.3
To converse	0.4	1.1
To produce verbalizations	0.2	0.0
Nonsocial Tasks		
To eat	1.1	2.9
To gain information (v)	19.4	8.4
To gain information (v & a)	11.3	11.2
live language directed to child	3.8	2.3
live language overheard by child	3.2	3.6
mechanical language	0.0	4.6
Sesame Street	4.3	0.0
Nontask	3.8	8.7
To pass time	3.2	4.1
To find something to do	0.4	0.0
To prepare for an activity	0.9	4.4
To construct a product	0.0	0.0
To choose	0.0	0.0
To procure an object	2.1	1.1
To engage in large muscle activity	0.6	0.5
To gain pleasure	0.4	4.9
To imitate	0.4	0.2
To pretend (role play)	5.6	0.8
To ease discomfort	0.0	0.4
To restore order	0.7	0.7
To relieve oneself	0.0	0.0
To dress/undress	0.3	0.0
To operate a mechanism	0.8	1.3
To explore	7.8	1.7
To improve a developing skill (mastery)	14.1	13.4
gross	11.1	1.4
fine	1.9	10.8
verbal	1.1	1.3
To eat and gain information (v)	1.4	1.2
To eat and gain information (v & a)	0.3	0.2
live language directed to child	0.4	0.2
overheard	0.0	0.1

SUBJECT #14

Subject #14 is a two-year-old SES Level IV predicted C boy who lives in a three-family apartment in a rather stark working-class neighborhood. The home is fairly roomy, nicely furnished, and kept spotlessly clean. Subject #14 has his own small bedroom apart from his 5½-year-old sister and 6-month-old baby brother.

He is a very active and vigorous child who causes much mischief for his often overwrought mother. She finds him to be a difficult child to handle and often refers to how much easier his more docile sister was to raise. He, in turn, is frustrated by the restrictions put on his activities (the neatness of the home is important to S's mother) and by the fact that he is usually excluded from his sister's "girlish" games. Sex-role differences are a recurring issue in this home. S's father is sometimes home during the day. At these times, he sides with his wife in restricting S's activities and admonishing him to behave.

S has few appropriate toys of his own and is encouraged to play outdoors on a small back porch or on the backyard swing set. He seems to be bored and frustrated, and subsequently takes his energies out in "mischief."

Summary of Test Scores

Subject #14   Group: Two-Year-Old Starters (n = 20)

Tests	Age of Testing (Months)	Score	Group Median
Bayley Mental Developmental Index	12	—	—
	24	86	101
Stanford-Binet IQ	36	81	117.5
WPPSI IQ	60	90	111
Language Test[1]	12	—	—
	15	—	—
	21	—	—
	24	30	30
	27	36	36
	30	42	40.5
	36	39	—
Abstract Abilities[2]	12	—	—
	15	—	—
	21	—	—
	24	6	5.5
	27	5	6
	30	5	6.5
	36	7	—
Discrimination Test[2]	12	—	—
	15	—	—
	21	—	—
	24	4.0	3.0
	27	3.0	3.0
	30	3.0	6.0
	36	6.0	—

[1] Scores in Months
[2] Scores in Level Achieved

Individual Subject Data 257

SOCIAL COMPETENCE FOR SUBJECT 14

```
                           T
GAIN         0XXXXXXXXXXXXXXXXXXXXXXXXXXXXXXXXXXXXXXXXXXXX
ADULT        0XXXXXXXXXXXXXXXXXXXXXXXXXXXXXXXXXXXXXXXXXXXXXXX
ATTENTION    0
                                     T
USE          0
ADULT        0XXXXXXXXXXXXXXXXXXXXXXXXXXXXXXXXXXXXXXXXXXXXXXXX
RESOURCE     0XXXXXXXXXXXXXXXXXXXXXXXXXXXXXXXXXXXXXXXXXXXXXXXXXX
             0            T
HOSTILITY,   0
AFFECTION    0XXXXXXXXXXXXXXXXXXXXXXXXX
TO ADULT     0XXXXXXXXXXXXXXXXXXXXXXXXX
                          T
             T
ROLE PLAY    0
             0
             T

PRIDE IN     T
PRODUCT      0
             0
             T
COMPETES     0   T
WITH         0XX
PEER         0XX
             0   T
HOSTILITY,   0    T
AFFECTION    0XXXXXXX
TO PEER      0XXXXXXX
             0    T
LEADS AND    0
FOLLOWS      0XX
PEER         0XX
             0

             0   1   2   3   4   5   6   7   8   9   10

             TOTAL SCORES    MEDIANS FOR 24/27 TWO YEAR STARTER CHILD.
               FOR S 14         FOR ALL SUBJECTS
ADULT COMPETENCE    28.2              23.2
PEER COMPETENCE      2.0               5.1
OVERALL COMPETENCE  30.3              28.6
```

T INDICATES THE MEDIAN FOR ALL SUBJECTS FOR EACH COMPETENCE FACTOR.

SOCIAL COMPETENCE FOR SUBJECT 14

```
                           T
GAIN         0XXXXXXXXXXXXXXXXXXXXXXXXXXXXXXXXXXXXXXXXXX
ADULT        0XXXXXXXXXXXXXXXXXXXXXXXXXXXXXXXXXXXXXXXXXXXX
ATTENTION    0
                        T
USE          0XXXXXXXXXXXX
ADULT        0XXXXXXXXXXXX
RESOURCE     0         T
                          T
HOSTILITY,   0XXXXXXXXXXXXXXXXXXXXXXXXXXXXXXXX
AFFECTION    0XXXXXXXXXXXXXXXXXXXXXXXXXXXXXXXX
TO ADULT     0            T
             T
ROLE PLAY    0XXXXX
             0XXXX
             T

PRIDE IN     0     T
PRODUCT      0
             0            T
             0
COMPETES     0   T
WITH         0
PEER         0
             0   T
HOSTILITY,   0            T
AFFECTION    0
TO PEER      0
             0            T
LEADS AND    0
FOLLOWS      0XXXXXXXXXXXX
PEER         0XXXXXXXXXXXX
             0   T

             0   1   2   3   4   5   6   7   8   9   10

             TOTAL SCORES    MEDIANS FOR 30/33 TWO YEAR STARTER CHILD.
               FOR S 14         FOR ALL SUBJECTS
ADULT COMPETENCE    26.5              24.0
PEER COMPETENCE      2.9              11.9
OVERALL COMPETENCE  29.5              28.9
```

T INDICATES THE MEDIAN FOR ALL SUBJECTS FOR EACH COMPETENCE FACTOR.

Subject #14

Social Tasks	% Duration	
	24-27 Months	30-33 Months
To please	1.6	0.3
To cooperate	2.8	3.4
To gain approval	1.5	0.2
To procure a service	4.6	4.1
To gain attention	3.9	5.9
To maintain social contact	10.4	7.9
To avoid unpleasant circumstances	0.7	2.4
To annoy	1.7	0.2
To direct	0.1	0.0
To assert self (protect domain)	2.6	4.3
To provide information	0.3	0.8
To compete	0.0	0.0
To reject overtures	0.0	0.0
To enjoy pets	0.0	0.0
To converse	1.6	1.1
To produce verbalizations	0.0	0.1
Nonsocial Tasks		
To eat	4.1	0.7
To gain information (v)	8.7	11.1
To gain information (v & a)	12.5	10.4
live language directed to child	4.5	3.2
live language overheard by child	0.9	1.0
mechanical language	6.0	5.3
Sesame Street	0.0	0.0
Nontask	7.6	12.2
To pass time	0.1	12.2
To find something to do	0.0	0.0
To prepare for an activity	3.1	1.8
To construct a product	0.0	0.0
To choose	0.0	0.2
To procure an object	1.9	1.3
To engage in large muscle activity	2.0	2.6
To gain pleasure	0.4	0.1
To imitate	0.6	0.1
To pretend (role play)	1.4	0.2
To ease discomfort	2.3	0.9
To restore order	0.8	1.1
To relieve oneself	0.7	0.0
To dress/undress	0.1	0.1
To operate a mechanism	1.0	0.2
To explore	4.4	5.1
To improve a developing skill (mastery)	11.5	6.3
gross	3.5	0.6
fine	0.5	5.7
verbal	7.5	0.0
To eat and gain information (v)	2.3	0.2
To eat and gain information (v & a)	0.9	0.1
live language directed to child	0.9	0.0
overheard	0.0	0.1

SUBJECT #16

Subject #16 is a one-year-old SES Level III predicted A boy. He has two older sisters, aged three and four. The family lives in a five-room apartment in an urban area. The father is at present attending college at night, and the mother hopes to go back to college to get her degree.

S is an active, curious child. Although there are few toys appropriate for a one-year-old, S keeps himself busy exploring household objects. However, his activities often get him into trouble, since he is usually one step behind his mother, undoing what she has just straightened.

S's mother is a warm, affectionate person who often finds herself exasperated by this active, assertive little boy.

Summary of Test Scores

Subject #16   Group: One-Year-Old Starters (n = 19)

Tests	Age at Testing (Months)	Score	Group Median
Bayley Mental Developmental Index	12	102	103
	24	127	112
Stanford-Binet IQ	36	127	113
WPPSI IQ	60	133	117.5
Language Test[1]	12	16	14
	15	18	16
	21	27	21
	24	42	36
	27	not tested	—
	30	45	43.5
	36	45	45
Abstract Abilities[2]	12	3	2
	15	1	2
	21	7	5
	24	7	6
	27	not tested	—
	30	7	7
	36	10	9
Discrimination Test[2]	12	2	1
	15	2	2
	21	3	3
	24	8	3.5
	27	not tested	—
	30	7	5
	36	8	8

[1] Scores in Months
[2] Scores in Level Achieved

Individual Subject Data   261

SOCIAL COMPETENCE FOR SUBJECT 16

```
GAIN              0
ADULT             OXXXXXXXXXXXXXXXXXXXT
ATTENTION         OXXXXXXXXXXXXXXXXXXX
                  0                                      T

USE               0                    T
ADULT             OXXXXXXXXXXXXXXXXXXXXXXXXXXXXXXXX
RESOURCE          OXXXXXXXXXXXXXXXXXXXXXXXXXXXXXXXX
                                      T

HOSTILITY,        0        T
AFFECTION         OXXXXXXXXXXXX
TO ADULT          OXXXXXXXXXXXX
                  0              T

ROLE PLAY         T
                  0
                  0
                  T

PRIDE IN          T
PRODUCT           0
                  0
                  T

COMPETES          0        T
WITH              0
PEER              0
                           T

HOSTILITY,        0   T
AFFECTION         0
TO PEER           0
                      T

LEADS AND         0 T
FOLLOWS           OXXXXX
PEER              OXXXXX
                  0 T
                  |---|---|---|---|---|---|---|---|---|---|
                  0   1   2   3   4   5   6   7   8   9   10
```

	TOTAL SCORES FOR S 16	MEDIANS AT 12/15 MONTHS FOR ALL SUBJECTS
ADULT COMPETENCE	18.0	13.8
PEER COMPETENCE	1.1	9.0
OVERALL COMPETENCE	19.1	20.5

T INDICATES THE MEDIAN FOR ALL SUBJECTS FOR EACH COMPETENCE FACTOR.

SOCIAL COMPETENCE FOR SUBJECT 16

```
GAIN              0
ADULT             OXXXXXXXXX  T
ATTENTION         OXXXXXXXXX
                  0              T

USE               0                               T
ADULT             OXXXXXXXXXXXXXXXXXXXXXXXXXXXXXXXXXXXXXXX
RESOURCE          OXXXXXXXXXXXXXXXXXXXXXXXXXXXXXXXXXXXXXXX
                  0                              T

HOSTILITY,        3        T
AFFECTION         OXXXXX
TO ADULT          OXXXXX
                  0            T

ROLE PLAY         0         T
                  0
                  0
                  T

PRIDE IN          0
PRODUCT           0
                  0
                  T

COMPETES          0                          T
WITH              OXXXXXXXXXXXXXXXXXXXXXXXXXXXXXXXXXXXXXXX
PEER              0                                  T

HOSTILITY,        0                T
AFFECTION         OXXXXXXXXXXXXX
TO PEER           OXXXXXXXXXXXXX
                  0                 T

LEADS AND         0
FOLLOWS           0
PEER              0
                  0
                  |---|---|---|---|---|---|---|---|---|---|
                  0   1   2   3   4   5   6   7   8   9   10
```

	TOTAL SCORES FOR S 16	MEDIANS AT 18/21 MONTHS FOR ALL SUBJECTS
ADULT COMPETENCE	9.3	22.2
PEER COMPETENCE	9.7	13.5
OVERALL COMPETENCE	18.9	23.5

T INDICATES THE MEDIAN FOR ALL SUBJECTS FOR EACH COMPETENCE FACTOR.

APPENDIX A

SOCIAL COMPETENCE FOR SUBJECT 16

```
GAIN           O                          T
ADULT          OXXXXXXXXXXXXXXXXXXXXX
ATTENTION      OXXXXXXXXXXXXXXXXXXXXX
               O                          T
-----------------------------------------------------------------
USE            O             T
ADULT          OXXXXXXXXXXXXXXXXXXXXXXXXXXXXXXXXXXXXXXXXXXXXXX
RESOURCE       OXXXXXXXXXXXXXXXXXXXXXXXXXXXXXXXXXXXXXXXXXXXXXX
               O             T
-----------------------------------------------------------------
HOSTILITY,     O             T
AFFECTION      OXX
TO ADULT       OXX
               O       T
-----------------------------------------------------------------
               O      T
ROLE PLAY      OXXXXXXXXXXXXXXXX
               OXXXXXXXXXXXXXXXX
               O      T
-----------------------------------------------------------------
               O   T
PRIDE IN       OXXXXXXXX
PRODUCT        OXXXXXXXX
               O   T
-----------------------------------------------------------------
COMPETES       O                                 T
WITH           OXXXXXXXXXXXXXXXXXXXXXXXXXXXXXXXXXXXXXXXXXXXXX
PEER           OXXXXXXXXXXXXXXXXXXXXXXXXXXXXXXXXXXXXXXXXXXXXX
               O                                 T
-----------------------------------------------------------------
HOSTILITY,     O                   T
AFFECTION      O
TO PEER        O
               O                   T
-----------------------------------------------------------------
LEADS AND      O        T
FOLLOWS        OXXXXXXXXXXXXX
PEER           OXXXXXXXXXXXXX
               O        T
-----------------------------------------------------------------
               0   1   2   3   4   5   6   7   8   9   10
```

	TOTAL SCORES FOR S 16	MEDIANS FOR 30/33 ONE YEAR STARTER CHILD. FOR ALL SUBJECTS
ADULT COMPETENCE	26.0	26.0
PEER COMPETENCE	12.3	12.2
OVERALL COMPETENCE	38.3	33.6

T INDICATES THE MEDIAN FOR ALL SUBJECTS FOR EACH COMPETENCE FACTOR.

Subject #16

Social Tasks	% Duration	
	12-15 Months	18-21 Months
To please	0.3	0.6
To cooperate	3.2	4.6
To gain approval	0.2	0.0
To procure a service	2.1	5.1
To gain attention	4.1	2.0
To maintain social contact	4.4	1.0
To avoid unpleasant circumstances	0.0	0.7
To annoy	0.4	1.0
To direct	0.0	0.4
To assert self (protect domain)	0.6	2.0
To provide information	0.0	0.0
To compete	0.0	0.0
To reject overtures	0.0	0.0
To enjoy pets	0.0	0.0
To converse	0.0	0.0
To produce verbalizations	0.0	0.2
Nonsocial Tasks		
To eat	10.7	10.5
To gain information (v)	16.1	8.6
To gain information (v & a)	6.2	5.7
live language directed to child	1.3	1.2
live language overheard by child	4.9	1.7
mechanical language	0.0	2.4
Sesame Street	0.0	0.4
Nontask	11.7	12.0
To pass time	1.6	3.0
To find something to do	2.3	0.1
To prepare for an activity	1.9	1.7
To construct a product	0.0	0.0
To choose	0.0	0.0
To procure an object	7.7	5.5
To engage in large muscle activity	0.0	0.7
To gain pleasure	0.0	0.1
To imitate	0.1	0.2
To pretend (role play)	0.0	0.0
To ease discomfort	1.3	0.4
To restore order	0.9	2.2
To relieve oneself	0.0	0.0
To dress/undress	0.0	0.2
To operate a mechanism	0.0	0.0
To explore	7.4	3.6
To improve a developing skill (mastery)	7.9	17.3
gross	4.5	7.9
fine	3.4	9.4
verbal	0.0	0.0
To eat and gain information (v)	5.4	3.7
To eat and gain information (v & a)	0.7	4.9
live language directed to child	0.8	0.4
overheard	0.0	0.1

SUBJECT #17

Subject #17 is a one-year-old SES Level I predicted A girl. She has an older sister, aged four. Both parents are college educated. S's mother continues her interest in art in a home studio. The family lives in a comfortable one-family home in an academic area.

S is a shy, watchful child whose early physical development was fairly slow. She spends most of her time with her mother, who is warm but reserved; verbal interaction between mother and child is not very high.

Subject has the run of the house. She has available a fair number of manipulative toys, such as small blocks, puzzles, and dolls. Both parents are at home a good deal of the time, and they are consistently affectionate and available to S, although they are not inclined to didactic interaction with her. In nice weather much of her playtime takes place outdoors, with mother gardening nearby.

Summary of Test Scores

Subject #17   Group: One-Year-Old Starters (n = 19)

Tests	Age at Testing (Months)	Score	Group Median
Bayley Mental Developmental Index	12	100	103
	24	137	112
Stanford-Binet IQ	36	139	113
WPPSI IQ	60	140	117.5
Language Test[1]	12	12	14
	15	14	16
	21	27	21
	24	36	36
	27	not tested	—
	30	48	43.5
	36	57	45
Abstract Abilities[2]	12	2	2
	15	3	2
	21	5	5
	24	6	6
	27	not tested	—
	30	7	7
	36	11	9
Discrimination Test[2]	12	1	1
	15	2	2
	21	6	3
	24	5	3.5
	27	not tested	—
	30	8	5
	36	8	8

[1] Scores in Months
[2] Scores in Level Achieved

APPENDIX A

SOCIAL COMPETENCE FOR SUBJECT 17

```
                                         T
GAIN              OXXXXXXXXXXXXXXXXXXXXX
ADULT             OXXXXXXXXXXXXXXXXXXXXXXX
ATTENTION         O                     T
                                 T
USE               OXXXXXXXXXXXXXXX
ADULT             OXXXXXXXXXXXXXX
RESOURCE          O              T
                         T
HOSTILITY,        OXXXXXXXXXXXXX
AFFECTION         OXXXXXXXXXXXX
TO ADULT          O         T
                  T
ROLE PLAY         O
                  O
                  T
                  T
PRIDE IN          O
PRODUCT           O
                  T
                      T
COMPETES          O
WITH              O
PEER              O T
                      T
HOSTILITY,        O
AFFECTION         O
TO PEER           O
                   T
LEADS AND         O
FOLLOWS           O
PEER              O T

                  0   1   2   3   4   5   6   7   8   9   10
```

	TOTAL SCORES FOR S 17	MEDIANS AT 12/15 MONTHS FOR ALL SUBJECTS
ADULT COMPETENCE	14.3	13.8
PEER COMPETENCE	0.0	9.0
OVERALL COMPETENCE	14.3	20.5

T INDICATES THE MEDIAN FOR ALL SUBJECTS FOR EACH COMPETENCE FACTOR.

SOCIAL COMPETENCE FOR SUBJECT 17

```
                          T
GAIN              OXXXXXXXX
ADULT             OXXXXXXXX
ATTENTION         O       T

USE               OXXXXXXXXXXXXXXXXXXXXXXXXXXXXXXXXXXX
ADULT             OXXXXXXXXXXXXXXXXXXXXXXXXXXXXXXXXXXXX
RESOURCE          O                                 T
                                                    T
HOSTILITY,        OXXXXXXXXXXXXXXXXXXX
AFFECTION         OXXXXXXXXXXXXXXXXXXX
TO ADULT*         O         T
                     T
ROLE PLAY         OXXXXXXXXXXXXX
                  OXXXXXXXXXXXX
                  O         T
                  T
PRIDE IN          O
PRODUCT           O
                  T
                              T
COMPETES          O
WITH              O           T
PEER              O
                              T
HOSTILITY,        O
AFFECTION         O
TO PEER           O
                              T
LEADS AND         O
FOLLOWS           O
PEER              O

                  0   1   2   3   4   5   6   7   8   9   10
```

	TOTAL SCORES FOR S 17	MEDIANS AT 18/21 MONTHS FOR ALL SUBJECTS
ADULT COMPETENCE	23.5	22.2
PEER COMPETENCE	0.0	13.5
OVERALL COMPETENCE	23.5	23.5

T INDICATES THE MEDIAN FOR ALL SUBJECTS FOR EACH COMPETENCE FACTOR.

SOCIAL COMPETENCE FOR SUBJECT 17

```
GAIN            O                           T
ADULT           OXXXXXXXXXXXXXXXXXXXXXXXXX
ATTENTION       OXXXXXXXXXXXXXXXXXXXXXXXX
                O                           T
---------------------------------------------------------------
USE             O               T
ADULT           OXXXXXXXXXXXXXXX
RESOURCE        OXXXXXXXXXXXXXXX
                O               T
---------------------------------------------------------------
HOSTILITY,      O               T
AFFECTION       OXXXXXXXXX
TO ADULT        OXXXXXXXXX
                O       T
---------------------------------------------------------------
                O       T
ROLE PLAY       OXXXXXXXXXXXXXXXXX
                OXXXXXXXXXXXXXXXXX
                O       T
---------------------------------------------------------------
                O    T
PRIDE IN        OXXXXXXXXX
PRODUCT         OXXXXXXXXX
                O    T
---------------------------------------------------------------
COMPETES        O                                  T
WITH            OXXXXXXXXXXXXXXXXXXXXXXXXXXXXXXXXXXXXXXXXXXXXXXX
PEER            OXXXXXXXXXXXXXXXXXXXXXXXXXXXXXXXXXXXXXXXXXXXXXXX
                O                                  T
---------------------------------------------------------------
HOSTILITY,      O                    T
AFFECTION       OXXXXXXXXXXXXXXXXXXXXXXXXXXXXXXXXXXX
TO PEER         OXXXXXXXXXXXXXXXXXXXXXXXXXXXXXXXXXXX
                O                    T
---------------------------------------------------------------
LEADS AND       O            T
FOLLOWS         OXXXXXXXXXXXXXXXXXXXXXXXXXXXXXXXXXXXXXXXXXXXXXX
PEER            OXXXXXXXXXXXXXXXXXXXXXXXXXXXXXXXXXXXXXXXXXXXXXX
                O            T
---------------------------------------------------------------
                0   1   2   3   4   5   6   7   8   9   10
```

	TOTAL SCORES FOR S 17	MEDIANS FOR 30/33 ONE YEAR STARTER CHILD. FOR ALL SUBJECTS
ADULT COMPETENCE	26.7	26.0
PEER COMPETENCE	26.7	12.2
OVERALL COMPETENCE	53.4	33.6

T INDICATES THE MEDIAN FOR ALL SUBJECTS FOR EACH COMPETENCE FACTOR.

Subject #17

Social Tasks	% Duration	
	12-15 Months	18-21 Months
To please	0.1	2.9
To cooperate	1.3	2.3
To gain approval	0.0	0.0
To procure a service	0.6	1.9
To gain attention	6.1	5.7
To maintain social contact	2.8	1.8
To avoid unpleasant circumstances	0.0	0.0
To annoy	0.0	0.2
To direct	0.0	0.1
To assert self (protect domain)	0.6	2.9
To provide information	0.0	0.0
To compete	0.0	0.0
To reject overtures	0.2	0.0
To enjoy pets	0.0	0.0
To converse	0.0	0.0
To produce verbalizations	0.0	0.0
Nonsocial Tasks		
To eat	4.1	9.6
To gain information (v)	39.6	14.8
To gain information (v & a)	4.2	2.3
live language directed to child	3.2	0.6
live language overheard by child	0.5	1.3
mechanical language	0.4	0.0
Sesame Street	0.0	0.0
Nontask	9.8	11.0
To pass time	0.5	3.2
To find something to do	0.0	0.0
To prepare for an activity	0.2	3.0
To construct a product	0.2	0.0
To choose	0.0	0.0
To procure an object	1.1	4.7
To engage in large muscle activity	0.0	0.0
To gain pleasure	0.0	0.0
To imitate	0.6	0.2
To pretend (role play)	0.0	3.3
To ease discomfort	0.3	0.5
To restore order	0.4	1.0
To relieve oneself	0.0	0.0
To dress/undress	0.0	1.2
To operate a mechanism	0.1	1.7
To explore	14.9	8.9
To improve a developing skill (mastery)	2.8	9.6
gross	1.1	0.0
fine	1.7	9.1
verbal	0.0	0.4
To eat and gain information (v)	8.5	2.7
To eat and gain information (v & a)	0.0	1.2
live language directed to child	0.0	0.8
overheard	0.0	0.5

SUBJECT #18

Subject #18 is a two-year-old SES Level III predicted A girl. She is the youngest of seven children ranging in age from two to twelve years. The family lives in a run-down, sparsely furnished house in an urban area. Both parents are very education oriented and spend a great deal of time interacting with their children.

S spends each morning alone with her mother while all the other children are in school. Mrs. C is totally available to S and serves as a playmate as well as a teacher. Most of the activities are centered around storybooks and coloring books. Other than books, there are very few toys available for S to play with.

Summary of Test Scores

Subject #18   Group: Two-Year-Old Starters (n = 20)

Tests	Age at Testing (Months)	Score	Group Median
Bayley Mental Developmental Index	12	—	—
	24	100	101
Stanford-Binet IQ	36	105	117.5
WPPSI IQ	60	109	111
Language Test[1]	12	—	—
	15	—	—
	21	—	—
	24	18	30
	27	27	36
	30	18	40.5
	36	39	—
Abstract Abilities[2]	12	—	—
	15	—	—
	21	—	—
	24	5	5.5
	27	6	6
	30	5	6.5
	36	9	—
Discrimination Test[2]	12	—	—
	15	—	—
	21	—	—
	24	2.0	3.0
	27	3.0	3.0
	30	0.0	6.0
	36	6.0	—

[1] Scores in Months
[2] Scores in Level Achieved

Individual Subject Data

SOCIAL COMPETENCE FOR SUBJECT 1H

```
                              T
GAIN         0XXXXXXXXXXXXXXXXXXXXXXXXXXXXXXXXXXX
ADULT        0XXXXXXXXXXXXXXXXXXXXXXXXXXXXXXXXXXXXXXX
ATTENTION    0                      T
             |----|----|----|----|----|----|----|----|----|----|
                              T
USE          0XXXXXXXXXXXXXXXXXXXXXXX
ADULT        0XXXXXXXXXXXXXXXXXXX
RESOURCE     0              T
             |----|----|----|----|----|----|----|----|----|----|
                          T
HOSTILITY,   0XXXXXXXXXXXXXXXXXXXXX
AFFECTION    0XXXXXXXXXXXXXXXX
TO ADULT     0                  T
             |----|----|----|----|----|----|----|----|----|----|
             T
ROLE PLAY    0
             0
             0
             T
             |----|----|----|----|----|----|----|----|----|----|
                      T
PRIDE IN     0XXXXXXXXXXXXXXXXXXXXXXXXXXXXXXXXXXXXXXXXXXXXX
PRODUCT      0XXXXXXXXXXXXXXXXXXXXXXXXXXXXXXXXXXXXXX
             0               T
             |----|----|----|----|----|----|----|----|----|----|
COMPETES     0  T
WITH         0
PEER         0
             T
             |----|----|----|----|----|----|----|----|----|----|
HOSTILITY,   0           T
AFFECTION    0
TO PEER      0
                 T
             |----|----|----|----|----|----|----|----|----|----|
LEADS AND    0   T
FOLLOWS      0
PEER         0
             T
             |----|----|----|----|----|----|----|----|----|----|
             0    1    2    3    4    5    6    7    8    9    10
```

	TOTAL SCORES FOR S 18	MEDIANS FOR 30/33 TWO YEAR STARTER CHILD. FOR ALL SUBJECTS
ADULT COMPETENCE	35.9	24.0
PEER COMPETENCE	0.0	11.9
OVERALL COMPETENCE	35.9	28.9

T INDICATES THE MEDIAN FOR ALL SUBJECTS FOR EACH COMPETENCE FACTOR.

SOCIAL COMPETENCE FOR SUBJECT 18

```
                          T
GAIN         0XXXXXXXXXXXXXXXXXXXXX
ADULT        0XXXXXXXXXXXXXXXXXXXX
ATTENTION    0               T
             |----|----|----|----|----|----|----|----|----|----|
                                        T
USE          0XXXXXXXXXXXXXXXXXXXXXXXXXXXXXXXXXXXXX
ADULT        0XXXXXXXXXXXXXXXXXXXXXXXXXXXXXXXXX
RESOURCE     0                     T
             |----|----|----|----|----|----|----|----|----|----|
                                      T
HOSTILITY,   0XXXXXXXXXXXXXXXXXXXXXXXXXXXXXX
AFFECTION    0XXXXXXXXXXXXXXXXXXXXXXXXXXXXX
TO ADULT     0                   T
             |----|----|----|----|----|----|----|----|----|----|
             T
ROLE PLAY    0
             0
             0
             T
             |----|----|----|----|----|----|----|----|----|----|
             T
PRIDE IN     0
PRODUCT      0
             0
             T
             |----|----|----|----|----|----|----|----|----|----|
COMPETES     0   T
WITH         0XX
PEER         0XX
             0  T
             |----|----|----|----|----|----|----|----|----|----|
HOSTILITY,   0    T
AFFECTION    0
TO PEER      0
             T
             |----|----|----|----|----|----|----|----|----|----|
LEADS AND    0         T
FOLLOWS      0
PEER         0    T
             T
             |----|----|----|----|----|----|----|----|----|----|
             0    1    2    3    4    5    6    7    8    9    10
```

	TOTAL SCORES FOR S 16	MEDIANS FOR 24/27 TWO YEAR STARTER CHILD. FOR ALL SUBJECTS
ADULT COMPETENCE	20.0	23.2
PEER COMPETENCE	0.4	5.1
OVERALL COMPETENCE	20.4	29.6

T INDICATES THE MEDIAN FOR ALL SUBJECTS FOR EACH COMPETENCE FACTOR.

Subject #18

Social Tasks	% Duration	
	24-27 Months	30-33 Months
To please	0.2	0.1
To cooperate	3.1	2.6
To gain approval	0.0	0.1
To procure a service	3.9	2.1
To gain attention	2.6	2.6
To maintain social contact	8.4	0.2
To avoid unpleasant circumstances	0.1	0.0
To annoy	0.0	0.0
To direct	0.3	5.8
To assert self (protect domain)	1.8	2.0
To provide information	0.2	1.3
To compete	1.2	0.0
To reject overtures	0.0	0.0
To enjoy pets	0.0	0.0
To converse	0.2	1.4
To produce verbalizations	0.0	0.2
Nonsocial Tasks		
To eat	12.0	3.2
To gain information (v)	13.8	13.2
To gain information (v & a)	9.4	10.2
live language directed to child	2.2	2.9
live language overheard by child	1.6	0.8
mechanical language	0.7	0.6
Sesame Street	3.8	4.6
Nontask	8.4	6.1
To pass time	2.4	2.3
To find something to do	0.3	0.0
To prepare for an activity	0.8	3.2
To construct a product	0.0	0.4
To choose	0.0	0.0
To procure an object	0.8	1.2
To engage in large muscle activity	0.0	0.0
To gain pleasure	0.0	0.0
To imitate	0.3	0.6
To pretend (role play)	2.7	1.3
To ease discomfort	0.4	0.2
To restore order	0.8	1.1
To relieve oneself	0.7	0.0
To dress/undress	0.0	0.0
To operate a mechanism	0.0	0.0
To explore	8.1	2.3
To improve a developing skill (mastery)	1.9	34.3
gross	0.5	0.1
fine	0.9	30.3
verbal	0.0	3.9
To eat and gain information (v)	6.3	1.0
To eat and gain information (v & a)	4.6	0.5
live language directed to child	4.7	0.1
overheard	0.0	0.0

SUBJECT #19

Subject #19 is a one-year-old SES Level I predicted A girl who is the youngest of three children. She has two sisters, aged five and seven. The family lives in a comfortable seven-room house in the suburbs of Boston. Both parents are professionally trained, although the mother does not work.

The subject is an attractive child who is under strict supervision much of the time, either in a playpen or gated off in one room. When allowed access to other areas of the house, she is watched rather closely by her mother when there is any likelihood of her "getting into" things.

Summary of Test Scores

Subject #19 **Group: One-Year-Old Starters (n = 19)**

Tests	Age at Testing (Months)	Score	Group Median
Bayley Mental Developmental Index	12	102	103
	24	127	112
Stanford-Binet IQ	36	120	113
WPPSI IQ	60	122	117.5
Language Test[1]	12	14	14
	15	16	16
	21	36	21
	24	36	36
	27	not tested	—
	30	42	43.5
	36	54	45
Abstract Abilities[2]	12	2	2
	15	1	2
	21	< 5	5
	24	7	6
	27	not tested	—
	30	7	7
	36	10	9
Discrimination Test[2]	12	2	1
	15	1	2
	21	2	3
	24	7	3.5
	27	not tested	—
	30	7	5
	36	8	8

[1] Scores in Months
[2] Scores in Level Achieved

Individual Subject Data

SOCIAL COMPETENCE FOR SUBJECT 19 (12/15 months)

```
                        0    1    2    3    4    5    6    7    8    9   10
GAIN
ADULT           OXXXX                T
ATTENTION       OXXXX
                0                         T

USE             O
ADULT           O                    T
RESOURCE        O
                O                              T

HOSTILITY,      O
AFFECTION       O                T
TO ADULT        O
                O                     T

ROLE PLAY       T
                O
                O
                T

PRIDE IN        T
PRODUCT         O
                O
                T

COMPETES        O
WITH            O               T
PEER            O
                O                   T

HOSTILITY,      O
AFFECTION       O           T
TO PEER         O
                O               T

LEADS AND       O
FOLLOWS         O      T
PEER            O
                O        T
```

	TOTAL SCORES FOR S 19	MEDIANS AT 12/15 MONTHS FOR ALL SUBJECTS
ADULT COMPETENCE	0.7	13.8
PEER COMPETENCE	0.0	9.0
OVERALL COMPETENCE	0.7	20.5

T INDICATES THE MEDIAN FOR ALL SUBJECTS FOR EACH COMPETENCE FACTOR.

SOCIAL COMPETENCE FOR SUBJECT 19 (18/21 months)

```
                        0    1    2    3    4    5    6    7    8    9   10
GAIN            O
ADULT           OXXXXXXX                 T
ATTENTION       OXXXXXX
                O                   T

USE             O
ADULT           OXXXXXXXXXXXXXX                   T
RESOURCE        OXXXXXXXXXXXXXX
                O                                T

HOSTILITY,      O                         T
AFFECTION       OXXXXXXXXXXX
TO ADULT        OXXXXXXXXXX
                O                 T

ROLE PLAY       O        T
                OXXXXXX
                OXXXXX
                O              T

PRIDE IN        T
PRODUCT         O
                O
                T

COMPETES        O
WITH            O                          T
PEER            O
                O                      T

HOSTILITY,      O
AFFECTION       O                    T
TO PEER         O
                O                  T

LEADS AND       O
FOLLOWS         O                    T
PEER            O
                O                 T
```

	TOTAL SCORES FOR S 19	MEDIANS AT 18/21 MONTHS FOR ALL SUBJECTS
ADULT COMPETENCE	16.2	22.2
PEER COMPETENCE	0.0	13.5
OVERALL COMPETENCE	16.2	23.5

T INDICATES THE MEDIAN FOR ALL SUBJECTS FOR EACH COMPETENCE FACTOR.

APPENDIX A

```
                    SOCIAL COMPETENCE FOR SUBJECT 19

    GAIN         O                       T
    ADULT        OXXXXXXXXXXXXXXX
    ATTENTION    OXXXXXXXXXXXXXXX
                 O                    T
    ----------------------------------------------------------------
    USE          O              T
    ADULT        OXXXXXXXXXXXXXXXXX
    RESOURCE     OXXXXXXXXXXXXXXXXX
                 O              T
    ----------------------------------------------------------------
    HOSTILITY,   O        T
    AFFECTION    OX
    TO ADULT     OX
                 O           T
    ----------------------------------------------------------------
                 O     T
    ROLE PLAY    O
                 O
                 O     T
    ----------------------------------------------------------------
                 O     T
    PRIDE IN     OXXXXXX
    PRODUCT      OXXXXXX
                 O     T
    ----------------------------------------------------------------
    COMPETES     O                            T
    WITH         O
    PEER         O
                 O                               T
    ----------------------------------------------------------------
    HOSTILITY,   O              T
    AFFECTION    O
    TO PEER      O
                 O                T
    ----------------------------------------------------------------
    LEADS AND    O        T
    FOLLOWS      O
    PEER         O
                 O           T
    ----------------------------------------------------------------
                 O   1   2   3   4   5   6   7   8   9   10
```

	TOTAL SCORES FOR S 19	MEDIANS FOR 30/33 ONE YEAR STARTER CHILD. FOR ALL SUBJECTS
ADULT COMPETENCE	12.1	26.0
PEER COMPETENCE	0.0	12.2
OVERALL COMPETENCE	12.1	33.6

T INDICATES THE MEDIAN FOR ALL SUBJECTS FOR EACH COMPETENCE FACTOR.

Subject #19

	% Duration	
Social Tasks	12-15 Months	18-21 Months
To please	0.6	1.6
To cooperate	2.2	8.1
To gain approval	0.1	0.0
To procure a service	0.4	0.9
To gain attention	1.2	2.6
To maintain social contact	2.3	6.7
To avoid unpleasant circumstances	0.0	0.0
To annoy	0.3	0.2
To direct	0.0	0.1
To assert self (protect domain)	0.4	1.3
To provide information	0.0	0.3
To compete	0.0	0.0
To reject overtures	0.0	0.2
To enjoy pets	0.0	0.0
To converse	0.0	0.0
To produce verbalizations	0.0	0.0
Nonsocial Tasks		
To eat	3.2	2.8
To gain information (v)	30.8	20.2
To gain information (v & a)	6.4	4.9
live language directed to child	4.3	4.0
live language overheard by child	1.4	0.8
mechanical language	0.7	0.0
Sesame Street	0.0	0.0
Nontask	12.2	11.8
To pass time	8.7	8.7
To find something to do	0.2	0.2
To prepare for an activity	2.2	2.1
To construct a product	0.0	0.0
To choose	0.0	0.0
To procure an object	3.3	2.2
To engage in large muscle activity	0.0	0.2
To gain pleasure	0.7	0.9
To imitate	0.1	1.7
To pretend (role play)	0.0	1.6
To ease discomfort	0.2	1.2
To restore order	1.2	0.7
To relieve oneself	0.0	0.0
To dress/undress	0.0	0.0
To operate a mechanism	0.1	0.3
To explore	17.0	2.5
To improve a developing skill (mastery)	5.7	14.3
gross	4.5	7.7
fine	1.2	5.7
verbal	0.0	0.9
To eat and gain information (v)	0.6	0.3
To eat and gain information (v & a)	0.0	0.0
live language directed to child	0.0	0.0
overheard	0.0	0.0

SUBJECT #20

Subject #20 is a one-year-old SES Level II predicted A girl. She has a 3-year-old sister and a 4½-year-old brother. The family owns their own home in a suburban area, but they have moved twice in the duration of the study.

S is a chubby little girl whose motor development was slow. She is growing up in a household devoted to supplying children with interesting things to do. The playroom is a beautifully stocked room, better equipped than many nursery schools. There are many materials that invite exploration—e.g., a large rack of wooden formboard puzzles, blocks of many types, mechanical toys, a large collection of sewing materials suitable for young children, a large collection of picture books. In addition, S's mother spontaneously takes part in many of S's activities, frequently explaining, expanding, naming, or counting for S.

Summary of Test Scores

Subject #20   Group: One-Year-Old Starters (n = 19)

Tests	Age at Testing (Months)	Score	Group Median
Bayley Mental Developmental Index	12	134	103
	24	132	112
Stanford-Binet IQ	36	142	113
WPPSI IQ	60	149	117.5
Language Test[1]	12	21	14
	15	24	16
	21	42	21
	24	39	36
	27	not tested	—
	30	54	43.5
	36	60	45
Abstract Abilities[2]	12	1	2
	15	2	2
	21	6	5
	24	7	6
	27	not tested	—
	30	7	7
	36	11	9
Discrimination Test[2]	12	3	1
	15	2	2
	21	3	3
	24	7	3.5
	27	not tested	—
	30	8	5
	36	8	8

[1] Scores in Months
[2] Scores in Level Achieved

APPENDIX A

SOCIAL COMPETENCE FOR SUBJECT 20

```
                              T
GAIN              O XXXXXXXXXXXXXXXXXXXXXXXXXXXXX
ADULT             O XXXXXXXXXXXXXXXXXXXXXXXXXXXXXXX
ATTENTION         O                T

                              T
USE               O XXXXXXXXXXXXXXXXXXXXXXXXXXXXXXXX
ADULT             O XXXXXXXXXXXXXXXXXXXXXXXXXXXXXXXXXXX
RESOURCE          O                            T

                     T
HOSTILITY,        O XXXXXXXXXXXXXXXXXXX
AFFECTION         O XXXXXXXXXXXXXXXXXXXXX
TO ADULT          O        T

                 T
ROLE PLAY     O
              O
                 T

                 T
PRIDE IN      O XXXXXXX
PRODUCT       O XXXXXX
                 T

COMPETES      O        T
WITH          O
PEER          O   T

HOSTILITY,    O   T
AFFECTION     O
TO PEER       O
                  T

LEADS AND     O   T
FOLLOWS       O
PEER          O
                 T

              0   1   2   3   4   5   6   7   8   9   10
```

	TOTAL SCORES FOR S 20	MEDIANS AT 12/15 MONTHS FOR ALL SUBJECTS
ADULT COMPETENCE	29.4	13.8
PEER COMPETENCE	0.0	9.0
OVERALL COMPETENCE	29.4	20.5

T INDICATES THE MEDIAN FOR ALL SUBJECTS FOR EACH COMPETENCE FACTOR.

SOCIAL COMPETENCE FOR SUBJECT 20

```
                              T
GAIN              O XXXXXXXXXXXXXXXXXX
ADULT             O XXXXXXXXXXXXXXXXXXXX
ATTENTION         O    T

                                                          T
USE               O XXXXXXXXXXXXXXXXXXXXXXXXXXXXXXXXXXXXXXXXXXXXX
ADULT             O XXXXXXXXXXXXXXXXXXXXXXXXXXXXXXXXXXXXXXXXXXXXXXX
RESOURCE          O                                 T

                              T
HOSTILITY,        O XXXXXXXXXXXXXXXXXXXXX
AFFECTION         O XXXXXXXXXXXXXXXXXXXXX
TO ADULT          O            T

                 T
ROLE PLAY     O XXXXXXXXXXX
              O XXXXXXXXXX
              O            T

              T
PRIDE IN      O
PRODUCT       O
              O
              T

COMPETES      O                      T
WITH          O XXX
PEER          O XXX
              O       T

HOSTILITY,    O                          T
AFFECTION     O XXXXXXXXXXXXXXXXXXXXXX
TO PEER       O XXXXXXXXXXXXXXXXXXXXXX
              O                    T

LEADS AND     O                            T
FOLLOWS       O XXXXXXXXXXXXXXXXXXXXXXXXXXXXXXXXXXXXXXXXX
PEER          O XXXXXXXXXXXXXXXXXXXXXXXXXXXXXXXXXXXXXXXXX
              O

              0   1   2   3   4   5   6   7   8   9   10
```

	TOTAL SCORES FOR S 20	MEDIANS AT 18/21 MONTHS FOR ALL SUBJECTS
ADULT COMPETENCE	27.6	22.2
PEER COMPETENCE	15.1	13.5
OVERALL COMPETENCE	42.7	23.5

T INDICATES THE MEDIAN FOR ALL SUBJECTS FOR EACH COMPETENCE FACTOR.

SOCIAL COMPETENCE FOR SUBJECT 20

```
GAIN            O                      T
ADULT           OXXXXXXXXXXXXXXXXXXXXX
ATTENTION       OXXXXXXXXXXXXXXXXXXXXX
                O                      T
-------------------------------------------------------------------
USE             O                T
ADULT           OXXXXXXXXXXXXXXXXXX
RESOURCE        OXXXXXXXXXXXXXXXXXX
                O                T
-------------------------------------------------------------------
HOSTILITY,      O           T
AFFECTION       OXXXXXXXXXXXXX
TO ADULT        OXXXXXXXXXXXXX
                O            T
-------------------------------------------------------------------
                O     T
ROLE PLAY       OXXXXXXXXXXXXXXXXXXXXXXXXXXXXXXXXXXXXXXXXXXXXXXXXXX
                OXXXXXXXXXXXXXXXXXXXXXXXXXXXXXXXXXXXXXXXXXXXXXXXXXX
                O     T
-------------------------------------------------------------------
                O   T
PRIDE IN        OXXXXXXXXXXXXXXXXXX
PRODUCT         OXXXXXXXXXXXXXXXXXX
                O   T
-------------------------------------------------------------------
COMPETES        O                            T
WITH            O
PEER            O
                O                              T
-------------------------------------------------------------------
HOSTILITY,      O               T
AFFECTION       O
TO PEER         O
                O                T
-------------------------------------------------------------------
LEADS AND       O         T
FOLLOWS         O
PEER            O
                O           T
-------------------------------------------------------------------
                0   1   2   3   4   5   6   7   8   9   10
```

	TOTAL SCORES FOR S 20	MEDIANS FOR 30/33 ONE YEAR STARTER CHILD. FOR ALL SUBJECTS
ADULT COMPETENCE	36.6	26.0
PEER COMPETENCE	0.0	12.2
OVERALL COMPETENCE	36.6	33.6

T INDICATES THE MEDIAN FOR ALL SUBJECTS FOR EACH COMPETENCE FACTOR.

Subject #20

Social Tasks	% Duration	
	12-15 Months	18-21 Months
To please	0.2	0.5
To cooperate	2.9	6.4
To gain approval	0.0	1.5
To procure a service	2.6	1.4
To gain attention	3.3	3.9
To maintain social contact	4.8	1.3
To avoid unpleasant circumstances	0.0	0.3
To annoy	0.0	0.0
To direct	0.0	0.7
To assert self (protect domain)	0.2	0.1
To provide information	0.0	0.3
To compete	0.0	0.0
To reject overtures	0.0	0.0
To enjoy pets	0.7	0.0
To converse	0.0	1.3
To produce verbalizations	0.0	0.0
Nonsocial Tasks		
To eat	3.1	3.0
To gain information (v)	34.3	15.7
To gain information (v & a)	12.5	13.4
live language directed to child	9.9	4.9
live language overheard by child	2.6	6.9
mechanical language	0.0	0.0
Sesame Street	0.0	0.0
Nontask	8.2	10.8
To pass time	1.6	7.7
To find something to do	0.0	0.2
To prepare for an activity	1.5	2.6
To construct a product	0.0	0.7
To choose	0.0	0.6
To procure an object	0.6	3.4
To engage in large muscle activity	0.0	0.2
To gain pleasure	3.2	0.0
To imitate	0.1	0.1
To pretend (role play)	0.0	1.8
To ease discomfort	1.4	0.5
To restore order	0.8	0.8
To relieve oneself	0.0	0.0
To dress/undress	0.0	0.5
To operate a mechanism	0.0	0.2
To explore	8.2	3.0
To improve a developing skill (mastery)	4.1	12.4
gross	1.9	1.3
fine	2.2	3.9
verbal	0.0	7.2
To eat and gain information (v)	4.8	0.9
To eat and gain information (v & a)	0.7	1.4
live language directed to child	0.8	0.2
overheard	0.0	1.2

SUBJECT #21

Subject #21 is a two-year-old SES Level I predicted A boy. The family lives in a lovely, spacious home with well-kept grounds. Both parents are college graduates, and the father has advanced degrees. The mother, a busy, energetic woman, spends most of her time with her children.

The child is a handsome, alert little boy who spends most mornings at home with his mother, while his four-year-old brother attends nursery school. There are many toys, books, and puzzles for him to play with, and he is usually busy with them. He has a playroom, but he usually plays in the general vicinity of his mother as she goes from room to room doing her chores. She is easily available to him and is often heard answering his questions or explaining something to him.

The child has access to all the rooms in the house but is not allowed to go outside unless someone is with him.

Summary of Test Scores

Subject #21   Group: Two-Year-Old Starters (n = 20)

Tests	Age at Testing (Months)	Score	Group Median
Bayley Mental Development Index	12 24	— 111	— 101
Stanford-Binet IQ	36	131	117.5
WPPSI IQ	60	134	111
Language Test[1]	12	—	—
	15	—	—
	21	—	—
	24	36	30
	27	51	36
	30	51	40.5
	36	60	—
Abstract Abilities[2]	12	—	—
	15	—	—
	21	—	—
	24	7	5.5
	27	7	6
	30	7	6.5
	36	10	—
Discrimination Test[2]	12	—	—
	15	—	—
	21	—	—
	24	3.0	3.0
	27	7.0	3.0
	30	8.0	6.0
	36	8.0	—

[1] Scores in Months
[2] Scores in Level Achieved

Individual Subject Data   285

SOCIAL COMPETENCE FOR SUBJECT 21

```
                              T
GAIN         OXXXXXXXXXXXXXXX
ADULT        OXXXXXXXXXXXXXX
ATTENTION    O                    T
             ---------------------------------------------
             O                       T
USE          OXXXXXXXXXXXXXXXXXXXXXXXXXXXXXX
ADULT        OXXXXXXXXXXXXXXXXXXXXXXXXXXXX
RESOURCE     O                           T
             ---------------------------------------------
             O                T
HOSTILITY,   OXXXXXXXXXXXXXXXXXX
AFFECTION    OXXXXXXXXXXXXXXX
TO ADULT     O         T
             ---------------------------------------------
             T
ROLE PLAY    OXXXXXXXXXXXX
             UXXXXXXXXXXX
             T
             ---------------------------------------------
             T
PRIDE IN     O
PRODUCT      O
             T
             ---------------------------------------------
             O  T
COMPETES     OXXXXXXXX
WITH         OXXXXXXX
PEER         O  T
             ---------------------------------------------
             O           T
HOSTILITY,   OXXXXXXXXXXXXXXXXXXXXXXXXX
AFFECTION    OXXXXXXXXXXXXXXXXXXXXXXXX
TO PEER      O        T
             ---------------------------------------------
             O                    T
LEADS AND    OXXXXXXXXXXXXXXXXXXXXXXXXXXX
FOLLOWS      OXXXXXXXXXXXXXXXXXXXXXXXXXX
PEER         O              T
             ---------------------------------------------
             0   1   2   3   4   5   6   7   8   9   10
```

	TOTAL SCORES FOR S 21	MEDIANS FOR 24/27 TWO YEAR STARTER CHILD. FOR ALL SUBJECTS
ADULT COMPETENCE	23.7	23.2
PEER COMPETENCE	11.9	5.1
OVERALL COMPETENCE	35.7	28.6

T INDICATES THE MEDIAN FOR ALL SUBJECTS FOR EACH COMPETENCE FACTOR.

SOCIAL COMPETENCE FOR SUBJECT 21

```
             O                    T
GAIN         OXXXXXXXXXXXXXX
ADULT        OXXXXXXXXXXXXXX
ATTENTION    O                  T
             ---------------------------------------------
             O                                  T
USE          OXXXXXXXXXXXXXXXXXXXXXXXXXXXXXXXXXXXXXXXXXXXXX
ADULT        OXXXXXXXXXXXXXXXXXXXXXXXXXXXXXXXXXXXXXXXXXXXXX
RESOURCE     O                         T
             ---------------------------------------------
             O           T
HOSTILITY,   O
AFFECTION    O
TO ADULT     O                   T
             ---------------------------------------------
             T
ROLE PLAY    O           T
             O
             T
             ---------------------------------------------
             O                     T
PRIDE IN     OXXXXXXXXXXXXXXXXXXXXX
PRODUCT      OXXXXXXXXXXXXXXXXXXXX
             O                      T
             ---------------------------------------------
             O    T
COMPETES     O
WITH         O
PEER         O    T
             ---------------------------------------------
             O                  T
HOSTILITY,   O
AFFECTION    O
TO PEER      O          T
             ---------------------------------------------
             O
LEADS AND    O                T
FOLLOWS      O
PEER         O
             ---------------------------------------------
             0   1   2   3   4   5   6   7   8   9   10
```

	TOTAL SCORES FOR S 21	MEDIANS FOR 30/33 TWO YEAR STARTER CHILD. FOR ALL SUBJECTS
ADULT COMPETENCE	21.5	24.0
PEER COMPETENCE	0.0	11.9
OVERALL COMPETENCE	21.5	28.9

T INDICATES THE MEDIAN FOR ALL SUBJECTS FOR EACH COMPETENCE FACTOR.

Subject #21

Social Tasks	% Duration	
	24-27 Months	30-33 Months
To please	0.6	0.1
To cooperate	6.7	6.5
To gain approval	1.0	0.0
To procure a service	2.4	1.4
To gain attention	1.7	1.3
To maintain social contact	5.9	2.6
To avoid unpleasant circumstances	0.0	0.0
To annoy	0.0	0.0
To direct	0.3	0.8
To assert self (protect domain)	1.0	0.9
To provide information	0.2	1.9
To compete	0.0	0.7
To reject overtures	0.0	0.0
To enjoy pets	0.0	0.0
To converse	1.1	5.9
To produce verbalizations	0.0	0.0
Nonsocial Tasks		
To eat	2.1	11.0
To gain information (v)	17.6	6.4
To gain information (v & a)	6.5	12.8
live language directed to child	5.8	9.4
live language overheard by child	0.7	2.7
mechanical language	0.0	0.0
Sesame Street	0.0	0.0
Nontask	6.5	5.3
To pass time	1.4	2.6
To find something to do	0.2	0.0
To prepare for an activity	1.8	4.6
To construct a product	2.5	0.0
To choose	0.0	0.5
To procure an object	1.4	1.6
To engage in large muscle activity	0.2	0.1
To gain pleasure	1.4	0.0
To imitate	2.9	1.7
To pretend (role play)	1.3	4.4
To ease discomfort	0.7	0.0
To restore order	0.7	3.5
To relieve oneself	0.0	0.0
To dress/undress	0.0	1.7
To operate a mechanism	0.8	0.0
To explore	4.2	3.8
To improve a developing skill (mastery)	23.2	9.0
gross	10.9	2.8
fine	6.9	5.7
verbal	4.8	0.5
To eat and gain information (v)	0.4	2.9
To eat and gain information (v & a)	0.2	3.7
live language directed to child	0.3	1.2
overheard	0.0	2.6

SUBJECT #22

Subject #22 is a two-year-old SES Level III predicted A girl. She is an attractive child who appears extremely capable. She is the youngest of three girls (ages 5½, 3, and 2) in a father-absent home. The family lives with relatives in a fairly comfortable seven-room house in a semiresidential area. The mother, who has completed one and a half years of college, takes care of the children during the day and has a job as a waitress in the evenings.

The general atmosphere in this home is warm and loving but not particularly child-centered. The mother encourages independence, although she will suggest activities for her daughter. The child has access to the whole house and is allowed to go out and play by herself with the neighborhood children.

Summary of Test Scores

Subject #22   Group: Two-Year-Old Starters (n = 20)

Tests	Age at Testing (Months)	Score	Group Median
Bayley Mental Development Index	12	—	—
	24	140	101
Stanford-Binet IQ	36	134	117.5
WPPSI IQ	60	not tested	111
Language Test[1]	12	—	—
	15	—	—
	21	—	—
	24	39	30
	27	48	36
	30	51	40.5
	36	60	—
Abstract Abilities[2]	12	—	—
	15	—	—
	21	—	—
	24	6	5.5
	27	7	6
	30	7	6.5
	36	11	—
Discrimination Test[2]	12	—	—
	15	—	—
	21	—	—
	24	3.0	3.0
	27	5.0	3.0
	30	8.0	6.0
	36	8.0	—

[1] Scores in Months
[2] Scores in Level Achieved

Individual Subject Data 289

SOCIAL COMPETENCE FOR SUBJECT 22

```
                              T
GAIN             OXXXXXXXXXXXXXXXXX
ADULT            OXXXXXXXXXXXXXXXXX
ATTENTION        O                 T
-----------------------------------------
                              T
USE              OXXXXXXXXXXXXXXXXXXXXX
ADULT            OXXXXXXXXXXXXXXXXXXXXX
RESOURCE         O                     T
-----------------------------------------
                   T
HOSTILITY,       OXXXXXXXXXXXXXXXXX
AFFECTION        OXXXXXXXXXXXXXXXXX
TO ADULT         O                T
-----------------------------------------
                 T
RULE PLAY        OXXXXXXXXXXXXXXXXXXXXXXXXXXXXXXXXXXXXXXXX
                 OXXXXXXXXXXXXXXXXXXXXXXXXXXXXXXXXXXXXXXXX
                 T
-----------------------------------------
                 T
PRIDE IN         OXXXXXXXXXXXXXXXXXXXXXXXXXXXXXXXXXXX
PRODUCT          OXXXXXXXXXXXXXXXXXXXXXXXXXXXXXXXXXXX
                 T
-----------------------------------------
COMPETES         O   T
WITH             OXX
PEER             OXX
                 O   T
-----------------------------------------
HOSTILITY,       O      T
AFFECTION        OXXXXXXXXXXXXXXXXX
TO PEER          OXXXXXXXXXXXXXXXXX
                 O      T
-----------------------------------------
                 O  T
LEADS AND        OXXXXXXXXXXXXXXXXX
FOLLOWS          OXXXXXXXXXXXXXXXXX
PEER             O  T
-----------------------------------------
                 0  1  2  3  4  5  6  7  8  9  10
```

	TOTAL SCORES FOR S 22	MEDIANS FOR 24/27 TWO YEAR STARTER CHILD. FOR ALL SUBJECTS
ADULT COMPETENCE	44.4	23.2
PEER COMPETENCE	4.1	5.1
OVERALL COMPETENCE	48.5	28.6

T INDICATES THE MEDIAN FOR ALL SUBJECTS FOR EACH COMPETENCE FACTOR.

SOCIAL COMPETENCE FOR SUBJECT 22

```
                              T
GAIN             OXXXXXXXXXXXXXXXXXXXXXXXXXXX
ADULT            OXXXXXXXXXXXXXXXXXXXXXXXXXXX
ATTENTION        O                          T
-----------------------------------------
                 O          T
USE              OXXXXXXXXXXX
ADULT            OXXXXXXXXXXX
RESOURCE         O          T
-----------------------------------------
HOSTILITY,       O
AFFECTION        OXXXXXXXXX
TO ADULT         OXXXXXXXXX
                 O         T
-----------------------------------------
                 T
RULE PLAY        O
                 O
                 T
-----------------------------------------
                 O          T
PRIDE IN         OXXXXXXXXXXXXXXXXXXXXXXXXX
PRODUCT          OXXXXXXXXXXXXXXXXXXXXXXXXX
                 O          T
-----------------------------------------
COMPETES         O   T
WITH             OXXX
PEER             OXXX
                 O   T
-----------------------------------------
HOSTILITY,       O         T
AFFECTION        OXXXXXXXX
TO PEER          OXXXXXXXX
                 O         T
-----------------------------------------
                 O   T
LEADS AND        OXXXXXX
FOLLOWS          OXXXXXX
PEER             O   T
-----------------------------------------
                 0  1  2  3  4  5  6  7  8  9  10
```

	TOTAL SCORES FOR S 22	MEDIANS FOR 30/33 TWO YEAR STARTER CHILD. FOR ALL SUBJECTS
ADULT COMPETENCE	25.0	24.0
PEER COMPETENCE	3.3	11.9
OVERALL COMPETENCE	28.4	28.9

T INDICATES THE MEDIAN FOR ALL SUBJECTS FOR EACH COMPETENCE FACTOR.

Subject #22

Social Tasks	% Duration	
	24-27 Months	30-33 Months
To please	0.2	0.1
To cooperate	6.3	2.7
To gain approval	0.0	0.6
To procure a service	1.9	0.9
To gain attention	3.0	0.3
To maintain social contact	3.4	1.1
To avoid unpleasant circumstances	0.0	0.5
To annoy	0.0	0.0
To direct	0.1	1.8
To assert self (protect domain)	1.1	0.1
To provide information	0.7	0.6
To compete	0.0	0.0
To reject overtures	0.0	0.0
To enjoy pets	0.0	0.0
To converse	0.4	0.3
To produce verbalizations	0.0	0.0
Nonsocial Tasks		
To eat	9.6	8.8
To gain information (v)	20.3	7.2
To gain information (v & a)	9.4	32.6
live language directed to child	5.1	3.3
live language overheard by child	2.9	2.1
mechanical language	0.0	0.2
Sesame Street	0.0	24.2
Nontask	6.4	5.1
To pass time	10.6	0.6
To find something to do	0.0	0.0
To prepare for an activity	2.7	2.6
To construct a product	0.0	1.9
To choose	0.0	0.0
To procure an object	1.3	4.7
To engage in large muscle activity	0.2	0.0
To gain pleasure	2.6	2.0
To imitate	1.2	0.2
To pretend (role play)	0.2	0.0
To ease discomfort	0.4	0.1
To restore order	1.0	1.4
To relieve oneself	0.8	0.0
To dress/undress	0.0	0.5
To operate a mechanism	0.2	0.2
To explore	7.2	2.2
To improve a developing skill (mastery)	2.4	13.3
gross	1.3	1.9
fine	1.1	10.9
verbal	0.0	0.5
To eat and gain information (v)	2.1	0.8
To eat and gain information (v & a)	1.3	4.3
live language directed to child	1.4	0.1
overheard	0.0	4.0

SUBJECT #24

Subject #24 is a one-year-old SES Level I predicted A boy. The family lives in a large, comfortable house in a prosperous suburban area. S has three older siblings ranging in age from three to eight. Both parents are physicians, but at present the mother is not practicing.

S's mother is a warm, energetic woman who is usually busy with household chores. Although the household is loosely organized from the adult point of view, for a child it is a lovely place to grow up. Every room on the first floor contains play equipment suitable to S's level of development. A hardwood ramp in the living room, propped against a table, is a challenge to climb on. Blocks and a well-stocked toy shelf in the dining room invite exploration. There are a variety of challenging toys in the kitchen (boxes with different-shaped holes for different-shaped objects; stacking toys; mechanical toys that require dexterity to operate). There is also a playpen in the kitchen that is full of toys, but S usually plays on the floor.

Subject #24 is a friendly child who goes about his business slowly and with deliberation. Once he starts to do something, he rarely gives up. He responds with great interest to his environment (his mastery score is the highest of all one-year-olds). His mother does not spend a lot of time in didactic type of interaction with him, but she is tuned in to the type of activities and materials that interest him. She invites exploratory behavior such as finding out what's inside the kitchen cabinets or playing with water and dishes in the kitchen sink. When S tries very hard to do something and runs into trouble, he receives ready attention and help from his mother, whether he needs assistance with a torn paper bag or with folding a paper bag and putting it away in the proper cupboard or with unfolding the paper liner from a box of animal crackers. Childish enterprises that might appear meaningless or inconsequential to many busy mothers receive ready support from this mother.

Summary of Test Scores

Subject #24   Group: One-Year-Old Starters (n = 19)

Tests	Age at Testing (Months)	Score	Group Median
Bayley Mental Developmental Index	12	107	103
	24	116	112
Stanford-Binet IQ	36	118	113
WPPSI IQ	60	123	117.5
Language Test[1]	12	10	14
	15	18	16
	21	24	21
	24	36	36
	27	not tested	—
	30	42	43.5
	36	51	45
Abstract Abilities[2]	12	2	2
	15	3	2
	21	6	5
	24	6	6
	27	not tested	—
	30	6	7
	36	10	9
Discrimination Test[2]	12	0	1
	15	2	2
	21	2	3
	24	3.5	3.5
	27	not tested	—
	30	7	5
	36	8	8

[1] Scores in Months
[2] Scores in Level Achieved

Individual Subject Data

SOCIAL COMPETENCE FOR SUBJECT 24

```
                              T
GAIN            OXXXXXXXXXXXXXXXXXXXXXXXXXXXXX
ADULT           OXXXXXXXXXXXXXXXXXXXXXXXXXXXXX
ATTENTION       O                T
                |
                              T
USE             OXXXXXXXXXXXXXXXXXXXXXXX
ADULT           OXXXXXXXXXXXXXXXXXXXXXX
RESOURCE        O       T
                |
                 T
HOSTILITY,      OXXXXXXXXXXX
AFFECTION       OXXXXXXXXXX
TO ADULT        O  T
                |
                T
ROLE PLAY       OXXXXXXXXXXXXXXXXXXXXXXXXXXXXXXXXXXXXXXXXXXXXXX
                OXXXXXXXXXXXXXXXXXXXXXXXXXXXXXXXXXXXXXXXXXXXXXX
                T
                |
                T
PRIDE IN        OXXXXXXXXXXXXXXXXXXXXXXXXXXXXXXXXXXXXXXXXXXXXXX
PRODUCT         OXXXXXXXXXXXXXXXXXXXXXXXXXXXXXXXXXXXXXXXXXXXXXX
                T
                |
COMPETES        O        T
WITH            O
PEER            O        T
                |
HOSTILITY,      O   T
AFFECTION       O
TO PEER         O       T
                |
LEADS AND       O   T
FOLLOWS         O
PEER            O   T
                |
                0---1---2---3---4---5---6---7---8---9---10

                TOTAL SCORES    MEDIANS AT 12/15 MONTHS
                  FOR S 24.        FOR ALL SUBJECTS

ADULT COMPETENCE      47.9              13.8
PEER COMPETENCE        0.0               9.0
OVERALL COMPETENCE    47.9              20.5
```

T INDICATES THE MEDIAN FOR ALL SUBJECTS FOR EACH COMPETENCE FACTOR.

SOCIAL COMPETENCE FOR SUBJECT 24

```
                      T
GAIN            OXXXXXXXXXX
ADULT           OXXXXXXXXXX
ATTENTION       O         T
                |
                                    T
USE             OXXXXXXXXXXXXXXXXXXXXXXXXXXXXXXXXXX
ADULT           OXXXXXXXXXXXXXXXXXXXXXXXXXXXXXXXXXX
RESOURCE        O                       T
                |
                       T
HOSTILITY,      OXXXXXXXXXXXXXX
AFFECTION       OXXXXXXXXXXXXXX
TO ADULT        O      T
                |
                  T
ROLE PLAY       OXXXXXX
                OXXXXXX
                O      T
                |
                T
PRIDE IN        OXXXXX
PRODUCT         OXXXXX
                T
                |
COMPETES        O               T
WITH            O
PEER            O               T
                |
HOSTILITY,      O           T
AFFECTION       O
TO PEER         O           T
                |
LEADS AND       O    T
FOLLOWS         O
PEER            O    T
                |
                0---1---2---3---4---5---6---7---8---9---10

                TOTAL SCORES    MEDIANS AT 18/21 MONTHS
                  FOR S 24         FOR ALL SUBJECTS

ADULT COMPETENCE      22.9              22.2
PEER COMPETENCE        0.0              13.5
OVERALL COMPETENCE    22.9              23.5
```

T INDICATES THE MEDIAN FOR ALL SUBJECTS FOR EACH COMPETENCE FACTOR.

APPENDIX A

SOCIAL COMPETENCE FOR SUBJECT 24

```
                          0                        T
GAIN          0XXXXXXXXXXXXXXXXXXXXXXXXXXXXXXXXXXXXXXXXXXXXX
ADULT         0XXXXXXXXXXXXXXXXXXXXXXXXXXXXXXXXXXXXXXXXXXXX
ATTENTION
                          0                    T
----------------------------------------------------------------
              0            T
USE           0XXXXXXXXXXXXXXXXXXXXXXXXXXXXXXXXXXXXXXXX
ADULT         0XXXXXXXXXXXXXXXXXXXXXXXXXXXXXXXXXXXXXX
RESOURCE
              0                T
----------------------------------------------------------------
HOSTILITY,    0            T
AFFECTION     0XXXXXXXXXXXXXXXXXXXXXXXXXXXXXXX
TO ADULT      0XXXXXXXXXXXXXXXXXXXXXXXXXXXXXXX
              0        T
----------------------------------------------------------------
              0        T
ROLE PLAY     0XXXXXXX
              0XXXXXXX
              0    T
----------------------------------------------------------------
              0    T
PRIDE IN      0XXXXXXXXXXXXXXXXXXXXXXXXXXXXXXXXXXXXXXXXXXXXXXXX
PRODUCT       0XXXXXXXXXXXXXXXXXXXXXXXXXXXXXXXXXXXXXXXXXXXXXXXX
              0    T
----------------------------------------------------------------
COMPETES      0                                T
WITH          0
PEER          0
              0                                    T
----------------------------------------------------------------
HOSTILITY,    0                    T
AFFECTION     0
TO PEER       0
              0                T
----------------------------------------------------------------
LEADS AND     0        T
FOLLOWS       0
PEER          0
              0    T
----------------------------------------------------------------
              0   1   2   3   4   5   6   7   8   9   10
```

	TOTAL SCORES FOR S 24	MEDIANS FOR 30/33 ONE YEAR STARTER CHILD. FOR ALL SUBJECTS
ADULT COMPETENCE	45.7	26.0
PEER COMPETENCE	0.0	12.2
OVERALL COMPETENCE	45.7	33.6

T INDICATES THE MEDIAN FOR ALL SUBJECTS FOR EACH COMPETENCE FACTOR.

Subject #24

	% Duration	
Social Tasks	12-15 Months	18-21 Months
To please	0.3	0.0
To cooperate	2.1	5.2
To gain approval	0.0	0.4
To procure a service	1.2	3.8
To gain attention	2.2	1.8
To maintain social contact	1.7	2.5
To avoid unpleasant circumstances	0.0	0.0
To annoy	0.1	0.0
To direct	0.0	0.0
To assert self (protect domain)	0.6	0.6
To provide information	0.0	0.4
To compete	0.0	0.0
To reject overtures	0.0	0.0
To enjoy pets	0.0	0.0
To converse	0.0	0.0
To produce verbalizations	0.0	0.0
Nonsocial Tasks		
To eat	4.7	8.8
To gain information (v)	14.4	10.6
To gain information (v & a)	5.8	2.3
live language directed to child	4.9	1.1
live language overheard by child	0.1	1.2
mechanical language	0.9	0.0
Sesame Street	0.0	0.0
Nontask	12.5	6.4
To pass time	0.5	4.1
To find something to do	0.3	0.0
To prepare for an activity	2.6	3.5
To construct a product	0.0	0.0
To choose	0.0	0.0
To procure an object	4.1	2.8
To engage in large muscle activity	0.0	0.0
To gain pleasure	0.0	0.0
To imitate	0.2	0.5
To pretend (role play)	0.0	0.0
To ease discomfort	0.5	0.3
To restore order	0.8	1.0
To relieve oneself	0.0	0.0
To dress/undress	0.0	0.0
To operate a mechanism	1.1	1.2
To explore	17.3	10.4
To improve a developing skill (mastery)	16.0	25.5
gross	9.5	2.5
fine	6.5	23.0
verbal	0.0	0.0
To eat and gain information (v)	8.1	4.5
To eat and gain information (v & a)	0.5	0.0
live language directed to child	0.6	0.1
overheard	0.0	0.0

SUBJECT #25

Subject #25 is a two-year-old SES Level IV predicted C boy. S has an older brother, age seven. The family lives in a sparsely furnished apartment in an urban area.

S is a very active, difficult child, and his mother is extremely ineffective in disciplining or redirecting S. There are few appropriate toys or objects for S to play with. S has frequent temper tantrums and engages in a great deal of mischievous behavior that he knows will upset his mother.

S is frequently left in the care of young, inappropriate babysitters who are incapable of handling his behavior. The atmosphere of the home was often hectic. Physical disarray was the rule rather than the exception.

Summary of Test Scores

Subject #25 Group: Two-Year-Old Starters (n = 20)

Tests	Age at Testing (Months)	Score	Group Median
Bayley Mental Development Index	12	—	—
	24	84	101
Stanford-Binet IQ	36	117	117.5
WPPSI IQ	60	116	111
Language Test[1]	12	—	—
	15	—	—
	21	—	—
	24	30	30
	27	36	36
	30	36	40.5
	36	51	—
Abstract Abilities[2]	12	—	—
	15	—	—
	21	—	—
	24	<5	5.5
	27	6	6
	30	7	6.5
	36	7	—
Discrimination Test[2]	12	—	—
	15	—	—
	21	—	—
	24	2.0	3.0
	27	3.0	3.0
	30	3.0	6.0
	36	8.0	—

[1] Scores in Months
[2] Scores in Level Achieved

APPENDIX A

SOCIAL COMPETENCE FOR SUBJECT 25

```
                      0         T
GAIN                  OXXXXXXXXXXXXXXXXXXXX
ADULT                 OXXXXXXXXXXXXXXXXXXXX
ATTENTION             O                 T
                      |---|---|---|---|---|---|---|---|---|---|
                      0         T
USE                   OXXXXXXXXXXXXXXXXXX
ADULT                 OXXXXXXXXXXXXXXXXXX
RESOURCE              O                      T
                      |---|---|---|---|---|---|---|---|---|---|
                      O         T
HOSTILITY,            OXXXXXXX
AFFECTION             OXXXXXXX
TO ADULT              O   T
                      |---|---|---|---|---|---|---|---|---|---|
                      T
ROLE PLAY             OXXXXXXXXXXXXXXXXXXXXXXXXX
                      OXXXXXXXXXXXXXXXXXXXXXXXXXXXXXX
                      |---|---|---|---|---|---|---|---|---|---|
                      T
PRIDE IN              O
PRODUCT               O
                      O   T
                      |---|---|---|---|---|---|---|---|---|---|
                      O   T
COMPETES              OXXXXXXX
WITH                  OXXXXXXX
PEER                  O   T
                      |---|---|---|---|---|---|---|---|---|---|
                      O        T
HOSTILITY,            OXXXXXXXXX
AFFECTION             OXXXXXXXXX
TO PEER               O    T
                      |---|---|---|---|---|---|---|---|---|---|
                      O   T
LEADS AND             OXXXXXXXXX
FOLLOWS               OXXXXXXXXX
PEER                  O    T
                      |---|---|---|---|---|---|---|---|---|---|
                      0   1   2   3   4   5   6   7   8   9   10
```

	TOTAL SCORES FOR S 25	MEDIANS FOR 24/27 TWO YEAR STARTER CHILD. FOR ALL SUBJECTS
ADULT COMPETENCE	22.4	23.2
PEER COMPETENCE	5.1	5.1
OVERALL COMPETENCE	27.4	28.6

T INDICATES THE MEDIAN FOR ALL SUBJECTS FOR EACH COMPETENCE FACTOR.

SOCIAL COMPETENCE FOR SUBJECT 25

```
                      O         T
GAIN                  OXXXXXXXXXXXXXXXXXXXX
ADULT                 OXXXXXXXXXXXXXXXXXXXX
ATTENTION             O                 T
                      |---|---|---|---|---|---|---|---|---|---|
                      O         T
USE                   OXXXXXXXXXXXXXXXXXXXX
ADULT                 OXXXXXXXXXXXXXXXXXXXX
RESOURCE              O                 T
                      |---|---|---|---|---|---|---|---|---|---|
                      O         T
HOSTILITY,            OXXXXXXXXXX
AFFECTION             OXXXXXXXXXX
TO ADULT              O         T
                      |---|---|---|---|---|---|---|---|---|---|
                      T
ROLE PLAY             O
                      O   T
                      |---|---|---|---|---|---|---|---|---|---|
                      O
PRIDE IN              O
PRODUCT               O
                      |---|---|---|---|---|---|---|---|---|---|
                      O   T
COMPETES              O
WITH                  O
PEER                  O   T
                      |---|---|---|---|---|---|---|---|---|---|
                      O            T
HOSTILITY,            O
AFFECTION             O
TO PEER               O       T
                      |---|---|---|---|---|---|---|---|---|---|
                      O      T
LEADS AND             O
FOLLOWS               O
PEER                  O
                      |---|---|---|---|---|---|---|---|---|---|
                      0   1   2   3   4   5   6   7   8   9   10
```

	TOTAL SCORES FOR S 25	MEDIANS FOR 30/33 TWO YEAR STARTER CHILD. FOR ALL SUBJECTS
ADULT COMPETENCE	13.9	24.0
PEER COMPETENCE	0.0	11.9
OVERALL COMPETENCE	13.9	28.9

T INDICATES THE MEDIAN FOR ALL SUBJECTS FOR EACH COMPETENCE FACTOR.

Subject #25

Social Tasks	% Duration	
	24-27 Months	30-33 Months
To please	0.5	0.0
To cooperate	3.7	4.0
To gain approval	0.0	0.8
To procure a service	2.4	4.4
To gain attention	3.9	3.3
To maintain social contact	6.2	1.5
To avoid unpleasant circumstances	0.1	0.0
To annoy	2.0	1.3
To direct	0.8	0.3
To assert self (protect domain)	2.1	1.3
To provide information	0.4	0.8
To compete	0.0	0.0
To reject overtures	1.7	0.1
To enjoy pets	0.0	0.0
To converse	0.0	2.4
To produce verbalizations	0.0	0.2
Nonsocial Tasks		
To eat	2.4	1.0
To gain information (v)	16.5	4.8
To gain information (v & a)	9.8	26.8
live language directed to child	3.1	3.1
live language overheard by child	1.8	1.8
mechanical language	10.5	10.5
Sesame Street	11.5	11.5
Nontask	11.2	7.2
To pass time	7.8	0.1
To find something to do	0.3	0.2
To prepare for an activity	1.3	3.7
To construct a product	0.0	5.6
To choose	0.0	0.0
To procure an object	2.1	5.5
To engage in large muscle activity	0.5	0.0
To gain pleasure	0.0	0.5
To imitate	0.1	0.0
To pretend (role play)	0.1	2.6
To ease discomfort	0.7	0.7
To restore order	0.5	0.9
To relieve oneself	0.0	0.3
To dress/undress	0.3	0.0
To operate a mechanism	0.2	1.2
To explore	12.2	5.4
To improve a developing skill (mastery)	6.9	11.4
gross	1.6	5.0
fine	5.3	6.1
verbal	0.0	0.3
To eat and gain information (v)	1.0	0.0
To eat and gain information (v & a)	0.3	0.8
live language directed to child	0.3	0.0
overheard	0.0	0.0

SUBJECT #27

Subject #27 is a two-year-old SES Level III predicted C boy who is the youngest of three children. His parents are divorced, and he lives with his mother and two sisters in a sizable but somewhat run-down two-family house on a dead-end street. The child is allowed access to all parts of the house and is allowed to go outside to play by himself. There are many toys available both inside and outside the house, although they are usually broken or missing some essential part. S is left unsupervised for long periods, during which time he may be playing, watching other children, or interacting with his sisters. His mother sporadically displays some interest in the child and occasionally speaks to him, but her reactions are erratic and unpredictable, and her moods are likely to shift markedly in the space of a short time.

Summary of Test Scores

Subject #27   **Group: Two-Year-Old Starters (n = 20)**

Tests	Age at Testing (Months)	Score	Group Median
Bayley Mental Development Index	12	—	—
	24	88	101
Stanford-Binet IQ	36	88	117.5
WPPSI IQ	60	99	111
Language Test[1]	12	—	—
	15	—	—
	21	—	—
	24	18	30
	27	30	36
	30	27	40.5
	36	39	—
Abstract Abilities[2]	12	—	—
	15	—	—
	21	—	—
	24	<5	5.5
	27	<5	6
	30	5	6.5
	36	8	—
Discrimination Test[2]	12	—	—
	15	—	—
	21	—	—
	24	2.0	3.0
	27	2.0	3.0
	30	3.5	6.0
	36	3.5	—

[1] Scores in Months
[2] Scores in Level Achieved

302 APPENDIX A

SOCIAL COMPETENCE FOR SUBJECT 27

```
                    0
GAIN                OXXXXXXXXXXXXXXXX      T
ADULT               OXXXXXXXXXXXXXXXX  T
ATTENTION           O

                    0
USE                 OXXXXXXXXXXXX          T
ADULT               OXXXXXXXXXXXX    T
RESOURCE            O

                    0
HOSTILITY,          OXXXXXXXXXXXX     T
AFFECTION           OXXXXXXXXXXXX         T
TO ADULT            O

                    T
ROLE PLAY           OXXXXXXXXXXX
                    OXXXXXXXXXXX
                    T

                    T
PRIDE IN            O
PRODUCT             O
                    T

                    O    T
COMPETES            OXXXXXXXXXXX
WITH                OXXXXXXXXXXX
PEER                O   T

                    O    T
HOSTILITY           OXXXXXX
AFFECTION           OXXXXXX
TO PEER             O     T

                    O       T
LEADS AND           OXXXX
FOLLOWS             OXXXX
PEER                O    T

                    0  1  2  3  4  5  6  7  8  9  10
```

	TOTAL SCORES FOR S 27	MEDIANS FOR 24/27 TWO YEAR STARTER CHILD. FOR ALL SUBJECTS
ADULT COMPETENCE	19.1	23.2
PEER COMPETENCE	4.3	5.1
OVERALL COMPETENCE	23.4	28.6

T INDICATES THE MEDIAN FOR ALL SUBJECTS FOR EACH COMPETENCE FACTOR.

SOCIAL COMPETENCE FOR SUBJECT 27

```
                    O                        T
GAIN                OXXXXX
ADULT               OXXXXX                T
ATTENTION           O

                    O
USE                 OX                       T
ADULT               OX                    T
RESOURCE            O

                    O                        T
HOSTILITY,          OXXXXXX
AFFECTION           OXXXXXX                T
TO ADULT            O

                    T
ROLE PLAY           O
                    O
                    T

                    O                         T
PRIDE IN            O
PRODUCT             O                      T

                    O    T
COMPETES            OXXXXXXXXXXXXXXXXXXXXXXXXXXXXXXXXXXXX
WITH                OXXXXXXXXXXXXXXXXXXXXXXXXXXXXXXXXXXXX
PEER                O    T

                    O                       T
HOSTILITY           OXXXXXXXXXXX
AFFECTION           OXXXXXXXXXXX                T
TO PEER             O

                    O        T
LEADS AND           OXXXXXXX
FOLLOWS             OXXXXXXX            T
PEER                O

                    0  1  2  3  4  5  6  7  8  9  10
```

	TOTAL SCORES FOR S 27	MEDIANS FOR 30/33 TWO YEAR STARTER CHILD. FOR ALL SUBJECTS
ADULT COMPETENCE	2.3	24.0
PEER COMPETENCE	12.6	11.9
OVERALL COMPETENCE	14.9	28.9

T INDICATES THE MEDIAN FOR ALL SUBJECTS FOR EACH COMPETENCE FACTOR.

Subject #27

Social Tasks	% Duration	
	24-27 Months	30-33 Months
To please	0.3	0.1
To cooperate	2.0	2.8
To gain approval	0.0	0.0
To procure a service	1.4	1.8
To gain attention	1.7	4.4
To maintain social contact	4.3	5.6
To avoid unpleasant circumstances	0.7	0.0
To annoy	0.4	0.4
To direct	0.0	0.0
To assert self (protect domain)	3.2	1.8
To provide information	0.0	0.0
To compete	0.0	0.6
To reject overtures	0.2	0.0
To enjoy pets	0.0	0.3
To converse	0.0	0.0
To produce verbalizations	0.0	0.0
Nonsocial Tasks		
To eat	1.6	3.3
To gain information (v)	13.7	17.6
To gain information (v & a)	2.1	7.4
live language directed to child	2.2	2.3
live language overheard by child	0.1	1.5
mechanical language	0.0	3.6
Sesame Street	0.0	0.0
Nontask	15.7	9.2
To pass time	0.1	0.7
To find something to do	0.0	0.1
To prepare for an activity	1.7	0.6
To construct a product	0.0	0.0
To choose	0.0	0.5
To procure an object	1.9	4.6
To engage in large muscle activity	4.9	0.0
To gain pleasure	0.0	0.0
To imitate	0.0	0.0
To pretend (role play)	1.6	2.6
To ease discomfort	0.6	1.1
To restore order	0.6	1.6
To relieve oneself	0.0	0.0
To dress/undress	0.7	0.3
To operate a mechanism	0.2	0.0
To explore	25.8	15.6
To improve a developing skill (mastery)	10.1	12.3
gross	8.8	1.2
fine	1.2	11.1
verbal	0.1	0.0
To eat and gain information (v)	1.3	1.1
To eat and gain information (v & a)	0.3	0.2
live language directed to child	0.4	0.2
overheard	0.0	0.0

SUBJECT #28

Subject #28 is a two-year-old SES Level III predicted C girl. She is the younger of two children. The family lives in a five-room upstairs apartment in a two-family house in a residential working-class area. The apartment is furnished with care and is always spotless.

Subject #28 is a pretty child with blond hair and blue eyes; she seems large for her age. She has access to the whole apartment but spends most of her time in the living room watching the television, which is on most of the day. She rarely interacts with her mother except for brief instances when her mother checks on her whereabouts in the apartment. Her mother rarely initiates any activities for her and seems pleased as long as she is quiet.

Summary of Test Scores

Subject #28 Group: Two-Year-Old Starters (n = 20)

Test	Age at Testing (Months)	Score	Group Median
Bayley Mental Development Index	12	—	—
	24	94	101
Stanford-Binet IQ	36	88	117.5
WPPSI IQ	60	95	111
Language Test[1]	12	—	—
	15	—	—
	21	—	—
	24	18	30
	27	27	36
	30	27	40.5
	36	39	—
Abstract Abilities[2]	12	—	—
	15	—	—
	21	—	—
	24	6	5.5
	27	5	6
	30	6	6.5
	36	7	—
Discrimination Test[2]	12	—	—
	15	—	—
	21	—	—
	24	3.0	3.0
	27	2.0	3.0
	30	6.0	6.0
	36	4.0	—

[1] Scores in Months
[2] Scores in Level Achieved

APPENDIX A

SOCIAL COMPETENCE FOR SUBJECT 28

```
GAIN              O                    T
ADULT             OXXXXXXX
ATTENTION         OXXXXXXX
                  O           T
------------------------------------------------
USE               O                    T
ADULT             OXXXXXXX
RESOURCE          OXXXXX
                  O               T
------------------------------------------------
HOSTILITY,        O           T
AFFECTION         OXXXXXXXXXXXX
TO ADULT          OXXXXXXXXXXX
                  O                T
------------------------------------------------
ROLE PLAY         T
                  O
                  O
                  O
                  T
------------------------------------------------
PRIDE IN          T
PRODUCT           O
                  O
                  O
                  T
------------------------------------------------
COMPETES          O    T
WITH              OXXXX
PEER              OXXXX
                  O  T
------------------------------------------------
HOSTILITY,        O    T
AFFECTION         OXXXXXXX
TO PEER           OXXXXXX
                  O    T
------------------------------------------------
LEADS AND         O        T
FOLLOWS           OXXXXXXXXXXXXXXXXXXX
PEER              OXXXXXXXXXXXXXXXXX
                  O        T

                  0  1  2  3  4  5  6  7  8  9  10
```

	TOTAL SCORES FOR S 28	MEDIANS FOR 24/27 TWO YEAR STARTER CHILD. FOR ALL SUBJECTS
ADULT COMPETENCE	9.3	23.2
PEER COMPETENCE	6.3	5.1
OVERALL COMPETENCE	15.5	28.6

T INDICATES THE MEDIAN FOR ALL SUBJECTS FOR EACH COMPETENCE FACTOR.

SOCIAL COMPETENCE FOR SUBJECT 28

```
GAIN              O
ADULT             OXXXXXXXXXXXX
ATTENTION         OXXXXXXXXXX
                  O
------------------------------------------------
USE               O                    T
ADULT             OXXXXXXXXXXXXXX
RESOURCE          OXXXXXXXXXXXXX
                  O                 T
------------------------------------------------
HOSTILITY,        O           T
AFFECTION         O
TO ADULT          O                T
------------------------------------------------
ROLE PLAY         T
                  O
                  O
                  T
------------------------------------------------
PRIDE IN          O                                T
PRODUCT           OXXXXXXXXXXXXXXXXXXXXXXXXXXXXXXXXX
                  OXXXXXXXXXXXXXXXXXXXXXXXXXXXXXXX
                  O
------------------------------------------------
COMPETES          O    T
WITH              O
PEER              O
                  O    T
------------------------------------------------
HOSTILITY,        O                T
AFFECTION         O
TO PEER           O              T
                  O
------------------------------------------------
LEADS AND         O        T
FOLLOWS           O
PEER              O        T
                  O

                  0  1  2  3  4  5  6  7  8  9  10
```

	TOTAL SCORES FOR S 28	MEDIANS FOR 30/33 TWO YEAR STARTER CHILD. FOR ALL SUBJECTS
ADULT COMPETENCE	17.4	24.0
PEER COMPETENCE	0.0	11.9
OVERALL COMPETENCE	17.4	28.9

T INDICATES THE MEDIAN FOR ALL SUBJECTS FOR EACH COMPETENCE FACTOR.

Subject #28

	% Duration	
Social Tasks	24-27 Months	30-33 Months
To please	0.3	0.0
To cooperate	1.3	0.7
To gain approval	0.0	0.0
To procure a service	2.1	1.9
To gain attention	5.1	0.7
To maintain social contact	7.2	0.0
To avoid unpleasant circumstances	0.3	0.0
To annoy	0.3	0.0
To direct	0.1	0.8
To assert self (protect domain)	3.7	2.9
To provide information	0.4	0.3
To compete	0.2	0.0
To reject overtures	0.1	0.0
To enjoy pets	0.0	0.0
To converse	0.2	0.1
To produce verbalizations	0.0	0.0
Nonsocial Tasks		
To eat	7.4	0.3
To gain information (v)	16.7	12.6
To gain information (v & a)	4.7	2.9
live language directed to child	0.7	0.7
live language overheard by child	2.1	0.7
mechanical language	1.4	1.5
Sesame Street	0.0	0.0
Nontask	21.2	18.2
To pass time	0.3	0.0
To find something to do	0.3	0.0
To prepare for an activity	0.3	1.7
To construct a product	0.0	0.0
To choose	0.7	0.0
To procure an object	2.5	1.8
To engage in large muscle activity	1.8	0.0
To gain pleasure	0.8	0.0
To imitate	1.9	1.0
To pretend (role play)	0.4	3.9
To ease discomfort	0.8	0.3
To restore order	2.4	2.1
To relieve oneself	0.0	1.7
To dress/undress	0.2	0.0
To operate a mechanism	0.0	1.0
To explore	4.0	22.1
To improve a developing skill (mastery)	10.6	21.1
gross	6.3	1.4
fine	2.3	19.7
verbal	2.0	0.0
To eat and gain information (v)	1.4	0.0
To eat and gain information (v & a)	0.0	1.8
live language directed to child	0.0	0.0
overheard	0.0	0.0

SUBJECT #30

Subject #30 is a two-year-old SES Level III predicted C girl. She is the youngest of eight children ranging from two to nine years of age. Neither parent completed high school. The family owns their home, a large, comfortable one-family house in a suburban area. The house is always impeccably clean and neat.

S is a pretty dark-haired child who is socially adept. The parents and children are very warm and affectionate with each other, and most interactions between the mother and S are affectionate teasing.

There are very few toys available for S to play with. Each morning she spends most of her time watching television or following her mother around while she does the household chores.

Although the social atmosphere in this household is remarkably pleasant, S's time is devoid of interesting activities aside from those of a social type.

Summary of Test Scores

Subject #30   Group: Two-Year-Old Starters (n = 20)

Tests	Age at Testing (Months)	Score	Group Median
Bayley Mental Development Index	12	—	—
	24	77	101
Stanford-Binet IQ	36	81	117.5
WPPSI IQ	60	99	111
Language Test[1]	12	—	—
	15	—	—
	21	—	—
	24	18	30
	27	21	36
	30	21	40.5
	36	39	—
Abstract Abilities[2]	12	—	—
	15	—	—
	21	—	—
	24	<5	5.5
	27	<5	6
	30	6	6.5
	36	6	—
Discrimination Test[2]	12	—	—
	15	—	—
	21	—	—
	24	3.0	3.0
	27	4.0	3.0
	30	7.0	6.0
	36	6.0	—

[1] Scores in Months
[2] Scores in Level Achieved

APPENDIX A

SOCIAL COMPETENCE FOR SUBJECT 30

```
                                                        T
GAIN            OXXXXXXXXXXXXXXXXXXXXXXXXXXXXX
ADULT           OXXXXXXXXXXXXXXXXXXXXXXXXXXXXXX
ATTENTION       O                      T
                                 T
USE             OXXXXXXXXXXXXXXXXXXXXXXXXXXX
ADULT           OXXXXXXXXXXXXXXXXXXXXXXX
RESOURCE                            T
                            T
HOSTILITY,      OXXXXXXXXXXXXXXXXXXXXXXXXXXXXXXXXXXXXXXXX
AFFECTION       OXXXXXXXXXXXXXXXXXXXXXXXXXXXXXXXXXXXXXXXXXXX
TO ADULT        O     T
                T
ROLE PLAY       O
                O
                T
                T
PRIDE IN        O
PRODUCT         O
                T
COMPETES        O    T
WITH            OXXXXX
PEER            OXXXX
                O  T
                        T
HOSTILITY,      OXXXXXXXXXXXXXXXXXXXXXXXXXXXXXXXXXXX
AFFECTION       OXXXXXXXXXXXXXXXXXXXXXXXXXXXXXXXXXXXXXX
TO PEER         O                   T
                    T
LEADS AND       OXXXXXXXXXXXXXXXXXXXXXXXXXXXXXXXX
FOLLOWS         OXXXXXXXXXXXXXXXXXXXXXXXXXXXXXXXXXXX
PEER            O           T

                0   1   2   3   4   5   6   7   8   9   10
```

	TOTAL SCORES FOR S 30	MEDIANS FOR 24/27 TWO YEAR STARTER CHILD. FOR ALL SUBJECTS
ADULT COMPETENCE	28.3	23.2
PEER COMPETENCE	20.7	5.1
OVERALL COMPETENCE	49.0	28.6

T INDICATES THE MEDIAN FOR ALL SUBJECTS FOR EACH COMPETENCE FACTOR.

SOCIAL COMPETENCE FOR SUBJECT 30

```
                            T
GAIN            OXXXXXXXXX
ADULT           OXXXXXXXXX
ATTENTION       O        T
                   T
USE             OXXXXXXX
ADULT           OXXXXXXX
RESOURCE        O
                                           T
HOSTILITY,      OXXXXXXXXXXXXXXXXXXXXXXXXXXXXXXXXXXXXXX
AFFECTION       OXXXXXXXXXXXXXXXXXXXXXXXXXXXXXXXXXXXXXXX
TO ADULT        O                    T
                T
ROLE PLAY       O
                O
                T
PRIDE IN        O
PRODUCT         O
                O
COMPETES        O  T
WITH            OXXX
PEER            OXXX
                O  T
                                T
HOSTILITY,      OXXXXXXXXXXXXXXXXXXXX
AFFECTION       OXXXXXXXXXXXXXXXXXXXX
TO PEER         O                 T
                                T
LEADS AND       OXXXXXXXXXXXXXXXXXXX
FOLLOWS         OXXXXXXXXXXXXXXXXXXX
PEER            O           T

                0   1   2   3   4   5   6   7   8   9   10
```

	TOTAL SCORES FOR S 30	MEDIANS FOR 30/33 TWO YEAR STARTER CHILD. FOR ALL SUBJECTS
ADULT COMPETENCE	15.4	24.0
PEER COMPETENCE	7.1	11.9
OVERALL COMPETENCE	22.5	28.9

T INDICATES THE MEDIAN FOR ALL SUBJECTS FOR EACH COMPETENCE FACTOR.

Subject #30

Social Tasks	% Duration	
	24-27 Months	30-33 Months
To please	0.4	0.5
To cooperate	5.4	3.7
To gain approval	0.2	0.1
To procure a service	3.0	1.9
To gain attention	3.9	5.9
To maintain social contact	8.4	6.3
To avoid unpleasant circumstances	0.2	0.0
To annoy	0.1	0.1
To direct	0.5	0.3
To assert self (protect domain)	2.6	1.0
To provide information	0.6	1.0
To compete	1.1	0.0
To reject overtures	0.0	0.1
To enjoy pets	0.0	0.0
To converse	0.0	0.4
To produce verbalizations	0.0	0.0
Nonsocial Tasks		
To eat	5.3	16.0
To gain information (v)	14.0	10.2
To gain information (v & a)	6.0	6.0
live language directed to child	1.3	1.7
live language overheard by child	3.3	3.2
mechanical language	0.0	0.5
Sesame Street	1.3	0.0
Nontask	12.7	6.7
To pass time	6.3	0.8
To find something to do	0.4	0.2
To prepare for an activity	1.2	1.3
To construct a product	0.0	1.7
To choose	0.0	0.0
To procure an object	0.6	3.7
To engage in large muscle activity	0.0	0.0
To gain pleasure	1.9	0.0
To imitate	0.5	0.1
To pretend (role play)	0.6	0.0
To ease discomfort	1.7	0.1
To restore order	0.6	1.8
To relieve oneself	0.1	6.1
To dress/undress	0.5	0.1
To operate a mechanism	0.3	0.2
To explore	8.4	6.2
To improve a developing skill (mastery)	3.6	6.8
gross	2.8	1.5
fine	0.3	4.4
verbal	0.5	1.0
To eat and gain information (v)	3.8	3.5
To eat and gain information (v & a)	0.0	2.0
live language directed to child	0.0	1.3
overheard	0.0	0.6

SUBJECT #31

Subject #31 is a one-year-old SES Level II predicted A boy who is the youngest of three boys. The family is composed of his parents and siblings, plus grandparents who live in the same building, as well as a babysitter who lives there too and appears to take almost full charge of the child. Although his parents are well educated and generally loving and interested in S, he is often in the care of the babysitter, who at best provides good caretaking but little stimulation. The child is rarely engaged in play but generally follows people (child or adult) from room to room, or looks for long periods out the window. The home atmosphere is quiet and controlled, and there are few, if any, available toys for S to play with. He is confined generally to one or two rooms, since there are unsafe stairways between various floors of the house.

Summary of Test Scores

Subject #31 Group: One-Year-Old Starters (n = 19)

Tests	Age at Testing (Months)	Score	Group Median
Bayley Mental Developmental Index	12	112	103
	24	108	112
Stanford-Binet IQ	36	118	113
WPPSI IQ	60	116	117.5
Language Test[1]	12	14	14
	15	16	16
	21	18	21
	24	21	36
	27	not tested	—
	30	36	43.5
	36	39	45
Abstract Abilities[2]	12	3	2
	15	3	2
	21	<5	5
	24	<5	6
	27	not tested	—
	30	7	7
	36	11	9
Discrimination Test[2]	12	2	1
	15	3	2
	21	4	3
	24	7	3.5
	27	not tested	—
	30	5	5
	36	8	8

[1] Scores in Months
[2] Scores in Level Achieved

Subject #31

Social Tasks	% Duration	
	12-15 Months	18-21 Months
To please	0.0	0.2
To cooperate	1.1	1.9
To gain approval	0.0	0.0
To procure a service	0.7	0.1
To gain attention	1.4	1.4
To maintain social contact	1.6	2.1
To avoid unpleasant circumstances	0.0	0.0
To annoy	0.0	0.0
To direct	0.0	0.0
To assert self (protect domain)	1.1	0.5
To provide information	0.0	0.0
To compete	0.0	0.0
To reject overtures	0.2	0.0
To enjoy pets	0.0	0.0
To converse	0.0	0.0
To produce verbalizations	0.0	0.0
Nonsocial Tasks		
To eat	11.7	11.9
To gain information (v)	16.1	14.4
To gain information (v & a)	2.1	10.0
live language directed to child	1.0	4.0
live language overheard by child	0.8	6.0
mechanical language	0.0	0.0
Sesame Street	0.0	0.0
Nontask	18.2	19.4
To pass time	5.3	6.6
To find something to do	1.0	0.3
To prepare for an activity	0.2	1.4
To construct a product	0.0	0.0
To choose	0.0	0.0
To procure an object	4.9	1.8
To engage in large muscle activity	0.0	0.0
To gain pleasure	0.7	0.1
To imitate	0.1	0.1
To pretend (role play)	0.0	0.5
To ease discomfort	1.7	1.0
To restore order	0.5	0.3
To relieve oneself	0.0	0.0
To dress/undress	0.0	0.0
To operate a mechanism	1.1	0.0
To explore	14.3	6.6
To improve a developing skill (mastery)	8.8	7.3
gross	5.5	3.4
fine	3.3	3.0
verbal	0.0	0.9
To eat and gain information (v)	4.7	5.2
To eat and gain information (v & a)	0.0	4.2
live language directed to child	0.0	0.0
overheard	0.0	4.2

Individual Subject Data   315

SOCIAL COMPETENCE FOR SUBJECT 31

```
                              T
GAIN             0XXX
ADULT            0XXX
ATTENTION        0                  T
                 ---------------------
                 0                     T
USE              0XXXXXXXXXXX
ADULT            0XXXXXXXXXX
RESOURCE         0                 T
                 ---------------------
                            T
HOSTILITY,       0XXXXXXX
AFFECTION        0XXXXXXX
TO ADULT         0            T
                 ---------------------
                 T
                 0
ROLE PLAY        0
                 0        T
                 ---------------------
                 T
PRIDE IN         0
PRODUCT          0
                 T
                 ---------------------
                 0          T
COMPETES         0XXXXXXX
WITH             0XXXXXXX
PEER             0   T
                 ---------------------
                             T
HOSTILITY,       0XXXXX
AFFECTION        0XXXXX
TO PEER          0      T
                 ---------------------
                 0  T
LEADS AND        0XXXXX
FOLLOWS          0XXXXX
PEER             0 T
                 ---------------------
                 0  1  2  3  4  5  6  7  8  9  10
```

	TOTAL SCORES FOR S 31	MEDIANS AT 12/15 MONTHS FOR ALL SUBJECTS
ADULT COMPETENCE	4.5	13.8
PEER COMPETENCE	3.4	9.0
OVERALL COMPETENCE	7.9	20.5

T INDICATES THE MEDIAN FOR ALL SUBJECTS FOR EACH COMPETENCE FACTOR.

SOCIAL COMPETENCE FOR SUBJECT 31

```
                 0            T
GAIN             0XXXXXXXXXXXXXXXXXXXXXXXX
ADULT            0XXXXXXXXXXXXXXXXXXXXXXXX
ATTENTION        0    T
                 ---------------------
                 0                          T
USE              0XXXXXXXXXXXXXXXXXXXXXXX
ADULT            0XXXXXXXXXXXXXXXXXXXXXXX
RESOURCE         0                   T
                 ---------------------
                 0          T
HOSTILITY,       0XXXXXX
AFFECTION        0XXXXXX
TO ADULT         0     T
                 ---------------------
                 0    T
                 0
ROLE PLAY        0
                 0  T
                 ---------------------
                 T
PRIDE IN         0
PRODUCT          0
                 0 T
                 ---------------------
                 0                    T
COMPETES         0
WITH             0
PEER             0
                 ---------------------
                 0                   T
HOSTILITY,       0XXXXXXXXXXXXXXXXXXX
AFFECTION        0XXXXXXXXXXXXXXXXXXX
TO PEER          0            T
                 ---------------------
                 0      T
LEADS AND        0XXX
FOLLOWS          0XXX
PEER             0
                 ---------------------
                 0  1  2  3  4  5  6  7  8  9  10
```

	TOTAL SCORES FOR S 31	MEDIANS AT 18/21 MONTHS FOR ALL SUBJECTS
ADULT COMPETENCE	15.6	22.2
PEER COMPETENCE	4.7	13.5
OVERALL COMPETENCE	20.2	23.5

T INDICATES THE MEDIAN FOR ALL SUBJECTS FOR EACH COMPETENCE FACTOR.

APPENDIX A

```
                    SOCIAL COMPETENCE FOR SUBJECT 31

GAIN            O                          T
ADULT           OXXXXXX
ATTENTION       OXXXXXX
                O                          T
------------------------------------------------------------------
USE             O              T
ADULT           OXXXXXXXX
RESOURCE        OXXXXXXXX
                O                T
------------------------------------------------------------------
HOSTILITY,      O         T
AFFECTION       O
TO ADULT        O
                O           T
------------------------------------------------------------------
                O      T
ROLE PLAY       OXXXXXXXXXXXXXXXXX
                OXXXXXXXXXXXXXXXXX
                O      T
------------------------------------------------------------------
                O    T
PRIDE IN        OXXXXXXXXX
PRODUCT         OXXXXXXXXX
                O    T
------------------------------------------------------------------
COMPETES        O                             T
WITH            O
PEER            O
                O                                T
------------------------------------------------------------------
HOSTILITY,      O              T
AFFECTION       O
TO PEER         O
                O                T
------------------------------------------------------------------
LEADS AND       O        T
FOLLOWS         O
PEER            O
                O         T
------------------------------------------------------------------
                O   1   2   3   4   5   6   7   8   9   10
```

	TOTAL SCORES FOR S 31	MEDIANS FOR 30/33 ONE YEAR STARTER CHILD FOR ALL SUBJECTS
ADULT COMPETENCE	16.0	26.0
PEER COMPETENCE	0.0	12.2
OVERALL COMPETENCE	16.0	33.6

T INDICATES THE MEDIAN FOR ALL SUBJECTS FOR EACH COMPETENCE FACTOR.

SUBJECT #32

Subject #32 is a one-year-old SES Level IV predicted A boy. He is the youngest child in a family of eight children ranging in age from one to nineteen years. The family owns their own home, a small house in south Boston that consists of seven rooms. Interior space is very limited. The house is nicely furnished and always neat. There is no yard. The neighborhood children play on the sidewalk. The first floor consists of three rooms: living room, kitchen, and bedroom. The kitchen is between the other two rooms, and it is the heart of the house. A large table takes up most of the space in the kitchen.

This subject is an ebullient little boy whose characteristic facial expression is one of good humor. He is very active (he learned to walk at the age of 9 months). He enjoys movement: climbing kitchen chairs, chasing his sister around the small living room, bouncing on the bed, walking up and down the kitchen table. Within the limits of the first floor, he is permitted maximum mobility. Both parents are permissive in regard to S's tendency to use family furniture for his own active purposes (the father has been observed twirling S on the lazy susan that is the centerpiece of the kitchen table.) The major limitation on the child's freedom is a gate across the stairway, which prevents him from getting to the second floor whenever he wants to do so (usually in order to keep up with a sibling).

The child's mornings are spent alone with his mother (all siblings are in school). At lunch time there is a high flow of people in and out: father, father's friends, brothers and sisters and their friends.

The atmosphere in this household is warm and congenial. The child's mother keeps an affectionate eye on him from the central vantage point of the kitchen. She checks up on him regularly but does not hover over him. Although she does not speak very much, she quietly encourages exploratory activities, such as finding out what's under the kitchen sink or what's behind the bed. When the child becomes overactive, his mother attempts to interest him in small toys (tops that spin, cars that wind) or quiet activities such as "reading" the newspaper on her lap. Although the child has been encouraged to watch "Sesame Street," so far he is not interested in sitting still and looking at a television screen.

Summary of Test Scores

Subject #32   Group: One-Year-Old Starters (n = 19)

Tests	Age at Testing (Months)	Score	Group Median
Bayley Mental Developmental Index	12	94	103
	24	108	112
Stanford-Binet IQ	36	93	113
WPPSI IQ	60	120	117.5
Language Test[1]	12	16	14
	15	16	16
	21	18	21
	24	24	36
	27	not tested	—
	30	39	43.5
	36	42	45
Abstract Abilities[2]	12	2	2
	15	3	2
	21	<5	5
	24	6	6
	27	not tested	—
	30	7	7
	36	8	9
Discrimination Test[2]	12	0	1
	15	0	2
	21	3.5	3
	24	2	3.5
	27	not tested	—
	30	3.5	5
	36	8	8[1]

[1] Scores in Months
[2] Scores in Level Achieved

Subject #32

	% Duration	
Social Tasks	12-15 Months	18-21 Months
To please	0.2	0.3
To cooperate	3.5	1.9
To gain approval	0.0	0.0
To procure a service	2.4	5.2
To gain attention	3.3	2.0
To maintain social contact	9.1	3.0
To avoid unpleasant circumstances	0.0	0.0
To annoy	0.2	0.3
To direct	1.9	0.6
To assert self (protect domain)	1.5	1.0
To provide information	0.0	0.0
To compete	0.0	0.0
To reject overtures	0.0	0.0
To enjoy pets	0.0	0.0
To converse	0.0	0.0
To produce verbalizations	0.0	0.0
Nonsocial Tasks		
To eat	4.9	13.3
To gain information (v)	13.2	10.5
To gain information (v & a)	8.2	7.8
live language directed to child	1.5	4.5
live language overheard by child	4.5	1.3
mechanical language	0.0	1.9
Sesame Street	1.3	0.0
Nontask	13.5	8.9
To pass time	2.5	4.3
To find something to do	0.6	0.0
To prepare for an activity	1.7	3.4
To construct a product	0.0	0.0
To choose	0.0	0.0
To procure an object	4.5	3.5
To engage in large muscle activity	1.5	0.3
To gain pleasure	0.0	0.0
To imitate	0.1	0.1
To pretend (role play)	0.0	2.6
To ease discomfort	1.0	0.3
To restore order	2.1	0.5
To relieve oneself	0.0	0.0
To dress/undress	0.0	0.0
To operate a mechanism	0.2	0.0
To explore	12.7	9.9
To improve a developing skill (mastery)	7.4	14.5
gross	6.7	7.3
fine	0.7	7.3
verbal	0.0	0.0
To eat and gain information (v)	2.5	0.8
To eat and gain information (v & a)	0.0	3.1
live language directed to child	0.0	0.6
overheard	0.0	0.0

APPENDIX A

SOCIAL COMPETENCE FOR SUBJECT 32

```
                        T
GAIN            0XXXXXXXXXXXXXXXXXXXXXXXXX
ADULT           0XXXXXXXXXXXXXXXXXXXXXXXXX
ATTENTION       0
                                            T
USE             0XXXXXXXXXXXXXXXXXXXXXXXXXXXXXXXXXXXXXXXXX
ADULT           0XXXXXXXXXXXXXXXXXXXXXXXXXXXXXXXXXXXXXXXXX
RESOURCE        0                   T
                            T
HOSTILITY,      0XXXXXXXXXXXXXXXXXXXXXX
AFFECTION       0XXXXXXXXXXXXXXXXXXXXXX
TO ADULT        0           T

                T
ROLE PLAY       0
                0
                    T
                T
PRIDE IN        0
PRODUCT         0
                    T

COMPETES        0           T
WITH            0
PEER            0       T

                        T
HOSTILITY,      0
AFFECTION       0
TO PEER         0   T

LEADS AND       0   T
FOLLOWS         0
PEER            0
                    T

                0   1   2   3   4   5   6   7   8   9   10

                    TOTAL SCORES    MEDIANS AT 12/15 MONTHS
                    FOR S 32        FOR ALL SUBJECTS
ADULT COMPETENCE    25.1            13.8
PEER COMPETENCE     0.0             9.0
OVERALL COMPETENCE  25.1            20.5
```

T INDICATES THE MEDIAN FOR ALL SUBJECTS FOR EACH COMPETENCE FACTOR.

SOCIAL COMPETENCE FOR SUBJECT 32

```
                        T
GAIN            0XXXXXXXXXXX
ADULT           0XXXXXXXXXXX
ATTENTION       0       T
                                                        T
USE             0XXXXXXXXXXXXXXXXXXXXXXXXXXXXXXXXXXXXXXXXXXX
ADULT           0XXXXXXXXXXXXXXXXXXXXXXXXXXXXXXXXXXXXXXXXXXX
RESOURCE        0                           T
                    T
HOSTILITY,      0XXXXXXXXXXX
AFFECTION       0XXXXXXXXXXX
TO ADULT        0   T

                T
ROLE PLAY       0XXXXXX
                0XXXXXX
                0   T

                T
PRIDE IN        0
PRODUCT         0
                0   T

COMPETES        0                       T
WITH            0
PEER            0               T

                                    T
HOSTILITY,      0
AFFECTION       0
TO PEER         0           T

LEADS AND       0                   T
FOLLOWS         0
PEER            0           T

                0   1   2   3   4   5   6   7   8   9   10

                    TOTAL SCORES    MEDIANS AT 18/21 MONTHS
                    FOR S 32        FOR ALL SUBJECTS
ADULT COMPETENCE    22.2            22.2
PEER COMPETENCE     0.0             13.5
OVERALL COMPETENCE  22.2            23.5
```

T INDICATES THE MEDIAN FOR ALL SUBJECTS FOR EACH COMPETENCE FACTOR.

SOCIAL COMPETENCE FOR SUBJECT 32

```
GAIN            O                    T
ADULT           OXXXXXXXXXXXXXXXXXXXXXXXXXXXXXXXXXXXXXXXXXXXXXXXXX
ATTENTION       OXXXXXXXXXXXXXXXXXXXXXXXXXXXXXXXXXXXXXXXXXXXXXXXXX
                O                    T
--------------------------------------------------------------------
USE             O             T
ADULT           OXXXXXXXX
RESOURCE        OXXXXXXXX
                O             T
--------------------------------------------------------------------
HOSTILITY,      O        T
AFFECTION       OXXXXXXXXXXX
TO ADULT        OXXXXXXXXXXX
                O        T
--------------------------------------------------------------------
                O        T
ROLE PLAY       OXXXXXXXX
                OXXXXXXXX
                O        T
--------------------------------------------------------------------
                O    T
PRIDE IN        O
PRODUCT         O
                O    T
--------------------------------------------------------------------
COMPETES        O                          T
WITH            O
PEER            O
                O                          T
--------------------------------------------------------------------
HOSTILITY,      O                T
AFFECTION       OXXXXXXXXXXXXXXXXXXXXXXXXXXXXXXXXXXXXXXXXXXXXXXXXX
TO PEER         OXXXXXXXXXXXXXXXXXXXXXXXXXXXXXXXXXXXXXXXXXXXXXXXXX
                O                T
--------------------------------------------------------------------
LEADS AND       O           T
FOLLOWS         OXXXXXXXXXXX
PEER            OXXXXXXXXXXX
                O           T
--------------------------------------------------------------------
                0   1   2   3   4   5   6   7   8   9   10
```

	TOTAL SCORES FOR S 32	MEDIANS FOR 30/33 ONE YEAR STARTER CHILD. FOR ALL SUBJECTS
ADULT COMPETENCE	23.5	26.0
PEER COMPETENCE	12.1	12.2
OVERALL COMPETENCE	35.7	33.6

T INDICATES THE MEDIAN FOR ALL SUBJECTS FOR EACH COMPETENCE FACTOR.

SUBJECT #33

Subject #33 is a two-year-old SES Level I predicted C boy. S has two older siblings, a five-year-old sister and an eight-year-old brother. The family lives in an upper-middle-class suburban area in a large, expensively furnished home. During most of our observations, S was left in the care of the live-in housekeeper, a strict young woman whose primary concern was keeping the home neat and clean. The child was routinely kept out of the dining and living rooms, which were usually immaculate.

S is an active, assertive little boy. Although there are ample toys available to S, he is rarely observed playing with them. Unfortunately, the mother structured most of our observations during the hours that "Sesame Street" was on, and consequently much of our observations center around S watching television.

Summary of Test Scores

Subject #33   Group: Two-Year-Old Starters (n = 20)

Tests	Age at Testing (Months)	Score	Group Median
Bayley Mental Development Index	12	—	—
	24	89	101
Stanford-Binet IQ	36	120	117.5
WPPSI IQ	60	118	111
Language Test[1]	12	—	—
	15	—	—
	21	—	—
	24	21	30
	27	21	36
	30	36	40.5
	36	42	—
Abstract Abilities[2]	12	—	—
	15	—	—
	21	—	—
	24	5	5.5
	27	<5	6
	30	6	6.5
	36	10	—
Discrimination Test[2]	12	—	—
	15	—	—
	21	—	—
	24	3.0	3.0
	27	2.0	3.0
	30	7.0	6.0
	36	8.0	—

[1] Scores in Months
[2] Scores in Level Achieved

324 APPENDIX A

SOCIAL COMPETENCE FOR SUBJECT 33

```
                          T
GAIN          0XXXXXXXXXXXXXXXXXXXXX
ADULT         0XXXXXXXXXXXXXXXXXXXXX
ATTENTION     0                T
------------------------------------
                              T
USE           0XXXXXXXXXXXXXXXX
ADULT         0XXXXXXXXXXXXXXXX
RESOURCE      0                 T
------------------------------------
HOSTILITY,    0           T
AFFECTION     0XXXXXXXXXXXX
TO ADULT      0XXXXXXXXXXXX
              0       T
------------------------------------
              T
RULE PLAY     0
              0
              0 T
------------------------------------
              T
PRIDE IN      0
PRODUCT       0
              0 T
------------------------------------
COMPETES      0  T
WITH          0
PEER          0
              0 T
------------------------------------
HOSTILITY,    0         T
AFFECTION     0XXXXXXXXX
TO PEER       0
              0      T
------------------------------------
LEADS AND     0
FOLLOWS       0     T
PEER          0
              0 T
------------------------------------
              0   1   2   3   4   5   6   7   8   9   10
```

	TOTAL SCORES FOR S 33	MEDIANS FOR 24/27 TWO YEAR STARTER CHILD. FOR ALL SUBJECTS
ADULT COMPETENCE	15.5	23.2
PEER COMPETENCE	0.0	5.1
OVERALL COMPETENCE	15.5	28.6

T INDICATES THE MEDIAN FOR ALL SUBJECTS FOR EACH COMPETENCE FACTOR.

SOCIAL COMPETENCE FOR SUBJECT 33

```
                           T
GAIN          0XXXXXXXXXXXXXXXXXXXX
ADULT         0XXXXXXXXXXXXXXXXXXXX
ATTENTION     0              T
------------------------------------
USE           0                T
ADULT         0XXXXXXX
RESOURCE      0XXXXXXX
              0          T
------------------------------------
HOSTILITY,    0          T
AFFECTION     0XX
TO ADULT      0XX
              0       T
------------------------------------
              T
RULE PLAY     0
              0
              0 T
------------------------------------
                                  T
PRIDE IN      0XXXXXXXXXXXXXXXXXXXX
PRODUCT       0XXXXXXXXXXXXXXXXXXXX
              0              T
------------------------------------
COMPETES      0  T
WITH          0
PEER          0 T
------------------------------------
HOSTILITY,    0           T
AFFECTION     0
TO PEER       0
              0      T
------------------------------------
LEADS AND     0        T
FOLLOWS       0
PEER          0
              0 T
------------------------------------
              0   1   2   3   4   5   6   7   8   9   10
```

	TOTAL SCORES FOR S 33	MEDIANS FOR 30/33 TWO YEAR STARTER CHILD. FOR ALL SUBJECTS
ADULT COMPETENCE	14.3	24.0
PEER COMPETENCE	0.0	11.9
OVERALL COMPETENCE	14.3	28.9

T INDICATES THE MEDIAN FOR ALL SUBJECTS FOR EACH COMPETENCE FACTOR.

Subject #33

	% Duration	
Social Tasks	24-27 Months	30-33 Months
To please	0.0	0.0
To cooperate	4.0	1.0
To gain approval	0.0	0.0
To procure a service	2.9	1.0
To gain attention	3.7	5.3
To maintain social contact	4.1	0.9
To avoid unpleasant circumstances	0.2	0.1
To annoy	0.0	0.0
To direct	0.8	0.9
To assert self (protect domain)	1.5	1.5
To provide information	0.1	0.5
To compete	0.0	0.0
To reject overtures	0.0	0.0
To enjoy pets	0.0	0.0
To converse	0.3	0.3
To produce verbalizations	0.0	0.0
Nonsocial Tasks		
To eat	1.2	1.6
To gain information (v)	9.5	7.4
To gain information (v & a)	46.4	24.4
live language directed to child	1.3	1.0
live language overheard by child	2.6	1.1
mechanical language	1.4	2.1
Sesame Street	40.5	17.1
Nontask	8.2	14.6
To pass time	5.8	5.7
To find something to do	0.0	0.6
To prepare for an activity	0.8	2.4
To construct a product	0.0	0.0
To choose	0.0	0.0
To procure an object	0.3	2.5
To engage in large muscle activity	0.0	0.0
To gain pleasure	0.0	0.0
To imitate	0.0	0.0
To pretend (role play)	0.0	3.1
To ease discomfort	0.9	0.6
To restore order	0.0	0.2
To relieve oneself	0.0	0.0
To dress/undress	0.0	0.5
To operate a mechanism	0.8	1.3
To explore	2.3	8.6
To improve a developing skill (mastery)	0.5	13.8
gross	0.2	8.5
fine	0.0	3.4
verbal	0.3	1.9
To eat and gain information (v)	0.3	0.2
To eat and gain information (v & a)	0.0	0.7
live language directed to child	0.0	0.0
overheard	0.0	0.6

SUBJECT #34

Subject #34 is a one-year-old SES Level IV predicted C boy. He is the youngest of three children. He has a seven-year-old brother and a four-year-old sister. The family lives in a seven-room apartment in a two-family house in a residential area of the city. The apartment is usually neat, but the furniture is quite worn.

This subject is a well-developed, alert little boy who spends the majority of each day alone in a playpen that takes up most of the space in the living room. The television is left on for him, and usually there are several toys in the playpen with him. His mother rarely interacts with him, but when she does, it is in an affectionate and playful manner. Although his four-year-old sister is also home all day, she rarely pays any attention to S.

Summary of Test Scores

Subject #34   Group: One-Year-Old Starters (n = 19)

Tests	Age at Testing (Months)	Score	Group Median
Bayley Mental Developmental Index	12	109	103
	24	66	112
Stanford-Binet IQ	36	57	113
WPPSI IQ	60	not tested	—
Language Test[1]	12	10	14
	15	10	16
	21	10	21
	24	10	36
	27	not tested	—
	30	12	43.5
	36	16	45
Abstract Abilities[2]	12	<1	2
	15	1	2
	21	<5	5
	24	<5	6
	27	not tested	—
	30	5	7
	36	5	9
Discrimination Test[2]	12	0	1
	15	0	2
	21	0	3
	24	3.5	3.5
	27	not tested	—
	30	2	5
	36	5	8

[1] Scores in Months
[2] Scores in Level Achieved

328 APPENDIX A

SOCIAL COMPETENCE FOR SUBJECT 34

```
                         T
GAIN           OXXX
ADULT          OXXX
ATTENTION      O            T

USE            O            T
ADULT          OXXXXXXXXXXXX
RESOURCE       OXXXXXXXXXXXX
               O       T

                   T
HOSTILITY,     O
AFFECTION      OXXXXXXXXXXXXXXXXXXX
TO ADULT       OXXXXXXXXXXXXXXXXXX
               O   T

               T
ROLE PLAY      O
               O
               O   T

               T
PRIDE IN       O
PRODUCT        O
               O T

COMPETES       O       T
WITH           O
PEER           O
               O   T

HOSTILITY,     O   T
AFFECTION      O
TO PEER        O
               O       T

LEADS AND      O   T
FOLLOWS        O
PEER           O T
               
               0   1   2   3   4   5   6   7   8   9   10
```

	TOTAL SCORES FOR S 34	MEDIANS AT 12/15 MONTHS FOR ALL SUBJECTS
ADULT COMPETENCE	8.5	13.8
PEER COMPETENCE	0.0	9.0
OVERALL COMPETENCE	8.5	20.5

T INDICATES THE MEDIAN FOR ALL SUBJECTS FOR EACH COMPETENCE FACTOR.

SOCIAL COMPETENCE FOR SUBJECT 34

```
GAIN           O
ADULT          O           T
ATTENTION      O       T
               O

USE            O                T
ADULT          OXXXXXXXXXX
RESOURCE       OXXXXXXXXXX       T
               O

HOSTILITY,     O            T
AFFECTION      OXXXXXXXXXXXXXXXXXXX
TO ADULT       OXXXXXXXXXXXXXXXXXXX
               O        T

ROLE PLAY      O        T
               O
               O    T
               O

PRIDE IN       T
PRODUCT        O
               O
               O T

COMPETES       O                T
WITH           OXXX
PEER           OXXX
               O                T

HOSTILITY,     O                T
AFFECTION      OXXXXXXXXXXXXXXXXXXXXX
TO PEER        OXXXXXXXXXXXXXXXXXXXXX
               O                T

LEADS AND      O            T
FOLLOWS        OXXX
PEER           OXXX
               O        T

               0   1   2   3   4   5   6   7   8   9   10
```

	TOTAL SCORES FOR S 34	MEDIANS AT 18/21 MONTHS FOR ALL SUBJECTS
ADULT COMPETENCE	5.7	22.2
PEER COMPETENCE	5.7	13.5
OVERALL COMPETENCE	11.4	23.5

T INDICATES THE MEDIAN FOR ALL SUBJECTS FOR EACH COMPETENCE FACTOR.

SOCIAL COMPETENCE FOR SUBJECT 34

```
GAIN              O                        T
ADULT             OXXXXXXXXXXXXXXXXXXXXXXXXXXXX
ATTENTION         OXXXXXXXXXXXXXXXXXXXXXXXXXXX
                  O                           T
-----------------------------------------------------------------
USE               O            T
ADULT             O
RESOURCE          O
                  O               T
-----------------------------------------------------------------
HOSTILITY,        O         T
AFFECTION         OXXXXXXXXXXXXXXXXXXXXXXXXXXXX
TO ADULT          OXXXXXXXXXXXXXXXXXXXXXXXXXXX
                  O          T
-----------------------------------------------------------------
                  O   T
ROLE PLAY         O
                  O
                  O   T
-----------------------------------------------------------------
                  O   T
PRIDE IN          O
PRODUCT           O
                  O   T
-----------------------------------------------------------------
COMPETES          O                              T
WITH              O
PEER              O
                  O                                T
-----------------------------------------------------------------
HOSTILITY,        O            T
AFFECTION         O
TO PEER           O
                  O               T
-----------------------------------------------------------------
LEADS AND         O        T
FOLLOWS           O
PEER              O
                  O         T
-----------------------------------------------------------------
                  0   1   2   3   4   5   6   7   8   9   10
```

	TOTAL SCORES FOR S 34	MEDIANS FOR 30/33 ONE YEAR STARTER CHILD. FOR ALL SUBJECTS
ADULT COMPETENCE	11.4	26.0
PEER COMPETENCE	0.0	12.2
OVERALL COMPETENCE	11.4	33.6

T INDICATES THE MEDIAN FOR ALL SUBJECTS FOR EACH COMPETENCE FACTOR.

Subject #34

	% Duration	
Social Tasks	12-15 Months	18-21 Months
To please	0.0	0.0
To cooperate	0.1	1.2
To gain approval	0.0	0.0
To procure a service	0.2	0.4
To gain attention	0.0	3.9
To maintain social contact	2.3	6.3
To avoid unpleasant circumstances	0.0	0.0
To annoy	0.0	0.0
To direct	0.0	0.0
To assert self (protect domain)	0.0	2.4
To provide information	0.0	0.0
To compete	0.0	0.0
To reject overtures	0.0	0.0
To enjoy pets	0.0	0.0
To converse	0.0	0.0
To produce verbalizations	0.0	0.0
Nonsocial Tasks		
To eat	1.5	3.9
To gain information (v)	8.2	5.3
To gain information (v & a)	17.6	14.9
live language directed to child	0.1	0.8
live language overheard by child	0.5	0.0
mechanical language	6.2	14.0
Sesame Street	10.4	0.0
Nontask	1.0	36.0
To pass time	37.1	2.8
To find something to do	0.0	0.0
To prepare for an activity	0.0	1.4
To construct a product	0.0	0.0
To choose	0.0	0.0
To procure an object	3.4	3.2
To engage in large muscle activity	0.3	0.0
To gain pleasure	0.6	0.0
To imitate	0.0	0.0
To pretend (role play)	0.0	0.0
To ease discomfort	0.5	0.0
To restore order	0.0	0.1
To relieve oneself	0.0	0.0
To dress/undress	0.0	0.0
To operate a mechanism	0.9	0.0
To explore	9.8	17.5
To improve a developing skill (mastery)	16.2	0.8
gross	7.7	0.8
fine	7.7	0.0
verbal	0.2	0.0
To eat and gain information (v)	0.0	0.0
To eat and gain information (v & a)	0.0	0.0
live language directed to child	0.0	0.0
overheard	0.0	0.0

SUBJECT #35

Subject #35 is a two-year-old SES Level III predicted A girl. The youngest child, she has four brothers and one sister. The next oldest child is two years older than S. S and her family live in a working-class section just outside the urban area in an eight-room house. The most striking aspect of subject #35's family life is the devotion and interest toward the children displayed by the lively and energetic mother. She participates actively in their daily lives, even to the extent of watching "Sesame Street" with her children and folding laundry nearby so as to interact fully with them. There is open communication among the family members, promoting a positive atmosphere for nurturing a developing child to his utmost potential.

Summary of Test Scores

Subject #35   Group: Two-Year-Old Starters (n = 20)

Tests	Age at Testing (Months)	Score	Group Median
Bayley Mental Developmental Index	12	—	—
	24	104	101
Stanford-Binet IQ	36	132	117.5
WPPSI IQ	60	124	111
Language Test[1]	12	—	—
	15	—	—
	21	—	—
	24	36	30
	27	42	36
	30	45	40.5
	36	54	—
Abstract Abilities[2]	12	—	—
	15	—	—
	21	—	—
	24	7	5.5
	27	7	6
	30	7	6.5
	36	11	—
Discrimination Test[2]	12	—	—
	15	—	—
	21	—	—
	24	6.0	3.0
	27	6.0	3.0
	30	6.0	6.0
	36	8.0	—

[1] Scores in Months
[2] Scores in Level Achieved

Individual Subject Data

SOCIAL COMPETENCE FOR SUBJECT 35

```
                       T
GAIN         O
ADULT        OXXXXXXXXXXXXXX
ATTENTION    OXXXXXXXXXXXXXX
             O        T
             ---------------
             O        T
USE          OXXXXXXXXXXXXXXXXXXXX
ADULT        OXXXXXXXXXXXXXXXXXXXXXXXX
RESOURCE     O                     T
             ---------------
HOSTILITY,   O          T
AFFECTION    O
TO ADULT     O          T
             ---------------
             T
ROLE PLAY    O
             O
             T
             ---------------
             T
PRIDE IN     OXXXX
PRODUCT      OXXX
             T
             ---------------
             O    T
COMPETES     OXX
WITH         OXX
PEER         O  T
             ---------------
HOSTILITY,   O       T
AFFECTION    O
TO PEER      O
                     T
             ---------------
             O       T
LEADS AND    OXXXXXXXXX
FOLLOWS      OXXXXXXXX
PEER         O     T
             ---------------
             0 1 2 3 4 5 6 7 8 9 10
```

	TOTAL SCORES FOR S 35	MEDIANS FOR 24/27 TWO YEAR STARTER CHILD. FOR ALL SUBJECTS
ADULT COMPETENCE	8.7	23.2
PEER COMPETENCE	2.3	5.1
OVERALL COMPETENCE	11.0	28.6

T INDICATES THE MEDIAN FOR ALL SUBJECTS FOR EACH COMPETENCE FACTOR.

SOCIAL COMPETENCE FOR SUBJECT 35

```
                       T
GAIN         O
ADULT        OXXXXXXXXXXXXXX
ATTENTION    OXXXXXXXXXXXXXX
             O        T
             ---------------
             O         T
USE          OXXXXXXXXXXXXXX
ADULT        OXXXXXXXXXXXXXX
RESOURCE     O         T
             ---------------
HOSTILITY,   O            T
AFFECTION    OXXXXXXXXXXXXXXXXXXXX
TO ADULT     OXXXXXXXXXXXXXXXXXXX
             O            T
             ---------------
             T
ROLE PLAY    O
             O
             T
             ---------------
             O             T
PRIDE IN     OXXXXXXXXXXXXXXXXXXX
PRODUCT      OXXXXXXXXXXXXXXXX
             O             T
             ---------------
             O  T
COMPETES     OXXXXXXXXXXXXXXXXXXXXXXXXXXXXX
WITH         OXXXXXXXXXXXXXXXXXXXXXXXXXXXXXX
PEER         O  T
             ---------------
HOSTILITY,   O          T
AFFECTION    OXXXXXXXXXXXXXX
TO PEER      OXXXXXXXXXXXXXX
             O          T
             ---------------
             O       T
LEADS AND    OXXXXXXXXXXX
FOLLOWS      OXXXXXXXXXXX
PEER         O       T
             ---------------
             0 1 2 3 4 5 6 7 8 9 10
```

	TOTAL SCORES FOR S 35	MEDIANS FOR 30/33 TWO YEAR STARTER CHILD. FOR ALL SUBJECTS
ADULT COMPETENCE	23.9	24.0
PEER COMPETENCE	11.0	11.9
OVERALL COMPETENCE	34.9	28.9

T INDICATES THE MEDIAN FOR ALL SUBJECTS FOR EACH COMPETENCE FACTOR.

Subject #35

Social Tasks	% Duration 24-27 Months	% Duration 30-33 Months
To please	0.3	0.0
To cooperate	4.0	4.9
To gain approval	0.0	0.0
To procure a service	2.1	1.2
To gain attention	1.0	1.1
To maintain social contact	0.0	7.4
To avoid unpleasant circumstances	0.0	0.0
To annoy	0.0	0.0
To direct	0.1	0.6
To assert self (protect domain)	0.8	1.3
To provide information	0.4	0.3
To compete	0.0	0.1
To reject overtures	0.0	0.0
To enjoy pets	0.0	0.0
To converse	0.2	0.8
To produce verbalizations	0.0	0.0
Nonsocial Tasks		
To eat	6.0	0.1
To gain information (v)	10.8	3.5
To gain information (v & a)	22.5	30.3
live language directed to child	4.0	3.7
live language overheard by child	1.5	7.9
mechanical language	0.0	2.3
Sesame Street	16.1	17.2
Nontask	3.6	4.2
To pass time	5.9	3.8
To find something to do	0.0	0.0
To prepare for an activity	3.7	2.3
To construct a product	0.2	0.0
To choose	0.0	0.0
To procure an object	2.8	1.6
To engage in large muscle activity	0.0	0.0
To gain pleasure	1.5	0.6
To imitate	0.1	0.0
To pretend (role play)	0.2	0.8
To ease discomfort	0.1	0.0
To restore order	0.2	0.0
To relieve oneself	0.0	0.0
To dress/undress	0.0	0.0
To operate a mechanism	0.0	0.0
To explore	8.4	1.7
To improve a developing skills (mastery)	11.4	32.6
gross	2.7	15.6
fine	8.7	17.1
verbal	0.0	0.0
To eat and gain information (v)	1.4	0.0
To eat and gain information (v & a)	8.2	0.2
live language directed to child	8.2	0.3
overheard	0.0	0.0

SUBJECT #36

Subject #36 is a two-year-old SES Level III predicted A boy who is the younger of two boys (brother is aged five). The family lives in a well-kept, small, four-room apartment in a working-class urban area. S has access to most areas of the apartment and is frequently engaged in play activities with his many toys, especially when his brother is at home.

S spends each morning alone with his mother, while his brother attends school. He stays close to her, following her around as she does her household chores.

S's mother is a warm person who is concerned about her children's development. Although her interaction with her children is limited, she keeps a close watch on their activities, disciplining them frequently with verbal reprimands.

Summary of Test Scores

Subject #36   Group: Two-Year-Old Starters (n = 20)

Tests	Age at Testing (Months)	Score	Group Median
Bayley Mental Development Index	12	—	—
	24	119	101
Stanford-Binet IQ	36	90	117.5
WPPSI IQ	60	110	111
Language Test[1]	12	—	—
	15	—	—
	21	—	—
	24	33	30
	27	36	36
	30	33	40.5
	36	39	—
Abstract Abilities[2]	12	—	—
	15	—	—
	21	—	—
	24	7	5.5
	27	7	6
	30	7	6.5
	36	8	—
Discrimination Test[2]	12	—	—
	15	—	—
	21	—	—
	24	4.0	3.0
	27	2.0	3.0
	30	4.0	6.0
	36	3.5	—

[1] Scores in Months
[2] Scores in Level Achieved

Individual Subject Data   337

SOCIAL COMPETENCE FOR SUBJECT 36

```
                    0             T
GAIN                OXXXXXXXXXXXXXXXXXXXXXXXXXX
ADULT               OXXXXXXXXXXXXXXXXXXXXXXXXX
ATTENTION                                   T
                    0
------------------------------------------------
                    0             T
USE                 OXXXXXXXXXXXXXX
ADULT               OXXXXXXXXXXXX
RESOURCE                       T
                    0
------------------------------------------------
                    0                    T
HOSTILITY,          OXXXXXXXXXXXXXXXXXXXXXXXXXXXXXXXX
AFFECTION           OXXXXXXXXXXXXXXXXXXXXXXXXXXXXXXX
TO ADULT                                    T
                    0
------------------------------------------------
                    T
                    0
ROLE PLAY           0
                    0
                    T
------------------------------------------------
                    0                    T
PRIDE IN            OXXXXXXXXXXXXXXXXXXXXXXXXXXXXXXXXXXXX
PRODUCT             OXXXXXXXXXXXXXXXXXXXXXXXXXXXXXXX
                                   T
                    0
------------------------------------------------
                    0  T
COMPETES            OXXXXXXXXXXXXXXXXXXXXXXXXXXXXXXXXXXXXXXXXX
WITH                OXXXXXXXXXXXXXXXXXXXXXXXXXXXXXXXXXXXXXXXXX
PEER                0   T
------------------------------------------------
                    0             T
HOSTILITY,          0X
AFFECTION           0X
TO PEER                      T
                    0
------------------------------------------------
                    0        T
LEADS AND           OXXXXXXXXXX
FOLLOWS             OXXXXXXXXX
PEER                      T
                    0
------------------------------------------------
                    0  1  2  3  4  5  6  7  8  9  10
```

	TOTAL SCORES FOR S 36	MEDIANS FOR 30/33 TWO YEAR STARTER CHILD. FOR ALL SUBJECTS
ADULT COMPETENCE	33.7	24.0
PEER COMPETENCE	12.2	11.9
OVERALL COMPETENCE	45.9	28.9

T INDICATES THE MEDIAN FOR ALL SUBJECTS FOR EACH COMPETENCE FACTOR.

SOCIAL COMPETENCE FOR SUBJECT 36

```
                    0             T
GAIN                OXXXXXXXXXXXXXXXXXXXXXX
ADULT               OXXXXXXXXXXXXXXXXXXXXX
ATTENTION                         T
                    0
------------------------------------------------
                    0                         T
USE                 OXXXXXXXXXXXXXXXXXXXXXXXXXXXXXXXX
ADULT               OXXXXXXXXXXXXXXXXXXXXXXXXXXXXXX
RESOURCE                                   T
                    0
------------------------------------------------
                    0                 T
HOSTILITY,          OXXXXXXXXXXXXXXXXXXXXXXXXXXXXXX
AFFECTION           OXXXXXXXXXXXXXXXXXXXXXXXXXXXXXXX
TO ADULT                                T
                    0
------------------------------------------------
                    T
                    0
ROLE PLAY           0
                    0
                    T
------------------------------------------------
                    T
                    0XXXXXXXXXXXX
PRIDE IN            0XXXXXXXXXXX
PRODUCT                    T
                    0
------------------------------------------------
                    0   T
COMPETES            0XX
WITH                0XX
PEER                0   T
------------------------------------------------
                    0    T
HOSTILITY,          0XXXXXXXX
AFFECTION           0XXXXXXXX
TO PEER                   T
                    0
------------------------------------------------
                    0
                    0XXXXXX
LEADS AND           0XXXXXX
FOLLOWS                  T
PEER                0
------------------------------------------------
                    0  1  2  3  4  5  6  7  8  9  10
```

	TOTAL SCORES FOR S 36	MEDIANS FOR 24/27 TWO YEAR STARTER CHILD. FOR ALL SUBJECTS
ADULT COMPETENCE	25.8	23.2
PEER COMPETENCE	3.3	5.1
OVERALL COMPETENCE	29.0	28.6

T INDICATES THE MEDIAN FOR ALL SUBJECTS FOR EACH COMPETENCE FACTOR.

Subject #36

Social Tasks	% Duration	
	24-27 Months	30-33 Months
To please	0.0	0.1
To cooperate	4.2	11.1
To gain approval	1.4	0.0
To procure a service	4.1	4.1
To gain attention	1.2	2.8
To maintain social contact	4.1	3.1
To avoid unpleasant circumstances	1.7	1.2
To annoy	2.5	0.0
To direct	2.2	1.0
To assert self (protect domain)	1.3	1.6
To provide information	0.1	0.9
To compete	0.0	0.0
To reject overtures	0.3	0.3
To enjoy pets	0.0	0.0
To converse	0.0	0.1
To produce verbalizations	0.0	0.2
Nonsocial Tasks		
To eat	8.1	7.3
To gain information (v)	9.6	4.5
To gain information (v & a)	2.1	2.3
live language directed to child	1.7	1.1
live language overheard by child	0.1	1.1
mechanical language	0.3	0.0
Sesame Street	0.0	0.0
Nontask	14.3	6.3
To pass time	3.5	1.3
To find something to do	0.0	0.0
To prepare for an activity	4.9	0.6
To construct a product	0.4	3.9
To choose	0.0	0.3
To procure an object	4.4	5.3
To engage in large muscle activity	0.0	0.1
To gain pleasure	0.8	2.5
To imitate	0.3	0.0
To pretend (role play)	0.9	0.0
To ease discomfort	0.0	0.0
To restore order	0.6	1.6
To relieve oneself	0.0	4.8
To dress/undress	0.0	0.0
To operate a mechanism	0.0	0.0
To explore	2.2	9.1
To improve a developing skill (mastery)	15.6	20.2
gross	8.7	14.6
fine	6.3	5.6
verbal	0.0	0.0
To eat and gain information (v)	4.2	1.8
To eat and gain information (v & a)	0.6	0.0
live language directed to child	0.0	0.0
overheard	0.4	0.1

SUBJECT #37

Subject #37 is a one-year-old SES Level V predicted C boy. He has two older siblings, aged two and five. The mother is divorced and raises the children alone. The family lives in rather modest circumstances, in a four-room apartment in a low-income housing project that is poorly kept; the apartment is equipped in a meager fashion to suit the needs of three young children. S, who is physically immature for his age, is kept in a playpen or jump seat for long periods, with the TV playing nearby. Interaction with his mother is of a playful and affectionate nature. Despite the meager physical surroundings, the child displays real interest in objects and toys, manipulating them for long periods when left to himself.

Summary of Test Scores

Subject #37   Group: One-Year-Old Starters (n = 19)

Tests	Age at Testing (Months)	Score	Group Median
Bayley Mental Developmental Index	12	50	103
	24	84	112
Stanford-Binet IQ	36	64	113
WPPSI IQ	60	109	117.5
Language Test[1]	12	10	14
	15	10	16
	21	14	21
	24	18	36
	27	not tested	—
	30	24	43.5
	36	36	45
Abstract Abilities[2]	12	2	2
	15	2	2
	21	5	5
	24	<5	6
	27	not tested	—
	30	<5	7
	36	7	9
Discrimination Test[2]	12	0	1
	15	0	2
	21	2	3
	24	2	3.5
	27	not tested	—
	30	2	5
	36	4	8

[1] Scores in Months
[2] Scores in Level Achieved

Individual Subject Data 341

SOCIAL COMPETENCE FOR SUBJECT 37

```
                      0   1   2   3   4   5   6   7   8   9   10
GAIN
ADULT         OXXXXXXXXXX       T
ATTENTION     OXXXXXXXXXX
              O                     T

USE           O
ADULT         OXXXXXX                   T
RESOURCE      OXXXXXX
              O                             T

HOSTILITY,    O                 T
AFFECTION     OXXXXXXXXXXXXXXXXXXXXXXXXXXXXXXXX
TO ADULT      OXXXXXXXXXXXXXXXXXXXXXXXXXXXXXXXXXXXXXXXXX
              O             T

ROLE PLAY     T
              O
              O
              O                 T

PRIDE IN      T
PRODUCT       O
              O
              O             T

COMPETES      O
WITH          O                         T
PEER          O
              O                     T

HOSTILITY,    O                 T
AFFECTION     OXXXXXXXXXXXXXXXXXXXXXXXXXXXXXX
TO PEER       O
              O             T

LEADS AND     O             T
FOLLOWS       O
PEER          O         T
              O
```

	TOTAL SCORES FOR S 37	MEDIANS AT 12/15 MONTHS FOR ALL SUBJECTS
ADULT COMPETENCE	17.5	13.8
PEER COMPETENCE	0.0	9.0
OVERALL COMPETENCE	17.5	20.5

T INDICATES THE MEDIAN FOR ALL SUBJECTS FOR EACH COMPETENCE FACTOR.

SOCIAL COMPETENCE FOR SUBJECT 37

```
                      0   1   2   3   4   5   6   7   8   9   10
GAIN          O
ADULT         OXXXXX           T
ATTENTION     OXXXXX
              O             T

USE           O
ADULT         OXXXXXXXXXXXXXXXXXXXXX       T
RESOURCE      OXXXXXXXXXXXXXXXXXX
              O                     T

HOSTILITY,    O             T
AFFECTION     OXXXXXXXXXXXXXXXXXXXXXXXXXXXXXXXXXXXXXXXXXXXXXXX
TO ADULT      OXXXXXXXXXXXXXXXXXXXXXXXXXXXXXXXXXXXXXXXXXXXXXX
              O                 T

ROLE PLAY     O                 T
              O
              O             T
              O

PRIDE IN      T
PRODUCT       O
              O
              O         T

COMPETES      O                                     T
WITH          OXXXXXXXXXXXXXXXXXXXXXXXXXXXXXXXXX
PEER          OXXXXXXXXXXXXXXXXXXXXXXXXXXXXXXX
              O                                 T

HOSTILITY,    O                         T
AFFECTION     OXXXXXXXXXXXXXXXXXXXXXXXXXXXXXXXXXXXXXXXXXXXXXX
TO PEER       OXXXXXXXXXXXXXXXXXXXXXXXXXXXXXXXXXXXXXXXXXXXX
              O                     T

LEADS AND     O                 T
FOLLOWS       OXXXXXXX
PEER          OXXXXXXX      T
              O
```

	TOTAL SCORES FOR S 37	MEDIANS AT 18/21 MONTHS FOR ALL SUBJECTS
ADULT COMPETENCE	15.4	22.2
PEER COMPETENCE	18.1	13.5
OVERALL COMPETENCE	33.5	23.5

T INDICATES THE MEDIAN FOR ALL SUBJECTS FOR EACH COMPETENCE FACTOR.

APPENDIX A

```
                    SOCIAL COMPETENCE FOR SUBJECT 37

GAIN           O                      T
ADULT          OXXXXXXXXXXXXXXXXXXXXXXXXXXXXXXXXXXX
ATTENTION      OXXXXXXXXXXXXXXXXXXXXXXXXXXXXXXXXXXX
               O                      T
-----------------------------------------------------------------
USE            O              T
ADULT          OXXXXXXXXX
RESOURCE       OXXXXXXXXX
               O              T
-----------------------------------------------------------------
HOSTILITY,     O       T
AFFECTION      OXXXXXXXXXXXXXXXXXXXXXXXXXXXXXXXXXXXXXXXX
TO ADULT       OXXXXXXXXXXXXXXXXXXXXXXXXXXXXXXXXXXXXXXXX
               O       T
-----------------------------------------------------------------
               O     T
RULE PLAY      OXXXXX
               OXXXXX
               O     T
-----------------------------------------------------------------
               O   T
PRIDE IN       OXXXXXXXXXXXXXXX
PRODUCT        OXXXXXXXXXXXXXXX
               O   T
-----------------------------------------------------------------
COMPETES       O                           T
WITH           OXXXXXXXXXXXXXXXXXXX
PEER           OXXXXXXXXXXXXXXXXXXX
               O                           T
-----------------------------------------------------------------
HOSTILITY,     O             T
AFFECTION      OXXXXX
TO PEER        OXXXXX
               O             T
-----------------------------------------------------------------
LEADS AND      O       T
FOLLOWS        O
PEER           O
               O     T
-----------------------------------------------------------------
               0   1   2   3   4   5   6   7   8   9   10
```

	TOTAL SCORES FOR S 37	MEDIANS FOR 30/33 ONE YEAR STARTER CHILD. FOR ALL SUBJECTS
ADULT COMPETENCE	32.0	26.0
PEER COMPETENCE	5.0	12.2
OVERALL COMPETENCE	37.0	33.6

T INDICATES THE MEDIAN FOR ALL SUBJECTS FOR EACH COMPETENCE FACTOR.

Subject #37

Social Tasks	% Duration	
	12-15 Months	18-21 Months
To please	0.0	0.0
To cooperate	6.5	5.8
To gain approval	0.0	0.0
To procure a service	0.3	1.1
To gain attention	0.3	0.9
To maintain social contact	1.6	1.6
To avoid unpleasant circumstances	0.0	0.0
To annoy	0.0	0.0
To direct	0.4	0.0
To assert self (protect domain)	1.0	0.0
To provide information	0.0	0.0
To compete	0.0	0.0
To reject overtures	0.0	0.0
To enjoy pets	0.0	0.0
To converse	0.0	0.0
To produce verbalizations	0.0	0.0
Nonsocial Tasks		
To eat	0.8	9.9
To gain information (v)	13.1	9.4
To gain information (v & a)	6.0	4.2
live language directed to child	1.2	2.8
live language overheard by child	0.3	0.4
mechanical language	4.6	0.0
Sesame Street	0.0	0.0
Nontask	13.3	25.9
To pass time	3.5	17.7
To find something to do	0.0	0.0
To prepare for an activity	0.0	0.7
To construct a product	0.0	0.0
To choose	0.0	0.0
To procure an object	4.2	2.8
To engage in large muscle activity	0.0	0.0
To gain pleasure	0.3	5.4
To imitate	0.0	0.8
To pretend (role play)	0.0	0.0
To ease discomfort	0.1	1.0
To restore order	0.0	0.2
To relieve oneself	0.0	0.0
To dress/undress	0.0	0.0
To operate a mechanism	0.6	0.3
To explore	25.3	9.9
To improve a developing skill (mastery)	14.5	1.7
gross	9.4	1.0
fine	5.1	0.7
verbal	0.0	0.0
To eat and gain information (v)	0.8	0.9
To eat and gain information (v & a)	6.4	0.0
live language directed to child	0.5	0.0
overheard	0.1	0.0

SUBJECT #38

Subject #38 is a two-year-old SES Level III predicted A boy who is the youngest of six children ranging in age from two to eight years. He lives in a small, somewhat disheveled apartment, in a run-down building in a working-class urban area. The home is not well equipped with toys, although there are some suitable objects for a child his age to use. However, subject #38 spends most of his time attending to his mother and her activities, occasionally imitating her household chores.

S's mother is a warm, energetic woman who seems able to cope with the many demands of a large family. She organizes the group activities such as eating and playing rather well, considering her limited resources.

Summary of Test Scores

Subject #38   Group: Two-Year-Old Starters (n = 20)

Tests	Age at Testing (Months)	Score	Group Median
Bayley Mental Development Index	12	—	—
	24	94	101
Stanford-Binet IQ	36	95	117.5
WPPSI IQ	60	102	111
Language Test[1]	12	—	—
	15	—	—
	21	—	—
	24	18	30
	27	30	36
	30	36	40.5
	36	42	—
Abstract Abilities[2]	12	—	—
	15	—	—
	21	—	—
	24	6	5.5
	27	6	6
	30	6	6.5
	36	8	—
Discrimination Test[2]	12	—	—
	15	—	—
	21	—	—
	24	0.0	3.0
	27	3.0	3.0
	30	1.0	6.0
	36	4.0	—

[1] Scores in Months
[2] Scores in Level Achieved

APPENDIX A

SOCIAL COMPETENCE FOR SUBJECT 38

```
                              T
GAIN              OXXXXXXXXXXXXXXXXXXXXXXX
ADULT             OXXXXXXXXXXXXXXXXXXXXXXX
ATTENTION         O                T
------------------------------------------
                                      T
USE               O
ADULT             OXXXXXXXXXXXXXXXXXXXXXXXXX
RESOURCE          OXXXXXXXXXXXXXXXXXXXXXXXXX
                  O                 T
------------------------------------------
                                T
HOSTILITY,        OXXXXXXXXXXXXXXXXXXXXXXX
AFFECTION         OXXXXXXXXXXXXXXXXXXXXXXX
TO ADULT          O              T
------------------------------------------
                  T
ROLE PLAY         OXXXXXXXXXXXXX
                  OXXXXXXXXXXXXX
                  T
------------------------------------------
                  T
PRIDE IN          O
PRODUCT           O
                  T
------------------------------------------
                  O  T
COMPETES          OXXXXXXX
WITH              OXXXXXXX
PEER              O  T
------------------------------------------
                  O T
HOSTILITY,        OXXXXXXXXXXXXXXXXXXXXXXXXXXXXXX
AFFECTION         OXXXXXXXXXXXXXXXXXXXXXXXXXXXXXX
TO PEER           O               T
------------------------------------------
                  O  T
LEADS AND         OXXXXXXXXXXXXXXX
FOLLOWS           OXXXXXXXXXXXXXXX
PEER              O  T
------------------------------------------
                  0  1  2  3  4  5  6  7  8  9  10
```

	TOTAL SCORES FOR S 38	MEDIANS FOR 24/27 TWO YEAR STARTER CHILD. FOR ALL SUBJECTS
ADULT COMPETENCE	27.2	23.2
PEER COMPETENCE	12.8	5.1
OVERALL COMPETENCE	40.0	28.6

T INDICATES THE MEDIAN FOR ALL SUBJECTS FOR EACH COMPETENCE FACTOR.

SOCIAL COMPETENCE FOR SUBJECT 38

```
                              T
GAIN              OXXXXXXXXXX
ADULT             OXXXXXXXXXX
ATTENTION         O             T
------------------------------------------
                                  T
USE               O
ADULT             OXXXXXXXXXXXXX
RESOURCE          OXXXXXXXXXXXXX
                  O                T
------------------------------------------
                         T
HOSTILITY,        O
AFFECTION         OXXXXXXX
TO ADULT          OXXXXXXX
                  O          T
------------------------------------------
                  T
ROLE PLAY         OXXXXXXXXXXXXXXXXXXXXXXXXXXXXXXXXXXXXXXXXX
                  OXXXXXXXXXXXXXXXXXXXXXXXXXXXXXXXXXXXXXXXXX
                                  T
------------------------------------------
                                      T
PRIDE IN          O
PRODUCT           OXXXXXXXXXXXXXXXXX
                  OXXXXXXXXXXXXXXXXX
                  O                 T
------------------------------------------
                  O  T
COMPETES          OXXXXXXXXX
WITH              OXXXXXXXXX
PEER              O  T
------------------------------------------
                              T
HOSTILITY,        O
AFFECTION         OXXXXXXXXXXXXXXXXXXXXXXXXXX
TO PEER           OXXXXXXXXXXXXXXXXXXXXXXXXXX
                  O             T
------------------------------------------
                  O                                          T
LEADS AND         OXXXXXXXXXXXXXXXXXXXXXXXXXXXXXXXXXXXXXXXXXXXXXXX
FOLLOWS           OXXXXXXXXXXXXXXXXXXXXXXXXXXXXXXXXXXXXXXXXXXXXXXX
PEER              O                              T
------------------------------------------
                  0  1  2  3  4  5  6  7  8  9  10
```

	TOTAL SCORES FOR S 38	MEDIANS FOR 30/33 TWO YEAR STARTER CHILD. FOR ALL SUBJECTS
ADULT COMPETENCE	32.4	24.0
PEER COMPETENCE	18.6	11.9
OVERALL COMPETENCE	50.9	28.9

T INDICATES THE MEDIAN FOR ALL SUBJECTS FOR EACH COMPETENCE FACTOR.

Subject #38

Social Tasks	% Duration	
	24-27 Months	30-33 Months
To please	0.1	0.0
To cooperate	5.8	3.5
To gain approval	0.0	0.0
To procure a service	2.7	2.2
To gain attention	3.8	6.7
To maintain social contact	5.9	8.2
To avoid unpleasant circumstances	0.4	0.0
To annoy	0.0	1.2
To direct	0.0	0.3
To assert self (protect domain)	0.9	2.0
To provide information	0.0	0.1
To compete	0.0	0.0
To reject overtures	0.8	0.3
To enjoy pets	0.0	0.0
To converse	0.0	0.0
To produce verbalizations	0.0	0.0
Nonsocial Tasks		
To eat	5.5	3.9
To gain information (v)	14.3	11.6
To gain information (v & a)	9.9	6.3
live language directed to child	1.8	1.7
live language overheard by child	3.4	2.8
mechanical language	4.3	1.8
Sesame Street	0.0	0.0
Nontask	13.9	33.0
To pass time	1.0	0.2
To find something to do	0.0	0.0
To prepare for an activity	0.6	1.5
To construct a product	0.0	0.0
To choose	0.0	0.0
To procure an object	2.7	2.5
To engage in large muscle activity	0.0	0.0
To gain pleasure	11.5	0.0
To imitate	0.2	2.8
To pretend (role play)	0.1	0.3
To ease discomfort	0.6	0.5
To restore order	2.0	0.6
To relieve oneself	0.0	0.0
To dress/undress	6.2	0.0
To operate a mechanism	0.0	0.0
To explore	4.3	0.9
To improve a developing skill (mastery)	6.0	6.2
gross	0.0	3.7
fine	6.0	2.6
verbal	0.0	0.0
To eat and gain information (v)	0.0	0.5
To eat and gain information (v & a)	0.4	0.5
live language directed to child	0.0	0.4
overheard	0.5	0.1

SUBJECT #39

Subject #39 is a two-year-old SES Level III predicted A boy. The family lived in a two-family house in an urban area. S has one older brother, age 4½; a new baby was born by the time S was 2½. There are many suitable toys available to S. This home is characterized by a quiet, calm, pleasant atmosphere. It is unusually well-kept, even though the child is allowed access to most of the space. S's mother seemed composed, warm, and well in control of the home.

Summary of Test Scores

Subject #39   **Group: Two-Year-Old Starters (n = 20)**

Tests	Age at Testing (Months)	Score	Group Median
Bayley Mental Development Index	12	—	—
	24	104	101
Stanford-Binet IQ	36	108	117.5
WPPSI IQ	60	106	111
Language Test[1]	12	—	—
	15	—	—
	21	—	—
	24	24	30
	27	36	36
	30	42	40.5
	36	48	—
Abstract Abilities[2]	12	—	—
	15	—	—
	21	—	—
	24	<5	5.5
	27	6	6
	30	7	6.5
	36	9	—
Discrimination Test[2]	12	—	—
	15	—	—
	21	—	—
	24	3.5	3.0
	27	3.5	3.0
	30	7.0	6.0
	36	8.0	—

[1] Scores in Months
[2] Scores in Level Achieved

350   APPENDIX A

SOCIAL COMPETENCE FOR SUBJECT 39

```
                               T
GAIN            0XXXXXXXXXXXXXXXXXXXXXXXXXXXXXXXXXXXXX
ADULT           0XXXXXXXXXXXXXXXXXXXXXXXXXXXXXXXXXXXXX
ATTENTION       0                 T
                                                  T
USE             0XXXXXXXXXXXXXXXXXXXXXXXXXX
ADULT           0XXXXXXXXXXXXXXXXXXXXXXXXXX
RESOURCE        0                        T

HOSTILITY,      0XXXXXXXXX         T
AFFECTION       0XXXXXXXXX
TO ADULT        0          T
                T
ROLE PLAY       0XXXXXXXXXXXXXXX
                0XXXXXXXXXXXXXXX
                           T
PRIDE IN        T
PRODUCT         0
                0
                T
COMPETES        0       T
WITH            0
PEER            0
                         T
HOSTILITY,      0                 T
AFFECTION       0
TO PEER         0       T

LEADS AND       0             T
FOLLOWS         0
PEER            0
                      T
                |---|---|---|---|---|---|---|---|---|---|
                0   1   2   3   4   5   6   7   8   9   10
```

	TOTAL SCORES FOR S 39	MEDIANS FOR 24/27 TWO YEAR STARTER CHILD. FOR ALL SUBJECTS
ADULT COMPETENCE	28.4	23.2
PEER COMPETENCE	0.0	5.1
OVERALL COMPETENCE	28.4	28.6

T INDICATES THE MEDIAN FOR ALL SUBJECTS FOR EACH COMPETENCE FACTOR.

SOCIAL COMPETENCE FOR SUBJECT 39

```
                                    T
GAIN            0XXXXXXXXXXXXXXXXXXXXXXXXXXXXXXXXXXXXXXXXXXXX
ADULT           0XXXXXXXXXXXXXXXXXXXXXXXXXXXXXXXXXXXXXXXXXXXX
ATTENTION       0                        T
                                       T
USE             0XXXXXXXXXXXXXXXXXXXXXXXXXX
ADULT           0XXXXXXXXXXXXXXXXXXXXXXXXXX
RESOURCE        0                              T

HOSTILITY,      0XXXXXXXXXXXXXXXXXXXXXXXXXXXXXXXXXXXX
AFFECTION       0XXXXXXXXXXXXXXXXXXXXXXXXXXXXXXXXXXXX
TO ADULT        0
                T
ROLE PLAY       0XXXXX
                0XXXXX
                T
                                                       T
PRIDE IN        0XXXXXXXXXXXXXXXXXXXXXXXXXXXXXXXXXXXXXXXXXXXXXXXX
PRODUCT         0XXXXXXXXXXXXXXXXXXXXXXXXXXXXXXXXXXXXXXXXXXXXXXXX
                0                    T

COMPETES        0   T
WITH            0
PEER            0   T

HOSTILITY,      0                    T
AFFECTION       0
TO PEER         0                T

LEADS AND       0             T
FOLLOWS         0
PEER            0        T
                |---|---|---|---|---|---|---|---|---|---|
                0   1   2   3   4   5   6   7   8   9   10
```

	TOTAL SCORES FOR S 39	MEDIANS FOR 30/33 TWO YEAR STARTER CHILD. FOR ALL SUBJECTS
ADULT COMPETENCE	45.7	24.0
PEER COMPETENCE	0.0	11.9
OVERALL COMPETENCE	45.7	28.9

T INDICATES THE MEDIAN FOR ALL SUBJECTS FOR EACH COMPETENCE FACTOR.

Subject #39

Social Tasks	% Duration	
	24-27 Months	30-33 Months
To please	0.2	0.0
To cooperate	4.7	4.2
To gain approval	0.0	1.4
To procure a service	4.2	1.0
To gain attention	3.2	3.1
To maintain social contact	4.1	0.4
To avoid unpleasant circumstances	0.2	0.0
To annoy	0.3	0.0
To direct	1.0	0.0
To assert self (protect domain)	1.4	0.0
To provide information	0.4	0.6
To compete	0.0	0.0
To reject overtures	0.0	0.0
To enjoy pets	0.0	0.0
To converse	0.0	0.4
To produce verbalizations	0.0	0.0
Nonsocial Tasks		
To eat	6.5	2.4
To gain information (v)	12.4	11.6
To gain information (v & a)	16.7	18.7
live language directed to child	7.5	5.7
live language overheard by child	4.2	8.7
mechanical language	3.0	0.8
Sesame Street	1.8	2.9
Nontask	7.2	4.3
To pass time	6.0	34.4
To find something to do	0.0	0.0
To prepare for an activity	3.5	1.9
To construct a product	0.0	2.3
To choose	0.0	0.0
To procure an object	2.2	2.1
To engage in large muscle activity	0.8	0.0
To gain pleasure	0.0	3.5
To imitate	0.1	0.7
To pretend (role play)	0.7	0.0
To ease discomfort	0.7	0.0
To restore order	0.0	0.0
To relieve oneself	0.0	0.0
To dress/undress	0.1	0.0
To operate a mechanism	1.6	0.3
To explore	5.0	0.8
To improve a developing skill (mastery)	11.6	6.0
gross	7.2	3.2
fine	4.4	2.8
verbal	0.5	0.0
To eat and gain information (v)	1.3	0.0
To eat and gain information (v & a)	2.4	0.0
live language directed to child	0.2	0.0
overheard	0.0	0.0

SUBJECT #40

Subject #40 is a one-year-old SES Level IV predicted C girl. S has two older siblings, ages four and six. The family rents an apartment in a two-family house in a working-class urban area. The apartment is poorly furnished. Although toys are available, they are usually broken and not suitable for a one-year-old.

S is a pleasant, active little girl. Both parents were usually home during the day, and S enjoyed interacting with them. She seems adept at making the most out of what is available to her in an apparently poor environment. The general tone of the home was invariably casual and friendly.

Summary of Test Scores

Subject #40   Group: One-Year-Old Starters (n = 19)

Tests	Age at Testing (Months)	Score	Group Median
Bayley Mental Developmental Index	12	122	103
	24	106	112
Stanford-Binet IQ	36	110	113
WPPSI IQ	60	106	117.5
Language Test[1]	12	16	14
	15	16	16
	21	18	21
	24	24	36
	27	33	—
	30	not tested	—
	36	54	45
Abstract Abilities[2]	12	3	2
	15	2	2
	21	5	5
	24	5	6
	27	6	—
	30	not tested	—
	36	9	9
Discrimination Test[2]	12	2	1
	15	0	2
	21	3	3
	24	4	3.5
	27	not tested	—
	30	6	5
	36	8	8

[1] Scores in Months
[2] Scores in Level Achieved

SOCIAL COMPETENCE FOR SUBJECT 40

```
                        0 XXXXXXXXXXXXXXX      T
GAIN                    0 XXXXXXXXXXXXXXX
ADULT                   0
ATTENTION                                T
                        -----------------------------------
                        0                       T
USE                     0 XXXXXXXXXXXXXXXXXXXXXXXXXXXXXXXXXX
ADULT                   0 XXXXXXXXXXXXXXXXXXXXXXXXXXXXXXXXXX
RESOURCE                0                              T
                        -----------------------------------
                        0         T
HOSTILITY,              0 XXXXX
AFFECTION               0 XXXXX
TO ADULT                0            T
                        -----------------------------------
                        T
                        0
ROLE PLAY               0
                        0 T
                        -----------------------------------
                        T
                        0
PRIDE IN                0
PRODUCT                 0 T
                        -----------------------------------
                        0         T
COMPETES                0 XXXXXXXXX
WITH                    0 XXXXXXXXX
PEER                    0       T
                        -----------------------------------
                        0 T
HOSTILITY,              0 XXXXXXX
AFFECTION               0 XXXXXXX
TO PEER                 0 T
                        -----------------------------------
                        0       T
LEADS AND               0 X
FOLLOWS                 0 X
PEER                    0  T
                        -----------------------------------
                        0   1   2   3   4   5   6   7   8   9   10
```

	TOTAL SCORES FOR S 40	MEDIANS AT 12/15 MONTHS FOR ALL SUBJECTS
ADULT COMPETENCE	12.6	13.8
PEER COMPETENCE	4.0	9.0
OVERALL COMPETENCE	16.6	20.5

T INDICATES THE MEDIAN FOR ALL SUBJECTS FOR EACH COMPETENCE FACTOR.

SOCIAL COMPETENCE FOR SUBJECT 40

```
                        0                        T
GAIN                    0 XXXXXXXXXXXXXXXXXXXXXXXXXXXXXXXX
ADULT                   0 XXXXXXXXXXXXXXXXXXXXXXXXXXXXXXXX
ATTENTION               0            T
                        -----------------------------------
                        0                    T
USE                     0 XXXXXXXXXXXXXXXXXXXXX
ADULT                   0 XXXXXXXXXXXXXXXXXXXXX
RESOURCE                0                 T
                        -----------------------------------
                        0         T
HOSTILITY,              0 XXXXXXXXXX
AFFECTION               0 XXXXXXXXXX
TO ADULT                0         T
                        -----------------------------------
                        0   T
                        0 XXXXXXXXXXXXXXXXXXXXXXX
ROLE PLAY               0 XXXXXXXXXXXXXXXXXXXXXXX
                        0          T
                        -----------------------------------
                        T
                        0
PRIDE IN                0
PRODUCT                 0 T
                        -----------------------------------
                        0                   T
COMPETES                0
WITH                    0
PEER                    0              T
                        -----------------------------------
                        0              T
HOSTILITY,              0
AFFECTION               0
TO PEER                 0       T
                        -----------------------------------
                        0          T
LEADS AND               0
FOLLOWS                 0
PEER                    0
                        -----------------------------------
                        0   1   2   3   4   5   6   7   8   9   10
```

	TOTAL SCORES FOR S 40	MEDIANS AT 18/21 MONTHS FOR ALL SUBJECTS
ADULT COMPETENCE	24.4	22.2
PEER COMPETENCE	0.0	13.5
OVERALL COMPETENCE	24.4	23.5

T INDICATES THE MEDIAN FOR ALL SUBJECTS FOR EACH COMPETENCE FACTOR.

SOCIAL COMPETENCE FOR SUBJECT 40

```
GAIN           O                 T
ADULT          OXXXXXXXXXXXXXXXXXXXXXXXXXXXXXXXXXXXXXX
ATTENTION      OXXXXXXXXXXXXXXXXXXXXXXXXXXXXXXXXXXXXXX
               O                 T
------------------------------------------------------
USE            O           T
ADULT          OXXXXXXXXXXXXXXXXXXXXXXXXXXXXXXXXXX
RESOURCE       OXXXXXXXXXXXXXXXXXXXXXXXXXXXXXXXXXX
               O           T
------------------------------------------------------
HOSTILITY,     O     T
AFFECTION      OXXXXXXXXXXXXXXXXXXXXXXXXXXXX
TO ADULT       OXXXXXXXXXXXXXXXXXXXXXXXXXXXX
               O     T
------------------------------------------------------
               O  T
ROLE PLAY      OXXXXXXXXXXXXXXXXXXXXXXXXXXXXXXXXXXXXXXXXXXXXX
               OXXXXXXXXXXXXXXXXXXXXXXXXXXXXXXXXXXXXXXXXXXXXX
               O  T
------------------------------------------------------
               O  T
PRIDE IN       O
PRODUCT        O
               O  T
------------------------------------------------------
COMPETES       O                           T
WITH           O
PEER           O
               O                           T
------------------------------------------------------
HOSTILITY,     O              T
AFFECTION      O
TO PEER        O
               O              T
------------------------------------------------------
LEADS AND      O       T
FOLLOWS        O
PEER           O
               O    T
------------------------------------------------------
               O   1   2   3   4   5   6   7   8   9   10
```

	TOTAL SCORES FOR S 40	MEDIANS FOR 30/33 ONE YEAR STARTER CHILD. FOR ALL SUBJECTS
ADULT COMPETENCE	37.0	26.0
PEER COMPETENCE	0.0	12.2
OVERALL COMPETENCE	37.0	33.6

T INDICATES THE MEDIAN FOR ALL SUBJECTS FOR EACH COMPETENCE FACTOR.

Subject #40

	% Duration	
Social Tasks	12-15 Months	18-21 Months
To please	0.1	0.0
To cooperate	3.3	1.6
To gain approval	0.0	0.0
To procure a service	1.0	0.0
To gain attention	2.3	0.2
To maintain social contact	2.8	2.8
To avoid unpleasant circumstances	0.0	0.0
To annoy	0.0	0.0
To direct	0.0	0.0
To assert self (protect domain)	0.8	3.0
To provide information	0.0	0.0
To compete	0.0	0.0
To reject overtures	0.0	0.0
To enjoy pets	0.0	0.0
To converse	0.0	0.0
To produce verbalizations	0.0	0.0
Nonsocial Tasks		
To eat	8.7	10.3
To gain information (v)	9.7	1.8
To gain information (v & a)	4.1	35.0
live language directed to child	2.4	5.9
live language overheard by child	0.9	0.0
mechanical language	0.8	7.2
Sesame Street	0.0	21.9
Nontask	29.4	16.2
To pass time	3.3	2.8
To find something to do	0.0	0.0
To prepare for an activity	1.7	1.2
To construct a product	0.0	0.0
To choose	0.0	0.0
To procure an object	1.9	1.6
To engage in large muscle activity	0.0	0.0
To gain pleasure	0.0	0.0
To imitate	0.0	0.0
To pretend (role play)	0.3	9.3
To ease discomfort	0.8	0.0
To restore order	0.8	0.8
To relieve oneself	0.0	0.0
To dress/undress	0.0	0.0
To operate a mechanism	0.0	1.8
To explore	19.6	8.5
To improve a developing skill (mastery)	6.3	0.8
gross	2.9	0.0
fine	2.4	0.8
verbal	0.1	0.0
To eat and gain information (v)	1.5	0.4
To eat and gain information (v & a)	0.4	1.6
live language directed to child	0.1	0.0
overheard	0.2	0.0

SUBJECT #41

Subject #41 is a one-year-old SES Level V predicted C girl who lives with two older brothers (ages five and six) and her parents in a low-income urban housing project. The apartment is crowded and, except for the living room, is poorly furnished. The home life in this family is unpredictable. The mother left home for fairly lengthy periods of time on two known occasions. During her absence, a grandmother and the father took over the household management. When the mother is home, she is moody and unpredictable. Although S is clearly her favorite, the mother engages in half-serious name-calling and threats. The mother is routinely verbally and physically harsh with the older children.

S is an appealing child who spent a considerable amount of time playing in her high chair. There were few toys or objects available to S. There were generally several pets in residence including a much-abused dog, a cat, and several tanks of fish.

Summary of Test Scores

Subject #41 Group: One-Year-Old Starters (n = 19)

Tests	Age at Testing (Months)	Score	Group Median
Bayley Mental Developmental Index	12	98	103
	24	91	112
Stanford-Binet IQ	36	76	113
WPPSI IQ	60	106	117.5
Language Test[1]	12	14	14
	15	16	16
	21	21	21
	24	24	36
	27	30	—
	30	not tested	—
	36	45	45
Abstract Abilities[2]	12	2	2
	15	2	2
	21	6	5
	24	5	6
	27	7	—
	30	not tested	—
	36	7	9
Discrimination Test[2]	12	1.0	1
	15	4.0	2
	21	3.0	3
	24	3.5	3.5
	27	not tested	—
	30	3.5	5
	36	5.0	8

[1] Scores in Months
[2] Scores in Level Achieved

SOCIAL COMPETENCE FOR SUBJECT 41

```
                           T
GAIN           OXXXXXXXXXXXXXXXXXX
ADULT          OXXXXXXXXXXXXXXXXXXX
ATTENTION      O                   T
               -------------------------------------
               O      T
USE            OXXX
ADULT          OXXX
RESOURCE       O              T
               -------------------------------------
                      T
HOSTILITY,     OXXXXXXXXXXXXXXXX
AFFECTION      OXXXXXXXXXXXXXXXX
TO ADULT       O                T
               -------------------------------------
               T
               O
ROLE PLAY      O
               T
               -------------------------------------
               T
PRIDE IN       O
PRODUCT        O
               T
               -------------------------------------
               O                              T
COMPETES       OXXXXXXXXXXXXXXXXXXXXXXXXXXXXXXXXX
WITH           OXXXXXXXXXXXXXXXXXXXXXXXXXXXXXXXXX
PEER           O   T
               -------------------------------------
               O     T
HOSTILITY,     OXXXXXXXXXXXXXXXXXXXXXXXXXXXXXXXX
AFFECTION      OXXXXXXXXXXXXXXXXXXXXXXXXXXXXXXXX
TO PEER        O             T
               -------------------------------------
               O  T
LEADS AND      OXXXXXXXXXXXXXXXXXXXXXXXXXXXXXX
FOLLOWS        OXXXXXXXXXXXXXXXXXXXXXXXXXXXXXX
PEER           O  T
               -------------------------------------
               0   1   2   3   4   5   6   7   8   9   10
```

	TOTAL SCORES FOR S 41	MEDIANS AT 12/15 MONTHS FOR ALL SUBJECTS
ADULT COMPETENCE	8.5	13.8
PEER COMPETENCE	30.0	9.0
OVERALL COMPETENCE	38.5	20.5

T INDICATES THE MEDIAN FOR ALL SUBJECTS FOR EACH COMPETENCE FACTOR.

SOCIAL COMPETENCE FOR SUBJECT 41

```
                           T
GAIN           OXXXXXXXX
ADULT          OXXXXXXXX
ATTENTION      O          T
               -------------------------------------
               O                            T
USE            OXXXXXXXXXXXXXXXXXXXXXXXXXXXX
ADULT          OXXXXXXXXXXXXXXXXXXXXXXXXXXXX
RESOURCE       O                             T
               -------------------------------------
               O   T
HOSTILITY,     OXXXXXXXXX
AFFECTION      OXXXXXXXXX
TO ADULT       O     T
               -------------------------------------
               O          T
               O
ROLE PLAY      O
               O     T
               -------------------------------------
               T
PRIDE IN       O
PRODUCT        O
               O
               T
               -------------------------------------
               T
COMPETES       O                  T
WITH           OXXXXXXXXX
PEER           OXXXXXXXXX
               O
               -------------------------------------
               O                                       T
HOSTILITY,     OXXXXXXXXXXXXXXXXXXXXXXXXXXXXXXXXXXXX
AFFECTION      OXXXXXXXXXXXXXXXXXXXXXXXXXXXXXXXXXXXX
TO PEER        O                       T
               -------------------------------------
               O                                              T
LEADS AND      OXXXXXXXXXXXXXXXXXXXXXXXXXXXXXXXXXXXXXXXXXXXXXX
FOLLOWS        OXXXXXXXXXXXXXXXXXXXXXXXXXXXXXXXXXXXXXXXXXXXXXX
PEER           O
               -------------------------------------
               0   1   2   3   4   5   6   7   8   9   10
```

	TOTAL SCORES FOR S 41	MEDIANS AT 18/21 MONTHS FOR ALL SUBJECTS
ADULT COMPETENCE	13.2	22.2
PEER COMPETENCE	16.8	13.5
OVERALL COMPETENCE	30.0	23.5

T INDICATES THE MEDIAN FOR ALL SUBJECTS FOR EACH COMPETENCE FACTOR.

APPENDIX A

SOCIAL COMPETENCE FOR SUBJECT 41

```
                    O                   T
GAIN                OXXXXXXXXXXXXXXXXXXXXXXXXXXX
ADULT               OXXXXXXXXXXXXXXXXXXXXXXXXXXX
ATTENTION           O                   T
-------------------------------------------------------------
USE                 O           T
ADULT               OXXXXXXXXXXXXX
RESOURCE            OXXXXXXXXXXXXX
                    O           T
-------------------------------------------------------------
HOSTILITY,          O     T
AFFECTION           OXXXXXXXXXXXXXXXXXXXXXXXXXXXXXXXXXXXXXXXXXXXXXXXXXX
TO ADULT            OXXXXXXXXXXXXXXXXXXXXXXXXXXXXXXXXXXXXXXXXXXXXXXXXXX
                    O     T
-------------------------------------------------------------
                    O    T
ROLE PLAY           OXXXXXXXXXXXXXXXXXXXXXXXXXXXXXXXXXXXX
                    OXXXXXXXXXXXXXXXXXXXXXXXXXXXXXXXXXXXX
                    O    T
-------------------------------------------------------------
                    O   T
PRIDE IN            OXXX
PRODUCT             OXXX
                    O   T
-------------------------------------------------------------
COMPETES            O                           T
WITH                O
PEER                O
                    O                              T
-------------------------------------------------------------
HOSTILITY,          O             T
AFFECTION           O
TO PEER             O
                    O             T
-------------------------------------------------------------
LEADS AND           O        T
FOLLOWS             O
PEER                O
                    O        T
-------------------------------------------------------------
                    0   1   2   3   4   5   6   7   8   9   10
```

	TOTAL SCORES FOR S 41	MEDIANS FOR 30/33 ONE YEAR STARTER CHILD. FOR ALL SUBJECTS
ADULT COMPETENCE	33.6	26.0
PEER COMPETENCE	0.0	12.2
OVERALL COMPETENCE	33.6	33.6

T INDICATES THE MEDIAN FOR ALL SUBJECTS FOR EACH COMPETENCE FACTOR.

Subject #41

Social Tasks	% Duration	
	12-15 Months	18-21 Months
To please	0.0	0.0
To cooperate	3.8	7.5
To gain approval	0.0	0.0
To procure a service	0.6	1.0
To gain attention	0.6	1.5
To maintain social contact	15.1	3.1
To avoid unpleasant circumstances	0.0	0.2
To annoy	0.0	0.0
To direct	0.0	0.4
To assert self (protect domain)	0.3	1.6
To provide information	0.3	0.0
To compete	0.0	0.0
To reject overtures	0.0	0.0
To enjoy pets	0.1	0.9
To converse	0.0	0.0
To produce verbalizations	0.0	0.0
Nonsocial Tasks		
To eat	19.5	16.4
To gain information (v)	5.1	12.0
To gain information (v & a)	2.8	6.0
live language directed to child	1.3	0.6
live language overheard by child	0.0	5.0
mechanical language	0.8	0.0
Sesame Street	0.0	0.4
Nontask	7.9	11.9
To pass time	13.5	0.4
To find something to do	0.0	0.0
To prepare for an activity	0.0	1.6
To construct a product	0.0	0.0
To choose	0.0	0.0
To procure an object	0.8	1.3
To engage in large muscle activity	0.0	0.0
To gain pleasure	0.0	0.0
To imitate	0.0	0.1
To pretend (role play)	0.3	2.7
To ease discomfort	0.2	1.2
To restore order	0.1	1.4
To relieve oneself	0.0	0.0
To dress/undress	0.0	0.0
To operate a mechanism	0.0	2.8
To explore	14.2	5.0
To improve a developing skill (mastery)	6.7	11.5
gross	5.1	1.6
fine	1.6	9.9
verbal	0.0	0.0
To eat and gain information (v)	3.6	4.4
To eat and gain information (v & a)	0.3	3.9
live language directed to child	0.1	0.0
overheard	0.3	4.0

SUBJECT #42

Subject #42 is a one-year-old SES Level III predicted C boy. S is the youngest of three children. This family, which consists of the parents, children, and grandfather, lives in a pleasant home in a suburban area. They own their home and are in the process of remodeling it themselves.

S is a quiet, friendly, and active child. Although toys are available downstairs in a playroom, S prefers to spend most of his time upstairs in the kitchen with his parents or outside watching his father make repairs on their house. He spends a good deal of time playing with objects, especially balls. Unlike in most families, this father is home most of each day because he works a late shift at his job. The atmosphere of the home is generally calm and happy.

Summary of Test Scores

Subject #42   Group: One-Year-Old Starters (n = 19)

Tests	Age at Testing (Months)	Score	Group Median
Bayley Mental Developmental Index	12	103	103
	24	94	112
Stanford-Binet IQ	36	98	113
WPPSI IQ	60	120	117.5
Language Test[1]	12	12	14
	15	16	16
	21	18	21
	24	24	36
	27	24	—
	30	not tested	—
	36	42	45
Abstract Abilities[2]	12	1	2
	15	1	2
	21	5	5
	24	6	6
	27	7	—
	30	not tested	—
	36	8	9
Discrimination Test[2]	12	0.0	1
	15	1.0	2
	21	2.0	3
	24	3.5	3.5
	27	not tested	—
	30	5.0	5
	36	8.0	8

[1] Scores in Months
[2] Scores in Level Achieved

364 APPENDIX A

SOCIAL COMPETENCE FOR SUBJECT 42

```
                                    T
GAIN              OXXXXXXXXXXXXXXXXXXXXX
ADULT             OXXXXXXXXXXXXXXXXXXXXX
ATTENTION         O                T
                  ----------------------
                                T
USE               OXXXXXXXXXXXXXX
ADULT             OXXXXXXXXXXXXXX
RESOURCE          O          T
                  ----------------------
                       T
HOSTILITY,        OXXXXXXXXXXXXXX
AFFECTION         OXXXXXXXXXXXXXX
TO ADULT          O        T
                  ----------------------
                  T
ROLE PLAY         O
                  O
                  O  T
                  ----------------------
                  T
PRIDE IN          O
PRODUCT           O
                  O  T
                  ----------------------
                    T
COMPETES          OXXXXXXXXXX
WITH              OXXXXXXXXXX
PEER              O      T
                  ----------------------
                  O  T
HOSTILITY,        OXXXXXX
AFFECTION         OXXXXXX
TO PEER           O  T
                  ----------------------
                  O  T
LEADS AND         O
FOLLOWS           O
PEER              O  T
                  ----------------------
                  0  1  2  3  4  5  6  7  8  9  10
```

	TOTAL SCORES FOR S 42	MEDIANS AT 12/15 MONTHS FOR ALL SUBJECTS
ADULT COMPETENCE	13.8	13.8
PEER COMPETENCE	3.7	9.0
OVERALL COMPETENCE	17.5	20.5

T INDICATES THE MEDIAN FOR ALL SUBJECTS FOR EACH COMPETENCE FACTOR.

SOCIAL COMPETENCE FOR SUBJECT 42

```
                                              T
GAIN              OXXXXXXXXXXXXXXXXXXXXXXXXXXXXX
ADULT             OXXXXXXXXXXXXXXXXXXXXXXXXXXXXX
ATTENTION         O                T
                  -------------------------------
                                           T
USE               OXXXXXXXXXXXXXXXXXXXXXXXX
ADULT             OXXXXXXXXXXXXXXXXXXXXXXXX
RESOURCE          O                T
                  -------------------------------
                            T
HOSTILITY,        OXXXXXXXXXXXXXXXXXXXXXX
AFFECTION         OXXXXXXXXXXXXXXXXXXXXXX
TO ADULT          O            T
                  -------------------------------
                  O  T
ROLE PLAY         O
                  O
                  O  T
                  -------------------------------
                  T
PRIDE IN          OXXXXX
PRODUCT           OXXXXX
                  O  T
                  -------------------------------
                  O            T
COMPETES          O
WITH              O
PEER              O  T
                  -------------------------------
                  O            T
HOSTILITY,        O
AFFECTION         O
TO PEER           O  T
                  -------------------------------
                  O      T
LEADS AND         O
FOLLOWS           O  T
PEER              O
                  -------------------------------
                  0  1  2  3  4  5  6  7  8  9  10
```

	TOTAL SCORES FOR S 42	MEDIANS AT 18/21 MONTHS FOR ALL SUBJECTS
ADULT COMPETENCE	20.1	22.2
PEER COMPETENCE	0.0	13.5
OVERALL COMPETENCE	20.1	23.5

T INDICATES THE MEDIAN FOR ALL SUBJECTS FOR EACH COMPETENCE FACTOR.

SOCIAL COMPETENCE FOR SUBJECT 42

```
GAIN           O                                    T
ADULT          OXXXXXXXXXXXXXXXXXXXXXXXX
ATTENTION      OXXXXXXXXXXXXXXXXXXXXXXXX
               O                                    T
-----------------------------------------------------------------------
USE            O                    T
ADULT          OXXXXXXXXX
RESOURCE       OXXXXXXXXX
               O                       T
-----------------------------------------------------------------------
HOSTILITY,     O            T
AFFECTION      OXXXXX
TO ADULT       OXXXXX
               O              T
-----------------------------------------------------------------------
               O       T
ROLE PLAY      OXXXX
               OXXXX
               O       T
-----------------------------------------------------------------------
               O    T
PRIDE IN       O
PRODUCT        O
               O    T
-----------------------------------------------------------------------
COMPETES       O                              T
WITH           O
PEER           O
               O                                 T
-----------------------------------------------------------------------
HOSTILITY,     O                    T
AFFECTION      O
TO PEER        O
               O                       T
-----------------------------------------------------------------------
LEADS AND      O           T
FOLLOWS        O
PEER           O
               O              T
-----------------------------------------------------------------------
               O   1   2   3   4   5   6   7   8   9   10
```

	TOTAL SCORES FOR S 42	MEDIANS FOR 30/33 ONE YEAR STARTER CHILD. FOR ALL SUBJECTS
ADULT COMPETENCE	8.3	26.0
PEER COMPETENCE	0.0	12.2
OVERALL COMPETENCE	8.3	33.6

T INDICATES THE MEDIAN FOR ALL SUBJECTS FOR EACH COMPETENCE FACTOR.

Subject #42

Social Tasks	% Duration	
	12-15 Months	18-21 Months
To please	0.0	0.0
To cooperate	2.0	1.9
To gain approval	0.0	0.0
To procure a service	1.1	1.0
To gain attention	2.1	3.7
To maintain social contact	0.3	0.0
To avoid unpleasant circumstances	0.0	0.0
To annoy	0.0	0.4
To direct	0.0	0.0
To assert self (protect domain)	1.0	0.0
To provide information	0.1	0.0
To compete	0.0	0.0
To reject overtures	0.0	0.0
To enjoy pets	0.3	0.4
To converse	0.0	0.0
To produce verbalizations	0.0	0.0
Nonsocial Tasks		
To eat	6.2	23.7
To gain information (v)	11.0	5.8
To gain information (v & a)	2.0	0.8
live language directed to child	0.4	0.8
live language overheard by child	0.8	0.0
mechanical language	0.4	0.0
Sesame Street	0.4	0.0
Nontask	12.4	10.8
To pass time	4.1	0.8
To find something to do	0.0	0.8
To prepare for an activity	1.3	3.3
To construct a product	0.0	0.0
To choose	0.0	0.0
To procure an object	4.0	5.2
To engage in large muscle activity	0.0	0.0
To gain pleasure	0.0	0.0
To imitate	0.0	0.0
To pretend (role play)	0.0	0.0
To ease discomfort	1.7	4.8
To restore order	0.8	0.0
To relieve oneself	0.0	0.0
To dress/undress	0.0	0.0
To operate a mechanism	0.0	0.0
To explore	8.0	1.2
To improve a developing skill (mastery)	32.1	27.1
gross	30.4	27.1
fine	1.7	0.0
verbal	0.0	0.0
To eat and gain information (v)	4.3	5.6
To eat and gain information (v & a)	2.3	0.4
live language directed to child	1.5	0.0
overheard	0.6	0.4

SUBJECT #43

Subject #43 is a one-year-old SES Level III predicted C boy. The family, which consists of the parents and three children, lives in a comfortable apartment in an urban area. There were many occasions during the first year of our observations when both parents were home, due to a temporary illness of the father. Later in the year, the family purchased a comfortable home in a suburban area.

S spent most of his time with his mother, playing near her or trying to involve her in his activity. There were sufficient toys available to S, although he was expected to play with them in whichever room they were in. The atmosphere of the home was neither tense nor totally calm. The home was generally well kept.

Summary of Test Scores

Subject #43   Group: One-Year-Old Starters (n = 19)

Tests	Age at Testing (Months)	Score	Group Median
Bayley Mental Developmental Index	12	97	103
	24	109	112
Stanford-Binet IQ	36	93	113
WPPSI IQ	60	116	117.5
Language Test[1]	12	14	14
	15	14	16
	21	18	21
	24	24	36
	27	24	—
	30	not tested	—
	36	33	45
Abstract Abilities[2]	12	1	2
	15	2	2
	21	<5	5
	24	<5	6
	27	6	—
	30	not tested	—
	36	8	9
Discrimination Test[2]	12	1.0	1
	15	1.0	2
	21	2.0	3
	24	3.5	3.5
	27	not tested	—
	30	3.0	5
	36	4.0	8

[1] Scores in Months
[2] Scores in Level Achieved

Individual Subject Data

SOCIAL COMPETENCE FOR SUBJECT 43

```
                                                    T
GAIN              OXXXXXXXXXXXXXXXXX
ADULT             OXXXXXXXXXXXXXXXX
ATTENTION         O                              T
                  -------------------------------------
                                                    T
USE               OXXXXXXXXXXXXXXXXXXXXXXXX
ADULT             OXXXXXXXXXXXXXXXXXXXXXXXXX
RESOURCE          O                                T
                  -------------------------------------
HOSTILITY,        O         T
AFFECTION         OXX
TO ADULT          OXX        T
                  O
                  -------------------------------------
                  T
ROLE PLAY         O
                  O
                  T
                  -------------------------------------
                  T
PRIDE IN          OXXXXXXXXX
PRODUCT           OXXXXXXXXX
                  T
                  -------------------------------------
                                  T
COMPETES          OXXXXXXXXX
WITH              OXXXXXXXXX
PEER              O      T
                  -------------------------------------
                  O       T
HOSTILITY,        OXXXXXXXXXXXXXXXXXXXXX
AFFECTION         OXXXXXXXXXXXXXXXXXXX
TO PEER           O    T
                  -------------------------------------
                  O   T
LEADS AND         OXXXXXXXXXXXXXXXXXXXXXXXX
FOLLOWS           OXXXXXXXXXXXXXXXXXXXX
PEER              O     T
                  -------------------------------------
                  0  1  2  3  4  5  6  7  8  9  10

                    TOTAL SCORES    MEDIANS AT 12/15 MONTHS
                       FOR S 43         FOR ALL SUBJECTS

ADULT COMPETENCE         9.2               13.8
PEER COMPETENCE         10.8                9.0
OVERALL COMPETENCE      20.0               20.5
```

T INDICATES THE MEDIAN FOR ALL SUBJECTS FOR EACH COMPETENCE FACTOR.

SOCIAL COMPETENCE FOR SUBJECT 43

```
                                   T
GAIN              OXXXXXXXXXXXXXXXXXXX
ADULT             OXXXXXXXXXXXXXXXXXX
ATTENTION         O                 T
                  -------------------------------------
                                                    T
USE               OXXXXXXXXXXXXXXXXXXXXX
ADULT             OXXXXXXXXXXXXXXXXXXXXX
RESOURCE          O                                 T
                  -------------------------------------
HOSTILITY,        O                T
AFFECTION         OXXXXXXX
TO ADULT          OXXXXXXX       T
                  O
                  -------------------------------------
                                 T
ROLE PLAY         OXXXXXXXXXXXXXXXXXXXXXXXXXXXXXXXXXXXXXXXXXXXXX
                  OXXXXXXXXXXXXXXXXXXXXXXXXXXXXXXXXXXXXXXXXXXXXX
                  O                T
                  -------------------------------------
                  T
PRIDE IN          OXXXXXXXXXXXXXXXXX
PRODUCT           OXXXXXXXXXXXXXXXXX
                  T
                  -------------------------------------
                                             T
COMPETES          O
WITH              O
PEER              O                       T
                  -------------------------------------
                                                 T
HOSTILITY,        O
AFFECTION         O
TO PEER           O                          T
                  -------------------------------------
                  O                          T
LEADS AND         O
FOLLOWS           O
PEER              O                   T
                  -------------------------------------
                  0  1  2  3  4  5  6  7  8  9  10

                    TOTAL SCORES    MEDIANS AT 18/21 MONTHS
                       FOR S 43         FOR ALL SUBJECTS

ADULT COMPETENCE        33.6               22.2
PEER COMPETENCE          0.0               13.5
OVERALL COMPETENCE      33.6               23.5
```

T INDICATES THE MEDIAN FOR ALL SUBJECTS FOR EACH COMPETENCE FACTOR.

APPENDIX A

SOCIAL COMPETENCE FOR SUBJECT 43

```
GAIN               O                        T
ADULT              OXXXXXXXXXXXXXXXXXXXXXXX
ATTENTION          OXXXXXXXXXXXXXXXXXXXXXXX
                   O                        T
-----------------------------------------------------------------
USE                O              T
ADULT              OXXXXXXXXXXXXXXXXXXXXXXXXXXXXXXXX
RESOURCE           OXXXXXXXXXXXXXXXXXXXXXXXXXXXXXXXX
                   O              T
-----------------------------------------------------------------
HOSTILITY,         O        T
AFFECTION          OXXXXXXXXXXX
TO ADULT           OXXXXXXXXXXX
                   O        T
-----------------------------------------------------------------
                   O   T
ROLE PLAY          OXXXXXXXXXXXXX
                   OXXXXXXXXXXXXX
                   O   T
-----------------------------------------------------------------
                   O  T
PRIDE IN           OXXXXXXXXXXXXXXXXXXXXXXXXXXXXXXXXXXXX
PRODUCT            OXXXXXXXXXXXXXXXXXXXXXXXXXXXXXXXXXXXX
                   O  T
-----------------------------------------------------------------
COMPETES           O                                 T
WITH               O
PEER               O
                   O                                 T
-----------------------------------------------------------------
HOSTILITY,         O             T
AFFECTION          O
TO PEER            O
                   O             T
-----------------------------------------------------------------
LEADS AND          O       T
FOLLOWS            O
PEER               O
                   O       T
-----------------------------------------------------------------
                   0   1   2   3   4   5   6   7   8   9   10
```

	TOTAL SCORES FOR S 43	MEDIANS FOR 30/33 ONE YEAR STARTER CHILD. FOR ALL SUBJECTS
ADULT COMPETENCE	33.9	26.0
PEER COMPETENCE	0.0	12.2
OVERALL COMPETENCE	33.9	33.6

T INDICATES THE MEDIAN FOR ALL SUBJECTS FOR EACH COMPETENCE FACTOR.

Subject #43

	% Duration	
Social Tasks	12-15 Months	18-21 Months
To please	0.0	0.0
To cooperate	1.3	0.7
To gain approval	0.0	0.0
To procure a service	0.2	0.7
To gain attention	2.9	2.6
To maintain social contact	1.4	3.7
To avoid unpleasant circumstances	0.0	0.0
To annoy	0.0	0.0
To direct	0.0	0.0
To assert self (protect domain)	0.8	1.1
To provide information	0.0	0.0
To compete	0.0	0.0
To reject overtures	0.0	0.0
To enjoy pets	0.0	0.0
To converse	0.4	0.0
To produce verbalizations	0.0	0.0
Nonsocial Tasks		
To eat	11.8	6.1
To gain information (v)	9.0	11.7
To gain information (v & a)	7.5	39.0
live language directed to child	1.3	2.4
live language overheard by child	0.6	0.4
mechanical language	5.2	0.7
Sesame Street	0.0	34.3
Nontask	13.5	3.7
To pass time	10.7	0.6
To find something to do	0.0	0.0
To prepare for an activity	1.0	1.8
To construct a product	0.0	0.0
To choose	0.0	0.0
To procure an object	6.2	2.6
To engage in large muscle activity	0.0	0.0
To gain pleasure	0.0	0.3
To imitate	0.0	0.0
To pretend (role play)	0.0	0.0
To ease discomfort	2.2	1.7
To restore order	0.0	0.0
To relieve oneself	0.0	0.0
To dress/undress	0.0	0.4
To operate a mechanism	0.0	0.0
To explore	12.8	8.2
To improve a developing skill (mastery)	9.0	2.5
gross	8.8	0.0
fine	0.2	1.8
verbal	0.0	0.7
To eat and gain information (v)	5.0	1.9
To eat and gain information (v & a)	3.7	10.3
live language directed to child	1.6	0.0
overheard	0.3	0.4

SUBJECT #44

Subject #44 is a one-year-old SES Level III predicted A girl. She has two older siblings, a five-year-old sister and a three-year-old brother. The family lives in a roomy, comfortable apartment in an urban area.

The children have ample toys, and S is given access to her siblings' toys as well as her own. The mother is a more serious, businesslike person than many of the other mothers. Her home is usually neatly kept, and she is generally there. She is quite strict with the older children and sets limits firmly for S. S is a cooperative, pleasant child who plays well by herself as well as with her older siblings.

Summary of Test Scores

Subject #44   Group: One-Year-Old Starters (n = 19)

Tests	Age at Testing (Months)	Score	Group Median
Bayley Mental Developmental Index	12	103	103
	24	132	112
Stanford-Binet IQ	36	113	113
WPPSI IQ	60	116	117.5
Language Test[1]	12	16	14
	15	16	16
	21	21	21
	24	33	36
	27	30	—
	30	39	43.5
	36	54	45
Abstract Abilities[2]	12	2	2
	15	3	2
	21	<5	5
	24	<5	6
	27	<5	—
	30	7	7
	36	9	9
Discrimination Test[2]	12	1.0	1
	15	2.0	2
	21	2.0	3
	24	2.0	3.5
	27	not tested	—
	30	3.5	5
	36	8.0	8

[1] Scores in Months
[2] Scores in Level Achieved

APPENDIX A

SOCIAL COMPETENCE FOR SUBJECT 44

```
                         0                                          T
GAIN                     OXXXXXXXXXXX
ADULT                    OXXXXXXXXXXX
ATTENTION                0                       T

                         0                                   T
USE                      OXXXXXXXXXXXXXXXXXXX
ADULT                    OXXXXXXXXXXXXXXXXXXX
RESOURCE                 0                            T

                         0         T
HOSTILITY,               OXXXXXXX
AFFECTION                OXXXXXXX
TO ADULT                 0              T

                         T
                         0
ROLE PLAY                0
                         0
                         T

                         T
PRIDE IN                 0
PRODUCT                  0
                         T

                         0         T
COMPETES                 OXXXXXXXXXXXXXXXXXXXXXXXXXXX
WITH                     OXXXXXXXXXXXXXXXXXXXXXXXXXXX
PEER                     0                   T

                         0    T
HOSTILITY,               OXXXXXX
AFFECTION                OXXXXXX
TO PEER                  0         T

                         0    T
LEADS AND                OXXXXXXXXXXX
FOLLOWS                  OXXXXXXXXXXX
PEER                     0    T

                         0  1  2  3  4  5  6  7  8  9  10
```

	TOTAL SCORES FOR S 44	MEDIANS AT 12/15 MONTHS FOR ALL SUBJECTS
ADULT COMPETENCE	11.6	13.8
PEER COMPETENCE	9.0	9.0
OVERALL COMPETENCE	20.5	20.5

T INDICATES THE MEDIAN FOR ALL SUBJECTS FOR EACH COMPETENCE FACTOR.

SOCIAL COMPETENCE FOR SUBJECT 44

```
                         0
GAIN                     OXXXXXXXXX
ADULT                    OXXXXXXXXX
ATTENTION                0                    T

                         0                                T
USE                      OXXXXXXXXXXXXXX
ADULT                    OXXXXXXXXXXXXXX
RESOURCE                 0                                       T

                         0                T
HOSTILITY,               OXXXXXXXX
AFFECTION                OXXXXXXXX
TO ADULT                 0         T

                         0    T
                         OXXXXXXXXXXXXXXXXXXXXXXXXXXXXXXXXXXXXXXXXXX
ROLE PLAY                OXXXXXXXXXXXXXXXXXXXXXXXXXXXXXXXXXXXXXXXXXX
                         0    T

                         T
PRIDE IN                 0
PRODUCT                  0
                         T

                         0                  T
COMPETES                 OXXXXXXXXXXXXXXXXXXXXXXXXXXXXXXXXXXXXXXXXXXXXX
WITH                     OXXXXXXXXXXXXXXXXXXXXXXXXXXXXXXXXXXXXXXXXXXXXX
PEER                     0              T

                         0                            T
HOSTILITY,               OXXXXXXXXXXXXXXXXXXXXXXXXXX
AFFECTION                OXXXXXXXXXXXXXXXXXXXXXXXXXX
TO PEER                  0                    T

                         0                            T
LEADS AND                OXXXXXXXXXXXXXXXXXXXXXXXXXXXXXXXXXX
FOLLOWS                  OXXXXXXXXXXXXXXXXXXXXXXXXXXXXXXXXXX
PEER                     0                T

                         0  1  2  3  4  5  6  7  8  9  10
```

	TOTAL SCORES FOR S 44	MEDIANS AT 18/21 MONTHS FOR ALL SUBJECTS
ADULT COMPETENCE	22.4	22.2
PEER COMPETENCE	22.3	13.5
OVERALL COMPETENCE	44.7	23.5

T INDICATES THE MEDIAN FOR ALL SUBJECTS FOR EACH COMPETENCE FACTOR.

Individual Subject Data

SOCIAL COMPETENCE FOR SUBJECT 44

```
GAIN          O                             T
ADULT         OXXXXXXXXXXXXXXXXXXX
ATTENTION     OXXXXXXXXXXXXXXXXXX
              O                        T
-----------------------------------------------------------------
USE           O                   T
ADULT         OXXXXXXXXXXXXXXX
RESOURCE      OXXXXXXXXXXXXXXX
              O                  T
-----------------------------------------------------------------
HOSTILITY,    O         T
AFFECTION     OXXX
TO ADULT      OXXX
              O             T
-----------------------------------------------------------------
              O     T
ROLE PLAY     OXXXXXXXXXXXX
              OXXXXXXXXXXXX
              O     T
-----------------------------------------------------------------
              O  T
PRIDE IN      O
PRODUCT       O
              O   T
-----------------------------------------------------------------
COMPETES      O                              T
WITH          O
PEER          O
              O                                 T
-----------------------------------------------------------------
HOSTILITY,    O                  T
AFFECTION     O
TO PEER       O
              O            T
-----------------------------------------------------------------
LEADS AND     O         T
FOLLOWS       O
PEER          O
              O     T
-----------------------------------------------------------------
              O    1    2    3    4    5    6    7    8    9    10
```

	TOTAL SCORES FOR S 44	MEDIANS FOR 30/33 ONE YEAR STARTER CHILD. FOR ALL SUBJECTS
ADULT COMPETENCE	14.0	26.0
PEER COMPETENCE	0.0	12.2
OVERALL COMPETENCE	14.0	33.6

T INDICATES THE MEDIAN FOR ALL SUBJECTS FOR EACH COMPETENCE FACTOR.

Subject #44

Social Tasks	% Duration	
	12-15 Months	18-21 Months
To please	1.0	0.0
To cooperate	4.0	3.9
To gain approval	0.0	0.0
To procure a service	1.2	1.2
To gain attention	4.7	2.5
To maintain social contact	3.2	6.7
To avoid unpleasant circumstances	0.0	0.0
To annoy	3.5	0.0
To direct	0.0	0.0
To assert self (protect domain)	0.3	2.0
To provide information	0.0	0.0
To compete	0.0	0.0
To reject overtures	0.1	0.0
To enjoy pets	0.0	0.0
To converse	0.0	0.0
To produce verbalizations	0.0	0.0
Nonsocial Tasks		
To eat	0.0	11.1
To gain information (v)	25.1	13.1
To gain information (v & a)	6.4	10.8
live language directed to child	1.7	1.1
live language overheard by child	4.6	3.4
mechanical language	0.1	6.3
Sesame Street	0.0	0.0
Nontask	12.2	18.1
To pass time	8.5	6.4
To find something to do	0.0	0.0
To prepare for an activity	0.4	3.8
To construct a product	0.0	0.0
To choose	0.0	0.0
To procure an object	2.4	3.3
To engage in large muscle activity	0.0	0.0
To gain pleasure	0.0	1.0
To imitate	0.0	1.9
To pretend (role play)	0.0	5.6
To ease discomfort	0.4	0.0
To restore order	1.2	0.5
To relieve oneself	0.0	0.0
To dress/undress	0.0	1.8
To operate a mechanism	0.0	0.4
To explore	9.4	0.4
To improve a developing skill (mastery)	13.5	3.8
gross	9.9	0.3
fine	2.5	3.3
verbal	1.1	0.2
To eat and gain information (v)	1.9	0.7
To eat and gain information (v & a)	0.1	1.1
live language directed to child	0.0	0.0
overheard	0.1	1.1

SUBJECT #45

Subject #45 is a one-year-old SES Level III predicted A girl. S has one older sibling, a three-year-old sister. The family lives in a small, crowded apartment in an urban area. The home always seems busy. There are generally several pets and several people moving through the five small rooms. A good deal of emphasis is placed on eating—on between-meal snacks and on preparation of meals. In general, the mood of the home is relaxed.

S is an active, curious child who has many toys available to her. The mother tries to restrict the children's play to the overcrowded bedroom that the girls share. The sibling relationship is marked by frequent squabbles and disputes over toys. By the time S is 2½ years old, the mother has given birth to another baby. Both the mother and the observers note that the S was particularly upset around the time of the birth of the new baby and during the months that follow. This appears to be reflected in her performance on the tests at age three.

Summary of Test Scores

Subject #45   Group: One-Year-Old Starters (n = 19)

Tests	Age at Testing (Months)	Score	Group Median
Bayley Mental Developmental Index	12	125	103
	24	96	112
Stanford-Binet IQ	36	76	113
WPPSI IQ	60	110	117.5
Language Test[1]	12	12	14
	15	16	16
	21	18	21
	24	18	36
	27	18	—
	30	not tested	—
	36	30	45
Abstract Abilities[2]	12	2	2
	15	1	2
	21	<5	5
	24	<5	6
	27	7	—
	30	not tested	—
	36	8	9
Discrimination Test[2]	12	2.0	1
	15	3.5	2
	21	3.5	3
	24	3.5	3.5
	27	not tested	—
	30	3.5	5
	36	7.0	8

[1] Scores in Months
[2] Scores in Level Achieved

Individual Subject Data

SOCIAL COMPETENCE FOR SUBJECT 45

```
                     0   1   2   3   4   5   6   7   8   9   10
GAIN              0XXXXXXXXXXXXX         T
ADULT             0XXXXXXXXXXXXX
ATTENTION         0                                  T

USE               0
ADULT             0XXXXXXXXXXX           T
RESOURCE          0XXXXXXXXXXX
                  0                  T

HOSTILITY,        0          T
AFFECTION         0XXXXX
TO ADULT          0XXXXX
                  0                T

ROLE PLAY         T
                  0
                  0
                  T

PRIDE IN          T
PRODUCT           0
                  0
                  T

COMPETES          0                T
WITH              0XXXXXXXXXXXXXXXXXXXXXXXXXXXXXXXXXX
PEER              0XXXXXXXXXXXXXXXXXXXXXXXXXXXXXXXXXX
                  0                   T

HOSTILITY,        0      T
AFFECTION         0XXXXXXXXXXXXXXXXXXXXXXXXXXXXXXXXXXXXXX
TO PEER           0XXXXXXXXXXXXXXXXXXXXXXXXXXXXXXXXXXXXXX
                  0          T

LEADS AND         0          T
FOLLOWS           0XXXXXXXXXX
PEER              0XXXXXXXXXX
                  0       T

                  0   1   2   3   4   5   6   7   8   9   10

                    TOTAL SCORES       MEDIANS AT 12/15 MONTHS
                     FOR S 45             FOR ALL SUBJECTS

ADULT COMPETENCE        6.4                   13.8
PEER COMPETENCE        19.6                    9.0
OVERALL COMPETENCE     26.0                   20.5
```

T INDICATES THE MEDIAN FOR ALL SUBJECTS FOR EACH COMPETENCE FACTOR.

SOCIAL COMPETENCE FOR SUBJECT 45

```
                     0   1   2   3   4   5   6   7   8   9   10
GAIN              0
ADULT             0XX                  T
ATTENTION         0XX               T
                  0

USE               0
ADULT             0
RESOURCE          0
                  0

HOSTILITY,        0
AFFECTION         0XXXXXX              T
TO ADULT          0XXXXXX
                  0                T

ROLE PLAY         0       T
                  0XXXXXXXXXXXXXXXXXXX
                  0XXXXXXXXXXXXXXXXXXX
                  0      T

PRIDE IN          T
PRODUCT           0
                  0
                  T

COMPETES          0                                      T
WITH              0XXXXXXXXXXXXXXXXXXXXXXXXXXXXXXXXXXXXXXXXXX
PEER              0XXXXXXXXXXXXXXXXXXXXXXXXXXXXXXXXXXXXXXXXXX
                  0                          T

HOSTILITY,        0
AFFECTION         0                                T
TO PEER           0                             T
                  0

LEADS AND         0                     T
FOLLOWS           0XXXXXXXXXXXXXXXXXXXXXXXXXXXXXXXXXXXXX
PEER              0XXXXXXXXXXXXXXXXXXXXXXXXXXXXXXXXXXXXX
                  0                 T

                  0   1   2   3   4   5   6   7   8   9   10

                    TOTAL SCORES       MEDIANS AT 18/21 MONTHS
                     FOR S 45             FOR ALL SUBJECTS

ADULT COMPETENCE        5.5                   22.2
PEER COMPETENCE        12.0                   13.5
OVERALL COMPETENCE     17.5                   23.5
```

T INDICATES THE MEDIAN FOR ALL SUBJECTS FOR EACH COMPETENCE FACTOR.

APPENDIX A

```
                    SOCIAL COMPETENCE FOR SUBJECT 45

GAIN            O                         T
ADULT           OXXXXXXXXXXXXXXXXX
ATTENTION       OXXXXXXXXXXXXXXXXX
                O                         T
-----------------------------------------------------------------
USE             O             T
ADULT           O
RESOURCE        O
                O              T
-----------------------------------------------------------------
HOSTILITY,      O        T
AFFECTION       OXXXXXXXX
TO ADULT        OXXXXXXXX
                O       T
-----------------------------------------------------------------
                O    T
ROLE PLAY       OXXXX
                OXXXX
                O     T
-----------------------------------------------------------------
                O  T
PRIDE IN        O
PRODUCT         O
                O  T
-----------------------------------------------------------------
COMPETES        O                              T
WITH            O
PEER            O
                O                                 T
-----------------------------------------------------------------
HOSTILITY,      O           T
AFFECTION       O
TO PEER         O
                O         T
-----------------------------------------------------------------
LEADS AND       O       T
FOLLOWS         O
PEER            O
                O    T
-----------------------------------------------------------------
                O   1   2   3   4   5   6   7   8   9   10
```

	TOTAL SCORES FOR S 45	MEDIANS FOR 30/33 ONE YEAR STARTER CHILD. FOR ALL SUBJECTS
ADULT COMPETENCE	5.8	26.0
PEER COMPETENCE	0.0	12.2
OVERALL COMPETENCE	5.8	33.6

T INDICATES THE MEDIAN FOR ALL SUBJECTS FOR EACH COMPETENCE FACTOR.

Subject #45

Social Tasks	% Duration	
	12-15 Months	18-21 Months
To please	0.2	0.0
To cooperate	3.7	3.3
To gain approval	0.0	0.0
To procure a service	0.1	0.0
To gain attention	0.8	0.4
To maintain social contact	0.6	1.7
To avoid unpleasant circumstances	0.1	0.0
To annoy	0.0	0.0
To direct	0.2	0.1
To assert self (protect domain)	0.8	1.9
To provide information	0.0	0.0
To compete	0.0	0.0
To reject overtures	0.0	0.0
To enjoy pets	0.3	6.3
To converse	0.0	0.0
To produce verbalizations	0.0	0.0
Nonsocial Tasks		
To eat	1.2	19.2
To gain information (v)	9.4	3.1
To gain information (v & a)	3.2	2.1
live language directed to child	1.0	0.4
live language overheard by child	0.4	1.7
mechanical language	0.0	0.0
Sesame Street	0.0	0.0
Nontask	30.5	26.2
To pass time	1.1	0.6
To find something to do	1.7	1.7
To prepare for an activity	1.5	0.6
To construct a product	0.0	0.0
To choose	0.4	0.0
To procure an object	9.4	1.2
To engage in large muscle activity	0.0	0.0
To gain pleasure	0.1	0.0
To imitate	0.2	0.6
To pretend (role play)	0.4	4.7
To ease discomfort	2.5	0.4
To restore order	2.5	0.0
To relieve oneself	0.0	0.0
To dress/undress	0.4	0.0
To operate a mechanism	1.0	0.7
To explore	12.5	2.2
To improve a developing skill (mastery)	15.3	16.1
gross	11.5	0.4
fine	2.6	15.7
verbal	1.2	0.0
To eat and gain information (v)	0.1	3.6
To eat and gain information (v & a)	0.0	0.4
live language directed to child	0.1	0.0
overheard	0.0	0.4

Appendix **B**

SUBSIDIARY ANALYSES

I. Social Competence

   Extreme Group Comparisons, Unmatched SES, *385*

   Task Data, 12-15 Months, *386*

   Task Data, 18-21 Months, *387*

II. Nonsocial Competence

   Extreme Group Comparisons, Unmatched SES, *388*

   Task Data, 12-15 Months, *390*

   Task Data, 18-21 Months, *391*

III. Overall Competence

   Extreme Group Comparisons, Partially Matched SES, *393*

   Task Data, 12-15 Months, *394*

   Task Data, 18-21 Months, *395*

TABLE 67. SES Characteristics of Children with Highest and Lowest Levels of Competence at Three Years of Age, Social Ranks (Unmatched SES Groups)

Achieved Competence Level	Hollingshead-Redlich SES Ratings* (# of Ss in Each Category)					
	I	II	III	IV	V	
Highest (n = 9)						Group Median
Female	2	1	0	1	1	
Male	1	1	1	0	1	II
Lowest (n = 5)						
Female	1	0	1	0	1	
Male	0	0	1	0	1	III

*Classes I and II are upper to middle classes; Classes III, IV, and V are middle to lower classes. A. B. Hollingshead and F. C. Redlich, *Social Class and Mental Illness* (New York: John Wiley and Sons, Inc., 1958).

TABLE 68. Task Experience of One-Year-Olds (12-15 Months), Extreme Group Comparisons, Social Competence (Unmatched SES Groups)

Social Tasks	Percent Time Spent in Activity (Group Medians)		
	Top 9	Bottom 5	U[1]
All social tasks	11.4	6.9	4.5*
To please	0.1	0.1	20.0
To cooperate	2.9	2.2	17.0
To procure a service	0.8	1.1	13.0
To gain attention	2.3	1.2	12.0
To maintain social contact	1.7	2.3	17.0
To assert self	0.6	0.5	19.5
Nonsocial Tasks			
To eat	4.5	3.2	21.0
To gain information (v)	14.4	11.0	18.0
To gain information (v & a)	5.8	3.3	17.0
live language directed to child	*3.2*	*1.0*	*9.0*
overheard language	*0.6*	*0.5*	*19.0*
mechanical langauge	*0.8*	*0.4*	*21.0*
Nontask	9.8	12.4	18.0
To pass time	3.3	4.1	17.0
To prepare for activity	1.0	1.5	17.5
To procure an object	2.3	3.4	13.0
To gain pleasure	0.0	0.6	12.5
To ease discomfort	0.5	0.7	14.5
To restore order	0.4	0.8	17.5
To operate a mechanism	0.1	0.1	20.5
To explore	14.9	12.5	12.0
Mastery	9.0	15.3	16.0
gross mastery	*6.4*	*7.7*	*19.0*
fine mastery	*2.4*	*2.2*	*21.0*
To eat and gain information (v)	5.0	0.6	8.0
To eat and gain information (v & a)	0.7	0.0	8.5
live language directed to child	*0.6*	*0.1*	*13.0*

[1] Mann-Whitney U two-tailed test of significance

*p ≤ .02

TABLE 69. Task Experiences of One-Year-Olds (18-21 Months), Extreme Group Comparisons, Social Competence (Unmatched SES Groups)

Social Tasks	Percent Time Spent in Activity (Group Medians)		
	Top 9	Bottom 5	U^1
All social tasks	16.2	14.2	21.0
To please	0.0	0.0	20.5
To cooperate	5.3	3.3	18.5
To gain approval	0.0	0.0	19.0
To procure a service	1.4	0.9	12.5
To gain attention	1.8	2.6	18.0
To maintain social contact	2.8	6.3	16.0
To direct	0.0	0.0	16.0
To assert self	1.1	1.5	20.0
Nonsocial Tasks			
To eat	9.1	12.0	16.0
To gain information (v)	11.7	5.8	19.5
To gain information (v & a)	6.0	4.5	15.0
live language directed to child	*2.4*	*0.8*	*14.0*
overheard language	*1.0*	*0.8*	*19.0*
mechanical language	*0.0*	*0.0*	*21.0*
Sesame Street	*0.0*	*0.0*	*12.5*
Nontask	11.0	16.7	10.5
To pass time	3.2	0.9	19.5
To prepare for activity	2.6	1.5	14.0
To procure an object	2.8	2.2	18.0
To engage in large muscle activity	0.0	0.0	22.0
To imitate	0.1	0.2	19.0
To pretend	1.8	1.6	21.0
To ease discomfort	0.8	0.4	21.0
To restore order	1.0	0.1	5.5*
To operate a mechanism	0.7	0.0	9.5
To explore	8.5	2.5	12.0
Mastery	11.5	8.0	21.0
gross mastery	*1.3*	*3.4*	*15.0*
fine mastery	*4.6*	*3.0*	*16.0*
verbal mastery	*0.2*	*0.0*	*20.0*
To eat and gain information (v)	1.9	2.9	21.5
To eat and gain information (v & a)	1.2	0.3	14.5
live language directed to child	*0.0*	*0.0*	*18.0*

[1] Mann-Whitney U two-tailed test of significance

*p ⩽ .05

TABLE 70. Source of Initiation of Tasks, Extreme Group Comparisons, Social Competence, All Tasks (Unmatched SES Groups)

Age (Months)	Group	Self		Mother		Other	
		Median	Significance of Difference	Median	Significance of Difference	Median	Significance of Difference
12-15	Most Competent (n = 9)	85.9		14.1		0.0	
	Least Competent (n = 5)	91.5	n.s.	7.9	n.s.	0.0	n.s.
18-21	Most Competent (n = 9)	89.1		9.0		0.0	
	Least Competent (n = 5)	85.0	n.s.	11.4	n.s.	0.0	n.s.

TABLE 71. Source of Initiation of Tasks, Extreme Group Comparisons, Social Competence, Social Tasks (Unmatched SES Groups)

Age (Months)	Group	Self		Mother		Other	
		Median	Significance of Difference	Median	Significance of Difference	Median	Significance of Difference
12-15	Most Competent (n = 9)	60.5		39.5		0.5	
	Least Competent (n = 5)	45.7	n.s.	54.3	n.s.	0.0	n.s.
18-21	Most Competent (n = 9)	58.9		38.9		0.0	
	Least Competent (n = 5)	61.6	n.s.	28.3	n.s.	0.0	n.s.

TABLE 72. Source of Initiation of Tasks, Extreme Group Comparisons, Social Competence, Nonsocial Tasks (Unmatched SES Groups)

Age (Months)	Group	Self		Mother		Other	
		Median	Significance of Difference	Median	Significance of Difference	Median	Significance of Difference
12-15	Most Competent (n = 9)	87.5		12.3		0.0	
			n.s.		n.s.		n.s.
	Least Competent (n = 5)	93.5		6.1		0.0	
18-21	Most Competent (n = 9)	94.0		6.0		0.0	
			n.s.		n.s.		n.s.
	Least Competent (n = 5)	90.1		9.2		0.0	

TABLE 73. SES Characteristics of Children with Highest and Lowest Levels of Competence at Three Years of Age, Nonsocial Ranks (Unmatched SES Groups)

Achieved Competence Level	Hollingshead-Redlich SES Ratings* (# of Ss in Each Category)					
	I	II	III	IV	V	
Highest (n = 9)						Group Median
Female	3	2	1	0	0	
Male	1	1	1	0	0	II
Lowest (n = 5)						
Female	0	0	1	0	1	
Male	0	0	1	1	1	IV

*Classes I and II are upper to middle classes; Classes III, IV, and V are middle to lower classes. A. B. Hollingshead and F. C. Redlich, *Social Class and Mental Illness* (New York: John Wiley and Son, Inc., 1958).

TABLE 74. Task Experiences of One-Year-Olds (12-15 Months), Extreme Group Comparisons, Nonsocial Competence (Unmatched SES Groups)

	Percent Time Spent in Activity (Group Medians)		
Social Tasks	Top 9	Bottom 5	U^1
All social tasks	11.7	7.0	11.0
To please	0.3	0.0	2.5**
To cooperate	2.9	3.7	21.5
To procure a service	1.2	0.2	6.0*
To gain attention	3.7	0.6	3.5**
To maintain social contact	2.3	1.6	18.5
To assert self	0.6	0.8	22.0
Nonsocial Tasks			
To eat	3.2	1.5	22.0
To gain information (v)	25.1	9.0	0.0***
To gain information (v & a)	6.4	6.0	18.0
live language directed to child	4.3	1.2	1.0***
overheard language	2.2	0.4	5.5
mechanical language	0.1	4.6	8.0
Nontask	9.8	13.3	16.5
To pass time	1.6	10.7	12.0
To prepare for activity	1.9	0.0	6.5
To procure an object	3.2	4.2	12.0
To gain pleasure	0.0	0.1	20.0
To ease discomfort	0.5	0.5	21.0
To restore order	0.8	0.0	9.0
To operate a mechanism	0.1	0.6	19.0
To explore	9.7	12.8	16.0
Mastery	8.5	14.5	13.0
gross mastery	6.4	8.8	13.0
fine mastery	2.5	2.6	20.0
To eat and gain information (v)	5.4	0.8	10.5
To eat and gain information (v & a)	0.5	0.3	21.0
live language directed to child	0.6	0.1	22.0

[1] Mann-Whitney U two-tailed test of significance

*p ≤ .05

**p ≤ .02

***p ≤ .002

TABLE 75. Task Experience of One-Year-Olds (18-21 Months), Extreme Group Comparisons, Nonsocial Competence (Unmatched SES Groups)

	Percent Time Spent in Activity (Group Medians)		
Social Tasks	Top 9	Bottom 5	U[1]
All social tasks	11.7	13.7	1.0***
To please	0.5	0.0	5.0**
To cooperate	5.2	3.3	15.0
To gain approval	0.2	0.0	10.0
To procure a service	1.7	0.7	5.0**
To gain attention	2.5	1.5	13.5
To maintain social contact	2.5	3.1	20.0
To direct	0.1	0.0	13.0
To assert self	1.8	1.6	19.5
Nonsocial Tasks			
To eat	9.1	9.9	14.0
To gain information (v)	12.1	9.4	10.0
To gain information (v & a)	5.7	6.0	20.0
live language directed to child	*1.3*	*0.8*	*11.5*
overheard language	*1.3*	*0.4*	*15.0*
mechanical language	*0.0*	*0.0*	*21.5*
Sesame Street	*0.0*	*0.0*	*18.0*
Nontask	11.0	25.9	12.0
To pass time	5.2	0.6	11.0
To prepare for activity	3.5	1.4	1.0***
To procure an object	3.4	2.6	4.5**
To engage in large muscle activity	0.2	0.0	10.0
To imitate	0.2	0.1	17.0
To pretend	1.6	0.0	17.0
To ease discomfort	0.5	1.0	15.5
To restore order	1.0	0.1	5.0**
To operate a mechanism	0.3	0.3	20.5
To explore	3.6	8.2	17.0
Mastery	14.3	2.5	8.0
gross mastery	*3.5*	*0.8*	*9.5*
fine mastery	*4.6*	*1.8*	*15.0*
verbal mastery	*0.5*	*0.0*	*10.0*
To eat and gain information (v)	1.0	1.9	21.5
To eat and gain information (v & a)	0.3	0.4	20.0
live language directed to child	*0.2*	*0.0*	*7.5*

[1] Mann-Whitney U two-tailed test of significance

*p ≤ .05
**p ≤ .02
***p ≤ .002

TABLE 76. **Source of Initiation of Tasks, Extreme Group Comparisons, Nonsocial Competence, All Tasks (Unmatched SES Groups)**

Age (Months)	Group	Self Median	Significance of Difference	Mother Median	Significance of Difference	Other Median	Significance of Difference
12-15	Most Competent (n = 9)	83.3		16.6		0.1	
			n.s.		n.s.		n.s.
	Least Competent (n = 5)	85.9		14.1		0.0	
18-21	Most Competent (n = 9)	87.1		12.4		0.0	
			n.s.		n.s.		n.s.
	Least Competent (n = 5)	89.0		9.5		0.0	

TABLE 77. **Source of Initiation of Tasks, Extreme Group Comparisons, Nonsocial Competence, Nonsocial Tasks (Unmatched SES Groups)**

Age (Months)	Group	Self Median	Significance of Difference	Mother Median	Significance of Difference	Other Median	Significance of Difference
12-15	Most Competent (n = 9)	86.5		13.5		0.0	
			n.s.		n.s.		n.s.
	Least Competent (n = 5)	87.5		12.3		0.0	
18-21	Most Competent (n = 9)	91.6		8.4		0.0	
			n.s.		n.s.		n.s.
	Least Competent (n = 5)	94.1		4.7		0.0	

TABLE 78. Source of Initiation of Tasks, Extreme Group Comparisons, Nonsocial Competence, Social Tasks (Unmatched SES Groups)

Age (Months)	Group	Self		Mother		Other	
		Median	Significance of Difference	Median	Significance of Difference	Median	Significance of Difference
12-15	Most Competent (n = 9)	68.4		28.2		1.4	
			n.s.		n.s.		n.s.
	Least Competent (n = 5)	45.7		54.3		0.0	
18-21	Most Competent (n = 9)	58.9		40.4		0.0	
			n.s.		n.s.		n.s.
	Least Competent (n = 5)	55.9		28.3		0.0	

TABLE 79. SES Characteristics of Children with Highest and Lowest Levels of Competence at Three Years of Age, Overall Ranks (Partially Matched for SES Groups)

Achieved Competence Level	Hollingshead-Redlich SES Rating* (# of Ss in Each Category)					
	I	II	III	IV	V	
Highest (n = 5)						Group Median
Female	0	2	0	1	0	
Male	0	1	1	0	0	II
Lowest (n = 5)						
Female	0	0	2	1	0	
Male	0	1	1	0	0	III

*Classes I and II are upper to middle classes; Classes III, IV, and V are middle to lower classes. A. B. Hollingshead and F. C. Redlich, *Social Class and Mental Illness* (New York: John Wiley and Sons, Inc., 1958).

TABLE 80. Task Experiences of One-Year-Olds (12-15 Months), Extreme Group Comparisons, Overall Competence (Partially Matched for SES Groups)

	Percent Time Spent in Activity (Group Medians)		
Social Tasks	Top 5	Bottom 5	U[1]
All social tasks	11.9	6.9	5.5
To please	0.1	0.1	8.5
To cooperate	3.2	2.5	8.0
To procure a service	1.3	1.1	7.5
To gain attention	3.2	2.0	8.0
To maintain social contact	2.7	1.5	9.5
To assert self	0.8	0.8	11.0
Nonsocial Tasks			
To eat	3.1	6.2	11.0
To gain information (v)	21.3	16.0	7.5
To gain information (v & a)	8.1	3.2	2.0*
live language directed to child	*6.9*	*1.0*	*2.0**
overheard language	*2.6*	*0.8*	*4.0*
mechanical language	*0.0*	*0.0*	*11.5*
Nontask	8.1	18.1	4.0
To pass time	1.6	4.0	11.0
To prepare for activity	1.9	1.3	5.5
To procure an object	1.8	3.9	6.0
To gain pleasure	0.6	0.0	10.0
To ease discomfort	1.3	1.6	10.0
To restore order	0.8	0.8	12.0
To operate a mechanism	0.0	0.0	10.5
To explore	8.2	12.5	8.0
Mastery	7.9	13.4	6.0
gross mastery	*4.5*	*9.9*	*7.0*
fine mastery	*2.4*	*2.5*	*11.5*
To eat and gain information (v)	4.8	4.3	10.0
To eat and gain information (v & a)	0.7	0.1	7.0
live language directed to child	*0.8*	*0.1*	*8.5*

[1] Mann-Whitney U two-tailed test of significance
*p ≤ .05

TABLE 81. Task Experience of One-Year-Olds (18-21 Months), Extreme Group Comparisons, Overall Competence (Partially Matched for SES Groups)

Social Tasks	Percent Time Spent in Activity (Group Medians)		
	Top 5	Bottom 5	U[1]
All social tasks	17.7	13.7	7.0
To please	0.4	0.0	4.0
To cooperate	5.2	3.3	6.5
To gain approval	1.1	0.0	8.0
To procure a service	2.0	1.0	4.5
To gain attention	1.9	2.0	12.0
To maintain social contact	1.2	2.1	9.0
To direct	0.4	0.0	3.0*
To assert self	2.0	1.5	7.0
To enjoy pets	0.0	0.4	7.0
Nonsocial Tasks			
To eat	10.3	11.9	0.0**
To gain information (v)	8.6	13.0	11.0
To gain information (v & a)	13.2	4.4	3.0*
live language directed to child	5.9	1.1	2.0*
overheard language	1.7	1.4	12.0
mechanical language	1.4	0.0	9.0
Sesame Street	1.4	0.0	5.0
Nontask	10.8	18.0	2.5
To pass time	5.2	0.8	8.0
To prepare for activity	2.5	1.5	8.0
To procure an object	3.6	1.8	7.0
To engage in large muscle activity	0.2	0.0	2.5*
To imitate	0.0	0.2	8.5
To pretend	0.8	3.1	11.5
To ease discomfort	0.3	0.4	11.0
To restore order	2.0	0.2	0.0**
To operate a mechanism	0.1	0.3	9.5
To explore	3.5	2.2	7.0
Mastery	12.3	7.9	11.5
gross mastery	3.5	3.4	11.0
fine mastery	4.0	3.0	8.0
verbal mastery	0.5	0.2	10.0
To eat and gain information (v)	1.0	3.6	6.0
To eat and gain information (v & a)	1.4	0.4	11.5
live language directed to child	0.3	0.0	6.5

[1] Mann-Whitney U two-tailed test of significance
*p ≤ .05
**p ≤ .01

TABLE 82. Source of Initiation of Tasks, Extreme Group Comparisons, Overall Competence, All Tasks (Partially Matched for SES Groups)

Age (Months)	Group	Self Median	Significance of Difference[1]	Mother Median	Significance of Difference	Other Median	Significance of Difference
12-15	Most Competent (n = 5)	82.1		17.0		0.4	
			p = .032		p = .056		n.s.
	Least Competent (n = 5)	91.6		7.2		0.0	
18-21	Most Competent (n = 5)	83.9		12.9		0.1	
			n.s.		n.s.		n.s.
	Least Competent (n = 5)	87.4		10.9		0.0	

[1] Mann-Whitney U test p values two-tailed.

TABLE 83. Source of Initiation of Tasks, Extreme Group Comparisons, Overall Competence, Social Tasks (Partially Matched for SES Groups)

Age (Months)	Group	Self Median	Significance of Difference[1]	Mother Median	Significance of Difference	Other Median	Significance of Difference
12-15	Most Competent (n = 5)	59.7		39.6		3.0	
			n.s.		n.s.		n.s.
	Least Competent (n = 5)	60.2		30.6		0.0	
18-21	Most Competent (n = 5)	58.3		41.7		0.5	
			n.s.		n.s.		n.s.
	Least Competent (n = 5)	61.6		27.7		0.0	

[1] Mann-Whitney U test p values two-tailed.

TABLE 84. Source of Initiation of Tasks, Extreme Group Comparisons, Overall Competence, Nonsocial Tasks (Partially Matched for SES Groups)

Age (Months)	Group	Self		Mother		Other	
		Median	Significance of Difference[1]	Median	Significance of Difference	Median	Significance of Difference
12-15	Most Competent (n = 5)	83.9		15.4		0.0	
			n.s.		n.s.		n.s.
	Least Competent (n = 5)	93.5		5.9		0.0	
18-21	Most Competent (n = 5)	88.4		10.9		0.0	
			n.s.		n.s.		n.s.
	Least Competent (n = 5)	90.8		7.0		0.0	

[1] Mann-Whitney U test p values two-tailed.

TABLE 85. Correlation Among Tasks at 12-15 Months and Achieved Levels of Competence, Controlling for SES Effects[1] (n = 19)

Social Tasks	Percent Time Spent in Activity (Group Median)	Correlation with Overall Competence[2] at Three Years of Age
All social tasks	10.3	−.50*
To please	0.1	−.07
To cooperate	2.8	−.34
To procure a service	1.0	−.41
To gain attention	2.2	−.33
To maintain social contact	2.2	−.39
To assert self	0.5	−.03
Nonsocial Tasks		
To eat	4.4	−.25
To gain information (v)	16.0	−.19
To gain information (v & a)	6.0	−.16
live language directed to child	1.7	−.53*
overheard language	0.8	−.22
mechanical language	0.2	.15
Nontask	12.2	.19
To pass time	3.4	.26
To prepare for activity	1.4	−.08
To procure an object	3.3	.42
To gain pleasure	0.0	−.12
To ease discomfort	0.6	.28
To restore order	0.7	.24
To operate a mechanism	0.1	.36
To explore	12.8	−.08
Mastery	8.7	.43
gross	0.7	.42
fine	2.4	−.06
To eat and gain information (v)	4.2	−.44
To eat and gain information (v & a)	0.3	−.20
live language directed to child	0.1	−.29

[1] The partial-correlation analysis described in the *Statistical Package for the Social Science* was utilized.

[2] The most competent child is ranked 1, and the least competent child is ranked 19. Therefore, the relationship of high competence and greater task duration is negative.

*p ≤ .05

TABLE 86. Correlation Among Tasks at 18-21 Months and Achieved Levels of Competence, Partially Controlling for SES Effects[1] (n = 19)

Social Tasks	Percent Time Spent in Activity (Group Median)	Correlation with Overall Competence[2] at Three Years of Age
All social tasks	16.2	−.09
To please	0.0	−.12
To cooperate	4.6	−.29
To gain approval	0.0	−.18
To procure a service	1.0	−.32
To gain attention	2.0	.07
To maintain social contact	2.8	.29
To direct	0.1	−.47*
To assert self	1.5	−.07
To enjoy pets	0.0	.43
Nonsocial Tasks		
To eat	10.3	.31
To gain information (v)	10.6	.04
To gain information (v & a)	6.0	−.33
live language directed to child	1.4	−.37
overheard language	1.3	−.16
mechanical language	0.0	.11
Sesame Street	0.0	−.27
Nontask	11.8	.57**
To pass time	3.2	−.07
To prepare for activity	2.0	−.24
To procure an object	3.1	−.25
To engage in large muscle activity	0.0	−.32
To imitate	0.0	.31
To pretend	1.5	−.15
To ease discomfort	0.4	.27
To restore order	0.6	−.61**
To operate a mechanism	0.2	−.44
To explore	6.6	−.07
Mastery	11.4	.05
gross	2.4	.21
fine	3.9	−.10
verbal	0.1	−.27
To eat and gain information (v)	1.9	.15
To eat and gain information (v & a)	0.4	−.21
live language directed to child	0.0	−.25

[1] The partial-correlation analysis described in the *Statistical Package for the Social Science* was utilized.

[2] The most competent child is ranked 1, and the least competent child is ranked 19. Therefore, the relationship of high competence and greater task duration is negative.

*p ⩽ .05
**p ⩽ .01

Appendix **C**

MEASUREMENT TECHNIQUES: MANUALS AND RELIABILITY STUDIES

Manual for Adult Assessment Scales, *403*
Manual for Assessing Social Abilities of
   One to Six Year Old Children, *431*
Manual for Testing the Language Ability of
   One to Three Year Old Children, *462*
Manual for Abstract Ability Test, *488*
Manual for Assessing the Discriminative Ability
   of One to Three Year Old Children, *512*

MANUAL FOR ADULT ASSESSMENT SCALES

by Burton L. White/Barbara Kaban/Bernice Shapiro/
Elizabeth Constable/Jane Attanucci

Purpose, *404*
Collecting the Raw Material, *404*
Coding the Data, *404*
Checklist I: Child-Adult Interaction, Subject Initiated, *406*
    Definitions of Child's Purposes
    Definitions of Adult's Response
Checklist II: Child-Adult Interaction, Adult Initiated, *410*
    Definitions of Adult's Purposes
    Definitions of Adult's Emotional Tone
Rating Scale I: Distal Adult Effects Definitions, *411*
Rating Scale II: Dimensions of Competence, *415*
    Social Abilities
    Nonsocial Abilities
Reliability of Adult Assessment Scales, *419*
Tables, *420*
Appendix to Adult Assessment Scales, *423*

Preschool Project, Laboratory of Human Development, Harvard University, Graduate School of Education, March, 1974, Revised March, 1975.

PURPOSE

These scales are to be used to produce quantifiable data on the details of the adult-child relationship as they relate to the focus of the Harvard Preschool Project—namely, the development of competence in young children. Since it is our thesis that competence by age three years depends heavily on experiences from birth on, we have developed these scales to monitor the performance of mothers, or of any caretakers, vis à vis their children aged 6-36 months.

The Adult Assessment Scales consist of the following:

Checklist I: Child-Adult Interaction, Subject Initiated.   This checklist is meant to score adult behavior in response to overtures by the child.

Checklist II: Child-Adult Interaction, Adult Initiated.   All adult-child behavior initiated by the adult is scored on this checklist.

Rating Scale I.   Distal adult effects upon the child, such as those due to the design and management of the environment, are to be scored on this rating scale.

Rating Scale II.   Encouragement or discouragement by the adult of the development of dimensions of competence in the child are scored.

COLLECTING THE RAW MATERIAL

1. An adult assessment data-collecting process is thirty minutes in length.

2. The observer should make a clear statement to the caretaker that she should try to ignore the observer's presence and carry on as normal. Conversation and additional interaction between observer and caretaker should be kept to a minimum during the actual data collection.

3. During this period the observer tape-records pertinent remarks about behavioral episodes involving caretaker and child as they occur naturally.

4. In recording, care should be taken to repeat into the tape recorder as much as possible of the actual language spoken by the adult to ensure ease of coding afterward

5. The observer stands between six and ten feet from the subject. This is to insure an appropriate vantage point with a minimum of direct interference by the observer, and to reduce (as far as possible) the distracting effect upon the caretaker and child.

6. A stop watch is used to time events to the nearest five seconds.

CODING THE DATA

1. The time and setting at the onset of the observation are to be noted on the front of the coding sheet.

2. The main difficulty in developing an instrument of this kind is the problem of the unit to be scored. We have chosen to record only episodes lasting

longer than three seconds, since brief episodes at times are likely to be unnoted by the observer.

3. Coding the tape-recorded material should take place as soon after the observation as possible.

4. Coded information is entered on Checklist I or II, depending on whether the episode was child or adult initiated (see pages 425-426).

5. The onset, duration, and purpose of each episode are noted on the coding sheet. On Checklist I the onset and duration of the adult response to overtures by the child are recorded. The onset and duration and purpose of the child's overture should also be recorded. On Checklist II, the onset, duration, purpose, and emotional tone of the adult-initiated episodes are recorded.

6. All obvious overtures by the subject to the adult should be coded, even if ignored or unnoticed by the adult.

7. The observer should be conservative about whether or not the child makes an overture. If the child merely moves in the direction of the adult (i.e., seeking proximity), the action should *not* be coded as an overture. When there is doubt about the occurrence of an overture, it should not be coded as such.

8. At times two brief episodes should be spanned. *Spanning* refers to the combining of events that occur very closely in time (within fifteen seconds of each other), and which are not separated by any other obvious interest of the person being observed. Such episodes have the same purpose. A child may make two attempts to *gain attention* within a fifteen-second interval. If the child does not pursue any other interest between these attempts, the entire fifteen-second unit should then be labeled *gain attention*.

9. Other types of closely spaced overtures include situations where the child has initiated a *gain attention* episode, then immediately initiates a *procure a service* episode. The *gain attention* episode should be *subsumed*, and the entire duration of the two interactions timed and coded as a *procure a service* episode. If the original purpose has been instrumental to the second purpose, then it is *subsumed* and labeled according to the second purpose.

10. Coding episodes which involve a shift in purpose by the initiator is very difficult. If there is an obvious change in direction of interest by the subject between two closely spaced overtures, they should not be spanned.

11. Whenever interactions occur between the child and an adult other than the primary caretaker, they are to be coded only if the adult is someone regularly seen by the child.

12. When routine caretaking such as feeding, diapering, washing, etc., takes place, the observer in coding should make a note of the onset, duration, emotional tone, and content of the routine caretaking event and record it on the Checklist II coding sheet. Although the caretaker's activity is necessarily dictated by the requirements of the job, resulting in little difference among caretakers, coding of the routine caretaking episode is necessary to describe adequately the amount of time the child and adult interacted during the thirty-

minute observation. There are times when the routine caretaking activity is accompanied by interesting or educational activities for the child (for example, language play, pointing out details of one kind or another). This information should be coded and included separately on the appropriate checklist.

13. If the child falls asleep or is put in for a nap during the observation, the observer should stop coding at the beginning of the sleep episode. The observer should wait at least ten minutes because often the child gets up shortly. If the child remains asleep, consider the observation complete with more than fifteen minutes.

14. After coding the two checklists as to purpose, duration, response, and content, the two rating scales (distal adult effects and dimensions of competence) should be completed (see pages 427-429).

CHECKLIST I: CHILD-ADULT INTERACTION, SUBJECT INITIATED

This section is, in our opinion, the most significant part of the adult assessment scale. Because of our previous research, we are most concerned with the response of the adult to overtures by children. Accordingly, eight categories for delineating the nature of the adult's response have been developed (see page 407-408). Children 6-36 months of age may have many different purposes in mind when they initiate an interaction. The apparent purpose of the child should be coded for Checklist I. For children 6-17 months of age, the following list seems to include all common purposes:

- to gain attention
- to procure a service
- to maintain social contact
- to ease discomfort
- to please
- to gain approval
- to annoy
- to direct/dominate/lead
- to compete/gain status

Definitions of Child's Purposes

1. *To Gain Attention**

a. To initiate social contact—e.g., calling to or touching the adult.

b. To maximize the chance of being noticed—e.g., banging on a feeding table and shouting.

c. To join a group—e.g., attempting to join mother and sibling's activity.

*This is the most frequently occurring behavior among 8-17-month-old children.

2. *To Procure a Service.* To try to obtain aid from another—e.g., asking for food or for help in mastering walking or climbing, or wanting to be read to, or requesting help with a toy. This behavior starts to emerge around 10 months of age. With a younger child, the desired service is often unclear, and the behavior should be coded as *gain attention* if there is any doubt.

3. *To Maintain Social Contact.* To be absorbed in insuring that a social contact continues—e.g., clinginess on the part of a young child, as when a child repeatedly wants to be close to and near the mother or repeatedly pursues the same tasks with the mother so as to keep her interested in him.

4. *To Ease Discomfort.* Purposeful behavior to alleviate physical or psychic discomfort in contrast to apparently aimless or habitual behavior—e.g., child dropping a toy on his foot, beginning to cry, and looking to his mother for comfort.

5. *To Please.* To attempt to obtain another's good favor by means of a sustained display of affection—e.g., repeatedly hugging mother spontaneously.

6. *To Gain Approval.* To ask (verbally or nonverbally) for favorable comment on a completed piece of work or on behavior—e.g., child attempting to climb something new by himself and looking up for mother's praise of his efforts.

7. *To Annoy.* To disturb another; to act in a manner designed to displease; to provoke by means of irritating teasing. This type of behavior emerges clearly in the period of negativism, when the child attempts to do things that he knows are not permitted—e.g., trying to get into the bathroom to play. The taunting of mothers that occurs in normal independence testing during this period should be scored as "to annoy."

8. *To Direct/Dominate/Lead.* To play the leader role; to demonstrate a process to another or to advise another; in short, to direct a specific activity of another. Although this behavior is rare with this age group, it is sometimes seen when a child initiates a specific game with his mother.

9. *To Compete/Gain Status.* This behavior is seen when a child attempts to gain the attention of his mother by competing with a sibling on whom she is focusing at the moment.

Definitions of Adult's Response

An adult may respond to or ignore an overture. If there is a response, the observer should record all relevant language on the part of the adult, so that each of the following eight aspects of the adult's response may be scored:

- timing and direction of the adult's response
- perception of the subject's need
- level of difficulty of words
- provision of related ideas
- complexity of language

- provision of encouragement and reinforcement of enthusiasm
- teaching of realistic limits
- satisfaction of the subject's needs

The exact onset and duration of each episode should be recorded accurately.

1. *Timing and Direction*

a. *Immediately.* The adult responds with words or actions within five seconds of child's overture. Record adult response onset to be the same as the onset of the overture, making the duration of the overture by the child *momentary.*

b. *Delayed.* The response occurs after 5 seconds. Record the onset of the adult response and the duration of the child's overture, thereby providing information on the length of the delay.

c. *No response.* The adult has either ignored or not been aware of the overture.

d. *Rejects.* The adult not only fails to act upon the child's overture but also makes known her dislike of, or lack of interest in, the child at that moment. She makes known her unwillingness to respond or interact at that moment. Record the onset and duration of child's overture.

2. *Perception of Subject's Need*

a. *Accurate.* The adult shows, either verbally or by her actions, that she is aware of the child's need of the moment. Sometimes the adult requires a bit more time to determine correctly the child's need.

b. *Partial.* When the adult can only determine to a limited extent what the child's need is, a score should be placed in this category.

c. *Not at all.* The adult either misperceives the child's need or is simply unaware of it. For example, a child may want a particular object, or need help in dealing with a sibling, but the caretaker fails to notice the child's concern of the moment.

3. *Level of Difficulty of Words**

a. *Appropriate.* The language uttered by the adult has to be more than two words and include a label where appropriate. Appropriate language should also include expressive language of more than two words, directed toward the child—e.g., "That is a big truck," "What a good boy you are!"

b. *Too complex.* The *meaning* of the adult's utterance depends on words that the child cannot understand.

c. *Too simple.* An utterance of one or two words and the absence of a label.

---

*The observer should make a point of repeating into the tape recorder as much of the adult's language during the observation as possible, in order to judge the average level of language used.

d. *Baby talk.* The adult uses nonstandard words or idiosyncratic sounds—e.g., "Is you a good boy?" "doggie woggie."

e. *None.* When no language is used during the interaction, code *none*.

4. *Provision of Related Ideas*

a. *Yes.* The scoring of this item depends on an adult's use of language. A one-word label, for example, is insufficient to code *yes*. The age of the child determines the scoring. With younger children (8-14 months), a verb added to a label is sufficient to be coded as a related idea. Example: Subject approaches the adult with a ball. The adult says, "Throw the ball." With older children (over 14 months), a more distantly related idea must be provided by the adult in order to code *yes*. Example: The subject approaches the adult with a ball and the adult says, "Bring me the pail and we'll throw the ball into it."

b. *No.* A one-word label should be coded *no*, as should the provision of an unrelated idea by an adult in response to a subject's overture. Example: The subject approaches an adult with a ball and the adult says, "Ball. Do you want a cookie?"

5. *Complexity of Language**

a. *Complex sentence.* A long sentence which expresses more than a single thought and which takes more than three seconds to express. Example: "Bring me the big red ball so we can play a game of catch together."

b. *Phrase or sentence.* A phrase or simple sentence expressing one thought and lasting less than three seconds. Example: "Bring mommy the book."

c. *One word.* This category is coded when the average level of language directed toward the child during the interaction consists of one-word utterances.

d. *None.* This is coded when no language is used during the interaction.

6. *Provision of Encouragement and Reinforcement of Enthusiasm*

a. *Yes.* Any positive verbal or physical response by an adult should be coded as encouraging and reinforcing to a subject. Examples: The subject throws a ball toward his mother. She rolls it back to him. The child is sitting with a picture book and calls to his mother, saying, "Doggie" (pointing to a picture of a dog in the book). The mother interrupts her work to look over and say, "That's a nice dog."

b. *No.* When an adult ignores a subject, verbally or physically, or actively discourages his behavior by verbal or physical means, *no* should be coded. Example: The child approaches his mother with a toy broom and shows it to her as she is sweeping in the kitchen. She ignores this overture, and says, "Get out of my way; don't step in the dirt."

c. *Inappropriate.* When the subject's purpose is *to ease discomfort* or *to annoy*, this category should be used to code an adult's response. Example: The subject drops a toy on his foot and begins to cry, approaching his mother

---

*Be sure to judge the average level of complexity during each episode.

for comfort. The mother picks him up and says some soothing words. Since there was no enthusiasm shown by the child in this situation, code *inappropriate*.

7. *Teaching of Realistic Limits.* The adult is often called upon to teach limits or impose restrictions on the child's behavior in situations involving safety or protection of breakables. At other times, an adult will have an opportunity to correct unrealistic goals being pursued by an infant or toddler. In addition, many social interactions between young children involve the setting of limits by the mother.

a. *Yes.* Example: The child begins to climb up on the kitchen table and indicates that he wants a cookie. His mother lifts him down and says, "You'll hurt yourself if you climb up there. Wait until after lunch for a cookie." The adult has clearly taught the child necessary limits. The verbal explanation is essential to differentiate *teaching* limits from control or merely *setting* limits.

b. *No.* Example: The child is seated on his mother's lap. She is drinking hot coffee. He indicates he wants some and she offers him a sip. She does not attempt to impose any limits on his behavior.

c. *Inappropriate.* Use this category when the question of safety, protection, or discipline is not an issue. Example: The child approaches his mother with a book and wants to be read to. She begins the story.

8. *Satisfaction of the Subject's Needs*

a. *Yes.* If the subject's original purpose is indeed satisfied by the adult's response, score this category *yes*. Example: The child wants to have a story read, and his mother complies.

b. *No.* If the subject is quieted or diverted by an adult's response, but the child's purpose is not satisfied, score this category *no*. If the adult rejects the subject's requests, or is unable to respond in a *procure a service* situation, score this category *no*. Example: The subject indicates to the adult that he wants something to eat. The adult says, "No, you'll be having lunch soon," and distracts the child with a toy.

c. *Partial.* If the subject's purpose is only partially satisfied by the adult's response, score this category *partial*. Example: The subject indicates he wants to reach for a pencil. The adult removes the pencil from reach and gives the child crayons.

CHECKLIST II: CHILD-ADULT INTERACTION, ADULT INITIATED

This checklist deals with episodes initiated by the adult. As with Checklist I, the exact onset and duration of each interaction should be recorded (within five seconds of accuracy), and the adult's behavior coded as to purpose, emotional tone, and content.

The following list includes all common adult purposes in their interactions with children 8-17 months old:

- to stimulate child
- to control—positive (distraction)
- to control—negative
- to provide routine caretaking

Definitions of Adult's Purposes

1. *To Stimulate Child.* The adult may attempt to stimulate the child's interest by various means—for example, by telling him something, by showing him or giving him objects, toys, books, etc., or by initiating an activity such as a game.

2. *To Control—Positive (distraction).* This form of control includes the following types of distraction:

   a. *To distract by stimulation.* When the adult attempts to control the child by shifting the child's focus, code *control—positive*. Example: The child is playing with a dangerous object, and the adult substitutes a toy.

   b. *To distract by affection.* When the adult uses social interaction such as kissing, holding, or cuddling, or other positive physical means to control the child's behavior, code this category.

   c. *To distract by non-stimulating means.* If the adult offers the subject a bottle or a cookie in order to control his behavior or to shift his attention from some undesirable act, code this category.

3. *To Control—Negative.* This category should be coded when the adult uses methods to control the child which are designed to simply terminate his behavior immediately without offering any explanation. Examples: (Verbal) "Don't do that," "Stop that"; (Physical) slapping or physically removing the child from the situation.

Definitions of Adult's Emotional Tone

Adults employ various emotional tones in dealing with children 8-17 months old. The following list combines commonly occurring adult emotional tones under three major headings: positive, negative, and neutral.

1. *Positive.* Code this category when the adult uses smiles, a friendly and encouraging tone, or other friendly gestures with the child.

2. *Negative.* Code this category when an adult is threatening, commanding, or rejecting in her behavior toward the child.

3. *Neutral.* Use of a matter-of-fact tone by the adult should be coded *neutral*.

RATING SCALE 1: DISTAL ADULT EFFECTS

The purpose of this scale is to rate the adult caretaker on her management of the child's daily activities and access to the environment. Some caretakers are skillful organizers and good designers who are able to provide interesting, safe environments for their children. Ratings are made on the following dimensions:

A. Design of the Home
  1. Procurement of Materials for the Subject's Use
  2. Safety Precautions
  3. Child-proofing
  4. Accessibility to Living Areas
B. Adult Effects
  1. Adult's Availability to Subject
  2. Adult's Scheduling of Daily Activities

This scale is used by the home visitor to monitor the manner in which mothers deal with issues of management in the home. Ratings should be made immediately after the visit, with explanatory comments added wherever possible. Ratings are made on a five-point scale; for purposes of brevity, the definitions that follow apply only to the two extreme ends of the scale. If no behavior has been observed relating to any specific category, check *no basis for rating*.

Definitions

A. *Design of the Home*

1. *Procurement of Materials for the Subject's Use*

Grossly suitable. The mother has made available toys and household objects which are suitable to the subject's age and level of development.

Grossly unsuitable. There is virtually a total absence of suitable toys or materials; or the mother has provided some toys and materials, but they are suited to much younger or much older children.

2. *Safety Precautions.* This item pertains to the protection of the young child from the ordinary dangers present in homes and apartments.

Excellent. The entire home has been made as safe as possible for the child, so that dependence on restrictive devices such as playpens or constant vigilance by the mother is unnecessary. Dangerous or harmful substances have been moved out of reach. The requirements for safety change with age and are repeatedly updated by the mother in advance of the child's growing abilities to crawl, pull to a stand, climb, and walk.

Grossly inadequate. Little or no attention has been paid to safety measures in the home, so that the child must be restricted to a confined space or endangered throughout the house. This type of mother is not aware of the child's propensities toward self-injury. She does not anticipate the child's growing motor abilities and therefore does not take precautions in advance of development. For example, she may not anticipate the child's ability to climb near open windows.

3. *Child-proofing.* This item pertains to the protection of the house *from* the child, the avoidance of destruction of breakables, and the reduction of unnecessary work in the home by means of careful planning of the environment, with appropriate changes made as the child develops new abilities.

Maximal child-proofing—maximal access. This rating is given when the caretaker enables the child to have maximum freedom in the house with minimum chance of breakage or destruction occurring. Breakable objects such as vases, lamps, and ashtrays have been removed, and books and materials from low shelves have been put away.

Maximal child-proofing—minimal access. Closing off entire areas of the home is one means by which this type of mother provides for child-proofing her home. The child is seriously impeded in his exploration attempts. The mother leaves breakables out and attempts to control the child's access to them by frequent admonitions.

Minimal child-proofing—maximal access. If access to most of the home is allowed but child-proofing has not been done and the mother depends on her own presence to protect the child and the house, this rating should be given.

4. *Accessibility to Living Area*

Maximum. This rating applies to the mother who allows her child access to as much of the house as possible. She skillfully manipulates materials and furnishings so that interesting areas are available and safe for the child, while assuming some supervision is needed at all times.

Minimum. The mother who restricts the child's area of activity for long periods of time—by keeping him, e.g., in a playpen, crib, walker—should be given a rating of *minimum*. The child is unable to play in certain areas that may interest him, and his scope for exploration is strictly limited.

B. *Adult Effects*

1. *Adult's Availability to the Subject*

Maximum. A mother scoring high on this dimension is available most of the time and frequently is in the same area as the child. Although she often is engaged in activities separate from the child's, she will interrupt her work to interact with the child at his request or signal. This type of mother is receptive to the child's social overtures, and also maintains a strong interest in his discoveries and accomplishments.

Minimum. Much of the time this mother is not in close physical proximity to the child and is therefore not available to help him with his activities.

2. *Adult's Scheduling of Daily Activities Which are Likely to Enhance Development*

Maximum. A mother who is able to use everyday situations to stimulate the child's awareness and attention should receive the highest rating on this dimension. Such a mother has an eye for novel or interesting objects and materials that will captivate and delight small children, and arranges the environment and activities to maximally challenge the child's curiosity. Such a mother seeks new situations and activities for both of them to experience as the child's needs change both inside and outside the home.

Minimum. A mother who scores low on this dimension seems unable to plan or schedule activities for the day. She waits until the child is in an obvious state of distress, boredom, or difficulty before she acts. She rarely initiates activities for the child and in general does not seem to know what to do with the child.

RATING SCALE II: DIMENSIONS OF COMPETENCE

From extensive observations of children, the Harvard Preschool Project has identified twenty characteristics of well-developed young children. Specific behaviors have been identified, such as getting an adult's attention, using adults as resources, etc.

The purpose of this scale is to rate the adult caretaker's behaviors in regard to the child's emerging competencies in both social and nonsocial areas. The response is rated either *excellent*, *average*, or *poor*. If no behavior has been observed relating to a dimension of competence, check the last box: *no basis for rating*.

Some of the dimensions defined below do not have direct implications for child-rearing practices in the 8-17-month period. However, the origins of most of these abilities are evident in the first three years of life, and they can be used as organizing factors around which to view and understand the child's development. Categories 1-11 are labeled *social abilities*; categories 12-20 are labeled *nonsocial abilities*.

Social Abilities

1. *To Get and Maintain the Attention of Adults in Socially Acceptable Ways.* If a mother usually gives her attention to the child when he makes overtures such as calling or signaling her, it will encourage the child to use positive rather than socially unacceptable means of getting an adult's attention as he grows older. Early in the 8-17-month age range the primary method the infant uses to gain attention is crying. If the mother lets the infant cry until he gets very agitated, she may be teaching him that the best way to get attention is through an extreme rather than a moderate overture. If she attends promptly to his overtures, the baby is encouraged in forming a close and appropriate bond with the mother. Nevertheless, mothers need not respond immediately on every single occasion, since the child will learn persistence as he gets older, especially if his attempts at gaining attention are usually successful.

2. *To Use Adults as Resources (After First Determining that a Task is Too Difficult).* The ability to make use of an adult in order to obtain or

achieve something by means of a verbal request or demand or a physical demonstration of his need. The child first determines he cannot do it alone, by either trying to or by thinking about the situation. If the mother routinely tries to adopt the point of view of the infant and generally makes herself available to assist, she can naturally guide the infant into the practice of using adults as resources. Example: The child is trying to stack one block on top of another. Because he is playing in his high chair he is dropping blocks often. He makes sounds to indicate that he wants his mother to pick up the blocks, which she does. After a while, the mother suggests he sit on the floor and moves both the child and the blocks to a more appropriate area.

In the 8-17-month age range the mother or substitute caretaker is obviously the major resource for the child's needs. However, during the first year or so of life, children do not often seem deliberately to be trying to use adults as resources. Starting early in the second year of life, infants usually begin to ask for help regularly.

 3.-4. *To Express Affection and Hostility to Adults.*

 7.-8. *To Express Affection and Hostility to Peers.* The ability to express warm, positive feelings and angry feelings toward another individual through verbal and/or physical means. For the most part, children express more affection than hostility during the 8-17-month period. They delight their parents with smiles, hugs, and verbal expressions of friendliness. However, all young children show occasional anger and hostility toward their parents and siblings. Indeed, we have found the ability to express anger (given provocation) toward a parent or siblings to be regularly associated with good development. From time to time, children will hit, grab, throw objects angrily, or have tantrums. The adult is best advised to handle this behavior as matter-of-factly as possible. Our effective parents are by no means *totally* indulgent in this area, however, Clear limits are set in regard to potentially dangerous or grossly antisocial behavior. The necessity for achieving a suitable level of autonomous behavior is strongly felt by most children in the second year (as reflected in the emergence of negativism) and is an important part of early normal development.

 5.-6. *To Lead and Follow Peers/Siblings.* The ability to assume control in peer-related activities—e.g., to give suggestions, to orient and direct, to set oneself up as a model for imitation. The ability to follow the lead of others—e.g., to follow suggestions. Most children in the 8-17-month age range are not capable of genuine give-and-take with a peer or sibling who is close in age. The first small leadership attempts may be directed toward the mother. Whenever possible, mothers should encourage such activities.

 9. *To Compete with Peers/Siblings.* The ability to engage in interpersonal contests regarding equipment, attention, or recognition. Although most young babies are not competitive in the ordinary sense, many do show signs of this ability as early as the second year of life, especially with older siblings around. Sometimes what looks like competitive activity is partly motivated by

hostility. A mother should try to encourage competition while discouraging the hostility.

10. *To Praise Oneself and/or Show Pride in One's Accomplishments.* The ability to express pride in something he has created, owns, or possesses at the moment, or something he is in the process of doing or has done. Children in the age range of 8-17 months will begin to show pride in themselves on occasion, beginning with very simple achievements that to them represent truly amazing feats. All such expressions of pride deserve the mother's encouragement and approval.

Effective mothers tend to encourage their children to complete what they have begun, and frequently give praise to their children, rewarding their efforts to master new skills or challenges. Such encouragement helps to build the child's sense of pride in himself and in his accomplishments.

11. *To Involve Oneself in Adult Role-Playing Behaviors or to Otherwise Express the Desire to Grow Up.* To act out a typical adult activity or verbally express a desire to grow up. To adopt make-believe roles where the child pictures himself as he would like to be when he is bigger and stronger. Although this form of behavior is rather rare among 8-17-month-olds, it will start to emerge at the end of the second year and should be encouraged by the mother. Children, as they become verbal, will behave in a fanciful manner at times. Adults entering into their "pretend" activities can use these as occasions to pique the child's curiosity and to bring humor into the situation.

Nonsocial Abilities

12. *Language Development.* The ability to understand words and phrases and to express oneself verbally. Very few infants younger than 8 months of age understand more than one or two words or phrases. Infants can recognize the sound of their mother's voice and do react differently to sounds varying in tone and volume.

In the 8-17-month age range the child's comprehension of language increases enormously, and he usually begins to use words to express himself. The mother should use the child's interest in specific objects or activities to extend his awareness and understanding of words and phrases. She should try to keep the content of her explanations appropriate to the child's level of development. For example, she should label objects regularly when the child is looking at pictures or handling a toy or household object, and perhaps include a remark or two about each item. As the child gets older, a mother should expand her communication, keeping her language natural and to the point. If a child loses interest in a topic, the mother should not insist on his attention. Most verbal comments by the mother to the child need not last more than twenty to thirty seconds but may last longer if the child continues to be interested.

Given access to a rich environment and an adult, locomoting infants will regularly seek adult attention for several purposes. They will call for assistance, for example, when something breaks or needs opening. On other occasions they will be excited about a discovery. At other times, infants will want comfort. Caretakers should use these opportunities to talk about whatever it is the *infant* is concerned with at the moment. The speech should be natural. No attempt should be made to prolong the event if the child seeks to end it.

Adults should occasionally initiate verbal contact with the infant in the normal course of events but should not monopolize the infant's time nor keep him from other things he would rather do.

Television probably will not harm the child, but it does not seem to interest children very much in the first year and a half of life.

Books and magazines are useful objects around which to focus conversations. Infants can learn to recognize objects, to talk about them, and to listen to brief informal comments about them, but a baby less than 18 months old should not be expected to sit still while a long story is told or read to him.

13. *The Ability to Sense Dissonance or Note Discrepancies.* The ability to indicate one's awareness of discrepancies, inconsistencies, and other forms of irregularity in the environment. The awareness is almost always expressed verbally but occasionally takes nonverbal forms as well. It is observable whenever a child comments upon some noticed irregularity. The affect that generally accompanies it usually involves mild confusion, a look of discovery, or a display of righteousness in pointing out and correcting the irregularity.

The origins of this ability may be as early as the time the infant discovers that sucking a pacifier does not result in milk entering his mouth, whereas sucking on the bottle nipple or the breast usually does. However, the above definition refers to the ability to notice irregularities at many levels, including things seen, done, or said; much of this ability is usually not evident until the child reaches 12-17 months of age. A mother should point out inconsistencies and oddities in everyday routines to the child. An example of a visible discrepancy might involve two objects which are identical except for one's having more dots than another, as in dominoes. An example of an oddity in a pattern of activity might involve any surprising event such as a double-yolked egg. A mother's aim should be to encourage her child to be a good observer.

14. *The Ability to Anticipate Consequences.* This is the ability to anticipate a probable effect on, or sequence to, whatever is currently occupying the attention of the child. This ability is usually expressed verbally but also takes nonverbal forms. It can take place in a social context or in relative isolation. It is not simply an awareness of a future event—e.g., "Tomorrow is Thursday"— but must somehow relate that event to a present condition. The relationship may be either causal—e.g., "If X, then Y"—or sequential—e.g., "Now 1, next 2." The second half of each relationship *must* be an anticipated future outcome. It cannot actually occur until after the child anticipates its occurrence.

This ability is usually not evident until the third year of life. However, if mothers make this type of verbal association to the child and allow the child to experience the consequences of his actions, it will probably help him understand cause-and-effect relationships. Example: letting a ten-month-old child hold his own cup and practice feeding himself despite the occasional spills, since this practice is likely to enhance his independence and help him learn what to expect.

15. *The Ability to Deal with Abstractions—i.e., Numbers, Letters, Rules.* The ability to use abstract concepts and symbols in ways that require building upon what is concretely present and showing mental organization of what is perceived. The term *concept* means "a mental state or process that refers to more than one object or experience"; the term *symbol* means "an object, expression, or responsive activity that replaces and becomes a representative substitute for another."

As the mother becomes aware of the child's level of intellectual development, she can structure brief play situations using objects of different shapes, color, or size, and point out characteristics of groups of objects that the child is ready to comprehend. During the child's second year, reading alphabet books and counting rhymes are good preparatory activities. The beginnings of abstract thinking abilities are very modest during infancy, but the process can be encouraged with frequent oral comments.

16. *The Ability to Take the Perspective of Another.* To show an understanding of how things look to another person whose position in space is different from the subject's or to show an understanding of a person's emotional state or mental attitude when different from the subject's (the opposite of egocentricity).

This ability does not ordinarily appear until the child is at least five years old. However, effective mothers themselves are likely to have the capacity to understand the perspectives of other people. When the child observes this kind of behavior on the part of his mother, he may be stimulated to adopt a similar style of behavior in his own peer interactions later on.

17. *The Ability to Make Interesting Associations.* When considering visible scenes, objects, or verbal descriptions, a child with this ability shows a capacity to produce related kinds of objects or themes from his own realm of past experience or from some imagined experience. These productions are characterized by the ingenuity of the relationships or the elaborateness of the representation. Another form of this attribute is the ability to build upon these events by assigning new and interesting labels to them or to build coherent stories around the presented elements.

The level at which this ability is defined presupposes verbal abilities well beyond that of most two-year-olds. However, if a mother responds to her child's statements or questions by adding associated ideas, she will help the child enlarge his own capacity to make interesting associations.

18. *The Ability to Plan and Carry Out Multistepped Activities.* This is an ability that does not emerge until the child's third year. However, the growth of this behavior is enhanced by letting a child have close contact with a person

who engages in multistepped activities—e.g., an older sibling planning a complicated construction or the mother preparing dinner. In this way the child grows in his awareness of how to organize sequences of behavior and models his behavior on those around him. Children who are regularly given the opportunity to solve some of their own problems show proficiency in planning and execution.

19. *The Ability to Use Resources Effectively.* The ability to select and organize materials and/or people to solve problems. An additional feature is the recognition of unusual uses of such resources.

Mothers who allow children to manipulate a great variety of objects and materials will find their child growing naturally in the ability to make effective and varied use of these things. On the other hand, children who are provided very limited access to materials such as paint, crayons, water, etc., often misuse them when they are given a chance to use such materials, or else do not develop as much interest in using such materials to create products. Mothers who demonstrate how and why things work will help their children in the effective use of resources.

20. *Attentional Ability—Dual Focus.* The ability to attend to two things simultaneously or in rapid alternation—i.e., the ability to concentrate on a proximal task and to remain aware of peripheral happenings; the ability to talk while carrying out another task.

When a mother talks to a child while the child is engaged in another activity, she encourages growth of his ability to focus on more than one thing at a time—on what he is actually doing and on what she is saying. As the child gets older, he will be able to monitor events in his environment at the same time that he is engaged in an activity of his own—thus making transitions easier to accomplish and making it easier to ward off distractions.

RELIABILITY OF ADULT ASSESSMENT SCALES

Six subjects were seen on the same occasions by two observers during August 1973. Four were boys, and two were girls, ranging in age from 11-14 months. Tables A-D summarize the percentage of agreement obtained on the various subject-initiated and adult-initiated categories. Medians for the group of six are included. Tables E and F summarize the percentage of agreement on

Subject	Age in Months	Sex
A	13	girl
B	14	girl
C	13	boy
D	14	boy
E	12	boy
F	11	boy

Rating Scales I and II. Raw data on each of the six subjects is also included. Observations were independently coded.

TABLE A. **Subject-Initiated Behavior: Medians, % of Agreement**

Number of Overtures	91.0
Time of Onset	71.0
Purpose	79.0
M's Response	
a. Timing and Direction	100.0
b. Perception of S's Need	96.0
c. Level of Difficulty of Words	77.5
d. Provision of Related Ideas	75.0
e. Complexity of Language	81.5
f. Provision of Encouragement	62.0
g. Teaching of Realistic Limits	92.5
h. Satisfaction of S's Needs	100.0

TABLE B. **Summary Table of Agreement on S-Initiated Behavior**

Category	Percentage of Agreement					
	Sub. A	Sub. B	Sub. C	Sub. D	Sub. E	Sub. F
Number of Overtures	100	93	88	80	81	100
Time of Onset	67	43-50	87	75	92	67
Purpose	70	83	85	67	75	100
M's Response						
a. Timing and Direction	100	83	100	100	100	100
b. Perception of S's Need	90	83	85	100	100	100
c. Level of Difficulty of Words	80	83	43	67	75	100
d. Provision of Related Ideas	90	83	28	67	67	100
e. Complexity of Language	80	83	28	33	83	100
f. Provision of Encouragement	50	67	57	33	83	100
g. Teaching of Realistic Limits	70	100	85	67	100	100
h. Satisfaction of S's Needs	80	100	100	100	100	100

TABLE C. **Mother-Initiated Behavior: Medians, % of Agreement**

Number of Overtures	95.0
Time of Onset	75.0
Purpose	100.0
Emotional Tone	92.5

TABLE D. Summary Table of Agreement on M-Initiated Behavior

Category	Percentage of Agreement					
	Sub. A	Sub. B	Sub. C	Sub. D	Sub. E	Sub. F
Number of Overtures	90	87.5	100	100	67	100
Time of Onset	75	25	71	80	75	100
Purpose	85	100	100	25	100	100
Emotional Tone	85	100	80	25	100	100

TABLE E. Group Percentage Agreements for Each Dimension on Rating Scale I: Distal Adult Effects

Distal Adult Effects	Raw Scores*	% Agreement
A. Design of Home		
1. Procurement of Materials	6/6	100
2. Safety Precautions	3/6	50
3. Child-proofing	6/6	100
4. Accessibility	6/6	100
B. Adult Effects		
1. Adult's Availability	6/6	100
2. Scheduling Activities	6/6	100
Median: 100%		

*Observer A/Observer B

TABLE F. Group Percentage Agreements for Each Dimension on Rating Scale II: Dimensions of Competence

	Dimensions of Competence	Raw Scores*	% Agreement
1.	To get and maintain the attention of adults	6/6	100
2.	To use adults as resources	6/6	100
3.	To express affection to adults	3/6	50
4.	To express hostility to adults	4/6	67
5.	To lead peers	6/6	100
6.	To follow peers	3/6	50
7.	To express affection to peers	4/6	67
8.	To express hostility to peers	4/6	67
9.	To compete	5/6	34
10.	To praise oneself or show pride in one's accomplishments	2/6	34
11.	To role play	6/6	100
12.	Language development	6/6	100
13.	To sense dissonance	6/6	100
14.	To anticipate consequences	5/6	84
15.	To deal with abstractions	6/6	100
16.	To take the perspective of another	6/6	100
17.	To make interesting associations	6/6	100
18.	To plan and carry out multistepped activities	6/6	100
19.	To use resources effectively	6/6	100
20.	To dual focus	6/6	100
	Median (20 dimensions): 100%		
	Median (13 dimensions)**: 84%		

*Observer A/Observer B

**Categories 13, 15, 16, 17, 18, 19, 20 omitted because they are never rated for children in this age range.

APPENDIX TO MANUAL FOR ADULT ASSESSMENT SCALES

by Burton L. White/Barbara Kaban/Bernice Shapiro/
Elizabeth Constable/Jane Attanucci

Preschool Project, Laboratory of Human Development, Harvard University, Graduate School of Education, March, 1974, Revised March, 1975.

ADULT ASSESSMENT SCALES, PRELIMINARY FORMS

Name _____

Date _____

Observer _____

Directions

The Adult Assessment Scales consist of the following:

1. Checklist I: Child-Adult Interaction, Subject Initiated
2. Checklist II: Child-Adult Interaction, Adult Initiated
3. Rating Scale I: Distal Adult Effects
4. Rating Scale II: Dimensions of Competence

An adult assessment visit will be thirty minutes in length. During this period as behaviors occur, the observer will check them off on Checklist I: Child-Adult Interaction, Subject Initiated, and on Checklist II: Child-Adult Interaction, Adult Initiated. Rating Scale I: Distal Adult Effects, and Rating Scale II: Dimensions of Competence, will be completed on the same day but after the observer has left the home. All four forms will be completed for each adult observation.

Setting at beginning of observation _____

_____

_____

Time at beginning of observation _____

CHECKLIST I: CHILD-ADULT INTERACTION, SUBJECT INITIATED
(Preliminary Form)

Overture begins at:								
Overture ends at:								
Duration of overture:								
Subject's purpose:								
A response begins at:								
A response ends at:								
Duration of response:								
1. Timing and direction of adult's response								
a. immediately								
b. delayed								
c. no response								
d. rejects								
2. Perception of subject's need								
a. accurate								
b. partial								
c. not at all								
3. Level of difficulty of words								
a. appropriate								
b. too complex								
c. too simple								
d. baby talk								
e. none								
4. Provision of related ideas								
a. yes								
b. no								
5. Complexity of language								
a. complex sent. > 3 sec.								
b. phrase/sent. < 3 sec.								
c. one word								
d. none								
6. Provision of encouragement and reinforcement of enthusiasm								
a. yes								
b. no								
c. inappropriate								

CHECKLIST I (continued)

7. Teaching of realistic limits
   a. yes
   b. no
   c. inappropriate
8. Satisfaction of subject's needs
   a. yes
   b. no
   c. partial

CHECKLIST II: CHILD-ADULT INTERACTION, ADULT INITIATED (Preliminary Form)

Episode begins at:

Number of seconds:

1. Purpose of the interaction
   a. to stimulate child
   b. to control—positive
   c. to control—negative
   d. routine caretaking

2. Emotional tone of the adult in interaction
   a. positive
   b. negative
   c. neutral

3. Content of interaction

RATING SCALE I: DISTAL ADULT EFFECTS (Preliminary Form)

A. Design of the home

  1. Procurement of materials for the subject's use

1	2	3	4	5	0
grossly suitable		average		grossly unsuitable	no basis for rating

  Comments: _____

  2. Safety precautions (safety to child)

1	2	3	4	5	0
excellent	above average	average	below average	grossly inadequate	no basis for rating

  Comments: _____

  3. Child-proofing (protection of breakables; avoiding destruction and unnecessary extra work)

1	2	3	4	5	0
maximal child-proofing— maximal access		minimal child-proofing— maximal access		maximal child-proofing— minimal access	no basis for rating

  Comments: _____

  4. Accessibility to living area

1	2	3	4	5	0
maximum	most of home	average	very little	minimum	no basis for rating

  Comments: _____

RATING SCALE I (continuted)

B. Adult effects

   1. Adult's availability to the subject

1	2	3	4	5	0
maximum	above average	average	below average	minimum	no basis for rating

   Comments: _____

   _____

   2. Adult's scheduling of daily activities which are likely to enhance or inhibit development

1	2	3	4	5	0
maximum	above average	average	below average	minimum	no basis for rating

   Comments: _____

   _____

RATING SCALE II: DIMENSIONS OF COMPETENCE (Preliminary Form)

Dimensions of Competence	Adult's Response			
	Excellent	Average	Poor	No Basis for Rating
1. To get and maintain attention of adults				
2. To use adults as resources				
3. To express affection to adults				
4. To express hostility to adults				
5. To lead peers				
6. To follow peers				
7. To express affection to peers				
8. To express hostility to peers				
9. To compete				
10. To praise oneself and/or show pride in one's accomplishments				
11. To role play				
12. Language development				
13. To sense dissonance				
14. To anticipate consequences				
15. To deal with abstractions				
16. To take the perspective of another				
17. To make interesting associations				
18. To plan and carry out multistepped activities				
19. To use resources effectively				
20. To demonstrate dual focus				

CATEGORIES FOR CHECKLIST I: CHILD-ADULT INTERACTION' SUBJECT INITIATED

Subject's Purpose	Abbreviation
To please	pl
To gain approval	gain app
To procure a service	proc serv
To gain attention	gain att
To maintain social contact	msc
To annoy	annoy
To direct/dominate/lead	direct
To compete/gain status	compete
To ease discomfort	ease disc

Comments:

MANUAL FOR ASSESSING SOCIAL ABILITIES OF ONE TO SIX YEAR OLD CHILDREN

by Bernice Shapiro * and Daniel Ogilvie*

Instructions, *432*
Extent of Coverage, *432*
Amount of Scoring, *432*
Independence of Categories, *433*
Reliability, *433*
Definitions of Categories in Checklist, *433*
    A. Categories for Interaction with Adults, *433*
    B. Categories for Interaction Between Peers, *443*
Checklist for Scoring Social Behavior, *450*
Social Competence: Scoring Information, *453*
Scoring Social Behavior Checklist, *453*
The Distribution Bonus, *455*
Social Behavior Reliability Procedures, *460*

---

*The original manual was written by Daniel Ogilvie and Bernice Shapiro in 1969, and subsequently has been appended April 1970, revised December 1973 and March 1974, and appended again October, 1974.

    Preschool Project, Laboratory of Human Development, Harvard University, Graduate School of Education, September 1969, Revised March 1974, Appended October 1974.

INSTRUCTIONS

In the process of developing and refining a system for scoring social behavior of children, a checklist has been constructed. Social behavior involving a child and and adult is recorded on the first page of the score sheet. Interactions between two or more peers or siblings are recorded on the second and third pages. The setting and ages of people present should be noted on the form, along with the date and time. An observation session is thirty minutes in length. The observer should stand between six and ten feet from the subject, and care is taken to minimize interference with, distraction of, and involvement with the subject.

EXTENT OF COVERAGE

It is important to note that no attempt has been made to score all social actions and interactions of children. As described elsewhere, great care has been taken to select variables which seem to us to differentiate well-developed children from poorly developed children. Hence, the observer should not expect to score all social behaviors. Some actions cannot be categorized and should not be "forced" into the checklist.

The social checklist may be used in observing behavior of children as young as 8 months old. Although many of the more mature forms of social action will not be observable until many months later, it is nevertheless possible to trace the development of rudimentary social action at these very young ages. It should be noted that the majority of categories describe child-initiated behavior. However, the compliance/noncompliance categories in particular depend on the mother's initiation.

AMOUNT OF SCORING

Each time a subject performs a scorable act, a slash mark is placed in the appropriate cell. For example, if S calls to an adult and the adult does not respond, a slash mark is placed in cell A.1, unsuccessful. If S calls again and A still does not repond, another slash is placed in the same cell. Slash marks are added each time S calls. If A eventually responds (A.1, successful) and S asks for a cracker, a slash mark is placed under A.3, Resource—seeks food. In another example, S is arguing with P. P hits S, and S responds with same (Score: B.11, physical). Several minutes later, S hits again (Score: B.11, physical), and seconds later throws a block at P (Score: B.11, physical). Episodes in sections A.1-5 and B.1-4, 12 and 13 should be scored according to whether they are successful or unsuccessful. Episodes in sections A.9 and B.11 should be scored according to whether they are verbal or physical.

Episodes in sections A.13 and A.14 are to be timed and given a score every five seconds. If a role play episode endures for forty seconds, eight slash marks should be placed in that cell. Episodes in other categories that endure for longer than five seconds should be given an additional slash mark every five seconds (example: a long crying episode in which S is seeking to use A as an emotional resource).

INDEPENDENCE OF CATEGORIES

An attempt has been made to describe each category with sufficient clarity to avoid both misscoring and multiple scoring. In a number of sections of the manual, categories likely to cause confusion are contrasted with related categories in an attempt to delineate category boundaries as carefully as possible. Each scorable act, then, should receive just *one* score. Multiple scoring of a single act is not allowed.

RELIABILITY

Reliability has been assessed by computing correlation coefficients on half-hour paired observations. Although this procedure does not directly determine, for example, if both observers simultaneously observe behavior A and score it in cell Z (only a minute-by-minute scoring breakdown could give that information), consistently high correlations obtained by observing a substantial number of children and rotating observers decrease the probability of chance agreements. In its current form, an overall correlation coefficient of .87 was computed on paired half-hour observations of twenty children aged three to six in seven preschools by six observers.

DEFINITIONS OF CATEGORIES IN CHECKLIST

A. Categories for Interaction with Adults

1. *Attention of Adult—Positive*

   a. Moves towards and stands or sits near A
   b. Touches A
   c. Calls to A
   d. Begins interaction with A
      (1) Shows something to A
      (2) Tells something to A

This section is meant to be scored when a child does something designed to get the attention of an adult whether it be the teacher, his mother, or a stranger. It does not matter for the purposes of this section what the child does once he has obtained the adult's attention. He may have no further end in mind, or he may go on to use the adult as a resource (see Section A.3), to attempt to control the adult (see Section A.5), or to express affection (see Section A.8).

We have found, after observing children between the ages of one and six, that the techniques children use to obtain the adult's attention can be grouped into six categories. Each of the six may be scored alone or in combination if S uses more than one technique when trying to get the adult's attention.

a. *Moves toward and stands or sits near A.* Child places himself in the vicinity of an adult and waits or expects to be noticed by the adult. No score should be given if S just happens to be near and shows no attention-seeking behavior.

b. *Touches A.* This is meant to include all instances of a child's touching A or pulling at A's clothing in order to make the adult aware of his presence and to attend to him. Excluded from this definition are those instances in which a child seeks physical contact or comfort from an adult (see Section A.4), as well as those in which a child expresses affection to an adult by touching him in some way (see Section A.8).

c. *Calls to A.* Any time a child calls out the adult's name or title ("Teacher"), or calls out "Mama" or its equivalent, he should receive a score here. Calls to A may also include yelling to A, whining, or speaking the adult's name. When a child both calls to an adult and touches the adult, he should receive two scores in this section. Each separate, discrete act is scored.

d. *Begins an interaction with A.*

(1) *Tells something to A*—In this category are included those times when a child initiates a conversation with an adult about things that the adult is not focused on at the moment. For example, in school a child might start to tell the teacher about something that went on at home or over the weekend, or he might talk about the weather or something he is doing. Generally, this will happen when an adult is nearby but doing something else; in order to get the adult to focus on him, a child might say, "I went to the zoo yesterday." The attempt to start a conversation is then interpreted as an attempt to get the attention of an adult. If the child uses the adult's name or touches her before saying "I went to the zoo," he would get a score for these specific actions as well.

(2) *Shows something to A*—This category is meant to cover those instances when a child shows something to an adult in order to begin an interaction or simply to be noticed. The child can show the adult practically anything; however, when the object is something the child has

just made or seems proud of (i.e., new clothes), this behavior should be scored in Section A.11, Pride in Product, or A.12, Pride in Attribute. Generally, the technique of showing something to an adult to begin an interaction will involve materials in the classroom—i.e., the hamsters or an interesting picture in a book. The object might also be something of no particular interest but is simply used as an excuse for a conversation, If the showing of an object does in fact lead to a conversation, the child should receive two scores.

2. *Attention of Adult—Negative* This section is meant to score those times when a child attempts to gain an adult's attention through negative behavior—for example, silliness, exaggerated actions, or misbehavior.

a. *Shows off.* This phrase should be interpreted in its everyday meaning—namely, silly or exaggerated behavior performed with the specific intent of drawing attention to oneself and—for the purposes of this category—drawing the attention of an adult. Showing off for the benefit of peers would not be scored here.

b. *Misbehaves.* This should also be interpreted in the everyday sense of the word, with the added feature of purposeful misbehaving in order to draw attention to oneself. Actions falling in to this category are closely related to showing off, but they have a more negative character to them. Examples include making loud noises, pounding on the table, etc., or, in the case of a younger child, doing something that has specifically been forbidden to him, such as moving the TV knobs clearly for the sake of getting attention.

3. *Uses Adult as a Resource—Instrumental*

   a. Seeks explanation or information
   b. Seeks A's judgment in peer dispute
   c. Seeks help with clothing
   d. Seeks help with equipment
   e. Seeks food

This section is intended to reflect the number of times a child is observed to make use of an adult in order to obtain something by means of a verbal request or demand, or by a physical demonstration of his need. His object may be to gain information, assistance, or food, and he may demonstrate this by declaring what he wants, making a request, making a demand, or by gesturing, acting out, or pointing. A request is any statement which can end in a question mark. Behavior in the form of demands or orders to any adult which do not relate to resources are to be scored under section A.5, Controls Adult. Verbal requests or demands may include crying, whining, monosyllabic utterances, babbling, and words or word strings. In scoring resource categories, we presume the child's need for help or assistance in doing something or obtaining something he cannot or will not do alone. We are interested in scoring all attempts made by the child in using the adult as resource. Sometimes a young child will appear to engage in controlling behavior in which he is demanding a particular resource (often a specific food) from an adult. It is more conservative to code this as A.3, Resource—instrumental, than A.5, Controls, since the child's ultimate purpose involves the resource rather than a desire to control A's behavior as an end in itself. The main distinction to note is whether a child is attempting to control another person for the purpose of *controlling* per se, or whether he is acting in order to achieve another ultimate purpose.

a. *Seeks explanation or information.* S requests clarification, asking A what something is used for, how it works, "What's that?" "When are we leaving?" "When is Daddy coming home?" "Is it my turn now?" "Do I have to clean up?" An infant may simply point to something to indicate a question he has.

b. *Seeks A's judgment in peer dispute.* S asks A for support in argument with peer concerning whose turn it is to use something. "He won't let me have a turn with the bicycle."

> S and P are having a dispute about whether S is her friend or her neighbor; finally S turns to A as if to ask for some support from her. A says to S, "You can be a friend and a neighbor." This settles the dispute.

c. *Seeks help with clothing.* In school settings, this behavior is often seen at recess time or at the end of the school day. S asks for assistance with zipper, hood, boots, etc. S may need help with smock, buttons, or dress-up costumes.

d. *Seeks help with equipment.* S asks A how to use something or to obtain something for him. S may need help setting up a new activity such as painting, may ask A to fix something, or to write his name on a painting.

> S asks, "Will you read this to me?" "May I go outside?" (S requires help opening the door).
>
> "May I hear my records now?" (S requires help operating record player).
>
> S asks M to separate toy soldiers which are stuck together.
>
> S is trying to erase a picture from his magic-sketch screen. He tries for a while, then turns to A saying, "I can't do it," and then hands the screen to A. A shakes it for him until the picture disappears.

e. *Seeks food or help with food.* Ordinarily during snack time, S requests more food, or during meal time S needs help with food (opening containers). S may request a drink during the morning. S may ask permission to have a cracker although he can obtain it by himself. A young child may occasionally be very demanding in trying to get a particular food from his mother. These demands are scored as resource attempts.

4. *Uses Adult as a Resourse—Emotional.* This section is intended to reflect the child's emotional dependency on an adult. Scores should be given whenever he demonstrates this dependency either verbally or physically.

Seeks comforting or reassurance. After a hurt or disappointment, S seeks A's aid, support, or affection; this should be distinguished from situations in which S demonstrates affection to A. General dependency manifested by seeking comfort can be scored in this section. For example, S runs to M when a stranger enters the home. An additional slash should be given for every five seconds that the episode endures.

5. *Controls Adults*

    a. Positve
    b. Neutral
    c. Negative

This section refers to those interactions in which the child attempts to control or influence the behavior of adults as an end in itself. The child's verbal or physical directives to A may be positive, neutral, or negative, depending upon the content of the directives and the style of delivery used. A child may control an adult affectionately, naturally (matter-of-factly), or in a hostile fashion. Directives may be verbal as well as nonverbal.

Section A.3, Uses Adult as Resource—Instrumental, precedes Controls Adults, and many behaviors classified under the former section could also be placed under the latter. The command, "Get me some juice," is clearly an attempt to control A, but it is also an attempt to use A as a resource.* Aside from very strongly worded commands like "shut up" or "go to hell" (statements that would be scored under Section A.9, Hostility), all remaining attempts at control are categorized under Section A.5.

"Come play with me."

"Be careful so you won't fall."

Father enters home, and S says, "Come with me." F asks, "What do you want?" S takes him by the hand, enthusiastically leads him to her room to point out a picture that she has drawn that day.

"Sit down."

"Close the door."

"Drink your coffee so we can go."

S dressed herself in slacks and a jersey. Her mother comes downstairs in a dress. S says, "But Mom, you had better wear slacks today because I have some on."

A baby sitter is putting away dishes and places a container in the wrong drawer. S shakes his head "no" and points to the correct drawer.

*To avoid double scoring, and to keep separate instances of controlling for the sake of *controlling*, actions intended to control the behavior of A in order to use A as a resource are categorized under section A-3.

> Mother is at the sink washing breakfast dishes. S crawls toward M and attempts to open the door beneath the sink where some pots and pans are stored. M does not realize she is in S's way and S shoves her leg.
>
> S inadvertantly knocks over a glass of water. Mother sponges the area but misses some of the water. S says, "Look, you didn't get some!" in a scolding voice. M returns to complete the job.
>
> S is in nursery school working with clay. He hears P in hallway calling for assistance in opening a door. S yells impatiently to T: "Miss B., you get that door! P is bothering me."
>
> M does not respond to being shoved by S. S pushes harder and screams "Ah!" M moves aside and says, "Oh, I'm sorry. Was I in your way?"

6. *Compliance with Adult's Directives.* This section is used to score those instances in which S *readily* complies with A's directive. Concentrate on verbal directives from M to S in scoring; eliminate physical directives such as M picking S up and placing him in a chair, or the many occasions when M changes diapers or dresses S. In general, whenever S shows a willingness to go along with a verbal suggestion, he should receive a score for compliance. Similarly, whenever resistance or defiance of a verbal demand is shown by S, he should receive a score for noncompliance.

> Mother says to Subject: "Go see if Joe's crying." S runs to living room and sits down by Joe.
>
> M says to S: "Climb up on your chair, it's lunchtime."
>
> In another example, M says to S: "Want to get Mommy a towel?" S goes into bedroom and returns with a dishcloth. M says: "That's a dishcloth, get me a towel." S returns with a bathroom towel.
>
> S is in kitchen while M is preparing supper. M says, "Please help Mommy set table." S opens silverware drawer and begins placing spoons, etc., on table.
>
> S and M are in S's room. M says, "Let's put away your blocks." S begins stacking blocks in block wagon.
>
> T says to S, "You may have only a tray at a time; put one back." S replaces the tray on its shelf.

7. *Noncompliance with Adult's Directives*

   a. Resistant—verbal
   b. Resistant—physical
   c. Disobeys or ignores

This section is used to score those times when S refuses to comply with A's directives. The refusals are scored in three categories.

   a. *Resistant—verbal.* All verbal noncompliance is scored in this category—for example, when S verbally says he does not want to do something suggested by A or verbally indicates through whining that he does not want to comply, such as in the following situations:

Mother tries to put S's snowsuit on him. S whines and does not help her.
Mother tells S it is time for his nap. S says "no" and whines.

b. *Resistant—physical.* This form of noncompliance may occur alone or along with verbal noncompliance. If both verbal and physical resistance occur, they are viewed as two discrete behaviors and warrant two scores under section A.7.

For example, when M tries to put S's snowsuit on him, S whines and hides his feet in such a way as to hinder the mother's putting his snowsuit on.

A tells S to play in another room. S does not move. A comes over to S and takes his hand. S drops to floor and lies limp in A's hand. A must pull S out of the room with no help from S.

c. *Disobeys or ignores.* The most obvious noncompliant behavior occurs when S actively disobeys A's directive by doing something else. Implied disobedience occurs when S ignores A's directive.

For example, T says to S: "Clean up now, S." S then reaches for additional blocks to add on to his building.

8. *Expresses Affection to Adults.*

a. Verbal
   (1) Smiles or laughs
   (2) Makes friendly statement
b. Physical
   (1) Touches
   (2) Shares or makes friendly gesture

The four subcategories under this section are intended to measure behaviors that "leave no doubt" in the observer's mind that affection is being expressed. Friendly statements made by S which attempt to control the behavior of A, such as "Sit next to me" or "Play with me" are scored under Section A.5, Controls Adult.

   a. *Verbal.*
      (1) *Smiles or laughs*—This category is reserved for instances in which S expresses focused pleasure to A in his presence. If A comes over to S and S looks up and smiles at A, S receives a score.
      (2) *Makes friendly statement.* Statements such as "I like you" or "You're nice" are statements of affection. As stated in the introduction to this section, certain friendly statements which are aimed at controlling the behavior of A ("Sit next to me") are scored under section A.5, Controls Adult.

b. *Physical.*
- (1) *Touches.* Expressions of physical affection to A, such as hugging, embracing, holding, and patting, are scored in this category. T is reading a story to a small group of children. S is standing next to T. As T reads, S puts his arm around T's shoulders.
- (2) *Shares or makes friendly gestures.* This category is used when S offers A a valued object (food, toy, game, etc.) or engages in behavior indicative of concern over the welfare or comfort of A (gets chair for A, retrieves dropped object).

The following form of social behavior is also classified by this category:

A is a guest who has just arrived at S's home. S immediately hands A a doll, paper clip, block, etc. Although one might be tempted to score this behavior in Section A.11, Shows Pride in Product or Possession, we have witnessed this sequence often enough to be convinced that the nature of the behavior is friendly and is often the child's way of saying, "I'll be your friend." On the other hand, if such behavior persists or if it begins after an extended visit, it is scored appropriately under Section A.11 or Section A.1, Attention of Adult, depending on other characteristics of the behavior.

9. *Expresses Hostility to Adult*

a. Verbal
b. Physical
   - (1) Hits, grabs, throws objects, etc.
   - (2) Tantrum
   - (3) Rejects physical affection

The categories under this section are types of behaviors that "leave no doubt" in the observer's mind that direct or displaced hostility to A is being expressed by S.

Often a thin line differentiates verbal hostility from verbal control of A (Section A.5). If the communication is phrased in terms of a demand intended to produce physical action or physical confinement on the part of A ("Leave me alone," "Get out of here," "Move!"), the behavior is scored under controlling (Section A.5).

- a. *Verbal.* Forthright statements of personal dislike ("I hate you"), strong and definite vocal rejections of A ("You're bad"), and other firmly stated expressions that betray momentary or long-standing dislike of A are one type of hostility S expresses to A.
- b. *Physical*
  - (1) *Hits, grabs, spits, etc.*—Hostile actions that entail direct physical contact (also near misses) are another type of hostility. Hitting, slapping, pulling hair, biting, spitting, kicking, thowing objects or toys are examples of behaviors that should be scored under Section A.9.

(2) *Tantrum*—More displaced patterns of hostile behavior are tantrums. Head banging, screaming, breath holding, various forms of writhing, or dumping food or objects intentionally and angrily onto the floor is scored here when the observer is convinced that such behavior is an alternative to more direct expression of anger toward A.

(3) *Rejects physical affection*—When an adult attempts to comfort a child by means of physical affection (hugs, touches, strokes) after a disappointment or mishap and the child withdraws from A or actively rejects the affection, a score for hostility is placed under this section. The physical affection expressed by the adult must be clear and direct, rather than a casual pat or touch.

10. *Imitation of Adult*

a. Imitates adult's statements
b. Imitates adult's actions

a. *Imitates A's statements.* When S directly repeats or imitates a statement made by an adult who is present, this behavior should be scored under section A.10.

b. *Imitates A's actions.* When S directly repeats or imitates an action done by an adult who is present, this behavior should be scored under section A.10.

T says to class, "It's clean-up time." S repeats, "It's clean-up time."

Mother is sweeping the floor, finishes, places broom against wall. S comes over to the broom, takes it, and sweeps the floor like mother did.

11. *Pride in Product—Creation.* This section is used to score those times when a child is pleased with something he has created and shows it in some way. Expressions of pride in product need not be verbal. The focus of such behavior can be to a peer, to A, to A and peers, or to self.

S finishes drawing a picture and holds it up in front of himself and smiles broadly.
S takes a clay figure he made over to T and shows it to her.
S says to P, "Look at my picture."

12. *Pride in Attribute—Possession, Action, or Boasting.* S may express pride in something he owns or possesses at the moment, (Possession), in something he is in the process of doing or has done (Action) or in something he claims he can do (Boasting).

"Look at my new car."
"This is a dress my mother made."
"Yesterday I made a big tower at home."
"I can hold six glasses in my hand at once."
"Teacher, I can climb up here."

13. *Adult Role Play.* S's role-playing behavior as an adult is scored under this section. Most of these instances will occur during a free-play situation. Sometimes, S might refer to his "growing up" in conversation. Occasionally S may take on the role of an animal which is analogous to a human role, such as Mamma or Pappa Bear in "The Three Bears." When this occurs, the observer can score S's role as adult role-playing. Time all role-playing episodes and give one check per five seconds of duration. If the episode lasts forty seconds, the number of checks would be eight.

   a. Dresses up like adult
   b. Plays adult role
   c. Expresses desire to grow up

   a. *Dresses like A.* Frequently, adult role-playing can be seen when S dresses up like an adult. S may put on an old pair of her mother's shoes. In school, S may wear a man's coat and hat. No verbal conversation is necessary for S to get a score.

   b. *Plays adult role.* When S plays an adult role, such as mother, father, teacher, policeman, or fireman, a score is placed in this section. Usually S will demonstrate an extended behavioral sequence while playing an adult role. That is, the observer may see or hear several cues indicating S is involved in adult role-playing.

   > S and P are in the doll corner. S puts on high heels and a woman's dress. She turns to P and says, "Go make your bed and then we will go to the store."

   c. *Expresses desire to grow up.* When S refers to his growing up, getting bigger and older, the reference is scored as an expression of the desire to grow up under section A.13. Such a comment can be made to a peer or an adult.

   > S to T: "My grandmother gave some earrings to my mother for me." T to S: "When can you wear them?" S to T: "When I get older, my mother says I can have them for my own."

14. *Child Role Play*

   a. Plays immature role
   b. Expresses desire to remain a child

   S's role-playing behavior as a baby or expressions of a desire to remain young or a child are scored under this section. Occasionally S may take on the role of an animal which is analogous to a human role such as Baby Bear in "The Three Bears." The observer can score such behavior as immature role-playing.

   a. *Plays immature role.* When S is playing an immature role, such as acting as a baby, his behavior is scored under section A.13. He may act or verbalize like a baby (crawling, babbling, fake crying) or allow himself to be treated as a baby.

> S and P are in the doll corner. P is the mother. S pretends to be the baby and allows himself to be wheeled around in the baby carriage.

b. *Expresses desire to remain a child.* This behavior is analogous to section A.13, except for the fact that S says something about being small, young, or a baby. This can occur in conversation with A or P or in role-playing.

> P says to S: "I'm a big ape." S replies to P, "I'm a little monkey and I'm scared." S says, "I'm little" or "I'm too small to do that."

B. Categories for Interaction Between Peers

1. *Attention of Peer*

  a. Moves toward and stands or sits near P
  b. Touches P
  c. Calls to P
  d. Begins interaction with P
   1. Shows something to P
   2. Tells something to P
  e. Shows off

This section is meant to score those times when a child does something designed to get the attention of a peer. It does not matter what occurs after the attention has been sought or obtained. The child may have no further end in mind, or he may go on to use the peer as a resource (Section B.2), attempt to lead the peer (Section B.3 or B.4), or express affection (Section B.10). Each of the following six categories may be scored alone or in combination with each other.

a. *Moves toward and stands or sits near P.* Child places himself in the vicinity of a peer and waits or expects to be noticed by the peer. No score should be given if S just happens to be near P and shows no attention-seeking behavior.

b. *Touches P.* This is meant to include all instances of a child's touching P or pulling at P's clothing in order to make the peer aware of his presence and to attend to him. Excluded from this definition are those instances in which a child seeks physical contact or comfort from a peer, as well as those in which a child expresses affection to a peer by touching him in some way (See Section B.10).

c. *Calls to P.*   Any time a child calls out the peer's name or title he should receive a score here. Calls to P may also include yelling to P, whining, or speaking the peer's name. When a child both calls to a peer and touches the peer, he should receive two scores in this section. Each separate, discrete act is scored.

d. *Begins an interaction with P*

(1) *Tells something to P*—In this category are included those times when a child initiates a conversation with a peer about things that the peer is not focused on at the moment. For example, in school a child might start to tell another student about something that went on at home or over the weekend, or he might talk about the weather or something he is doing. Generally, this will happen when a peer is nearby but doing something else, and, in order to get his friend to focus on him, a child might say, "I went to the zoo yesterday." The attempt to start a conversation is then interpreted as an attempt to get the attention of a peer. If the child uses the peer's name or touches him before saying, "I went to the zoo," he would get a score for these specific actions as well.

(2) *Shows something to P*—This category is meant to cover those instances when a child shows something to a peer in order to begin an interaction or simply to be noticed. The child can show the peer practically anything; however, when the object is something the child has just made or seems to be proud of (i.e., new clothes), this behavior should be scored in Section A.11, Pride in Product, or A.12, Pride in Attribute. Generally the technique of showing something to a peer to begin an interaction will involve materials in the classroom—i.e., the hamsters or an interesting picture in a book. The object might also be something of no particular interest but is simply used as an excuse for a conversation. If the showing of an object does in fact lead to a conversation, the child should receive two scores.

e. *Shows off.*   This phrase should be interpreted in its everyday meaning—namely, silly or exaggerated behavior performed with the specific intent of drawing attention to oneself and—for the purposes of this category—drawing the attention of a peer. Showing off for the benefit of an adult would not be scored here.

2. *Peer as a Resource—Instrumental*

   a. Seeks explanation or information
   b. Seeks P's judgment in dispute
   c. Seeks help with clothing
   d. Seeks help with equipment

This section reflects S's tendency to use peers or siblings as a means of obtaining information or help. It is intended for situations in which S makes a request or poses a question to a peer, makes a demand or statement, or otherwise indicates a need or desire for help or information.

a. *Seeks explanation or information.*

"What are you doing?" "Why are you doing it that way?" "Where are my clocks?" S: "Where's the hammer?" to peer, as they are searching for some toys in a box. "May I play with that after you?" "Can I sit next to you?"

b. *Seeks P's judgment in dispute.*

S brings in peer B when S cannot convince peer A of something.
S seeks support for his position. S asks peer A for support during argument with peer B.

c. *Seeks help with clothing.*

S asks peer instead of T to tie shoe, etc. S: "Can you tie my shoe?"

d. *Seeks help with equipment.*

S requests peer's help in obtaining a toy or asks for demonstration of how to work something. S asks peer to put record on phonograph.
S has been trying to erase another picture from his magic sketch screen. He turns to P and says, "I can't do this; you know." Peer ignores him.
S asks peer to pour juice for him.

3. *Leads in Peer Activities—Positive or Neutral*

4. *Leads in Peer Activities—Negative.* These sections refer to those interactions in which the child attempts to control or influence the behavior of his peers. In order to avoid double scoring, actions which are intended to control the behavior of a peer in order to obtain a resource are scored under B.2, Uses Peer as a Resource, rather than here; strongly worded commands which indicate hostility are scored under B.11, Expresses Hostility to Peers.

The child's verbal or physical directive to a peer may be positive, neutral, or negative, depending upon the content of the directive and the affect expressed by the style of delivery or tone of the child's communication—that is, whether the directive given is affectionate, matter-of-fact, or hostile.

"Come over to my house after school."
"Sit next to me."
S and P are playing catch in a driveway. The ball goes into the street. P starts to go after it. S says, "Be careful! If you go into the street, you might get hurt by a car."
"Sit down."
"Close the door."

> S and P are playing on the jungle gym. S is sitting at the top and says to P, "Come up here."
>
> "Give him back his truck!"
>
> S says to P, "Get off my blanket!"

5. *Being a Model.* In addition to verbal and physical directives, a child may exert influence or control over peers through a modeling process. Any attempt to set himself up as a model for peer behavior, when unaccompanied by a directive, is scored under Section B.5, Serves as a Model for Peer.

> S and P are playing with blocks while sitting on the floor. S gets up and runs to the piano. He pounds on the keys, and P follows him and also pounds on the keys. S then goes to the clothes corner and selects a fireman's hat which he puts on his head. P comes after him and says, "I'll be a fireman, too," and he also puts a fireman's hat on his head.
>
> S and P are sitting at a table playing with clay. S says, "I think I'll make an elephant" and proceeds to do so. P watches S and follows his exact procedure as he also makes an elephant.

6. *Follows Lead of Peer—Verbal Directions.* This section is concerned with the instances in which S follows the lead of a peer, including direct imitations and more subtle following behaviors. We have classified three types of following behaviors:

a. *What to do.* This reaction is scored as following P's lead when S responds to a direction given by a peer.

> P: "Let's play ball here." S joins P and plays ball.

b. *How to do something.* When S does an activity according to P's directions of *how* to do it, this behavior is scored as following the lead of a peer.

> P: "Throw the ball like this." S does what P directs him to do.
>
> S is coloring. P walks over to S and says, "Use this crayon now." S follows P's directions.

c. *Follows but modifies.* When S follows the basic idea P suggests but modifies it, his behavior is scored under this section.

> P: "Let's play ball here." S: "Let's play ball outside."
>
> P: "Let's build a house." S: "Let's make it a teepee."

7. *Follows Lead of Peer—Peer Gives No Directions.* This section lists five possible reactions S may give to P's physical or verbal *behavior* (exclusive of directions scored in section B.6).

a. Involved observation
b. Verbally supports peer's statement
c. Follows peer around
d. Joins peers engaged in specific activity

a. *Involved observation.* When S is obviously "caught up" visually with peer's behavior, he gets a score under this section.

> S watches intently as P paints, for example.

b. *Verbally supports peer's statement.* When a peer says something and S verbally supports P's comment, a score is placed under this section.

> P, when listening to a record of *Peter and the Wolf,* says, "Oh, this is really scary." S says, "Oh, I'm scared."
>
> Peer A says to Peer B "You're scribbling!" Peer B answers, "I am not." S says, "You are too!"

c. *Follows peer around.* S's behavior is scored when he literally follows a peer around inside or outside. There is no additional interaction. S is just a tag-along.

d. *Joins peers engaged in specific activity.* When S sees peers doing something and joins them in their activity, his behavior is scored as following peer's behavior. He may or may not have been doing something else before he joins the peer or peers.

> S sees peers looking at hamsters. He walks over to them and joins them in looking at the hamsters.

8. *Refuses to Follow or Ignores Peer's Directions.* This section is used to tabulate S's refusals to follow a peer's directions. For example:

> Peer and S are building with blocks. P says, "Put that block up here, okay?" S says, "No more up there."
>
> S is coloring. P walks over to S and says, "Let's play in the doll corner." S continues to color.

9. *Imitation of Peer.* We are interested in scoring all immediate peer imitation here, whether it be repetition of words, sentences, gestures, or a sequence of behavior. The model and the behavior copied should be noted as well as in scoring.

Repeats sound or action. When S repeats a sound or action done first by P, his behavior is scored as following peer's behavior. The observer will also score the instances when S slightly modifies P's sound or action.

P says, "Bang, bang." S a few moments later says, "Bang, bang, bang."

P shakes head in time to music. S, who has been watching P, starts to shake her head and moves her arms in time as well.

10. *Expresses Affection to Peers*

a. Verbal
   (1) Smiles or laughs
   (2) Makes friendly statement
b. Physical—touches (hugs)
c. Offers help or shares

This section is intended to measure direct verbal or physical expressions of affection to peers. Criteria for scoring such behavior are very similar to those stated in Section A.8, Expresses Affection to Adults—that is, behavior which leaves no doubt in the observer's mind that affection is being expressed. Friendly statements which attempt to control the behavior of a peer such as, "Sit next to me" or "Come play with me" are scored in Section B.3, Leads in Peer Activities.

a. *Verbal.*

(1) *Smiles or laughs*—When S expresses focused pleasure to a peer in his presence by smiling at him or by friendly laughing with him, the behavior is scored as expressing affection.

A peer comes over to S, and S looks up and smiles at P.

(2) *Makes friendly statement*

S and P are looking at a book together when S says to P, "I like you; you're my best friend."

In another example, S and P are on swings and P says to S, "I like you." S smiles and says, "I like you, too."

b. *Physical—touches (hugs).*

S and P are listening to a story when S puts his arm around P's shoulder. This is scored as physical affection. Behaviors such as hugging, patting, embracing, holding hands are scored as expressions of affection.

c. *Offers help or shares.* When S offers P a valued object (game, toy, food, etc.) or engages in behavior indicative of concern over the welfare or comfort of P (gets crayons for P, retrieves a dropped object, helps P put on his shoes), this behavior is scored as expressing affection to P.

11. *Expresses Hostility to Peers*

    a. Verbal
    b. Physical
        (1) Hits, grabs, spits, etc.
        (2) Physically disrupts peers' activity
        (3) Refuses to share
        (4) Rejects physical affection

This section is intended to measure direct verbal or physical expressions of hostility to peers. Criteria for scoring such behavior are very similar to those stated in Section A.9, Expresses Hostility to Adults—that is, behavior which leaves no doubt in the observer's mind that hostility is being expressed.

    a. *Verbal.* Forthright statements of personal dislike ("I hate you"), strong and definite vocal rejections of a peer ("You're not my friend"), and other firmly stated expressions that betray momentary or long-standing dislike of P are scored as expressions of hostility to peers.
        Often a thin line differentiates verbal hostility from negative verbal directing of peers (Section B.4). If the communication is phrased in terms of a demand intended to produce physical action or physical confinement on the part of P ("Leave me alone"; "Get out of here"; "You can't play with us"; "Move!"), the behavior is scored as giving direction (Section B.4).
    b. *Physical.*
        (1) *Hits, grabs, spits, etc.*—Hostile actions that entail direct physical contact (also near misses) fall into this category. Hitting, slapping, pulling hair, biting, spitting, kicking, throwing objects or toys are examples of behaviors scored as physical hostility.
        (2) *Physically disrupts peers' activity*—A group of peers is building an elaborate block structure when S attempts to join them. P says to S, "You can't play with us," to which S responds by knocking down the structure.
        (3) *Refuses to share*—S is coloring at a table when P arrives with a sheet of paper and asks to share the crayons. S refuses, saying, "I'm using them now; you can't have any."
        (4) *Rejects physical affection*—S and P are lining up to go outside. T tells class to choose partners. P takes S's hand; S pulls away.

12. *Competes with Peers for Adult's Attention.* S's overt competitive behavior is scored in this section. Unlike some of the other sections, this one demands on-the-spot interpretation of the behavior with the aid of situational and behavioral cues. Often competitive behavior can be seen as S and P try to use the same toy or to get A's attention; however, the observer should decide whether or not the competition is overtly present and then score the behavior in the most appropriate section. Often S will compete for A's attention with one or more peers. This can occur in a didactic situation when S wants to say something to T. Or S can begin a conversation with T who is paying attention to someone else; this is scored as competition.

450   APPENDIX C

T is reading to the class. She asks, "What happens next?" S and several peers wave their hands trying to get T's attention so they can give the answer. In another example T is tying P's shoelace and S approaches and says, "He has new shoes on." S receives a score under B.12.

13. *Competes for equipment.* A common source of competition is over equipment. This competition may be a silent tug-of-war over a toy, a verbal argument, or a combination of verbal and physical competition. S may or may not have possession of the item at first.

S and P both want to ride on a swing in the playground. They run to it, and both pull at it. P lets go. S swings.

P (or S) has a ball. S (or P) tries to take it away; after some words and pulling, S (or P) gains possession of the ball.

CHECKLIST FOR SCORING SOCIAL BEHAVIOR

Name_____ Date and Time_____

Code #_____ Age_____ Place of Obs._____Observer_____

A. Categories for Interaction Between Child and Adult

  1. Attention of Adult—Positive
     (Examples of behavior to be scored: Moves toward and stands or sits near A; touches A; calls to A; shows something to A; tells something to A)

Successful	Unsuccessful
10	12

  2. Attention of Adult—Negative
     (Shows offs; misbehaves)

Successful	Unsuccessful
14	16

  3. Uses Adult as a Resource—Instrumental
     (Seeks explanation or information; seeks A's judgment in peer dispute; seeks A's help with clothing, equipment, or food)

Successful	Unsuccessful
18	20

  4. Uses Adult as a Resource—Emotional
     (Seeks comforting; seeks reassurance)

Successful	Unsuccessful
22	24

  5. Controls Adult—Positive, Neutral, or Negative
     (Directs A in a positive, neutral, or negative manner)

Successful	Unsuccessful
26	28

  6. Compliance with Adult's Directives
     (Readily follows A's directives)

	30

CHECKLIST FOR SCORING SOCIAL BEHAVIOR (continued)

7. Noncompliance with Adult's Directives
   (Resists either verbally or physically; disobeys, ignores)

32

8. Expresses Affection to Adult
   (Verbal affection: smiles, laughs, makes friendly statement; physical affection: touches, hugs, shares, makes friendly gesture)

34

9. Expresses Hostility to Adult
   (Verbal: rejections or expressions of dislike, physical: hits, grabs, throws object, tantrum, rejects physical affection)

Verbal	Physical
36	38

10. Imitation of Adult
    (Direct imitation of A's statement or action)

Verbal	Physical	Unspecif.
40	42	44

11. Pride in Product—Creation
    (Expresses pride in a creation S has completed, to self, peer, or adult)

46

12. Pride in Attribute
    (Expresses pride in possessions or actions; boasting)

48

13. Adult Role Play
    (Dresses up like adult; plays adult role; expresses desire to grow up)

50

14. Child Role Play
    (Plays immature role; expresses desire to remain a child)

52

Note: Please list comments about this subject on reverse side.

B. Categories for Interaction Between Peers

1. Attention of Peer
   (Moves toward and stands or sits near P; touches P; calls to P; shows something to P; tells something to P; shows off)

Successful	Unsuccessful
10	12

2. Uses Peer as a Resource—Instrumental
   (Seeks explanation or information; seeks P's help with clothing or equipment)

Successful	Unsuccessful
14	16

CHECKLIST FOR SCORING SOCIAL BEHAVIOR (continued)

3. Leads in Peer Activities—Positive or Neutral
   (Directs P in a positive or neutral manner)

Successful	Unsuccessful
18	20

4. Leads in Peer Activities—Negative
   (Directs P in a negative manner)

Successful	Unsuccessful
22	24

5. Serves as a Model for Peer
   (Situations where S is copied by P without having given P any directions to do so)

26

6. Follows Lead of Peers—Peer gives S Verbal Directions
   (Follows P in what to do or how to do something; follows but modifies peer's directions)

28

7. Follows Lead of Peers — Peer gives No Verbal Directions
   (Involved observation; verbally supports peer's statement; follows peer around; joins peer or group engaged in specific activity)

30

8. Refuses to Follow Peer's Directions
   (Resists, refuses, disobeys, or ignores peer's directions)

32

9. Imitation of Peer
   (Repeats sound or action of peer—e.g., word, phrase, sentence, gesture, sequence of behavior in game, etc.)

WHO	WHAT
34	FV
36	FP
38	MV
40	MP

10. Expresses Affection to Peer
    (Verbal: smiles, laughs, makes friendly statement; physical: touches, hugs, offers help or sharing)

42

11. Expresses Hostility to Peers
    (Verbal: hostile or resistant statements; physical: hits, grabs, spits, physically disrupts peer's activity (equipment), refuses to share, rejects physical affection)

VERBAL	PHYSICAL
44	46

12. Competes with Peer for Adult's Attention
    (Talks about materials or peers in which A is showing an interest; tries to be picked by A for a specific task)

Successful	Unsuccessful
48	50

13. Competes with Peer for Equipment
    (Verbal or physical competition over classroom objects or equipment)

Successful	Unsuccessful
52	54

SOCIAL COMPETENCE: SCORING INFORMATION

After having collected data on the social behavior of children aged one to three years for a period of one year, we needed to calculate indices of social competence for each child. Using the original eight dimensions of social competence that formed the basis for the Social Behavior Checklist, we derived a scoring system based in part on raw frequencies and in part on bonuses for favorable ratios of positive to negative and successful to unsuccessful behaviors. To be exact, the following discussion shows, for each dimension, what elements contributed to the overall competence scores.

Each of the eight dimensions of social competence is scored for each subject. One-year-olds' scores are computed separately from two-year-olds'. Raw scores are converted to standard scores, with the maximum score in each age group (one's and two's) receiving 10 points, and the intervening scores proportioned between 0 and 10. The adult competence score consists of five dimensions: gaining the attention of an adult, using an adult as a resource, expressing affection and hostility to adults, showing pride in product, and adult role play. The peer competence score consists of three dimensions: leading and following, expressing affection and hostility, and competing for equipment and for adult's attention. Peer competence scores were computed only where sufficient interaction warranted their inclusion; that is, if during at least 60 percent of the time a child was observed he was in the presence of peers, then his peer score was computed. For children with both adult and peer scores, a combined index of social competence is computed based on all eight dimensions.

In summary, scores on all dimensions are converted to standard scores which range from 0 to 10. The maximum adult competence score is 50; the maximum peer competence score is 30; the maximum combined score is 80.

SCORING SOCIAL BEHAVIOR CHECKLIST

Getting an Adult's Attention

From a psychological point of view, the ability to get an adult's attention through socially acceptable means is one factor contributing heavily to the social competence score. The frequency of successful socially acceptable attempts is noted; if success outweighs lack of success on this dimension, a bonus of two points is added. The actual ratio of success to lack of success is added to the score (with a maximum ratio of five); if total frequency of positive attention-getting attempts is greater than total frequency of negative attention-getting attempts, then a bonus of two points is added. Finally, the ratio of positive to negative attention-getting attempts is entered into the score. These elements are then added to produce a score on dimension one: getting an adult's attention.

Using an Adult as a Resource

If a child shows success in utilizing an adult as a resource, either instrumentally or emotionally, then the total frequency of such success is added to his competence score and receives greatest weight; furthermore, a bonus of two points accrues if success outweighs failure in using an adult instrumentally; next, a two-point bonus is added for success outweighing failure in using an adult as an emotional resource; then the ratio of success to failure is entered in using an adult instrumentally (with a maximum ratio of five); the ratio of using the adult as an instrumental as opposed to an emotional resource is then added to the competence score for dimension two, using an adult as a resource.

Expressing Affection and Hostility to an Adult

The child's ability to express *both* affection and hostility is viewed as a manifestation of social competence. The total frequency of affection scores is added if the scores for affection outweigh the hostility scores, then the frequency of hostility scores is added; the presence of hostility scores receives a bonus of two points, and the ratio of affection to hostility is entered, with a maximum ratio of five. This method insures equal weighting of affection and hostility.

Showing Pride in Product

This dimension of social competence has been weighted equally in the scoring system, despite its lower frequency overall. Expressions of pride in creations, possessions, or actions are added to a subject's score in their raw frequency form.

Adult Role Play

Although also less frequent in its occurrence, this dimension like showing pride in product, is given equal weight in the scoring system, with total frequency of such scores entered into the competence score.

Leading and Following: Peers and Children

The ability to lead and follow others (children are under age seven; peers are age mates) is another dimension of social competence. The frequency of positive (or neutral) leadership attempts, combined with the frequency of following (with or without verbal directions) other children, forms one part of this score and receives greatest weight; furthermore, if successful leadership attempts (positive, neutral, or negative) outnumbers unsuccessful attempts, a bonus of two points accrues; the ratio of success to failure in leadership attempts is added (with a maximum ratio of five); and finally, the subject received a bonus of two points if overall leadership attempts outweighed the following behavior.

Expressing Affection and Hostility to Peers and Children

The subject's total affection frequency was entered, followed by a bonus for expression of hostility and the inclusion of the ratio of affection to hostility. The frequency of hostility scores is entered only if affection scores are present.

Competition with Peers and Children

The score for competition consists of the number of successful attempts at competing for adult's attention and for equipment, plus the ratio of success to failure in competition attempts.

THE DISTRIBUTION BONUS

For children between 8 and 36 months of age, the final step in determining the social competence score requires consideration of the breadth of such abilities.

The social behaviors of competent three to six year old children were the source of our definition of social competence. We listed eight social skills because they were *each* commonly seen in *all* of the well-developed children we studied. Some weight therefore has been given to the factor of *distribution* of social abilities as well as to the extent of the individual abilities. Very often children under three years of age have too little experience with children their own age to indicate their social abilities with peers. This necessitates concentrating the assessment process for young children on the five dimensions of social competence shown by such children in interactions with adults or older children.

After calculating standard scores for each of the adult-oriented social competencies, a credit for representation across categories is added as follows: 12 points for scoring 1 or more points in five categories, 8 points for scoring in four categories, and 4 points for scoring in three categories. For example, a child scoring 25 points in three categories gets a 4-point bonus, bringing his score to 29 points, while a child scoring 25 points in five categories gets a 12-point bonus, raising his score to 37 points.

In summary, scores on the five adult dimensions are converted to standard scores which range from 0 to 10. A bonus is then added to reflect the breadth of social skills. Including the bonus for representation in all five dimensions, the maximum adult social competence score is 62 points.

APPENDIX C

COMPETENCE FACTORS

For Col. # headings, see Social Behavior Checklist numbers entered in boxes on following page)

Subject: _____ Age: _____ Cycle: _____

Type A (Col 9 = 0 or blank)	Type B (Col 9 = 1, 2, 3, 4, 5)
Col: 10 12 14 16 18 20 22 24 34 36 38 46	Col: 18 20 22 24 28 30 42 44 46 48 50
Total _ _ _ _ _ _ _ _ _ _ _ _	Total _ _ _ _ _ _ _ _ _ _ _
Col: 48 50	Col: 52 54
Total _ _	Total _ _

10 ▷ _____
if 10 > 12, 2 ▷ _____
10/12 > ▷   0 > ____ > 5
if 10 + 12 > 14 + 16, 2 ▷ _____
10 + 12/14 + 16 ▷   0 > ____ > 5
A = Attention of Adult _____

18 + 22 ▷ _____
18 > 20, 2 ▷ _____
18/20 ▷   0 > ____ > 5
if 20 > 24, 2 ▷ _____
18 + 20/22 + 24 ▷   0 > ____ > 5
R = Using Adult as a Resource _____

34 ▷ _____
if 34 − 36 − 38 > 0, 36 + 38 ▷ _____
if 36 + 38 > 2, 2 ▷ _____
34/36 + 38 ▷   0 > ____ > 5
RA = Expression of Affection and Hostility to Adults _____

PP = 46 + 48 _____
PP = Pride in Product

RP = 50 _____
RP = Role Play

---

18 + 20 + 28 + 30 ▷ _____
if 18 + 22 > 20 + 24, 2 ▷ _____
18 + 22/20 + 24 ▷   0 > ____ > 5
if 18 + 20 + 22 + 24 > 28 + 30, 2 ⤋ _____
LF = Leading and Following Peers and Children _____

42 ▷ _____
if 42 − 44 − 46 > 0, 44 + 46 ⤋ _____
if 44 + 46 > 2, 2 ▷ _____
42/44 + 46 ▷   0 > ____ > 5
RP = Expression of Affection and Hostility to Peers and Children

48 + 52 ▷ _____
48 + 52/50 + 54 ▷   0 > ____ > 5
C = Competition with Peers and Children

	A	R	HA	RP	PP	HP	LF	C	Competence
RAW	__	__	__	__	__	__	__	__ =	____
Weight	__	__	__	__	__	__	__	__	
Corrected	__	__	__	__	__	__	__	__ =	____

SOCIAL BEHAVIOR—RELIABILITY PROCEDURES (SEPTEMBER 1969)

In order to ascertain interobserver agreement on the Social Behavior Checklist, simultaneous observations were performed on twenty children in seven preschools by six observers working in pairs. These subjects ranged in age from three to six. Each observation lasted thirty minutes and took place during the second half of October 1968. A Pearson Product-Moment correlation was calculated for each pair of observations, with results shown below. Overall agreement for the group was .867.

	Subject	Interobserver Agreement
A	3-year-old boy	.991
B	3-year-old girl	.983
C	4-year-old boy	.920
D	4-year-old girl	.976
E	5-year-old boy	.837
F	5-year-old girl	.954
G	6-year-old boy	.658
H	6-year-old girl	.839
I	3-year-old boy	.846
J	3-year-old girl	.902
K	4-year-old boy	.850
L	4-year-old girl	.711
M	5-year-old boy	.843
N	5-year-old girl	.929
O	6-year-old boy	.601
P	6-year-old girl	.894
Q	3-year-old boy	.917
R	4-year-old girl	.936
S	5-year-old boy	.873
T	6-year-old girl	.883
Overall agreement for subjects "3-6" years old:		.867

SOCIAL BEHAVIOR—ADDITIONAL RELIABILITY PROCEDURES (FEBRUARY 1970)

In order to ascertain interobserver agreement on the Social Behavior Checklist, simultaneous observations by two observers were carried out on ten subjects between the ages of one and three years. Each observation lasted thirty minutes and took place during the week of December 8, 1970, in the child's home. The following table shows individual and overall Pearson Product-Moment correlations for both one to two year olds and two to three year olds.

Subject	Interobserver Agreement	Overall Agreement for Subjects 1-2 Years
A boy 13 months	1.00	
B boy 17 months	.860	
C girl 15 months	.628	.850
D boy 17 months	.854	
E boy 13 months	.906	

Subject	Interobserver Agreement	Overall Agreement for Subjects 2-3 Years
A girl 35 months	.868	
B boy 34 months	.909	
C boy 26 months	.822	.835
D girl 25 months	.943	
E girl 29 months	.635	

		Overall Agreement for Subjects 1-3 Years
		.843

SOCIAL BEHAVIOR—ADDITIONAL RELIABILITY PROCEDURES (APRIL 1970)

In April 1970 a reliability study on the social checklist was conducted by Observers A and B. Six children (three one-year-olds, three two-year-olds) were observed for a half hour each by the two observers. A Pearson Product-Moment correlation coefficient was calculated from each set of data. The mean correlation for the six subjects was .93. The correlation coefficient for each subject follows:

	Subject	r
A	1-year-old boy	.95
B	2-year-old girl	.92
C	1-year-old girl	.88
D	1-year-old girl	.95
E	2-year-old girl	.90
F	2-year-old boy	.97

SOCIAL BEHAVIOR—ADDITIONAL RELIABILITY PROCEDURES

Interobserver agreement using the Social Behavior Checklist was ascertained by comparing the frequencies for each category of behavior during a series of ten thirty-minute observations of children one to three years old. The checklist consists of twenty-seven categories, 14 of which pertain to adult-child interaction and the other 13 of which concern child-child interaction. If a child was seen in a situation involving only himself and his mother, only twenty categories were used to compute reliability; otherwise forty categories were considered in the calculations. On the basis of these checkmarks, Pearson Product-Moment correlations were computed for paired observations, as explained earlier.

SOCIAL BEHAVIOR—ADDITIONAL RELIABILITY PROCEDURES

In order to ascertain interobserver agreement on the Social Behavior Checklist, simultaneous observations by two observers were carried out on six subjects between the ages of 8 and 16 months. Each observation lasting one-half hour took place during the week of October 28, 1974, in the child's home. The following table shows individual pairs and overall Pearson Product-Moment correlations for the six subjects.

	Subject		Interobserver Agreement
A	girl	12 months	.90
B	boy	16 months	.90
C	boy	11 months	.99
D	boy	8 months	.92
E	boy	11 months	.96
F	boy	8 months	.98
Overall agreement for 8 to 16 month old subjects:			.942

The above simultaneous observations were also analyzed for reliability using the analysis of variance method prescribed by Winer (1962). The reader may refer to Winer for the most complete description of the procedure.

For each pair of raters gathering social behavior data on the checklist, entries were made of the percentage of success to total entries for the following categories: attention, resource (instrumental), resource (emotional). The percentage of compliance-noncompliance was used, as well as percentage of affection scores. Imitation was included since there were entries made, but role play and expressions of pride were omitted due to low frequencies. The following table shows results when estimating reliability by means of analysis of variance, giving the following entries: reliability unadjusted for differences among raters both for the mean of two raters and for a single rating, and reliability adjusted for differences among raters both for the mean of two raters and for a single rating. Scores on these categories range from .62 to 1.00.

Estimation of Reliability by Analysis of Variance Table for Social Behavior Instrument

Item	Reliability Unadjusted for Differences Among Raters						Reliability Adjusted to Differences Among Raters					
	Mean of Two Raters			Single Rating			Mean of Two Raters			Single Rating		
	Raters 1 & 2	Raters 1 & 3		Raters 1 & 2	Raters 1 & 3		Raters 1 & 2	Raters 1 & 3		Raters 1 & 2	Raters 1 & 3	
Adult Attention—Positive	1.00	.94		.99	.88		1.00	.93		.99	.86	
Adult Attention—Negative	.99	.99		.99	.98		.99	.99		.99	.98	
Instrumental Resource—Adult	.99	.97		.98	.95		.99	.97		.98	.94	
Emotional Resource—Adult	.99	1.00		.98	.99		.99	1.00		.98	.99	
Compliance/Noncompliance	.90	.93		.82	.88		.92	.96		.85	.93	
Affection/Hostility—Adult	.99	.97		.99	.94		.99	.98		.98	.95	
Imitation*	.76	.99		.62	.98		.76	.99		.62	.98	

*No entries for Role Play or Pride occurred.

MANUAL FOR TESTING THE LANGUAGE ABILITY OF ONE TO THREE YEAR OLD CHILDREN

by Janice Marmor/Elizabeth Constable

Introduction, *463*
Procedure for Language Testing: 12-24 Months, *463*
Procedure for Language Testing: 24-36 Months, *465*
Test Materials, *468*
Sample Data Sheets, *471*
    12-24 Months
    24-36 Months
Scoring System, *480*
Reliability Studies, *482*

Preschool Project, Laboratory of Human Development, Harvard University, Graduate School of Education, April 1971, Revised November 1975 by Ingrid Stocking and Eugenia Ware.

INTRODUCTION

The following procedures have been devised to test the receptive-language ability of children between the ages of 12 and 36 months. In the 12-24-month-old group, the tests measure the ability to understand vocabulary words and to follow verbal instructions. The vocabulary items are based on the Pacific Expressive Vocabulary Objects as described by Meyers.* The procedure consists of responding to simple object labels and to more difficult labels for classes of objects by identifying their referent objects. The items in the instructions section test the ability to follow simple, familiar commands or to carry out more complex sequences of behavior.

The test battery for the 24-36-month-old group is also receptive in nature and includes the Ammons Full-Range Picture Vocabulary Test,† the Pacific Expressive Vocabulary Objects from Meyers, and a grammar test roughly adapted from Bellugi-Klima's Grammatical Comprehension Tests.‡ The Meyers test is used only in the event that the Ammons FRPVT proves to be too difficult.

Procedures and scoring information are contained in the general instructions for each test. Sample data sheets are also included.

I. PROCEDURE FOR LANGUAGE TESTING: 12-24 MONTHS

1. Allow about ten minutes to get to know the mother and the child, and to briefly explain objectives and testing procedure to the mother, since she will be serving as examiner with your assistance.

2. If the child is less than 15 months of age, get a detailed inventory from the mother of the child's receptive vocabulary including names of toys and household objects, foods, body parts, other family members, and so forth. Second, get an inventory of instructions which the child is likely to be able to understand and follow, including daily activities and games (turn off the light, throw me the ball), chores for mother (bring me a diaper), and grooming activities (brush your hair). A checklist of some common object names and activities is included in the data sheet to facilitate this process.

3. Explain to the mother not to use gestures when she is giving instructions to the child. For example, if the instruction is "give me the ball" she

---

* C. E. Meyers, et al., "Four Ability-Factor Hypotheses at Three Preliterate Levels in Normal and Retarded Children" (monograph of the Society for Research in Child Development, 1964), 29, (5), 62-68.

† R. B. Ammons and J. C. Holmes, "The Full-Range Picture Vocabulary Test: III. Results for a Preschool-Age Population," *Child Development*, 1949, 20, 5014.

‡ U. Bellugi-Klima, "Grammatical Comprehension Tests" mimeographed, March 1968.

must not put her hand out to take it. If a gesture is used, the child may be responding to the gesture rather than to the words.

4. The testing procedure should be informal and flexible in order to take advantage of the child's momentary inclinations. Do not upset the child by working against his inclinations. Rather, attempt to utilize these inclinations in the testing situation. For example, if while testing a child on item A2 (labeling classes of unfamiliar objects), he shows a particular interest in the balls, utilize this situation to test his capacity to understand instructions (Part B) by saying, "Throw the ball to me" or "Give the ball to Mommy."

5. Although it seems to be easier to begin testing with vocabulary items, the order of testing is not immutable. Some children are more amenable to following instructions and will simultaneously display an understanding of object names while carrying out instructions.

6. Be sure not to test the child beyond the minimum criterion necessary to pass any one item. This will tire the child needlessly.

7. If the validity of the child's response to any one item is in question, repeat that item later in the testing period.

A. Vocabulary—"Meyers Test"

1. Depending on information procured from the mother, begin testing with either item A1 or A2. This will most likely vary with age of subjects, the 12 to 14 month-olds starting with A1, the 15 to 24 month-olds starting with A2.

2. *When beginning with A1 (simple labeling):* If convenient, arrange some of the objects listed on the data sheet on the floor in front of the subject, and have the mother ask of each item in turn, "Where is the _____?" "Show me the _____," or "Point to the _____," and so forth. Any clear means which the subject uses to identify the desired object is acceptable. Make use of natural situations as much as possible. For example, if the child spontaneously picks up a ball, ask him to "put the ball in the cup" rather than to "show me the cup." (This will illustrate an understanding of the word "cup," but not necessarily "ball," since the subject is already holding the ball.)

If the mother indicates that the child can identify objects in another room, move around the house and have the mother ask the child to identify the objects. For item A1, five objects must be labeled correctly before moving to A2. If A1 is not completed correctly, move on to B1 (simple instructions).

3. *A2 (labeling classes of objects):* Arrange two examples of each of the following items on the floor in front of the subject: ball, cup, keys, glasses, pencil, spoon, toothbrush. Be sure *not* to remove each object as it is identified, for this will diminish the size of the object pool, making each subsequent identification easier. However, if the subject has latched onto a favorite object which distracts him from the task at hand, try to replace it with something less troublesome. If the subject is not interested in these items, substitute the

subject's own toys. Four classes must be labeled correctly for full credit. Move on to item B2.

B. Capacity to Understand Instructions

Making use of the home environment and its natural situation is particularly recommended for testing understanding of instructions. For example, if the child is standing up, ask him to sit down; if he is thirsty, ask him where the milk is. Lamps can be turned on and off, and doors opened and closed upon request. An onlooking sibling is often an appropriate examiner for certain instructions such as "give me a kiss," "bring me the ball," etc. Always remember that we are trying to test comprehension rather than compliance. If the child clearly demonstrates understanding of an instruction but balks in the middle of its performance, he may still be credited on the item (e.g., the mother says "Give me the ball," and the child says, "No," and puts the ball behind his back.)

1. *B1 (simple familiar instructions):* The mother asks the child to perform at least four simple, familiar actions—e.g. wave bye-bye, stand up, sit down. If these are completed correctly, go on to B2. If not, conclude testing at this point.

2. *B2 (complex familiar instructions):* The child performs an action related to a specific object *toward which his attention was not already directed.* For example, "Kiss me" is a complex instruction (B2). The child has to stop what he's doing and come to give the kiss to a particular person. If, however, he is standing close and interacting with the object of the kiss prior to bestowing it, the action is scored as a simple instruction (B1). Similarly, if the child is holding a ball and looking at the mother and she says, "Give me the ball," the action cannot be scored as a complex instruction. If, on the other hand, the child is stumbling around the room with the ball and not attending to the mother and *then* she says, "Give me the ball," the action may be scored as complex (B2). Four instructions must be correctly followed before moving on to item B3. If B2 is not performed correctly, conclude testing at this point.

3. *B3 (unfamiliar instructions):* Select two objects which the subject can identify correctly, and instruct him to carry out two instructions with each item. ("Bring _____ to the door; put _____ on the chair," etc., see data sheet). A correct score means that the subject correctly followed four instructions. A partial score means that the subject followed two instructions with the same object.

II. PROCEDURE FOR LANGUAGE TESTING: 24-36 MONTHS

1. Allow five to ten minutes to get to know the mother and the child, and to briefly explain the objectives of the test.

2. If the mother is to serve as examiner (this is usually necessary only when the subject is very shy or uncooperative for the examiner), explain that the examiner will set up each testing situation (holding up the Ammons cards, or arranging the props for the grammar test) and will say the vocabulary word or grammatical statement for each item. Each word or statement is then to be repeated, verbatim, by the mother to the child. Be sure the mother understands this. The mother should also be told that three repetitions are allowed. It is sometimes comforting for the child if he sits on the mother's lap.

3. Be sure your materials are organized and compartmentalized beforehand and are accessible in the order in which they are used.

A. Ammons Vocabulary Test

Begin testing with the Ammons Full-Range Picture Vocabulary Test. Follow the instructions included with the Ammons Plates. For this age range, most plates contain only one or two appropriate items, although occasionally there will be more than two that are appropriate. On the other hand, some plates will have no appropriate items—i.e., Form A, Plate 1: "pie," "window"; Plate 2: nothing appropriate. If subject succeeds readily with easiest items, administer item for next age level—i.e., on Form A, Plate 1, if "pie" (1.7) and "window" (1.7) are answered easily, try "seed" (6.5) and "sill" (6.7) before going on to Plate 2. See data sheet for list of items to be administered. Those which are checked (✓) should always be given. Words marked with a dash (—) should be given when checked items above are answered correctly.

B. Meyers Vocabulary Test

This test will be used *only* when a score of less than 6 correct is obtained on the Ammons Vocabulary Test. In administering the Meyers Vocabulary Items, arrange two examples of each of the following items on the floor in front of the subject: ball, cup, keys, glasses, pencil, spoon, toothbrush. Have the mother ask of each kind of item, "Where is the _____?" "Show me _____," or "Point to the _____," and so forth. In order to receive credit for having identified a class of any particular item, the subject must identify *both* examples; i.e., when the subject successfully points to one ball, the mother says, "Now show me another one," or "Point to the other ball." Be sure *not* to remove each object as it is identified, for this will diminish the size of the object pool, making each subsequent identification easier. Four classes must be identified correctly for the child to pass the item.

C. Grammar Test

1. Before administering the grammar test, read through the items several times and become familiar with the toy props to be used for each item. This

is necessary to prevent errors and confusion during the testing session. Make sure the equipment is complete (see list of test materials) and easily accessible during the testing session. If possible, the examiner and the subject should sit at a table or desk, and make use of the table surface for setting up each item. If this is not convenient, the bare floor can be used.*

2. If the mother is being used as examiner, ask her to repeat each item to the subject verbatim as the examiner says it after the examiner arranges props. This should be done consistently throughout the testing session. Three repetitions are permitted. If an answer is ambiguous but has already been given three trials, mark it as questionable and come back to it later.

3. Follow instructions for each item as described in the grammar test and record "+" for correct completion and "0" for incorrect answer in scoring column to the left of the items. *Note:* Several items consist of two parts, both of which must be answered correctly for credit to be received. After scoring an item, mark its validity (high or low) in the validity column.

4. If at any time during testing three items are failed consecutively, discontinue testing.

5. If the subject has been tested on a previous occasion and has passed at Level III, give him credit for Levels I and II and begin testing at item 14 (Level III).

6. In order to avoid tiring or boring the subject, test only for the minimum number of items necessary to pass each level. If the first five levels are completed correctly, extra credit items (27-30, Level VI) should be administered.

7. Children in this age range tend to tire quickly or get bored. The order of testing is not crucial. For example, if a child shows particular interest in certain objects, it is permissible to vary the order of the items to accommodate the child's interest. Again, if an item is presented to the subject, and he is not interested, leave it and come back to it later in the test.

8. With children in this age range, it is often necessary to change an item to accommodate the child's inclinations and interest in a particular object. Such changes are permissible *only* so long as the grammatical structure of the item is *not* altered. For example, item 24 ("Put the ball *between* the cup and the box") could legitimately be changed to: "Put the ball *between* the mommy and the daddy" if the child is particularly interested in playing with the dolls.

---

*Some children are distracted by the toy props, while others are very shy or negative. In these situations, positive reinforcement in the form of raisins or miniature marshmallows cut in fourths may prove useful. Ask the mother's permission first and use these sparingly so that the child is not satiated. A note of caution: Be certain not to let child or siblings see these treats before you are ready to use them.

TEST MATERIALS

12-24 Months

Meyers objects

2 red rubber balls: 3 inches in diameter, 2 inches in diameter
2 cups: same size (about 4 inches high), different colors
2 sets of keys
2 pairs of sunglasses
2 pencils: different colors
2 teaspoons: one colored plastic, one metal
2 toothbrushes: different colors

24-36 Months

a. *Ammons Full-Range Picture Vocabulary Test*

   Plates used: 1, 3, 6, 8, 9, 10, 11, 12, 13, 15, 16

b. *Meyers objects* (as above for 12-24 months)

c. *Grammar test*

   2 red rubber balls (see above, Meyers objects)
   2 cups (see above, Meyers objects)
   5 dolls resembling father, mother, big boy, little boy, baby girl
   2 boxes approximately 8 inches x 3 inches x 3 inches
   2 blond dolls (4 inches tall with movable limbs)
   Make a hat for one doll (for item 28) with an elastic band
   Cardboard, 8½ inches x 11 inches, with the following pictures:
      bowl of cereal
      3 shoes grouped together
      small picture of a dog (Snoopy)
      piece of cake
      half grapefruit (or orange)
      cat's head
      chocolate pudding in stem glass
   3 pieces pink cardboard (or pink file cards), 3 inches x 5 inches, with blue yarn pasted on (see illustrations, next page)
   3 thin (¼ inch diameter) different colored wooden sticks of varying lengths (4-8 inches) (e.g., Tinkertoys)
   2 thick (½ inch diameter) different colored wooden sticks of the same length, no longer than 6 inches
   plastic horse with cowboy that fits on
   2 deer or 2 sheep

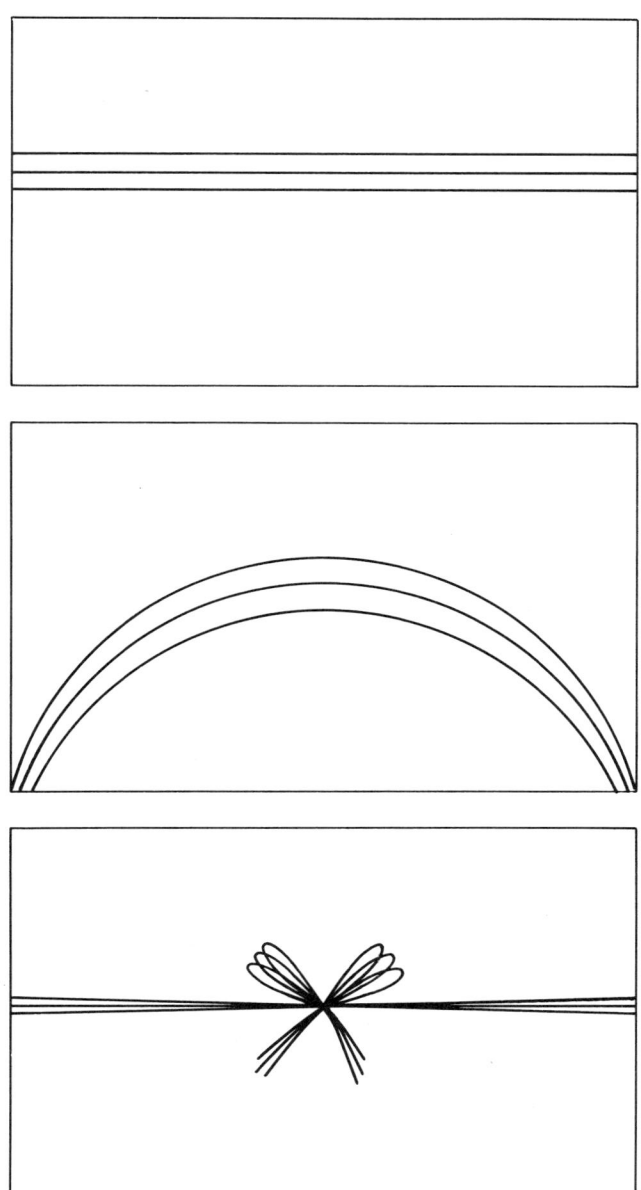

Diagrams For Cards With Yarn

470   APPENDIX C

12-24 months

Name _____   Code _____

Tester _____   Sex _____

Birth Date ____/____/____   Age ____/____
                                Yrs.   Mos.

Test Date ____/____/____

Score:

Vocabulary _____   Instructions _____

Pass Level _____   Developmental Age _____

Comments:

INVENTORY CHECKLIST

Show following list to mother to help her think of words and expressions her child is familiar with:

Vocabulary Words

____ ball	____ cookie	____ radio	____ brother
____ cup	____ apple	____ record	____ mommy
____ keys	____ carrot	____ music	____ daddy
____ glasses	____ snack	____ picture	____ boy
____ spoon	____ drink	____ book	____ girl
____ toothbrush	____ juice	____ magazine	____ doggy
____ coat	____ pillow	____ newspaper	____ cat
____ hat	____ bed	____ phone	____ kitty
____ jacket	____ blanket	____ telephone	____ pussycat
____ shoe	____ chair	____ soap	____ pony
____ socks	____ highchair	____ washcloth	____ horse
____ water	____ crib	____ towel	____ car
____ milk	____ table	____ doll	____ bus
____ cereal	____ television	____ baby	____ train
____ cracker	____ TV	____ sister	____ stove

(cont.)

Testing for Language Ability   471

INVENTORY CHECKLIST (cont.)

_____ refrigerator	_____ eye	_____ teeth	_____ fingers
_____ brush	_____ nose	_____ tongue	_____ bellybutton
_____ comb	_____ mouth	_____ feet	
_____ blocks	_____ hair	_____ toes	

Instructions

_____ come here	_____ kiss	_____ put away
_____ give me	_____ lie down	_____ get up
_____ bring me	_____ go to sleep	_____ brush, comb hair
_____ get me	_____ walk	_____ do you want a cookie, juice
_____ stand up	_____ run	_____ bring me a diaper
_____ sit down	_____ don't run	_____ open, close the door
_____ put away	_____ listen	_____ sit down on the chair
_____ pull	_____ show me	_____ wave bye-bye
_____ push	_____ where is	_____ stop
_____ hug	_____ fall down	_____ turn on, off (the light)

A. RECEPTIVE-LANGUAGE CHECKLIST AND DATA SHEET

Knows *simple word or label*; i.e., mama, bottle, cup, show, doggie.
Child must know five labels.

VALIDITY

	object	label		object	label
1.	_____	: _____	4.	_____	: _____
2.	_____	: _____	5.	_____	: _____
3.	_____	: _____			

Item 1.

Knows *classes for objects* (may be chosen by mother or child, or use Meyers objects).

Score (0, +)   *response*

	1.		1.	Item 2.
	2.		2.	

	1.		1.
	2.		2.

	1.
	2.

response

BALL	1.	PENCIL	1.
	2.		2.

CUP	1.	SPOON	1.
	2.		2.

KEYS	1.	TOOTHBRUSH	1.
	2.		2.

GLASSES	1.
	2.

B. INSTRUCTIONS

Understands *simple familiar instructions* (requiring only a single discrete action). Child must respond to four instructions which mother indicates are familiar—e.g., wave bye-bye; stop it; sit down; get up; come here.

VALIDITY

Item 1.

Score (0, 1, 2)   *instruction*   *response*

☐ 1.

☐ 2.

☐ 3.

Understands *complex familiar instructions* for actions related to a specific object toward which the child's attention was not already directed. Child must respond to four instructions which mother indicates are familiar—e.g., get me _____ ; go to your room; give _____ to mommy; put _____ over there; bring _____ to the lady.

Item 2.

Score (0, 1, 2)   *instruction*   *response*

☐ 1.

☐ 2.

☐ 3.

☐ 4.

APPENDIX C

Can carry out matrix of *unfamiliar instructions* using experimenter's *or* child's own toys. Use any two toys known to S in carrying out two unfamiliar instructions; use each toy in each instruction, for a total of four responses. Instructions must include prepositional phrases.

Sample instructions:

Put keys, ball under the table, on the chair, on Mommy's head, in Mommy's lap, in your bed, on Daddy's desk, etc.

Take/bring ball, keys into the kitchen, to the door, to the chair, etc.

VALIDITY

Item 3.

OBJECT score (0, 1, 2)   instruction   response

☐ ——————————————— 1.

1. ___

☐ ——————————————— 2.

_____

☐ ——————————————— 3.

2. ___.

☐ ——————————————— 4.

_____

SCORING: VOCABULARY AND INSTRUCTIONS
(Language, 12-24 mos.)

VOCABULARY

0 = Does not respond to language at all
1 = Knows five names but not classes of own toys
2 = Knows four classes of own or experimenter's toys

INSTRUCTIONS

0 = Unable to follow even simplest instructions
1 = Follows four simple familiar instructions
2 = Completely follows four complex familiar instructions
3 = Follows two unfamiliar instructions with the same object
4 = Completely follows matrix of unfamiliar instructions with two objects

Vocab. + Instruct.	Pass Level	Dev. Age
0 + 0	0	10 mos.
0 + 1	I	12 mos.
1 + 0	I	12 mos.
1 + 1	II	14 mos.
1 + 2	III	16 mos.*
2 + 1	III	16 mos.
2 + 2	IV	18 mos.
2 + 3	V	21 mos.
2 + 4	VI	24 mos.

*Scored as 17 months on earlier data sheets (before 9/70).

24-36 months

Name _____   Code _____

Tester _____   Sex _____

Birth date _____   Age _____
                                                        Yrs.   Mos.

Test date _____

SCORE:		Total Score	Pass Level	Devel. Age
	AMMONS			
	MEYERS VOCABULARY			
	GRAMMAR			

OVERALL SCORE: _____

COMMENTS:

(Language, 24-36 months)
AMMONS FULL-RANGE PICTURE VOCABULARY TEST
Answer Sheet—Form A

√ = Always include this item.
- = Include this item when checked items on plate have been answered correctly.

Plate 1
√ pie (1.7)
√ window (1.7)
- seed (6.5)
- sill (6.7)
transparent (13.3)
rectangular (14.7)
sector (16.0)
illumination (16.0)
culinary (17.2)
egress (A6.3)

Plate 2
athletes (8.6)
competition (15.0)
revelry (A4.0)
ebullience (A6.4)

Plate 3
√ counter (4.0)
√ pump (4.4)
- clerk (6.4)
sport (7.6)
recreation (10.8)
pugnacity (16.9)
replenishment (A3.1)
retaliation (A4.1)

Plate 4
shrubbery (9.8)
dwelling (11.7)

Plate 5
surf (12.5)
isolation (12.9)

Plate 6
√ horse (1.5)
√ wagon (2.3)
- insect (6.7)
transportation (8.6)
antiquated (A3.8)

Plate 7
discussion (7.7)
skill (10.9)
amour (13.8)

Plate 8
√ firecracker (2.7)
√ clothes (3.0)
-- explosion
clean (5.5)
dehydration (A4.3)

Plate 9
√ farm (4.1)
currency (12.2)
tranquility (16.5)
agrarian (A6.2)

Plate 10
√ furniture (4.4)
- steel (6.0)
refreshment (6.2)
liquid (7.3)
container (9.5)
centigrade (14.5)

Plate 11
√ clock (1.6)
√ locket (3.0)
√ numbers (3.4)
engraving (9.8)

Plate 12
√ hot (5.2)
fear (7.4)
nutrition (10.4)
gorging (12.8)
poverty (13.9)
mastication (A2.6)
itinerant (A4.5)
coercion (A4.6)
corpulence (A5.5)
insatiable (A5.6)

Plate 13
√ telephone (2.1)
√ crying (2.9)
√ accident (3.0)
vehicles (9.5)
destruction (10.0)
portrait (10.2)
communication (10.6)
consolation (13.4)
negligence (14.3)
bereaved (15.4)
deleterious (A6.2)

Plate 14
danger (5.6)

Plate 15
√ bed (1.6)
√ newspaper (2.5)
anaesthesia (11.7)
immersion (14.6)
displacement (A5.0)
perusing (A5.0)

Plate 16
√ propellers (3.7)
harbor (8.1)
locomotive (8.2)
nautical (16.5)

	Pass Level	Develop. Age (Months)
0-6	0	18
6-8	I	24
9-11	II	30
12-15	III	36
16	IV	42
17-18	V	48
19-20	VI	54
21+	VII	60

MEYERS VOCABULARY TEST

To be used only when a score of less than 6 correct is obtained on the Ammons Vocabulary Test.

Arrange *two* examples of each of the following items on floor or table in front of S and say, "Where is the _____ ?" then, "Can you show me another _____ ?". S must identify both examples.

BALL _____

CUP _____

SPOON _____

KEYS _____

PENCIL _____

EYEGLASSES _____

TOOTHBRUSH _____

Total Correct _____

GRAMMAR TEST

VALIDITY	SCORING	
		I. pass = 5/6 correct
	1.	
	2.	
	3.	
	4.	
	5.	
	6.	
		II. pass = 5/7 correct
	7.	

I. E sits with S at a table or on bare floor, puts out two balls and two cups, and places one ball in one cup and says:

    1. Take the ball *out* of the cup.
    2. Put the ball *in* the cup.
    3. Point to *your* head.

Arrange one cup upside down, the other right side up:

    4. Put the ball *on* the cup (or *on* the chair, etc.).

Put out boy, daddy, and girl doll. Arrange boy and girl in standing position about two inches apart, facing each other:

    5. Stand the cup *in front of* the doll.
    6. Show me how the girl *hugs* the boy.

    7. Touch the daddy *of* the boy.

(cont.)

GRAMMAR TEST (cont.)

VALIDITY		SCORING	
	8.		8. Touch *his* head. (S may touch head of either male doll).
	9.		9. Touch the *daddy's boy*.
	10.		10. Show me how the girl touches *herself*.

Leave dolls in background and bring out cup, box, and balls. Arrange cup and box four inches apart. Place one ball next to cup, the other ball distant from cup and box but still in plain view:

	11.		11. Move the ball *toward* the cup; now move the ball toward the box.
	12.		12. Stand the cup *behind* the boy.
	13.		13. Point to *my* head.
		III. pass = 5/7 correct	

Arrange the dolls in two groups—2 in one group and 1 in the other group:

	14.		14. Give me the *doll*. Give me the *dolls*.

Bring out the two blond dolls and the small boy doll and arrange all dolls in one group in front of S:

	15.		15. Point to the doll that *is* sitting. Point to the doll that *isn't* sitting.

Bring out the two balls, cup, and box:

	16.		16. Give the *little* boy the *little* ball. Give the *big* boy the *big* ball.
	17.		17. Give me a cup *and* a ball.

Arrange cup and box about four inches apart. Place one ball next to cup and other ball distant from cup and box but still in plain view:

	18.		18. Move the ball *away from* the cup.
	19.		19. Give me *either* a cup *or* a box.

Leave balls, cups, and box in background and bring out pictures (on cardboard) and three pink cards with blue yarn attached. Show S cards first:

	20.		20. Show me the one that is *tied*. Show me the one that is *untied*.

GRAMMAR TEST (cont.)

VALIDITY	SCORING	
		IV. pass = 2/3 correct
21.		
22.		
23.		
		V. pass = 2/3 correct
24.		
25.		
26.		
		VI. pass = 2/4 correct
27.		
28.		
29.		
30.		

21. Point to the ones you *can* eat.
    Point to the ones you *can't* eat.

Bring out the boy doll, girl doll, and daddy doll:

22. Show me how the doll *jumps*.
    Show me how the dolls *jump*.

Put away dolls, leave out balls, box, and cups, and take out bundles of sticks. Hold purple one and arrange others on table:

23. Give me a stick that is *longer and thinner* than this one.

Arrange two cups and one box in a row, each about two inches apart. Give S a ball:

24. Put the ball *between* the cup and the box.
25. Give me a stick that is *shorter than* this (purple) one.
26. Give me something that is *neither* a ball *nor* a cup.

Ask the following items *only* if *all* the above levels (I-V) have been passed:

Put out one boy doll and two girl dolls:

27. Make the boy hit one of the girls.
    Make the girl that the boy hit run away.

Put out the doll with the hat and show S how the hat can be taken on and off. E takes off hat and says to make this story:

28. *Before* she put on her hat, she sat down.

Show S the cowboy and horse and how they move. E tells S to make this story:

29. *After* he went for a ride, he took a walk.

Put out two deer (or two sheep):

30. Show me how the deer *lies* down.
    Show me how the deer *lie* down.

GRAMMAR TEST—LEVELS OF DIFFICULTY*
Totals correct per level

I.	II.	III.
1. out	7. daddy of	14. doll/dolls
2. in	8. his	15. is/isn't
3. your	9. daddy's boy	16. little/big
4. on	10. touches herself	17. and
5. in front of	11. toward	18. away from
6. girl hugs the boy	12. behind	19. either, or
	13. my	20. tied/untied
Pass = 5 out of 6 correct	p = 5/7 correct	p = 5/7 correct

IV.	V.	VI.
21. can/can't	24. between	27. hit/girl that boy hit
22. jump/jumps	25. shorter than	28. before
23. longer and thinner	26. neither, nor	29. after
		30. lies/lie
p = 2 out of 3 correct	p = 2/3 correct	p = 2/4 correct

	Pass Level		Developmental Age
TOTALS: 0.	_____	=	18 mos.
I.	_____	=	24
II.	_____	=	36
III.	_____	=	42
IV.	_____	=	48
V.	_____	=	54
VI.	_____	=	60
PASS LEVEL	_____	=	_____

*Each level can be passed with a lower score than the criterion listed above IF additional items at a higher level are also passed. For Levels I, II, and III, S must pass 2 items at the next highest level OR 1 item which is two levels higher. For Levels IV and V, S must pass one additional item at any higher level. I.e., Susie passes 5 items at Level I but only 4 items at Level II. However, she also passes 2 items at Level III. Although she doesn't meet the 5 out of 7 criterion for a Level II pass, the additional items passed at Level III give her a legitimate Level II pass. The same outcome would result if Susie had passed 4 items at Level II, none at Level III, and 1 item at Level IV.

SCORING SYSTEM

12-24 Months

The final score earned on the language test for one-year-olds is based on the combined score for Vocabulary and Instructions. Scores are expressed as developmental age equivalents, in months, ranging from Level I (= 10 months) for the subject who cannot follow any instructions and does not demonstrate a knowledge of any vocabulary words to Level VI (= 24 months), the score given to subjects who can identify objects from their class label and can completely follow a sequence of unfamiliar instructions. This scoring system is outlined in detail on page 475.

24-36 Months

The final score earned on the language test for two-year-olds is based on an average of the Ammons Vocabulary score (or the "Meyers Test," in the case where this is used instead; see page 477) and the score on the grammar items. On the Ammons Test, the score is based on the total number of words correctly identified, as summarized on page 476.

Scoring of the grammar items is somewhat more complex. The score is based on the highest level of difficulty which the subject can master. For example, to pass Level I, a subject must correctly complete 5 out of 6 Level I items. To pass Level V, he must complete 2 out of 3 Level V items. Because the test items are arranged in order of increasing difficulty, it is presumed that a child who passes items at Level V can also pass most items in Levels I-IV. A detailed outline of this scoring system is presented on page 477 and summarized on page 482.

Scoring System—12-24 Months

Vocabulary and Instructions

Scoring Level	Developmental Age	Definition
0	10 mos.	0 = Does not respond to language at all 0 = Unable to follow even simplest instructions
I	12 mos.	1 = Knows some names but not classes of own toys 0 = Unable to follow even simplest instructions
II	14 mos.	1 = Knows some names but not classes of own toys 1 = Follows simple familiar instructions
III	16 mos.	1 = Knows some names but not classes of own toys 2 = Completely follows instructions calling for familiar sequences of behavior
IV	18 mos.	2 = Knows classes of own or experimenter's toys 2 = Completely follows instructions calling for familiar sequences of behavior
V	21 mos.	2 = Knows classes of own or experimenter's toys 3 = Partially follows unfamiliar instructions
VI	24 mos.+	2 = Knows classes of own or experimenter's toys 4 = Completely follows matrix of unfamiliar instructions

The final score on the Language Test for 24 to 36 month olds is expressed as a developmental age equivalent based on the average of the development-age scores on the Ammons Vocabulary and on the grammar test.

Scoring System—24-36 Months

Ammons Vocabulary and Grammar Items

	Pass Level	Developmental Age	Criteria for Pass
Ammons	0	18 mos.	0-6 words passed
	I	24	6-8
	II	30	9-11
	III	36	12-15
	IV	42	16
	V	48	17-18
	VI	54	19-20
	VII	60	21+
Meyers		18 mos.	4 classes of toys passed
Grammar*	0	18 mos.	Less than 5 items passed
	I	24	5 out of 6 items passed
	II	36	5 out of 7
	III	42	5 out of 7
	IV	48	2 out of 3
	V	54	2 out of 3
	VI	60	2 out of 4

*See footnote, page 000, for further scoring details.

RELIABILITY RUN—LANGUAGE TEST BATTERY

An interobserver reliability study on the Language Test Battery was run between observers Bud White and Janice Marmor in December 1969. A total of ten subjects were used, five 12 to 24 month olds and five 24 to 36 month olds. Each subject was seen on two separate occasions, once by Marmor and once by White. An attempt was made to schedule both visits to any one subject at the same time of day, and to balance first-time visits equally between the two observers. All observations were completed within a two-week time period.

Two statistical tests of correlation were used to determine the level of reliability achieved: the Pearson Product-Moment correlation statistic and the Spearman Rank correlation coefficient. In each case, four correlations were performed: an overall correlation using all ten subjects, and three subtest correlations for the 12 to 24 month old group, the Ammons scores, and the grammar test.

Table I lists the results of these tests. In all cases, reliability was found to exceed $r = 0.900$. Raw scores are listed on pages 483-487. All scores are developmental age equivalents, in months.

TABLE I

	SPEARMAN			PEARSON		
	N	r_s	sig.	df	r_p	sig.
Overall correlation	10	0.993	.01	8	0.978	.01
12 to 24 month olds	5	0.973	.05	3	0.928	.05
Ammons test	5	0.916	.05	3	0.900	.05
Grammar test	5	0.916	.05	3	0.969	.05

Reliability Run Scores—Language Test Battery
(All scores in months)

Subjects	C.A.	Overall Score		12-24 Months		Ammons		Grammar	
	Mos.	White	Marmor	White	Marmor	White	Marmor	White	Marmor
1	12	16	14	16	14				
2	12.5	12	14	12	14				
3	19.5	21	21	21	21				
4	20	21	21	21	21				
5	22	18	18	18	18				
6	24	30	33			36	42	24	24
7	25.5	36	45			36	54	36	36
8	29.5	57	54			66	66	48	42
9	33.5	57	57			66	66	48	48
10	34.5	45	51			42	54	48	48

Pearson Product-Moment Correlation

Overall Reliability—10 Subjects—12-36 Months

$$r = \frac{N \Sigma XY - \Sigma X \Sigma Y}{\sqrt{[N \Sigma X^2 - (\Sigma X)^2] [N \Sigma Y - (\Sigma Y)^2]}}$$

S's	X	Y	X^2	Y^2	XY
1	16	14	256	196	224
2	12	14	144	196	168
3	21	21	441	441	441
4	21	21	441	441	441
5	18	18	324	324	324
6	30	33	900	1089	990
7	36	45	1296	2025	1620
8	57	54	3249	2916	3078
9	57	57	3249	3249	3249
10	45	51	2025	2601	2295
	313	328	12325	13478	12830
N = 10	ΣX	ΣY	ΣX^2	ΣY^2	ΣXY

1. *Overall Pearson*

$$r = \frac{[10(12830)] - [(313)(328)]}{\sqrt{[10(12325) - (313)^2][10(13478) - (328)^2]}}$$

$$= \frac{128{,}300 - 102{,}664}{\sqrt{(123{,}250 - 97{,}969) \times (134{,}780 - 107{,}584)}}$$

$$r = \frac{25{,}636}{\sqrt{(25{,}281)(27{,}196)}} = \frac{25{,}636}{\sqrt{687{,}542{,}076}} = \frac{25{,}636}{26{,}221.0} = .978$$

Overall Pearson $\quad r = 0.978$

12-24 Months, Pearson

S's	X	Y	X^2	Y^2	XY
1	16	14	256	196	224
2	12	14	144	196	168
3	21	21	441	441	441
4	21	21	441	441	441
5	18	18	324	324	324
	88	88	1606	1598	1598
N = 5	ΣX	ΣY	ΣX^2	ΣY^2	ΣXY

$$r = \frac{[5(1598)] - [(88)(88)]}{\sqrt{[5(1606) - (88)^2][5(1598) - (88)^2]}} = \frac{7790 - 7744}{\sqrt{[8030 - 7744][7790 - 7744]}}$$

$$r = \frac{246}{\sqrt{(286)(246)}} = \frac{246}{\sqrt{70356}} = \frac{246}{265.3} = .928$$

12-24 months Pearson $\quad r = 0.928$

Pearson: *Ammons*

S's	X	Y	X^2	Y^2	XY
6	36	42	1296	1764	1512
7	36	54	1296	2916	1944
8	66	66	4356	4356	4356
9	66	66	4356	4356	4356
10	42	54	1764	2916	2268
	246	282	13068	16308	14436
N = 5	ΣX	ΣY	ΣX^2	ΣY^2	ΣXY

$$r = \frac{5(14{,}436) - (246)(282)}{\sqrt{[5(13{,}068) - (246)^2][5(16{,}308) - (282)^2]}} = \frac{72{,}180 - 69{,}372}{\sqrt{(65{,}340 - 60{,}516)(81{,}540 - 79{,}524)}}$$

$$r = \frac{2{,}808}{\sqrt{(4{,}824)(2{,}016)}} = \frac{2{,}808}{\sqrt{9{,}725{,}184}} = \frac{2{,}808}{3{,}118.5} = 0.9004$$

Ammons Pearson $r = 0.900$

Pearson: *Grammar*

S's	X	Y	X^2	Y^2	XY
6	24	24	576	576	576
7	36	36	1296	1296	1296
8	48	42	2304	1764	2016
9	48	48	2304	2304	2304
10	48	48	2304	2304	2304
	204	198	8784	8244	8496
N = 5	ΣX	ΣY	ΣX^2	ΣY^2	ΣXY

$$r = \frac{[5(8496)] - [(204)(198)]}{\sqrt{[5(8784) - (204)^2][5(8244) - (198)^2]}}$$

$$r = \frac{42{,}480 - 40{,}392}{\sqrt{(43{,}920 - 41{,}616)(41{,}220 - 39{,}204)}} = \frac{2{,}088}{\sqrt{(2{,}304)(2{,}016)}}$$

$$r = \frac{2{,}088}{\sqrt{4{,}644{,}864}} = \frac{2{,}088}{2{,}155.2} = .96882$$

Pearson Grammar $r = 0.969$

Spearman Rank Correlation Coefficients

	Scores		Ranks			
S's	BW	JM	BW	JM	d_i	d_i^2
1	16	14	2	1.5	.5	.25
2	12	14	1	1.5	−.5	.25
3	21	21	4.5	4.5	0	0
4	21	21	4.5	4.5	0	0
5	18	18	3	3	0	0
6	30	33	6	6	0	0
7	36	45	7	7	0	0
8	57	54	9.5	9	.5	.25
9	57	57	9.5	10	−.5	.25
10	45	51	8	8	0	0
$N = 10$					$\Sigma d_i^2 = 1.0$	

.011 Overall r_s = .993
.052 12-24 mos. r_s = .973
n.s.3. Ammons r_s = .805
.054 Grammar r_s = .913

(1) Overall Reliability Using Spearman (All 10 S's)

$$r_s = \frac{\Sigma x^2 + \Sigma y^2 - \Sigma d^2}{2\sqrt{\Sigma x^2 \, \Sigma y^2}}$$

$$\Sigma x^2 = \frac{N^3 - N}{12} - \Sigma\left(\frac{t^3 - t}{12}\right)$$

$$\Sigma x^2 = \frac{990}{12} - \frac{6}{12} + \frac{6}{12} = 82.5 - 1.0 = 81.5$$

$\Sigma y^2 = 81.5$

$$\frac{81.5 + 81.5 - 1.0}{2\sqrt{(81.5)(81.5)}} = \frac{162}{163}$$

$\Sigma d^2 = 1.0$

Overall $r_s = .993$ sig. at <.01 level

(2) Spearman: *12-24 months*

$$\Sigma x^2 = \frac{(5)^3 - 5}{12} - \left(\frac{2^3 - 2}{12}\right) = \frac{125 - 5}{12} = \frac{6}{12} = 9.5$$

$$\Sigma y^2 + \frac{(5)^3 - 5}{12} - \left(\frac{2^2 - 2}{12} + \frac{2^2 - 2}{12}\right) = \frac{125 - 5}{12} - 1.0 = 9.0$$

$$r_s = \frac{9.5 + 9.0 - .50}{2\sqrt{(9.5)(9.0)}} = \frac{18}{2(9.25)} = \frac{18}{18.50} = .973$$

$r_s = .973$ 12-24 mos. sig. at <.05

(3) Spearman: *Ammons*

	Scores		Ranks			
S's	BW	JM	BW	JM	d_i	d_i^2
6	36	42	1.5	1	.5	.25
7	36	54	1.5	2.5	−1.0	1.00
8	66	66	4.5	4.5	0	0
9	66	66	4.5	4.5	0	0
10	42	54	3	2.5	.5	.25
N = 5				$\Sigma d_i^2 = 1.50$		

$$r_s = \frac{9.0 + 9.0 - 1.50}{2\sqrt{(9.0)(9.0)}} = \frac{16.5}{18} = 0.9166$$

$r_s = 0.917$ Ammons   sig. at $<.05$

(4) Spearman: *Grammar*

	Scores		Ranks			
S's	BW	JM	BW	JM	d_i	d_i^2
6	24	24	1	1	0	0
7	36	36	2	2	0	0
8	48	42	4	3	1	1.0
9	48	48	4	4.5	−.5	.25
10	48	48	4	4.5	−.5	.25
N = 5				$\Sigma d_i^2 = 1.50$		

$$\Sigma x^2 = \frac{(5)^3 - 5}{12} - \left(\frac{3^3 - 3}{12}\right) = 10 - 2 = 8.0$$

$$\Sigma y^2 = \frac{(5)^3 - 5}{12} - \left(\frac{2^2 - 2}{12}\right) = 10 - .5 = 9.5$$

$$r_s = \frac{8.0 + 9.5 - 1.50}{2\sqrt{(8.0)(9.5)}} = \frac{16}{(2)(8.72)} = \frac{16}{17.44} = .9174$$

$r_s = .917$ Grammar   sig. at $<.05$ level

MANUAL FOR ABSTRACT ABILITY TEST

by Bernice Shapiro / Barbara Kaban

Introduction, *489*
Levels I-IV, General Instructions, *489*
Objects Used, *491*
Screens Used, *491*
Test Administration, *491*
Levels V-VIII, General Instructions, *496*
Description of Pattern-Completion Items, *497*
Picture-Completion Items, *499*
Form-Color Matching Items, *500*
Reliability Studies, *501*
Scoring Forms and Procedures, *503*

Preschool Project, Laboratory of Human Development, Harvard University, Graduate School of Education, Revised April, 1976.

INTRODUCTION

The Harvard Preschool Project Test of Abstract Abilities assesses a child's ability to deal with abstractions between the ages of one and three. Eight levels of development have been designated based on our experience with infants and preschoolers taking these test items. Levels I through IV correspond to developmental ages 12.5 months through 21 months; Levels V through VIII correspond to ages 21.5 months through 36 months. Items for Levels I through IV were selected from scales I and V of the Hunt-Uzgiris Scales of Infant Development;* items for Levels V through VIII were selected from the Pacific Test Series† and the Stanford-Binet Intelligence Scales.‡

LEVELS I-IV, GENERAL INSTRUCTIONS

All test items are grouped according to developmental levels (see Table I). Each developmental level consists of four items, and a subject must pass three out of four items to score at a particular level. When testing a subject between 12 and 36 months, it is advisable to begin the test one level below his or her chronological age. Discontinue testing when the subject fails two items at any level.

Any child who scores at the 36-month level should be given a full-scale Stanford-Binet Intelligence Test. We recommend the WPPSI° for children performing at or above the four-year level.

Since these situations are presented to children varying considerably in age, certain adjustments in procedure are helpful with younger and older children. Younger children are more likely to become frustrated during testing, and it is necessary to check repeatedly for their interest in the object being used as well as for their attention to the task. For example, failure to follow the successive displacements of the object during the examiner's demonstration would certainly lead to failure on the item. Since children often tend to be impatient and start the search immediately, it is necessary to make sure that they have observed all the displacements. In contrast, older children may become bored with the simple hidings, and if such a reaction is sensed, we recommend that you reduce the number of trials with the simple hidings to a minimum. The cooperation of older children is often improved by helping

---

*I. T. Uzgiris and J. McV. Hunt, *Assessment in Infancy* (University of Illinois Press, 1975).
† Pacific Test Series.
‡ Stanford-Binet Intelligence Scale, revised version by Samuel R. Pinneau, Lewis M. Terman, and Maud A. Merrill (Boston: Houghton Mifflin Co., 1960).
° Wechsler Preschool and Primary Scales of Intelligence, by David Wechsler (New York: Psychological Corporation, 1967).

Abstract Abilities Test Items (Levels I-IV)

Level	Developmental Age*	Items to Be Administered
I	Below 12.5 months	1. Finding an object hidden under one of two screens 2. Finding an object hidden under one of two screens alternately 3. Finding an object hidden under one of three screens 4. Recognizing the reverse side of objects
II	12.5 months	1. Finding an object after successive visible displacements 2. Finding an object hidden in a container that is covered by superimposed screens 3. Following an object through a series of invisible displacements 4. Dropping objects in order to study their trajectories
III	14.5 months	1. Following an object through one hidden displacement with one screen 2. Following an object through one hidden displacement with two screens 3. Following an object through one hidden displacement with three screens 4. Understanding equilibrium
IV	18-21 months	1. Developing representation of a series of displacements 2. Understanding the relationships of the container and contained 3. Understanding gravity 4. Recognizing the absence of familiar persons

*The developmental levels designated here were derived from the testing of infants and preschoolers during the course of research investigations done by the Harvard Preschool Project, and hence do not represent standardized scores. The levels are suggestive of the developmental ages noted. Further normative sampling procedures are necessary.

them view the testing as a game and permitting them a turn at hiding the object if they so desire.

The object chosen for these situations should be one in which the child shows strong interest; otherwise, one cannot be sure whether the child gives up the search because he has lost interest in it or because he is unable to follow the displacements. It is permissible to change objects at any point. However, it is important to recognize that loss of interest may signify that the task has become too difficult. If the examiner suspects that the child is losing interest due to the difficulty of the task, he should hide the same object in a simpler way (i.e., in a way that the child was previously able to handle) and observe whether the child will then search for it. If the child is still interested in the object, he will usually search for it in the easier situation. The repeated disappearance of a desired object often proves frustrating to young children. When it seems that the loss of interest in an object may be due to frustration, permit the child to play with the object for a minute or two and observe whether interest is restored. On the other hand, if the need to relinquish the object after each trial appears to be causing the frustration, it is best to pick up the object as soon as the child removes the screen and begins to reach for it, without actually permitting the child to obtain the object each time.

OBJECTS USED

Practically any object in which the child shows strong interest may be used, as long as it is small enough to be completely covered by each of the screens without bulging too conspicuously. Objects such as a small doll, a red car, a plastic flower have been used successfully. Food such as cereal or candy may also be used.

SCREENS USED

Three screens are needed. They have to be large enough to cover the hidden object. They should be unattractive in themselves, and should differ enough to permit the child to tell one from the other. A large, white, nontransparent scarf, a piece of cloth printed in a small pale pattern, a square pillow covered with dull corduroy, and a piece of drably colored cloth have all been used as screens. *Note:* It is important to differentiate the search for the hidden object from pulling at the screen out of desire to play with the screen itself. In general, if the child has demonstrated a desire for the object before it was hidden and reaches for it either while lifting the screen off or immediately after pulling the screen off, one may assume that the child is searching for the hidden object. On the other hand, if the child lifts the screen and holds it for a considerable length of time before reaching for the now-exposed object, possibly even directing attention to the screen, one may guess that the child has lifted the screen for its own sake.

TEST ADMINISTRATION

Level I Items

1. *Finding an Object Hidden Under One of Two Screens (Doll, Flower, Food).* If the child obtains the object in two out of three trials when it is hidden under a single screen, place a second screen on the opposite side of the child during the last trial of hiding the object under the first screen, and then hide the object under the second screen. Observe the child's reaction. To repeat

the trial, hide the object under the second screen two more times, and then switch to hiding the object under the first screen and count this last trial as a repeat. Observe the child's behavior and rate according to the following:

    a. loses interest in the object
    b. searches for the object where it was found previously—i.e., under the first screen
*c. searches for the object where it is observed to be hidden—i.e., under the second screen

2. *Finding an Object Hidden Under One of Two Screens Alternately (Doll, Car, Flower, Food).* If the child searches correctly at least twice in the presence of two screens, hide the object under the first and second screen alternately, three to five times, and observe the child's behavior:

    a. becomes perplexed and loses interest in object
    b. searches haphazardly under one or both screens
*c. searches correctly under either of the two screens

3. *Finding an Object Hidden Under One of Three Screens (Doll, Car, Flower, Food).* If the child searches correctly in at least three trials when the object is hidden under one of two screens, introduce a third screen in front of the child and hide the object under each of the three screens, in a random fashion, five to seven times, or until the child's behavior appears clear:

    a. loses interest in the object
    b. searches haphazardly under some or all screens
*c. searches directly under the correct screen

4. *Recognizing the Reverse Side of Objects (Object with Definite Reverse Sides—Animal or Rattle).* Have the child sitting up. Take an object with a definite reverse side in which the child shows some interest, such as the plastic animal or the baby's bottle. Hold the object in front of the child within his reach, with its "right" side facing him. When the child begins to reach for the object, quickly reverse it, so that the child would be faced with the other side of the object (repeat once or twice). Observe the child's reaction to the reversal:

    a. continues to reach and grasps the object
    b. withdraws hands and shows evidence of surprise at the reversal
*c. grasps the object, but turns it to the "right" side immediately each time or turns the object over several times looking at it intently

---

*For each item written at each level, asterisk denotes correct response.

Level II Items

1. *Finding an Object After Successive Visible Displacements (Necklace, Doll, Car, Flower, Food).* Arrange three screens in front of the child, all within his reach. Take an object in which the child shows a strong interest and hold it in such a way that the hand does *not* cover the object. Hide it successively under each of the three screens by moving the hand along the path of the screens—i.e., so that the object becomes hidden under one screen and then reappears in the space between the screens and again becomes hidden as the hand passes under another screen. Leave the object under the last screen. Observe where the child searches for the object. If the child finds the object directly under the last screen, change the position of the screens by making the last screen the first, to check for preference for any particular screen. If the child again searches correctly, on the next trial, change the direction of the path followed by the hand in order to check for a position preference. Repeat the hiding three to five times and note the child's reaction each time.

    a. does not follow the object through the successive hidings
    b. searches only under the first screen which hides the object
    c. searches under the screen where the object was found on the previous trial
    d. searches under all screens haphazardly
    e. searches under all screens in the order of hiding
 *f. searches directly under the last screen in the series

Note: It is permissible to interrupt the series at this point.

2. *Finding an Object Hidden in a Container which is Covered by Superimposed Screens (Object in Box Under Screen).* Take an object in which the child is interested and place it inside a box with an easily removable cover, or wrap it in one of the screens, and then proceed to cover the hidden object by stacking the remaining screens over it. Observe the child's reaction.

    a. loses interest in the object
    b. gives up search after removing one or all of the superimposed screens
 *c. persists in searching and obtains the object

Note: It is not only permissible, but desirable, to interrupt this series occasionally. If all the situations are presented in sequence, the child often shows what may be termed a generalization reaction to "lift all screens in sight." This leads to some search behavior among children who are really unable to handle an invisible displacement. If it is unfeasible to intersperse other test situations, a break for some free play would be desirable.

3. *Following an Object Through a Series of Invisible Displacements:*

Following an Object Through a Series of Invisible Displacements in Sequence (Object Hidden in Hand Under Last of Three Screens). Arrange three screens on a sound-absorbing surface in front of the child. Use an object small enough to be hidden in the closed hand, such as a small doll, a plastic flower, etc., in which the child shows interest. Use the hand rather than the box to produce the invisible displacement. While the child watches, hide the object in the closed hand and then hide the hand under each of the three screens in succession, leaving the object under the last of the screens. Make sure the child is paying attention throughout the whole procedure and that the object is not visible in the hand when the hand appears in the spaces between the screens. Show the child that your hand is empty after the last replacement. Observe the child's search for the object. Repeat at least three times always taking the same path and leaving the object under the screen.

    a. searches only in the examiner's hand
    b. searches only under the first screen in the series
*c. searches under all screens in the same order as followed by the examiner's hand
*d. searches directly under the last screen

Note: To check whether the child searches under the last screen due to some position preference, reverse the path of hidings, so that the first screen becomes last. Repeat at least three times. To check whether the child prefers the screen which happens to be the last one in the series, change the order of the screens but continue hiding the object along the same path.

    4. *Interest in the Phenomenon of the Fall:*

Dropping Objects in Order to Study Their Trajectories (Box Filled with Small Objects). Have the child sit in a highchair and present him with a box filled with small objects. Observe the child's play with these objects.

    a. does not drop any of the objects
    b. drops several objects repeatedly but pays little attention to where they fall
*c. drops several objects repeatedly and looks down to see where they fall

Level III Items

1. *Following an Object Through One Hidden Displacement with Two Screens (Object in Box Under Second Screen, Remove Box).* If the child succeeds in finding the hidden object at least twice with one screen, place a second screen beside the first one and proceed to hide the object *in the same manner* under the second screen. Observe the child's search. To repeat, hide the object under the second screen at least three times and then switch back to hiding it under the first screen.

    a. searches only in the box
    b. searches under the screen where the object was previously found
*c. searches under the correct screen

2. *Following the Object Through One Hidden Displacement with Two Screens Used Alternately (Object in Box Under One of Two Screens, Remove Box).* If the child succeeds in finding the object with two screens at least twice, hide it in the same manner under the two screens *alternately*. Repeat three to five times.

    a. loses interest in the object
    b. searches haphazardly under the two screens
*c. searches directly under the correct screen

3. *Following an Object Through One Hidden Displacement with Three Screens (Object in Box Under One of Three Screens, Remove Box).* If the child succeeds in finding the object with two screens used alternately, introduce a third screen and hide the object in the same manner under each of the three screens in a random fashion. Repeat five times.

    a. loses interest in the object
    b. searches haphazardly under all three screens
*c. searches directly under the correct screen

4. *Understanding Equilibrium (Small Blocks).* Present the child with several blocks and observe his play with them. If the child does not proceed to build with the blocks spontaneously, demonstrate by building a tower of three blocks. If the child develops a game of scattering the examiner's tower, knock the tower down before the child scatters it. Observe the child's play with the blocks.

    a. does not build a tower
*b. approximates two blocks, but does not leave one on top
*c. builds a tower of at least two blocks

Level IV Items

1. *Developing Representation of a Series of Displacements (Object Hidden in Hand Under First of Three Screens).* If the child searches directly under the last screen of a series of invisible displacements, leave the screens in the same order, but hide the object under the first screen in the path, while continuing the movements of the now empty hand in the same manner under all the screens. Observe the child's search.

    a. searches only under the last screen and gives up
    b. searches haphazardly under all three screens
*c. searches systematically from the last screen to the first in reverse order

2. *Development of Understanding of Relationships Between Objects:*

Understanding the Relationship of the Container and Contained (Small Beads and Container). Present the child with some small objects, such as several blocks, and a container. If the child does not initiate play with both the objects and the container spontaneously, place the objects into the container, without permitting the child to see the procedure, and present the infant with the objects and the container once more. Observe the child's play.

- a. does not place the objects into the container
- b. places the objects into the container and takes them out one by one
- *c. turns the container over and dumps out the contents

3. *Understanding Gravity (Car on Incline).* Make an incline by propping a piece of cardboard in a low box. Take an object which would easily roll down the incline, such as a small car, and demonstrate that it rolls down the incline by itself. Present the object to the child and observe his behavior.

- a. plays with the object without using the incline
- b. guides the object down the incline
- *c. permits the object to roll down the incline

4. *Recognizing the Absence of Familiar Persons (Asks Whereabouts of Familiar Person Such as Brother or Sister).* Find out from the person taking care of the child which member of the family is not present and ask the child where that person is, or to be taken to that person. Observe the child's actions and his reply.

- a. does not comprehend the question
- b. goes to look for that person
- *c. indicates knowledge of the absence of that person by pointing to the outside, saying "gone," "bye-bye," etc.

LEVELS V-VIII, GENERAL INSTRUCTIONS

Levels V through VIII make use of three-dimensional materials which require that the child complete various patterns and puzzles, and match abstract form. Each level consists of four items (see Table II). The instructions that follow are given for each type of item. In actual practice the examiner should administer the items according to the developmental levels and proceed according to the subject's ability to pass three out of four items at a given level.

Abstract Abilities Test Items (Levels V-VIII)

Level	Developmental Age*	Items to Be Administered
V	21.5 months	A 1. Pattern completion #1—green square B 2. Pattern completion #2—purple wedge C 3. Picture completion #1—dog D 4. Picture completion #2—duck
VI	25.5 months	A 1. Pattern completion #3—red wedge B 2. Pattern completion #4—black triangle C 3. Picture completion #3—baby D 4. Form and color matching #1—red circle
VII	31 months	A 1. Picture completion #4—giraffe B 2. Picture completion #5—boat C 3. Form and color matching #2—red circle D 4. Form and color matching #3—black circle
VIII	36 months	A 1. Pattern completion #5—blue half circle B 2. Form and color matching #4—yellow rhombus C 3. Block building: bridge D 4. Picture memories

*The developmental levels designated here were derived from the testing of infants and preschoolers during the course of research investigations done by the Harvard Preschool Project, and hence do not represent standardized scores. The levels are suggestive of the developmental ages noted. Further normative sampling procedures are necessary.

DESCRIPTION OF PATTERN-COMPLETION ITEMS

Level V Items

Sample A. Pink (triangle):
    dem (1) purple square
    dem (2) pink triangle
    dem (3) green circle
    adm (1) green circle
    adm (2) pink triangle
    adm (3) purple square

Card 1. Green (square):
    (1) green square
    (2) red circle
    (3) yellow triangle

Card 2: Purple (wedge):
    (1) purple wedge (4 x 2 inches at ends, side slightly over 4 inches.)
    (2) yellow circle
    (3) red square

Level VI Items

Sample B. Blue (quarter circle):   dem (1) pink quarter circle
dem (2) blue quarter circle
dem (3) black circle
adm (1) black circle
adm (2) blue quarter circle
adm (3) pink quarter circle

Card 3. Red (wedge):   (1) red wedge
(2) yellow circle
(3) green wedge

Card 4. Black (triangle):   (1) black triangle
(2) yellow half circle
(3) white triangle

Level VIII Items

Card 5. Blue (half circle):   (1) blue half circle
(2) purple half circle
(3) red rectangle (2 x 4 inches)

Materials

Seven colored corrugated boards are needed, 9 x 12 inches, each with a cutout from the middle of a 12-inch side. Each cutout is 4 inches at the outside edge and 4 inches deep, regardless of its form. The forms are squares, semicircles, quarter circles, triangles, and wedges. For each board there are three smaller pieces, one of which is the cutout (having the same form and color obviously fitting), and two of which are "wrong." S is to fit the correct one. In items 1 and 2 the correct choice is the only one of the three with both correct form and correct color. In Item 3-5 one of the "wrongs" has the *same form* but the *wrong color.*

Procedure

In each case, *place the large card with the cutout side facing S, and the three choices between S and the large card.* Using sample card A with the cutout portion facing S, place the response items on the same side as the cutout section following the number series (1, 2, 3) on the back of each response choice. Use numbers for demonstration ("dem.") and after showing the correct response, replace all choices in the order required for administration ("adm.") to the subject. Ask S to *"put the one that fits here"* (point to cutout portion). *Help S*

Abstract Ability Test **499**

to place his choice if he demonstrates some motor difficulty in handling and placing his responses in the large cards. Compliment S on making a correct choice when applicable. Correct all errors and explain verbally the reason for choosing the response item.

Administer items 1 and 2 using the number series (1, 2, 3) on the back of the responses for the layout. Demonstrate sample card 2 by showing approval for correct choice made by S. Follow procedure as above using Sample B before items 3 and 4.

Allow a reasonable length of time for S to make corrections in his responses, distinguishing carefully between S's trying out and his seeming to have made a final choice. Avoid glances of doubt, or motions of hesitation which might cue S that his selection is wrong, but avoid also too quick a conclusion of a set lest he be viewing his results with an eye to correction.

The cards and their associated cutout choices are listed on page 000. Choices (1), (2), and (3) refer to left-right arrangement to E of the three choices when placed between the large card and S.

In the case of wedges, triangles, half circles, and quarter circles where rotation would affect difficulty, the item is always placed with narrower or curved side toward the large card, as though cut from it and moved away without rotation action.

Score: Give 1 point for correct choice.

Time: No time limit.

Note: It is not necessary for the correct response to fit perfectly into cutout portion in order to receive score. If S hands his choice to E, place in cutout position and comment or make correction.

PICTURE-COMPLETION ITEMS

Pictures 1-5 are pairs of colored pictures mounted on heavy board, each 3¾ x 4½ inches. Both pictures in picture pair 1 are cut in half, with an irregular cut to permit E to demonstrate how S should bring his pieces together to make a complete picture. One member of each of picture pairs 2-5 is cut into two pieces, the other left intact as the model for S to produce.

Pictures 1-5: Place segments of picture in front of S one picture at a time. Demonstrate item 1 only. On items 2-5 show E's uncut picture and ask S to make his picture look the same. Make corrections on all errors or non-completions.

Level 5 items: #1 and #2 (dog; duck)
Level 6 items: #3 (baby)
Level 7 items: #4 and #5 (giraffe; boat)

Directions for placement of parts, items 1 to 3: Place top edge and bottom edge of picture on a horizontal *plane* (line) in front of S. *Items 4 and 5:* Place top and bottom edges approximately 2 inches apart on a vertical plane (line) in front of S.

Score: Give 1 point for each correctly completed picture.
Time: No time limit.

FORM-COLOR MATCHING ITEMS

Materials

Four boards of 1/8-inch masonite, 3 x 12 inches, are needed. On one end is one 1/4-inch plywood figure, the model, surfaced with adhesive-backed shelf paper. On the other end are two figures, one of which is the same form and color as the one on the first end. The figures are circles with diameters of 2½ inches; rhombuses with sides of 1¼ inch and angles of 60 degrees and 120 degrees, with a 60-degree angle at the bottom; and squares with sides of 2½ inches; stars with 2¼ inches between alternate points. Below are the shapes and colors of the figures from left to right.

	Board Model	Choices	
Sample:	red circle	red circle	green rhombus
Level 6:	red circle	green rhombus	red circle
Level 7:	red circle	red circle	green rhombus
	black circle	black circle	pink star
Level 8:	yellow rhombus	yellow rhombus	black circle

Procedure

Place the board directly in front of S with the choices (to E's left) covered by a manila strip, 3½ inches x 6 inches. Say, *"See this one?"* Point to the left figure (to E's right) and say, *"Find it over here."* Expose the covered choices.

Use sample board A as a demonstration. If necessary, guide S's hand to the correct choice. Present the series rapidly and encourage S to choose quickly. Correct each mistake quickly. Credit immediate self-corrections.

Score: Count each identification. One point for each correct response in test series.

See Stanford-Binet Manual (Form L-M) for specific instructions on administering the following selected items:

Year III (pages 72-73 in Binet Manual)
#3: Block Building: Bridge
#4: Picture Memories

RELIABILITY STUDIES

In October 1975 a test-retest reliability study was conducted on the revised form of the Abstract Abilities Test. Each child was tested twice by two different examiners during the third week of October 1975. The overall agreement in test scores was .98 using a Pearson Product-Moment correlation. Specific scores follow for each subject:

| Subjects | | Score | Score |
Age	Sex	Examiner A	Examiner B
29 mos.	M	Level 8	Level 8
24 mos.	M	Level 4	Level 4
24 mos.	F	Level 6	Level 6
23 mos.	F	Level 5	Level 4
15 mos.	F	Level 3	Level 3
12 mos.	F	Level 3	Level 2
15 mos.	F	Level 3	Level 2
15 mos.	M	Level −12.5 mos.	Level −12.5 mos.
20 mos.	M	Level 4	Level 4
15 mos.	M	Level 3	Level 3
23 mos.	F	Level 4	Level 4

In April 1974 a test-retest reliability study was conducted on the second half of the Abstract Abilities Test. Five subjects, between the ages of 24 and 36 months, were seen on two separate occasions by each examiner. The overall agreement using a Pearson Product-Moment correlation, was .90. Specific scores follow for each subject:

	Examiner A	Examiner B			
	X	Y	X^2	Y^2	XY
Michelle	20.5	20.5	420.25	420.25	420.25
Kirsten	28.5	28.5	812.25	812.25	812.25
Lesley	28.5	28.5	812.25	812.25	812.25
Barbara	20.5	24.5	420.25	600.25	502.25
Nick	24.5	24.5	600.25	600.25	600.25
	122.5	126.5	3,065.25	3,245.25	3,147.25

$$r = \frac{5(3147.25) - 15{,}496.25}{\sqrt{[5(3{,}065.25) - (122.5)^2][5(3{,}245.25) - (126.5)^2]}}$$

$$r = \frac{15{,}736.25 - 15{,}496.25}{\sqrt{[15{,}326.25 - 15{,}006.25][16{,}226.25 - 16{,}002.25]}}$$

$$r = \frac{240}{\sqrt{(320)(224)}} = \frac{240}{\sqrt{71{,}680}}$$

$$r = \frac{240}{268} = .90$$

Ten subjects ranging in age from 10 to 35 months were examined twice within twenty-four to forty-eight hours by two examiners. Subjects were seen in their own homes with their mothers present on January 13 and 14, 1970. Their scores, expressed as developmental age equivalents, follow:

	Examiner 1	Examiner 2
Subject A—17 mos. boy	15 mos.	15 mos.
Subject B—10 mos. boy	8 mos.	11 mos.
Subject C—10 mos. girl	15 mos.	15 mos.
Subject D—11 mos. girl	11 mos.	11 mos.
Subject E—12 mos. boy	15 mos.	11 mos.
Subject F—29 mos. boy	32 mos.	32 mos.
Subject G—31 mos. boy	28 mos.	28 mos.
Subject H—35 mos. girl	28 mos.	28 mos.
Subject I—26 mos. boy	28 mos.	28 mos.
Subject J—26 mos. girl	24 mos.	24 mos.

A Pearson Product-Moment correlation was calculated. Test-retest reliability was .79.

HUNT-UZGIRIS SCALE—SCORE SHEET

NAME _____ AGE ____ DATE _____ EXAMINER _____ SCORE _____

Level I Items

1. *Following an object through a complete disappearance:*

    Finding an object hidden under one of two screens (necklace, doll, car, flower) (food)
    a. loses interest in the object
    b. searches for the object where it was previously found—i.e., under the first screen
    *c. searches for the object where it is observed to be hidden—i.e., under the second screen

2. *Finding an object hidden under one of two screens alternately (necklace, doll, car, flower) (food)*
    a. becomes perplexed and loses interest in object
    b. searches haphazardly under one or both screens
    *c. searches correctly under either of the two screens

3. *Finding an object hidden under one of three screens (necklace, doll, car, flower) (food)*
    a. loses interest in the object
    b. searches haphazardly under some or all screens
    *c. searches directly under the correct screen

4. *Recognizing the reverse side of objects (object with definite reverse side—animal or rattle)*
    a. continues to reach and grasp the object
    b. withdraws hands and shows evidence of surprise at the reversal
    *c. grasps the object, but turns it to the "right" side immediately each time or turns the object over several times looking at it intently

Level II Items

1. *Finding an object after successive visible displacements (necklace, doll, car, flower, food)*
    a. does not follow the object through the successive hidings
    b. searches only under the first screen which hides the object
    c. searches under the screen where the object was found on the previous trial
    d. searches under all screens haphazardly
    e. searches under all screens in the order of hiding
    *f. searches directly under the last screen in the series

*For each item written at each level, asterisk denotes correct response.

2. *Finding an object hidden in a container which is covered by superimposed screens (object in box under screen)*
   a. loses interest in the object
   b. gives up search after removing one or all of the superimposed screens
   *c. persists in searching and obtains the object

3. *Following an object through a series of invisible displacements:*

   Following an object through a series of invisible displacements in sequence (object hidden in hand under last of three screens)
   a. searches only in the examiner's hand
   b. searches only under the first screen in the series
   *c. searches under all screens in the same order as followed by the examiner's hand

4. *Interest in the phenomenon of the fall:*

   Dropping objects in order to study their trajectories (box filled with small objects)
   a. does not drop any of the objects
   b. drops several objects repeatedly but pays little attention to where they fall
   *c. drops several objects repeatedly and looks down to see where they fall

Level III Items

1. *Following an object through one hidden displacement with two screens (object in box under second screen, remove box)*
   a. searches only in the box
   b. searches under the screen where the object was previously found
   *c. searches under the correct screen

2. *Following the object through one hidden displacement with two screens used alternately (object in box under one of two screens, remove box)*
   a. loses interest in the object
   b. searches haphazardly under the two screens
   *c. searches directly under the correct screen

3. *Following an object through one hidden displacement with three screens (object in box under one of three screens, remove box)*
   a. loses interest in the object
   b. searches haphazardly under all three screens
   *c. searches directly under the correct screen

4. *Understanding equilibrium (small blocks)*
   a. does not build a tower
   *b. approximates two blocks, but does not leave one on top
   *c. builds a tower of at least two blocks

*For each item written at each level, asterisk denotes correct response.

Level IV Items

1. *Developing representation of a series of displacements (object hidden in hand under first of three screens)*
   a. searches only under the last screen and gives up
   b. searches haphazardly under all three screens
   *c. searches systematically from the last screen to the first in reverse order

2. *Development of understanding of relationships between objects:*

   Understanding the relationship of the container and contained (small beads and container)
   a. does not place the objects into the container
   b. places the objects into the container and takes them out one by one
   *c. places the objects into the container and turns the container in order to remove the objects

3. *Understanding gravity (car on incline)*
   a. plays with the object without using the incline
   b. guides the object down the incline
   *c. permits the object to roll down the incline

4. *Recognizing the absence of familiar persons (ask whereabouts of familiar person such as brother or sister)*
   a. does not comprehend the question
   b. goes to look for that person
   *c. indicates knowledge of the absence of that person by pointing to the outside, saying "gone," "bye-bye," etc.

*For each item written at each level, asterisk denotes correct response.

APPENDIX C

PACIFIC PATTERN AND PICTURE COMPLETION

Score Sheet

NAME _____ AGE _____ DATE _____ EXAMINER _____ SCORE _____

		Correct	Incorrect
			1 point each

Place sample card A with 3 choices in numerical order and demonstrate.

Sample A. Pink triangle (no score)

Change order of choices and ask S to put the one that fits there, pointing to gap.

Level V Items

1. Green square — 1 ☐ 0 ☐

Correct all errors explaining correct choice. Help S place the form if he shows some motor difficulty but has indicated correct choice.

2. Purple wedge — 1 ☐ 0 ☐

Level VI Items

Allow one demonstration trial; let S place correct choice; then rearrange the choices.

Sample B. Blue quadrant (no score)

3. Red Wedge — 1 ☐ 0 ☐

4. Black Triangle — 1 ☐ 0 ☐

Level VIII Items

5. Blue Oval — 1 ☐ 0 ☐

PACIFIC PATTERN AND PICTURE COMPLETION (continued)

Puzzles. Correct all errors or incompletions.

		Item Number	Correct	Incorrect
Level V Items				
1. Dog	Place E's and S's segments. Demonstrate with E's. Ask S to "Make yours just like mine."	1. Dog	1 ☐	0 ☐
2. Duck	Place uncut pictures in front of E, pieces before S.	2. Duck	1 ☐	0 ☐
Level VI Items			1 ☐	0 ☐
3. Baby		3. Baby		
Level VII Items			1 ☐	0 ☐
4. Giraffe		4. Giraffe		
5. Boat		5. Boat	1 ☐	0 ☐

PACIFIC FORM AND COLOR MATCHING—SCORE SHEET

NAME_____ AGE_____ DATE_____ EXAMINER_____ SCORE_____

Place board in front of S, with choices covered by a manila strip. Say, "See this" (uncover choices); "Find it over here." Use the first few as demonstrations and place at the end: Begin when S seems to have the response set. One point for each correct response.

Level VI Items

	Correct	Incorrect
Sample A	1 ☐	0 ☐
1. red circle		

Level VII Items

2. red circle	1 ☐	0 ☐
3. black circle	1 ☐	0 ☐

Level VIII Items

4. yellow rhombus	1 ☐	0 ☐

Level VIII Items

Binet Items

III 3	Pass	Fail
III 4	Pass	Fail

SUMMARY, LEVELS V-VIII

NAME _____ AGE ____ DATE ____ EXAMINER _____ SCORE* ____

Level V Items	Item Number	Correct	Incorrect
Pattern Completion	1.	1 ☐	0 ☐
	2.	1 ☐	0 ☐
Picture Completion	1.	1 ☐	0 ☐
	2.	1 ☐	0 ☐
Level VI Items			
Pattern Completion	3.	1 ☐	0 ☐
	4.	1 ☐	0 ☐
Picture Completion	3.	1 ☐	0 ☐
Form and Color Matching	1.	1 ☐	0 ☐
Level VII Items			
Picture Completion	4.	1 ☐	0 ☐
	5.	1 ☐	0 ☐
Form and Color Matching	2.	1 ☐	0 ☐
	3.	1 ☐	0 ☐

*To pass at any given level, 3 out of 4 items must be correct.

SUMMARY, LEVELS V-VIII (continued)

Level VIII Items	Item Number	Correct 1	Incorrect 0
Pattern Completion	5.	☐	☐
Form and Color Matching	4.	☐	☐
Binet III, 3	3.	☐	☐
Binet III, 4	4.	☐	☐

(See Manual for WPPSI Test)

Level 9	Items	passing WPPSI at	42 mos.
Level 10	Items	passing WPPSI at	48 mos.
Level 11	Items	passing WPPSI at	54 mos.
Level 12	Items	passing WPPSI at	60 mos.

Scoring Abstract Abilities Test

Hunt-Uzgiris Items	Score Needed	Level*
Level I Items 1 2 3 4	3 out of 4 items correct	Level I (less than 12.5 mos. of age)
Level II Items 1 2 3 4	3 out of 4 items correct	Level II (12.5 mos.)
Level III Items 1 2 3 4	3 out of 4 items correct	Level III (14.5 mos.)
Level IV Items 1 2 3 4	3 out of 4 items correct	Level IV (18-21 mos.)

*This preliminary scoring of the Abstract Abilities Test is based on items passed at each age level by the median number of subjects who took the test. One feature of the scoring system is that it is relatively easy for a subject to achieve the level closest to his true age, but difficult to achieve the next highest age level.

Scoring Abstract Abilities Test (continued)

Pacific Items

Level V Items				
Patterns	Pictures		3 out of 4	Level V
1	1		items correct	(21.5 mos.)
2	2			

Level VI Items		Form and Color		
Patterns	Pictures	Matching	3 out of 4	Level VI
3	3	1	items correct	(25.5 mos.)
4				

Level VII Items		Form and Color		
	Pictures	Matching	3 out of 4	Level VII
	4	2	items correct	(31 mos.)
	5	3		

Level VIII Items		Form and Color		
Patterns		Matching	3 out of 4	Level VIII**
5	Binet Items	4	items correct	(36 mos.)
	III #3, #4			

**Any child who scores at the 36-month level on the Abstract Abilities Test should be given a full Stanford-Binet Intelligence Test. For developmental levels at or above four years we recommend using the WPPSI in place of the Binet for testing children. The following levels are to be used in scoring.

        level 9 = passing WPPSI at 42 mos.
        level 10 = passing WPPSI at 48 mos.
        level 11 = passing WPPSI at 54 mos.
        level 12 = passing WPPSI at 60 mos.

MANUAL FOR ASSESSING THE DISCRIMINATIVE ABILITY OF ONE TO THREE YEAR OLD CHILDREN

by Barbara Koslowski/Barbara Kaban

Introduction, *513*
Materials, *513*
Procedure, *513*
Criterion, *518*
Scoring, *520*
Reliability Studies, *520*

Preschool Project, Laboratory of Human Development, Harvard University, Graduate School of Education, Revised May 1976.

INTRODUCTION

This test has been developed by the Harvard Preschool Project as one of a battery of new assessment techniques for children in the one to three years age range. A preliminary finding of the project's research is that talented three to six-year-old children are good observers. Such children notice small discrepancies in physical appearances, in the following of rules, in statements of logic, etc., sooner than do their peers. In order to assess the development of this ability, we developed a simple test of the capacity to note discrepancies in physical appearances.

MATERIALS

The materials for this test consist of nine pairs of cups. For the first three pairs, the relevant cues are rather gross differences between two objects:

1. a small bright red cup vs. a dull green cup about three times as large as the red cup
2. two opaque, white plastic cups, one about three times as large as the other
3. two opaque, plastic cups identical except for color.

The remaining pairs of stimuli present much finer differences. The stimuli consist of pairs of identical opaque white cups with the appropriate block shapes pasted on them (see Figures A and B).

PROCEDURE

The examiner should allow at least ten minutes for the child to get used to E before beginning the test session. The aim is not to present the child with the test and then see how much of it he completes spontaneously. Rather, the examiner should try to induce the child to perform to his full capacity. (Some suggestions for eliciting maximum performance from young children can be found under "Reinforcement.")

The mother is asked to stay in the same room, although she need not sit right next to the child. In fact, the situation is often less testlike if she goes about her usual activities, providing they are not too distracting.

A child in the 12 to 24 month age range should be seated in a highchair if one is available. An older child (24-36 months) should sit at a table with the examiner opposite. If an older child uses a highchair regularly, use it in the testing situation. If no table or highchair is readily available, the box which contains the test materials doubles as a table.

It is often difficult to hold a young child's attention for more than ten minutes in this testing situation. Thus, speed and organization on the part of E are essential. S should not be put in the highchair until E is ready to begin testing. Organize the pairs of stimuli before S is put in the highchair. Seek the mother's help in determining what reinforcement should be used.

After establishing rapport, give the child some cereal or a raisin, etc. (see "Reinforcement"). This is done to spark his interest, to ascertain which, if any, he has a preference for, and to give him the idea that the reward is his—that he is to look for it. After this, each pair of stimuli is presented for a training session followed immediately by a testing session.

With any child younger than 24 months, start with stimulus pair #1. By 24 months of age, the first stimulus pair can be omitted, and the training may begin with pair #2. A 36-month-old child can be started with pair #3 1/2.

The rewarded member of each pair is as follows:

Stimulus Pair	Rewarded Member
1	small red container
2	the smaller of the two containers
3	white container

(The same small, white container is thus the rewarded member of both pair 2 and pair 3. Although this is unorthodox, it was reasoned that, in both cases, in order to choose the rewarded container, the child would first have to discriminate it from the nonrewarded one—and his discriminative ability is the prime concern of this test.) Level 3 1/2 represents one full level above level 3 for scoring purposes. For level 3 1/2 through level 8, use member A of each pair for the reward member (see Figures A and B).

Training

The child is allowed to play with the two test objects for a while. If the objects in question happen to be a pair of cups with black stimulus patterns and if S shows a preference for one of them, that cup is the one used to cover the reward. For the rare cases in which the child shows no preference, and for the three easiest pairs, follow the instructions presented above.

If cups are used on a training level, E points to the patterns on both cups, tracing the general outline with his fingers, and making certain that the child is looking at the patterns. To avoid an uncomfortable silence, he usually accompanies the gestures with statements like "See," "See the picture," "This one goes like this," etc. As a general rule, whenever oral language is used, it is kept to a minimum and consists of simple words: ball, circle, a lot, only one, etc.

Each stimulus pair is presented for three training trials. The right-left position of the positive stimulus is alternated during these three trials. Each trial

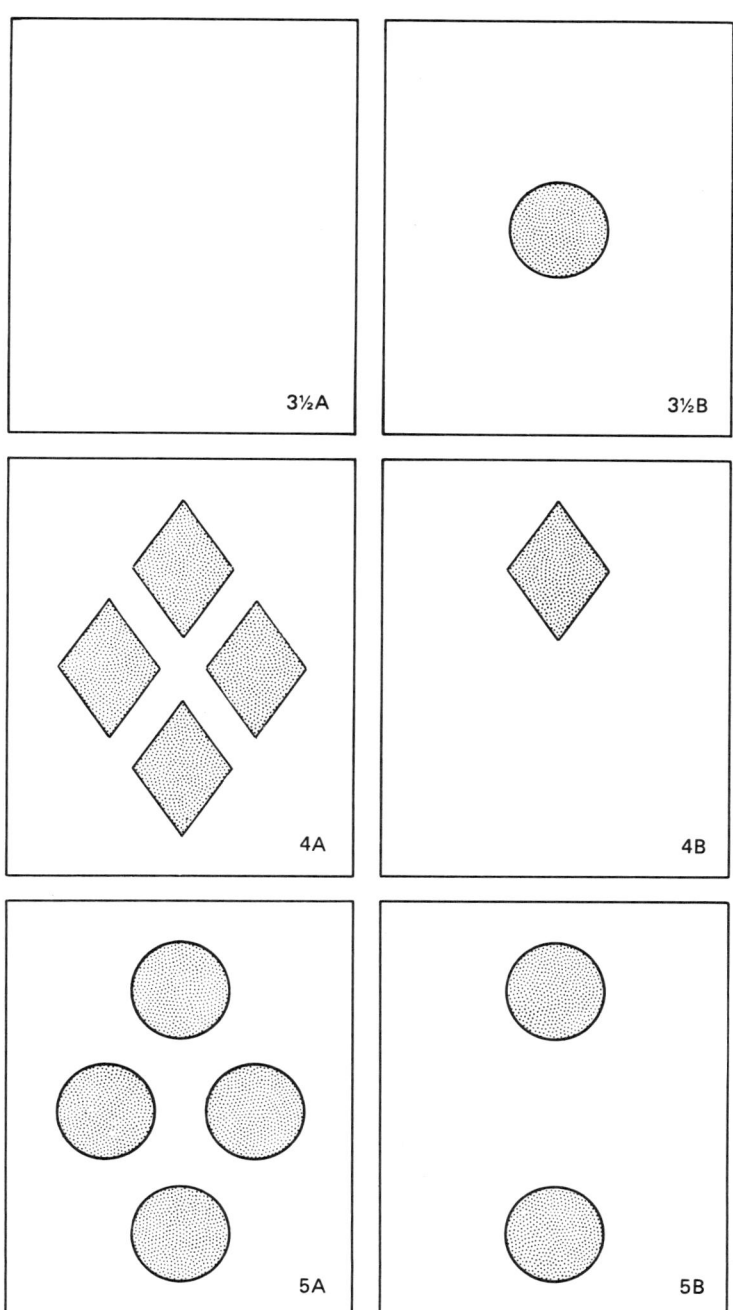

Figure A. Stimulus patterns 3½, 4, 5

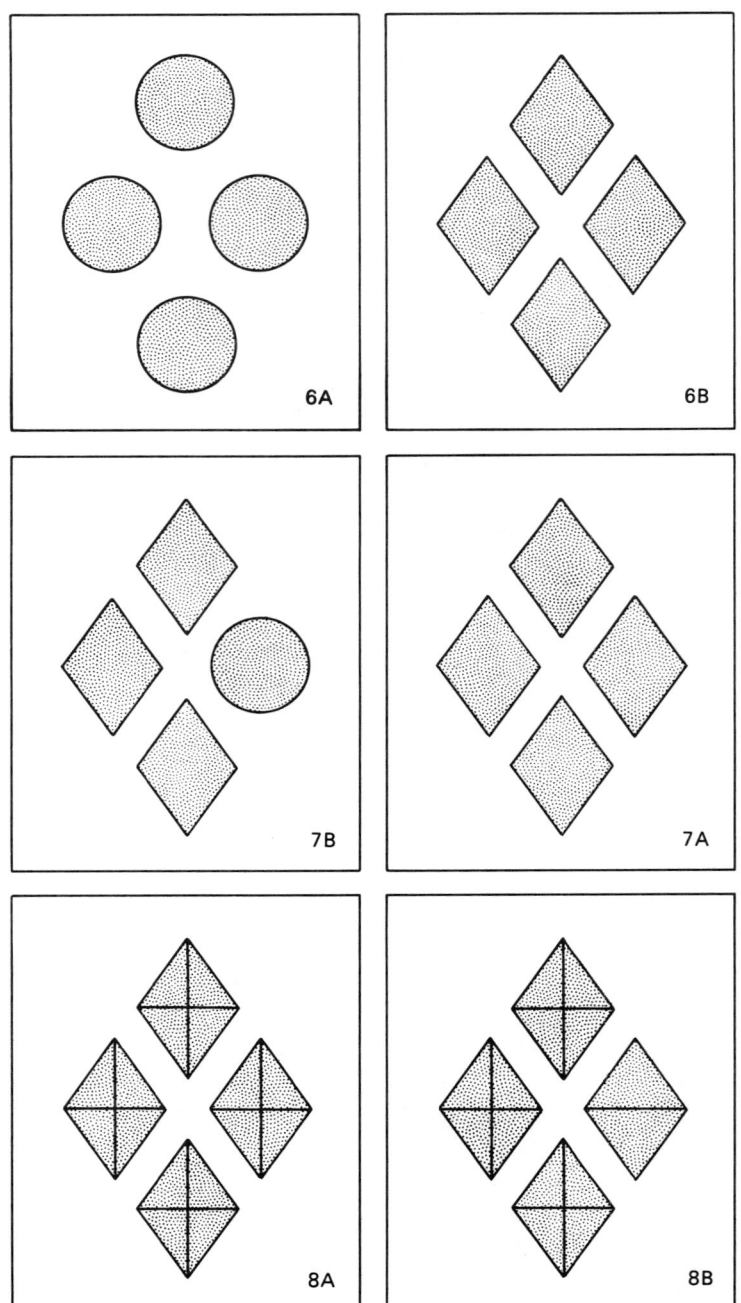

Figure B. Stimulus patterns 6, 7, 8

proceeds as follows. The examiner shows the child the food, points to or outlines the positive pattern, and hides the food under the positive cup. He makes certain that the child looks at the pattern and then at the food rather than just at the part of the table where the food is placed.

After the child finds and eats his reward, the examiner makes certain the child continues to watch while he changes the position of the stimuli (saying something like "Now I'm going to move it" or, "Now it's going over here," points to the positive stimulus, and hides the reward just as above.

Note that after each training trial, the positions of the test objects are alternated *before* the reward is hidden.*

Testing

During testing a screen (a piece of cardboard 8½ inches x 11 inches) is placed in front of the test objects before the reward is hidden.

Two points should be noted here: The first has to do with changing the position of the objects. Before the screen is put in front of the test objects, their R-L position is disrupted. E either holds the positive one while he brings the screen down, or else places one object on top of the other while the screen is brought down. If this is not done, some children automatically choose the *place* at which the reward was last hidden.

The second point has to do with alternating. Within any three consecutive, correct trials (i.e., within criterion) one must omit the possibility that the child is responding to an alternation rule. Thus, in any three consecutive, correct trials place the positive stimulus in one of the following example patterns: R-R-L or R-L-L. After presenting each pair of test objects, the examiner scores the child's performance on the scoring sheet.

Reinforcement

Three types of edible rewards are used for all children: raisins cut in half; miniature marshmallows cut into quarters; or pieces of sweet, dry cereal such as Captain Crunch or Apple Jacks.

Two points should be noted here: If the child's attention or enthusiasm seems to be waning, one quite reliable way of increasing it is to change the reinforcement or (if it does not seem likely that the child will lose his appetite) to hide two different types of reinforcement on each trial.

Although many children will work ad infinitum for bits of food, some children require a bit more enticement to show what they can do. These are

---

*If the examiner hides the reward and *then* alternates the positions of the test objects, some children have a tendency to do the following: They designate the *place* where they saw the reward hidden—i.e., the place now occupied by the incorrect test object.

some suggestions which have worked in the past. They have been used both singly and in combination:

1. The mother may know whether the child has a strong preference for a particular kind of food and can usually be counted on to provide some.
2. Social rewards are often more valuable than any kind of food. To this end, being enthusiastic helps in that children are particularly responsive to applause, cheers, bursts of "Good!" "Very nice!" pats on the head, and hugs.
3. Some children who find little pleasure in eating the reinforcement find true joy in collecting it. Such children are given a cup and told that they can "save" their raisins, etc., in the cup. The examiner augments this game with statements like, "Boy, you really have a lot in that cup," "That's really good," "Would you like to find some more for your cup?" etc.
4. One little girl who was delighted with her recent proficiency in using language was more than willing to play if each correct choice was followed by a word she did not know: super, groovy, stupendous, etc. A little boy first became excited by the game when each correct choice was followed by a raisin *and* a piece of cereal, a combination which the examiner called a "little breakfast."
5. If all else fails, the examiner might try hiding his or her jewelry—an earring, bracelet, cuff link, tie clasp, etc.

Feedback

Whenever S chooses the negative object of a pair, the examiner does the following: He does *not* allow S to lift the positive object. He points to the table where the negative object was and says, in a mildly woeful voice, "Oh! Too bad. No raisins. See! The raisins are over here, under this one" (as he lifts the positive object and points to the reward). He points to the pattern on the cup and to the food, and then covers the reinforcement with the cup a few times to convey the fact that the reinforcement was under the positive object.

If the child then reaches for the reward, the examiner *usually* shakes his head and says, "No, I have to hide it again." An exception to this rule is made when it is clear that a child who guesses wrong is genuinely trying to learn how to play the game (as opposed to being interested only in getting the reward), and when such a child shows extreme disappointment in not being rewarded for a wrong choice.

CRITERION

The criterion for passing each level is three consecutive correct trials out of seven. A trial ends when the child deliberately designates his choice in *any* of the following ways: pointing to, labeling, touching, or picking up one of the objects. If he picks up both objects, the trial is scored as incorrect.*

A certain pattern of responding is given special consideration during the testing. This pattern is shown by a child who seems to be using gestures to eliminate the negative object. During training, it is obvious that he is attending closely. Yet, on each trial, he *consistently* touches or points to the negative object and then picks up the positive one. During testing, he does the same thing. Since his behavior is consistent, and since he does the same thing during training, the examiner should alter the criterion for the end of a trial to reflect this pattern of responding.

If, with seven trials, S is unable to reach criterion on a given stimulus pair, he is given the next most difficult pair to make certain he has reached his limit. Once the child has failed two consecutive pairs of stimuli, the testing is stopped.

Controlling Impulsiveness**

Occasionally, children show a tendency to lunge, at random, for a stimulus as soon as the screen is raised. To control for this, when E lifts the screen, he sees to it that the stimuli are too far away for the child to reach. After S has had a chance to look at them, E moves both stimuli toward him and allows him to choose one.

If the table area is too small to permit the above, E might try lightly holding back the child's arms for a few seconds, or, with a verbal child, E might simply say, "Now wait a minute and look at them before you pick one."

If there is no table area, the surface on which the stimuli are placed can itself be moved away from, and then back close to the child.

---

*The second special type of child is one who is very unsure of himself. During training, even though he is attending, he consistently designates the correct stimulus and, then, looks up at E and does not pick up the designated stimulus until E confirms his choice. Since what is involved is his lack of confidence rather than his lack of ability, the usual testing procedure is to continue either nodding or saying, "Yes, that's right," after S points to the correct stimulus. A fairly successful strategy one can try during training with this type of child is to ask her if her dolly, doggy, puppet, etc., can find the raisin. This low-confidence child is distinguished from one who is guessing by his behavior during training. A child who is guessing becomes unsure of himself only during testing. He does not need encouragement during training.

**We realize that the classical studies of discrimination learning do not try to eliminate this variable. Rather, they regard it as one of the many obstacles the child should overcome on his own. However, the present test is aimed at assessing the child's discriminative capacity in the absence of interference.

SCORING

On the scoring sheet, the stimulus number (A or B) and the number of trials is recorded for each level. Also recorded are the number of correct trials and the validity of the child's response to the particular item.

SCORING SHEET

Examiner: _____   Age: _____

Subject: _____   Level Passed: _____

Date Tested: _____

Level	Stimulus #	# Trials	Correct?	Valid?
1				
2				
3				
3 1/2				
4				
5				
6				
7				
8				

Additional Comments:

RELIABILITY STUDIES

Summary of the Reliability Studies of the Test of Discriminative Abilities

In order to determine whether the discrimination-learning procedure yields a measure of the child's discriminative ability that is relatively independent of the examiner, two examiners tested each of ten children. Five of the children were first tested by Examiner A; five were first tested by Examiner B. With one exception, there was a 48-hour interval between the two test sessions. For each child, both sessions occurred at the same time of day and in the same physical setting (either at a table or on the floor). In addition, both examiners started each child at the same level of stimulus difficulty.

The data from one of the originally scheduled children was discarded because her home situation made it impossible to test her reliably. The ten children whose results were used were of the following ages: 11, 11, 12, 22, 23, 24, 26, 27, 31, and 36 months.

The Pearson Product-Moment correlation of the scores obtained by the two examiners was .90.

Reliability Study of the Discrimination-Learning Instrument (Cognitive I)

An interobserver reliability study of the Discrimination Learning Instrument (also known as the Discrepancies Test) was conducted in August 1971 by two examiners. Eight subjects ranging in age from 12 to 35 months were seen twice over a period of three weeks. Subjects were tested in their own homes, with mother present, on two separate occasions, once by each examiner. Testing sessions lasted 20 to 40 minutes. For each child, the two sessions were scheduled about one week apart, at approximately the same time of day and in the same physical setting (in a highchair, on a table, on the floor). In addition, first-time visits were balanced equally between the two examiners.

The Pearson Product-Moment correlation of the scores obtained by the two examiners was 0.98.

Subject	Age in Months	X	Y	X^2	Y^2	XY
1	35	8	8	64	64	64
2	22	3	3	9	9	9
3	31	7	6	49	36	42
4	12	1	2	1	4	2
5	34	7	7	49	49	49
6	16	3	3	9	9	9
7	16	4	4	16	16	16
8	14	2	2	4	4	4
	$\Sigma =$	35	35	201	191	195

$$r = \frac{N\Sigma XY - \Sigma X \Sigma Y}{\sqrt{[N\Sigma X^2 - (\Sigma X)^2][N\Sigma Y^2 - (\Sigma Y)^2]}}$$

$$r = \frac{8(195) - (35)(35)}{\sqrt{[8(201) - (35)^2][8(191) - (35)^2]}} = \frac{335}{\sqrt{(383)(303)}}$$

$$= \frac{335}{340.7} = 0.983$$

Summary of a Reliability Study of the Discrimination-Learning Procedure

In this reliability eight subjects between 15 and 35 months were tested on two separate occasions, once by Examiner A and once by Examiner B. Both testing sessions were scheduled at the same time of day one week apart. The first-time visits were equally balanced between the two testers.

The Pearson Product-Moment correlation of the scores obtained by the two examiners was .95.

Subject	Age in Months	E.C. X	I.S. Y	X^2	Y^2	XY
1	15 1/2	1	2	1	4	2
2	22	2	4	4	16	8
3	21	2	3	4	9	6
4	35	8	8	64	64	64
5	15	1	2	1	4	2
6	23	3	3	9	9	9
7	31	6	8	36	64	48
8	27	3	3	9	9	9
	Σ =	26	33	128	179	148

$$r = \frac{[n(xy) - (x)(y)]}{\sqrt{[n(x^2) - (x)^2][n(y^2) - (y)^2]}}$$

$$= \frac{[8(148) - (26)(33)]}{\sqrt{[8(128) - (26)^2][8(179) - (33)^2]}}$$

$$= \frac{1184 - 858}{\sqrt{[1024 - 676][1432 - 1089]}}$$

$$= \frac{326}{\sqrt{(348)(343)}} = \frac{326}{\sqrt{118,364}} = \frac{326}{344} = .947$$

Appendix

A TRAINING PROGRAM TO ASSIST PEOPLE IN EDUCATING INFANTS

*by Burton L. White/Barbara Kaban,
Bernice Shapiro/Elizabeth Constable*

Introduction, *525*
Group and Home Visit Content, Introductory Period (5-8 Months), *525*
Group Visit Content, Core Period (8-17 Months), *535*
Home Visit Format and Questions (8-17 Months), *540-47*
Sample Home Visit Reports (8-17 Months), *547*

Preschool Project, Laboratory of Human Development, Harvard University, Graduate School of Education, March, 1974.

INTRODUCTION

The training package reflects the work we have done for the past eighteen months on translating hypotheses about effective child-rearing practices into a workable program for average families. Many of the details of the program (e.g., home visit questions) evolved as we worked with the pilot family group. The present training package reflects the curriculum which seemed to be most sensitive to the needs of the families and also represents the most effective methods for communicating our information.

The pilot study consisted of two segments: the 5-8 month introductory period and the 8-12 month core period. The purpose of the 5-8 month period was to introduce the families to the fields of child development research and early education, and to the staff. Four group meetings were held at the university. Each group meeting was followed by a home visit (see Schedule I). The purposes of the home visit were to review the content of the group meeting and to begin to adjust our program to the individual circumstances of each family.

Outlines of the group and home visit activities during the 5-8-month period can be found on pages 525-535. Sample tape recordings are also available.

During the 8-17 month period we concentrated on guiding each family toward patterning the daily fabric of the child's experience in a manner consistent with our hypotheses about effective child-rearing practices. Home visits occurred at two-week intervals. After each visit, staff members collected evaluation and monitoring data. Group visits were used less frequently during this phase of the program (at 10, 13, and 16 months) (see Schedule II). Outlines of those group meetings may be found on pages 535-540. Sample tape recordings of these sessions are available.

After each home visit the staff member wrote a brief summary report (see pages 547-559). Outlines of the home visit format during the 8-17 month period can be found on pages 540-547. Sample tape recordings are available.

GROUP AND HOME VISIT CONTENT, INTRODUCTORY PERIOD (5-8 MONTHS)

Group Session #1

I. We have always begun formal education no earlier than six years of age, but children are learning many things from birth such as:
   A. Language: The majority of ordinary language that most of us use is learned in the preschool years.
   B. Social Skills: A child learns how to get along with others through his early social relationships, especially through his relationship with his mother.
   C. Learning to learn: Children may not be able to solve a great many problems by age three but they have learned the tools for solving problems.

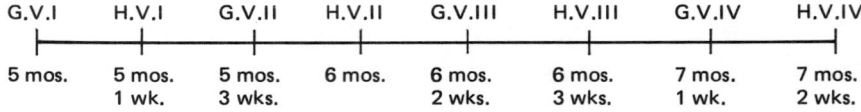

Chronological Age of Child (5-8 Months)

CODE: G.V. = Group Visit
H.V. = Home Visit

Schedule I

    D. Motivation: All babies are curious, but this curiosity is often stifled by the time a child starts school.

II. Is it important to get good preschool development?
    A. A well-developed child, one who likes himself and can get along with adults and other children, will probably do better at learning in school than the child who is overly shy or overly aggressive.
    B. Remedial programs such as Headstart and Follow-Through have not been very successful. Age three is probably too late to make up for poor preschool development.

III. Do most children get good preschool development?
    A. It may be that the child who does well in school at age six was better endowed when he came into the world. It is *not* the case that every child is born equal.
    B. The majority of children are considered "average" at age six. It may be the case that most of these children could have gotten more out of the preschool years.

IV. Why don't we have children getting the best early experiences which might lead to the best early development?

Until recently, educators and psychologists did not pay much attention to the preschool years. Consequently, little was known about the different experiences children are exposed to during the preschool years and the differential effects they have on development.

V. New ideas in education
    A. Public school systems are beginning to look downward to the preschool years. California has recently made public school education available to four-year olds.
    B. The more we concentrate on the early years, the more people will start examining the effects of different homes on children. For example:
        1. Dr. R. Heber studied the effects of placing retarded mothers' children in a day-care center from infancy. When control subjects who had been raised in their homes by their retarded mothers were compared to the subjects who had received the experimental treatment, a significant difference in achievement

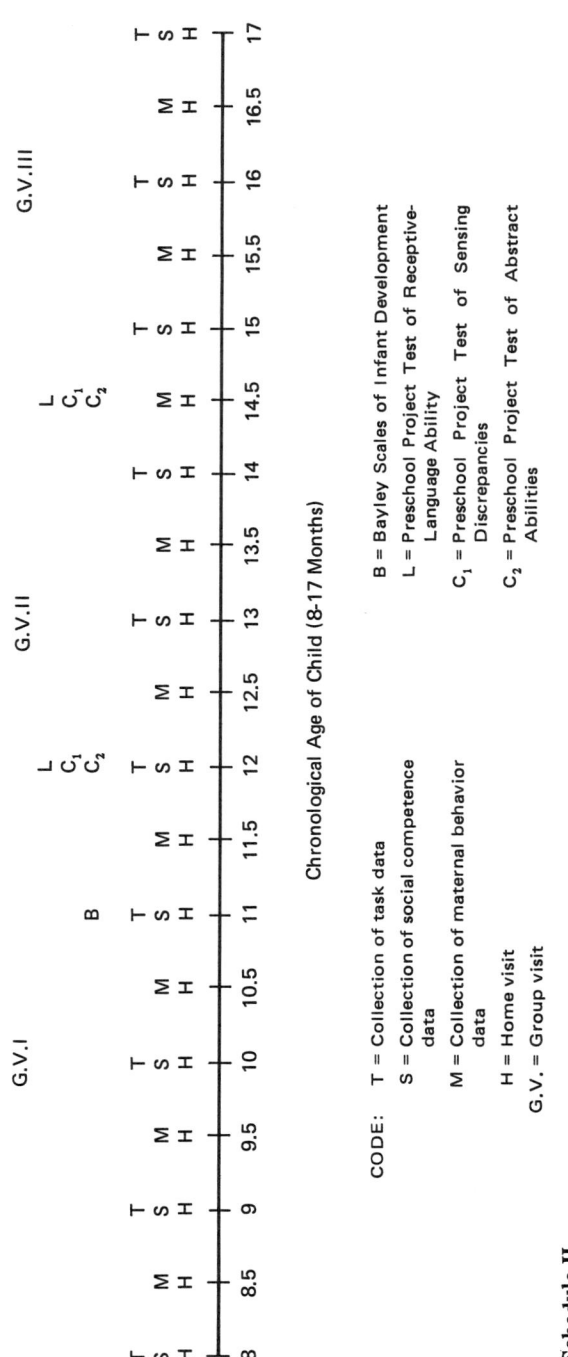

Schedule II

was found at 45 months of age (the experimental group scored 33 IQ points higher).*
2. An Iowa judge placed the children of a retarded couple in a foster home.

VI. The ideas in early development which have had the greatest influence on theories of child development in the last few decades are:
A. Piaget: A Swiss psychologist who was interested in the growth of intelligence from birth to adolescence, including problem solving and foundations of intellectual development.
B. Ethologists: They study animal life and its relationship to human behavior.
C. Freud: A psychoanalyst who studied emotional disturbances in personality development (major themes: the development of sexuality; aggression).

VII. The Preschool Project: the case for the special importance of the 8-16 month period.
A. We will try to tell you about development so that your child will get as much as possible out of the first years. We also feel you will find it a more interesting job and more fun by knowing more about children's development.
B. In our study of the differences between a group of children who were developing beautifully and a group who were developing poorly we found that most families do a fine job until a child gets to crawling age (approximately 8 months).
C. At this stage families begin to vary importantly in the effectiveness of their child-rearing patterns. The difficulties appear to arise as the child begins to move around and, consequently, can get hurt or create clutter.
D. Mothers who handle the danger and extra work by restricting their children seem to have children who develop less well. Mothers who handle the danger by child-proofing the house and are willing to do the extra work created by a child who is allowed to satisfy his curiosity seem to have better developing children.

VIII. Film: *Object Permanence* by Dr. J. McV. Hunt.

Film Report

Title: Object Permanence
Narrator: Dr. J. Hunt
Length: Approximately 35 minutes (black and white)

*R. Heber, and H. Garber, "An Experiment in the Prevention of Cultural-Familial Mental Retardation (Paper Presented at the second congress of the International Association for the Scientific Study of Mental Deficiency, Warsaw, August 1970).

Topics covered: This film illustrates Piaget's ideas about the development of object permanence in young children. The *ages* of the children seen range from a few weeks to approximately 18 months. The children are seen being tested in their own homes. The development of object permanence is illustrated by showing the children in logical age sequence, youngest to oldest.

Instructions: Omit the first eight (approximately) minutes of the film. This is an introduction showing Hunt and Uzguris. It is too complicated and technical for this audience. Instead, give a brief introduction before screening, mentioning Piaget and the concept of object permanence. Show 10-15 minutes of the remainder of the film.

Group Session #2

I. What is the Preschool Project all about?
   A. Most people seem to do a good job during the first 8 to 12 months. Most of the problems (e.g., feeding, sleeping, and teething problems) don't seem to require any special knowledge in order to cope with them. Unfortunately, some children begin to lose ground during the second year of life.
   B. The major predictors of future development are the child's ability to understand language and his social development.
      1. The ability to understand language begins to develop at about 8 months of age and progresses until at about three years of age the child will be able to understand most of the language he will use in ordinary adult conversation. The ability to produce language varies greatly and is not as good a predictor of future development in the first three years.
      2. Social development progresses through stages (e.g., no smiling at birth, indiscriminate regular smiling at 3-4 months, smiling more readily at mother at 4 months, and stranger wariness at 7-9 months), and the relationship a child establishes with his mother becomes the basis for his future relationships with other adults (teachers) and children.

II. What does the Preschool Project have to offer?
   A. In the past, advice from "experts" has not been particularly dependable. There have been many changes of opinions regarding the best procedures for child-rearing (e.g., for toilet training).
   B. The Preschool Project studied the differences between a group of well-developed children and a group of poorly developed children. We observed both kinds of children in their own homes during their second and third years. The difference in their development often seemed to be related to the way the mothers handled the children and structured their lives. The more effective mothers were less restrictive, were good at guessing what the children wanted,

and were also able to say "no" when the children were making unreasonable demands.
  C. We will provide you with your own private consultant to talk to about your children.
III. There are two major ideas which help explain much of what babies do in this age range.
  A. Babies at 8 months of age are very curious about the world around them, and that curiosity is the source of learning and development. Mothers should encourage the development of curiosity since curiosity is the basis for learning.
  B. Babies at 8 months of age are becoming very interested in their mother's behavior. They focus a lot of attention on her and learn to depend on her for the satisfaction of their needs, for protection, for affection, and for guidance. How the mother responds has a great influence on how the baby learns to get along with other people later in life.
IV. Other ideas of significance are:
  A. Babies are learning to control their bodies and progress from crawling, to cruising, to walking, to climbing, and to running.
  B. Babies are very much interested in small detailed objects with moving parts (e.g., keys, hinges, balls).
V. The well-developed child at three years of age exhibits the following abilities:
  A. To get and maintain attention of adults
  B. To use adults as resources
  C. To express affection to adults
  D. To express hostility to adults
  E. To lead peers
  F. To follow peers
  G. To express affection to peers
  H. To express hostility to peers
  I. To compete
  J. To prove oneself or show pride in one's accomplishments
  K. Role play
  L. Language development
  M. To sense dissonance
  N. To anticipate consequences
  O. To deal with abstractions
  P. To take the perspective of another
  Q. To make interesting associations
  R. To plan and carry out multistepped activities
  S. To use resources effectively
  T. To dual focus
VI. Film: *Emotional Ties in Infancy*, from the Parent and Child Center Series, by Dr. Joseph Stone.

Film Report

Title: Emotional Ties in Infancy
Film maker: From the Parent and Child Center Series (Vassar College), directed by Dr. Joseph Stone
Length: 12 minutes (black and white)
Topics covered: The main concepts illustrated in this film are *attachment* of the child to the primary caretaker and *distrust* of strangers. *Settings:* (1) Attachment and temporary distrust of strangers is shown in a home-reared child. (2) Three institutionally reared children are shown in an experimental situation. Varying degrees of attachment and distrust of strangers are illustrated.
Age range of children: 9-12 months
Instructions: Screen the entire film. Give a brief introduction before screening and define attachment and distrust of strangers, and note the settings to be seen in the film. Also mention that the film was made for viewing by people working in institutions and that technical words are used in the film. After the screening, invite the audience to ask questions.

Group Session #3

I. There are three ways of discussing goals for infants in the 8-16 month age range.
   A. The dimensions of competence describe a well-developed child at three years of age. They consist of the following abilities:
      1. To get and maintain attention of adults
      2. To use adults as resources
      3. To express affection to adults
      4. To express hostility to adults
      5. To lead peers
      6. To follow peers
      7. To express affection to peers
      8. To express hostility to peers
      9. To compete
      10. To praise oneself or show pride in one's accomplishments
      11. Role play
      12. Language development
      13. To sense dissonance
      14. To anticipate consequences
      15. To deal with abstractions
      16. To take the perspective of another
      17. To make interesting associations
      18. To plan and carry out multistepped activities
      19. To use resources effectively
      20. To dual focus

B. Four prerequisite skills for later learning are:
   1. Language: Language understanding begins at approximately 7-9 months of age and proceeds rapidly to three years of age when a child will know most of the language he will use in ordinary adult conversations. The primary way to develop language well is for the mother to talk to the child at the right time and in the right way.
   2. Curiosity: An infant is a very curious human being. Ideally that curiosity should get deeper and stronger, but many mothers stifle curiosity because they are protecting the child and/or the house. Stifling curiosity can lead to the child's having undue interest in the mother or too little interest in the mother.
   3. Learning to learn: Learning the alphabet or to count is not as important as learning the basic way to approach problems. Example: The first time a child does a puzzle it takes him a very long time. Each time he does that puzzle it will take him less time. When he gets a new puzzle it will not take him as long as the first time he did the first puzzle because he has learned something about how to do puzzles.
   4. Social Skills and attachment: A child needs to get through the first three years with a healthy attachment to his mother. The social patterns that he develops with his mother will serve as the basis for his social interaction with other adults and children.
C. A balance between the child's interest in his mother and his interest in exploring the rest of the world: Almost all children at 8-9 months have a balance between attachment to their mother and curiosity. Often by two years of age this balance no longer exists.

II. The activities that babies are primarily interested in during the 8-16 month period are:
   A. Gross motor activities: One of the compelling activities for young babies is mastering the use of their bodies; e.g., they progress from leg extension, to crawling, to pulling to stand, to cruising, to walking, to running, and to climbing.
   B. Exploring the properties of objects: Children in this age range will spend a great deal of time exploring small, detailed, interestingly shaped objects and will be fascinated by the movement of objects (e.g., a ping-pong ball bouncing on a wooden floor) and by objects with moving parts such as hinges or bottles and caps.
   C. Learning about mother: The mother's reactions to the child's overtures and her response to his interest in the social and object world will greatly shape his behavior.
   D. Learning about themselves: As the child reaches the age of 15 months, he begins increasingly to assert his independence and individuality. This period is often referred to as the stage of negativism (due to the child's frequent use of the word "no").

E. Language: Mastering the understanding and use of language is critical for the child's development. The language used by the mother must be meaningful to the child, but mothers should not underestimate the amount of language a child can understand by 16 months of age.
III. Film: First half of *Learning to Learn in Infancy*, from the Parent and Child Center Series, by Dr. Joseph Stone.

Film Report

Title: Learning to Learn in Infancy
Film maker: From the Parent and Child Center Series (Vassar College), directed by Joseph Stone
Length: 30 minutes (black and white)
Topics covered: The following topics are stressed in this film:

1. Learning begins early in life.
2. The key to learning is curiosity.
3. Young babies are explorers.
4. Exploring leads to curiosity.
5. Human relationships are essential to learning.
6. Communications (that is, language) and imitation are important to learning.

Settings: The above topics are illustrated showing children who are being reared in institutions. There are brief scenes showing home-reared children.
Age Range: 6 weeks to 20 months
Instructions: Since this is a long film, the impact of the subject matter is conveyed more strongly if the film is divided into two 15-minute segments, and screened on separate occasions. Give a brief introduction mentioning the main concepts dealt with in the film. Encourage questions from the audience.

Group Session #4

I. General guidelines for effective child-rearing practices:
   A. Provide access to as much of the house as possible so that the child has the maximum opportunity to exercise his curiosity and explore his world.
   B. Provide a wide range of materials for the child to explore. You don't have to spend a lot of money on toys. Children in this age range are fascinated by common household objects—e.g., plastic jars with covers, a big plastic container filled with smaller interesting objects, a baby-proofed kitchen cabinet filled with pots and pans or canned goods.
   C. Spend at least half of your child's waking hours available to him. That does not mean you have to hover over him constantly but

that you should be nearby to provide the attention, support or assistance he may need.
II. If you are available and your child is given access to a large area and a wide variety of materials, it is inevitable that he will make overtures to you. The following is a list of recommended ways to respond to your child's overtures:
   A. Respond promptly as often as possible.
   B. Respond favorably.
   C. Make some effort to understand what the child is trying to do.
   D. Set limits; do not give in to unreasonable requests.
   E. Provide encouragement as often as possible.
   F. Provide enthusiasm as often as possible.
   G. Provide assistance as often as possible.
   H. Use words as often as possible.
   I. Use words that the child understands or words that are a little too hard for him.
   J. Use words to provide a related idea or two.
   K. Do not prolong the episode if the child wants to leave; the interchange will often last less than one minute.
   L. Encourage "pretend" activities.
III. The above practices refer to situations in which the child initiates interaction with the mother. Mothers we have observed usually initiate interactions with their children if:
   A. The child seems bored; the mother will provide things for him to do.
   B. The child is misbehaving; the mother will discipline him firmly and consistently.
   C. The child is trying to do something new which may be unsafe (e.g., stair climbing); the mother will watch rather than stop him. Children are more careful than most people realize.
IV. We've been talking about things for mothers to do. The following is a list of practices for mothers to avoid.
   A. Don't cage your child or confine him regularly for long periods.
   B. Don't allow your child to concentrate his energies on you to the point where he spends most of his time following you around or staying near you, especially in the second year of life.
   C. Don't allow tantrums.
   D. Don't worry that your baby won't love you if you say "no" from time to time.
   E. Especially from the middle of the second year when your baby may start becoming negative with you, don't try to win all the fights with him.
   F. Don't try to prevent the baby from cluttering the house; it's an inevitable sign of a healthy, curious baby.
   G. Don't be overprotective; babies are more careful than you think.

A Training Program to Assist People in Educating Infants   535

   H. Don't overpower him; let him do what he wants to do as often as possible.
   I. Don't make yourself largely unavailable to the baby during this period of his life.
   J. Don't bore your baby if you can avoid it.
   K. Don't worry about when he learns to read, count numbers, or say the alphabet. Don't even worry if he's slow to talk as long as he seems to understand more and more language as he grows.
   L. Don't try to force toilet training. By the time he's two or over it will be easy to do.
   M. Don't let your baby think the whole world was made just for him.
V. Film: Second half of *Learning to Learn in Infancy*, from the Parent and Child Center Series, by Dr. Joseph Stone.

Home Visit Questions

General Format of Questions

1. What has the subject been doing lately?
2. Has there been anything new in the subject's behavior since our last visit?
3. Is there anything you would like to bring up as a concern at this time?

GROUP VISIT CONTENT, CORE PERIOD
(8-17* MONTHS)

Group Visit #1

I. Purposes of the group visits during the remainder of the project:
   A. General purposes

Some activities are best done in the group setting—e.g., hearing parents remark about concerns that other parents are currently coping with, introducing group information on topics that help an individual family compare their own situation with that of others in a less confronting manner than the home visit format allows.

Any activity that can be successfully done in a group setting is cheaper in time and money that way; e.g., films can be shown much more easily to a group at the institution than in homes.

---

*During September 1973, as several babies reached 14 and 15 months of age, we noted that the onset of negativism seemed slightly later than we had expected it to be. In order to provide assistance to families in coping with negativism and in order to be able to observe the evolution of family adaptions, we extended the final time of the project home visit program from 16 to 17 months.

In addition, fathers can be present more easily at evening group meetings.
- B. Specific purposes

The relationship of the 8-17 month period to the 5-8 month period can be reviewed simultaneously for all parents.

The staff can present their summarized views on:

What's happening in the lives of the babies during the 8-11 month period.

What kinds of helpful information are appropriate for this kind of period.

What kinds of practices to avoid.

II. Recurring themes of concern to us as cited in home visit reports
- A. Problems of hostility on the part of the next oldest child toward the baby.
- B. The advisability of more appropriate language activities by mother with babies.
- C. A need for more effort by mothers to tune in on the baby's needs, interests, and capabilities.
- D. Overrestrictiveness by mothers of babies' exploratory efforts.
- E. Overprotectiveness.
- F. Overconcern with the neatness of the house to the possible detriment of the baby's exploration.
- G. A greater need to protect the house from the child.
- H. A greater need to protect the child from the house.
- I. A need for a better understanding of the relationships among the child's need to explore and to practice crawling and climbing and the problem of providing maximum access to the living area.

III. The Movie: *Abby's First Two Years*

[We decided that this movie was not worth using, but we would recommend that another be used.]

IV. Discussion and Final Comments

Group Visit #2

I. Introduction

Review of:
- A. Where Group Visit #2 fits into the total program.
- B. The agenda for the evening.
- C. Announcement of special feedback sessions when each child is 12½ months old. Such sessions, in response to requests by three parents, will inform parents of patterns of test scores of their children and also of their own child-rearing behavior.

II. New Business—Emergents (10-12 Months)
   A. Walking
   B. Climbing 12-inch units.
   C. A diversity of reasons for overtures to the mother.
   D. Stabilization of patterns of undesirable behavior from older child to the subject. Reduction of difficulties in this area.
   E. The subject's tendencies to express anger at others.
   F. Outdoor summer activities.
   G. Imitation of sounds and gestures.
   H. Teasing games with others.
   I. Self-feeding skills.
   J. The decline in use of playpens.
   K. The decline in stranger anxiety.
   L. The first clear attempts to ask another for help.
   M. Favorite places.
   N. Favorite activities.
   O. Favorite objects.
   P. Dangerous tendencies, plus the danger of ingesting poisonous substances.
III. The Immediate Future
   A. The dawning of a sense of self.
   B. Negativism (15-21 months).
IV. Review of Three Ways of Viewing Educational Goals for This Program
   A. Encouraging development of competencies listed earlier.
   B. The four major educational processes:
      1. Language.
      2. Social attachment.
      3. Curiosity.
      4. Learning to learn.
   C. An appropriate balance of interest by the child between interest in mother and exploration of the rest of the world.
V. Film: First half of *Four Families*, Margaret Mead, National Film Board of Canada
   A. Child-rearing in India.
   B. Child-rearing in France.

Film Report

Title: Four Families
Film maker: Canadian Broadcasting Commission
Narrator: Margaret Mead
Length: This film is in two parts, each 30 minutes in length. Part I shows two families, one in India and one in France; Part II shows families in Japan and Canada. (black and white)

Topics covered: An attempt has been made to select four comparable rural families. Each family is filmed in similar *settings*. These include scenes depicting preparation of food, eating, bathing, division of labor, and layout of the house. Attitudes toward and methods of child-rearing are also shown. These include punishment, roles of older children, toys. The relationship between child-rearing and national characteristics is stressed, and comparisons and contrasts are pointed out concerning the four countries presented.

Age range of children: Each family consists of a baby of approximately 10 months, two older siblings, and two parents. (The Japanese family also includes the children's paternal grandparents.)

Instructions: Screen each part of this film on separate occasions. Give a brief introduction and allow time for discussion after the film.

Group Visit #3

I. Introduction
   Review of:
   A. The agenda for the evening.
   B. The schedule for the next year re: cessation of home visits at 17 months and follow-up contact at 22-27 months.

II. Emergents (Subjects ranged in age from 8-14 months.)
   A. All subjects do the following:
      1. Imitate sounds and gestures.
      2. Say 3-5 words.
      3. Play games (e.g., peek-a-boo).
      4. Express affection to adults (particularly to the mother).
      5. Express anger to parents and siblings.
      6. Climb up stairs; however, there is no report of any subject being able to climb *down* stairs.
      7. Experience minimal or no stranger anxiety.
   B. Gross motor development
      1. 8 of the 11 subjects are presently walking unaided.
      2. 10 of the 11 subjects can climb 12 inches or more.
      3. 7 of the 11 subjects can ride wheeled bikes, horses, or ducks.
   C. Language development
      1. 10 of the 11 subjects can identify five or more objects.
      2. 9 of the 11 subjects can follow simple instructions.
      3. 5 of the 11 subjects can follow instructions calling for a familiar sequence of behavior.
   D. Procuring a service
      1. 7 of the 11 subjects ask for help by pointing.
      2. 7 of the 11 subjects ask for help by calling the mother.
      3. 4 of the 11 subjects ask for help by leading the mother by the hand.
      4. 3 of the 11 subjects ask for help by bringing the object to the mother.

E. Self-feeding
   1. 10 of the 11 subjects use a spoon.
   2. 9 of the 11 subjects drink from a cup.
F. Restrictiveness
   1. 9 of the 11 subjects no longer use a playpen when indoors.
   2. 8 of the 11 subjects no longer use a playpen when outdoors.
G. Most frequently mentioned favorite objects:
   ball (6 subjects)
   animals (6 subjects)
H. Most frequently mentioned favorite places:
   bathroom (10 subjects)
   outdoors (11 subjects)

III. Recurrent themes perceived by staff—The following is an updated report on some of the recurrent themes that were emphasized earlier. The numbers in parentheses are the frequencies found at the last analysis of this date.
   A. Problem with older child
      no: 9   improved: 1   yes: 1 (4)
   B. Sibling relationships
      good: 7   competitive: 3 (1)   aggressive: 1
   C. Need for safety precautions
      yes: 4 (4)   no: 7
   D. Mother is overprotective.
      yes: 2 (3)   no: 9.
   E. Mother uses restrictive devices.
      yes: 2(2)   no: 9
   F. Need for more language by mother to subject
      yes: 2 (2)   no: 7   no evidence in reports: 2

IV. Expected Emergents (15-36 months)
   A. Negativism
   B. Social abilities
      1. To lead and follow peers.
      2. To express affection and hostility to peers.
      3. To compete with peers.
      4. To praise oneself or show pride in one's accomplishments.
      5. To involve oneself in adult role-playing behaviors or to otherwise express the desire to grow up.
   C. Nonsocial abilities
      1. Linguistic competence.
      2. The ability to sense dissonance or to note discrepancies.
      3. The ability to anticipate consequences.
      4. The ability to plan and carry out multistepped activities.

V. Film: Second half of *Four Families*, Margaret Mead, National Film Board of Canada
   A. Child-rearing in Japan
   B. Child-rearing in Canada

HOME VISIT FORMAT

8-11 Months

I. Opening
   Questions:
   How are things going?
   Are there any complaints?
   Is there anything about (the next oldest child's name)'s behavior that you'd like to discuss?
II. Goals
   A. Discussion of the emerging dimensions of competence
      1. To get and maintain attention of adults
      2. Language
      3. To use adults as a resource
      4. To express affection to adults
   B. Prerequisite learnings of the preschool period
      1. Curiosity: Babies are very curious about the world around them and that curiosity is the source of learning and development. Ideally, curiosity should get deeper and stronger but many mothers stifle curiosity because they are protecting the child and/or the house. Stifling curiosity can lead to the child's having undue interest in the mother or too little interest in the mother.
      2. Receptive Language: The ability to understand language begins to develop at about 8 months of age and progresses until at about three years of age the child will be able to understand most of the language he will use in ordinary adult conversations. The primary way to develop language well is for the mother to talk to the child, primarily when the child makes an overture to her. At that time the mother should use words the child will understand or words that are a little too hard for him, should provide a related idea or two, and should not prolong the episode if the child wants to leave. The interchange will often last less than one minute.
   C. Balance of social and nonsocial interests: If a child is given maximum opportunity to exercise his curiosity and explore his world, and if his mother is available to provide the attention, support, or assistance the child may need, the child will strike a good balance between his social and nonsocial interests.
III. Particular interests of the child
   A. Gross motor activities: One of the most compelling activities for young babies is mastering the use of their bodies; e.g., they progress from leg extension, to crawling, to pulling to stand, to cruising, to walking, to running, and to climbing.
   B. Exploring the properties of objects: Children in this age range will spend a great deal of time exploring small, detailed, interestingly

shaped objects and will be fascinated by the movement of objects (e.g., a ping-pong ball bouncing on a wooden floor) and by objects with moving parts such as hinges or bottles and caps.
   C. Games—e.g., pat-a-cake, bye-bye, and peek-a-boo
IV. Practices for mothers to avoid
   A. Don't cage your child or confine him or her regularly for long periods.
   B. Don't worry that your baby won't love you if you say "no" from time to time.
   C. Don't try to prevent baby from cluttering house; it's an inevitable sign of a healthy, curious baby.
   D. Don't be overprotective; babies are more careful than you think.
   E. Don't make yourself largely unavailable to baby during this period.
V. Reactions to approaches made by child.
   A. Respond promptly.
   B. Respond favorably.
   C. Make some effort to understand what baby is trying to do.
   D. Set limits.
   E. Provide encouragement.
   F. Provide enthusiasm.
   G. Provide assistance as often as possible.
   H. Use words as often as possible.
   I. Use words that the child understands or that are a little too hard for him.
   J. Use words to provide a related idea or two.
   K. Don't prolong the episode if baby wants to leave.
   L. Encourage pretend activities.
VI. Mother-initiated interaction
   A. Provide things for baby to do if he seems bored.
   B. Be a firm disciplinarian.
VII. Recurrent themes
   A. Concerns about the older child
      1. Punishment/discipline/control
      2. Guidelines for preparing activities and materials
   B. The dimensions of competence
      1. Language development and the mother's role in language development
      2. Attention-seeking behavior and the mother's response
   C. Child-proofing and safety precautions
   D. Gross motor development
   E. Restrictiveness
VIII. Previews of coming attractions

11-14 Months

I. Opening
   Questions:
   How are things going?
   Are there any complaints?
II. Goals
   A. Discussion of the emerging dimensions of competence
      1. Language
      2. To express affection and hostility to adults and siblings
      3. To use adults as resources
      4. To praise oneself or show pride in one's accomplishments
   B. Prerequisite learnings of the preschool period
      1. Language: The ability to understand language begins to develop at about 8 months of age and progresses until at about three years of age the child will be able to understand most of the language he will use in ordinary adult conversations. The ability to produce language varies greatly and is not as good a predictor of future development in the first three years. The primary way to develop language well is for the mother to talk to the child, primarily when the child makes an overture to her. At that time the mother should use words the child will understand or words that are a little too hard for him, and should provide a related idea or two, and should not prolong the episode if the child wants to leave. The interchange will often last less than one minute.
      2. Learning to learn: Learning the alphabet or to count is not as important as learning the basic way to approach problems. Example: The first time a child does a puzzle it takes him a very long time. Each time he does that puzzle it will take him less time. When he gets a new puzzle, it will not take him as long as the first time he did the first puzzle because he has learned something about how to do puzzles.
   C. Balance of social and nonsocial interests: If a child is given maximum opportunity to exercise his curiosity and explore his world, and if his mother is available to provide the attention, support, or assistance the child may need, the child will strike a good balance between his social and nonsocial interests.
III. Particular interests of the child:
   A. Learning about mother: The mother's reactions to the child's overtures and her response to his interest in the social and object world will greatly shape his behavior.
   B. Exploration and mastery of object world: Provide a wide range of materials for the child to explore and master. You don't have to spend a lot of money on toys. Children in this age range are fascinated by

common household objects—e.g., plastic jars with covers, a big plastic container filled with smaller interesting objects, a baby-proofed kitchen cabinet filled with pots and pans or canned goods.
IV. Practices for mothers to avoid
   A. Don't allow your child to concentrate his energies on you to the point where he spends most of his time following you around or staying near you.
   B. Don't overpower him; let him do what he wants to do as often as possible.
   C. Don't bore your baby if you can avoid it.
   D. Don't let your baby think the whole world was made for him.
V. Reactions to approaches made by child
   A. Respond promptly.
   B. Respond favorably.
   C. Make some effort to understand what baby is trying to do.
   D. Set limits.
   E. Provide encouragement.
   F. Provide enthusiasm.
   G. Provide assistance as often as possible.
   H. Use words as often as possible.
   I. Use words that the child understands or that are a little too hard for him.
   J. Use words to provide a related idea or two.
   K. Don't prolong the episode if baby wants to leave.
   L. Encourage pretend activities.
VI. Mother-initiated interaction
   A. Provide things for baby to do if he seems bored.
   B. Be a firm disciplinarian.
VII. Recurrent themes

14-17 Months

I. Opening
   Questions:
   How are things going?
   Are there any complaints?
   Is there anything about (next oldest child's name)'s behavior that you'd like to discuss?
II. Goals
   A. Discussion of the dimensions of competence
      1. Language
      2. To express hostility to adults
      3. To sense dissonance

            4. To anticipate consequences
            5. To deal with abstractions
        B. Prerequisite learnings of the preschool period.
           Learning to learn
        C. Social skills
           Emerging negativism
   III. Particular interests of the child
        A. Learning about himself (emerging negativism)
        B. Exploration and mastery of the object world
   IV. Practices for mothers to avoid
        A. Don't allow tantrums.
        B. Especially from the middle of the second year when your baby may start becoming negative with you, don't try to win all the fights with him.
        C. Don't worry about when he learns to read or count numbers or say the alphabet. Don't even worry if he's slow to talk as long as he seems to understand more and more language as he grows.
        D. Don't try to force toilet training.
    V. Reactions to approaches made by child
        A. Respond promptly.
        B. Respond favorably.
        C. Make some effort to understand what baby is trying to do.
        D. Set limits.
        E. Provide encouragement.
        F. Provide enthusiasm.
        G. Provide assistance as often as possible.
        H. Use words as often as possible.
        I. Use words that the child understands or that are a little too hard for him.
        J. Use words to provide a related idea or two.
        K. Don't prolong the episode if baby wants to leave.
        L. Encourage pretend activities.
   VI. Mother-initiated interaction
        A. Provide things for baby to do if he seems bored.
        B. Be a firm disciplinarian.

HOME VISIT QUESTIONS

8-11 Months

A. Standard Questions (to be asked by each visitor routinely at the beginning of the visit)

1. Favorites
   a. What are S's favorite activities?
   b. What are S's favorite places?
   c. What are S's favorite objects, toys?
2. Emergents
   What new behaviors has S shown since our last visit?
3. Concerns
   a. Is there any specific cause for concern on your part in terms of S's behavior?
   b. Is there anything you want to discuss?

B. Particular Questions (Relevant to S's age)
   1. Motor Abilities
      a. Does S cruise, pull to a stand, walk with help?
      b. Does S use the playpen at all?
      c. How high can S climb?
      d. Has the living area been adequately child-proofed and made as safe as possible for this age infant?
   2. Social Abilities
      a. Does S play games with you?
      b. Does S show stranger anxiety?
      c. Does S show affection and/or anger to you?
      d. Does S imitate sounds or gestures?
   3. Daily Scheduling and Care
      a. What is S's general pattern of eating and sleeping at this age?
      b. Does S drink from a cup? Eat finger foods?
   4. Language
      What particular sounds does S use?

C. Individual Family Concerns
   Are there any particular problems you would like to discuss?

11-14 Months

A. Standard Questions (to be asked by each visitor routinely at the beginning of the visit)
   1. Favorites
      a. What are S's favorite activities?
      b. What are S's favorite places?
      c. What are S's favorite objects, toys?
   2. Emergents
      What new behaviors has S shown since our last visit?
   3. Concerns
      a. Is there any specific cause for concern on your part in terms of S's behavior?
      b. Is there anything you want to discuss?

B. Particular Questions (Relevant to S's age)
   1. Development of Social Abilities
      a. Does S indicate when he needs help? How?
      b. Does S show affection to adults? to siblings?
      c. Has stranger anxiety subsided?
      d. Does S show anger to mother or to siblings?
   2. Language
      Does S use sounds and words to indicate objects?
   3. Motor Abilities
      a. How high an object can S climb?
      b. Does S walk unaided? Since when?
      c. Are there any safety or child-proofing concerns that you want to discuss?
   4. Daily Scheduling and Care
      a. What is the general pattern of eating, sleeping, and outings now that S is _____ months old?
      b. Does S feed himself, use a cup, a spoon?
      c. What are S's food preferences?
C. Individual Family Concerns
   Are there any particular problems you would like to discuss?

14-17 Months

A. Standard Questions (to be asked by each visitor routinely at the beginning of the visit)
   1. Favorites
      a. What are S's favorite activities?
      b. What are S's favorite places?
      c. What are S's favorite objects, toys?
   2. Emergents
      What new behaviors has S shown since our last visit?
   3. Concerns
      a. Is there any specific cause for concern on your part in terms of S's behavior?
      b. Is there anything you want to discuss?
B. Particular Questions (Relevant to S's age)
   1. Negativism
      a. Is S throwing his weight around?
      b. Does S seem fascinated with the word *no*?
      c. Does S test limits, such as by disobeying for the sake of disobeying?
   2. Language
      Does S use any new words?
   3. Motor Abilities
      a. Can S climb all things in the house?

b. Can S ride wheeled toys?
   c. Does S go outside to parks or gardens?
  4. Development of Self
   a. Does S show hurt feelings?
   b. Does S initiate new activities with older siblings and with parents?
  5. Safety
   Has the problem of accidental poisoning been adequately dealt with? [National Statistics]
C. Individual Family Concerns
 Hostility of older sibling toward baby: reemergence of conflict with siblings?

SAMPLE HOME VISIT REPORTS

The following reports were written by various staff members after visits to the home of Mrs. X whose second child was born 6-1-72. The older brother is referred to as PM_3 (male peer, age 3). These reports were written informally to maintain interstaff communication.

Home Visit #1 (5-8 Months)

Observer: B.W.
Date: 11/15/72
Age: 5½ months

Comments about first group meeting: It was fine, "not over my head." She tried a few exercises from the film.

Content: The plan was to introduce the dimensions of competence. Discussion was achieved on the following three only:

  1. getting and maintaining attention
  2. expressing hostility and affection ["saying *friendly* or *unfriendly* things"]
  3. role play ["make-believe"]

Special topics: Mrs. X has had pressure to toilet-train her older child very early (one year or so), from her parents or in-laws. She was much relieved when I supported her resistance to the idea.

Comments of E:

  1. This mother talks a great deal and often about the older child. In particular, she believes she was too harsh and punishing with him.

2. The older brother is alert, asks many questions, and seems to want a lot of attention.

Home Visit #2 (5-8 Months)

Observer: B.K.
Date: 1/5/73
Time: 11:30
Age   7 months

Setting: Mrs. X, PM$_3$, and subject were home. The radio and the TV were on. We were all in the kitchen which is a large, comfortable room. The children have a lot of toys and playing space available to them in the kitchen.

General comments: It is very hard to get a word in once Mrs. X begins talking. She is more interested in the opportunity to express her concerns than in the subject matter we are presenting. I was supposed to cover the Group II Session, but she found it almost impossible to sit and listen. I got through the barest outline and then let her talk.

Specific topics discussed:

1. To gain attention.   Mrs. X related this more to PM$_3$ but she said she really found it useful to try and think why he is doing something. She said she and her husband are having discussions now about what the children do and why. She is trying to get her husband to be less strict with PM$_3$.
2. Restrictiveness.   Mrs. X contrasted PM$_3$ and S in that PM$_3$ was kept in his highchair or crib most of the time. S was on the floor or in his walker and free to roam while I was there. She feels that S is much more curious and alert than PM$_3$ was at this age.
3. Distraction.   Mrs. X commented that S cries when she takes something away from him. I suggested that if she offers him something else first she will probably have less difficulty taking something away. I suggested that this type of redirection of S's interest might be useful with PM$_3$ as well.

Home Visit #3 (8-17 Months)

Observer: B.K.
Date: 2/23/73
Time: Noon
Age: 8 months, 3 weeks

Setting: S was being fed when I arrived. PM$_3$ was upstairs taking a nap (he joined us after about 30 minutes).

Discussion Points:

1. Language—I explained and demonstrated how to accompany S's interest in objects and toys with brief verbal statements.
2. PM_3's attention span.

General Comments:

1. S is able to spend a lot of time by himself exploring objects. Mrs. X has arranged the environment nicely and allows him a lot of freedom.
2. Mrs. X talks to S a lot but not always appropriately. (She commented that when Dr. White was in her house she felt self-conscious and didn't talk to S).
3. I told her not to expect PM_3 to spend a long time (1-2 hours) with any particular activity; that 10-20 minutes is a long time for a child his age. She found this reassuring.
4. S enjoys having PM_3 around and watches his brother constantly.

Data: A task social observation was done.

Home Visit #4 (8-17 Months)

Observer: B.K.
Date: 3/22/73
Time: 10 a.m.
Age: 9 months, 3 weeks

Setting: Mother, PM, and subject were home. PM was watching "Sesame Street," and S was playing on the kitchen floor. He seemed tired and cranky today.

Topics:

1. Language. Mrs. X is labeling objects for and talking to S in a consistent and effective manner. I told her that her language was appropriate and frequent enough and encouraged her to continue.
2. Curiosity. S is "getting into everything." I explained that we were happy to hear this since it meant that he was curious and allowed to satisfy his curiosity through exploration. I encouraged this, although reiterating the fact that she can and should set reasonable limits.
3. Gross motor development. S is pulling himself up to a standing position and tries to climb on furniture, etc. Mrs. X noted this and expressed concern about his safety. I encouraged her to allow him to try.
4. Task and social observations were done.
5. Mrs. X said an evening meeting is fine and that her husband would like to attend.

General comments:

1. Mrs. X seems to be having fewer problems with PM.
2. Mrs. X has really begun to tune in to S's behavior and look at what he is trying to do. I was very impressed today with her language and with her ability to correctly perceive S's interest or needs. Our group discussions and home visits have definitely altered Mrs. X's behavior with her child.
3. Mrs. X and her husband are concerned that S might become a "brat" because he's allowed too much freedom, etc. ("We're doing things very differently than what we did with PM"). I stressed the fact that they should set limits and that the children we've observed were not "brats" and, in fact, were easier to get along with, etc.

Home Visit #5 (8-17 Months)

Observer: B.S.
Date: 4/9/73
Age: 10 months, 1 week

Comments: This home visit was the occasion for a first trial of the revised Adult Assessment Scales utilizing the five-second rule and incoporating the language guidelines. E.C. and I felt it went poorly due to the large amount of double coding of abilities and language and the necessity for shifting attention from category to category when there is a lot of interaction. Worst of all, Mrs. X spent the full twenty-five minutes feeding S and this made the occasion rather a biased one for our purposes. Since she timed the ending of the meal with the ending of our observation, and there was a friend of hers present, this was not an ideal observation in terms of naturalness of behavior captured.

Mrs. X was rather more controlling than usual today, going so far as to control every morsel of pizza that passed S's lips, encouraging him to bite (his food) repeatedly, and trying to keep him neat and clean. This woman has a neatness hangup. She related a story of how she held S on her lap for one hour before going to a birthday party so he would stay clean, and then held him on her lap for 3 hours while there because no baby chair was available. In addition she bemoaned her "dirty" floors (they are nearly spotless) and in general is compulsive on this score. She does try to let S wear old clothes at home so he will get a chance to crawl about, but mentioned plans for restricting his access to the kitchen and den as he gets more mobile. She claimed one of her problems was with "discipline" and getting S to understand what was "off limits" (the TV, the bathroom, etc.). Mrs. X will need additional help overcoming her compulsive restrictive tendencies. Otherwise things are going well and S appeared content and pleased.

Topics covered: Access to parts of house; discipline and control; child-proofing; communication and language—S's efforts to verbalize; sibling relationships have improved and things are going well.

A Training Program to Assist People in Educating Infants 551

Home Visit #8 (8-17 Months)

Observer: B.K.
Date: 5/17/73
Age: 11 months, 2 weeks

Mrs. X was getting PM dressed to go out in the backyard. He spent the entire visit outside, playing happily. M reports that he spends most of his time outdoors and gets upset when it is time to come in. The baby practiced climbing but was not particularly interested in toys. His favorite household object is a spoon. S also gets to go out in the afternoons and M reports that he plays happily and doesn't seem as interested in her when he is outside. M was very pleased that he was playing in the sandbox but not eating the sand.

Topics discussed:

1. Gross motor development. S can climb up on a kitchen chair.
2. Imitation. S imitates simple actions and sounds.
3. Language. S doesn't say any words but seems to try to say G.T., Ma, and Da-da. M reports proudly that he understands the word *no*.
4. Feeding. S can feed himself using his fingers. He is less successful with a spoon but does get opportunities to try. M doesn't encourage the use of a cup because she feels it is easier to use a bottle.
5. Medical problems. S has an appointment to see a foot specialist next week. His feet turn in very badly and the pediatrician recommended a specialist.

General comments:

1. Things seem to be fine here.
2. M said she wants to wait a couple of years before she has another baby, but that they definitely want at least one more.
3. M is thinking about nursery school for PM for next year.

Home Visit #9 (8-17 Months)

Observer: E.C.
Date: 5/31/73
Time: 9:00 a.m.
Age: 12 months

Setting: In kitchen with M and S. PM (3½) also at home, watching TV and occasionally coming to the kitchen to check on the proceedings there.

552   APPENDIX D

Coverage:

1. Gross motor development
   a. climbs onto couch (about 24"), stairs
   b. sometimes walks aided
   c. cruises
   d. prefers crawling
   e. S has been to a specialist about his feet, has had X-rays, etc. Mrs. X hopes to get the results next week.
2. Favorite places.   Playing outside in yard; likes the sandbox and swing.
3. Sibling relationship.   According to Mrs. X, "fantastic." However, I did observe that PM does occasionally push S.
4. Imitation.   Sounds and gestures.
5. Stranger anxiety.   S is not completely over his fear of strangers. M says he is "coming around."
6. Playpen
   a. is still used for short periods when M is particularly busy.
   b. Also, M has erected 2 gates: one a kitchen door which leads into the living room and one to prevent him going up the stairs.
7. Interest in toys.   Mrs. X reported that S is no longer so interested in toys, but prefers to crawl around and explore the house and household objects.

Home Visit #10 (8-17 Months)

Observer: B.W.
Date: 6/4/73
Age: 1 year, 3 days old

Setting: At home in the kitchen with many, many toys on the floor, etc., and a gate to the living room and stairs.

Coverage:

1. Favorite objects.   A large metal spoon!
2. Problems.   Very few.
   a. Subject has begun to test authority. He will repeat forbidden approaches, and when admonished he dissolves into tears.
   b. Lately, he gets up in the middle of the evening occasionally.
3. Motor development.   He cruises, and he climbs a great deal (twelve-inch unit). Two nights ago, under supervision, he climbed all the way to the third floor. He has taken a *few steps* unaided.
4. Stranger Anxiety.   He still shows some, although it is clearly decreasing.
5. Anger.   "He has a temper now." "He beat up on his brother."
6. Favorite places.   The kitchen, the windows, back yard. He likes the bathroom and the foot of the stairs, but is *forbidden both*.*

*Balance of interest between mother and the rest of the world. Fine.

7. Language. Not much happening. He knows his name, "no," and perhaps "Give me a kiss."
8. Access. Now that there is a gate on the stairs, he can use all of the apartment except the bathroom, *unless* he is very dirty. If so, he cannot use the living room. He goes outside to the back yard a great deal.
9. Asking for help. Not sure.
10. Showing pride. No.
11. PM's behavior to subject. Somewhat more roughhousing, but generally very good.

Home Visit #11 (8-17 Months)

Observer: B.S.
Date: 6/27/73
Time: 11:00 a.m.
Age: 12 months, 3½ weeks

Today we reported to Mrs. X on S's progress to date and she was quite pleased with the results. We visited during a time when there were several house guests; a sister-in-law was present during our discussion and joined in at the end of the visit for an additional half-hour chat about her work as a public health nurse in California with Mexican families. Mrs. X was quite proud of S's achievements and requested that I repeat some of the comments her sister-in-law had missed.

(The visit took place the morning after a group visit, and Mrs. X reported that she and Mrs. Y spent two hours talking in the parking lot after the meeting ended!)

Coverage:

1. S will be showing increased noncompliance soon and this should be realized.
2. S has responded favorably to all the guests and is over stranger anxiety.
3. He shows anger when removed from the area at the bottom of the stairs, as well as when a toy or object is removed.
4. He enjoys bouncing on a riding horse in his bedroom.
5. He is very mother oriented today, making repeated overtures for attention, and crying occasionally (could be the guests?).
6. S's ability as a climber has been noted; he climbs stairs, chairs, and the chain link fence.

12½-month feedback report to M

Tests:
Dissonance: Level 0
Bayley 6 mos.: 100 motor, 100 mental
      10 mos.: 106 motor, 104 mental

554 APPENDIX D

Language 12 mos.: I–12 mos. level
Abstract Abilities 12 mos.: VI–15.5 mos. level

Language:

1. knows some names but not classes of own toys (11).
2. understands simple, familiar instructions requiring only a single discrete change in behavior (4).

Abstract Abilities

1. visual pursuit and object permanence: can search when there are invisible displacements in a series.
2. construction of object in space: understands relationships, equilibrium, gravity, detours, absence (brother hides toys under chairs; he's been trained).

HOME VISIT HIGHLIGHTS:

1. Improvement noted in PM's behavior in mother's handling of him—more realistic.
2. Increase in *freedom* with S—less restrictiveness noted.
3. Mrs. X *well tuned-in* to S's overtures, although he makes relatively few.
4. *Curiosity, exploration,* and *self-motivated play* have all been progressing nicely.
5. Dimensions of competence have progressed well, with language input showing the most improvement. Mrs. X has shown a marked ability to correctly perceive S's interests and needs.
6. S's love of *physical mobility;* good *peer relationships; imitation* and *games;* outdoor play; self-*feeding;* growth of *temper; testing* authority; *reduced stranger anxiety.*

SOCIAL INSTRUMENT

Most frequent categories (5 observations):

*Compliance	22
Emotional Resource (comforting, reassurance)	15
*Noncompliance	12
Attention (Pos)	9
Affection A	9
Resource A	8
Imitation A	6

Imitation P discussed—beginning now

| Follows P | 15 (all on one day) |
| Affection P | 2 (all on one day) |

*Good Balance

More occurs than was noted on forms. S beginning to hit PM, but PM doesn't hit back.

Home Visit #13 (8-17 Months)

Observer: B.W.
Date: 7/27/73
Time: 3:05 p.m.
Age: just under 14 months
(b.d. 6/1/72)
Tape Available

Setting: In kitchen, children upstairs resting

Coverage:

1. GV: M enjoyed it.
2. S is now affectionate.
3. He "recognizes certain people"; e.g., *crazy about F; in-laws at house in Maine; he's very sociable.*
4. Stranger anxiety: shyness in second year.
5. Lots of sounds but few that can be understood.
6. He had a big fight with PM a week ago, but generally they get along very well.
7. Climbs anything in the house; house is safety proofed.
8. Access to house. He has a few "no" areas—e.g., the bar and bathroom—but most of the house is available to him.
9. Teething
10. Negativism. Doesn't like to have things taken away from him.
11. Thinking. Starting now, memory growing.
12. Clings to M when he needs a nap: otherwise plays well by himself.
13. *Discipline*. M feels more comfortable with S than with PM.
14. TV. Color and music, cartoons, commercials; but not usually for very long (only 1 time to date)
15. Times are great except on long rides in car or up country where he had to be confined to a playpen for many hours.
16. Discussed movie on attachment in connection with playpens. A 14-month-old *should* be upset when kept in a playpen for more than one hour.
17. Anything puzzling or need talking about? No.
18. Loves to climb stairs, but can only come down 3 or 4 steps.

Comments: All is well.

Home Visit #14 (8-17 Months)

Observer: E.C.
Date: 8/20/73
Time: 9:30 a.m.
Age: 14½ months

Setting: In the yard: M, S and PM

Coverage:

1. Gross motor development. S began walking unaided the day prior to this visit. He seems to be enjoying practicing this new skill. M says he climbs a lot; climbs up stairs but not down.
2. Language development. Understands many instructions. Says "dadda," "Mumma," "D-D." Babbling a lot.
3. Anger. M reports S's temper is being exhibited more often of late—e.g., when he is interrupted in his activities; if an object or toy is taken away from him.
4. Discipline. Gets "spanked" for hitting his brother or when he hits his mother. Whines and fusses when M says "no" sharply.
5. Asking for help. Points sometimes, makes noises, bangs on the table with his hand; whines, says "Mumma" and "Dadda."
6. Sibling relationship. Good; M reports very little competition between the two boys.
7. New interest. Animals—particularly dogs. (The Xs are considering buying a dog.)
8. Favorite toy. Ball
9. Favorite place. Yard
10. Favorite activity. Walking; climbing the stairs

General Comments: Everything seems to be going along well in this home. Mrs. X was eager to express how pleased she is with being part of this study. She says she has learned a lot and now is able to observe and understand many of the things we have been talking about over the last few months. She is sorry that the study will soon be ending.

Home Visit #17 (8-17 Months)

Observer: B.S.
Date: 9/25/73
Time: 1:00 p.m.
Age: 15¾ months

Setting: In kitchen with M, PM, and friends.

Coverage: The most recent news about the X household concerns Mrs. X's recent hospitalization for four days for removal of an abcess. As well, her husband has been laid off his job again and they are in some financial difficulty since the hospital insurance may not cover her recent surgery. Mrs. X is also dieting and has lost fifteen pounds, intending to continue for another ten pounds or so. She also has bronchitis. Despite the sound of the above notes, she was in good spirits and the visit went rather well. She reported that S is doing well and PM seemed fine, despite an accident involving wetting his trousers which she handled rather harshly. There were friends visiting during my visit, and S had recently awakened from a nap and spent most of the time eating in his highchair.

1. Motor abilities. S walks well, has started to run, and can climb out of his crib now. He enjoys riding toys.
2. Negativism. The onset of negativism has occured, and S flaunts parental authority when a direct request is made of him. He doesn't respond to swats on the bottom and hits back when struck by M. He does show hurt feelings when yelled at by his father.
3. Family planning. Mrs. X stated her intention to have no more children since two friends' babies were recently born with hyaline membrane disease.
4. Favorite places. Bathroom (door is kept locked), where he recently climbed into a tub of water fully clothed; also yard.
5. Favorite activity. Eating; it's his favorite kind of fun, preferred over toys.
6. Favorite object. His brother's motorcycle rider.
7. New activities. Watching TV, especially cartoons and "Sesame Street." He watches his brother to see when to laugh. [This emergent should be noted for some of our other subjects.]
8. Language. He understands everything but says relatively few words clearly, although he babbles in a sentencelike form rather often.
9. Safety. The kitchen chairs tip over easily when he climbs up and leans over. He does not attempt to walk down stairs yet. He has climbed out of crib onto his jumping horse, and this is a potential danger early in the morning. He is also able to descend from his highchair alone if M allows it.

Comments: Mrs. X seems to be doing well with both children, although she is still inclined to be a bit harsh with PM. It will be interesting to see how hard she comes down on S during this present phase of assertiveness.

Home Visit #19 (8-17 Months)

Observer: E.C.
Date: 10/19/73
Time: 9:30 a.m.
Age: 16½ months

Coverage: Mrs. X reports several changes in S's behavior during the last couple of weeks. *Negativism* has increased. He is *asserting himself* much more and *testing limits*. Mrs. X says *distraction* works most of the time. She also tries smacking his hand in an attempt to discipline. She freely admits this method does not work most of the time. We discussed various methods of discipline and also the need for firmness and consistency. *Sibling problems* have emerged again. Most of the difficulties are initiated by S, not PM. He hits PM without provocation, competes for M's attention, copies almost everything PM does, fights over toys, etc. PM will often come to M for help in these situations rather than fighting back. In the area of *language development*, progress is good. His vocabulary includes "who's there," "come in," "D.D.," "Mama," "Dada," "pupi" (puppy), "car." *Favorite places* include outside and living room (where there are many forbidden objects within his reach); *favorite activity* is dancing; *favorite thing* is the puppy. He also climbs everything. S shows *hurt feelings* usually only toward father. S does initiate games. An *emergent* mentioned by M is that S is now trying to do things like dressing and undressing himself.

General Comments: S is a very appealing child, despite negativism. Mrs. X seems to be handling and surviving negativism quite well. PM seems to be bearing the brunt of a lot of S's negativistic behavior. It will be interesting to watch the sibling relationship here.

Home Visit #20 (8-17 Months)

Observer: B.K.
Date: 10/31/73
Time: 10:00 a.m.
Age: 17 months

Setting: In the kitchen: M and S

Coverage: Since this was the final fivit, I intended to give M a full report on S's 14½-month test scores and the observational data. However, M was totally preoccupied with problems concerning the teen-agers in her community and spent most of the time talking about her role as "pseudoparent" to a group of approximately 8-10 adolescents. Each time I tried to bring the discussion back to S, she listened politely for about one minute and then turned the conversation back to the original topic. Basically, M is not having much difficulty with S at this point in time, and is quite comfortable with his progress. I did manage to report that he was scoring at or above the group median on the Preschool tests at 14½ months and reviewed the tentative schedule for the follow-up study (20-27 months). During our conversation, S was actively engaged in exploration of toys and household objects and gross motor mastery. He showed some signs of negativism (i.e., testing behavior) which M handled easily and firmly. M reported that his favorite activity was "getting into everything," but that he showed no consistent preference for one toy or household object.

Everything seems fine here.

Index

Abstract ability, in longitudinal experiment, 35-36, 55, 87, 93, 102-3
  manual for, 488-501, 502-11
  reliability of test for, 501-2
Adaptation indices, Escalona's, 118
Adult Assessment Scales, 6, 173-75, 189
  manual for, 403-19, 423-30
  reliability of, 419-22
Age:
  to begin work with children, 166-68
  most stressful, 126
Ammons, R. B., 463
Anastasi, A., 195
Annoying, in longitudinal experiment, 132, 139
Asserting oneself, in longitudinal experiment, 97, 112, 136
Attanucci, Jane, 403, 423
Avoiding unpleasant circumstances, in longitudinal experiment, 132

Barker, Roger, 66, 115, 126, 187, 188, 190
Baron, F., 195
Bayley, Nancy, 166
Bayley Mental Index, 37, 38, 41, 55, 145-46, 148-49, 189

Bayley Tests of Mental Development, 16, 37, 118
Behavior episode units, in Caldwell scale, 122
Bell, T. H., 199
Bellugi-Klima, U., 463
Berkeley Growth Study, 39, 116, 120
Binet test, *see* Stanford-Binet Intelligence Scale
Birch, H. F., 116
Blacks, in longitudinal experiment, 118-19
Bloom, Benjamin, 200
Bored children, 155, 157, 158
Bowlby, J., 166, 193
Bronfenbrenner, U., 199
Bronson, W. C., 117, 121, 124
Brown, D. G., 195
Brown, R. E., 166
Bühler, Charlotte, 189

Caldwell, B., 6, 117-19, 123-26
Caldwell Approach Scale, 121-22
California First Year Mental Scale, 116
Car seat, child in, 100
Carew, J. V., 119-21, 124, 125
Categories of infant behavior in various studies, 121-23

561

562 INDEX

Cattell scale, 118
Characterological outcomes, Sander's project on, 118
Checklist for Scoring Social Behavior, 29
Chess, S., 116
Child-rearing
  conclusions from experiment on, 150-57
  experiment training program for, 176-81
    manual for, 523-47
    sample home visit reports from, 547-59
  general guidelines on, 157-59
  generating hypotheses about, 26, 69, 77-78
  See also Infant education
Clarke-Stewart, A. K., 67, 70, 117-26, 188
Cluttering the house by child, 158
Comparative experiment, 163-69
Competence
  definition of
    development of, 117-18
    "fully competent," 62-63
    original study, 8-11
  effects of experience on, 140-48
  in longitudinal experiment, *see* Longitudinal natural experiment
  rating scale for, 142-44
  use of term, 4
Conditioning studies, 114
Constable, Elizabeth, 403, 423, 452, 523
Constructing products, in longitudinal experiment, 74, 133
Conversing, in longitudinal experiment, 73, 133
Cooperating, in longitudinal experiment, 70, 72, 96, 100-102, 129, 136
Curiosity, development of, 167
  educational foundation for, 177
  lack of ability to assess, 189-90
  UNESCO report on, 200
Curricula, "written," 66

Denver scale, 189
Directing the behavior of others, in longitudinal experiment, 95, 96, 100-103, 133, 139
Disciplining child, 156-57, 158
Discriminative ability, manual for assessing, 512-20
  reliability study for, 520-22
Dissonance, sensing of, in longitudinal experiment, 34-35, 45-47, 53-54, 87-88, 93, 103
Dollinow, Phyllis, 152, 188
DQ scale, 36, 37

Early education, *see* Infant education

Easing discomfort, in longitudinal experiment, 85
Eating, in longitudinal experiment, 74, 93, 95, 97, 100-102, 133, 136, 139
Eating and gaining information (visual and auditory), in longitudinal experiment, 87, 135
Eating and listening to live language, in longitudinal experiment, 93, 101-3, 136, 137, 139
Eating and looking, in longitudinal experiment, 133, 139
Eating and overhearing live language, in longitudinal experiment, 133
Eating and steady staring, in longitudinal experiment, 84, 86, 111, 130
Ecological psychology, 66, 115
Educability
  in competence study, 9
  dropping of term, 4
Empty time, *see* Nontask behavior
Engaging in large muscle activity, *see* Large muscle activity
Engaging in role play, in longitudinal study, 58, 59
Enjoying pets, in longitudinal study, 136
Environmental factors, 66, 115
  general questions on, 186-87
  in longitudinal study, 75-149
    experiences at 12-15 months, 78-94, 110-14
    experiences at 18-21 months, 94-110
  subgroup for, 172
Environmental Force Unit, 122, 189
Erikson, Erik, 190, 197, 198
Escalone, S., 115, 117, 118, 120
Ethology, 186, 190
Experiences of children
  data on, from longitudinal experiment, 70-74
  effects of, on competence at five years of age, 140-48
  validity of data on, 65-70
  See also Infant education
Experiments, *see* Comparative experiment; Longitudinal natural experiment
Exploratory behavior
  child's need for, 157
  items suitable for, 155
  in longitudinal experiment, 85, 87, 93, 130, 146-48
  in other studies, 125-26
Expressing hostility or affection, in longitudinal experiment, 58, 59
Expressing pride in achievement, in longitudinal experiment, 38, 48, 57-59

Father, infant's interaction with, 72*n*

Fine motor mastery, *see* Motor mastery
Frederickson, John, 77
Freud, Sigmund, 197
Full-time job by person responsible for child, 158
"Fully competent," definition of, 62-63

Gaining approval, in longitudinal experiment, 103
Gaining attention in socially acceptable ways (attempting to gain attention)
  good development and, 152
  in longitudinal experiment, 38, 48, 50, 52, 57-59, 78, 86, 87, 93, 101, 112, 145
Gaining information (auditory and visual) in longitudinal experiment, 74, 84, 135
Gaining information (visual) (through steady staring; *includes* simple steady staring)
  good development and, 152
  in longitudinal experiment, 70, 72, 74, 78, 81, 84, 86, 93, 100-103, 113, 129, 130, 133, 136, 145-47
  in other studies, 125
Garber, H., 528n
Gesell, A., 36, 189
Golden, M., 36, 165, 198
Griffith scale, 189
Gross motor mastery, *see* Motor mastery
Guidance Study, 39, 116, 119-20
Guidelines for child-rearing, 157-59
Guidubaldi, J., 28

Halpern, Florence, 33, 166
Harvard Preschool Project, *see* Preschool Project
Head Start, 3-4, 39, 66, 119
Heber, R., 528n
Henderson, R. W., 195
Hinde, Robert A., 66, 188
Hollingshead, A. B., 9, 10, 49n, 76n, 128, 131, 132, 199
Holmes, J. C., 463
Home visits
  sample reports of, 547-59
  scheduling of, 67, 121
Honzik, Marjorie, 116
Hospitalism, 193
Hunt, J. McV., 36, 37, 39, 86, 114, 164, 195, 198, 489

Index of Social Position, 19
Infant education, 4
  conclusions about, 192-200
  evaluations of programs for, 66
  See also Child-rearing

Intelligence (intellectual development)
  educational foundations for development of, 177
  in longitudinal experiment, 35-38, 47-48, 55
  Piaget on, 171
  See also Abstract ability
Intelligence tests
  general assessment of, 194-96
  intercorrelations among scores of, 148-49
  longitudinal-experiment scores of, 195
  social competence scores compared to, 196
Interaction, *see* Adult Assessment Scales; Social interaction
Interactionalism, 115
Israel, kibbutz life in, 197

Jensen, A. R., 4, 15
Jones, H. E., 195

Kaban, Barbara, 70, 403, 423, 488, 512, 523
Kagan, J., 116
Kibbutz life, 197
Kitchens of effective child-rearers, 155
Koslowski, Barbara, 512
Kretsch, Esther, 176

LaCrosse, Robert, 172
Language
  age of adults' using of, to children, 194
  age of first learning of, 167
  difficulty of assessing development of, 189
  educational foundation of development of, 177
  guideline on, 159
  in longitudinal experiment
    development of language, 73, 74, 86-87, 93, 102
    manual for testing, 462-82
    reliability study, 482-87
    See also Receptive-language development
  UNESCO report on, 200
Large muscle activity, in longitudinal experiment, 96, 97, 100-103
Learning events, 115
Lee, Patrick, 11n
Lewin, Kurt, 66, 115, 126, 187-90
Lieberman, Marcus, 77
Light, Richard, 77
Listening to language from all sources, in longitudinal experiment, 133
Live language directed to child
  in Clarke-Stewart study, 126

564 INDEX

Live language directed to child (cont'd)
  good development and, 152-53
  in longitudinal experiment, 78, 79, 84, 85, 87, 95, 97, 100, 102, 103, 111, 113, 129, 130, 139, 145-47
Live language overheard by child, in longitudinal experiment, 78, 79, 86, 87, 95, 101, 103, 129, 136
Longitudinal natural experiment, 15-159
  central purpose of, 121
  conclusions from, 150-57
  data collection schedule in, 16-17
  design of, 15-16, 171-72
  development of competence in, 27-64
    interim achievement data (partially matched groups), 48-57
    interim achievement data (unmatched groups), 27-38
    primary outcome data, 62-64
    primary outcome data (partially matched groups), 57-62
    primary outcome data (unmatched groups), 39-48
  environmental factors in, 75-149
    experiences at 12-15 months, 78-94, 110-14
    experiences at 18-21 months, 94-110
    subgroup for, 172
  guidelines for childrearing from, 157-59
  intelligence test scores in, 194-95
  manuals for, see Manuals
  nonsocial competence in, 85, 93, 97-101
  patterns of experience in, 65-74
    problems involved, 65-70
  predicted vs. achieved competence levels in, 39-42
  reliability studies of, see Reliability studies
  results on competence in, 27-33, 42-44, 50-52, 57-58
    compared to intelligence scores, 196
  staff subgroups in, 170-72
  subjects in, 17-24
    demographic information, 20-23
    individual data, 205-381
    SES, 19, 24
  subsidiary analysis of competence in, 383-99
  tape recorder in, 123-24
Longitudinal studies (in general)
  comparison of findings of, 124-27
  history of, 116-17
  small number of, 185, 187
Lorenz, K., 186

MacFarlane, 166
Maintaining social contact, in longitudinal experiment, 93, 112, 114, 132, 136

Make-believe, see Pretend behavior
Manuals
  for abstract ability test, 488-501, 502-11
  for Adult Assessment Scales, 403-19, 423-30
  for assessing discriminative ability, 512-20
  for assessing social abilities, 431-56
  for testing language ability, 462-82
  for training program, 523-47
Marmor, Janice, 462, 482
Mason, William, 188
Mastery behavior
  in longitudinal experiment, 74, 78, 79, 87, 101, 103, 113, 135, 136
  See also Motor mastery
Materials for child to explore, 155, 157
Meyers, C. E., 36, 47, 463
Mother
  infant's interaction with
    in longitudinal experiment, 72
    in other studies, 125
  studies on separation of infant from, 193
Motor mastery (includes gross, fine motor mastery)
  good development and, 154
  in longitudinal experiment, 86, 87, 93-97, 101, 103, 111, 130, 133, 136-37, 139
Movies in experimental training program, 177
Murphy, Lois, 8
Muscle skills, see Motor mastery

"Naps," good development and, 153-54
National Institutes of Child Health and Human Development, 185
National Institutes of Mental Health, 185
Nature-nurture controversy, 187-88, 192, 193
Nonsocial abilities, in longitudinal experiment, 40-41, 58-62
Nonsocial competence, in longitudinal experiment, 85, 93, 97-101
Nonsocial experiences, pattern of, in longitudinal experiment, 73-74
Nonsocial tasks, initiation of, 81, 96
Nontask behavior (empty time), in longitudinal experiment, 74, 84, 86-87, 95-97, 101-3, 130, 146, 147
  earlier passing time and, 153-54

Observer effect, 67, 120
  See also Process monitoring
Office of Child Development, 27, 176, 185
Ogilvie, Daniel, 11n, 27n, 431

Operating a mechanism, in longitudinal experiment, 102, 130, 133, 136, 139
Overpowering the child, 158
Overprotectiveness, 158

Pacific Expressive Vocabulary Objects, 463
Pacific Test Series, 489
Parent-Child Centers, 39
Pasamanick, B., 37
Passing time
  good development and, 153-54
  in longitudinal experiment, 74, 84, 93, 94, 100, 102, 103, 111, 113, 139
Pathological development, studies of, 187
Pavlov, I., 114
Peabody Picture Vocabulary Test, 9
Piaget, J., 36, 65, 115, 124-25, 168, 171, 186, 197-98, 200
Playpen confinement, 94, 111
  good development and, 153-54, 158, 194
Pleasing, in longitudinal experiment, 78, 82, 84-85, 95, 96, 100-103, 112, 128, 130, 135, 136
Preparing for activities, in longitudinal experiment, 86, 87, 93, 95-97, 100-103, 114, 130, 133
Preschool education, see Infant education
Preschool Project, 4-7, 119-22
  compared to other projects, 124-27
  liabilities of, 124
  See also Longitudinal natural experiment
Pretend behavior, in longitudinal experiment, 74, 102, 133, 136, 139
Primates, young, staring behavior by, 152
Process monitoring
  data from, 70-74
  importance of, 114-24
  problems of, 66-70
Procuring objects
  good development and, 154
  in longitudinal experiment, 78, 79, 85, 87, 93, 94, 97, 100-103, 111-113, 130, 136
Procuring services
  good development and, 151-52
  in longitudinal experiment, 73, 78, 79, 83-87, 93, 95, 96, 100-103, 111, 112, 133, 136, 139
Project Follow-Through, 4
Project Head Start, 3-4, 39, 66, 119
Providing information, in longitudinal experiment, 73, 133, 139
Psychological life-space, 115
Psychological research, assessment problems in, 195-96

Psychology
  ecological, 66, 115
  topological, 115

Receptive-language development, in longitudinal experiment, 6, 33-34, 44-45, 52-53
Redlich, F. C., see Hollingshead, A. B.
Reliability studies, 123
  for abstract ability test, 520-22
  of Adult Assessment Scales, 419-22
  for assessing social abilities, 433, 457-61
  for discriminative ability test, 520-22
  of Language Test Battery, 482-87
Research on child development
  lack of, 185
  lack of design and statistical analysis for, 190
  various professions in, 190-91
  See also Comparative experiment; Longitudinal natural experiment; Longitudinal studies
Resisting domination, in longitudinal experiment, 97
Restoring order, in longitudinal experiment, 87, 97, 100-103, 130
Restriction of infant, see Playpen confinement
Rorschach test, 195

Sander, L. W., 117, 118, 126
Schaefer, Earl, 26, 33, 166
Schoggen, Maxine, 115, 117, 119, 124, 126, 187, 188
Schoggen, Philip, 115, 117, 119, 124, 126, 187, 188
Seeking approval, in longitudinal experiment, 96, 101, 102, 130
Seeking attention, in longitudinal experiment, 79, 85-87, 109, 111, 129, 130, 146, 147
Seeking services, see Procuring services
Seeking to maintain social contact, in longitudinal experiment, 100
Sensing dissonance, see Dissonance, sensing of
SES, see Socioeconomic status
"Sesame Street" (TV program), in longitudinal experiment, 68, 74, 86, 130, 153
Setting limits for child, 156-57
Sex differences, in longitudinal experiment, 133-40
Shapiro, Bernice Broyde, 11n, 27n, 70, 403, 423, 431, 488, 523
Skinner, B. F., 114
Social abilities, manual for assessing, 431-56
  reliability of, 433, 457-61

Social attention, 126
Social competence, *see* Competence; *and topics in* Longitudinal natural experiment
Social Competence Rating Scale, 142-44
Social interaction with children
    amount of time necessary for, 151
    of effective child-rearer, 155-56, 158
    by fathers, 72*n*
    by mothers
        in longitudinal experiment, 72
        in other studies, 125
Social skills and attachment development, educational foundation for, 177
Social tasks, initiation of, in longitudinal experiment, 72, 81, 96
Socioeconomic status (SESO, in longitudinal experiment, 19, 24, 75-77
    analysis of effects of, 127-33
    bias in, 124
    cases especially sought out, 118-19
Spitz, Rene A., 126, 193
Stanford-Binet Intelligence Scale, 6, 41-42, 85-86, 93, 101-2, 113, 145-46, 148-49, 194, 489
Statistical analysis, lack of, 190
Steady staring, *see* Gaining information (visual)
Stocking, Ingrid, 462
Stone, Joseph, 197
Stream of behavior, 66
Stream of experience
    ability to sample, 188
    data from, 70-74, 121
    monitoring of, 66-70, 114-24
Syracuse University, 118

Tantrums, 158
Tape recorder for observations, 123-24
TAT (Thematic Apperception Test), 195
Television viewing
    in Clarke-Stewart study, 126
    in longitudinal experiment, 126, 130, 136, 152-53
    See also "Sesame Street"
Terman, L. M., 8*n*

Test scores, repeated testing and, 165
Tests, intelligence, *see* Intelligence tests
Thomas, A., 115
Thorndike, E. L., 114
Thought, abstract, *see* Abstract ability
Tinbergen, N., 186
Toilet training, 159
Topological psychology, 115
Training program (for parents), 176-81
    manual for, 523-47
    sample home visit reports from, 547-59
Training programs (for staff), lack of, 190
Twin studies, 187-88

UNESCO report on preschool education, 199-200
Unsafe actions of child, 158
Using adult as resource, in longitudinal study, 38, 48, 50, 52, 57-59, 84, 111
Uzgiris, I. C., 36, 489

Verbal mastery, in longitudinal experiment, 100-103, 130, 133
Vineland Social Maturity Scale, 189

Wachs, T. D., 36
Walker, D., 27
Ware, Eugenia, 462
Watts, Jean Carew, 6-7, 172
Wechsler Preschool and Primary Scales of Intelligence (WPPSI), 6, 9, 78, 141, 144-49, 194-95, 489
Wenar, C., 70*n*, 117, 119, 124, 125
White, B. L., 36, 70, 166, 172, 403, 423, 482, 523
Whiting, B., 66
Whiting, J., 66
Winer, B. J., 460
World Health Organization, 166, 193
Wright, Herbert, 66, 115, 126, 187, 188, 190
Written records in infant-behavior studies, 123-24

Yarrow, L. J., 117-19, 121, 124

DATE DUE

AUG 11 '80			
NOV 18 '91			
OCT 8 '90			
GAYLORD			PRINTED IN U.S.A.